Legal Ethics, Second Edition

KENT D. KAUFFMAN

DELMAR
CENGAGE Learning

Australia • Brazil • Japan • Korea • Mexico • Singapore • Spain • United Kingdom • United States

DELMAR
CENGAGE Learning™

Legal Ethics, Second Edition
Kent D. Kauffman

Vice President, Career and Professional Editorial: Dave Garza

Director of Learning Solutions: Sandy Clark

Acquisitions Editor: Shelley Esposito

Managing Editor: Larry Main

Product Manager: Melissa Riveglia

Editorial Assistant: Lyss Zaza

Vice President, Career and Professional Marketing: Jennifer McAvey

Marketing Director: Debbie Yarnell

Marketing Manager: Erin Brennan

Marketing Coordinator: Jonathan Sheehan

Production Director: Wendy Troeger

Production Manager: Mark Bernard

Content Project Manager: Steven Couse

Art Director: Joy Kocsis

Technology Project Manager: Tom Smith

Production Technology Analyst: Thomas Stover

For product information and technology assistance, contact us at
Cengage Learning Customer & Sales Support, 1-800-354-9706
For permission to use material from this text or product, submit all requests online at **cengage.com/permissions**
Further permissions questions can be emailed to
permissionrequest@cengage.com

Library of Congress Control Number: 2008930300

ISBN-13: 978-1-4283-0410-9

ISBN-10: 1-4283-0410-X

Delmar Cengage Learning
5 Maxwell Drive
Clifton Park, NY 12065-2919
USA

Cengage Learning is a leading provider of customized learning solutions with office locations around the globe, including Singapore, the United Kingdom, Australia, Mexico, Brazil, and Japan. Locate your local office at: **international.cengage.com/region**

Cengage Learning products are represented in Canada by Nelson Education, Ltd.

For your lifelong learning solutions, visit **delmar.cengage.com**

Visit our corporate website at **cengage.com**

NOTICE TO THE READER

Publisher does not warrant or guarantee any of the products described herein or perform any independent analysis in connection with any of the product information contained herein. Publisher does not assume, and expressly disclaims, any obligation to obtain and include information other than that provided to it by the manufacturer. The reader is expressly warned to consider and adopt all safety precautions that might be indicated by the activities herein and to avoid all potential hazards. By following the instructions contained herein, the reader willingly assumes all risks in connection with such instructions. The publisher makes no representation or warranties of any kind, including but not limited to, the warranties of fitness for particular purpose or merchantability, nor are any such representations implied with respect to the material set forth herein, and the publisher takes no responsibility with respect to such material. The publisher shall not be liable for any special, consequential, or exemplary damages resulting, in whole or part, from the readers' use of, or reliance upon, this material.

Printed in Canada
1 2 3 4 5 X X 10 09 08

Dedication

This second edition is dedicated to Reagan, my little son.
Daily I am refreshed by your laughter.

Contents

CHAPTER 2 Paralegals and Their Profession 36

CHAPTER 6 Advertising and Solicitation 314

Preface

It has been said of the über-brilliant Mozart that once he placed a note on the musical staff, there it was almost certain to stay, not because the eighteenth century composer lacked an eraser, but because his talent was so great that perfection was achieved on the first attempt. Thankfully, for the rest of us mere mortals, there is a wonderful thing called a second edition. It is my hope that the second edition of *Legal Ethics* achieves its aim: to more clearly and vibrantly explain the key professional responsibility topics and issues facing those who work in a law office.

Legal Ethics springs from the author's first experiences teaching a legal ethics course at his college and discussing with his students what they liked and did not like about their course.

ORGANIZATION

The chapter topics in the book logically progress in the following order: an examination of how lawyers are regulated; a history and overview of the paralegal profession; the unauthorized practice of law; confidentiality and attorney-client privilege; conflicts of interest; advertising and solicitation; legal fees and fee sharing with paralegals and legal assistants; and miscellaneous ethics issues. Many of these issues have to do with litigation, including competence, truthfulness, malpractice liability for the non-lawyer, and pro bono services. Special attention is paid to particularly thorny issues, such as the following: whether paralegals and legal assistants should be licensed; whether independent-contracting paralegals engage in the unauthorized practice of law; the work product rule as it applies to non-lawyer employees; the hidden risk of violating confidentiality because of "metadata" in electronic documents; imputed disqualification and screening for paralegals and legal assistants; fee sharing between lawyers and paralegals; the recovery of paralegal and legal assistant fees under statutes that only explicitly provide for the recovery of lawyer's fees; malpractice liability risks for paralegals; and the specific issues that apply to those who work in prosecuting attorney's offices.

PEDAGOGY

Legal Ethics, 2nd Edition provides a fresh approach to the study of the significant professional responsibility issues facing the legal profession. Starting with the premise that students should not be "talked down to," and because non-lawyer employees are required to act with the same professional care as if they are lawyers, the text provides a thorough and substantive analysis of the major principles that affect how the practice of law is regulated. And because lawyers are responsible for the conduct of their non-lawyer employees, the text then applies those major principles to lawyers as well as to paralegals. Supporting citations to federal and state statutes and case law, as well as national, state, and local ethics opinions are provided in-text.

Because studying ethics rules can be tedious, *Legal Ethics, 2nd Edition* gives the reader a variety of methods designed to improve understanding and interest. It begins by explaining how one becomes licensed to practice law, how the American Bar Association affects the practice of law, and how the behavior of lawyers is regulated. To provide an example of how the lawyer-disciplinary process works, a thorough and provocative look at the disbarment proceedings against former President Bill Clinton is presented in the first chapter. Other real-world examples and hypotheticals are provided throughout the chapters to facilitate a better grasp on the technical material. Over 60 visual aids have been added to the second edition, so that critical and difficult concepts can be better understood and retained. Vignettes of lawyer or paralegal misbehavior, all of them true and some of them quite odd, have been placed throughout the second edition to enliven the reading experience. Hypothetical scenarios that tie real-world issues to current ethics rules have been added to the end of each chapter to help students review the material in an alternative manner while preparing for what might be faced at work. Case law is provided immediately following the material it is designed to amplify, and the case questions are framed to promote both the understanding of the legal analysis, as well as the cultivation of the reader's own opinions.

Review questions at the end of the chapter, called "Points to Ponder," will, if studied, enable students to easily get outstanding grades on any quizzes or tests and will serve as a springboard for further, independent study, if desired. The presidents of both the National Federation of Paralegals and the National Association of Legal Assistants have each written an essay specifically for the text—found in the last chapter—on what makes a paralegal or legal assistant professional and competent. And there is a legal ethics movie guide, updated with more movies for the second edition, where the author discusses over 20 movies that have a connection to legal ethics or the practice of law. Readers from any jurisdiction will benefit by reading and relying on *Legal Ethics, 2nd Edition*.

FEATURES

There are four notable, new features for the second edition.

- "Not Quite Lincoln" sections are true stories of lawyer or paralegal misbehavior— the really reprehensible or just plain bizarre examples. There are three to five

"Not Quite Lincoln" sections in every chapter, placed where they fit best. Each has been written and presented in the text to look like newspaper articles, which they almost are, except they are just for fun.

- "Ethics in Action" sections are detailed hypothetical scenarios that will improve the reader's understanding of each chapter, as well as the reader's analytical skills. There are five to eight of these hypothetical scenarios at the end of every chapter, and they can be used either to stimulate class discussion or for out-of-class assignments.

- A Student CD-ROM accompanies the second edition, providing more ethics hypotheticals and dialogues.

- An Online Companion for the second edition will be available on the Cengage Web site (http://www.paralegal.delmar.cengage.com), giving students more information, Web links, and sample quiz questions with answers.

Beyond the brand new features and the updates, the second edition has many other attributes that distinguish this book from other legal ethics books, including the following:

- A discussion of the latest trends affecting the paralegal/legal assistant profession, including the controversial subjects of the licensing and certification of paralegals, the application of the recent changes to the federal overtime pay requirements, and recent paralegal/legal assistant compensation information.

- A current analysis of Ethics 2000, providing explanations in each substantive chapter on the correlative changes to the ABA model Rules of Professional Conduct, many of which have been adopted by most of the country's jurisdictions.

- Explanations of the key distinctions between the ABA Model Rules of Professional Conduct and the ABA Model Code of Professional Responsibility.

- Exhibits designed to help explain some of the more difficult concepts in the book, including the unauthorized practice of law, confidentiality, the work product rule, conflicts of interest, lawyer and non-lawyer screening, lawyer advertising and solicitation, and fee sharing with and fee recovery of paralegals and legal assistants.

- Dozens of real-life examples of lawyer and paralegal misbehaviors provided throughout the chapters, and with case law citations, which help breathe life into the ethics rules.

- A discussion of the disbarment proceedings against President Clinton and F. Lee Bailey, and the role President Nixon played in legal ethics courses.

- A discussion of news events of famous and infamous people who relate to the chapter topics, including Bill and Hillary Clinton, Vince Foster and Kenneth Starr, Martha Stewart, Dr. Phil, Bill Gates, super-attorney David Boies, and Mike Nifong, the former prosecutor in the Duke Lacrosse case.

- Essays by the current presidents of the National Association of Legal Assistants and the National Federation of Paralegal Associations.

- The latest versions of the significant ethics codes for paralegals and legal assistants.

- Inclusion of current and classic case law, which help the reader see how courts interpret and apply the ethics rules to lawyers and their non-lawyer employees.

- Even more margin-placed definitions of key legal words used in the text, and an accompanying glossary.

- Legal ethics Web sites and links strategically placed throughout the chapters, as well as an accompanying legal ethics Web site directory, focusing on the Web addresses of state bar associations, national paralegal associations, and key ethics Web sites.

- An updated legal ethics movie guide that summarizes and reviews movies such *Erin Brockovich*, *A Civil Action*, *The Rainmaker*, *Changing Lanes*, and *Michael Clayton*.

Ancillary Materials

This new edition is accompanied by a support package that will assist students in learning and aid instructors in teaching.

Instructor's Manual

There is an accompanying instructor's manual, written by the author and updated for the second edition. The instructor's manual will significantly assist in class preparation because it has features such chapter outlines, teaching suggestions, and full case briefs for all the case law in the text. The instructor's manual also includes answers for the questions that follow the case law, as well as the chapter review questions, called "Points to Ponder." The instructor's manual also contains complete test banks for each chapter, including essay questions and accompanying answers. Because of the text's organization and chapter sequence, professors and instructors will be able to logically divide the material into either a traditional sixteen-week, or shorter, semester.

Student CD-ROM

The new accompanying CD-ROM provides spirited, scripted dialogues that challenge the reader to think about key portions of the material discussed in each chapter. Each dialogue concludes with thought-provoking application questions.

Instructor's eResource CD-ROM

The new e-Resource component provides instructors with all the tools they need in one convenient CD-ROM. Instructors will find that this resource provides them with a turnkey solution to help them teach by making available PowerPoint® slides for each chapter, a Computerized Test Bank, and an electronic version of the Instructor's Manual. All of these Instructor materials are also posted on our Web site, in the Online Resources section.

Online Companion™

Through the Online Companion, students have access to Web links and sample quiz questions with answers. The Online Companion™ can be found at http://www.paralegal .delmar.cengage.com in the Online Companion™ section of the Web site.

Web page—Come visit our Web site at http://www.paralegal.delmar .cengage.com, where you will find valuable information such as hot links and sample materials to download, as well as other Delmar Cengage Learning products.

Please note that the Internet resources are of a time-sensitive nature and URL addresses may often change or might be deleted.

ACKNOWLEDGMENTS

This second edition, as with the first, would not have been possible without the help of many, and they deserve to be thanked in print. First, to Shelley Esposito, the acquisitions editor, thank you for your expertise in shepherding and guiding this book through the multi-year gestation required of textbook publishing. To Melissa Riveglia, the developmental editor, thank you for your insight in managing the nuts and bolts of putting a second edition together. To editorial assistant Lyss Zaza, thank you for ably helping me with much of what is wrongly referred to as the "small stuff." And to Melissa Berry and the other fantastic members of GEX Publishing Services, who worked so efficiently and pleasantly at turning the fragments of a manuscript into an attractive book, many thanks.

I greatly appreciate that copyright holders graciously allowed me to use some of their materials, including ethics codes, as appendixes, exhibits, or articles. Thank you to the American Bar Association, the Florida Bar, the Indiana Continuing Legal Education Forum, the National Federation of Paralegal Associations, and the National Association of Legal Assistants.

Tita Brewster, ACP, President of the National Association of Legal Assistants, and Anita G. Hayworth, RP, President of the National Federation of Paralegal Associations, graciously provided essays on professionalism for Chapter 8. Also they kindly provided many answers to my questions about their organizations. They are admirable leaders of their organizations.

Thank you to the following reviewers of the second edition manuscript:

Bernard Behrend
Duquesne University
Pittsburgh, PA

Jonathan Bent
Keiser University
West Palm Beach, FL

S. Whittington Brown
Pulaski Technical College
North Little Rock, AR

Mary Conwell
Edison College
Fort Myers, FL

Matthew Cornick
Clayton State University
Morrow, GA

Jane McElligott
Kaplan University
Boise, ID

Kathleen Fisher
National Center for Paralegal Training
Atlanta, GA

Giselle Franco
Keiser University
Miami, FL

Diane Pevar
Manor College
Jenkintown, PA

Anita Whitby
Kaplan University
Ft. Lauderdale, FL

Two former students of mine deserve special praise for volunteering their time to help me in critical ways. Michelle Roberts conducted hours of research, searching for lawyer discipline cases—including those involving paralegals and legal assistants. Much of her research proved fruitful, because many of the "Not Quite Lincoln" pieces were the result of cases she mailed to me from her home in Oklahoma. Amanda Friend spent many late nights on the Internet, helping to find Web sites that might be fitting additions to the chapters and ancillary materials. Their generosity of spirit and time is rare and very much appreciated.

Chuck Kidd of the Indiana Disciplinary Commission has been instrumental in answering a multitude of questions, lending his sage advice, and serving as a sounding board. It is an honor to have had someone of his caliber give me his time. Bob Colestock has for over a decade occupied a special place in my professional life, even from states away. But more important than mentor and the giver of fabulous advice is the title I give Bob that is more fitting: friend.

And to my luminous wife Karen—whose everlasting encouragement made the first and second editions of this text possible, and whose Job-like patience ensured that they could be written from home, at night, and on weekends—thank you.

ABOUT THE AUTHOR

Kent Kauffman, Esq., is the Paralegal Studies Program Chair at Ivy Tech Community College, in Fort Wayne, Indiana, where he teaches legal ethics, legal research and writing, business law, criminal law, constitutional law, and alternative dispute resolution. He is a *summa cum laude* graduate of Temple University, and a graduate of The Dickinson School of Law of the Pennsylvania State University, and is licensed to practice law in Indiana. Mr. Kauffman is also the author of *The Legal Movie Guide: Key Scenes for the College Class*. He has also taught political science and elements of law at Indiana University—Purdue University, Fort Wayne, is a multiple recipient of *Who's Who Among America's Teachers*, and is a recipient of *Who's Who in American Law*.

Table of Cases

CHAPTER 1

Lawyers, Legal Assistants, and the Regulation of the Legal Profession

INTRODUCTION

Admit it—you like lawyer jokes. In fact, if you were paid $10 for every lawyer joke you could think of off the top of your head, you could probably make enough money to buy this textbook. Why are lawyer jokes so prevalent, so much a part of our culture, that books and Web sites are dedicated solely to poke fun at lawyers? Is it because lawyer jokes are especially hilarious, better than those standard jokes about certain religious officials sitting in a bar or stuck on a lifeboat, or the tired jokes about mentally challenged, fair-haired women? Or is it because lawyers remain one of the last groups in American society—the other group being politicians, who just happen to be mostly lawyers—that can still be safely lampooned? Generally, most jokes or insults about groups have fallen out of favor under the scrutiny of political correctness and a heightened awareness of unkindness, but jokes about lawyers abound.

For more lawyer jokes and cartoons that anyone thought could be categorized, check out the aptly titled following link: http://www.lawyer-jokes.us/.

According to the American Bar Association Market Research Department, in 2006 there were 1,116,967 lawyers in the country and, unfortunately for the legal profession, lawyer jokes may be born more out of ire, rather than good-natured humor. In fact, in April 2002, the Litigation Section of the American Bar Association released the results of two surveys it commissioned from the Chicago research firm of Leo J. Shapiro & Associates. The survey asked non-lawyer respondents to rate various occupations, in terms of public confidence. The results from a survey done before the September 11 attacks show that only the news media was held in greater disregard than lawyers, while doctors were held in highest regard. When the survey was done a few months after September

> "The first thing we do, let's kill all the lawyers."
>
> **WILLIAM SHAKESPEARE**
> *KING HENRY VI* **(1591)**

> "What do you call one thousand lawyers at the bottom of the ocean? A good start."
>
> **SOURCE UNKNOWN**

11, the news media got out of the public confidence cellar by jumping one place ahead of the legal profession. It is sad that many respondents referred to lawyers as greedy and corrupt, and only 29 percent of the respondents from the April 2001 survey agreed with the following statement: "The legal profession does a good job of disciplining lawyers." In addition, dispelling the armchair wisdom that perceptions are influenced by the boorish and cartoonish behavior of lawyers on television shows, there was no significant difference in opinion between those respondents who did and did not watch *Ally McBeal* or *The Practice*. How interesting it is that doctors—who often get sued by their patients for malpractice and have an average income almost twice that of lawyers—are thought of so highly that they ranked first on the respect-in-the-professions survey, while lawyers —many of whom represent those patients in their malpractice claims—are thought of so negatively. See Exhibit 1–1 for more on the American Bar Association (ABA) survey on the public's perception of lawyers.

Many people think that William Shakespeare said, "Let's kill all the lawyers." He did not. However, he did write it in 1591 for Dick the Butcher, who said the infamous line in Act IV, Scene II, of the play *King Henry VI, Part II*. That line has aroused controversy concerning whether it was meant as a humorous smear or a sly compliment. Some say Shakespeare was using an evil character like Dick the Butcher to express Shakespeare's own disdain of lawyers. Others, however, believe the line is complimentary. That is because Dick the Butcher thought that murdering all the lawyers would guarantee success in the evil plans conspired by

---

EXHIBIT I–I   ABA SURVEY ON THE PERCEPTIONS OF THE LEGAL PROFESSION

Percent of Respondents Agreeing with the Following Statements:

Lawyers are more interested in winning than in seeing that justice is served.	74%
Lawyers spend too much time finding technicalities to get criminals released.	73%
Lawyers are more interested in making money than in serving their clients.	69%
Most lawyers are concerned more with their own self-promotion than their clients' best interests.	57%
We would be better off with fewer lawyers.	51%
Lawyers do not keep their clients informed of the progress of their case.	40%
Most lawyers try to serve the public interests well.	39%
The best lawyers are elected to serve as judges.	28%
The legal profession does a good job disciplining lawyers.	26%

Source: April 2001 ABA survey conducted by Leo J. Shapiro & Associates, http://www.abanet.org/litigation/lawyers/public_standing.pdf.

Jack Cade, the anarchist leader of the gang to which Dick the Butcher belonged. By getting the lawyers out of the way first, injustice could then be allowed to prevail. How ironic it is that a line that launched a thousand smirks might, in fact, have been intended as a badge of honor for the legal profession.

If Shakespeare were alive today, he might have written the less violent line, "First let's jail all the lawyers," because sometimes when lawyers end up behind bars, something that rarely occurs, the results can benefit us all. In much the same way that the placement of a life-saving traffic light at a dangerous country intersection is often the result of the carnage of a horrific accident, the creation of legal ethics courses in American law schools is largely a fortuitous result of the Watergate scandal. What might have gone unnoticed in the months following that national crisis and presidential pardon was that dozens of lawyers—most of them government lawyers—were the focus of attorney disciplinary charges. Many of those charges resulted in disbarments for those involved, including G. Gordon Liddy (chief planner of the Watergate break-in), John Dean (chief plotter of Watergate and its cover-up), and Richard Nixon (commander in chief). The collective embarrassment and hand-wringing by the legal profession and the American Bar Association that ensued did have a position outcome, however. It led to a realization that a formal emphasis on ethics and professional responsibility was needed in the curricula of America's law schools. So if you are taking your own ethics course while reading this book, thank the late President Nixon for what you are about to encounter.

Does any book about legal ethics need to be longer than a postcard? Is "legal ethics" really an oxymoron? Do lawyers deserve the ill will heaped upon them? Perhaps. But if such a negative stereotype is deserved, then should those who work for lawyers be guilty by association? No, at least not yet. Not until such guilt is earned—which, it is hoped, will be never.

Paralegals and legal assistants continue to become more of an integral part of the legal team. Where once attorneys considered that there was a divide between themselves and everyone else in the firm, a bridge has been built and paralegals cross that bridge every day. When a paralegal is used effectively, he does substantive legal work, not solely clerical tasks. Interviewing, case management, research, and writing are just some of the functions in which legal assistants can engage, thereby allowing attorneys to work on other projects. However, with more responsibility in the law office comes a recognition that paralegals need to be fully acquainted with the same rules of ethics (commonly called rules of professional responsibility or professional conduct) that their supervising attorneys are obligated to follow, or else the belief that paralegals are professionals might prove incorrect.

To put the legal assistant's role and ethical obligations in perspective, it is necessary that we first examine how one becomes a lawyer and then determine what rules of ethics are incumbent on that profession. The subsequent chapters will analyze specific themes of the ethics rules, with emphasis on how they affect paralegals. Throughout this book, the terms *paralegal* and *legal assistant* will be used interchangeably, as they are often considered synonymous, with some regions in the United States preferring one title over the other. (However, not all groups consider the terms equally, as will be discussed in Chapter 2.)

WHO REGULATES LAWYERS AND THE PRACTICE OF LAW?

Once one graduates from law school, having endured years of torture, tedium, and triviality, the next step is to take—and pass—the bar exam. The practice of law is jurisdiction-specific; there is no such thing as a national bar exam. An applicant to the bar must take the bar exam of the state (including the District of Columbia) where one wants to be licensed to practice law. There are few exceptions; one of those would be if an attorney has passed a **multi-state bar exam**. Where jurisdictions allow out-of-state applicants to be licensed, those jurisdictions will likely use the Multistate Bar Exam (MBE) and the Multistate Essay Exam (MEE), both created by the National Conference of Bar Examiners. These exams test the applicant's general knowledge about particular subjects of the law without regard to state specifics and peculiarities. Those exams have scaled scores (similar to a curve), and just a few jurisdictions will license an attorney based solely on the applicant's MBE score without requiring the applicant to take a concurrent or separate bar exam. For example, the District of Columbia will admit someone to the practice of law if the applicant has graduated from an ABA-approved law school, has a scaled MBE score of 133, and has passed his jurisdiction's written bar exam at the time he requests to be admitted in Washington, D.C. Attorneys also can seek permission to practice law on a limited basis in another jurisdiction by seeking permission from that jurisdiction's highest court, which is called *pro hac vice.*

Despite the jokes made about lawyer ethics, a premium is placed on ethics as a prerequisite to being admitted to the bar. As part of applying for permission to take the bar exam, an applicant must be found morally fit to practice law, and permission can be refused based on prior conduct, including having a felony conviction. Recently, state bar associations have begun to debate whether members of hate groups who advocate violence toward others should be denied entrance into the bar. Some have argued that one cannot swear to uphold the Constitution—which is part of the lawyer's oath—and, at the same time, seek to deny, by violence or other methods, the constitutional rights of others.

Beyond the bar exam, applicants to practice law in every jurisdiction but the state of Washington must also pass a legal ethics exam, which can be taken before the applicant takes the bar exam. This exam, the Multistate Professional Responsibility Exam (MPRE), also created by the National Conference of Bar Examiners, questions the applicant's specific knowledge and application of the rules of professional responsibility. The exam is also scaled and, depending on the jurisdiction, a passing score ranges from 75 to 86. So, after paying one's

▓ **multi-state bar exam**

A bar exam that allows the successful applicant to be licensed in more than one jurisdiction. Such an exam is a result of a reciprocity agreement between the jurisdictions.

examination fees, passing the bar exam (which in many jurisdictions is a multi-day, essay extravaganza), passing the ethics exam, and paying the appropriate court membership fees, the applicant now becomes an attorney and is obligated by the oath of admission to the bar to honor his jurisdiction's rules of ethics.

Passing the bar exam, by the way, is no walk in the park. Although it is human nature to exaggerate the difficulty of accomplishing something even mildly difficult, many smart and diligent people who take the bar exam fail on their first or second attempt (or more). Passing rates vary jurisdictionally, and some jurisdictions have notoriously difficult rates. New York's 2005 pass rate for those taking its bar exam in February was 47 percent, while Utah's 2005 pass rate in February was 85 percent. That does not mean that New York law students are

NOT QUITE LINCOLN

"If This Law Practice Thing Doesn't Work Out, I Can Always Go Back to Divinity School"

James Hamm's 2004 Character and Fitness Report, filed with the Arizona State Bar Committee on Character and Fitness, had one fact on it that, it is hoped, rarely appears: Hamm had committed first-degree murder in 1974. When he was a 26-year-old divinity school dropout, Hamm began selling marijuana. Hamm and an accomplice shot and killed two unsuspecting customers, as part of a plan to rob them during a sale. Hamm shot one of the victims in the back of the head. Having pled guilty to first-degree murder, he was sentenced to life in prison with no chance of parole for 25 years. But, after earning a college degree from behind bars, getting married, and founding a prison reform advocacy group, Hamm's sentence was commuted in 1989, and he was released in 1992. He graduated from the Arizona University College of Law, and he passed the bar exam in 1999. However,

when his admission to the bar was denied in 2004 on character and fitness grounds, he appealed to the Arizona Supreme Court.

Acknowledging that it had found no case where a first-degree murderer had been admitted to the bar of any state, the Court nonetheless inquired into whether Hamm was fully rehabilitated. The Court concluded that Hamm had not met the high burden. The Court also took note that not only did Hamm still seem to shift the blame for the murders (three were killed), but he also had never paid any child support to his former wife for a child born in 1969.

In fact, Hamm argued—in a way that shows he at least thought like a lawyer—he had never received the final divorce decree, even though he had been arrested in 1973 for failing to pay child support. James Hamm's admission to the Arizona Bar was denied on lack of demonstrating good moral character.

not as smart as those in Utah (although the former might have more study distractions). Evidence of that is John F. Kennedy, Jr., who was the object of jokes and ridicule after failing the New York bar exam twice. However, he was never considered anything but intelligent, courteous, and ethical during his life, which was tragically cut short by a plane crash in 1998. See Exhibit 1–2 for a few bar exam statistics.

NOT QUITE LINCOLN

"If This Law Practice Thing Doesn't Work Out, I Can Always Go Back to Teaching."

William Vaughn's fifth application to the Oklahoma Board of Bar Examiners was denied in 1988 on grounds that he lacked sufficient moral character and fitness for the practice of law. It is too bad unmitigated gall was not considered an element of character. Vaughn would have nailed that.

It seems that, during the course of Vaughn's career as a high school teacher, he was believed to have had sexual relationships in 1983 and 1984 with two 14-year-old female students. He was arrested and charged with sodomy and statutory rape in the first instance.

Vaughn argued that because all charges against him were eventually dropped, he was being unfairly judged by the Board of Bar Examiners. The Oklahoma Supreme Court saw things a bit differently, and agreed with the Board that Vaughn lacked the requisite moral character.

Exercising his constitutional right against self-incrimination, Vaughn refused to discuss with the Board of Bar Examiners the circumstances surrounding the charges brought against him. (Those charges also eventually resulted in his dismissal from his school on grounds of moral turpitude.) Vaughn then argued that the dropped charges tend to show that he did not commit the acts that led to his arrest. On paper, that sounds pretty good. However, the overwhelming evidence showed that in the first instance Vaughn had written love letters to the girl, had promised to marry her, and had sexual relations with her.

However, due to pretrial maneuvering by the defense and the victim's unwillingness to testify after the first preliminary hearing, the charges were dropped.

Then, Vaughn used the same tactics all over again, with another 14-year old girl, who he helped run away from home for a time. And just for good measure, one of Vaughn's two character witnesses testified at Vaughn's character and fitness hearing that she did not think there was anything improper about a 28-year-old man dating a 14-year-old girl. It was no surprise when the Oklahoma Supreme Court affirmed the Board's denial of Vaughn's application.

EXHIBIT I–2   SAMPLE SELECTION OF THOSE WHO TOOK AND PASSED THE 2005 BAR EXAM

Jurisdiction and Length of Exam	Took the February Bar	Passed the February Bar	Took the July Bar	Passed the July Bar	Total Number of Applicants and Those Who Passed	Total Passing Percentage
Alaska/2.5 days	52	44	70	39	132/83	63%
California/3 days	4,520	1,810	8,343	4,072	12,863/5,882	46%
Illinois/2 days	1,059	734	2,813	2,274	3,872/3,008	78%
New York/2 days	3,213	1,525	10,175	6,809	13,388/8,334	62%
South Carolina/2 days	178	134	390	318	568/452	80%

Source: National Conference of Bar Examiners 2005 Statistics

Depending on where lawyers practice, they might need to keep a copy of another set of rules in their offices. They will first have consulted the Admission and Discipline Rules, which procedurally control how one might get into (and get kicked out of) the bar, and the Rules of Professional Conduct, which control how lawyers (and their paralegals and legal assistants) are to behave professionally. In addition to the just-stated rules, many state and local bar associations have passed codes or creeds of civility or courtesy. Such codes or creeds might be a sincere attempt to combat the contemptible opinion of lawyers held by many of those who are not the parents of lawyers. These nonbinding codes are those to which lawyers should aspire. They include standards or maxims that focus on how lawyers should agree to treat one another, judges, their clients, and the general public in the course of their professional lives. Washington, D.C., the city with the most lawyers per capita in the world, has a civility code worthy of the bureaucracy and legalese that makes that city run. That code has nine separate portions, each with its own rules of civility, along with a preamble that is six full paragraphs.

By contrast, Alabama (the first state with a formal code of ethics) has a State Bar Code of Professional Courtesy that has 19 sentence-length directives, including: "A lawyer should always be punctual." The Boston Bar Association Civility Standards for Civil Litigation has a section that concerns depositions, and part of it states, "A lawyer should not inquire into a deponent's personal affairs or question a deponent's integrity where such inquiry is irrelevant to the subject matter of the deposition." Included in the Virginia Bar Association Creed is a statement on the treatment lawyers should accord each other, which states, "As a professional, I should always: 1. Attempt to determine compatible dates with opposing counsel before scheduling motions, meetings and depositions... 9.

Avoid personal criticism of another lawyer." And the Beverly Hills Bar Association Guidelines of Professional Courtesy announces its opposition to unnecessarily emptying an opponent's pockets when it says, "I will advise my client that I will not engage in tactics intended to delay unreasonably resolution of the matter or to harass, abuse or drain the other party's financial resources."

State and local bar associations do not regulate their members' conduct the way the courts do, but bar associations have a role in discipline in several ways. First, a bar association has its own membership bylaws and can sanction its members for bylaw violations. Second, a bar association can contact its jurisdiction's highest court (the regulating court) to make recommendations regarding the regulation of the practice of law, including the unauthorized practice of law. Some jurisdictions have a **unified bar association**, which means that membership is required upon being granted a law license. More than 30 states have such associations, which are also known as integrated bar associations. Other jurisdictions make the decision to join the bar association a voluntary one.

WHAT ARE RULES OF ETHICS?

Rules of ethics, more formally known as rules of professional responsibility or professional conduct, are those rules created by the American Bar Association (ABA), the largest and most powerful national bar association in America. Founded in New York in 1878 and headquartered in Chicago, Illinois, the ABA has over 400,000 members. The ABA's first set of ethics rules was its Canons of Professional Ethics in 1908, which was based in large part on the Alabama Bar Association Code of Ethics, from 1887. The inspiration for Alabama's Code of Ethics can be traced to the lectures of Judge George Sharswood in the 1850s; Sharswood's lectures were later published as a book, *Professional Ethics*.

In 1969, the ABA adopted the Model Code of Professional Responsibility. The Model Code was organized by three distinctions: Canons, which were general statements of ethical ideals; Ethical Considerations, which were aspirational statements associated with the Canons and signified as *EC*; and Disciplinary Rules, which were the mandatory portions of the Model Code and signified by *DR*.

In 1983, and after a six-year process, the ABA adopted the Model Rules of Professional Conduct, designed to replace the Model Code of Professional Responsibility. Formatted differently and with some substantive changes, the Model Rules consist of mandatory rules, followed by advisory paragraphs, called **comments**.

In 1997, the ABA Commission on Evaluation of the Model Rules of Professional Conduct, more commonly known as the Ethics 2000 Commission, was appointed to put forward a report concerning revising the Model Rules. The Ethics 2000 Commission issued a report in November 2000, and then issued its final report in August 2001. Some of the proposals in the two reports included

■ unified bar association

A bar association whose members must join upon being admitted to the practice of law in a particular jurisdiction. It is also known as an integrated bar association.

■ comments

In this context, a comment is the official commentary of the rules committee that follows specific rules of court. Comments are designed to give meaning to the specific rules.

allowing more discretion for attorneys to disclose client confidences, requiring all fee agreements to be in writing, expressly banning sexual relationships between lawyers and clients, and prohibiting real-time Internet solicitation of clients. None of the Ethics 2000 proposals would go into effect until the governing body of the ABA, known as the ABA House of Delegates, specifically adopted the proposals.

At the August 2001 meeting of the ABA House of Delegates, and also at the February 2002 mid-year meeting of the ABA House of Delegates, the delegates voted on and approved many of the recommendations of the Ethics 2000 Commission. Some of the Ethics 2000 proposals rejected by the House of Delegates included declining to require that lawyers put all fee agreements with their clients in writing, and declining to expand a lawyer's discretion to reveal confidential information to the extent proposed by the Ethics 2000 Commission. The ABA House of Delegates voted on further amendments to Ethics 2000 in 2003. These amendments concerned reassessing the lawyer's ethical responsibility in a corporate environment, with the ABA approving more exceptions to the rules on confidentiality, thus allowing a lawyer to disclose client confidences when the lawyer's services have resulted in the client committing fraud, in turn resulting in substantial injury. *See* ABA MR 1.6 (b), and 1.13. Throughout this book's chapters that concern specific ethics issues, the Ethics 200 proposals and changes to the corresponding parts of the ABA Model Rules will be discussed. Please see Exhibit 1-3 for a family tree of legal ethics.

It is important to understand that the ABA's various sets of ethics rules are not operative on lawyers, even those who are members of the ABA. This is because the ABA, being a private organization, does not license attorneys. The rules that apply to any lawyer are the particular ABA version that has been

---

EXHIBIT I–3   A LEGAL ETHICS GENEALOGY

- 1850s   Alabama Judge George Sharswood's lectures lead to the book, *Professional Ethics*

- 1887   Alabama Bar Association Code of Ethics

- 1908   ABA Canons of Professional Ethics

- 1969   ABA Model Code of Professional Responsibility

- 1983   ABA Model Rules of Professional Conduct

- 1997   ABA Ethics 2000 Commission created

- 2002   ABA House of Delegates votes on the Ethics 2000 recommendations

- 2003   ABA House of Delegates votes on a few Ethics 2000 Amendments

■ jurisdiction

In this context, jurisdiction means a particular place over which a court has authority, usually a state.

adopted by the highest appellate court in the state where a lawyer is licensed. A state Supreme Court, having **jurisdiction** over its lawyers and their professional behavior, always has the authority to change the language of an ABA ethics rule it chooses to adopt or to refuse to adopt certain parts of the ABA ethics rules. For example, Florida's Rules of Professional Conduct are based on the ABA Model Rules. However, Florida's rule on the solicitation of clients differs from the ABA Model Rules version in that it prohibits a lawyer from contacting in writing a prospective personal injury client for 30 days after an accident. Florida Rules of Professional Conduct, Rule 4–7.4(b)(1)(A). Once adopted by a jurisdiction, though, a jurisdiction's rules of conduct are the ones that jurisdiction's attorneys must follow, and not the ABA's rules. According to the 2001 edition of the *ABA Compendium of Professional Responsibility Rules and Standards,* 42 states, the District of Columbia, and the Virgin Islands have ethics codes based on the ABA's Model Rules of Professional Conduct. Iowa, Nebraska, New York, Ohio, Oregon, and Puerto Rico have ethics codes that are based on the ABA's Model Code of Professional Responsibility. But by 2007, states such as Iowa (in 2005), Nebraska (in 2005), Ohio (in 2007), and Oregon (in 2005) had joined the overwhelming majority and adopted the ABA Model Rules and its format. See Exhibit 1–4 for jurisdictions and their sources of ethics rules.

The process of shelving the ABA Model Code and adopting a version of the ABA Model Rules often involves the state's Supreme Court appointing an ad hoc committee to investigate and report on the prospects of adopting a new and different set of ethics rules. The committee's positive report will be made available to the state bar association and its members, so they can comment on that report. Eventually, the regulating court will vote to adopt the new ethics rules and set an effective date for the new rules, which is usually January 1st of the year after the court's final decision. Ohio's new ethics rules have been prepared in a reader-friendly way that makes the transition from the Model Code to the Model Rules quite smooth for such a full-scale change. At the conclusion of each rule, in not only an official Comment (in keeping with the Model Rules format), but also in a section that compares the new rule to its ancestor—the official ABA Model Rule version—there is an accounting for any changes made to the "model" by the Ohio Supreme Court.

Rules of professional responsibility, being adopted by state Supreme Courts instead of passed by legislatures, are **rules of court**, rather than statutes. Be advised, though, that some jurisdictions have placed their lawyer ethics codes in their statutory codes. For instance, New York's Code of Professional Responsibility is located in the Appendix of the "Judiciary Law" section of the New York Statutes. The more common kinds of rules of court with which legal and paralegal students are familiar include rules of trial procedure, rules of appellate procedure, and rules of evidence. A student who truly wants to grasp the principles in this textbook must, in addition to reading it, study his or her own state's rules of professional responsibility. The nuances of those rules instruct legal assistants how to protect their professionalism and, most critically, the

■ rules of court

Sets of rules that are adopted by the highest appellate court of a jurisdiction and apply to the practice of law, unlike statutes, which are passed by a legislature and apply to all.

licenses of their employers. Such protection is important because, as discussed in detail in Chapter 2, supervising attorneys are responsible for the conduct of their non-lawyer employees and assistants.

When studying your jurisdiction's rules of court, it is always preferable to use an **annotated** rules of court, as opposed to an official set of rules. Both sets have the same rules in them, but an annotated rules of court (similar to an annotated statutory code), which is published by a company instead of the government, contains more than just the rules. Following the rules and comments are case summaries—specific to that jurisdiction—that correspond to the particular rule. For instance, if you are using an annotated version when looking at your state's rule on solicitation (likely to be Rule 7.3 if your state has adopted the ABA Model Rules), you can find summaries of cases in your state, with their citations, that have interpreted the meaning of the rule on solicitation. By measuring all three angles to this triangle—the rules, the official commentary, and any cases interpreting the rules—you will find yourself as capable as any lawyer of understanding the significance of professional ethics.

■ **annotated**

When a rule of court or statute is annotated, that means it is privately published and comes with research material in addition to the statute or rule.

EXHIBIT 1–4 JURISDICTIONS AND THEIR SOURCE OF ATTORNEY ETHICS RULES

Jurisdictions Not Following The Format Of The ABA Model Code Or Model Rules	Jurisdictions Following The Format Of The ABA Model Code	Jurisdictions Following The Format Of The ABA Model Rules
California (but it is considering adopting the Model Rules)	**New York** (but it is considering adopting the Model Rules)	**Every Other Jurisdiction**
Maine (but it is considering adopting the Model Rules)	**Puerto Rico**	

A SUMMARY OF THE DISCIPLINARY PROCESS

Although not identical in every jurisdiction, the disciplinary process generally includes four similar components: complaint, investigation, prosecution, and appeal. Anyone can file a complaint against an attorney, called a **grievance**, with the **disciplinary commission**, or similarly titled agency, of that attorney's jurisdiction. While it is natural to think of a disgruntled client filing a grievance, fellow attorneys, judges, bar associations, and even members of the public also may and do file them. Regardless of who makes the complaint, all grievances are formally made in writing and under oath. Jurisdictions often provide **immunity** to those who file grievances, which protects those persons filing from being sued by those against whom they have complained. And as interpreted by many courts, the doctrine of immunity protects grievants from being sued for defamation if their complaints are false, intentional or otherwise. For an example of the unintended blessing of immunity, see the *Not Quite Lincoln*

■ **grievance**

One's allegation that something denies some equitable or legal right, or causes injustice.

■ **disciplinary commission**

A panel consisting mostly of lawyers and authorized by a state's highest court to investigate and prosecute lawyer misconduct.

■ immunity

A grant of protection made by prosecutors to witnesses, which prevents them from being prosecuted for their testimony or written statements, except where their assertions are lies.

in Chapter 2. That section relates the story of the paralegal who filed false charges with the state bar against her former boss as revenge because he fired her after a week of employment. Anonymous complaints might be made against an attorney, but any consequent grievance would have to be formally filed by a jurisdiction's disciplinary commission, which has the authority, on its own initiative, to file a grievance against an attorney. An example of an anonymous complaint would be if one attorney believes another's Yellow Pages advertisement violates the rules on advertising, and then cuts the ad out and mails it to the disciplinary commission.

Once filed with a state's disciplinary commission, it is the task of that agency, generally operating under the authority of that state's highest court, to investigate the allegation. If a complaint is groundless on its face, or without merit, the commission then disposes of it. For example, if a client files a grievance against his or her lawyer, complaining that the fees were too high, that type of complaint is likely to be dismissed unless something in the grievance shows a fee that was unreasonable. (See Chapter 7 on what makes a fee reasonable.) It is obvious that we all would prefer to pay less for every product or service we have purchased, especially when those products or services do not meet our lofty expectations. However, when a grievance warrants investigation, the disciplinary commission notifies the attorney that he or she is the subject of a grievance. The lawyer is then required to respond in writing to the investigative team. At this stage, it is advisable that the lawyer hire legal representation because occasionally a lawyer will land himself in trouble after writing an obscenity-laced, incomplete, or even damning answer to the charges the irate lawyer thinks are unfounded. During this phase, members of the disciplinary commission gather facts related to the grievance in conjunction with the lawyer's response.

■ adjudication

The process of formally resolving a controversy, based on evidence presented.

If the commission finds after its investigation that there is reasonable cause to believe the attorney committed the alleged misconduct, the commission will file a formal complaint against the attorney. Attorneys from the disciplinary commission act in the **adjudication** similarly to prosecuting attorneys, and lawyers who are the subject of formal ethics charges would be remiss not to have representation by this time. This brings to mind the tired but true cliché: "He who represents himself has a fool for a client." A special hearing officer, often a judge, will be appointed to preside over the eventual disciplinary hearing and the accompanying evidentiary disputes. If the attorney is found to be in violation of the rules, then a sanction will be recommended. Sanctions can range from a reprimand (private or public) to suspension or disbarment. When an attorney is suspended for a short term (less than six months), reinstatement usually occurs automatically at the conclusion of the suspension. When more severe violations result in a long-term suspension, the attorney must apply for reinstatement at the suspension's end. Disbarment usually means forever, but some jurisdictions, such as Florida, allow a disbarred attorney to apply for readmission to the bar some years after the disbarment.

Disciplinary sanctions are generally not final until they have been approved by the highest court in the jurisdiction (i.e., the state Supreme Court), because that court has authority over the lawyers licensed in its jurisdiction. Furthermore, an attorney has the right to appeal any finding of misconduct and/or sanction issued against him. Results of those appeals can range from approving the hearing officer's findings and sanction, rejecting them completely (including when the hearing officer finds in favor of the attorney), or agreeing with the "verdict" while altering the recommended discipline. When the appellate court renders its decision, the opinion it provides serves two purposes: first, to explain to the attorney the basis for the court's decision; and, second, to make precedent so that other attorneys in the jurisdiction—and their paralegals and legal assistants—can better understand how to follow the legal ethics rules. Please see Exhibit 1-5 for a summary of the common types of attorney discipline.

EXHIBIT 1–5   TYPES OF ATTORNEY DISCIPLINE

- **Reprimand or Censure**
  For slight infractions, the attorney's name might be protected from disclosure (For example, In Re Anonymous)

- **Short Suspension**
  Usually, the attorney's reinstatement is automatic after the suspension

- **Significant Suspension**
  Usually, the attorney needs to apply for reinstatement

- **Disbarment**
  Disbarment is not always permanent (Florida has a five year disbarment option)

WHY DOESN'T THE LEGISLATURE REGULATE THE PRACTICE OF LAW?

Much of the law that regulates the daily lives of citizens is statutory, coming from the legislature. Trades and occupations, such as construction, and professions, such as medicine, are regulated by a variety of legislative and administrative rules. But the legal profession is different. With limited exceptions, state Supreme Courts, rather than legislatures, regulate the practice of law. There are two primary reasons for this. One reason is connected to the fact that courts are composed of lawyers, and the second concerns the principle of **judicial review**.

The first reason seems obvious. Lawyers become judges, and judges work in courts. Even though most lawsuits are settled before trial and many lawyers are not litigators, everything a lawyer does for a client may end up in a court. Because

judicial review
The doctrine from *Marbury v. Madison* that gives appellate courts the right to review the constitutionality of the acts of the legislative and executive branches, in addition to reviewing the decision of lower courts.

the practice of law is very much like a regulated monopoly (one cannot do legal work for someone else without first being licensed to engage in the practice of law), then tradition dictates that courts will be the most appropriate regulator of the legal profession. In fact, some state constitutions grant their state's highest court the power to set the requirements for the right to practice law. For example, the Indiana constitution, in the fourth section of Article Seven, grants the Indiana Supreme Court the exclusive right to regulate the practice of law.

That, however, does not explain why legislatures rarely intrude into the regulation of the practice of law. After all, state legislatures are filled with lawyers, so it would seem that they would also be inherently knowledgeable about the legal profession. Furthermore, nothing requires legislators to have worked in the construction industry, for example, in order to have the right to draft laws concerning the construction industry. This brings us to judicial review, a hallowed doctrine in constitutional law with which all legal students should be acquainted. The doctrine of judicial review comes from *Marbury v. Madison* 5 U.S. 137 (1803), a case whose significance is not to be underestimated and is worthy of background explanation.

The U.S. Constitution replaced the Articles of Confederation as the first document governing the country. Two camps opposed each other in the constitutional ratification fight: **federalists**, who believed in the need for a powerful, even unlimited federal government; and **antifederalists**, who did not. The second president, John Adams, was a federalist who, as he was leaving office, appointed a number of federalist judges after Congress passed what became known as the "Midnight Judges Act." After Thomas Jefferson, an antifederalist, took office as the third president, it was discovered that some of those judges had yet to have their official commissions (documents of employment) delivered to them, an oversight by Adam's secretary of state. President Jefferson ordered his secretary of state, James Madison (father of the Constitution), to refuse delivery of the seals, thereby keeping some of Adams's federalist judges off the federal bench. William Marbury was one of those judges. He had been given a justice of the peace job in the District of Columbia, and, like any good American, he sued. But he took his lawsuit directly to the United States Supreme Court, rather than to a federal, trial court.

The Supreme Court was led by its federalist Chief Justice, John Marshall, whose opinion alone in *Marbury v. Madison* makes him, according to some, the most powerful Chief Justice ever. Justice Marshall decided the case in a most unusual way. He first declared Marbury right in his assertion that he had been wrongfully denied his federal job, but then declared him the loser under a line of reasoning that we know as "judicial review." Marshall declared that a federal statute passed in 1789 authorized Marbury to bring his suit originally to the Supreme Court, whereas the Constitution gives the Supreme Court authority over such a suit only in its appellate function. Setting up such a self-opposing premise allowed Marshall to debate the question of which is superior—the Constitution, or an act of Congress that contradicts the Constitution? Chief

■ **federalists**

A founding father who believed in the need for the federal government to have unlimited power, as designed in the Constitution.

■ **antifederalists**

A founding father who opposed the design of the Constitution because it provided for an unlimited federal government.

Justice Marshall argued that because America's new government was based on a written constitution, the Constitution must be higher than a federal statute, whose existence flows from the Constitution. He viewed the Constitution as "superior . . . law, unchangeable by ordinary means." *Marbury*, at 177. Therefore, the statute in question must be invalid because it contradicts the Constitution.

Another question presented in *Marbury* was whether the Supreme Court had the power to declare a statute unconstitutional, because the Supreme Court was given authority in the Constitution over lower courts, but not another branch of government such as Congress. Marshall resolved this question in favor of the Supreme Court by declaring that, "[I]t is emphatically the province and duty of the judicial department to say what the law is. . . . If two laws conflict with each other, the courts must decide on the operation of each. . . . *This is the very essence of judicial duty.*" *Marbury*, at 177, 178. (Emphasis added.) And that is the doctrine of judicial review. The U.S. Supreme Court, in *Marbury v. Madison*, created a power for itself not granted to it in the Constitution, but not questioned since 1803, holding that it had ultimate authority over any law, whatever the source.

How does that apply to the regulation of the practice of law? First, judicial review is a doctrine whose scope extends to state Supreme Courts, giving them the power to declare state laws void. Second, because the practice of law is regulated on a state level, rather than a national level, state Supreme Courts grant their own lawyers—and perhaps paralegals some day—the right to practice law. Therefore, when a state legislature passes a law dealing with lawyers, the right to practice law, or the expansion of the rights of non-lawyers to engage in certain legal transactions, it is likely that the Supreme Court of that state will strike down the statute as an impermissible intrusion into the Supreme Court's business. Keep this in mind, and you will better understand how the regulation of the practice of law is unlike that of any other occupation or profession.

Poor old Marbury never did get his justice of the peace job, because after Jefferson served two terms as president, James Madison was elected, then reelected to the Presidency. Madison never granted to Marbury that which Jefferson had originally ordered to be denied. Those are the breaks, as they say, in the world of political patronage. And in the spirit of Paul Harvey, here is the twist to *Marbury v. Madison*: President Adams's secretary of state, the one who neglected to deliver the judicial commission to William Marbury, was none other than John Marshall, the Chief Justice. Perhaps that makes Marbury's decision to go directly to the Supreme Court more logical. Considering that Marbury brought his case to the Court in 1801, it might seem curious that the decision was not handed down until 1803. However, Chief Justice Marshall's infamous opinion in *Marbury* was not delayed due to court congestion, but was actually delivered about a month after the conclusion of the case. So rancorous was the fighting between Marshall's federalists and Jefferson's antifederalists that the Supreme Court was actually closed for 14 months after Marbury filed suit. The closure was due to a law passed in 1801 that nearly stripped the federalist Supreme Court of its official sessions. Politics has always been a contact sport.

NOT QUITE LINCOLN

"May It Please the Court" Was Not Meant to Be Taken Literally."

While watching a grandfather's emotional testimony in a murder case of his grandchild in 2003, jurors thought they heard a whooshing sound. It sounded like a blood pressure cuff was being pumped.

During a break in the trial, a police officer who also overheard the sound approached Oklahoma Judge Donald Thomson's bench. The police officer found a penis-enlargement pump behind the bench.

How can we conclude that it belonged to Judge Thomson? It was his courtroom. Also, the judge's long-time court reporter Lisa Foster confirmed it was his. Foster, who wept during her testimony at Thomson's 2006 indecent exposure trial, said she had personally seen him use it on himself during court on many occasions, starting in 2000.

Jurors from Judge Thomson's court testified that they saw and heard him using it on himself during trials. In addition, tape recordings of two trials in 2003 capture the pumping sounds.

There was even testimony by witnesses that they had observed Judge Thomson conduct trials while taking his shoes off and shining them, clipping his toenails, and spitting tobacco.

What defense did this 23-year judge and former state representative make to such bizarre and grotesque charges? His lawyer claimed the pump was a gag gift from the judge's best friend, and the judge just happened to keep the gift at his bench, but that he never used it during court. Furthermore, the defense claimed the former jurors, from their location in the jury box, could never have seen Judge Thomson using the pump—not exactly a sterling endorsement of the device. And, of course, the defense claimed Judge Thomson was the victim of a political smear by Lisa Foster and the local police.

After five hours of deliberation, the jury, who were seen giggling and guffawing throughout the trial, found Judge Thomson guilty on all four counts of indecent exposure. He was sentenced to four years in prison.

If more salacious details are sought on the self-help judge, they can be found at The Smoking Gun, the great Web site custodian of celebrity or notorious legal information and public records: http://www.smokinggun.com.

NOT QUITE LINCOLN

What If the Looks on Their Faces Were Pity Instead of Shock?

The women of Columbus, Ohio, have nothing to fear, or perhaps mock, any longer, now that the self-exposing photographer who had been harassing them has been arrested, zipped up, and convicted. For 18 months, this perverted performance artist was photographing the immediate reactions of women to whom he had exposed himself, while wearing only a knit cap for the disguise and sneakers for the getaway.

The most telling exposure was that the naked flasher, finally arrested in 2003 in an alley behind a Kroger's grocery store, was an attorney. By day, Stephen P. Linnen worked as deputy counsel for the Ohio Republican Caucus at the statehouse in Columbus. By night, he roamed the streets looking for victims for his photo album, some of whom he also touched during those encounters. Linnen pleaded guilty to 53 misdemeanors of exposing himself, and was sentenced to 18 months at a work release center.

Throughout the criminal, and disciplinary proceedings, he claimed—and who would not —that he suffered from a sexual addiction, and that the stress of his job caused the peculiar relief he exhaustingly sought. These alibis were unpersuasive to the Ohio Board of Commissioners on Grievances and Discipline. The unconvinced commissioners noted Linnen's refusal to take the medications prescribed for his claimed sex addiction, as well as his lack of accepting responsibility for traumatizing his victims. The board recommended to the Ohio Supreme Court in 2006 that Mr. Linnen be indefinitely suspended.

HOW TO BRIEF A CASE

Few things annoy legal students more than being assigned cases to brief. That is an understandable reaction because briefing cases is tedious. It requires one to read case law very carefully, often more than once, and often using highlighters. Then it requires the reader to analyze the case, making judgment calls in choosing the portions that are relevant for the reader's needs. Finally, it requires the reader to turn those judgment calls into a coherent, summary form that expresses the essence of the judge's opinion. And that is exactly why case briefing is so important. In a **common law** country, such as America, case law will always be the ultimate answer to any legal question. Therefore, appellate cases will always need to be read and understood. And, at a pragmatic level, the better one gets at legal analysis, the more valuable one becomes, and nothing sharpens

■ **common law**

This phrase has three related definitions. In this context, common law refers to judge-made law, or the process whereby appellate courts make precedent that lower courts must follow. Because of our colonial history with England, America is known as a common law country.

one's legal analysis skills more than briefing cases. As you read the cases in the chapters, understand that they are presented for two reasons: to help you understand how courts interpret the rules of professional responsibility and to help bring those dry rules to life. Be aware that even though a case in the text might have come from your jurisdiction, it does not mean that that case is still followed in its original form or even followed at all.

Like making omelets, everyone has their own method on how to brief cases. My view is that a case brief should consist of five elements: facts, issue, holding, reasoning, and decision. A sixth element could be the dissent, but not all cases have a dissenting opinion. As these elements are explained, bear in mind that your instructor might have a different view on the format of a case brief.

The Facts

Law does not occur in a vacuum. A good case brief starts with its facts section, but to be "brief," a facts section should include only the key facts. As a rule of thumb, key facts are those whose existence not only places the case in a context, but also helps to shape the case's outcome. How is that determined? It is done through careful reading. As you examine the facts from a case in order to brief it, ask yourself if the court could have reached its decision without that fact being in existence. If not, that usually indicates a key fact that should be in your brief.

The Issue

The issue is the brain center of a case brief and the hardest part of a brief to grasp. A good issue asks a legal question, not an "outcome" question. An issue is about what the court has to grapple with in the appeal, not about who wins or loses. A good issue also incorporates some of the key facts into its wording. You know you have written a good issue when it stands on its own—when it, by itself, would allow a reader who has not read the case to still get an understanding of it. Write your issue in the form of a question. Do not be alarmed if your issue reads differently from someone else's, because issues can convey the same legal question but be expressed in different ways.

The Holding

For a case brief, the holding should simply answer the question presented in the issue in as short a method as possible. On a formal level, however, a holding is the pronouncement of law issued by the court's majority opinion; it is the precedent. The holding in a case brief, however, should just answer the issue.

The Reasoning

The reasoning section is the heart of the brief. A good reasoning section tells the reader why the court did what it did or how it reached its conclusion. Because appellate courts most often reach their conclusions through relying on case law, then a question is often raised concerning whether a reasoning section should include case citations. It generally should not, because citations, by themselves, explain nothing. Instead of citations, a reasoning section should give the principles from the precedent cited in the case. Sometimes courts use prominent legal doctrines, commonly called **black letter law**, as the foundation on which their reasoning is built. A court's reasoning is often in the latter part of the opinion and usually makes reference to the facts in the earlier part of the opinion. Likewise, your reasoning section should revisit integral facts in order to summarize the court's analysis.

The Decision

The decision section is procedural in nature. Appellate courts do one of four things with a case: **affirm**, **reverse**, **remand**, or **vacate**. At times, however, courts do more than one of the preceding options in the same opinion. One can usually find the court's decision at either the beginning or the end of the case. If a disciplinary sanction against an attorney is stated or upheld, it is wise to include that sanction in your decision.

Please read the following case twice. Then, try briefing it along the left half of one or two pages of paper, leaving the right half of the paper open. This visual method will allow you to include on the right half of the same section of the brief any critical elements discussed in class that you may have missed, as well as any class notes associated with that case. When you are done briefing the case, look at the following page in the text. There you will find a sample brief of the case. The sample brief will be in italics, with some instructional comments placed in brackets. Compare your brief to the sample for similarities. On a final note, the more one briefs cases, the faster and better one gets at it, so hang in there.

■ black letter law

Legal principles that have become so accepted and unequivocal that they are cited as truisms.

■ affirm

The decision of an appellate court that maintains the status quo and keeps the lower court's decision in place.

■ reverse

The opposite of affirm.

■ remand

A remand occurs when an appellate court sends at least part of an appeal back to a lower court to reexamine the evidence or damages in light of the higher court's decision.

■ vacate

Similar to a remand, but sometimes a higher court vacates a lower court's decision to temporarily set a matter aside with instructions that the lower court rewrite its opinion in light of the higher court's opinion.

CASE LAW   *In the Matter of Anonymous*

689 N.E.2d 434 (Ind. 1997)

PER CURIAM.

Lawyers who advertise that they are "specialists" in a particular area of the law must comply with the provisions of Ind.Admission and Discipline Rule 30. The respondent in this disciplinary action failed to comply with those provisions and for that misconduct will receive a private reprimand. Herein, we set forth the facts and circumstances of this case in order to educate the bar with respect to provisions regarding lawyer specialist certification, while preserving the private nature of the admonishment.

The Commission charged the respondent with violating Rule 7.4(a) of the *Rules of Professional Conduct for Attorneys at Law* by claiming, in an advertisement, that he was a specialist in personal injury law when in fact he was not so certified. Pursuant to Ind. Admission and Discipline Rule 23, Section 11, the respondent and the Commission have agreed that the respondent engaged in misconduct and that a private reprimand is an appropriate sanction. That agreement is now before us for approval.

The parties agree that in 1995, the respondent purchased advertising time on a radio station and provided text for an advertisement of his law office. The text he submitted for the ad was culled from "canned" advertisements the respondent purchased from a legal periodical several years before. The respondent allowed his office manager to send the material to the radio station without first reviewing its contents. On March 15, 1995, the radio station broadcast the advertisement, which stated that the respondent "specialize[d] in personal injury cases." At the time the advertisement aired, the respondent was not certified as a specialist in any area of the law under Ind.Admission and Discipline Rule 30.

Indiana Professional Conduct Rule 7.4(a) provides that lawyers may not express or imply any particular expertise except that authorized by Prof.Cond.R. 7.4(b), which in turn allows certification as a specialist only when authorized by the provisions of Admis.Disc.R. 30. Admission and Discipline Rule 30 provides, in relevant part:

Section 5. Qualification Standards for Certification. -(a) To be recognized as certified in a field of law in the State of Indiana, the lawyer must be duly admitted to the bar of this state, in active status, and in good standing, throughout the period for which the certification is granted. (b) The lawyer must be certified by an ICO [independent certifying organization] approved by CLE [Commission for Continuing Legal Education], and must be in full compliance with the Indiana Bar Certification Review Plan, the rules and policies of the ICO and the rules and policies of CLE.

At the time the respondent's radio advertisement aired, he was not certified as a specialist in the area of personal injury law pursuant to Admis.Disc.R. 30. We therefore find that he violated Prof.Cond.R. 7.4(a) by expressing an expertise when he was not certified as a specialist pursuant to Admis.Disc.R.30. We find that a private reprimand is appropriate in

(continues)

CASE LAW *In the Matter of Anonymous* (continued)

this case largely because the respondent's misconduct was unintentional. The offending content of the advertisement made its way on air due to the respondent's failure to review the material prior to submitting it to the radio station. We therefore view his misconduct as less culpable than if he had knowingly submitted a wrongful advertisement. It is, therefore, ordered that the tendered *Settlement of Circumstances and Conditional Agreement for Discipline* is approved, and accordingly, the respondent is to be given a private reprimand.

SAMPLE BRIEF *In the Matter of Anonymous*

689 N.E.2d 434 (Ind. 1997)

Facts: *The Disciplinary Commission charged an attorney with violating Rule 7.4 of the Indiana Rules Professional Conduct. In 1995, the attorney paid for a radio commercial to advertise his services. The text for his radio spot came from "canned" advertisements he had previously purchased from a legal periodical. The advertisement was given to the radio station by the attorney's paralegal before the attorney reviewed it. The ad stated that the attorney "specialized in personal injury cases." At the time the commercial aired, attorney was not certified as a specialist under Indiana law.*

[Notice that the attorney's name is not listed in this case; this is an example of private discipline. Also, this case is not on appeal to the Indiana Supreme Court because the attorney and the disciplinary commission agreed to the facts and a sanction. The Supreme Court has this case in order to approve the sanction. Your facts should show that the lawyer placed an ad that implied he was a specialist when, at the time of the ad's publication, he was not certified, as required by Rule 7.4. The sample facts section includes the facts about the paralegal because it is *of* importance to know that the lawyer is responsible for the mistake of his employees. Moreover, maybe the paralegal would not have sent the ad at all if he or she had been more aware of the Indiana Rules of Professional Conduct.]

Issue: *When an attorney uses an advertisement that states he "specializes" in some area of the law, is the that equivalent under the rules of professional responsibility to stating he is a "specialist"?*

[Because this is not a traditional appeal, there is no "legal conflict" as earlier described. That makes the issue a bit harder to find. So, instead, craft an issue that would come out of the case if the attorney here was disputing the findings of the disciplinary commission. What would that be? Namely, that he did not say he was a specialist, but that he was specialized, which might mean that he does a lot of a certain kind of cases. Do not forget to use key facts in your issue so that it can stand securely by itself.]

(continues)

SAMPLE BRIEF   *In the Matter of Anonymous* (continued)

Holding:	*Yes.*
	[A reading of the case shows that the attorney did violate the advertising rules, so the answer to our issue is yes.]
Reasoning:	*Rule 7.4 states that one cannot even imply he is a specialist unless he is certified as a specialist, as allowed by Admission Rule 30. That rule says that in order to be certified as a specialist, an attorney must be certified by an independent certifying organization that has been approved by the Indiana Commission for Legal Education. Since the attorney's ad said he specialized in personal injury law, it implied he was a specialist. And, at the time of the ad's broadcast, he was not certified, as required.*
	[This is a case brief, so do not include all of the court's explanation, including copying all of the language from the two rules (MR 7.4, and A&D Rule 30(5)), but include enough to leave you with a definitive explanation. The key to this reasoning section is to close the loop, to show in your brief why the attorney violated the advertising and specialization rules, not to restate that he did violate them, failing to include any of the details.]
Decision:	*The Court agreed that a private reprimand was sufficient here, since the attorney unintentionally violated the advertising and specialization rules.*
	[In attorney discipline cases, the decision will usually include a sanction, or approval of a sanction, unless the Court finds that the rules were not violated. Here, your decision should state why a minimal sanction was given because that shows how intent to break the rules affects a court's sanctioning process.]

A CASE STUDY IN LAWYER DISCIPLINE: THE DISBARMENT PROCEEDINGS AGAINST WILLIAM JEFFERSON CLINTON

■ independent counsel

A special prosecutor, authorized by specific statute with a broad scope of authority to investigate and, if necessary, criminally prosecute high government officials.

On January 19, 2001, the day before leaving office, President Clinton reached a written agreement with Robert Ray, the **independent counsel** who succeeded Kenneth Starr and was in charge of the criminal investigation of what has commonly been called the "Whitewater Matter." That agreement involved President Clinton acknowledging that he misled federal judge Susan Webber Wright, the trial judge overseeing the lawsuit of Paula Jones, filed in 1994 and accusing the president of sexually harassing Ms. Jones in a hotel room in Little Rock when he was governor of Arkansas. The agreement reached between the president and the independent counsel called for the president to pay a $25,000 fine and prevented the president from being criminally charged with obstruction of justice and perjury after leaving office. The agreement also allowed the president to bring a conclusion to the disbarment proceeding pending against him in Arkansas. On that same day, a statement, signed by the president and filed in Little Rock, Arkansas, acknowledged that he "knowingly gave evasive and misleading answers" in his **deposition** from the Paula Jones lawsuit and that his behavior was "prejudicial to the administration of justice." In exchange for admitting such behavior, the president agreed to have his law license suspended for five years.

Then, in October 2001, the U.S. Supreme Court suspended President Clinton from practicing before it and gave the president 40 days to respond by showing cause why he should not be permanently disbarred by the high court. Although President Clinton had never argued a case before the Supreme Court, membership alone is considered a high honor. Initially, President Clinton's lawyer, David Kendall, promised that a response to the Court would be forthcoming, but on November 9, the president formally resigned from the Supreme Court bar. Although many pundits believed it impossible for the president to have been convicted had he been indicted by the special prosecutor, the issue of whether President Clinton would (or should) have been disbarred from the Arkansas bar—which was the recommendation of the Arkansas disciplinary panel—is also likely to be debated for quite some time.

The Background to the Disciplinary Charges

Part of the discovery process in Paula Jones's sexual harassment lawsuit against the president included depositions. At his January 17, 1998, deposition, when asked about his relationship with Monica Lewinsky, the president declared under oath that he had had no sexual relationship with Lewinsky. Furthermore, Ms. Lewinsky put forward an **affidavit** stating the same. Months later, and after giving testimony to the Whitewater grand jury, President Clinton admitted he had been misleading regarding his relationship with Ms. Lewinsky. In April 1999, Judge Weber Wright then held the president in **contempt** for what she found to be his "intentionally false" testimony, rebuking him sharply in her contempt order, fining him $90,000 in attorneys' fees and court costs, and referring the matter to the Arkansas Supreme Court Committee on Professional Conduct. Although being given the opportunity by the nature of Judge Weber Wright's order, the president did not appeal her sanction. Ironically, one year earlier, on April 1, 1998, the Jones lawsuit came to a conclusion when Judge Weber Wright granted the president's motion for **summary judgment**, dismissing the case. Eventually, the president settled with Ms. Jones in November 1998 (while Ms. Jones's appeal of the summary judgment was with the Eighth Circuit Court of Appeals), paying her $850,000.

deposition

A litigation discovery device, similar to testifying at trial, whereby the deponent is put under oath and subject to lawyer's questions. Depositions occur in law offices or conference rooms, but not in courtrooms.

affidavit

A written statement of declaration made under oath and very often in the course of litigation.

contempt

Also known as contempt of court, this is an act or omission that tends to obstruct the administration of justice or shows disrespect for the court; it can include disobeying the instructions or orders of the court.

summary judgment

A litigation strategy in which a trial is prevented because the judge dismisses the case due to two prerequisites: (a) there are no material facts concerning the case that are in disagreement by both parties; and (b) the law applying to the case is on the side of the party who has asked the judge for a summary judgment.

The Nature of the Disciplinary Charges

After its investigation, the Arkansas Supreme Court Committee on Professional Conduct recommended to the Arkansas Supreme Court in May 2000 that President Clinton be disbarred. The committee's letter to the Arkansas Supreme Court stated that a majority of the committee found "that certain of the attorney's conduct as demonstrated in the complaints constituted serious misconduct in violation of Rule 8.4(c) and 8.4(d) of the Arkansas Model Rules of Professional Conduct." The rule in question to which the committee made reference states, "It is professional misconduct for a lawyer to: (c) engage in conduct involving dishonesty, fraud, deceit or misrepresentation; (d) engage in conduct that is prejudicial to the administration of justice." Because the Model Rules (or state versions of them) have official comments that follow specific rules, it is interesting to notice some of the language in the Comment to Rule 8.4.

Paragraph 1 of that Comment notes that "some matters of personal morality, such as adultery and comparable offenses . . . have no specific connection to the fitness for the practice of law." That paragraph then speaks to the kind of morality with which the Rules are concerned. "Offenses involving violence, dishonesty, breach of trust, or serious interference with the administration of justice are in that category." Ironically, Paragraph 3 of that Comment states, "Lawyers holding public office assume legal responsibilities going beyond those of other citizens. A lawyer's abuse of public office can suggest an inability to fulfill the professional role of an attorney."

The Debate over Disbarment

While it is hard to separate the legal issues from the political issues in a case such as this, the question of whether it would have been appropriate to disbar President Clinton provides a fascinating framework for analyzing lawyer discipline. Those who were in favor of disbarment have made a few key points:

- *A Lawyer Lied under Oath.* Bill Clinton is an attorney, and anything short of disbarment would be an insufficient deterrent to both lawyers and non-lawyers who might also consider lying under oath. If lying under oath is not interference with the administration of justice, then what is? Those who commit perjury can be charged with a crime, so why should the president not be disbarred?

- *This Lawyer Is Also the President.* President Richard Nixon lost his New York law license due to his deception, even though he was never under oath when he made misleading or false statements. Remember that the Comment to Rule 8.4 states that lawyers holding public office should be held to a higher standard and that no lawyer can hold any higher public office than president of the United States. Before becoming president,

Clinton was an Arkansas law professor, Arkansas attorney general, and also governor, and thus should be more than cognizant of the ramifications of lying under oath.

- *The Arkansas Disciplinary Commission Recommended Disbarment.* According to Howard Brill, an ethics professor at the University of Arkansas Law School (and former colleague of the president), the Arkansas Supreme Court very often upholds the recommendation of a disciplinary panel. Furthermore, the Arkansas Supreme Court, in a recent opinion on lawyer ethics, quoted another state Supreme Court by stating, "There simply is 'no place in the law for a man or woman who cannot tell the truth, even when his or her own interests are involved.'" *Shochet v. Arkansas Board of Law Examiners*, 979 S.W.2d 888, at 894 (Ark. 1998). And because the president never appealed the contempt sanction of Judge Weber Wright, which was a harsh condemnation against his false testimony, how could the president argue that he should not be disbarred because he did not lie?

Those who would oppose the disbarment of the president make arguments that are equally compelling:

- *The President Never Lied.* David Kendall, the president's lawyer in this matter, always maintained that President Clinton gave evasive answers in that deposition, but not legally false answers. Furthermore, the president did not commit perjury, even assuming he lied. Because the Lewinsky relationship was determined to be irrelevant to the Jones lawsuit—one that was ultimately dismissed—then President Clinton's misleading statements were not material to the case and, therefore, not perjury.

- *The President's Statements in That Deposition Concerned His Private Life.* Although a public figure, President Clinton's consensual relationship with Ms. Lewinsky has no bearing whatsoever on anything related to his law license. In fact, the Comment to Rule 8.4, under which the president was charged, clearly states that personal issues of morality, such as adultery, are not a specific concern of the Arkansas Model Rules of Professional Responsibility. Therefore, even if the president did lie, such a lie had nothing to do with him as a lawyer, but rather concerned him as a man, who would naturally be evasive in these circumstances.

- *The President Was Acting as a Client, Not as a Lawyer.* Beyond the fact that Mr. Clinton's obfuscation was of a personal nature, it was made in his role as a witness, not as a lawyer. Because the president was not representing himself in the lawsuit, one could not even make the leap of an argument that he, as a lawyer, assisted himself, as a witness, in deceiving the court. The rules of professional responsibility apply to lawyers acting as lawyers, which was not the case here.

If possible, put aside your political ideologies and personal opinions of President Clinton. Now, revisit the issues and choose the disciplinary sanction: disbarment, suspension, or reprimand. While a five-year suspension and disbarment from the U.S. Supreme Court bar are undoubtedly heavy sanctions, those sanction have a practical mootness, because there is no indication that the former president, now living both in Washington, D.C., and in the New York City region, will be practicing law in Arkansas or arguing cases before the U.S. Supreme Court. Examine your own state's rules of professional responsibility for its version of Rule 8.4, or DR 1–102(A) for those in a Model Code jurisdiction. If you use an annotated Rules of Court, such as those published by West Legal Studies, then read the annotations that follow that Rule's Comment to see if there are any cases in your state on lawyers being disbarred for lying, whether or not under oath.

In the following case, the New Jersey Supreme Court disbarred a lawyer for misappropriating his clients' funds. While reading it, notice that the Court is perplexed about how the attorney's alcoholism affected the Court's decision to disbar him.

CASE LAW *In the Matter of Hein*

516 A.2d 1105 (N.J.1986)

PER CURIAM.

This matter arises from a report of the Disciplinary Review Board (DRB) recommending disbarment of respondent. The recommendation is based upon its finding of multiple instances of misconduct involving neglect of clients' matters, misrepresentation of the status of matters, and, most significantly, two instances of misappropriation of clients' funds. Based upon our independent review of the record, we are clearly convinced that respondent engaged in the described conduct and that the ethical infractions warrant the discipline recommended.

Respondent was admitted to the bar in 1976. He opened an office for the practice of law as a sole practitioner. He practiced without incident until 1979, when the first of these incidents involving neglect arose. The problem matters continued into 1980 and were concluded in August 1981, when respondent closed his office. Various complaints were filed against him, including certain matters that were resolved without a finding of disciplinary infraction. He was suspended on September 28, 1982, for failure to answer the complaints. Respondent made no answer to any of the disciplinary complaints until January 11, 1983, when he appeared at a hearing conducted by the District III Ethics Committee (Ocean/ Burlington). At that time, he substantially conceded the matters set forth in the complaints and attributed his failings to very serious drinking problems.

(continues)

CASE LAW *In the Matter of Hein* (continued)

The DRB made detailed findings with respect to the several incidents as to which it sustained the District Ethics Committee's presentment of unethical conduct. Those findings may be summarized as follows: three clients gave retainers to respondent to represent them in matrimonial matters. Despite receipt of the retainers, respondent failed to file the requested complaints or to prosecute the parties' claims. He misrepresented the status of the file to one client. Another client retained him to handle various tax and commercial matters, to collect rents, and to prepare and file an income tax return. Respondent failed to file the tax return, to respond to inquiries about the matters, and to turn over $174 in rent receipts. In another instance, respondent was found to have aided a non-lawyer in the practice of law by reviewing bankruptcy petitions that the non-lawyer was preparing for filing. The non-lawyer signed respondent's name to the petitions without his consent.

The matter of gravest consequence to us and the ethics panels is a matter in which respondent was given a power-of-attorney, by clients who were in the military service, to collect the proceeds of a second mortgage. The clients had to leave the state before the matter could be resolved. Respondent collected almost $1,400 due on the mortgage but never responded to the clients' inquiries about the status of the matter and never turned the proceeds over to the clients. When the clients learned from the mortgagor that she had paid the mortgage balance to respondent, this complaint ensued.

It is plain that respondent exhibited a pattern of neglect in his handling of legal matters generally, in violation of DR 6–101(A)(2); that he failed to carry out his clients' contracts of employment, in violation of DR 7–101(A)(2); and that he misrepresented the status of various matters to his clients, in violation of DR 1–102(A)(4). Standing alone, these incidents would probably not warrant disbarment since they occurred during a relatively brief period of respondent's career and were influenced, at least in part, by respondent's dependence upon alcohol during the period. . . . However, we remain gravely troubled by the misappropriation of clients' funds. Respondent acknowledges that he collected about $1,400 on behalf of the clients and that these funds were converted to his own use. This evidence clearly established that respondent unlawfully appropriated clients' funds. Although the amounts involved do not evidence a course of magnitude, there is no suggestion in the proofs that it was an unintentional misuse of clients' funds through neglect, *In re Hennessy*, 93 N.J. 358, 461 A.2d 156 (1983), or through misunderstanding, *In re Hollendonner*, 102 N.J. 21, 504 A.2d 1174 (1985).

Respondent, in a quite appealing sense of candor, admitted to the District Ethics Committee that, with certain exceptions not relative to our disposition, the allegations are essentially true. When asked if there was anything he would like to say by way of mitigation, he told the committee that he had "very serious drinking problems" and "that I didn't have enough sense to seek help when I should have. . . . I thought I was succeeding. But it did not succeed. It got progressively worse." His final comments were:

(continues)

CASE LAW *In the Matter of Hein* (continued)

MR. HEIN: I would like to add for what it is worth, I am sorry for the other members of the Bar. I cast a bad look on lawyers for doing this. But it got out of my control.

MR. BEGLEY: That is a nice thing to say. But you have to try to think about yourself and straighten your own life out.

MR. HEIN: That is why I am here today. I just want to get this all resolved and I will never practice law again. But at least I will be able to live with myself again.

How far we should look behind such an uncounseled admission concerns us deeply. Unfortunately, respondent did not appear before the DRB. It acted on his matter on the record before it. Before us, respondent was represented by counsel who forcefully argued that his misconduct was causally related to his alcohol dependency and that his alcoholism should be a mitigating factor that would avoid the extreme sanction of *In re Wilson*, 81 N.J. 451, 409 A.2d 1153 (1979). . . .

To some extent a similar effect on perception, cognition and character may be caused by financial reverses, especially when that results in extreme hardship to respondent's family. It is not unusual in these cases to find such hardship, at least as perceived by most respondents. Yet we disbar invariably. It is difficult to rationalize a lesser discipline where alcohol is the cause—especially in view of the often related factors of financial reverses, failure in the profession, family hardship, and ultimately misappropriation.

We recognize, as respondent argues, that alcoholism is indeed not a defect in character. The public policy of the State of New Jersey recognizes alcoholism as a disease and an alcoholic as a sick person. See, e.g., N.J.S.A. 26:2B–7 (alcoholics "should be afforded a continuum of treatment" rather than subjected to criminal prosecution). The course that we have pursued in disciplinary matters is premised on the proposition that in our discipline of attorneys our goal is not punishment but protection of the public. *In re Goldstein*, 97 N.J. 545, 547-48, 482 A.2d 942 (1984); *In re Jacob*, 95 N.J. 132, 138, 469 A.2d 498 (1984). There may be circumstances in which an attorney's loss of competency, comprehension, or will may be of such magnitude that it would excuse or mitigate conduct that was otherwise knowing and purposeful. See *In re Jacob*, supra, 95 N.J. at 137, 469 A.2d 498.

We have carefully tested against the Jacob standard the proofs submitted by the respondent consisting of evidence of his seeking treatment at a rehabilitation center, expert analysis and expert opinion with respect to his condition, and personal affidavits from himself, his wife, and an employee. These documents do demonstrate an alcohol dependency, but they do not demonstrate to us the kind of loss of competency, comprehension, or will that can excuse the misconduct. Respondent's expert described the normal progression of alcohol dependency to the point where "there is a disruption eventually of the normal critical thinking and in concern and judgment in his perception of daily living and in the accomplishment of skills in his particular profession." He concluded

(continues)

CASE LAW *In the Matter of Hein* (continued)

that respondent "has gone through all the expected stages of drug abuse. . . . There is no question, in my opinion, that there is a direct causal relationship between the progressive disease of alcoholism and the loss of critical care and judgment affecting [respondent's] practice of law."

In this case the evidence falls short, however, of suggesting that at the time the mortgage proceeds were converted to respondent's use, he was unable to comprehend the nature of his act or lacked the capacity to form the requisite intent. In addition, it does not appear that he was continually in a dependent state, since he was able to attend to his practice. We must, however, accept, as respondent's expert points out, that the alcoholic becomes skilled at concealing the impairment. Respondent's secretary candidly stated that she was surprised that he could function as he did. These psychological states are extremely difficult for us to resolve. We do not purport here to determine definitively the effect alcohol dependency can have upon the volitional state of an individual. We have only the legal standard to guide us. We wish that we knew more.

Until we know more, perhaps until science and society know more, we shall continue to disbar in these cases. We believe that to do less will inevitably erode the Wilson rule and the confidence of the public in the Bar and in this Court. We believe that public attitudes towards alcoholics and addicts have changed, that they are much more compassionate, and almost totally nonpunitive, and that the members of the public have recognized more and more that they are dealing more with a disease than with a crime. Nevertheless we do not believe that that sympathy extends to the point of lowering the barriers to the protection we have attempted to give to that portion of the public who are clients, especially clients who entrust their money to lawyers.

The circumstance of the rehabilitated alcoholic or addict is deeply troubling to us. He has presumably recovered from the condition that contributed to cause his clients harm, and he will probably never again do any harm. But many of the lawyers, nonalcoholic, nonaddicted, disbarred by us for misappropriation would probably never again misappropriate. Indeed the probabilities may be even greater. Yet we disbar. That individual harshness—and so it is in most cases—is justified only if we are right about the devastating effect misappropriation—unless so treated— has on the public's confidence in the Bar and in this Court. Our primary concern must remain protection of the public interest and maintenance of the confidence of the public and the integrity of the Bar.

There may come a time when knowledge of the effect of drugs or alcohol, or other dependency upon the ability of individuals to conform their conduct to a norm, may lead us to alter our current view. Programs may be developed in conjunction with the Bar and the involved professionals that will promise the avoidance of public injury with the concurrent rehabilitation of dependent attorneys. We have seen, as they attest, that dependent

(continues)

attorneys become skilled at deception, not only of others, but of themselves. The best help is self-help, but others may be able to detect the need and help attorneys to take the first step to recovery. Under such programs an attorney could demonstrate commitment to a firm plan of recovery from the disease or condition. That in turn could assure the Court, and therefore the public, of the individual's ability to practice under circumstances or conditions that will assure public confidence until the disease or defect was arrested. For now, we find it difficult to exonerate the conduct influenced by the compulsion of alcohol dependency as contrasted with the compulsion to preserve one's family or assist another in a time of extreme need. . . .

Upon consideration of all the circumstances, we conclude that the appropriate discipline is disbarment. We direct further that respondent reimburse the Ethics Financial Committee for appropriate administrative costs.

Case Questions

1. What were the attorney's acts of misconduct? Which of those acts really bothered the Court?

2. If the attorney originally told the ethics committee that he was never going to practice law again, why did he fight the disbarment? Do you think his change of heart made his original declaration a lie?

3. What makes alcoholism, or other chemical addictions, a mitigating factor in attorney discipline?

4. Do you think addictions should be mitigating factors for surgeons or air traffic controllers who have committed wrongful professional acts? Why or why not?

5. Why did the Court disbar the attorney?

FINAL THOUGHTS ON THE ABA'S ROLE IN REGULATING LAWYERS

The ABA, like state and local bar associations, issues its own ethics opinions. These ethics opinions are meant to interpret the ABA Model Code of Professional Responsibility or the ABA Model Rules of Professional Conduct, depending on the date of the ethics opinion. Because the ABA is a private association and does not license lawyers, these ethics opinions are advisory only and do not have the force of law. In fact, in a 1998 case (discussing "inadvertent disclosure" is an important topic covered in detail in Chapter 4), the Texas Supreme Court stated that ABA ethics opinions are just that, advisory opinions that have no direct bearing on the behavior of Texas attorneys. *In re Meador*, 969

S.W.2d 346, 350. (Tex. 1998). Although ethics opinions are advisory in nature, because of the ABA's significance, its ethics opinions are important, and very often other bar associations make references to ABA opinions. ABA ethics opinions come with two possible labels: Formal and Informal. And according to the Rules of Procedure of the ABA's Model Rules of Professional Conduct, the distinction between the two is that, "[f]ormal Opinions are those upon subjects the [Rules of Procedure] Committee determines to be of widespread interest or unusual importance." Certain ABA ethics opinions are cited throughout the chapters of this book.

The ABA has also issued a document called "The ABA Standards for Imposing Lawyer Sanctions," which was revised in 1992 and establishes a blueprint upon which regulating courts can and do rely when considering imposing sanctions of lawyers. Included in the ABA's document are reasons for disciplining lawyers and categories of ethical duties violated by malfeasant lawyers, of which the most serious duty to be violated is one owed to a client. The ABA standards also specifically address four factors that should be considered when determining what level of sanction should be administered, and which are the following: (1) the duty violated; (2) the lawyer's mental state; (3) the potential or actual injury caused by the lawyer's misconduct; and (4) the existence of aggravating or mitigating factors. ABA Standards 3.0. Included in the aggravating circumstances are selfish or dishonest motives, multiple offenses, a refusal to acknowledge wrongfulness, and substantial experience in the practice of law. ABA Standards 9.22. Included in the mitigating circumstances are the lawyer's reputation for having a good character, recovery from a chemical dependency that caused the misconduct, and a lack of a prior disciplinary record. ABA Standards 9.32. Some regulating courts look to the ABA Standards for guidance when disciplining their lawyers, and others direct their disciplinary panels to follow the ABA Standards in their proceedings. *See In re Conduct of Wittemyer*, 980 P.2d 148 (Or. 1999); *Grievance Administrator v. Lopatin*, 612 N.W.2d 120 (Mich. 2000).

NOT QUITE LINCOLN

"No, Son...I told You NOT to Send That by Registered Mail!!"

Bob Castleman of Pocahontas, Arkansas, surrendered his law license to the Arkansas Supreme Court in July 2004 for what one could safely infer was in lieu of disbarment.

It seems that Bob and his son Robert were not getting along so well with a Mr. Albert Staton, who was unhappy with an ATV purchase he had made from the younger Castleman.

Eschewing the burning bag of doggie doo or toilet papering the Staton's property, Bob and Robert decided to send a message to Albert—literally. But there were two problems with what they mailed Mr. Staton. The first problem, but not the least, was that inside the package sent to Staton was a live, three-foot-long copperhead snake. The second problem was that Mrs. Staton got the mail that day. Imagine her surprise. Fortunately for Mrs. Staton, the snake did not bite her after popping out of the box. Unfortunately for the snake, a sheriff's deputy dispatched it. After being charged with the accurately titled crime of sending a threatening communication through the mail, Bob Castleman pled guilty in January 2004. However, his sentence was delayed after he tested positive for marijuana. Eventually, Castleman was sentenced to two years in prison, and at his sentencing he said, "I am an educated idiot." There is no word on whether PETA spoke on behalf of the dead snake.

SUMMARY

Lawyers are licensed to practice law on a jurisdiction-specific basis by the highest courts in their jurisdictions. Those courts set the prerequisites for those who want to practice law in their jurisdictions, one of which is the requirement that once admitted to the bar, an attorney is obligated to follow the rules of professional conduct that have been adopted. Such rules of conduct originate from the American Bar Association, which created the Model Code of Professional Responsibility, and then replaced it with the Model Rules of Professional Conduct in 1983. The Ethics 2000 Commission of the ABA then revised the ABA Model Rules, and the ABA House of Delegates accepted many of the commission's recommendations were. Also, many jurisdictions that are "Model Rules" jurisdictions have adopted many of the Ethics 2000 revisions.

An attorney who violates the rules of conduct in his jurisdiction is subject to discipline by the court that granted that attorney's law license, after an investigation by a disciplinary commission and a hearing. Sanctions can range from a reprimand to disbarment. All findings of misconduct can be appealed to that jurisdiction's highest court. Rules of professional responsibility are given fuller meaning in two, primary ways. First, each rule is accompanied by its official commentary. Second, case law interprets the rules by applying them to specific situations. Finally, state bar associations and the American Bar Association issue ethics opinions that answer questions regarding the interpretation of the rules of ethics. Although these ethics opinions do not have the effect of law (as do rules and appellate court opinions), they offer valuable insight to lawyers and are occasionally cited by courts.

Paralegals and legal assistants also must abide by their jurisdictions' rules of lawyer ethics. Because non-lawyer employees engage in substantive legal work, they face many of the same types of dilemmas lawyers face, and that requires non-lawyer employees to have a sufficient understanding of what is appropriate, professional conduct. While not directly responsible to a court for violations of professional ethics rules, paralegals are indirectly responsible, because attorneys are accountable for the misconduct of their paralegals and legal assistants.

ETHICS IN ACTION

1. Roberta has been a member of her state's bar for about 15 years, practicing criminal defense. She has always thought of herself as a free thinker and open-minded, and is opposed to the death penalty and government intrusion into one's personal life. Although she was horrified by the murderous acts of September 11, she has become equally angered by what she believes is the U.S. government's destructive response, and its "war on terror." Roberta has written letters to the editor of her local newspaper, railing against the justice department and the president, and has spoken out against the loss of civil liberties to various, like-minded organizations. As a protest against the government's monitoring of its citizens' activities, she made a $1,000 contribution to a known terrorist group connected to Al Qaeda. The contribution was made through the group's Web site. The FBI noted her contribution, and she is being charged with a Patriot Act crime. Also, her state's disciplinary commission is attempting to disbar her for supporting the activities of a terrorist group whose stated aim is to destroy America.

   After examining your jurisdiction's Admission and Discipline Rules (particularly the rule on the attorney's oath), do you think that Roberta's actions, motivated more by protest than support, should get her disbarred since she cannot support the U.S. Constitution and financially assist a group who is trying to tear up the Constitution, one American at a time? Or, do you think she has free speech right that protects her against disbarment?

2. John is a fantastic lawyer who works for a corporate law firm. He went to the right schools and belongs to the right clubs and has joined the right legal associations in his conservative legal community. What nobody knows about John is that he smokes marijuana, a habit he picked up at one of those right schools he attended. It did not prevent him from graduating magna cum laude, getting into a first-tier law school, or landing a six-figure income. In fact, he is on track to become a partner, and is well respected by his colleagues and clients. Because John does not want to get caught buying pot from an undercover friend, he has grown it in his basement for a few years. However, an untimely leak in his kitchen on Thanksgiving Eve led to a plumber making an untimely visit to John's basement. The plumber had gone to college too, and he knew John was not growing basil down there, so he called his cousin who

(continues)

ETHICS IN ACTION   *(continued)*

works for the sheriff's department. Now, John has an arrest record, an impromptu meeting with the managing partner, and a letter from the professional responsibility committee, which is accusing him of violating the ethics code.

What rules from your jurisdiction's ethics code would be implicated by John's behavior? What sanction would you give him for his illegal activities? Research your jurisdiction's case law to see if there are any cases of lawyers being sanctioned for using illegal drugs, particularly where the drug use had no adverse effects on the lawyer's work.

3. Emily is applying for admission to the bar. But she has one slight problem. Despite having good grades and references from law school and taking a bar review course, she is a convicted felon. She knows that the application requires her to list and explain any criminal past. Emily knows that character and fitness to practice law is, at least officially, as important to being eligible to sit for the bar exam as is graduating from law school, and she is aware that the admissions committee will discover her felony if she fails to include it on her application. When she was 19, Emily hit another driver while driving drunk. To make matters worse, she fled the scene of the accident, and when arrested, she initially claimed that she was at a movie in another town at the time of the accident. She was convicted and sentenced to six months in prison, although she could have received four years. It was during her incarceration that she got the desire to go to law school, and has since stopped drinking alcohol. But she is worried about being denied the chance to sit for the bar exam because of her past.

Examine your jurisdiction's admission rules and corresponding comments and decide whether Emily's criminal past shows her to be lacking the character or fitness required of an attorney. Are there any cases in your jurisdiction on the issue of what it means to have the kind of character—or lack thereof—needed to be found fit to practice law?

■ POINTS TO PONDER

1. Generally, how does one become a lawyer?

2. Examine the Rules of Court for your jurisdiction to determine how someone from your jurisdiction is admitted to practice law.

3. What is the difference between the bar exam, the Multistate Bar Exam, and the Multistate Professional Responsibility Exam?

4. Why is it that the ABA's rules of conduct do not apply to lawyers?

5. Are your jurisdiction's rules based on the ABA Model Code or the ABA Model Rules?

6. Does your jurisdiction's rules of lawyer conduct have a section for legal assistants?

7. Do you know if attorneys in your jurisdiction must join the bar association?

8. What sanctions are available to be used against an attorney who is found to be in violation of his jurisdiction's rules of conduct?

9. Why do state legislatures usually stay out of the regulation of the legal profession?

10. What is the significance of *Marbury v. Madison*? (Honestly, it really is significant.)

11. Why is it important for all non-lawyer employees in a legal office, especially paralegals, to have a working knowledge of their jurisdiction's rules of lawyer conduct?

12. Do you think President Clinton should have been disbarred? Why or why not?

■ KEY CONCEPTS

ABA House of Delegates

ABA Model Code of Professional Responsibility

ABA Model Rules of Professional Conduct

American Bar Association (ABA)

Case brief

Disbarment

Disciplinary commission

Ethics opinions

Ethics 2000 Commission

Impeachment

Judicial review

Jurisdiction

Rules of court

■ KEY TERMS

adjudication	contempt	jurisdiction
affidavit	deposition	multi-state bar exam
affirm	disciplinary commission	remand
annotated	federalists	reverse
antifederalists	grievance	rules of court
black letter law	immunity	summary judgment
comments	independent counsel	unified bar association
common law	judicial review	vacate

Online Companion™
For additional resources, please go to
http://www.paralegal.delmar.cengage.com

Student CD-ROM
For additional materials, please go to the
CD in this book.

2

Paralegals and Their Profession

INTRODUCTION

What makes an occupation a profession? A professional athlete is one who gets paid to play, but does that make the sport a profession? The clergy, doctors, and lawyers work in what are classically referred to as professions, yet all of those professions involve many aspects that arguably make them businesses. Whatever makes something a profession today, one of the historical, distinguishing features of a profession is that entry into it requires successful completion of two prerequisites: high levels of education and licensure.

"All professions are a conspiracy against the laity." This stinging line was written over a century ago by Irish playwright and Nobel Prize winner George Bernard Shaw in the play, *The Doctor's Dilemma*. The dilemma to which the title refers involves a British doctor's duty to help his patients, and his incentive to perform surgeries that only help his bank account. No doubt Shaw's pro-socialism views contributed to his artistic themes, but something remains to be said about the economic control wielded by professions over those who are to be served. For instance, in Las Vegas, one must obtain a license to work as an interior designer and move any furniture taller than 69 inches, because such effort is considered "space planning." (Thank God for futons.)

That brings us to the paralegal. Some would say that paralegals are professionals because they engage in substantive legal work on behalf of attorneys, who are professionals. Others would say that even if paralegals are to be distinguished from other support staff, such as secretaries and receptionists, they cannot be considered professionals unless they are licensed. Still others would say that paralegal certification, rather than licensure, is a sufficient benchmark. Concerning the ethical obligations of paralegals, there is some inconsistency, as was discussed in Chapter 1, in that paralegals are obligated to obey the ethics rules of lawyers, even though many legal assistants have yet to be granted traditional membership in state bar associations. This chapter will examine the history of paralegalism, paralegal associations, the debate concerning licensure versus certification, the dynamics of lawyer supervision and paralegal discipline, legal assistants joining state bar associations, overtime pay for legal assistants, and disbarred lawyers working as legal assistants.

A SHORT HISTORY OF LEGAL ASSISTING

Plenty of people, most of them women, were doing paralegal-type work long before the terms *legal assistant* or *paralegal* were coined. Curiously enough, Della Street, who worked so loyally all those years for Perry Mason, might be considered America's first legal assistant. Perry Mason was the first, famous television drama lawyer, whose fictional series ran for almost a decade, starting in the late 1950's. Although she may have been thought of as Perry Mason's secretary, she did a lot more than answer the phone: she worked with clients; she engaged in investigations, and, on occasion, she went to court with Perry. As peculiar as that comparison may seem, the fact remains that her depiction on a television show from the 1950s is evidence that the growing opportunities for legal assistants since the days of Della Street, including formally recognizing non-lawyer employees as paralegals, are a result of an evolution whose beginnings may have gone unnoticed.

The distinguishing feature between a secretary and a paralegal is not the level of their education, but the level of their participation in the services rendered for the client. As the last half of the twentieth century progressed, the reality was that there were a growing number of non-lawyer employees in law offices, as well as in the legal departments of corporations and government agencies, who engaged in substantive legal work for their supervising attorneys. Certainly, a significant reason for this shift was that legal services could be delivered in a more cost-efficient manner if non-lawyers were trained to do the work of lawyers. The client's bill would then be smaller, because a non-lawyer's billing rate is less than that of an **associate**. Associates report to their supervising partner, or partnership mentor, or a **partner**. Likewise, the firm could increase its productivity by deploying its lawyers to other billable endeavors while its skilled, non-lawyer employees were used in their expanded roles. Increased productivity leads to increased profitability, while at the same time clients get smaller bills due to the expanded role of the lower-billing, non-lawyer employees. This is known as a classic win-win outcome.

Recognizing this evolution, in 1968 the American Bar Association (ABA) created a committee known as the Special Committee on Lay Assistants for Lawyers. It was organized to encourage the use of non-lawyer employees in legal employment and to develop initiatives to promote cost-effective methods to deliver legal services. The committee's name was changed in 1971 to the Special Committee on Legal

associate
A lawyer in a law firm who has not reached partnership status, but may be on a partnership track.

partner
A lawyer who has been granted ownership status in a firm, having been voted in as a partner by the other partners. Partners generally share in the firm's profits.

Assistants, and its role was expanded to include studying the tasks undertaken by legal assistants in other professions, the training given to them for those tasks, and the education available for legal assistants. By 1975, the ABA gave permanent status to the committee, renaming it the Standing Committee on Legal Assistants (SCOLA). The ABA authorized the committee to determine curriculum guidelines appropriate for legal assistant education as well as to grant ABA approval to legal assistant programs, of which there are about 260 such programs in America. In 2003, SCOLA changed its name to the Standing Committee on Paralegals (SCOP).

In 1991, SCOLA issued the American Bar Association Model Guidelines for the Utilization of Legal Assistant Services (located in Appendix A). As stated in the Preamble to the ABA Model Guidelines, the purpose of SCOLA's efforts was to assist states that did not yet have guidelines for the use of legal assistants in adopting such guidelines, as well as to assist, for revision purposes, the 17 states that already had paralegal or legal assistant guidelines. (In fact, Florida had addressed the use of legal assistants in 1976, when its Supreme Court adopted amendments to its Code of Professional Responsibility. *In re Petition to Amend Code of Professional Responsibility*, 327 So.2d 13 (Fla. 1976). That same year, Michigan adopted Guidelines for the Utilization of Legal Assistant Services. SCOLA acknowledged that the ABA Model Guidelines were drafted to conform with the ABA's Model Rules of Professional Conduct. The Guidelines have a similar format to the model rules in that the Model Guidelines have declarative statements (the specific guidelines), followed by explanatory paragraphs (the comments to the guidelines). While specifically addressing the use of legal assistants, the ABA Model Guidelines are written to and for lawyers because the Model Guidelines address how lawyers can appropriately and ethically utilize legal assistants in their profession.

In 2003, The Standing Committee on Paralegals recommended changes to the Model Guidelines on the Use of Legal Assistant Services, and those changes were adopted by the ABA House of Delegates in 2004. In summary, the changes were stylistic and the most significant change was that the rules now use the word "paralegal" instead of "legal assistant," which makes the new title "The Model Guidelines on the Use of Paralegal Services." Also, references to the lawyer's (and paralegal's) duty to follow the ABA Model Rules of Professional Conduct have been changed to reflect the lawyer's (and paralegal's) duty to follow the rules of conduct operable in the lawyer's jurisdiction. See Exhibit 2–1 on the history of paralegalism.

The ABA's Web site has a Web page specifically dedicated to paralegals and legal assistants (http://www.abanet.org/legalservices/paralegals/, see also Appendix E). There, one can learn about ABA-approved paralegal education programs, access information concerning the ABA's position on paralegals, gather career-related information, and order paralegal-related publications.

The American Association for Paralegal Education (AAfPE), founded in 1981 and headquartered in Mt. Royal, New Jersey, is a national organization serving the needs of educational institutions that offer paralegal education. Their

---

EXHIBIT 2-1 A SHORT HISTORY OF PARALEGALISM

- 1968: The ABA creates the Special Committee on Lay Assistants for Lawyers
- 1971: The name is changed to the Special Committee on Legal Assistants
- 1975: The name is changed to the Standing Committee on Legal Assistants (SCOLA)
- 1986: The ABA adopts a definition of a legal assistant
- 1991: SCOLA issues the Model Guidelines for the Utilization of Legal Assistant Services
- 1997: The ABA modifies its legal assistant definition
- 2003: SCOLA changes its name to the Standing Committee on Paralegals (SCOP)
- 2004: ABA adopts changes to the Model Guidelines

Web site is http://www.aafpe.org/. Like the ABA, the AAfPE provides guidelines on appropriate paralegal curricula and grants institutional membership status to paralegal programs that are either ABA approved or in substantial compliance with ABA guidelines and also are accredited by a nationally recognized accrediting agency. Presently, there are over 300 such programs in America. Legal education programs that fail to qualify for institutional membership can be granted associate membership in the AAfPE upon providing evidence that their education programs meet six listed objectives. The objectives include providing a well-designed curriculum as well as providing sufficient instructor-student interaction and access to legal research library facilities. Paralegal programs that are institutional members can induct their best students into *Lambda Epsilon Chi* (LEX), a national paralegal honor society that has stringent eligibility standards and an exclusive membership.

The AAfPE has developed a model paralegal curriculum that it believes qualified paralegal programs should offer. The curriculum includes a minimum of 18 general education credits and electives such as accounting, business, or computer classes. An AAfPE membership core curriculum should include legal research, legal writing, litigation, legal ethics, computer applications in the law, and an internship. The AAfPE also recommends a minimum of 18 credit hours of core courses, as well as specialty courses, such as Wills, Criminal Law, or Bankruptcy. All courses in an AAfPE membership curriculum are supposed to develop "Core Competencies for Paralegals," which are specific skills and types of knowledge the AAfPE recommends a paralegal graduate should possess. The skills section of the core competencies includes the following: critical thinking skills, general communication skills, legal research and writing skills, and interviewing skills. The knowledge section of the Core Competencies includes the following: organization and operation of the legal system, the paralegal profession and ethical obligations, torts, and litigation procedures.

The AAfPE publishes *The Paralegal Educator*, a magazine for its members. It also periodically surveys paralegal program directors on their views on issues facing paralegal education. Some of the more recent surveys have concerned whether paralegal programs are considering changing the name of their programs to more neutral titles, such as legal studies. Other recent surveys have inquired about the propriety and extent of distance learning courses offered in paralegal programs.

The International Paralegal Management Association (IPMA) is an organization dedicated to serving the needs of those who manage legal assistants; IPMA refers to them as legal assistant management professionals. Founded in 1984 as the Legal Assistant Management Association (LAMA) and located in Avondale Estates, Georgia, LAMA changed its name to IPMA in 2005, in part to reflect that "paralegal" is used more often than "legal assistant" by colleges, the ABA, and within the legal industry. Part of IPMA's goals include "be[ing] the primary provider of information and educational resources on legal assistant management" and "promot[ing] the value of the legal assistant manager's role in the delivery of legal services." There are over 550 IPMA members in America and Canada. IPMA has four membership categories, the highest being reserved for those responsible for managerial duties specifically related to legal assistants. Among the services provided, IPMA publishes a magazine, *Paralegal Management*, and conducts surveys related to paralegal compensation, as well as legal assistant utilization.

Their Web site is http://www.paralegalmanagement.org/ipma/index.asp.

PARALEGAL ASSOCIATIONS

Paralegals can get involved in their profession by joining paralegal or legal assistant organizations. These organizations provide various benefits, including employment assistance and networking opportunities, continuing legal education, and professional ethics education. At the national level, there are two leading organizations: the National Federation of Paralegal Associations and the National Association of Legal Assistants.

The National Federation of Paralegal Associations

The National Federation of Paralegal Associations (NFPA), founded in 1974, is headquartered in Edmonds, Washington. It has approximately 11,000 members, who in turn belong to 50 regional NFPA associations. The NFPA publishes its own magazine, *The National Paralegal Reporter*, and has a Web site, http://www.paralegals.org, that provides extensive information on the paralegal profession and information considered valuable to NFPA members. Memberships can be obtained by working paralegals (who must provide a resume and letter from their supervising lawyer affirming the paralegal status of the applicant), students (who must provide transcripts), and organizations that support paralegals and paralegal education.

The NFPA created its own rules of ethics, the NFPA Model Code of Ethics and Professional Responsibility and Guidelines for Enforcement (located in Appendix B). Within this code are the NFPA Model Disciplinary Rules and Ethical Considerations, adopted in 1997 and amended in 2006, which replaced NFPA's Model Code of Ethics, adopted in 1993, which in turn had replaced its Affirmation of Professional Responsibility, adopted in 1987. The NFPA Model Code of Ethics and Professional Responsibility consists of eight sets of rules, each with its own Ethical Considerations. In addition, the NFPA issues its own Informal Ethics and Disciplinary Opinions, which have a similar appearance to the ethics opinions issued by the ABA, or various state bar associations. For example, an NFPA ethics opinion in 2006 addressed whether a paralegal could continue to work during the time her supervising lawyer was suspended from the practice of law. *NFPA Informal Ethics and Disciplinary Opinion No. 06-03.*

In 2002, NFPA conference delegates voted to change NFPA's definition of a paralegal by removing the term "legal assistant." The term was removed from the definition because NFPA policy makers believe that too many law firms call their secretaries "legal assistants." NFPA's decision to exclusively use "paralegal" was forward-thinking because, as already mentioned, the ABA and LAMA followed suit a few years later and removed "legal assistant" from their titles and ethical guidelines. When making the definitional change, NFPA announced that its membership policy would extend membership to those who call themselves legal assistants, provided they meet NFPA's paralegal standard.

The NFPA offers its own certification exam, known as the Paralegal Advanced Competency Exam (PACE). Designed to test the competency of experienced paralegals, PACE is a four-hour, computer-generated exam, which is offered in two tiers. Tier I consists of general legal knowledge and legal ethics questions, and Tier II consists of legal specialty questions. To be eligible to take either tier, an applicant must meet any of the following prerequisites: At least four years of paralegal experience by December 31, 2000; *or* an institutionally approved associate's degree in paralegal studies and six years of paralegal experience; *or* an institutionally accredited bachelor's degree in any field of study and three years of paralegal experience; *or* both an associate's degree in paralegal studies and a bachelor's degree in any field and two years of paralegal experience. Successful completion of PACE allows a paralegal to use the title PACE-Registered Paralegal, or RP. Continuing legal education is required to maintain the designation, including 12 hours of credits every two years, including one ethics hour. If, however, an applicant for the PACE certification has a felony conviction, or is under suspension from any other registration or licensing entity, then the applicant is disqualified from eligibility.

The National Association of Legal Assistants

The National Association of Legal Assistants (NALA) was founded in 1975 and is headquartered in Tulsa, Oklahoma. Through its 90 affiliated associations, there are approximately 18,000 members. The NALA publishes its own magazine, *Facts and Findings*, and has its own Web site, http://www.nala.org. NALA's Web site is a clearinghouse for all things related to legal assisting. Members also are provided access to the NALA Campus and NALA Net File. The former provides on-line continuing legal education opportunities and self-study courses, and the latter offers NALA members an on-line conference center and a unique research site consisting of legislation, court decisions, and ethics opinions that concern paralegals and legal assistants. NALA acknowledges the distinctions some paralegal groups have made between "paralegal" and "legal assistant," but believes that both terms continue to be used interchangeably enough to allow their synonymous use; NALA generally does so on its Web site and in its materials.

NALA has two sources of ethics guidelines. The NALA Code of Ethics and Professional Responsibility (located in Appendix D), first adopted in 1975 and revised on four occasions, most recently in 2007, consists of nine canons of aspiration-linked statements of professional ethics. The NALA Model Standards and Guidelines for the Utilization of Legal Assistants (located in Appendix C), first adopted in 1984 and revised several times, most recently in 2007, is a declaration concerning how a legal assistant may be used, and is written in reference to existing law dealing with paralegals and legal assistants.

NALA also has its own certification process available to its members, the NALA Certified Legal Assistant (CLA) Program, which began in 1976 and is now also designated the Certified Paralegal (CP) program. The CLA/CP exam is a two-day, comprehensive exam on federal law and procedure. The exam consists of the following major subject areas: communications; legal research; ethics; human relations and interviewing techniques; judgment and analytical ability; and legal terminology. The seventh subject area consists of five "mini-exams," one of which is the American Legal System; the applicant chooses the remaining four from a list of legal specialty areas, which include contracts, criminal law and procedure, family law, and litigation. Fewer than half of all participants pass all seven sections of the exam in their first sitting. As of February 2006, there were approximately 13,000 CLAs or CPs. Certified Legal Assistants must earn an average of 10 continuing legal education credits per year; one must be a legal ethics credit. In addition, there are three state-specific advanced CLA exams. California has an advanced paralegal specialty certification mechanism, which is a Web-based program created in conjunction with NALA and the California Association of Paralegal Associations. Legal assistants in Florida and Louisiana can sit for certification exams that test applicants on their state's substantive and procedural law. To be eligible to sit for Florida's and Louisiana's state-specific exams, applicants must first have passed the national CLA exam. Legal assistants and paralegals in North Carolina and Texas may sit for CLA/CP exams based on those states' laws.

NALA also offers a CLA/CP Advanced Certification Program for those who have reached CLA status and want to be certified in one of seven specialty areas. Formerly, the program was called CLA Specialty Program, but it was revised in spring 2006 after a few years of study and debate. One significant change in the new Advanced Certification Program is the shift to a curriculum-based Internet learning and assessment process. As of February 2006, there are over 1100 CLA/CP specialists.

The eligibility requirements for taking the CLA exam are one of three alternatives. The first alternative requires that the applicant for the CLA exam has graduated from a legal assistant program that is either institutionally accredited, ABA approved, or has a minimum of 60 semester hours. At least 15 of those semester hours must consist of substantive legal courses. The eligibility prerequisites provide the chance for paralegal students—most likely near graduation—to sit for the CLA, similar to the experience of law school graduates who sit for the bar exam without any experience requirements. The second alternative involves the applicant having a bachelor's degree in any major, plus one year's experience as a legal assistant (15 semester hours of substantive legal courses are considered equivalent to one year's experience). For the third alternative, the applicant must have a high school diploma and seven years of legal assistant experience under the supervision of an attorney, as well as 20 hours of continuing legal education credits completed within two years of the date of the CLA examination. See Exhibit 2–2 on the significant paralegal ethics codes.

EXHIBIT 2–2   SIGNIFICANT PARALEGAL/LEGAL ASSISTANT ETHICS CODES

- American Bar Association Guidelines for the Utilization of Paralegal Services (1991, revised 2004)

- NALA Model Standards and Guidelines for Utilization of Legal Assistants (1997)

- NALA Code of Ethics and Professional Responsibility (1995, revised 2007)

- NFPA Model Code of Ethics and Professional Responsibility and Guidelines for Enforcement (1997, updated 2002)
  - NFPA Model Disciplinary Rules and Ethical Considerations
  - NFPA Guidelines for the Enforcement of the Model Code of Ethics and Professional Responsibility

PARALEGAL COMPENSATION

Once a new occupational category is created, it can then be analyzed to track employment trends. It probably is no surprise that computer jobs (such as computer engineers and systems analysts) have the highest projections of employment growth. However, according to the Bureau of Labor Statistics, an agency of the U.S. Department of Labor, the paralegal and legal assistant field is projected to grow 28 percent by 2014, as compared to 2004. This rate is considered much faster than average. The Department of Labor's projections for paralegal employment between 2000 and 2010 are that the profession will grow faster than average, which, coupled with the projected increase by 2014, means an employment increase of 21 to 35 percent. Furthermore, those projections concern traditional legal jobs—in law firms and the like. In addition, students with legal educations are becoming more valuable in alternative careers where their critical thinking skills, communication skills, and their understanding of the legal system and legal research can be quite valuable in business, public relations, politics, education, and human resources.

Paralegal compensation is both a complicated and a serious issue. Because the paralegal field is relatively small (compared to other, more mature occupations), average compensation figures can be less than conclusive if they come from too small a sample size or if the respondents to a salary survey do not represent the class of paralegals as a whole, and particularly if a majority of respondents have worked as paralegals for many years. Also, wages and other forms of compensation for legal jobs are higher in larger markets and larger firms, and wages for legal jobs in federal agencies are higher than in state and local agencies.

Nevertheless, there are some averages to consider. According to the *Bureau of Labor Statistics 2005 National Occupational Employment and Wage Estimates*, the mean (or average) annual paralegal wage was $43,510, while the median (midpoint) annual paralegal wage was $41,170. These numbers indicate a noticeable increase from the 1999 statistics, in which the mean annual paralegal wage was $36,550 and the median annual paralegal wage was $34,090. According to the *Occupational Employment and Wage Estimates*, the jurisdictions with the highest annual mean paralegal wages were California (in first place with $50,810), and Massachusetts, the District of Columbia, New York, and Connecticut. But before turning in your resignation notice, packing your car, and moving to greener pastures, be aware that those places have the highest costs of living, the highest average home prices, and some of the highest state and local taxes in the country. See Exhibit 2–3 on paralegal pay.

According to the *National Federation of Paralegal Associations 2006 Compensation and Benefits Report Executive Summary*, a survey to which 1,468 NFPA members responded, the mean paralegal salary was $50,496, and the median salary was $49,000. One-third of the respondents reported receiving an annual bonus, of which the average was $2,994. The average respondent to the 2006 NFPA survey

EXHIBIT 2–3   PARALEGAL PAY

Source	Mean	Median		
Bureau of Labor Statistics (2005):	$43,510	$4,170		
		Average	**Bonus**	
NFPA (2006):		$50,496	$2,994	
NALA (2008):		$48,211	$3,808	
IPMA (2006):		$53,500	$2,500	

was a white woman with 11 years of paralegal experience. The NFPA data also include information on other compensation-related and job-satisfaction issues (for example, overtime pay, retirement benefits, billable hours), as well as the geographical locations and educational backgrounds of the survey respondents (http://www.paralegals.org/associations. Then search for the salary survey executive summary inside that link.).

And, according to the *National Association of Legal Assistants 2008 National Utilization and Compensation Report*, the average paralegal/legal assistant salary was $48,211, with an average bonus of $3,808. The NALA report is an extensive document, consisting of multiple reports, and even includes compensation averages within types of legal specialties, with average years of legal experience being 18, and average years of employment with current employer being eight (http://www.nala.org/Survey_Table.htm).

The International Paralegal Management Association, in conjunction with the famed law firm-consulting group, Altman Weil, Inc., also conducts compensation surveys. *The IPMA/Altman Weil 2007 Annual Compensation Survey for Paralegals/Legal Assistants and Managers*, based on responses from 274 law firms and 78 law departments, showed that paralegals earned an average of $53,500 and a bonus of $2,500. That survey showed that the highest paid paralegals, at an average salary of $69,675, work in the practice area of intellectual property (copyrights, trademarks, patents). Because all of the previously cited sources report different salary and bonus figures, to gain a greater appreciation of the significance of the numbers, examine in detail all of the noted compensation surveys. Bear in mind that survey data, including data mined from a large pool of residents, reflect those who responded to the survey, and do not necessarily reflect on the association members as a whole or on all paralegals across the country.

NOT QUITE LINCOLN

"Can I Get a Reference Letter from You, or Must I File a False Claim with the Disciplinary Commission?"

Seven days were enough for John Carter, partner in the Boca Raton law firm of Carter & Thomas, to realize that the firm's new legal secretary Bryce Rutherford had to go. Insubordination and incompetence can cause that reaction. Had he known what she had in store for him, he might have paid her the ridiculous severance package she demanded, or at least thrown a going-away party. Had she known what he had in store for her, she might have thought twice about filing false charges against him with the Florida Bar. Her retaliation for his refusal to pay her $2000-demand for unpaid overtime was a mistake. When she was fired in 2001, Ms. Rutherford accused her former boss of forging a guardianship client's signature on a court document. The result of the investigation into the disciplinary complaint was a quick dismissal because the charges were groundless. Mr. Carter then sued Ms. Rutherford for malicious prosecution, defamation, and tortuous interference with a business relationship. When he realized that Florida law provides absolute immunity to anyone who makes accusations against an attorney to the Florida Bar, Carter dropped his lawsuit against Ms. Rutherford, but not his fight. He went to the Broward County State Attorney's Office and got the prosecutor to bring perjury charges against Ms. Rutherford because her false allegations were made in writing under oath. Conviction of that charge could lead to a five-year prison sentence. Ms. Rutherford defended herself procedurally by clinging to *Tobkin v. Jarboe*, the 1998 Florida Supreme Court case that established the absolute immunity doctrine that earlier proved so valuable to her. But, the Florida Fourth District Court of Appeal disagreed, concluding in 2004 that *Tobkin* extended only to civil cases, not criminal prosecutions. The court noted that to hold otherwise would render meaningless the requirement in the Florida Bar Rules that complaints against lawyers be made in writing and "under oath." The criminal charges against Rutherford were reinstated.

THE GREAT DEBATE: LICENSURE VERSUS CERTIFICATION

As explained in Chapter 1, a person is not an attorney by virtue of graduating from law school. Only after being licensed in the jurisdiction whose bar exam and ethics exam they pass does a person become an attorney. Likewise, doctors and ministers are required to be licensed. Licensing is mandatory in a profession, and the methods of licensure are, with the obvious exception of ministers, determined and managed by governmental authority. Certification, on the other hand, is a voluntary method of formally standardizing competence or proficiency, and is usually a title granted by private organizations.

Minimum Qualifications: When Does One Become a Paralegal?

The paralegal presently exists in a no-man's-land, where almost nothing prevents a person from claiming to be a paralegal or legal assistant. While that may seem a tad curious, this structure flows naturally from the genesis of paralegalism, but also is a structure the legal community has yet to alter. The ABA first adopted a definition of a legal assistant in February 1986. According to the minutes of its Board of Governors, the definition is the following:

"A legal assistant is a person, qualified through education, training, or work experience, who is employed or retained by a lawyer, law office, governmental agency, or other entity in a capacity or function which involves the performance under the ultimate direction and supervision of an attorney, or specifically delegated substantive legal work, which work, for the most part, requires a sufficient knowledge of legal concepts that, absent such assistant, the attorney would perform the task."

In 1997, the ABA House of Delegates adopted the current ABA definition of a legal assistant or paralegal. The current definition, drafted by the-then ABA Standing Committee on Legal Assistants (SCOLA), is the following:

"A legal assistant or paralegal is a person, qualified by education, training, or work experience, who is employed or retained by a lawyer, law office, corporation, governmental agency, or other entity, and who performs specifically delegated substantive legal work for which a lawyer is responsible."

Even though the ABA's original definition of a legal assistant noted that a legal assistant works under the supervision of an attorney, that idea is not determinate, because every non-lawyer in a law firm—from the receptionist to the secretary to the billing department—ultimately works under the supervision of an attorney.

Does education make one an authentic paralegal? Not necessarily. Although the trend is that legal assistants should have at least some legal education at the college level (ideally a degree), many of the first paralegals were not educated beyond high school, and almost no one working as a paralegal at that time had any legal education. Decades ago, almost no legal courses were offered at the college level, so it was nearly impossible to study the law without attending law school. And, where rules of courts or statutes define paralegals, often those definitions do not require a certain level of education, much less a degree.

Instead, education is cast as an option of eligibility, because the definitions generally focus on "*someone who is qualified through education, training, or work experience...*" as is stated in the ABA definition. [Emphasis added.]

As discussed in Chapter 1, state legislatures generally defer to their judicial counterparts when it comes to regulating lawyers and the practice of law. Likewise, many state supreme courts include paralegal codes of conduct into their already-created schemes by incorporating into their rules that govern lawyers those ethics rules that concern paralegals. The use of the word *rules* is tricky because—as is discussed later in the chapter—paralegals and legal assistants, as outsiders, cannot be sanctioned for violating the rules of lawyer conduct. Furthermore, there are no "rules" concerning paralegals or legal assistants in either the ABA Model Code or ABA Model Rules, the sources for the lawyer conduct rules. Very often the word *guidelines*, as in "Guidelines for the Use of Paralegals," is used in the rules of professional conduct.

Some state legislatures, however, use their lawmaking power to formally define what it means to be a paralegal. California, Illinois, Indiana, Maine, and South Dakota are states where the legislative definitions of a legal assistant or paralegal are synonymous with the definition created by the ABA Standing Committee on Paralegals. Cal. Bus. And Prof. Code § 6450; 5 Ill. Comp. Stat. 70/ 1.35; Ind. Code § 1–1–4–6(a); Me. Rev. Stat. tit. 4, § 921; S. D. Codified Laws § 16–18–34. In addition, Maine provides for a fine of $1,000 against anyone who unlawfully uses the title of paralegal or legal assistant. Me. Rev. Stat. tit. 4, § 922 (2). Alabama's statutory definition of "Legal Service Provider" is directed to those licensed to practice law, but also includes "legal assistants" and "paralegals." However, Alabama does not delineate what makes a person a legal assistant or paralegal. Ala. Code § 6-5-572(2).

Some states define a paralegal or legal assistant in their supreme court-created rules of court or bar association rules. North Dakota's definition of a legal assistant is found in the "Terms" section of its rules of professional conduct; the definition states the following:

"Legal Assistant" (or paralegal) means a person who assists lawyers in the delivery of legal services, and who through formal education, training, or experience, has knowledge and expertise regarding the legal system and substantive and procedural law, which qualifies the person to do work of a legal nature under the direct supervision of a licensed lawyer."

Other states also define a legal assistant or paralegal in their rules of court. Kentucky defines a paralegal in the Preliminary Statement of Rule 3.700, titled "Rules Relating to Paralegals," located in the Kentucky Rules of the Supreme Court. New Mexico defines a legal assistant in Rule 20–102 in a set of its rules of court entitled "Rules Governing Legal Assistant Services." Rhode Island's definition is located in Provisional Order No. 18—Use of Legal Assistants, which follows the Comment to Rule 5.5 of the Rhode Island Rules of Professional Conduct.

Some state bar associations issue definitions of legal assistant or paralegal. The Oklahoma Bar Association Board of Governors adopted a legal assistant definition in 2000 that is much like the ABA's current definition. The Virginia State Bar Association's Standing Committee on the Unauthorized Practice of Law issued a formal statement in 1995 that recommended all Virginia lawyers make reasonable efforts to ensure their paralegals conform their conduct to the Educational Standards and Professional Responsibility Guidelines of the Virginia Alliance of Legal Assistant Associations, thereby incorporating the definition of the standards and guidelines. Moreover, West Virginia's governor restated the SCOLA definition of a legal assistant in a proclamation of Legal Assistant Day, on May 19, 2000.

Some states, such as South Dakota, even establish minimum qualifications for a paralegal or legal assistant (*see* S. D. Codified Laws § 16–18–34.1). But even when a state provides a definition and minimum qualifications, those minimum qualifications are usually not contingent on one uniform prerequisite, including a legal education. South Dakota provides seven options for meeting the minimum qualifications required of a legal assistant, some of which are met by experience only, some of which are met through legal education, but all of which at a minimum require a high school diploma or GED (*Id*).

Consider California's scheme for regulating paralegals, for instance. California defines a paralegal as the following:

"[a] Person who holds himself or herself out to be a paralegal, who is qualified by education, training, or work experience, who either contracts with or is employed by an attorney, law firm, corporation, governmental agency, or other entity, and who performs substantial legal work under the direction and supervision of an active member of the State Bar of California, as defined in Section 6060, or an attorney practicing law in the federal courts of this state, that has been specifically delegated by the attorney to him or her." Cal. Bus & Prof. Code § 6450(a).

A later section within the statute establishes minimum qualifications and requires a paralegal to possess one of four prerequisites: (1) a certificate from an ABA-approved paralegal program; (2) a certificate of completion from an accredited paralegal program that requires at least 24 legal credits; (3) at least a baccalaureate degree in any subject, with at least one year of experience working for a California attorney who has at least three years of legal experience and a letter from that attorney stating that the person is qualified to perform legal tasks; or (4) a high school diploma or general equivalency diploma (GED), with at least three years of experience working for a California attorney who has at least three years of legal experience and with a letter from that attorney stating that the person is qualified to perform legal tasks. § 6450(c). Although the California statute does allow one to be considered a paralegal without any accredited college education, that method is effectively tolled by a required completion date of December 31, 2003. § 6450(c)(4). California paralegals are also required to earn continuing legal education credits, including legal ethics credits § 6450(d), and are prohibited from identifying themselves as paralegals unless they meet one of the previously described qualifications. §6452. California makes no distinction between "paralegal" or "legal assistant," or even "attorney assistant," *§6454*, and provides for steep penalties (including the possibility of jail) for those who violate key provisions of the paralegal laws, §6455(b)). However, California exempts state-employed paralegals from the application of all the statutes regulating paralegals. *§6456.*

Does certification make one a paralegal? As mentioned earlier, NFPA and NALA have certification programs. Other groups do as well, including the American Alliance of Paralegals (AAPL) and the NALS (known as The Association for Legal Professionals). But certification, in almost all cases, could not make someone a paralegal. For example, the NFPA's certification program requires an applicant to have paralegal experience, and the NALA's certification program encourages experience as a viable prerequisite. So, in most cases, one must first be working as a paralegal to be eligible to be a certified paralegal. While lack of a certification title may affect one's pay or promotion, it does not prevent one from being a paralegal, because *the root of any paralegal definition, whether legislatively or judicially created, is the employment of one as a paralegal or legal assistant.* [See Exhibit 2–4 on what makes one a paralegal.]

An example of the dilemma faced by bar associations and courts over issues such as state-run certification can be found in Hawaii and Indiana. Hawaii has considered certification of its paralegals since 2000, when court staff of the Hawaii Supreme Court, prompted in part by the desire to promote greater competency in the paralegal profession, proposed rules that would require certification of paralegals. The Hawaii Supreme Court then asked the Hawaii State Bar Association (HSBA) for official comments on the proposals, and a special task force was formed. The task force rejected the call for mandatory

---

EXHIBIT 2–4   WHAT MAKES SOMEONE A PARALEGAL?

- **Education?**
  No – although it has become a practical necessity.

- **Certification?**
  No – although it can be earned from NALA and NFPA.

- **Licensure?**
  No – although it might some day.

- **Membership?**
  No – although paralegals and legal assistants may join the ABA, paralegal organizations, and various state and local bar associations.

Then, what does make someone a paralegal?

Employment as a paralegal or legal assistant

certification, but asked the Court for time to consider the idea of voluntary certification. More study and reflection was given, and by June 2002, this HSBA special committee acknowledged that it had failed to reach a consensus on voluntary certification. They recommended that no rule amendments concerning paralegal certification be adopted.

Indiana has been considering since 2004 to have a paralegal certification program that would fall under the regulatory arm of the Indiana Supreme Court. Proposed initially as a paralegal "registration" mechanism, and eventually titled "certification," Indiana's method for formalizing paralegal competency was drafted as a new part to Rule 2.2 of that state's Admission and Discipline Rules. Borrowing heavily from the architecture of the state bar association's paralegal membership admission materials, the state's Supreme Court certification program required certified paralegals to meet an alternative of educational or experimental qualifications, establish that they do substantive legal work for Indiana attorneys, earn annual continuing legal education credits (including ethics), and pay their fees. But, after years of revising the language in the rule, and submitting it for comment to the members of the Indiana State Bar Association as well as to key paralegal groups in the state, the proposal was tabled in 2006 due to a claimed lack of understanding about its ramifications.

North Carolina, on the other hand, has quite an extensive, voluntary certification program that is the result of much deliberation and the approval of the North Carolina Supreme Court in 2004. As of 2005, paralegals may seek to be certified, but those who do not may still be called "paralegal" or "legal assistant" and may do the same work as those who are certified. During the first two years of the program, current paralegals could be grandfathered in if they possessed either of the NALA's or NFPA's certifications and had worked in North Carolina for at least 2000 hours in two years prior to applying, or had graduated from a "qualified paralegal program" and had worked at least 2000 hours and gained paralegal experience in the two years prior to applying. Even paralegals with only a high school diploma can be grandfathered in if they have worked at least 5000 hours in the paralegal field in the five years prior to admission, and have taken at least three hours of ethics continuing education (CLE) credits. Beginning in 2007, all North Carolina paralegals desiring to be certified must meet education requirements *and* must pass North Carolina's certification exam. All certified paralegals—grandfathered or otherwise—must earn six hours of CLE credits annually, of which one credit must be ethics.

Florida also joined the exclusive ranks of jurisdictions that have a paralegal registration system. Similarly to North Carolina, Florida uses the term registration rather than certification. In late 2007, the Florida Supreme Court adopted the proposed rules of the Florida Bar, with some modifications, providing for voluntary paralegal registration with the Florida Supreme Court. What began in 2005 as a legislative attempt heavily opposed by the Florida Bar, concluded as a mechanism under the auspices of the Florida Supreme Court, which, in its opinion, declared that the outcome was not the "regulation" of the paralegal profession. Rather, the new rules, found in the new Chapter 20 of the Rules Regulating the Florida Bar, and which went into effect March 1, 2008, provide a forum for paralegals to establish their bona fide qualifications (college degrees, working experience, and/or certifications) in exchange for the privilege of referring to themselves as registered paralegals, provided they agree to follow Florida's ethics rules. Even assuming the eligibility requirements have been met, the registration rules deny eligibility to, among others, disbarred or suspended lawyers, convicted felons whose civil rights have not been restored, those found to have committed the unauthorized practice of law "in any jurisdiction," and those who fail to complete their annual, continuing legal education credits requirement of 30 credits every three years (and which include ethics credits). The specific ethics rules for registered paralegals are specified rules regarding the unauthorized practice, confidentiality, conflicts of interest, and lawyer-supervised maxims found in traditional paralegal ethics codes. One rule worth noting requires registered paralegals to contact the Florida Bar when other registered paralegals have violated the ethics code or any other of the paralegal registration rules. Florida Rules of Court, Rule 20-7.1(h).

The Licensing of Paralegals: Not Yet

It might seem logical to suppose that paralegals must be licensed in the jurisdictions where they work, particularly because the ideal role for paralegals is to engage in substantive legal tasks, limited only by those that would constitute the unauthorized practice of law. That, however, is not the case.

The Standing Committee on Paralegals

It may be a surprise to find out that, at the time of this writing, no state regulates paralegals to the point of licensing them. It may be a greater surprise to find out that the ABA's Standing Committee on Paralegals opposes paralegal licensure. The Standing Committee on Paralegals has twice issued formal policy statements opposing the licensing of paralegals, in 1975 and 1986. On both occasions, SCOP concluded that licensure was unnecessary because paralegals are required to work under the direct supervision of attorneys, as well as to follow the rules of professional responsibility that govern the attorneys for whom they work. Because lawyers are professionally responsible for the work of their non-lawyer employees, the committee believes that regulating paralegals is unnecessary.

The ABA revisited the issue in the 1990s and, after a lengthy study and investigation, confirmed its earlier position against paralegal licensing. However, the ABA adopted a revised legal assistant/paralegal definition in 1997, using the phrase, "for which a lawyer is responsible" to replace the prior language of "under the ultimate direction and supervision of an attorney." Notice that even though the ABA opposes paralegal licensing, its revised paralegal definition shows a loosening of the historical grip on the role of paralegals and legal assistants.

The National Association of Legal Assistants

The National Association of Legal Assistants opposes paralegal licensing. In summary, NALA has not yet seen a licensing proposal that, in the opinion of NALA and its members, does not create undue increase in legal costs being passed on to consumers, unfairly limit entry for new paralegals, and fail to allow an expansion of the role of paralegals and legal assistants. NALA restated its opposition after the New Jersey Supreme Court Committee on Paralegal Education and Regulation issued a report in 1998 concerning the use of paralegals, which included the recommendation of paralegal licensure. That committee was formed as a result of a 1992 New Jersey Supreme Court decision, *In re Ethics Opinion No. 24 of the Committee on the Unauthorized Practice of Law*, 607 A.2d 962 (N.J. 1992), that concerned using independent contractor paralegals. (That case is presented in Chapter 3.) NALA issued its own response report in 1999, in which it stated its opposition to paralegal licensure. Specifically, NALA's response stated that licensing of paralegals would harm the expansion of the paralegal profession, as well as be anti-competitive. One aspect of the New Jersey report that NALA found unfair was that New Jersey's licensing scheme required a post–high school education. NALA's response was that a legal education, without any paralegal experience, is an insufficient measure of competence. An overview of the NALA response follows: there is no demonstrable evidence of a need for paralegal licensing; paralegal licensing would increase the costs of paralegal services to legal employers; such increased costs would then be passed on to the general public; and licensing would unduly limit the growth and evolution of the paralegal profession. In May 1999, the New Jersey Supreme Court issued an administrative determinations report that rejected its committee's proposal concerning paralegal licensure and regulation, finding that the supervision of paralegals is best left to attorneys.

The National Federation of Paralegal Associations

The National Federation of Paralegal Associations does endorse paralegal licensure. In 1992, the NFPA adopted a regulation that stated it is in favor of state-by-state licensing, particularly licensing that would be consistent with NFPA's two-tier certification program. Specifically, the NFPA resolution states that it may support paralegal licensing in a state where the majority of voting NFPA members in that state support such licensing and as long as the criteria for licensing are consistent with NFPA policy. When the New Jersey Supreme Court was considering the licensure and regulation of paralegals, NFPA issued its own response to the recommendation report, stating that it was "generally in favor of a paralegal licensing scheme that would provide for an expanded role of paralegals."

In 1995, NFPA issued its "Model Act for Paralegal Licensure," which is a lengthy document that, according to its preamble, "is provided for assistance in developing and drafting Paralegal Licensure legislation and reflects NFPA's policy on paralegal regulation." Intended to serve as a blueprint for jurisdictions considering licensing its paralegals, the Act has the appearance of a statutory chapter, complete with its own parts and subparts. To be licensed under the NFPA Model Act, a person must have a sufficient moral character, pass a legal exam, *and* have at least a bachelor's degree.

More information on the NFPA Model Act can be found on the NFPA Web site, http://www.paralegals.org.

What Does the Future of Licensing Portend? Wisconsin Might Have the Answer

At least one state—Wisconsin—has ruminated on the idea of actually licensing its paralegals. Since 1996, the state's Paralegal Practice Task Force has investigated—and then has recommended—licensure for its paralegals. Lest one think that the word "licensure" is a synonym for the less demanding "certification," the Task Force definition of paralegal states in part, "no individual shall use the title 'paralegal' in this state unless that person is licensed under this chapter." Wisconsin Paralegal Practice Task Force Final Report, p. 5, January 2004. So, no licensure, no employment.

Eligibility for licensure is found in one of the two traditional imperatives: education or experience; but experience alone is a dying requisite. Under the Task Force's plan for licensure, one who wants to be a paralegal must meet minimum educational requirements at the post-secondary level at either an ABA-approved program, or one that is a member of the American Association for Paralegal Education (AAfPE). In summary, the applicant must have at least 18 credits with a C or better in certain courses, including ethics. The other alternative, which will go the way of the mastodon, allows an applicant with only a high school degree to seek licensure based on previous paralegal work experience. That requirement is set at 4800 hours of experience in the five years prior to applying for licensure, and such experience must be documented by those attorneys who employed the applicant during those hours. In addition, this type applicant must have completed three hours of ethics CLEs before applying for licensure. This experience-only alternative is a grandfathering provision, and will end three years after the licensure mechanism is in effect.

Similarly to what would-be attorneys face, applicants for licensure can be denied admission if they have been convicted of crimes involving "moral turpitude," or if they "lack good moral character." Likewise, continuing legal education credits are required to maintain one's license. Unfortunately, for those in Wisconsin and elsewhere who long for progress within the profession, since the Task Force issued its final report in 2004, and the public was invited to give its opinion on the proposals, the Wisconsin Supreme Court has taken no further action on this matter, as of this text's publication.

Is Certification the Alternative to Licensure?

As noted, the powers that be seem to oppose paralegal licensure; the National Federation of Paralegal Associations is the only exception. Why is the idea of licensure opposed? Many states require day care providers, as well as those who cut and style hair, to be licensed. Every state requires that schoolteachers have at least a bachelor's degree and be licensed in the states in which they teach—people cannot be schoolteachers simply because they have lots of experience with children. And yet, in a peculiar anomaly, while few states require that a person meet any prerequisite to work as paralegal, the two national certification programs originally required years of experience as a prerequisite to certification eligibility. Eventually, after a grandfathering period waned, both certification programs instituted a mandatory educational component in conjunction with paralegal experience.

Herein lies the paradox: A) there is rarely anything official that one must do to be a paralegal, other than be employed as a legal assistant; B) the American Bar Association, the most powerful force for change in the legal profession, opposes the licensing of paralegals, yet at the same time continues to ask states to consider expanding paralegal roles; and, C) increasingly, the ability to obtain employment as a legal assistant and also be promoted requires that one have a certain level of formal education, and then become certified by one of two private, unregulated organizations that determine the certification worthiness of those working in a field alongside licensed (i.e., regulated) attorneys.

The Ohio State Bar Association has a voluntary paralegal certification program. Applicants must complete the online application and pass the certification exam (a refresher is course available). Continuing legal education credits, including ethics credits, are required once certification status has been reached. For more information on the Ohio certification program, a paralegal certification link can be found on the Ohio State Bar Association Web site: http://www.ohiobar.org/. See Exhibit 2–5 on the difference between paralegal licensure and certification.

The Arguments in Opposition to Paralegal Licensure

Those who oppose paralegal licensure make three primary arguments. First is the view that there is no demonstrable evidence that licensure is necessary. Because paralegals work under the supervision of lawyers who are regulated by their jurisdictions' rules of ethics and discipline and who also are responsible for the conduct of their non-lawyer employees, it would be redundant to license paralegals. That argument has history on its side and is bolstered by the recognition that in the last few decades, improvements in the delivery of legal services have come without the licensing of paralegals.

Second, the licensing of paralegals would cause the costs of legal services to greatly increase, thereby hurting the very clients who most benefit from the increased use of paralegals. Using a paralegal reduces the client's bill because a

EXHIBIT 2–5   PARALEGAL LICENSING: ARGUMENTS ON BOTH SIDES

Licensing Is Unnecessary	Licensing Is Necessary
There is no need to alter the status quo, which has worked since the beginning.	The status quo should change as the profession evolves.
Licensing would drive up legal costs because paralegals would expect more pay.	Increased costs, if any, would not be prohibitive, but would still be cheaper than lawyers' fees.
Licensing would prevent some paralegals from entering the job market.	Licensing should prevent unqualified persons from entering the job market.

paralegal is paid less than a lawyer. The law firm bills the client for paralegal work at a lower rate than if a lawyer had done the work. Therefore, if paralegals were licensed, the increased costs of obtaining licensure (and increased prestige) would be passed along to clients, whose bills would then be higher, not because of increased effort, but increased status.

Third, licensing paralegals would unfairly prevent some from entering a field that would earn them a living wage. Access to employment is a critical issue in a free-market economy, and even regarding conflicts of interests (to be discussed in Chapter 5), some states provide more leniency to paralegals, in contrast to lawyers, partly because of the desire to provide them greater access to legal employment.

The Arguments in Support of Paralegal Licensure

The proponents of paralegal licensure make the following arguments. First, they argue that paralegals need real regulation by the bar. In the last 40 years, the paralegal field has grown from being an oddity (at least to traditionalists who believed that there was no role in a law office for a "para"-legal), to a curiosity, and then to a vibrant segment of the legal profession. As this occupation moves out of its infancy, the next logical step is to institute some licensing mechanism.

Second, there is no evidence that licensing will prohibitively increase legal costs. Certainly, the ABA has not considered the likelihood of increased costs to the public due to the influx of graduates of ABA-approved paralegal programs. Note that such programs have endured an arduous approval process. Likewise, certifications cost considerable sums (membership fees, testing fees, continuing legal education fees, and opportunity costs), and a promoted benefit of any certification program is higher income to the certified paralegal or legal assistant. Presumably, state-specific certification, in those states that provide for it, also would result in even more prestige and accompanying financial benefits.

Furthermore, as earlier stated, some form of a college degree is required to sit for either the PACE or CLA certification exam. Perhaps more important than the pursuit of knowledge, the most compelling reason for getting a college degree (and incurring the debt that often comes with it) is the presumption of higher starting and continuing wages.

Third, a licensing procedure would prevent some people from entering a field for which they are unsuitable. Plenty of people are denied entrance into their desired employment choice because they lack certain skills. The legal assistant field should not protect deficient paralegals at the expense of clients. Some people might say that legal assistants would command greater respect if the general public understood that those who call themselves legal assistants have officially earned the privilege of that title. See Exhibit 2–6 on the differences between paralegal licensure and certification.

EXHIBIT 2–6 KEY DIFFERENCES BETWEEN LAW LICENSURE AND PARALEGAL CERTIFICATION	
Licensure	**Certification**
Licensure is mandatory.	Certification is voluntary.
Licensure is determined and regulated by government.	Certification is determined and regulated by private groups.
Applicants must possess law degrees.	Applicants do not always have to possess four-year degrees.
Members are held to legally required standards.	Members are held to internally required standards.
Licensure is valid only in the jurisdiction granting the license.	Certification is valid nationally.

PARALEGAL DISCIPLINE: IS IT POSSIBLE TO SANCTION A PARALEGAL?

A basic question of life in an orderly society concerns what makes something law. Tradition, custom, and ritual may share some of the same attributes as law, but they are not law. All of the aforementioned involve some level of planning, order, and an agreed way of doing things, but law includes an aspect that distinguishes it from all else—penalty. Law is organization plus penalty. Although obeying the law may be virtuous, it is rare that virtue causes people to obey the law. It is the risk of a ticket and higher insurance rates that keeps us driving as close to the speed limit as we dare. It is the risk of an Internal Revenue Service audit that might catch an intentional evasion of taxes that leads us to report our income accurately. While the chances of getting a ticket or getting audited are statistically rare, the fact that they are possibilities is the stick, and not the carrot, that keeps us—at least most of us—in line.

Paralegal Associations Can Sanction Their Members

If a paralegal belongs to a national, state, or local paralegal association, then failure to abide by the association's sets of rules can result in some form of a sanction—penalty. For instance, the NALA Rules for Disciplinary Proceedings list three nonexclusive sanctions against its Certified Legal Assistants found to be in violation of NALA ethics standards: a formal caution, a suspension of CLA designation, and a revocation of CLA designation. And Rule 2.7(a) of the NFPA Guidelines for the Enforcement of the Model Code of Ethics and Professional Responsibility lists five possible sanctions that can be issued against its rules violators, including suspension from the NFPA and fines. Furthermore, both the NALA and NFPA will revoke the CLA or PACE certifications of their members who are subsequently convicted of a felony or equivalent crime.

The NFPA issues its own Informal Ethics Opinions, which have a similar appearance to the ethics opinions issued by state bar associations. Responding to questions by its members, the NFPA Informal Ethics Opinions interpret the NFPA Model Code of Ethics and Professional Responsibility. For instance, a 2005 NFPA opinion discussed the propriety of disbarred attorneys teaching paralegal classes or working as paralegals (which is discussed later in this chapter; NFPA Informal Ethics and Disciplinary Opinion No. 05-2). However, such opinions do not have the effect of law, and by contacting the NFPA for guidance, the interested party warrants that he or she will refuse to hold the NFPA liable for any consequences resulting from relying on the ethics opinion.

■ **malfeasance**

A wrongful or unlawful act.

■ **respondeat superior**

A Latin phrase that means "let the superior reply." This is a legal doctrine that makes employers (or principals) liable for the misconduct of their employees (or agents) that is committed within the scope of the employment.

The Lawyer's Duty of Supervision: The Stick, Not the Carrot

As long as paralegals are unlicensed, then their misconduct or **malfeasance** will be laid at the feet of their employing lawyers, assuming the misconduct is within the scope of their employment. Because paralegals and legal assistants are not licensed to practice law, they cannot be professionally disciplined for violating the rules of conduct, even though those rules apply to them by virtue of their professional relationship to licensed attorneys. Therefore, lawyers pay the price for the errors of their legal assistants. Such is the scheme in place due to the general principles of *respondeat superior* and the rules of professional responsibility.

The ABA Model Rules make *respondeat superior* expressly clear in the Ethics 2000 version of Rule 5.3, which is titled "Responsibilities Regarding Nonlawyer Assistants." MR 5.3(a) requires partners and those lawyers with comparable managerial authority to make reasonable efforts to ensure that their law firms have taken steps to ensure that their non-lawyer employees or assistants conduct themselves compatibly with the same obligations as lawyers. This rule is the key to the professional life of the legal assistant because, by implication, it requires paralegals and legal assistants in ABA Model Rules jurisdictions to learn, understand, and follow the operative rules of attorney conduct. This rule expresses, almost in passing, the need for all nonlegal employees to study their operative attorney's rules of conduct; those rules, after all, are the only rules that apply to the supervisors of non-lawyer employees.

MR 5.3(b) requires supervising lawyers to make reasonable efforts to ensure that their non-lawyer assistants comply with the professional obligations of lawyers. This rule makes it incumbent upon the firm to formally acquaint their legal assistants with those operative rules of professional responsibility. Preferably, such rules would be made known at a newly hired legal assistant's orientation.

MR 5.3(c) closes the loop by stating:

A lawyer shall be responsible for conduct of such a person that would be a violation of the Rules of Professional Conduct if engaged in by a lawyer if:

1. the lawyer orders or, with the knowledge of the specific conduct, ratifies the conduct involved; or

2. the lawyer is a partner in the law firm in which the person is employed, or has direct supervisory authority over the person, and knows of the conduct at a time when its consequences can be avoided or mitigated but fails to take reasonable remedial action.

Why is it important that a legal assistant know the operative rules of professional responsibility? It is important because any paralegal's supervising lawyer will be sanctioned for the misconduct of that legal assistant, with limited exceptions. Lawyers will even be sanctioned for the clerical errors of their paralegals. For instance, in an Iowa case, a criminal defense lawyer put forward a motion to dismiss his client's charges because the indictment was not brought within 45 days of arrest. However, the legal assistant who prepared the motion mistook the date of the alleged crime for the date of arrest, which made the motion misleading, and the lawyer (who failed to read his legal assistant's work) was suspended. *Iowa Supreme Court Bd. of Professional Ethics and Conduct v. Ackerman*, 611 N.W.2d 473 (Iowa 2000).

The older ABA Model Code of Professional Responsibility lacked a general directive such as MR 5.3, but it had specific directives. For instance, DR 4-101(D) stated that an attorney "shall exercise reasonable care to prevent his employees, associates, and others whose services are utilized by him from disclosing or using confidences or secrets of a client." Guideline 1 of the ABA Model Guidelines for

NOT QUITE LINCOLN

Well, at Least Nobody Sent a Snake in the Mail

Karen Milner's disbarment in 2001 should have been a surprise to no one, including her paralegal Matthew Kemp. This Colorado attorney was found to have engaged in 14 different instances of professional misconduct, ranging from neglecting client matters, charging an unreasonable fee, engaging in conduct involving misrepresentation and deceit, failing to keep her clients reasonably informed about their cases, as well as failing to adequately supervise her non-lawyer employee, whom she also assisted in the unauthorized practice of law. Kemp's involvement in the matters is particularly disturbing and provides more anecdotal evidence for the argument that paralegals should also be disciplined for their own malfeasance. A prospective client seeking custody of his children went to Milner's office and was interviewed by Kemp, who not only took the case in Milner's absence, but also took a retainer. What wasn't taken were notes of the interview, because Milner had no idea she had been retained when the client appeared at the office on the day of the first court appearance. After a month of enduring more incompetent representation, the client fired Milner by letter, and asked for the return of his case file. The letter and request were ignored. The client threatened to picket outside Milner's office if he didn't get his file. Milner then sent a letter to the client. The letter noted the client was being fired because he threatened his ex-wife, which was a lie. When the client's ex-wife saw the letter, she contacted social services and obtained custody of the children. Then, the client's case was dismissed for lack of any prosecution. And in an attempt to poison a new well, Kemp contacted the former client's new attorney to say that he directly heard the former client make threats against his ex-wife and children, another falsehood. And still the file was not returned. As part of the disbarment order, Milner was required to pay restitution to that client, as well as three others.

the Utilization of Legal Assistant Services puts the burden on lawyers, making them responsible for "all of the professional actions of a legal assistant performing legal assistant services at the lawyer's direction."

Distinct from the ethics rules, lawyers could be held responsible for their paralegals' conduct because of legislation that mandates such responsibility. Such is the case in California, where one statute that concerns paralegals states that a lawyer who uses a paralegal "is liable for any harm caused as the result of the paralegal's negligence, misconduct, or violation of [the statutes on paralegals]." Cal. Bus & Prof. Code § 6452(b). Notice that this burden of responsibility is broader than established in Model Rule 5.3, which makes a lawyer responsible for the paralegal's misconduct when the lawyer has some direct hand in the misconduct—either through ordering or ratifying it—or when the lawyer does nothing to amend for or lessen the misconduct. California's standard is more in line with the ABA Model Guideline for the Utilization of Paralegal Services, whose first Guideline makes a lawyer responsible for "all of the professional actions of the paralegal performing services at the lawyers direction..." See Exhibit 2–7 on the lawyer's duty of supervision.

When a paralegal lacks appropriate supervision and engages in conduct that hurts the client, the following case shows the common result—the paralegal's supervising lawyer will be held accountable.

EXHIBIT 2–7   THE LAWYER'S DUTY OF SUPERVISION

- ABA Model Rule 5.3 makes a lawyer responsible for the legal assistant's misconduct when the lawyer orders it, ratifies it, or fails to mitigate (lessen) its consequences.

- ABA Model Guideline I makes a lawyer responsible for all of the professional actions of a legal assistant performed at the lawyer's direction.

- The case law makes a lawyer responsible for failing to adequately supervise his or her legal assistant.

CASE LAW *Musselman v. Willoughby*

337 S.E. 2d 724 (Va. 1985)

This is an attorney malpractice case arising from a real estate transaction. The lawyer represented a corporate client and employed an untrained paralegal who played a significant role in the closing of the transaction.

The relevant facts mainly are undisputed. Appellee Willoughby Corporation, the plaintiff below, was formed in September 1974 by a large number of holders of O'Neill Enterprises, Inc., real estate bonds which had been secured by undeveloped land known as the "Willoughby Tract," lying in the City of Charlottesville and Albemarle County. When O'Neill Enterprises defaulted and went into bankruptcy, the bondholders formed Willoughby Corporation (hereinafter, the Corporation) in order to sell or develop the property to recoup their investments. Appellant Robert M. Musselman, a defendant below, represented the bondholders in formation of the Corporation. He became attorney for the Corporation and also served as its Secretary. He was not a member of the Board of Directors. The daily operations of the Corporation were handled from defendant's law

(continues)

CASE LAW *Musselman v. Willoughby* (continued)

office by defendant's employees. One director testified that Musselman took "a very dominant role in the affairs of the corporation" and that the Board looked to defendant for "guidance and leadership." Upon formation of the Corporation, several tracts of land, residential and commercial, were combined. One of the parcels, an 11.5-acre commercial piece known as Parcel 9, is the subject of this controversy.

In 1976, aware that the Board of Directors wished to sell a portion of the Willoughby Tract, defendant contacted Thomas J. Chandler, Jr., a local real estate broker, who obtained an offer to purchase Parcel 9. The offer was made by Charles W. Hurt, a medical doctor who had been a real estate developer in the Charlottesville and Albemarle County area for a number of years. Initially, Hurt offered to pay $200,000 for the land. The realtor completed a standard form purchase contract dated March 26, 1976 reciting that amount and, as instructed by Hurt, showed the purchaser to be "Charles Wm. Hurt or Assign." The proposal was delivered to defendant who later asked the realtor to attend a special meeting of the Board of Directors, held at Musselman's law office on April 9, 1976.

Among those present at the meeting were the following Board members: Charles J. Frankel, President, a medical doctor who held a law degree; John H. Robinson; and William Massie Smith, an attorney. Defendant attended along with Chandler and consultants in the fields of finance and real estate. The Board minutes of the meeting show that Chandler "presented" Hurt's offer to the Board at the meeting and that the Board fully considered "the advantages and disadvantages" of the proposed sale. The Board decided to accept the offer subject to several modifications, to which Hurt later agreed.

Subsequently, another standard form purchase contract for $215,000 was completed dated May 6, 1976. The purchaser was shown to be "Charles Wm. Hurt or Assigns." The contract provided that the purchaser pay $45,000 cash by the time of closing, scheduled for March 1, 1977, and the balance of $170,000 evidenced by a deferred purchase money note secured by a deed of trust, the terms of which were set forth in an addendum attached to the contract. The contract was executed by Hurt, by Musselman on behalf of the Corporation as corporate Secretary, and by the realtor.

The closing did not occur on March 1, 1977. The delay was attributed, in part, to a disagreement between Hurt's attorney and Musselman about the matter of interest on the debt as it related to the availability of sewer service to the property. The delay in closing was a subject of discussion during a meeting of the Board of Directors on September 1, 1977. Directors present at that meeting were Frankel, Clifford C. Fox, and Lloyd T. Smith, Jr., an attorney with extensive experience in real estate matters. Also present were Musselman and one Stanley K. Joynes, III. Joynes had been employed by Musselman in June 1977. Joynes had just graduated from college but had no formal training either as a lawyer or a paralegal. His main responsibility, under Musselman's direction, was to "shepherd the Willoughby

(continues)

Project along." Joynes attended his first Board meeting in July 1977 and was chosen Assistant Secretary of the Corporation. In the course of the September 1977 Board meeting, defendant was directed to close the Hurt transaction "as soon as possible." Three weeks later, Stuart F. Carwile, Hurt's attorney, notified Musselman by letter dated September 22, 1977 that his client desired to take title to Parcel 9 as follows: "Stuart F. Carwile and David W. Kudravetz, as trustees for the Fifth Street Land Trust, pursuant to the terms of a certain land trust agreement dated 22 September 1977." Carwile advised that after Musselman submitted a draft of the deed, Carwile would forward the proposed deed of trust and note for defendant's approval.

The paralegal then prepared the deed, with "some assistance" from other employees of defendant, in accordance with Carwile's request showing the Land Trust as grantee. Joynes arranged for Frankel to execute the deed, dated October 5, 1977, and on that day participated with Carwile in the closing of the transaction. Musselman was out of town on business on both October 4th and 5th. In the course of the closing on October 5th, the paralegal accepted the deed of trust, and other closing documents prepared by Carwile, which specifically exculpated Hurt from personal liability in the transaction as beneficiary under the land trust.

At this point, we note several important undisputed facts. First, the Board of Directors, upon being advised that Hurt, a man of substantial wealth, was to be the purchaser of Parcel 9, intended to rely on Hurt's potential personal liability as a part of the security for payment of the deferred purchase price. Second, Musselman maintained in his trial testimony that he was authorized by the Board to execute the contract of sale on behalf of the Corporation, and this was not contradicted by any witnesses. In addition, Musselman testified that Joynes, the paralegal, represented the Corporation at the closing, acting within his authority as an employee of defendant. Also, none of the Board members, prior to closing, ever examined either the proposed contract of March 26 or the final contract dated May 6. Moreover, no member of the Board knew before closing that the contract showed the purchaser to be "Hurt or Assigns." In addition, Musselman always was of opinion that the foregoing language in the contract authorized Hurt to escape personal liability under the contract by assigning his rights in the contract to whomever he chose. Also, Musselman never called the language to the Board's attention or explained its meaning to the Board. Finally, the fact that the closing documents exculpated Hurt from personal liability as beneficiary under the land trust was never revealed or explained to the Board of Directors prior to closing.

The Board of Directors met on October 6, the day after closing. Directors present were Frankel, Fox, and Lloyd T. Smith, Jr. Joynes and Musselman were also present, among others. The paralegal reported that the sale of Parcel 9 was complete. When a question arose about the date from which interest was to run, Smith asked to see Musselman's file

(continues)

CASE LAW *Musselman v. Willoughby* *(continued)*

and discovered that the property had been conveyed to a land trust and not to Hurt. He examined the note, saw that Hurt had not endorsed it, and thought the situation was "just frightening." Smith also examined the other closing documents and saw they specifically provided that Hurt would have no personal liability. Smith next observed the provisions dealing with release of large portions of the property from the lien of the deed of trust upon receipt of the down payment of $45,000 and he was "really concerned." As a result of the discussion at that meeting, "Musselman stated that he would speak with Dr. Hurt and his attorney . . . in an attempt to clear up these problems." The contract of sale was not exhibited to the Board until the following meeting and no discussion had taken place during the October meeting about the "or Assigns" language . . . .

The Land Trust defaulted under the terms of the $170,000 note in respect to an interest payment due on April 1, 1978. Subsequently, this action to recover the principal sum, plus interest, due under the real estate transaction was filed in September 1978 in numerous counts against Hurt and Musselman. The proceeding against Hurt was severed and he was eventually dismissed by the trial court as a party defendant.

The Corporation's action against Musselman was based on alternative theories. The plaintiff charged that defendant breached certain fiduciary duties in his capacity as an officer of the Corporation. In addition, the Corporation alleged that Musselman, in his capacity as attorney for the Corporation, was negligent and breached his fiduciary duty as counsel to the Corporation. At the March 1982 trial, the jury was permitted, under the instructions, to find against defendant in his capacity either as attorney, or as an officer of the Corporation, or as both attorney and officer. The jury found against defendant in his capacity as attorney only and fixed the damages, which were not in dispute, at $243,722.99. This sum represented the principal amount due on the obligation, plus interest through the last day of trial. The trial court entered judgment on the verdict in June 1982, and we awarded defendant this appeal in July 1983.

On appeal, defendant understandably does not seriously contend that the evidence was insufficient to raise a jury question on the issue of negligence and breach of fiduciary duty in his capacity as an attorney. Under the circumstances, Musselman had a duty to disclose anything known to him which might affect his client's decision "whether or how to act." *Owen v. Shelton*, 221 Va. 1051, 1054, 277 S.E.2d 189, 191 (1981) (applying the rule in the case of a real estate broker). See *Allen Realty v. Holbert*, 227 Va. 441, 446-47, 318 S.E.2d 592, 595 (1984) (applying the rule in the case of accountants). And, contrary to defendant's assertion, a lawyer is not relieved of such duty owed to a corporate client merely because some members of the board of directors are attorneys. Of course, an attorney acting as counsel for a corporate client is not required to explain to the board of directors every

(continues)

CASE LAW *Musselman v. Willoughby* (continued)

sentence in a standard form land contract. But the attorney has a duty to disclose information necessary to enable the client to understand those contract provisions that have the potential for affecting the client adversely.

In the present case, the evidence showed that defendant failed to advise the Board before closing that the crucial "or Assigns" language was in the contract, and failed to explain the legal effect of the language when, in defendant's opinion, use of the language enabled Hurt to escape personal liability, a consideration of prime importance to the Board in view of the manner in which the deal was structured. In addition, the evidence demonstrated that Musselman permitted an untrained paralegal to accept formulation of final documents that further exculpated Hurt, without bringing such documents to the Board for approval. In sum, the evidence was sufficient to support the jury's finding that defendant breached his duty as an attorney to adequately inform his client and that such breach was a proximate cause of plaintiff 's loss.

Inexplicably, defendant's main contentions on appeal are based on the faulty premise that he lacked corporate authority to act in executing the contract containing the "or Assigns" language and in completing the conveyance to a land trust, while, in the process, exculpating Hurt from personal liability. This argument is totally inconsistent with defendant's trial testimony that he did, in fact, have authority to execute the contract. It is also at odds with the uncontroverted evidence about defendant's "dominant role" in acting for the Corporation. This idea relies on the following circular reasoning: Even though specifically empowered to execute the contract, defendant had no authority to permit conveyance to a land trust, because the Board of Directors was unaware of the crucial contract provisions, which Musselman had the duty to disclose to the Board in his capacity as attorney....

There is no merit to this argument. Musselman, being authorized to execute the contract and to close the transaction, had the responsibility as counsel to advise his client, immediately upon discovery of the "problem," that it should attempt to rescind the transaction, if we assume an attempt at rescission would have been successful. Instead, defendant at no time advised the Board of Directors that it should pursue rescission. At the meeting on October 6, the day after closing, Musselman merely stated that he would "attempt to clear up these problems" by speaking with Hurt and his attorney. At the next Board meeting, Musselman only promised to perform further research on the "or Assigns" question. All the while, the Board justifiably expected that the transaction would be satisfactorily completed and that Hurt would consent to become personally bound in the event of default....

For these reasons, the judgment of the trial court will be Affirmed.

(continues)

CASE LAW *Musselman v. Willoughby* (continued)

Case Questions

1. Why did the court refer to the paralegal, Stanley K. Joynes III, as having no formal training as a paralegal if he had a college degree? If Joynes had been trained, would that have helped in this case?

2. According to the Court, why was the corporation willing to sell the land to Dr. Hurt?

3. What did Musselman do, or not do, that caused the corporation for which he served as attorney and an officer to sue him?

4. What did Musselman's paralegal do that contributed to Musselman's liability?

5. How was it that the paralegal's work was unsupervised?

6. If two members of the corporation's board were also attorneys, why were they not responsible for the losses suffered when the purchaser of Parcel 9 defaulted?

Although lawyers are professionally responsible for the conduct of their non-lawyer assistants, it is not always the case that lawyers will be liable for every misstep taken by those who work for them. The duty of supervision is not automatically violated when associates, paralegals, or secretaries do that which they knew, or should have known, was not to be done. Instead, courts focus on what methods were in place to ensure appropriate conduct or what remedial measures were taken once any mistake was discovered. For example, when a Colorado paralegal grew tired of a client's ceaseless phone calls to the firm (concerning a matter the lawyer had neglected), the paralegal told the client to "stop calling and bitching." Although her supervising lawyer was charged with violating Rule 5.3 because of the intemperate remark, the Hearing Board dismissed that charge, finding that a single outburst, even one lacking in tact, did not implicate the supervisory obligation of that rule. However, that was a small victory for the attorney because he was disbarred in the same case for other violations. (*People v. Milner,* 35 P.3d 670 (Colo. O.P.D.J. 2001).

Occasionally, a paralegal's conduct is blatantly unethical or even criminal. If such conduct is found to be outside the scope of employment, or if the conduct is so wildly inappropriate that no reasonable supervisory methods could have prevented it, the supervising lawyer will not be liable. For example, in a Connecticut case, an attorney's investigator took an illegal kickback from a client when transferring the proceeds from a settlement to the client. The attorney was accused of violating the duty of supervision. Rule 5.3(b) and (c). However, the Court ruled in favor of the attorney because he had no knowledge of the illegal kickback, nor had he ratified it, and there was no evidence to show how his supervision, or lack thereof, contributed to his employee's wrongful behavior. *Statewide Grievance Committee v. Pinciaro,* No. CV 970396643S, 1997 WL 155370 (Conn. Super. Ct. Mar. 21, 1997).

In the following case, an attorney ran his law practice like a fast-food restaurant and was then accused of a variety of ethics violations, one of which involved his failure to adequately represent a client after the attorney's paralegal was neglectful.

CASE LAW *Attorney Grievance Commission of Maryland v. Ficker*

706 A.2d 1045 (Md. 1998)

The complaints against Ficker arise largely from alleged deficiencies in the way he ran his office—principally in the way he kept track of cases and assigned them to associates. In 1990, we reprimanded Ficker for a similar inattention to detail that, as in some of the instant cases, led to a failure to appear in court for two scheduled trials or hearings. *Attorney Griev. Comm'n v. Ficker,* 319 Md. 305, 572 A.2d 501 (1990) (Ficker I).

Ficker was admitted to practice in 1973. In 1986, when his earlier troubles surfaced, he was a solo practitioner who operated out of an office in Bethesda and was assisted by a clerk with no legal training. As we pointed out in Ficker I, he maintained no diary or tickler system, and his only schedule of court dates was a large desk calendar. Id. at 308, 572 A.2d 501. By 1988, when the current charges began to arise, he had three offices—one in Bethesda, one in College Park, and one in Frederick. His practice was a high-volume one that concentrated on serious traffic violations, often alcohol-related. He estimated that, in 1988–91, he handled between 750 and 850 cases a year. He had cases throughout the State but practiced primarily in Montgomery, Prince George's, and Frederick Counties. To assist him in maintaining that practice, Ficker hired various associates, none of whom, according to this record, remained in his employ very long or consistently. Stephen Allen was employed as Ficker's first associate in June, 1988. In August, 1989, Ficker hired a second associate, Denise Banjavic. Banjavic quit five months later, in January, 1990, and was replaced by B. Edward McClellan and Thomas Mooney. A month later, Allen left, after 19 months; he was replaced, in March, 1990, by David Saslaw and Noreen Nelligan. McClellan left in February, 1991 (13 months); Mooney left in March, 1992 (26 months). Saslaw and Nelligan left for a time but later returned. Ficker apparently did not have a secretary but instead employed one non-lawyer assistant. His first assistant was Art Williams; after Mr. Williams, who was then in his seventies, suffered a stroke in 1989, Ficker employed Alex Burfield, a law student, to replace him. . . .

With this general background, we shall turn to the eight complaints made against Ficker. [The only complaint against Ficker that is relevant here, in this edited version of the case, is one made by Ms. Theo Dylewski.] In October, 1987, Ms. Dylewski met Ficker in the lobby

(continues)

of the Holiday Inn in Frederick and retained him to represent her in connection with a charge of driving while intoxicated. She paid him $100 toward a $650 fee but received neither a receipt nor a written retainer agreement. Trial was scheduled in the District Court in Frederick County for March 2, 1988; Ficker formally entered his appearance in November, 1987.

Ms. Dylewski testified before the AGC Inquiry Panel that she called Ficker's office in late January or early February to advise that she would be in Florida on March 2 and to request that the trial be postponed. She thought that she spoke to Ficker himself and that he told her a postponement would not be a problem, but that, if it were, he would let her know. Ficker said that he had no recollection of speaking with Ms. Dylewski about a postponement. He testified that, a day or two before the trial date, his assistant Art Williams told him that Ms. Dylewski had called and said that she wanted to be in Florida on the day of trial. He had no recollection of speaking with Ms. Dylewski at that point but said that he "probably" tried to reach her. Mr. Williams, who was 81 when he testified in this matter in 1995, said that he had no recollection of Ms. Dylewski but asserted that he would never, on his own, advise a client of Ficker's that a postponement would be granted or that it was all right not to show up for trial. He acknowledged that one of his duties was to answer the telephone and take messages, and that, if a client called and said that she needed a postponement, he would tell Ficker about it.

Ficker appeared in court on the trial date and orally requested a continuance, informing the court that his employee had informed him that his client wanted to be in Florida. He said that he did not file a motion in advance because (1) he had experienced difficulty in getting postponements in the District Court in Frederick, and (2) he had no idea of "why she wasn't going to be in court or indeed if it was a sure thing that she wasn't going to be in court." When the prosecutor objected to a continuance, the court denied the request and issued a bench warrant for Ms. Dylewski. Ficker said that, upon returning to his office, he called the number he had for Ms. Dylewski and left a message with "someone" that a bench warrant had been issued. Ms. Dylewski testified that her first awareness of the warrant was on April 8, after she had returned from Florida, when her husband informed her that the State Police had been to her home to serve the warrant. She called Ficker, who advised her to surrender herself. Upon the advice of a District Court clerk, she wrote a letter to the judge explaining the circumstances, and, eventually, the warrant was withdrawn. Ms. Dylewski later retained other counsel. Ficker never refunded the $100.

(continues)

CASE LAW *Attorney Grievance Commission of Maryland v. Ficker (continued)*

AGC charged Ficker with violations of MLRPC Rules 1.1 (requiring the provision of competent representation), 1.3 (requiring a lawyer to act with reasonable diligence and promptness), 1.4 (requiring a lawyer to keep a client reasonably informed about the status of a matter), 5.3 (requiring a lawyer to provide proper supervision over non-lawyer assistants), and 8.4(d) (engaging in conduct prejudicial to the administration of justice).

On the evidence presented, Judge Ferretti said that he could not find by clear and convincing evidence that Ms. Dylewski spoke personally with Ficker when she called his office in January or February. He did find, however, that Ficker was informed of her request for a continuance at least three or four days before the scheduled trial date. Judge Ferretti concluded that, as "a written request for a continuance might have been consented to by the State," by failing to file a motion for continuance at that time, Ficker did not act with reasonable diligence and promptness in representing Ms. Dylewski, in violation of MLRPC 1.3. He concluded further that, in failing to communicate with his client in a reasonably prompt manner, he also violated MLRPC 1.4(a) and 1.4(b). The court found no violation of MLRPC Rule 1.1 and no violations of MLRPC Rules 5.3or 8.4(c), by not having a better management system in place or by not properly supervising Mr. Williams. . . .

AGC excepted to the court's failure to find a violation of Rule 5.3. . . . AGC . . . urges that, if Ficker did not know of his client's situation until three or four days before trial, that was because he did not have in place proper measures to assure that Mr. Williams would do his job properly, and that that failure constitutes a violation of Rule 5.3. . . .

We find no merit in AGC's exception with respect to MLRPC Rule 5.3 in this matter. That rule provides, in relevant part, that a lawyer having direct supervisory authority over a non-lawyer shall make reasonable efforts to ensure that the non-lawyer's conduct is compatible with the professional obligations of the lawyer. AGC notes that, if Ms. Dylewski did not talk to Ficker, she spoke with Mr. Williams, among whose duties were answering the telephone and taking messages. Its position is that Ficker should have had in place some procedure to assure that Williams would, in a timely manner, relay any message he received from Ms. Dylewski. Judge Ferretti found that no tickler or calendaring system would have prevented the lapse in question. It was simply a matter of Mr. Williams apparently not timely relaying a call, which he acknowledged was his duty to do. There is no evidence in this record that that was a persistent problem with respect to Mr. Williams, and we are not prepared to conclude, on this record, that one missed communication, even though significant, constitutes a violation of MLRPC Rule 5.3.

[Ficker was charged with many ethics violations in connection with eight clients, and was found to be in violation of most of the remaining charges not appearing here. As a result of those violations, he was indefinitely suspended from the practice of law with a right to reapply for admission following 120 days after his suspension began.]

(continues)

Case Questions

1. If Ficker's client was harmed by the communication breakdown, then why did the Court find no Rule 5.3 violation?

2. Because Mr. Williams, Ficker's non-lawyer assistant, failed to relay a client message, and then Ficker was not found in violation, why did the Court fail to find Williams in violation and sanction him?

3. Do you think the result would have been different if Ms. Dylewski had been arrested, placed in jail, and then while in jail, been beaten or sexually assaulted?

In another case from Maryland, eerily reminiscent of *Ficker,* an even more neglectful lawyer who assigned many cases to his associates and assistants was charged with violating Maryland's version of 5.3 (among many disciplinary charges) because an unidentified assistant told one of the attorney's clients that attending his own criminal trial was unnecessary. Following that advice, the client failed to appear and a bench warrant was issued for the man's arrest. Upon hearing about the warrant, the client turned himself in and was jailed for two days. As part of the Maryland Court of Appeals' disciplinary action against the attorney for his various violations, the Court noted that the attorney failed to follow 5.3 by neglecting to have reasonable procedures in place ensuring that his staff would accurately inform clients of the status of their matters. *Attorney Grievance Comm'n v. Mooney,* 753 A.2d 117, 36. (MD. 2000).

Can a Legal Assistant Be Directly Sanctioned by a Court?

■ **cause of action**
Facts that are sufficient to entitle a party to claim a legal wrong, entitling the claimant to a remedy. Lawsuits are based on causes of action and can be dismissed if they fail to state a cause of action.

If a legal assistant misses the statute of limitations by neglecting to file a pleading on time, or if a legal assistant drafts a complaint that fails to state a **cause of action**—thereby resulting in the defendant succeeding in its motion to dismiss —that negligence is the attorney's negligence for two reasons. First, the kind of work that is properly delegated to an attorney must also be properly supervised. If a paralegal fails to draft a complaint competently, it is really the attorney who has failed, because the attorney's signature on the complaint, in compliance with what is commonly Rule 11 of most rules of civil procedure, is evidence that the attorney has "officially" prepared the complaint and is responsible for its contents. Likewise, if a paralegal places an attorney advertisement that violates that jurisdiction's rules on advertising, the attorney is responsible for failure to properly supervise their paralegal. That is the message of Model Rule 5.3. In fact, the end of the official Comments to MR 5.3 states, "The measures employed in supervising nonlawyers should take account of the fact that *they do not have legal training and are not subject to professional discipline*" (emphasis added).

The second reason is subtler. A lawyer is also subject to discipline for a paralegal's misconduct because it would be quite difficult for a state supreme court to discipline a paralegal for failing to obey rules that apply only to licensed attorneys. As explained in Chapter 1, any jurisdiction's rules of professional responsibility apply to a person after that jurisdiction's admission and discipline rules have first been met. If a person is subject to professional discipline, it is because he or she has first been admitted to the bar, which then makes the rules of conduct obligatory.

Many jurisdictions do make their rules of conduct applicable to paralegals, either directly through the incorporation of Model Rule 5.3, or indirectly by adopting some form of the ABA Model Guidelines. For instance, New Mexico's rules for lawyer conduct include Rule 5.3, and separate rules for the use of paralegals also exist. In these rules, lawyers are obligated to make sure that their paralegals do nothing that, if done by lawyers, would violate the New Mexico Rules of Professional Conduct. N.M. Rules Governing Legal Assistant Services, Rule 20–114. But, Rule 20-112 explicitly makes paralegals directly accountable to their supervising attorneys.

Maine's definition of a paralegal is almost identical to the ABA's definition, with the exception that Maine's definition uses "paralegal" and "legal assistant" synonymously. ME. Rev. Stat. tit. 4, § 921. And section 922 provides for up to a $1000 penalty for any person who uses the titles "paralegal" or "legal assistant" without meeting the definition in section 921. Indiana's Guidelines on the use of Non-Lawyer Assistants, found at the end of its Rules of Professional Conduct, require an Indiana paralegal and legal assistant to obey the Indiana Rules of Professional Conduct. Indiana Guidelines on the Use of Non-Lawyer Assistants, Guideline 9.10 (j). Curiously, before 2005, Guideline 9.10(j) required Indiana non-lawyer employees to follow both the ABA Model Rules of Conduct *and* the ABA Model Code of Professional Responsibility. Not only would it have been difficult to find a copy of the 1969 ABA Model Code, it would have been practically impossible to be governed by both sets of rules because, in some areas, such as confidentiality, incompatible distinctions exist between the Model Code and Model Rules. Furthermore, Indiana attorneys are governed only by the Indiana Rules of Professional Conduct, a fact not lost on the Indiana Supreme Court when it amended Guideline 9.10(j) in 2005.

There is, however, a two-step method of sanction that can be used directly against non-lawyers, although its use is rare. The first is the issuance of an **injunction**. If, for instance, a non-lawyer is engaging in the unauthorized practice of law, a court could issue an injunction against that person, ordering them to cease from such unauthorized conduct. And, in the event the non-lawyer disobeys the injunction, a court could hold the non-lawyer in contempt, resulting in a fine or other punishment. Michigan not only issues injunctions against those who have

■ **injunction**
A court order forbidding a party to do something or ordering them to start doing something.

engaged in the unauthorized practice of law, it also posts notice of those injunctions on its state bar Web site. The list is updated every two years and includes a quick description of the activities that gave rise to the permanent injunctions: http://www.michbar.org/ (then search inside "professional/injunctions").

The following case involves a self-styled, independent paralegal in South Carolina who was sued by the state attorney general for the unauthorized practice of law.

CASE LAW *State v. Robinson*

468 S.E.2d 290 (S.C. 1996) MOORE, Justice.

This case is before us in our original jurisdiction. The State seeks an injunction prohibiting the unauthorized practice of law and solicitation of clients by defendant Robinson. We grant the injunction as follows.

FACTS

This case was referred to a special master to make findings of fact and conclusions of law. After two evidentiary hearings, the master made findings of fact including the following: 1) Robinson is not licensed or qualified to practice law; 2) he has a business license from Anderson County and advertises in the yellow pages as a "paralegal"; 3) Robinson performs services without attorney supervision; 4) he has represented more than sixteen clients in court; 5) when appearing in family or circuit court, Robinson does not charge a fee to his clients but requires reimbursement for costs; 6) Robinson obtains leave of court to appear pursuant to S.C.Code Ann. § 40–5–80 (1986); and 7) Robinson gives legal advice.

The master concluded as a matter of law that Robinson's appearances in court did not constitute the unauthorized practice of law because he sought and obtained leave of court in each instance. He found, however, that Robinson's solicitation of clients, giving of legal advice, and preparation and filing of legal documents constituted the unauthorized practice of law and recommended Robinson be enjoined from engaging in these activities. Neither the State nor Robinson takes exception to any of the master's findings of fact.

ISSUES

1. Does Robinson have a first amendment right to advertise himself as a paralegal?

2. Are giving legal advice and preparing legal documents activities authorized under § 40–5–80?

DISCUSSION

The advertisement in question here is a yellow pages listing under "Paralegals" that reads as follows:

Robinson Melvin J "IF YOUR CIVIL RIGHTS HAVE BEEN VIOLATED—CALL ME." 1612 E River St. . . . 224-7800

Robinson also has a business card he distributes with the same message on it. His business card and letterhead refer to him as "Paralegal Consultant."

(continues)

CASE LAW *State v. Robinson* (continued)

It is undisputed the First Amendment does not protect commercial speech that is false, deceptive, or misleading. *Zauderer v. The Office of Disciplinary Counsel*, 471 U.S. 626, 105 S.Ct. 2265, 85 L.Ed.2d 652 (1985). Robinson contends, however, that advertising himself as a paralegal is not false since there are no regulations requiring any qualifications to be a paralegal in this State. This Court has addressed the function of a paralegal in *In re: Easler*, 275 S.C. 400, 272 S.E.2d 32 (1980):

Paralegals are routinely employed by licensed attorneys to assist in the preparation of legal documents such as deeds and mortgages. The activities of a paralegal do not constitute the practice of law as long as they are limited to work of a preparatory nature, such as legal research, investigation, or the composition of legal documents, which enable the licensed attorney-employer to carry a given matter to a conclusion through his own examination, approval or additional effort. Id. at 400, 272 S.E.2d at 32–33

While there are no regulations dealing specifically with paralegals, requiring a paralegal to work under the supervision of a licensed attorney ensures control over his or her activities by making the supervising attorney responsible. See Rule 5.3 of the Rules of Professional Conduct, Rule 407 SCACR (supervising attorney is responsible for work of nonlawyer employees). Accordingly, to legitimately provide services as a paralegal, one must work in conjunction with a licensed attorney. Robinson's advertisement as a paralegal is false since his work product is admittedly not subject to the supervision of a licensed attorney.

Further, the ad's statement, "If your civil rights have been violated—call me," is an unlawful solicitation. It is unlawful for one who is not a licensed attorney to solicit the cause of another person. S.C.Code Ann. § 40–5–310 (Supp.1994). We find Robinson should be enjoined from advertising himself as a paralegal or soliciting the representation of others.

Next, Robinson contends he should not be enjoined from giving legal advice and preparing legal documents since he obtains the right to represent others by leave of court under § 40–5–80. That section is entitled, "Citizens not prevented from appearing in person or for others without reward" and provides:

This chapter shall not be construed so as to prevent a citizen from prosecuting or defending his own cause, if he so desires, or the cause of another, with leave of the court first had and obtained; provided, that he declare on oath, if required, that he neither has accepted nor will accept or take any fee, gratuity or reward on account of such prosecution or defense or for any other matter relating to the cause. (emphasis added)[1]

Robinson argues "defending or prosecuting" necessarily includes giving legal advice and preparing and filing legal papers and therefore the leave granted by the court includes leave to engage in these activities. This Court has defined the practice of law to include the preparation and filing of legal documents involving the giving of advice, consultation, explanation, or recommendations on matters of law. *State v. Despain*, 319 S.C. 317,

(continues)

CASE LAW   *State v. Robinson* (continued)

460 S.E.2d 576 (1995); *State v. Buyers Service Co.,* 292 S.C. 426, 357 S.E.2d 15 (1987). Clearly, one defending or prosecuting a cause of action must engage in these activities. We note, however, the express language of § 40–5–80 requires that leave be obtained first. The record indicates Robinson does not always obtain leave before giving advice and preparing pleadings. Accordingly, we find Robinson should be enjoined from preparing and filing legal documents and giving legal advice unless he first obtains leave of court pursuant to § 40–5–80. Further, we emphasize that it is within the trial judge's sound discretion whether to allow such representation.

INJUNCTION ISSUED.

FINNEY, C.J., and TOAL, WALLER and BURNETT, JJ., concur.

[1]This Court has also construed § 40-5-80 to allow a non-lawyer officer, agent, or employee to represent a business in civil magistrate's court for compensation. In re: Unauthorized Practice of Law Rules, 309 S.C. 304, 422 S.E.2d 123 (1992).

Case Questions

1. What specific conduct of Robinson's was the state trying to stop?

2. Why did the state Supreme Court agree that Robinson was not engaging in the unauthorized practice of law by representing others in state trial courts?

3. What two things were wrong with Robinson's Yellow pages advertisement? Could he safely advertise after the Court's decision?

4. In light of the fact that there were no formal requirements about what made someone a paralegal, what did the Court say was conclusive as to whether someone is a paralegal?

5. Did the Court discipline Robinson for his unauthorized practice of law or his false advertising?

After reading *Robinson*, one might wonder whether a statute that allows a person to be someone else's lawyer, even if that person is unpaid and gets court permission, leaves the door wide open for abuse—charging exorbitant expenses in lieu of a fee or incompetent representation. Of course, incompetent representation in court by a non-lawyer could result in the disgruntled client suing the non-lawyer representative for malpractice, which is discussed in Chapter 8. Whether prompted by the South Carolina Bar Association or judges who had to deal with non-lawyer representatives, in 2002 South Carolina's legislature amended § 40-5-80 so drastically that it now only states, "This chapter may not be construed so as to prevent a citizen from prosecuting or defending his own cause, if he so desires."

NOT QUITE LINCOLN

This Paralegal Would Have Really Gone Places Had She Worked at Enron.

You have to hand it to Phoebe Nicholson, a former paralegal at Honeywell International, a Fortune 500 corporation. She may have been a grifter and an embarrassment to honest paralegals everywhere, but at least she is no slouch. The scheme she concocted that netted her almost $600,000 from her own employer was reminiscent of the film *Catch Me If You Can.* And just fill in your favorite punch line, realizing the irony of Ms. Nichols spending much of her ill-gotten gain on psychics. While working as a paralegal in the corporate law department in 2002 and 2003, Ms. Nichols issued Honeywell seven counterfeit legal bills from the firm of Fish & Neave, a national patent firm that had done legal work for the company in the past. She then forged her boss's approval on the bills and convinced Honeywell's accounting department to give the checks to her personally, rather than mail them, so she could deliver them to Fish & Neave. Are you with me so far? Simultaneously, she applied for and received a business certificate from the state of New York for a law firm named "Fish Neave" (deleting the &); she listed herself as the firm's owner, which allowed her to open a bank account in the same name. When Honeywell gave her the checks for Fish & Neave, Ms. Nicholson deposited them in her Fish Neave bank account. If it weren't for a scrupulous bank employee who noticed the ever-so-slight discrepancy, Ms. Nicholson might have gotten away with her intricate scheme. But maybe not, because she was also caught in another fraud in which she lied about her job status and income at Honeywell to fraudulently obtain a bank loan of over $500,000. In 2005, Ms. Nicholson was convicted of identity theft and fraud, ordered to pay restitution of $1.3 million, and sentenced to three to nine years in prison.

MISCELLANEOUS ISSUES FOR THE PARALEGAL PROFESSION

Most professions have certain work-related issues that are peculiar to that profession. Three issues relevant to the ever-changing paralegal profession are whether paralegals must be paid overtime, whether suspended or disbarred lawyers should be allowed to work as paralegals, and whether paralegals may join state and local bar associations.

Salary versus Overtime Pay: Does That Make One a "Professional?"

Few issues are more contentious and subject to curious interpretations of the law than whether law firms and other legal employers are required to pay their paralegals and legal assistants overtime compensation. One characteristic of professionals is that their pay is not generally tied to their hours worked. Professionals are salaried personnel and it is not required that they be paid overtime. According to the Fair Labor Standards Act, overtime pay must be paid to employees, unless the employees qualify as being "exempt" from the overtime requirements. *See* 29 U.S.C. §§ 201–219. The Department of Labor has the authority to interpret those statutes by drafting regulations that specifically cover many industries and occupations. Many of those regulations were substantially revised and went into effect August 23, 2004 and included revisions of the regulations that implicate paralegals.

Lawyers are exempt employees, falling under the learned professions exemption of the Act. 29 C.F.R. § 541.301 (2006). To be considered a professional, an employee's primary duty must be the performance of work requiring knowledge of an advanced type in a field of science or learning customarily acquired by a prolonged course of specialized intellectual instruction. The primary duty test includes these elements:

1. The employee must perform work requiring advanced knowledge;

2. The advanced knowledge must be customarily acquired by a prolonged course of specialized intellectual instruction. *Id.*

Section 301(d) strikes at paralegals who have become skilled solely through experience, in that it finds that the professional exemption "does not apply to occupations in which most employees have acquired their skill by experience rather than by advanced specialized intellectual instruction." More specifically, section 304 states that a bona fide legal professional is one who holds a valid law license and who is actually practicing that profession. 29 C.F.R. § 541.304(a)(1).

Do paralegals qualify as being exempt from overtime pay requirements? That depends on whom you ask. Despite changes in the regulations, including those specifically addressed to paralegals, many law firms still view their paralegals and legal assistants differently than does the Department of Labor. Before the 2004 revisions, the now-repealed 29 C.F.R. § 541.314, which covered the professional exemptions (lawyers, doctors, educators), stated those exemptions do not apply to employees in related professions who "...merely serve these professions."

Confusion over the prior version of the regulations led to multiple interpretations, so the Department of Labor tightened the language, leaving little doubt that the United States government considers that paralegals deserve overtime pay. Section 314(e)(7) directly addresses paralegals and legal assistants, finding that they "generally do not qualify as exempt learning professionals because an advanced specialized academic degree is not a standard prerequisite for entry into the field." Later, however, that subsection acknowledges that some paralegals possess four-year degrees or higher, and it then provides a limited, learned professional exemption of "paralegals who possess advanced specialized degrees in other professional fields and *apply advanced knowledge in that field* in the performance of their duties." (Emphasis added.) *Id.* To illustrate the meaning of the sentence, the regulation mentions someone who would be exempt from the overtime requirement: an engineer who is working as a paralegal, giving expert advice on product liability or patent matters. This example provides little leeway for firms to classify their paralegals and legal assistants as exempt from overtime pay, at least under the learned professional exemption, which is the most natural exemption for such employees.

The Department of Labor issues opinion letters written to answer questions about the regulations. A few opinion letters sent after the regulations changed in 2004 affirm the Department of Labor's conclusion that paralegals must be paid overtime. In an opinion letter issued December 16, 2005, a law firm asked whether any of its six paralegals could be exempt from overtime pay under either the professional or administrative exemptions (discussed later in this chapter). Noting that the paralegals' educations ranged from associate's degrees to an MBA, the Department of Labor still ruled against the firm on the professions exemption, finding that only the paralegal with the MBA (and who passed the CPA exam) might qualify as exempt, except that paralegal was a conventional paralegal who did not use her MBA in a distinct or expert fashion at the firm. FLSA 2005-54 (December 16, 2005). Other opinion letters issued in 2005 and 2006 reaffirm the view that paralegals are not exempt from overtime pay. FLSA 2005-9 (January 7, 2005), FLSA 2006-27 (July 24, 2006).

A 1986 opinion letter issued under the former overtime exemption rules considered the question of whether a paralegal with an educational certificate (after six months of study) qualified as nonexempt under the professional employee exception. The letter declared that such an educational level "would not qualify as a prolonged course of specialized, intellectual instruction as required by . . . § 541.3(a)." FLSA–1035 (August 18, 1986).

Then why not classify a paralegal as exempt on a different basis? Two other exemptions might apply: the administrative exemption or the executive exemption. The administrative exemption applies to those employees whose office or nonmanual work is directly related to the firm's management policies or business operations, and who regularly exercise independent judgment and discretion with respect to matters of significance. 29 C.F.R. § 541.200(a)(2, and 3) (2006). Section 2003 lists 10 examples of occupations that might qualify under the administrative exemption, from claim adjusters to human resource managers to purchasing agents. But nowhere is a paralegal listed. Assuming that a paralegal's work qualifies as being "directly related to the firm's management policies," may a paralegal exercise the kind of independent judgment required? According to a 1994 opinion letter issued by the Department of Labor, paralegals do not qualify as being exempt under the administrative exemption because they do not exercise the discretion and independent judgment approved by the regulation and, therefore, must be paid overtime. FLSA-1369 (November 10, 1994). The Department of Labor opinion letters discussed earlier, written after the 2004 revisions, also applied the administrative exemptions and likewise concluded that they provided no safe harbor to the inquiring law firms that wanted to sidestep the overtime requirements.

The final possible exemption category is for those who are executives. *See* 29 C.F.R. § 541.100 (2006). This exemption applies to those who have key management authority over the "enterprise," who regularly oversee the work of at least two employees, and who have considerable influence in hiring and firing decisions. *Id.* Some believe the executive exemption applies to *certain* paralegals, because some of them do have supervisory roles over other paralegals, legal assistants, and other non-lawyer personnel. In fact, the International Paralegal Management Association, discussed earlier in the chapter, was organized to meet the needs of such law firm employees. However, to qualify as an executive under this exemption, this paralegal would need to be empowered to direct the management of the firm or a permanent subdivision. Later regulations amplify the meaning of terms used in those prerequisites. *See* 29 C.F.R. §§ 541.101–106 (2006). See Exhibit 2–8 on key overtime exemptions under federal labor law.

Employers and employees may not agree to opt out of the overtime pay requirements by waiving the overtime pay rights granted by federal law. Willful violations of the overtime pay requirements can subject the employer to a $10,000 dollar fine and, possibly, incarceration. 29 C.F.R. § 778.102 (2001); 29 U.S.C. § 216(a). In a warning to any overtime-dodging employers, 29 C.F.R. § 541.2

EXHIBIT 2–8   KEY OVERTIME PAY EXEMPTIONS UNDER FEDERAL LABOR LAW

The Executive Exemption (29 C.F.R. § 541.100)	The Administrative Exemption (29 C.F.R. § 541.200 and 201)	The Professional Exemption (29 C.F.R. § 541.300 and 301)
• Employed as a bona fide executive and paid not less than $455 per week • Primary duty is management of the enterprise • Customarily and regularly directs the work of at least two employees • Has the authority to hire and fire	• Employed in a bona fide administrative capacity and paid not less than $455 per week • Primary duty is performing nonmanual work directly related to management...of the employer or employer's customers • Exercising discretion and independent judgment with matters of significance	• Employed in a bona fide professional capacity and paid not less than $455 per week • Primary duty is performing work that requires advanced knowledge...that is acquired by a prolonged course of specialized intellectual instruction • Intellectual in character and consistently exercising discretion and judgment

cautions that "[a] job title alone is insufficient to establish the exempt status of any employee." Exemptions must be individually based on an employee's pay and the application of the exemption regulations. *Id.* However, due to the fact-specific nature of the professional, administrative, or executive exemptions—as well as the ways in which law firms might interpret the federal regulations—it is likely that some law firms might classify at least some of their paralegals as exempt, thereby sidestepping the overtime pay requirement.

In a federal case in 1994, the Department of Labor sought the payment of $40,000 in back overtime pay for paralegals from the law firm of Page & Addison. *Reich v. Page & Addison,* No. 91–CV–2655-P (N.D. Tex, March 9, 1994). The jury, however, found that 10 paralegals from Page & Addison were exempt from the overtime pay requirements of the Fair Labor Standards Act. They agreed with the law firm's argument that the administrative exemption (independent judgment test) applied to their paralegals. The Department of Labor eventually dropped its appeal, so the decision stood. However, the decision—based on the specific facts presented in the litigation—has no value as precedent because the case got no higher than a trial court.

Philosophically, it might negatively affect the recognition of paralegals and legal assistants as professionals if they are treated as secretaries for overtime purposes, regardless of whether they might make more money being paid overtime. On the other hand, nurses are nonexempt employees who are paid overtime, and that fact does not seem to hinder the nursing reputation in the United States. The NFPA does not take an official position on whether paralegals are exempt from the requirement of overtime pay, but it has issued a variety of reports on the subject, and has a detailed portion of its Web site dedicated to the overtime issue. According to the *NFPA 2006 Paralegal Compensation and Benefits Report,* 35 percent of the respondents were considered exempt employees, a considerable drop from the prior survey, conducted before the overtime regulations were revised in 2004, which noted that 47 percent of the respondents were not paid overtime by their law firms. NALA's *2008 National Utilization and Compensation Survey Report* showed that 25 percent of the respondents were never paid overtime, while the 2004 survey listed 37 percent of the respondents as never having been paid overtime. Again, that is a significant reduction, which may be due to the intervening tightening of the federal overtime regulations. NALA issued a press release following the Page & Addison decision, summarizing the case and stating that the NALA membership was divided on the issue of exempt versus nonexempt employment status. After surveying its membership, the NALA found that many members depended on the overtime pay, while other members believed that being exempt from overtime pay was an appropriate mark of a professional.

Disbarred or Suspended Lawyers Working as Paralegals

An issue of growing concern to paralegals and paralegal associations is whether lawyers who have been disbarred, or are serving a suspension, can be employed as paralegals. As discussed in Chapter 1, disbarment occurs for extreme professional misconduct, certain kinds of criminal conduct, or excessive violations of the rules of professional responsibility. Suspensions can occur for a variety of intentional and unintentional acts of misconduct and can range from a month to a few years. To be disbarred is to receive the scarlet letter of misbehavior. That does not necessarily mean, however, that a disbarred attorney has a monumental lack of knowledge regarding the law. Incompetence is why there are malpractice cases; impropriety is why there are disciplinary cases. It might seem that working as a paralegal after being disbarred or while serving a suspension would be a natural employment option. Who would know better about substantive legal work—the kind of work paralegals and legal assistants are educated and trained to do—than those who were at one time lawyers?

Should lawyers, no matter their abilities, be allowed to work in the law in a non-lawyer capacity if they have been found unfit to practice law, even if temporarily? As expected, paralegal associations are opposed to sanctioned lawyers working as paralegals. They argue that the reputation of paralegals is severely damaged by allowing unethical lawyers to become paralegals. This is especially true because paralegals are expected to behave ethically and have their own sets of ethics rules, while sanctioned lawyers have already proven themselves unethical. In fact, the National Federation of Paralegal Associations has its own character and fitness criteria that preclude disbarred or suspended lawyers from becoming NFPA members, and the National Association of Legal Assistants forbids those convicted of felonies from becoming association members. Furthermore, it is argued that clients will be confused about the proper role of the sanctioned lawyer, which in turn might lead to the unauthorized practice of law. There is also a thorny employment opportunity issue at stake—there will be fewer jobs for paralegals if they will have to compete with women and men who have law degrees and practice experience.

Some states expressly prohibit disbarred or suspended lawyers being employed as legal assistants. Indiana and Illinois require lawyers who have been disbarred or suspended for at least six months to make sure they do not give any impression that they work as legal assistants. Indiana Admission and Discipline Rules, Rule 23(26)(b); Illinois Supreme Court Rules, Rule 764(b). Guideline 10 of the Rhode Island Guidelines on the Utilization of Legal Assistants states, "A lawyer shall not use or employ as a legal assistant any attorney who has been suspended or disbarred pursuant to an order of this court, or an attorney who has resigned in this or any other jurisdiction for reasons related to a breach of ethical conduct." Massachusetts forbids its lawyers who have been disbarred or suspended or who have resigned their license due to misconduct allegations from working as paralegals. Massachusetts S.J.C. Rule 4:01, § 17(7). New Jersey prohibits its lawyers from employing any disbarred or suspended lawyers. New Jersey S.C.R. 1:20-20(a).

Other states that have similar prohibitions in their rules of court (or by ethics opinions) include Maryland, South Carolina, Tennessee, Washington, and Wisconsin. Louisiana, a state that in the past tacitly allowed suspended lawyers to work as paralegals, no longer does. Revisions to Rule 5.5 (on the Unauthorized Practice of Law) of Louisiana's Rules of Professional conduct prohibit an attorney from employing a disbarred attorney, and allow a suspended lawyer to be hired by an attorney only if the hiring attorney files with the Disciplinary Counsel the proper employment registration that, *inter alia*, describes how the suspended lawyer will be used and compensated. Prior to these rule changes, Louisiana reached no conclusion on the legality of suspended lawyers working as paralegals for other lawyers, but it did engage in inquiries about the activities of such paralegals, including possible unauthorized practice of law activities. See *In re Elkins*, 700 S.2d 211 (La. 1997).

Perhaps surprisingly, there are quite a few states that do permit disbarred lawyers to work as paralegals. For instance, an opinion of the General Counsel for the Alabama State Bar not only took the position that disbarred or suspended Alabama lawyers may work as legal assistants, but also stated (without citations) that a majority of states allow the same thing. 58 Ala. Law. 106 (1997). An Alabama Disciplinary Commission Ethics Opinion issued in 1996 also addressed the issue, concluding that such sanctioned lawyers (including those who are on inactive status due to psychological or addiction disabilities) may work as paralegals or in other law office capacities, subject to seven conditions, which include not having any client contact whatsoever, not attending any court proceedings with their supervising lawyers, and not having any access to client funds. Ala. Ethics Op. 1996-08 (1996).

Delaware and Kansas also allow disbarred or suspended lawyers to work as paralegals, but in contrast with traditional paralegals, sanctioned lawyers working as paralegals are not allowed to have any client contact. See *Matter of Frabizzio*, 508 A.2d 468 (Del.1986); *Matter of Wilkinson*, 834 P.2d 1356 (Kan.1992). In fact, restrictions on client contact seem to be a common limitation placed on disbarred or suspended lawyers who are allowed to work as paralegals. Iowa's Rules of Court allow suspended attorneys to work as legal assistants, provided they do not have direct client contact. See Iowa Court Rule 35.12(4). The Pennsylvania Supreme Court amended Rule 217 of its Rules of Disciplinary Enforcement in 2000 to allow formerly admitted attorneys to work in law firms and engage in paralegal work, provided that they work under the direct supervision of a member in good standing of the Pennsylvania Bar, who is designated as the supervising attorney of the formerly admitted attorney. There are some limitations placed on such formerly admitted attorneys, including that they may not have any direct contact with or perform any law-related services for any clients who were clients before such attorneys were disbarred. See Pa. Rules of Disciplinary Enforcement, Rule 217(j). And, South Dakota initially forbids disbarred or suspended lawyers from working as legal assistants, but then allows them to apply to the South Dakota Supreme Court for permission to work as legal assistants. See S. D. Codified Laws §§ 16–18–34.4 and 16–18–34.5. Other states that allow disbarred or suspended lawyers to work as paralegals include Alaska, California, Colorado, Connecticut, the District of Columbia, Florida, Georgia, Hawaii, Kansas, Ohio, Oklahoma, Oregon, Texas, Utah, Virginia, West Virginia, and Wyoming.

Paralegals and Legal Assistants Joining State Bar Associations

Even though a paralegal must obey the rules of professional conduct in the jurisdiction in which the legal assistant is employed, that paralegal is usually on the outside looking in at the organization whose rules he or she is supposed to follow. Legal assistants have historically been unwelcome as members in state bar associations because admission to a state bar association is generally contingent on being licensed to practice law. Furthermore, because paralegals are unlicensed, it is uncertain as to what prerequisites would determine eligibility and what role paralegals would have in state bar associations. It must be emphasized that where those jurisdictions allow non-lawyers to join bar associations, that does not make those non-lawyers members of the bar, because being a member of the bar is different from being a member of the bar association.

The American Bar Association allows non-lawyers to become members. Beyond allowing law students to join, the ABA has an associate membership category for those whose careers are connected to the law, which expressly includes paralegals and legal assistants. Such a membership provides many of the privileges and benefits that are afforded to ABA members who are attorneys. And even those who are simply interested in the law but have no academic or employment connection to it may join the ABA. See the following link for more information on joining the ABA: http://www.abanet.org/join/.

Fortunately, state bar associations have in the past few decades begun to allow paralegals and legal assistants to join their ranks, usually as part of a section within the bar association, or as a division of the bar association. Texas is thought to be the first state to allow paralegals and legal assistants entrance into its state bar association, having created its Paralegal Division of the Texas State Bar in 1981, originally called the Legal Assistant Division. The originally stated purpose of the Paralegal Division (The Division) was "to enhance paralegals' participation in the administration of justice, professional responsibility and public service in cooperation with the State Bar of Texas." The membership classifications range from "active members" to "student members. To qualify as an active member, the legal assistant must be: A) professionally employed as a legal assistant under the direct supervision of a licensed attorney, performing substantial legal work 80 percent of the time; and B) also meet one of eight options, ranging from being certified (by the Texas Board of Legal Specialization, the NALA, or the NFPA), to having completed varying levels of collegiate legal study accompanied with corresponding years of paralegal experience, to having no legal education but having at least three years of paralegal experience and ten hours of continuing legal education credits. An active member is entitled to vote on Division matters and is subject to professional discipline, including expulsion from the division for a variety of criminal acts, engaging in the unauthorized practice of law, or violating the Code of Ethics of the Paralegal Division. The Division has a board of directors and holds an annual meeting at the same time the Texas Bar holds its annual meeting, and publishes an official periodical, *The Texas Paralegal Journal.*

Other state bar associations also allow membership for legal assistants. The Illinois State Bar Association has a membership category for law office administrators and legal assistants who may join the bar association with the required sponsorship of an active lawyer-member. The Indiana State Bar Association voted in the fall of 2001 to allow legal assistants to become affiliate members, beginning in 2002. Indiana legal assistants must meet certain entrance requirements, including establishing that at least 70 percent of their work is substantive legal work. Maryland's State Bar Association also decided in 2001 to allow paralegals and law firm administrators to join as associate members, provided they are sponsored by an active attorney-member of the MSBA. Michigan's Bar Association Bylaws, Article I, Section 6, allow currently employed or retained legal assistants who meet a combination of educational or experiential prerequisites to become a "Legal Assistant Affiliate Member" of the Michigan State Bar Association. Once members, legal assistants can join the Legal Assistant Section of the State Bar of Michigan, which has its own set of bylaws. In 1998, the Montana Bar Association created a Paralegal Section and started allowing paralegals to join the following year. Applicants for membership must meet postsecondary educational requirements and sign a statement promising to follow the Montana Rules of Professional Conduct. After one year in the Paralegal Section, members must then earn 10 approved hours of continuing legal education credits. It is interesting that one of the professed reasons for creating the Paralegal Section was to stem the tide of the unauthorized practice of law by independent paralegals in Montana. The New Jersey State Bar Association allows legal assistants to become nonvoting members, provided they are employed as legal assistants, as described by the Association's bylaws. Like Texas, New Mexico has a Legal Assistant Division in its state bar association, with its own set of bylaws, a code of ethics, and continuing legal education requirements (12 annual hours, one of which must be an ethics hour). The Ohio State Bar Association also allows paralegals to become members if they are employed by members in good standing of the bar association. And, as earlier discussed, Ohio provides a voluntary paralegal certification program.

In summary, the trend within the legal profession is to allow—and often invite—paralegals and legal assistants to join state and local bar associations. In keeping with the evolving notion of the paralegal as one uniquely qualified by education and training to engage in substantive legal tasks on behalf of a licensed attorney, membership comes with the twin duties of observing the operative ethics guidelines and earning continuing legal education credits.

SUMMARY

People have worked as paralegals and legal assistants for years before the legal profession formally acknowledged the occupation. The American Bar Association first got involved in the late 1960s by creating a committee to study the role and regulation of paralegals. That committee is now known as the Standing Committee on Paralegals (SCOP), and it encourages the use of paralegals and legal assistants, as well as establishes guidelines for appropriate curricula for colleges that offer paralegal programs. The American Association for Paralegal Education (AAfPE) is a national organization that also promotes educational standards for paralegal programs. According to the Department of Labor, paralegalism is an occupational category that is expected to grow much faster than average over the next decade.

There are two significant national paralegal organizations: the National Federation of Paralegal Associations and the National Association of Legal Assistants. Both organizations have thousands of members who are in regional or local associations, and both have their own sets of ethics rules that members are expected to follow. The NFPA has its own certification program, the Paralegal Advanced Certification Examination (PACE), which members are entitled to take if they meet the educational and work experience prerequisites. The NALA also has its own certification program, the Certified Legal Assistant program (CLA) or Certified Paralegal exam (CP), which its members are entitled to take if they meet the educational and work experience prerequisites. Members of NFPA and NALA are subject to discipline from their respective organizations for violations of their codes of ethics.

Paralegalism is largely an unregulated profession, and those states that define a paralegal or legal assistant rarely do so in such a way as to require any education or training. No state licenses paralegals, and with few exceptions, the certification programs in existence are voluntary and unconnected to any state bar. The American Bar Association's SCOP is opposed to the licensure of paralegals, believing that it is unnecessary because paralegals work under the supervision of lawyers who are licensed. SCOP also believes that licensure will unduly increase the cost of legal services. The NALA does not favor legal assistant licensing, but the NFPA is in favor of it.

Because paralegals work under the supervision—or on the behalf—of lawyers, the ethics rules make supervising lawyers personally responsible for the misconduct of their paralegals. ABA Model Rule 5.3 requires that supervising lawyers and those with comparable managerial authority ensure that the actions of their non-lawyer assistants be compatible with the professional ethics standards of lawyers. Model Rule 5.3 also makes supervisory lawyers responsible for the conduct of their non-lawyer assistants. Because paralegals and legal assistants are unlicensed by state supreme courts, it is difficult for such courts or their disciplinary committees to sanction legal assistants for professional misconduct. One possible exception would be if a court were to hold a paralegal in contempt for violating an injunction ordering a paralegal or other non-lawyer to stop engaging in the unauthorized practice of law. And, the associations can sanction members of legal associations for violating association rules. Such sanctions can include fines and membership suspensions.

According to federal labor law, including the 2004 revisions of the exempt/nonexempt status regulations, paralegals are not considered exempt from overtime pay requirements under either the professional, administrative, or executive exemptions. The regulations provide an exception for those paralegals having advanced degrees who apply that knowledge distinctly in the performance of their paralegal duties. Some jurisdictions allow suspended or disbarred attorneys to work as paralegals, although client contact is generally prohibited. Increasingly, state bar associations have begun to allow paralegals to become members, and a few state bar associations have created legal assistant divisions within their state bar associations.

ETHICS IN ACTION

1. Robin and Iris met each other for the first time waiting in line at a sidewalk lunch truck near their downtown offices. They both work for lawyers in the same building a few blocks away, but on different floors. Interested by the fact that they both work for sole practitioners, they began comparing their jobs. Robin works for a personal injury lawyer who limits his practice to medical malpractice. Robin's boss will not call her a paralegal or allow her to have a business card because he fears that will force him to pay Robin a higher wage. For similar reasons, he also frowns on Robin taking any college classes. He insists she refer to herself as a secretary, and in addition to her clerical duties, Robin does some drafting of pleadings, motions, and pretrial orders, contacts insurance company representatives regarding medical bills, and is the primary contact person for her boss's clients. Iris works for a lawyer who calls Iris "my

(continues)

ETHICS IN ACTION *(continued)*

paralegal," and provides Iris with her own business card. Iris has a 60-credit, accredited paralegal degree and belongs to the National Federation of Paralegal Associations. Iris's job consists of answering the phone and taking messages, running documents to the courthouse, and typing the tape-recorded work her boss creates.

Which of these women is a paralegal? Why?

2. Brittany works at a law firm that represents criminal defendants. One day, while her boss was at a hearing, a client accused of arson stopped by unannounced. Although Brittany had little contact with this client, she was aware that he might have some psychological difficulties. During the course of the conversation, he told her, "If that assistant D.A.'s house burns down tonight, don't be surprised." He then laughed and said before walking out the door, "I've seen a couple John Grisham movies; you have to keep that a secret, don't you?" Brittany is serious about her ethical duties and belongs to the NFPA, whose ethics code says in EC-1.33(f), "If a paralegal possesses knowledge of future criminal activity, that knowledge must be reported to the appropriate authority immediately." Brittany also knows that her jurisdiction's lawyer ethics code states in Rule 1.6 that an attorney *may* breach client confidentiality in order to prevent a client from committing a crime likely to cause serious bodily injury or death.

What should she do? If she refuses to call the police, should she be sanctioned by the NFPA?

3. Tina's paralegal duties include the management of her firm's client trust account (which is discussed in detail in Chapter 7). When funds such as advance payments or settlement distributions come into the firm, Tina takes the money and deposits it in the client trust account. Eventually, when money is to be paid from the account, she disburses those funds and keeps detailed records. Tina, who has managed the trust account for about two years, has an accounting background and was trained by the firm on how to keep proper trust account records. A few months ago, she stole five hundred dollars from the account to pay a personal medical bill. A collection agency had been contacting her at home. She had just received a small raise at work, but it was not enough to pay the bill. When the bank noticed the discrepancy, it contacted the state bar, which audited the trust account. After the investigation, the disciplinary commission instituted a charge against Tina's supervising lawyer for failing to adequately supervise Tina.

In light of Guideline 1 of the ABA Model Guidelines for the Utilization of Paralegal Service and Model Rule 5.3, do you think the lawyer should be held personally responsible for Tina's embezzlement?

(continues)

ETHICS IN ACTION *(continued)*

4. Aaron is a legal assistant at a law firm with seven attorneys. He works for an associate attorney and that attorney's supervising partner. Generally, the partner assigns her case files to Aaron, but the associate is allowed to assign tasks to Aaron if the associate first gets the partner's approval. Recently, Aaron has been drafting pleadings and client letters for the associate, as well as forging the associate's signature on those documents. This was done at the request of the associate attorney, who has a large case load and is trying to cut corners while still billing the hours required from someone who hopes to make partner eventually. The supervising partner is blissfully unaware of these deceitful activities.

    If the disciplinary commission of his jurisdiction discovers Aaron's unlawful activity, who will be disciplined: Aaron, the associate, or the partner? Does it matter whether you analyze this situation under Ethics 200 version of Model Rule 5.3 or under its prior version?

5. Hillary was suspended from the practice of law for one year because she was found to have repeatedly ignored client matters and was caught cheating on her taxes. To pay her IRS penalties and the costs associated with her disciplinary proceeding, Hillary needs to work. However, all that she knows is the law. She is hoping to work as a paralegal during her suspension. She has been offered two positions: one with a lawyer in her firm; and, another with a lawyer she knows from law school.

    If Hillary lived in your jurisdiction, could she work as a paralegal during her suspension? If so, under what conditions? Do you know where to look for the answer?

■ POINTS TO PONDER

1. What distinguishes a paralegal or legal assistant from other law office personnel, such as secretaries or receptionists?

2. When did paralegalism start to be recognized as a separate legal occupation?

3. What role does the American Bar Association play in the paralegal field?

4. If you are a student in a legal studies department, is your department's curriculum consistent with SCOP or AAfPE guidelines?

5. Does your state define "paralegal" or "legal assistant" in its state code or rules of court? If so, is the definition broad or narrow?

6. Do your state's attorney rules of professional conduct have any rules or guidelines specifically addressed to the use of paralegals?

7. Do your state's rules of professional conduct have the ABA Ethics 2000 version of Rule 5.3?

8. Are you a member, or do you know any members, of either the NFPA or NALA? If so, what are the benefits of being in either organization?

9. If paralegals must comply with their state's attorney rules of ethics, why do the national paralegal organizations have their own rules of ethics?

10. Assuming there is a conflict between the attorney rules of ethics in a paralegal's jurisdiction and the ethics rules for the paralegal association to which that paralegal belongs, which rule should be followed? Why?

11. What prerequisites must be met for a paralegal to have a certification designation, under the auspices of either the NFPA or NALA?

12. Do you think it is fair that a person must have working experience in order to sit for a certification exam?

13. Do you think it is fair that one must, with limited exceptions, have a bachelor's degree in order to sit for a certification exam?

14. Does your state offer any state-specific certifications?

15. What are the pros and cons of paralegal licensure?

16. Are there any other considerations regarding paralegal licensure not mentioned in the chapter?

17. Do you oppose or favor paralegal licensure? Why?

18. Why are attorneys responsible for the misconduct of their non-lawyer assistants, including paralegals?

19. When would a lawyer be excused from either professional discipline or personal liability for the misconduct of the lawyer's non-lawyer assistants?

20. Why is it that courts do not sanction paralegals for violations of their jurisdiction's rules of professional conduct?

21. What, under federal labor law, determines whether someone should be paid overtime?

22. Regardless of the financial benefits of overtime pay, do you think legal assistants should be exempted from overtime pay under any of the federal exemptions?

23. Do you think suspended lawyers should be allowed to work as paralegals? Why or why not?

24. Does your state have any rule or statute that concerns suspended or disbarred lawyers working as paralegals? Should either category of lawyers be allowed to work as paralegals?

25. Does your state or local bar association provide for legal assistant membership? If so, are there any continuing legal education requirements for legal assistants who are members?

KEY CONCEPTS

ABA Model Guidelines for the Utilization of Paralegal Services

ABA Model Rule 5.3

ABA Standing Committee on Paralegals

American Association for Paralegal Education (AAfPE)

Certified Legal Assistant (CLA)/Certified Paralegal (CP)

Exempt employee

International Paralegal Management Association (IPMA)

NALA Code of Ethics and Professional Responsibility

NALA Model Standards and Guidelines for Utilization of Legal Assistants

National Association of Legal Assistants

National Federation of Paralegal Associations (NFPA)

NFPA Model Code of Ethics and Professional Responsibility and Guidelines for Enforcement

Paralegal Advanced Competency Exam (PACE)

Paralegal/legal assistant certification

Paralegal/legal assistant licensure

Respondeat superior

Scope of employment doctrine

KEY TERMS

associate

cause of action

injunction

malfeasance

partner

respondeat superior

Online Companion™
For additional resources, please go to
http://www.paralegal.delmar.cengage.com

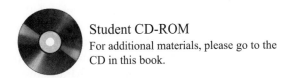

Student CD-ROM
For additional materials, please go to the
CD in this book.

The Unauthorized Practice of Law

INTRODUCTION

Although Rachel enjoys her job as a paralegal, she feels conflicted about the fact that many people she knows could not afford the services of her firm, or any law firm for that matter. She believes that paralegals should be licensed to independently engage in certain legal services such as basic will drafting, no-fault divorces, and typical landlord/tenant dispute resolutions. Rachel has become a source of information for her neighborhood friends—and their friends—who seek her help on all kinds of legal matters, and is torn between lending a helping hand and violating her professional responsibilities. What can Rachel do to assist her friends without crossing the line and engaging in the unauthorized practice of law?

Few subjects related to the legal profession are as fraught with uncertainty as the unauthorized practice of law (UPL). Much of the subject, perhaps too much, is gray and the lines of demarcation often move like a sundial. Yet almost no subject other than UPL is more important to paralegals and lawyers alike from an ethics perspective. Lawyers can be disciplined for assisting someone in engaging in the unauthorized practice of law, even if their efforts are unintentional. Paralegals face issues every day that require them to walk a fine line between doing good work and doing too much good. Companies, such as banks and real estate companies, and even legal self-help publishing companies can be sued by state bar associations for intruding into the practice of law. Private citizens who have no formal connection to the legal profession can find themselves the target of a bar association investigation, or charged with civil or criminal violations of unauthorized practice of law statutes. This chapter will focus on what traditionally constitutes the practice of law, what kinds of laws are in place to prohibit UPL, what kinds of activities paralegals are usually prohibited from performing, and what kinds of activities paralegals can safely perform. The chapter will close with a discussion on the subject of independent-contracting paralegals.

WHAT IS THE PRACTICE OF LAW?

It is one thing to say that a person must be licensed in a jurisdiction in order to be called a lawyer. It is another thing to define the practice of law, particularly because those who are not supposed to engage in it need to know where the boundaries are. While it is intuitive to expect that the practice of law would be defined in a specific rule or statute (statutory law is sometimes referred to as **positive law**), that is not the case in many states. Even though every state has some statute prohibiting the unauthorized practice of law—usually making it a **misdemeanor** unless fraud is involved—less than a majority of states have statutes that specifically define the practice of law. As described in Chapter 1, legislatures rarely get involved in regulating the practice of law, leaving those tasks to the appropriate appellate court. According to a 1997 study by the ABA State Legislative Clearinghouse, only 12 states and the District of Columbia define the practice of law by statute or rule of court. But, more than a decade later, approximately 19 states define the practice of law in either of those methods. For example, Rhode Island's statute (R.I. Gen. Laws § 11–27–2) defines the practice of law in this manner:

> The term "practice of law" as used in this chapter shall be deemed to mean the doing of any act for another person usually done by attorneys at law in the course of their profession, and without limiting this generality, shall be deemed to include the following:
>
> (1) The appearance or acting as the attorney, solicitor, or representative of another person before any court, referee, master, auditor, division, department, commission, board, judicial person, or body authorized or constituted by law to determine any question of law or fact or to exercise any judicial power, or the preparation of pleadings or other legal papers incident to any action or other proceeding of any kind before or to be brought before the court or other body;
>
> (2) The giving or tendering to another person for a consideration, direct or indirect, of any advice or counsel pertaining to a law question or a court action or judicial proceeding brought or to be brought;

▥ **positive law**
A phrase that refers to law made through political, governmental means.

▥ **misdemeanor**
Generally, a lower classified crime, in comparison to a felony.

(3) The undertaking or acting as a representative or on behalf of another person to commence, settle, compromise, adjust, or dispose of any civil or criminal case or cause of action;

(4) The preparation or drafting for another person of a will, codicil, corporation organization, amendment, or qualification papers, or any instrument which requires legal knowledge and capacity and is usually prepared by attorneys at law.

Washington State's rules of professional conduct provides a general definition which states, "[t]he practice of law is the application of legal principles and judgment with regard to the circumstances or objectives of another entity or person(s) which require the knowledge and skill of a person trained in the law." Washington Court Rules, General Rule 24(a). The rule then goes on to list nonexclusive behaviors that constitute the practice of law, including giving legal advice and representing others in court. *Id.*

The majority of states still do not define the practice of law by positive law, but instead choose to rely upon the fabric of their common law to fashion a working definition. Hawaii's view on the subject is typical of other jurisdictions. In a case concerning the practice of law, the Hawaii Supreme Court quoted a state senate committee which noted "[a]ttempts to define the practice of law in terms of enumerating the specific types of services that come within the phrase are fruitless because new developments in society, whether legislative, social, or scientific in nature, continually create new concepts and new legal problems." *Fought & Co., Inc. v. Steel Engineering and Erection, Inc.*, 951 p.2d 487 (Hawaii 1998).

At one time, one could be an attorney without having a formal, legal education. (Thomas Jefferson, lawyer, author of the Declaration of Independence, president, and founder of the University of Virginia, did attend The College of William and Mary for two years, but his legal education was one of personal study under the tutelage of the famous Virginia attorney George Wythe. And, Abraham Lincoln, perhaps the most admired figure in American history, was an outstanding Illinois lawyer who never attended college, much less law school.) State courts determined what one needed to do to be eligible to practice law and, as an extension, defined what it meant to be an attorney. Therefore, in many jurisdictions, case law is the starting place for determining what the practice of law is.

It is interesting that many of those cases that define the practice of law involve activities that courts found to be the *unauthorized* practice of law. The foundational cases are usually older ones, and a Vermont case serves as a good example. In *In re Flint*, 8 A.2d 655 (Vt. 1937), Flint was found in contempt of court for engaging in the unauthorized practice of law for negotiating a settlement between two prospective litigants. Flint, who was a sheriff and a law student, arrested a Mr. Pike. During the trip to the jail, the two started discussing some romantic letters Pike had found that a Mr. Whipple had written to Mrs.

Pike. Pike then asked Flint about what could be done (at that time, a spouse could sue his or her spouse's lover for "alienation of affections"). After putting Pike in a cell, Flint started to advise him about threatening Whipple with a lawsuit and then went to Whipple, advising him about settling a possible lawsuit with Pike. After some jailhouse negotiations, in which Flint told each man a different story about what he thought the case was worth, he got the two men to settle any future lawsuit about Pike's wife for $1,000 and he retained $200 for his efforts. After being accused of the unauthorized practice of law, Flint claimed he was not acting as a lawyer because, he said, he only told the men what he would do if he were in their shoes. The court found that unpersuasive, finding that he gave legal advice to the men in that he advised them on the settlement of a legal claim and took a fee for doing so. *Flint* at 657. The court also cited similar cases from other jurisdictions, including one where another court, explaining what it means to practice law, stated, "...when one undertakes to give counsel as to legal status or rights in respect to a pending claim, he is performing a special function reserved for attorneys at law, as much as diagnosis, prognosis, and prescriptions are within the special field of medicine." *Fink v. Peden*, 17 N.E.2d 95, 96 (Ind. 1938). (It does seem odd that a case from 1937 would cite a case from 1938, but it was done.)

NOT QUITE LINCOLN

Law School Is for Losers, I Guess

Maybe Jonathan "Johnny Kane" Harris of Philadelphia never heard the axiom credited to Abraham Lincoln: "He who represents himself has a fool for a client." Or perhaps Harris never knew of the status accorded a "Philadelphia lawyer," a term which can be found in the dictionary, stemming from a reputation that trails back to the colonial days. That lofty reputation took a mortal blow when in 2003 the 34-year-old high school dropout represented himself in three criminal trials over a three-month period. He won an acquittal every time, including a death penalty, first-degree murder case. Ignorance is such bliss. Imagine three juries failing to give the convictions implored of them by professionally educated and trained prosecutors, facing a *pro se* defendant who knew nothing about the discovery process, the trial rules, or the rules of evidence. Well, maybe a little more than nothing. As reported by the *Philadelphia Daily News*, Jonathan Harris was believed to be the first person to successfully defend himself in a murder trial in Philadelphia in many years. To be fair to the hapless prosecutors who struck out against him, some would say that a *pro se* defendant has a slight advantage, particularly if he is as eloquent as Harris was thought to be. Without a defense lawyer at his table to take on the government, the *pro se* defendant can milk his underdog status for all it is worth. And sometimes, that defendant will get free legal help from a trial judge who might periodically cut some procedural slack. After the most recent acquittal in the capital murder case, Harris was scheduled to be tried in two more felony cases in Philadelphia's Court of Common Pleas. If he wins those cases, the University of Pennsylvania Law School might be considering hiring a faculty member who has no transcripts.

■ **adjudication**

The process of formally resolving a controversy, based on evidence presented.

■ **pleadings**

Formal allegations of facts that consist of the plaintiff's claim (the complaint) or the defendant's response (the answer).

■ **motions**

Formal applications to a court (such as a motion for summary judgment), requesting the court to issue an order.

An examination of the case law and rules of court leads to a few, general principles. First, representing someone in court, including small claims court, is the practice of law. Second, representing someone in an administrative **adjudication** is the practice of law. Third, giving legal advice to someone is the practice of law. Fourth, drafting or completing transactional documents, such as wills, and litigation documents, such as **pleadings** or **motions**, is the practice of law. And fifth, negotiating on behalf of someone in situations where that person's legal rights (including the right to sue) are involved is the practice of law. See Exhibit 3–1 on what constitutes the practice of law.

That, however, does not end the inquiry, since the previous list is neither exclusive nor self-explanatory. Furthermore, to state what activities constitute the practice of law also requires one to determine what kinds of people can engage in those activities. Lawyers in good standing can do everything on the list in Exhibit 3–1. Lawyers who are serving a period of suspension can do nothing on the list. Law students are allowed to practice on a limited basis if they meet the prerequisites stated in their state's Admission and Discipline rules. Those prerequisites usually include completing the second year of law school, completing a legal ethics course, and being certified by their law school's dean as approved for limited licensure. Then, such a law student can practice only under the direct supervision of an attorney who agrees to bear responsibility for the student's work. Law graduates who are awaiting the results of the bar exam can also practice under similar constraints.

Paralegals can engage in some of those activities in two ways. First, paralegals can engage in certain activities, such as drafting pleadings or assisting clients with discovery requests under the condition that their work is conducted under the supervision of an attorney who takes official responsibility for the work, often as

---

EXHIBIT 3–1   WHAT IS THE PRACTICE OF LAW?

- Representing Someone in Court
- Giving Legal Advice
- Drafting and Executing Legal Documents
- Negotiating on Behalf of Someone's Legal Rights

evidenced by his signature on the work product. The effective use of supervised paralegals is the essence of the ABA's Model Guidelines for the Utilization of Paralegal Services. And as will be discussed later, federal, state, and local laws have granted to non-lawyers, including those who are not legal assistants, the right to engage in certain legal activities, including some activities listed previously. See Exhibit 3–2 on the Paralegal's Place in the Practice of Law.

Believing that the changing environment of the practice of law called for an examination of whether the ABA should create a uniform definition of the practice of law, the ABA Board of Governors impaneled an entity, The Model Task Force on the Model Definition of the Practice of Law, to work on creating such a definition. Included in the ABA's stated purposes behind the task force's directive was the realization that there is increasing activity of non-lawyers providing services to the public that are difficult to characterize as legal services. The task force released a draft definition in September 2002, seeking comments and suggestions on it by December 2002.

The U.S. Justice Department and the Federal Trade Commission responded in writing to the ABA, expressing the opinion that the ABA's definition violates antitrust law by prohibiting the activities of non-lawyer service providers, including real estate brokers and banks, as well as those that sell legal forms or self-help books to the public. In February 2003, a public hearing was held on the model definition at the ABA Midyear meeting.

Notice that the draft definition of the practice of law does cover the work of paralegals and legal assistants in section (d), but it does so without stating that the work of paralegals and legal assistants is the practice of law.

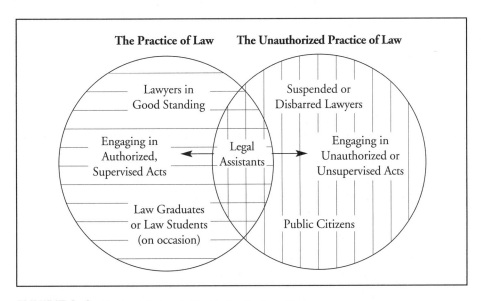

EXHIBIT 3–2 The Legal Assistant's Place in the Practice of Law

(a) The practice of law shall be performed only by those authorized by the highest court of this jurisdiction.

(b) Definitions:

    (1) The 'practice of law' is the application of legal principles and judgment with regard to the circumstances or objectives of a person that require the knowledge and skill of a person trained in the law.

    (2) 'Person' includes the plural as well as the singular and denotes an individual or any legal or commercial entity.

    (3) 'Adjudicative body' includes a court, a mediator, an arbitrator or a legislative body, administrative agency or other body acting in an adjudicative capacity. A legislative body, administrative agency or other body acts in an adjudicative capacity when a neutral official, after the presentation of evidence or legal argument by a party or parties, will render a binding legal judgment directly affecting a party's interests in a particular matter.

(c) A person is presumed to be practicing law when engaging in any of the following conduct on behalf of another:

    (1) Giving advice or counsel to persons as to their legal rights or responsibilities or to those of others;

    (2) Selecting, drafting, or completing legal documents or agreements that affect the legal rights of a person;

    (3) Representing a person before an adjudicative body, including, but not limited to, preparing or filing documents or conducting discovery; or

    (4) Negotiating legal rights or responsibilities on behalf of a person.

(d) Exceptions and exclusions: Whether or not they constitute the practice of law, the following are permitted:

    (1) Practicing law authorized by a limited license to practice;

    (2) Pro se representation;

    (3) Serving as a mediator, arbitrator, conciliator or facilitator; and

(4) Providing services under the supervision of a lawyer in compliance with the Rules of Professional Conduct.

(e) Any person engaged in the practice of law shall be held to the same standard of care and duty of loyalty to the client independent of whether the person is authorized to practice law in this jurisdiction. With regard to the exceptions and exclusions listed in paragraph (d), if the person providing the services is a nonlawyer, the person shall disclose that fact in writing. In the case of an entity engaged in the practice of law, the liability of the entity is unlimited and the liability of its constituent members is limited to those persons participating in such conduct and those persons who had knowledge of the conduct and failed to take remedial action immediately upon discovery of same.

(f) If a person who is not authorized to practice law is engaged in the practice of law, that person shall be subject to the civil and criminal penalties of this jurisdiction.

At this point, it can be said that the unauthorized practice of law occurs when: (a) a private citizen engages in activities that are only allowed to be done by attorneys; (b) a paralegal exceeds his or her authority as defined by local law and rules of court; and (c) an attorney engages in otherwise lawful behavior during a period of suspension or disbarment.

After much hand wringing, more criticism from many corners of the legal profession, and more reflection, the task force reconvened and dropped its recommended model definition on the practice of law, replacing it in August 2003 with what might be called a revised definition. This version, found in a new task force resolution, simply states that every jurisdiction should adopt a definition of the practice of law, which, according to the task force, "should include the basic premise that the practice of law is the application of legal principles and judgment to the circumstances or objectives of another person or entity." The revised definition seems more like a common law principle (found in all those state cases holding that a singular definition of the practice of law is unwise) than the type of definition containing the kind of teeth the ABA originally hoped would be found sharp enough to be adopted by the states. For more information on the task force's opinion on this matter, please consult the task force's 2003 report to the ABA House of Delegates, which can be found by searching the ABA's Web site at http://www.abanet.org.

So, where does that leave us, besides a little confused? At this point, it can be said that the unauthorized practice of law occurs when: (a) a private citizen engages in activities that are only allowed to be done by attorneys; (b) a paralegal exceeds his or her authority as defined by local law and rules of court; and (c) an attorney engages in otherwise lawful behavior during a period of suspension or disbarment. See Exhibit 3–3 on when the unauthorized practice of law occurs.

> **EXHIBIT 3–3**   UPL OCCURS WHEN...
>
> - Non-lawyers engage in acts that only lawyers are allowed to do
> - Paralegals exceed their authority, as defined by applicable law
> - Attorneys practice law while suspended or disbarred

The following case shows a fourth possibility of the unauthorized practice of law. In the case, an attorney kept his law office open during the period of a short suspension and then unintentionally involved his legal staff in the unauthorized practice of law. While reading the case, pay close attention to the court's expansion of the definition of the practice of law.

CASE LAW *In Re Thonert*

693 N.E.2d 559 (Ind. 1998)

PER CURIAM.

Lawyers who have been suspended from the practice of law may not allow their nonlawyer staff to continue to actively operate their law office and conduct business on behalf of clients during the period of suspension. On July 3, 1997, this Court suspended the respondent, Richard J. Thonert, for a period of thirty days, beginning August 11, 1997, and ending September 10, 1997, for violations of the Rules of Professional Conduct for Attorneys at Law. *Matter of Thonert*, 682 N.E2d 522 (Ind. 1997). That order specified that the respondent would be automatically reinstated to the practice of law, provided he pay the costs of the underlying proceeding and comply with the requirements of Admis.Disc.R. 23(4)(c). On September 2, 1997, the Commission filed its Verified Objection to Automatic Reinstatement stating that during the period of his suspension, the respondent engaged or attempted to engage in the practice of law by acting through non-attorney employees of his office. On September 10, 1997, this Court stayed the respondent's automatic reinstatement pending consideration of the Commission's objections. Thereafter, the parties filed stipulations of fact and a joint petition for ruling. Each fully briefed its position. On October 17, 1997, this Court issued an Order Imposing Additional Suspension and Lifting Stay of Automatic Reinstatement, finding that the respondent "violated the order of suspension and that an additional period of suspension, with automatic reinstatement, is warranted." Accordingly, we extended the respondent's suspension from September 10, 1997, until October 17, 1997. This opinion more fully sets forth the facts and circumstances of this case and our analysis underlying our decision to extend his suspension.

(continues)

CASE LAW *In Re Thonert* (continued)

I. FACTS

Adopting the parties' stipulations, we now find that the respondent is a solo practitioner with a law office located in Fort Wayne, Indiana. At relevant times, the respondent employed a four-person non-lawyer support staff. The respondent's law practice is one of high volume and relies heavily on the support staff to process paperwork. Much of the practice in routine matters is systematized, relying on support staff to generate the appropriate paperwork upon the occurrence of certain events. On some routine matters, support staff members sign the respondent's name to legal documents. Occasionally, this is done without the respondent's input or review. Prior to his disciplinary suspension on August 11, 1997, the respondent filed motions to continue all matters that were set for hearing or trial during his period of suspension, arranged for another attorney to speak with his clients during that time and to cover any court hearings for which a continuance could not be obtained or which arose during the suspension, and informed his staff that he could not practice law during the suspension. He informed his staff that any questions they had should be directed to specific attorneys the respondent had arranged to be available for consultation.

The respondent was in his office periodically between the effective date of his suspension and August 25, 1997, after which he left the state to visit with relatives. Various questions arose among his staff about what they could and could not do during the period of suspension. For answers, they contacted the office of the respondent's personal attorney. An associate in that office called the respondent and advised him generally as to what actions his support staff could take during the period of suspension. The respondent recorded the conversation and allowed his staff to listen to the tape. He then told his staff members that they were not to provide legal advice to clients, but that they could keep clients informed of court dates or other matters that occurred in their cases, that if they had questions they should contact the attorney with whom the respondent had arranged for them to speak, and that the designation "Attorney at Law" should be removed from the office letterhead. In signed correspondence, the respondent directed them to write "Secretary to Richard J. Thonert." Projects the respondent instructed his staff to undertake during the period of suspension included going through old accounts receivable and sending out new statements, organizing the office, and closing old files. He gave them no specific instructions concerning the preparation and processing of routine forms and correspondence. During the suspension, several clients in fact spoke with the attorney to whom they were referred. That attorney appeared in court on numerous matters, on behalf of the respondent's clients.

While in his office during the period of suspension, the respondent reviewed incoming mail and dictated "informational" letters to clients. The letters, signed by the secretaries, advised of court hearings or other matters relative to specific cases. His staff produced,

(continues)

CASE LAW *In Re Thonert* (continued)

signed and dispersed form letters advising clients of documents received during the suspension period. The respondent stipulated that not only did he believe that he and his staff were permitted to provide such information to clients, but also that his failure to do so could expose him to further disciplinary action. If a matter on an existing case needed to be continued or some other action was needed, the respondent directed his staff to contact the referral attorney to handle the matter. In some instances, the respondent and/or his staff prepared motions or other documentation and forwarded them to the attorney for signature and filing. If an existing client presented a new matter, or if a potential new client contacted the office, the person either was directed to another attorney or was scheduled to meet with the respondent after the period of suspension expired.

On August 8, 1997, a member of the respondent's support staff prepared and sent a letter to a deputy prosecuting attorney in Allen County requesting his support in a motion for sentence modification. Attached to the letter was a proposed petition for modification of sentence, an agreed entry, and a status report from the client's probation officer. This correspondence was a duplicate of an earlier, pre-suspension request which the respondent had sent to the prosecutor but which the prosecutor apparently had not acknowledged. On August 18, 1997, a member of the respondent's support staff sent a letter to another of the respondent's clients enclosing a charging information and providing instructions relating to discovery material which had been received from the prosecutor in the case. The support staff person indicated that it was the usual practice in the respondent's office to forward to clients discovery materials and other pleadings received by the respondent. The respondent dictated similar letters during his suspension for signature and dispersal by his clerical staff.

On August 20, 1997, a member of the respondent's support staff called the Wells County Prosecutor's Office asking about discovery, charging documents, cause numbers, and hearing dates relative to a criminal action pending against one of the respondent's clients. The call was to follow up on similar inquiries made by the respondent to the prosecutor's office prior to his suspension. On August 21, 1997, a member of the respondent's support staff prepared and sent a letter to an Allen County deputy prosecuting attorney requesting that the prosecutor agree to modify the conviction of another of the respondent's clients from a Class D felony to a Class A misdemeanor. Attached to the letter was a petition, an agreed entry, and a status report from the probation officer. The correspondence was essentially a duplicate of a prior request made by the respondent to the deputy prosecutor.

On August 25, 1997, a member of the respondent's support staff sent a letter to a Wells County deputy prosecuting attorney concerning one of the respondent's clients. The letter stated, in relevant part:

Dear [Deputy Prosecuting Attorney]:

(continues)

In Re Thonert (continued)

I am writing concerning [client]. His present driving status is HTV [habitual traffic violator]. In order for him to become reinstated, it would be necessary to set aside one or more of the above-referred convictions.

If vacating one or more of these convictions would be acceptable to your office, I am enclosing the following documents:

1. Copy of [client's] Driver's Record

2. Agreed Entry/Order After you have the opportunity to review your file, please send a letter concerning your position in this matter to our office. I remain,

Very truly yours,

[Secretary] Secretary to Richard J. Thonert

The support staff person signing the letter considered the act of producing and dispersing the letter a routine "clerical" task.

On August 26, 1997, a member of the respondent's support staff prepared and sent a letter to an Allen County deputy prosecuting attorney requesting that the prosecutor agree to a petition for post-conviction relief to vacate and set aside a prior traffic offense against another of the respondent's clients. Attached to the letter was a petition for post-conviction relief, an agreed entry, and a proposed order. Again, the correspondence essentially was a duplicate of a request made by the respondent prior to his suspension. The respondent stipulates that numerous other documents similar to those identified above were produced and sent by his staff during his period of suspension. The respondent's bookkeeper received on his behalf no legal fees on new matters during his period of suspension.

On September 7, 1997, after learning that his automatic reinstatement had been stayed upon the Commission's objections, the respondent met with his staff and informed them that the letters mailed to the deputy prosecutors and others went beyond informing clients of the status of their cases, that they should not have been sent, and that they could not continue to be sent during the period of his suspension. The respondent then arranged for the referral attorney to completely supervise the respondent's office pending his reinstatement.

II. COMMISSION'S ALLEGATIONS

In its Verified Objection, the Commission concluded that the respondent "attempted to circumvent this Court's order of suspension from the practice of law by continuing to actively operate his law office and conduct business on behalf of clients during the period of suspension." Specifically, the Commission contends that the respondent's law office engaged in the unauthorized practice of law during the respondent's period of suspension. The respondent argues that it was not his intention to violate this Court's order of suspension

(continues)

CASE LAW *In Re Thonert* (continued)

and that his intention only was to allow his staff to continue to disperse routine correspondence and information to clients and adverse parties as it systematically did before he was suspended.

III. DISCUSSION

This Court has noted that

The core element of practicing law is the giving of legal advice to a client and the placing of oneself in the very sensitive relationship wherein the confidence of the client, and the management of his affairs is left totally in the hands of the attorney. The undertaking to minister to the legal problems of another creates an attorney-client relationship with regard to whether the services are actually performed by the one so undertaking the responsibility or are delegated or subcontracted to another. It is the opinion of this Court that merely entering into such a relationship constitutes the practice, of law. . . . The conducting of the business management of a law practice, in conjunction with that practice, constitutes the practice of law [emphasis added]. *Matter of Perrello*, 270 Ind. 390, 398, 386 N.E.2d 174, 179 (1979)

We have also said that "[to] practice law is to carry on the business of an attorney at law," and "to make it one's business to act for, and by the warrant of, others in legal formalities, negotiations, or proceedings." *Fink v. Peden*, 214 Ind. 584, 17 N.E.2d 95 (1938). A person who gives legal advice to clients and transacts business for them in matters connected with the law is engaged in the practice of law. *State ex rel. Pearson v. Gould*, 437 N. E.2d 41 (Ind. 1982). Thus, the practice of law is not defined only as the giving of legal advice or acting in a representative capacity—it also had been extended by this Court to conducting the business management of a law practice.

It is undisputed that the respondent's non-lawyer support staff produced motions, proposed entries, and correspondence seeking legal relief on behalf of clients and sent them to opposing counsel. It is also undisputed that the staff informed clients of upcoming hearing dates, provided instructions to them for answering formal discovery requests and, in a general sense, advised them of the status of their legal proceedings. We find that the communications to public officials undertaken in a representative capacity by the members of the respondent's support staff during his period of suspension, which sought to obtain benefits for individuals represented by the respondent, constituted the practice of law. Likewise, the production and communication of motions, pleadings, and proposed agreed entries, done without the supervision of an attorney licensed to practice in this state, constituted the unauthorized practice of law. Pursuant to court rule, legal assistants may perform services only under the direct supervision of a lawyer authorized to practice in this state. See Guideline 9.1: Use of Legal Assistants. A lawyer is responsible for all of the professional actions of a legal assistant performing legal assistant services at the lawyer's

(continues)

CASE LAW *In Re Thonert* (continued)

direction and should take reasonable measures to ensure that the legal assistant's conduct is consistent with the lawyer's obligations under the Rules of Professional Conduct. Id. The respondent himself admits that his staff should not have contacted deputy prosecuting attorneys asking that the state agree to sentence modifications or post-conviction relief and that they should not have sent discovery to clients with instructions as to how to begin preparing factual responses. He states that he should have given clearer and more thorough advice and instruction to his staff about what it could and could not do during his suspension.

The respondent was responsible for ensuring that his staff was adequately informed about what it could and could not do while he was suspended. Guideline 9.I; see also Ind. Professional Conduct Rule 5.3. The order imposing his initial suspension was filed July 3, 1997, with the suspension effective August 11. The purpose of the delay between issuance of the order and the effective date of the suspension was to give the respondent time to make arrangements for the care of his clients' legal needs, both substantive and ministerial, to be placed in the expert hands or under the supervision of a licensed attorney. He failed to make adequate arrangements or provide sufficient explanation until his staff had engaged in the unauthorized practice of law. His failure to do so placed his clients at great risk by allowing their cases to be handled by those not trained in the law and licensed to practice.

This case also included less obvious instances of misconduct. The fact that the respondent allowed his support staff to continue "to carry on the business of an attorney at law," i.e., to inform clients of upcoming hearing dates, to apprise them of the status of their legal matters, etc., without the direct supervision of a licensed attorney, constituted the unauthorized practice of law. We caution that to allow non-lawyer staff any contact with clients about the legal status of their cases in the absence of a lawyer's supervision risks harm to the legal rights of the clients. By this decision today, we do not mean to imply that lawyers who have been suspended from the practice of law should simply "walk away" from the practice of law to the detriment of their clients; instead, lawyers should make arrangements for all client needs arising during the period of suspension to be handled by or under the direct supervision of a licensed attorney, or inform all clients who do not choose to use the services of the referral attorney to seek substitute legal counsel of their choice. Admis.Disc.Rule 23(26)(c).

We note, however, that the respondent made a good-faith effort to inform his employees of what they could and could not do during his suspension. When he learned of their communications with clients and prosecutors, he immediately took action to correct the wrongful conduct. He has also expressed sincere remorse for his actions. Because the respondent apparently did not intend to circumvent our July 3, 1997, order of suspension, we find that the brief extension of the suspension already imposed is a sufficient sanction for

(continues)

> **CASE LAW** *In Re Thonert* (continued)
>
> his misconduct during his period of suspension. The respondent is also admonished of his
> obligations to comply with the duties of disbarred or suspended attorneys set forth in
> Admis.Disc.R. 23(26)(b) and discussed in this Court's recent opinions in *Matter of DeLoney*,
> 689 N.E.2d 431 (Ind. 1997), *Matter of Thonert*, 682 N.E.2d 522, etc.
>
> **Case Questions**
>
> 1. Did attorney Thonert's paralegals engage in the unauthorized practice of law, did the
>   attorney do so, or did they all do so?
>
> 2. What category of behavior has this court added to the more common definition of
>   the practice of law?
>
> 3. If there was another attorney upon whom the suspended attorney's legal staff relied
>   during the attorney's suspension, then how were the staff's activities unauthorized?
>
> 4. Do you think the attorney knowingly contributed to the unauthorized practice of
>   law?
>
> 5. Based on the court's reasoning, what would you say a legal assistant could do during
>   the suspension (or even vacation) of his or her supervising attorney?

EXISTING RULES THAT PROHIBIT THE UNAUTHORIZED PRACTICE OF LAW

Although the unauthorized practice of law may be loosely defined, it is certainly specifically forbidden. A variety of statutes, attorney rules of professional responsibility, and paralegal rules of professional responsibility prohibit the unauthorized practice of law, which also includes assisting someone who is engaging in it.

Statutes Prohibit UPL

It is against the law for someone who is not an attorney to practice law. But if someone is not an attorney, then that person is obviously not a member of the bar. How then does the bar, and its rules of conduct, control that person's behavior? It can be very difficult to do so. But there is a trump card—legislation. All jurisdictions have statutes in place that prohibit the unauthorized practice of law. As an example, Florida's unauthorized practice statute states the following:

Any person not licensed or otherwise authorized by the Supreme Court of Florida who shall practice law or assume or hold himself or herself out to the public as qualified to practice in this state, or who willfully pretends to be, or willfully takes or uses any name, title, addition, or description implying that he or she is qualified, or recognized by law as qualified, to act as a lawyer in this state, and any person entitled to practice who shall violate any provisions of this chapter, shall be guilty of a misdemeanor of the first degree, punishable as provided in s. 775.082, s. 775.083, or s. 775.084. Fla. Stat. ch. 454.23. According to s. 775.082, the incarceration for a first-degree misdemeanor conviction can be as long as one year; and, according to s. 775.083, the fine for a first-degree misdemeanor conviction can be as high as $1,000.

A reading of the preceding Florida statute shows that not just intentionally misleading, lawyer-like activity is illegal, but also illegal is the unintentional, unauthorized practice of law. The serious implication of that statute's wording means that one can be guilty of violating the law without trying or even realizing it, and that includes paralegals. In addition, the statute covers attorneys who might violate other related laws, including practicing law while suspended (ch. 454.31) and assisting disbarred or suspended lawyers in the practice of law. The fact that a first-time offender of the unauthorized practice statute is unlikely to be sentenced to a prison term or get a steep fine does not lessen the gravity of that statute; it is a serious thing to practice law without a license.

Statutes that make the unauthorized practice of law a crime necessitate the action of a prosecutor to enforce the law. In addition to a local prosecutor's office, a state attorney general's office can bring charges against a violator. Because consumer protection is part of the role of an attorney general's office, such enforcement could occur if that office believed the violator was engaging in fraud in connection with acting as an attorney.

Attorney Rules of Professional Conduct Prohibit UPL

The ABA Model Rules of Professional Conduct and the ABA Model Code of Professional Responsibility prohibit the unauthorized practice of law. However, the focus of those rules is on preventing those persons who are under the lawyer's authority from the unauthorized practice of law.

As discussed in Chapter 2, the Ethics 2000 version of the ABA Model Rule 5.3 concerns the supervision of non-lawyer assistants in the law firm, and states:

With respect to a nonlawyer employed or retained by or associated with a lawyer:

(a) A partner, and a lawyer who individually or together with other lawyers possess comparable managerial authority in a firm shall make reasonable efforts to ensure that the law firm has in effect measures giving reasonable assurance that the person's conduct is compatible with the professional obligations of the lawyer;

(b) A lawyer having direct supervisory authority over the nonlawyer shall make reasonable efforts to ensure that the person's conduct is compatible with the professional obligations of the lawyer; and

(c) A lawyer shall be responsible for conduct of such a person that would be a violation of the Rules of Professional Conduct if engaged in by a lawyer if:

> (1) the lawyer orders or, with the knowledge of the specific conduct, ratifies the conduct involved; or

> (2) the lawyer is a partner or has comparable managerial authority in the law firm in which the person is employed, or has direct supervisory authority over the person, and knows of the conduct at a time when its consequences can be avoided or mitigated but fails to take reasonable remedial action.

This rule emphasizes three things: design, supervision, and responsibility. Rule 5.3(a) requires the management of the firm to have in place a scheme for ensuring that the professional conduct of non-lawyer employees rises to the ethical standards required of lawyers in the firm. Rule 5.3(b) requires a lawyer in the firm to directly supervise the work of the non-lawyer for the purposes of maintaining standards of professional conduct. And, Rule 5.3(c) makes the supervisory lawyer responsible for any misconduct of the non-lawyer if the lawyer causes it to occur, does nothing to prevent its occurrence, or does nothing to minimize the damage of its occurrence. Even though its connection is indirect, this rule concerns the unauthorized practice of law because it makes the firm responsible for all unethical conduct committed by its paralegals.

The ABA Model Code has no provision similar to MR 5.3, but Disciplinary Rule (DR) 4–101 states that a lawyer "shall exercise reasonable care to prevent his employees, associates, and others whose services are utilized by him from disclosing or using confidences or secrets of a client..." Also, DR 7–107(J) states that a lawyer "shall exercise reasonable care to prevent his employees and associates from making an extrajudicial statement that he would be prohibited from making..."

The unauthorized practice of law is directly addressed in ABA Model Rule 5.5, which was revised in August 2002. That revision included having "Multijurisdictional Practice of Law" added to its title. The portion that most closely concerns paralegals is 5.5(a), which says "A lawyer shall not practice law in a jurisdiction in violation of the regulation of the legal profession in that jurisdiction, *or assist another in doing so.*" (Emphasis added.) The former version of that rule addressed non-lawyers and UPL in 5.5(b). There are some new Comments to the Ethics 2000 version of 5.5, including a sentence in one Comment that implies the use of independent contracting paralegals, as well as acknowledges the allowance of limited, legal services providers: "Lawyers also may assist independent nonlawyers, such as paraprofessionals, who are authorized by the law of jurisdiction to provide particular law-related services."

The Official Comments to MR 5.5 acknowledge that the definition of the practice of law is not uniform throughout the country, but it advises lawyers to avoid assisting someone in unauthorized practice, whatever the definition. If a lawyer were to assist a paralegal in the unauthorized practice of law, such assistance would be a violation of both 5.3 (failure to adequately supervise non-lawyer employees) and 5.5 (assisting a non-lawyer in the unauthorized practice of law). See Exhibit 3–4 on the two critical ways a paralegal might commit the unauthorized practice of law.

Canon 3 of the ABA Model Code states, "A Lawyer Should Assist in Preventing the Unauthorized Practice of Law." Ethical Consideration 3–5 acknowledges the difficulty of having a uniform definition of the practice of law by providing, "It is neither necessary nor desirable to attempt the formulation of a single, specific definition of what constitutes the practice of law." And EC 3–6 positively addresses paralegals engaging in substantive legal work by stating, "[s]uch delegation is proper if the lawyer maintains a direct relationship with his client, supervises the delegated work, and has complete professional responsibility for the work product. This delegation enables a lawyer to render legal service more economically and efficiently." DR 3–101(A), which is almost identical to Model Rule 5.5(b), states, "[a] lawyer shall not aid a non-lawyer in the unauthorized practice of law."

EXHIBIT 3–4   TWO WAYS THAT PARALEGALS MIGHT ENGAGE IN UPL

- Engaging in legal work that is _Unsupervised_
  - Paralegals and legal assistants may only do substantive legal work when it is properly supervised.

- Engaging in legal work that is _Unauthorized_
  - Paralegals and legal assistants may not do certain types of substantive legal work, regardless of whether it is supervised.

Paralegal Codes of Conduct Prohibit UPL

It is no surprise that all the significant national codes of conduct which have been created by or for paralegals specifically address the significant ethical problem of engaging in the unauthorized practice of law.

The ABA Model Guidelines for the Utilization of Paralegal Services

As stated in Chapter 2, the ABA Model Guidelines for the Utilization of Paralegal Services is written to and for lawyers and is an adjunct to the Model Rules of Professional Conduct. However, the guidelines are not additional rules;

hence, the operative word is '*Guidelines.*' And, because these guidelines are addressed specifically to the role of the paralegal, a discussion of them is included in this section on paralegal codes of conduct. The ABA Model Guidelines have four guidelines that deal with the unauthorized practice of law.

Guideline 1 obligates a lawyer to "take reasonable measures to ensure that the paralegal's conduct is consistent with the lawyer's obligations under the rules of professional conduct of the jurisdiction in which the lawyer practices." How does this relate to the unauthorized practice of law? It does so because one of the ABA Model Rules, 5.3 (previously addressed), requires attorneys to ensure that those who work for them do so in a manner consistent with the lawyer's professional responsibility obligations under the Model Rules. Therefore, if a paralegal engages in the unauthorized practice of law, the paralegal's supervising lawyer will be responsible for such misconduct.

Guideline 2 is an interesting guideline. It provides that a lawyer may allow a paralegal to engage in substantive legal work, the kind traditionally done by lawyers, provided that two conditions are met. The first condition requires the lawyer to be responsible for the paralegal's work, while the second condition prohibits the lawyer from authorizing the paralegal to do anything that the law (including rules of ethics) says may not be done by non-lawyers. The Comment to Guideline 2 acknowledges what has already been discussed, which is that most jurisdictions do not affirmatively define the practice of law. As such, the Comment emphasizes the need for lawyers to be aware of what is allowed to be delegated to paralegals in their jurisdiction, and to recognize that the activities of legal assistants who are engaging in properly delegated work must be supervised. (The Comment cites a case exemplifying that principle, *Musselman v. Willoughby Corporation*, which is included in Chapter 2.)

Guideline 3 lists three activities for which a paralegal may not be responsible: (1) establishing the attorney-client relationship; (2) establishing the fees to be charged; and (3) issuing a legal opinion to a client. Although these activities will be discussed later in this chapter, it can be noted at this point that the theme associated with these activities is that the lawyer must maintain a direct relationship with the client. The Comment also states that a lawyer would not be in violation of the guideline if a paralegal *assists* the lawyer in establishing client relationships, fees, or rendering legal opinions. (Emphasis added.)

Guideline 4 concerns appearances of impropriety by putting into the lawyer's hands the duty to inform all relevant parties—clients, courts, and other lawyers—that the lawyer's paralegal is not a licensed attorney. The Comment avoids requiring a particular method of communicating this fact, but reiterates that it must be done so that no one, particularly a client, is confused about the status of a paralegal. The Comment also gives its approval to paralegal-signed correspondence if the status of the paralegal is clearly given.

The NFPA Model Disciplinary Rules and Ethical Considerations

Rule 1.8 of the NFPA Model Disciplinary Rules and Ethical Considerations (formally titled as such, but inside the NFPA Model Code) specifically addresses the issue by stating, "A paralegal shall not engage in the unauthorized practice of law." Its corresponding ethical consideration, EC 1.8(a), then states, "A paralegal shall comply with the applicable legal authority governing the unauthorized practice of law." However, it does not define unauthorized practice. Other rules in the NFPA Model Disciplinary Rules and Ethical Considerations indirectly concern the unauthorized practice of law. Rule 1.3 requires that paralegals "...maintain a high standard of professional conduct." EC–1.3(b) states, "A paralegal shall avoid impropriety and the appearance of impropriety." And Rule 1.7 requires that a paralegal's title "be fully disclosed."

NALA Code of Ethics and Professional Responsibility

The NALA Code consists of Canons without commentary or ethical considerations. Canon 1 leaves no doubt concerning the unauthorized practice of law: "A legal assistant must not perform any of the duties that attorneys only may perform nor take any actions that attorneys may not take." Canon 3 prohibits the unauthorized practice activities previously listed in the ABA Guidelines for the Utilization of Legal Assistant Services, but it also includes a prohibition of any activity (even the encouragement of it) "which *could* constitute the unauthorized practice of law." (Emphasis added.) Such a broad construction shows that the spirit of the Canon, as well as its language, should direct a legal assistant's behavior.

Canon 4 advises a legal assistant against giving any independent legal judgment in place of an attorney. And Canon 5 requires disclosure of non-lawyer status to even the general public and cautions prudence when one is considering how extensively a client may be assisted in the absence of the attorney. Canons 3–5 make reference to the NALA Model Standards and Guidelines for Utilization of Legal Assistants. There, one can find many of the same prohibitions listed in the ABA Guidelines for the Utilization of Legal Assistant Services, the NFPA Model Code of Ethics and Professional Responsibility, and the NALA Code of Ethics.

The NALA Model Standards and Guidelines for the Utilization of Legal Assistants

The NALA Model Standards and Guidelines, as stated in its introduction, "represent a statement of how the legal assistant may function." It is similar to the ABA Model Guidelines in that it is a comprehensive document with rule-like text, commentary, and citations. NALA's Guideline 2 surveys the unauthorized practice of law landscape in the following specific and general manner:

Legal assistants should not do the following:

1. Establish attorney-client relationships; set legal fees; give legal opinions or advice; or represent a client before a court, unless authorized to do so by said court, nor

2. Engage in, encourage, or contribute to any act which could constitute that unauthorized practice of law.

The preceding specific prohibitions will be discussed at length in the next section of the chapter. Guideline 5 lists nine activities that legal assistants may perform under the supervision of an attorney. Included on that list are client interviewing, document and correspondence drafting, and discovery device summarizations, including depositions. Permitted paralegal activities will also be examined later in the chapter.

WHAT ACTIVITIES ARE PARALEGALS PROHIBITED FROM PERFORMING?

Broad principles must be supported with specific guidelines to be effective. General statements against the unauthorized practice of law, such as those previously discussed, take shape in specific prohibitions. Four categories of prohibitions will be discussed. The first three consist of the holy grail of unauthorized practice and are found in every code of legal ethics: giving legal advice, establishing the attorney-client relationship, and establishing fees. The fourth category includes miscellaneous prohibited activities, some of which are not prohibited everywhere all the time. Readers are encouraged to examine the hypothetical scenarios for this chapter in light of the following sections on paralegal prohibitions. Because so much of unauthorized practice inhabits the gray zone, reasonable paralegals and lawyers might disagree about the conclusions reached in hypothetical scenarios.

Giving Legal Advice

The cornerstone for any discussion on the unauthorized practice of law has to be that non-lawyers must not give legal advice, or even appear to do so. All paralegals should know this obvious platitude by heart. But what does it really mean to give legal advice? It would certainly include, for instance, informing a corporate client being sued for negligence due to the act of one of its employees that the doctrine of *respondeat superior* will result in the corporation being liable. It would also include telling someone that he cannot file a lawsuit because the statute of limitations has run out. But does giving legal advice include answering a friend's question about whether that friend's pension is protected from his spouse in the event of a divorce? What about answering a friend's question about getting out of an apartment lease early?

The finer points of the definition of legal advice may vary from jurisdiction to jurisdiction, but there is a consistent theme, which is that *giving legal advice involves applying the law, including legal principles, to a specific fact pattern.* Clients see attorneys when something has happened or is about to happen to them, good or bad. They want to start a business; they want to adopt a baby; they want to sue someone; or perhaps they have been sued. These situations require the professional judgment of an attorney, and even if a non-lawyer knows the correct statute or other rule that would apply, the non-lawyer should not get involved without the supervising attorney's direction and supervision. Similarly, a nurse might know, based upon his education and experience, that a patient has a particular illness, yet the nurse should not give a diagnosis.

A unique dilemma can arise when paralegals are used effectively. The client who has repeated contact with an able paralegal might seek the advice of the paralegal rather than the lawyer, particularly when the client realizes that phone calls to the paralegal cost less than phone calls to the lawyer. Unless the lawyer has sufficiently explained the role of the paralegal to the client during the initial consultation, the client probably is unaware that the paralegal is not authorized to answer the client's legal questions. Also, the client might not realize that certain questions call for an answer that would qualify as legal advice. For instance, it is natural for someone accused of a crime to be curious about the possible punishment. Many prison sentences are standardized, and a legal assistant might know that a particular first offense would result in a fine only. However, the legal assistant should refuse to answer the question: "How much time will I get if I'm convicted?"

What about outside the law office? The answer is the same: paralegals may not give legal advice to anyone. Applying the law to a friend's problem is as inappropriate as doing the same for a paying client. Even helping someone who is representing himself is highly likely to be inappropriate. Although it is a more tempting violation, it would not qualify as pro bono activity. So, what is there to do? How can you be helpful and responsible? First, answering a general legal question not tied to someone's situation is allowable (although it may be unadvisable, because being wrong is worse than not answering). Second, nothing prohibits anyone who knows how to read the law from showing it to others. Statutes, cases, and regulations are all available for public viewing. It is absolutely appropriate to help someone find a statute or a case, as long as neither the statute's nor case's meaning is applied to the friend's problem.

One exception to the prohibition against non-lawyers giving legal advice concerns legal representation behind bars. Jailhouse lawyers, as they are commonly called, are not lawyers at all, but inmates who assist other inmates in the preparation of their appeals or other lawsuits. Such assistance is clearly the unauthorized practice of law, except that is specifically allowed as an exception to the prohibition against UPL by the United States Supreme Court in *Johnson v. Avery*, 393 U.S. 484 (1969).

Establishing the Attorney-Client Relationship

Imagine an attorney attending a Christmas party. While at the eggnog bowl, someone asks the attorney about whether a person has a case for age discrimination if, after being fired, a younger person is hired as a replacement. Has that attorney acquired a new client if he answers the question? Not usually, although some courts have recently started to focus on what was the reasonable belief of the other party, rather than the attorney's belief, when determining at what point the attorney-client relationship has attached. (See Chapters 4 and 5 on when the attorney-client relationship has attached for client confidentiality and conflicts of interest purposes.)

The more common scenario for establishing the attorney-client relationship involves the lawyer, in his or her office, agreeing to take someone's case. One of the substantive tasks for a paralegal who is being used effectively is client interviewing, including taking part in the initial interview. When interviewing any prospective clients, it is important that paralegals neither express nor imply whether prospective clients have a good case or the kind of case their firm will take. Because the establishment of the attorney-client relationship can occur in the absence of a written agreement, and because appearances can be viewed as reality, the paralegal must delicately, but firmly, defer to the attorney any questions concerning whether the firm will take a case. Of course, deference cannot be made when an attorney operates such a shoddy practice that his clients are led to believe they are being interviewed by, and that their cases are being handled by, the firm's lawyers, when in fact all work is being done by unsupervised legal assistants, some of whom are staked out at a chiropractic clinic in order to sign up clients. *In re Robinson*, 495 S.E.2d 28 (Ga. 1998).

Establishing Legal Fees

As with the attorney-client relationship, the operative word is *establish*. Establishing fees is closely connected to establishing the attorney-client relationship because both actions involve statements that carry with them an implication of professional judgment, the kind that only licensed attorneys are authorized to make. When a fee agreement has been reached, there is a presumption that the client trusts the attorney's expertise in how the client's fees have been determined, particularly because the rules on legal fees prescribe what must be in a free agreement and which fee agreements must be in writing and signed by the client. (See Chapter 7 for more information on legal fees.) However, assuming the firm allows it, paralegals can answer certain fee-related questions, such as those regarding a lawyer's hourly rate. If the firm has a flat fee for certain standardized services, a paralegal would be allowed to state that flat fee without violating the prohibition on establishing fees. Also, a paralegal could explain to a client how costs and expenses differ from legal fees. But the establishment of fees would occur if a paralegal were to tell a client, or a prospective client, how much a particular legal service will, or is likely to, cost, because those types of statements have a ring of authoritative projection. See Exhibit 3–5 on the major categories for paralegals and the unauthorized practice of law.

EXHIBIT 3–5 THE BIG THREE: WHAT PARALEGALS MAY NOT DO		
Give Legal Advice	Establish the Attorney-Client Relationship	Establish Legal Fees
Applying the law to a specific fact pattern	*Stating or implying that the lawyer will take the prospective client's case*	*Stating or implying that an agreement on fee arrangements has been reached*

Miscellaneous Prohibitions

The three general prohibitions discussed earlier do not complete the picture on UPL. There are additional specific types of conduct that would also constitute UPL if engaged in by paralegals. Knowing and understanding the following miscellaneous prohibitions might even be more valuable than knowing the general prohibitions, because the specific prohibitions are situational.

Representation in Court

It almost goes without saying that no one without a license to practice law can represent anyone else in any court proceedings. Such representation would certainly be the unauthorized practice of law, because courtroom advocacy is an integral part of the practice of law. Courtrooms are the final arbiters of interpersonal conflict, and those peculiar rules of trial procedure and evidence are so important to the process that the decisions made at trial concerning those rules often form the bases for any appeals that are filed. Serving as someone's advocate in a trial or appellate court is so much a part of the lawyer culture that it is what most people think of when they imagine what lawyers do, even though the majority of lawyers are not trial lawyers.

Paralegals are also generally not allowed to represent others in small claims court. *See* Iowa Supreme Court Board of Professional Ethics and Conduct, Op. 88–18 (1989) and 89–30 (1990). California, however, does allow non-lawyers who have been adequately trained to serve as small claims advisors—at no charge—to litigants in small claims court. Cal. Rules of Court, Rule 1725. And Michigan prohibits small claims litigants from using attorneys (unless the actual litigant is an attorney), although it does not expressly prohibit the use of non-lawyer representatives in small claims court. Mich. Comp. Laws §§ 600.8401–600.8427.

■ **pro se**

A Latin phrase that refers to one representing oneself in a legal matter.

A person does have the right to represent himself or herself in litigation **pro se**, even if that is a bad idea. In fact, that right to self-representation in federal court is granted by statute and case law. 28 U.S.C. § 1654; *Farretta v. California*, 422 U.S. 806 (1975). A question that often arises in the pro se discussion is whether someone who is not a lawyer can help someone else in a pro se matter. Although an argument could be made that helping someone who is pro se is not the same as serving as someone's lawyer, the right to proceed pro se does not extend to helping someone else who is proceeding pro se, and that includes representing a spouse or other family member. See Osei-Afriyie by *Osei-Afriyie v. Medical College of Pennsylvania*, 937 F.2d 876 (3rd Cir. 1991) (where the court ruled that a father could represent himself, but not his children); *Johnson v. Ivimey*, 488 A.2d 1275 (Conn.App.1985) (where the court allowed a husband to represent himself, but not his wife). However, the general principle against non-lawyers representing others in court can be affected by specific exceptions, such as the South Carolina statute, discussed in the *Robinson* case from Chapter 2, which, until 2002, allowed

NOT QUITE LINCOLN

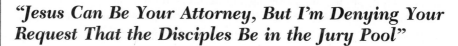

"Jesus Can Be Your Attorney, But I'm Denying Your Request That the Disciples Be in the Jury Pool"

Richard John Adams of Missouri was pulled over in 2002 for speeding and failing to wear a seatbelt. Adams requested a jury trial, but while awaiting that court date he was accused of a more serious crime, threatening a judge. Adams put in writing the threat he previously made in court to the judge and, at that point, the prosecutor dropped the moving violations charges and began a new prosecution. The case moved through two counties and four judges, no doubt due to Mr. Adams' strident and vocal opinions on the judicial system. Adams, a self-described patriot and Christian, considered lawyers to be devils because he believed the Missouri Bar Association "created the Federal reserve through their unconstitutional statutes and case laws." So, it came as no shock that Adams wanted nothing to do with a defense lawyer. The shock came when Adams told the trial judge at a pretrial hearing that he wanted Jesus Christ to be his trial attorney, and listed his "Christian brother" Lee Constance as co-counsel. The court accepted Adams' request for divine representation, but refused to allow Mr. Constance's involvement because he was not licensed to practice law. Considering the faith Adam's placed in his trial counsel, one would suppose Adams was quite shocked to hear the jury's guilty verdict on both counts of threatening a judge.

a non-lawyer to represent others in court if he or she is granted permission by the judge, and if the non-lawyer promises to conduct the representation without any compensation.

When non-lawyers get caught engaging in illegal court representation, courts will issue injunctions against them. Unfortunately, however, the issuing courts often mistakenly refer to the non-lawyers as paralegals: *Housing Authority of Charleston v. Key*, 572 S.E.2d 284 (S.C. 2002) (Non-lawyer with a paralegal certificate who had been unemployed for years and had no address or telephone number and had filed pleadings for others and represented them in a hearing); *Columbus Association v. Purcell*, 760 N.E.2d 817 (Ohio 2002) (Non-lawyer fraudulently filed independent-contracting paralegal registration statement with probate court and attempted to settle a minor's claim with an insurance company, including applying for a $3,500 "paralegal" fee).

NOT QUITE LINCOLN

"Hi, I'm Deck Shifflet, Paralawyer, and I'll Be Conducting Your Defense Today"

As the cliché says, life imitates art. Yet sometimes it's the other way around. In the 1997 film *Rainmaker*, one of the most charming characters was actor Danny DeVito's Deck Shifflet. Shifflet, the six-time loser of the Tennessee bar exam and a self-proclaimed "paralawyer," helps the innocent Rudy Baylor (Matt Damon) find his way through his first case, and in so doing, helps Rudy lose his naiveté. One of the more glaring ethics violations in the film occurs when Deck covers for Rudy, who is late to court, by conducting part of the big trial.

In an Ohio courtroom in 1989, a larger transgression occurred when an attorney allowed a non-lawyer assistant to make the opening statement and examine witnesses in a felony case. Worse still, the lawyer also referred, in his closing argument, to his non-lawyer assistant as "my partner."

What is not surprising is that the client was convicted. What is surprising is why attorney Stanlee E. Culbreath committed such a fraud with Michael E. Samuels, a man who would later (in 1993) be denied admission to the Ohio Bar for reasons including unresolved drug and alcohol addictions, financial irresponsibility, lying on his application, and (drum roll, please) for committing the unauthorized practice of law when he was a law clerk. Even after the conviction in the trial partially conducted by a non-lawyer, Culbreath didn't tell his client the truth about Samuels, and allowed Samuels to later represent the client in a civil matter. When the client discovered the truth, he successfully moved to have his conviction set aside, and sued for return of the $10,000 in legal feeds he paid Culbreath. When the Ohio Supreme Court eventually heard the matter, it suspended Culbreath for six months.

Paralegals may attend trials with attorneys from their firms and assist them without fear of engaging in the unauthorized practice of law. Such assistance, including keeping track of documentary evidence, is not unauthorized practice because it is not representation. Instead, it is support of the representation. A Virginia ethics opinion even states that a non-lawyer may appear in court on behalf of someone else for the limited purpose of providing dates for scheduling a trial. Virginia Bar Association Unauthorized Practice Committee, Op. 64 (1984). At the other end of the spectrum, Iowa only allows a paralegal to sit with a bankruptcy client at a bankruptcy hearing if the client's lawyer is also present at the counsel's table. Iowa Supreme Court Board of Professional Ethics and Conduct, Op. 92–24 (1993). And the 7th Circuit Court of Appeals ruled in 2006 that a paralegal may not appear at a **status conference** in the absence of the supervising attorney. *Harrington v. City of Chicago*, 433 F.3d 542 (7th Cir. 2006).

An exception to the preceding prohibition on paralegals making court appearances on behalf of clients can be found in an Arizona ethics opinion. That opinion approves of an attorney delegating to a paralegal who is also a licensed tribal advocate the authority to represent clients before an Indian Tribal Court. This opinion states that the jurisdiction of Tribal Courts is outside the jurisdiction of the Arizona court system. Therefore, the attorney would not be assisting a non-lawyer in the unauthorized practice of law (ER 5.5 of the Arizona Rules of Professional Conduct) when allowing the paralegal to practice in a Tribal Court. State Bar of Arizona, Ethics Op. 99–13 (1999).

Depositions

Closely related to court representation is the conducting of a deposition, something else a paralegal is not allowed to do. A deposition is similar to a trial in the sense that it is a recorded event and the deponent, like a witness, is put under oath and subject to direct and cross-examination. A deposition requires sufficient legal skill both in asking the questions and in listening to the responses. Furthermore, a lawyer representing a deponent has the right to raise objections to certain questions, and the decision to object requires legal judgment. Even if an attorney had a prepared list of questions for a deposition, and had instructed his or her legal assistant to ask only what was on the list, the very act of reading the questions to a deponent would be the unauthorized practice of law, because the legal assistant would be in control of the deposition. See *State v. Foster*, 674 So.2d 747 (Fla. Dist. Ct. App. 1996), where a husband and wife paralegal business were found to have violated Florida's statute on the unauthorized practice of law by, among other things, engaging in depositions on behalf of their clients. However, as is the case with court appearances, paralegals may attend depositions and assist attorneys by, for example, helping them manage the order of issues to be covered.

A variety of jurisdictions have issued ethics opinions disapproving of paralegals, or other non-lawyers, conducting depositions. *See* Colorado Bar Association, Formal Ethics Op. 79 (1989); Iowa Supreme Court Board of

■ **status conference**

A pretrial meeting required under the federal rules of procedure and many state and local procedure rules, attended by the attorney, and designed to inform the trial court of where things are in the pretrial stage (discovery, witnesses, settlement negotiations, estimated length of a trial).

Professional Ethics and Conduct, Op. 96–03 (1996); North Carolina Bar Association, Ethics Op. 183 (1994); Oregon Bar Association, Ethics Op. 449 (1980); Pennsylvania Bar Association, Ethics Op. 87–127 (1987). (This ethics opinion states that a paralegal may not even read deposition questions that have been prepared by an attorney, even if the client and opposing counsel approve.)

Not even law students are cut any slack when it comes to conducting depositions. Kentucky issued an ethics opinion on the subject of non-lawyers conducting depositions and determined that a lawyer could not delegate the task of taking depositions to non-lawyer employees, including law school graduates who have yet to pass the bar exam. Kentucky State Bar Association, Ethics Op. 341 (1990). Pennsylvania also reached the same conclusion about law students conducting depositions (in this instance, a third-year law student, ranked fifth in the graduating class), and later reaffirmed the position with respect to paralegals. Pennsylvania Bar Association, Ethics Op. 91–137 (1991) and Op. 98–75 (1998).

Alternative Dispute Resolution

Alternative dispute resolution (ADR) has become so prevalent in America that many jurisdictions have some form of rules of court for ADR that are distinct from their rules of trial procedure. **Mediation** is one of the major forms of ADR and the process whereby a neutral third party (the mediator) assists the litigants in resolving their dispute through management of a semi-formalized bargaining process. Mediation is used more and more each year. Although non-lawyers can conduct certain kinds of mediation, lawyers trained in mediation generally conduct mediations connected to legal disputes.

Paralegals are generally prohibited from conducting legal mediations or representing clients at mediations because, even though mediation is a conflict resolution form that is wholly distinct in kind from litigation, a mediation that flows from litigation or prospective litigation involves the settling of claims and rights that are legal in nature.

A few jurisdictions have specifically discussed the role of non-lawyers in mediations. A Rhode Island ethics opinion states that a lawyer may not form an association with a non-lawyer to provide mediation services. Rhode Island State Bar Association, Op. 87–3 (1988). An Indiana ethics opinion dealt with a question concerning the appropriateness of paralegals conducting pre-suit mediation. While approving of paralegals attending mediations in an attorney-assistance role, the committee decided that a lawyer could not delegate to a paralegal the role of representing a client in pre-suit mediation. Because of the nature of mediation, its decisional flexibility, and the need of legal analysis in settlement evaluations, the committee considered that only lawyers would be appropriate to have such direct client contact. Indiana State Bar Association, Ethics Op. 1 (1997). However, the opinion did state that, with proper supervision and client consent, a lawyer could delegate to a paralegal the authority to engage in pre-suit negotiations on behalf of the client.

▓ **alternative dispute resolution (adr)**

Method of resolving conflict outside the traditional method of litigation and a trial. Forms of ADR include negotiation, mediation, and arbitration.

▓ **mediation**

A form of ADR in which a third party, known as a neutral, assists the opposing parties in the process of trying to reach a settlement.

As stated, specific exceptions trump general prohibitions, and Florida provides a specific exception. Its Small Claims Court Rules allow a non-lawyer to represent a party to a small claims mediation, provided the court is not opposed and the non-lawyer representative has the party's written authority to appear on his behalf. Florida Small Claims Rule 7.090(f). In Maine, a bill was put forward that would have allowed paralegals with degrees from accredited colleges to represent parties in alternative dispute resolutions and small claims matters (Maine H.P. 861 (1987)). However, it received an "ought not to pass" recommendation from the legislature's judiciary committee, and it ultimately did not pass. A North Dakota ethics opinion discussing the allowable role of suspended lawyers concluded that such a lawyer may act as a mediator during his or her suspension, provided he is on the North Dakota list of approved mediators. State Bar Association of North Dakota, Ethics Opinion 01–02 (2001).

Considering that the ABA is often the precursor to change, in the near future non-lawyers might be granted broader opportunities to engage in mediation. In February 2002, the ABA Section of Dispute Resolution issued its "Resolution on Mediation and the Unauthorized Practice of Law," in which it states that mediation is not the practice of law. Included in the Dispute Resolution Section's statement was the Section's belief that, "...statutes and regulations should be interpreted and applied in such a manner as to *permit all individuals, regardless of whether they are lawyers, to serve as mediators*." (Emphasis added.) For more on the subject, consult the ABA resolution, which can be found by searching the ABA Web site at http://www.abanet.org.

Regardless of whether jurisdictions follow suit and make it easier for non-lawyers to serve as mediators, that would have no effect on whether non-lawyers would be authorized to act as client representatives at mediations involving legal disputes. This is because representing someone else in a legal dispute is generally allowed for lawyers only.

Executions of Wills and the Selling of Legal Documents

Paralegals may not execute wills. They may, however, assist lawyers in serving clients with estate-planning needs, gathering financial information, collecting records, and even helping with the drafting of wills and other estate-planning documents. A paralegal may also serve as an attesting witness to a will, but the execution of a will is a formal transaction that affects the legal rights of others and must be conducted by an attorney.

Closely related to executing wills is the practice of selling will kits or other estate-planning devices. Many jurisdictions are opposed to non-lawyers having anything to do with such forms, particularly selling them to the public or assisting members of the public in completing them. *See* Illinois State Bar Association, Advisory Op. 95–7 (1995) (although this opinion specifically stated that accountants could only type and file articles of incorporation for their clients, because anything more would be the unauthorized practice of law, its decision is equally applicable to paralegals); Ohio S. Ct. Board of Board of Commissioners on Grievances and Discipline, Op. 92–15 (1992); Tenn. Op. Atty. Gen. No. 92–02 (1992) (this opinion also disapproves of non-lawyers providing bankruptcy petitions, divorce petitions, and prenuptial agreements).

Nevada dealt with the issue of typing services in *Greenwell v. State Bar of Nevada*, 836 P.2d 70 (Nev. 1992), where the Nevada Bar Association sought a permanent injunction against a typing business. The typing business, which originally typed documents for lawyers, was typing legal documents for the public and providing legal advice to its customers. The typing service's defense was that state precedent provided an exception to unauthorized practice for the delivery of simple legal services when lawyers are unavailable. The court was moved by that argument to the point of ordering the bar association to investigate the problem of the unavailability of legal services for the poor. However the court still determined that the activities of the typing business were the unauthorized practice of law, and permanently enjoined the business from doing anything other than typing.

California, on the other hand, does have a set of statutes that allows certain individuals, known as "legal document assistants," to sell self-help legal services to members of the public who are representing themselves pro se. Such self-help services include typing legal forms for others, as well as providing general legal information that has been written by an attorney and making published legal documents available to those who are representing themselves in legal matters. Legal document assistants must register, according to the statutes' prerequisites (which include educational pre-requisites), and post a $25,000 dollar **surety bond**. A later statute prohibits legal document assistants from giving legal advice to their customers. *See* Cal. Bus. & Prof. Code §§ 6400–6415. Whatever California's legal document assistants statutes stand for, officially, they do not allow one to render independent paralegal services to the public, at least the kind of services that involve exercising any intellectual judgment or giving legal advice. One should contrast California's view on typing services with Nevada's view, as well as Florida's view, expressed in *Florida Bar v. Catarcio*, discussed later in the chapter.

The South Carolina Supreme Court dealt with a paralegal who invoked the court's **original jurisdiction**, in *Doe v. Condon*, 532 S.E.2d 879 (S.C. 2000), asking whether the paralegal, who was employed by an attorney, could conduct estate-planning seminars outside the presence of the attorney, and whether the paralegal could meet privately at the attorney's office with the attorney's clients and answer their general questions about wills and other estate-planning devices. Although the court approved of the paralegal interviewing clients and gathering estate-planning information from them, it ruled against the paralegal on all of his requests. Specifically, the court found that the paralegal would be engaging in the unauthorized practice of law because what he wanted to do—give estate-planning seminars and answer client questions about estate matters—constituted the giving of legal advice. Although the paralegal claimed that he was only dispensing general information in his seminars, the court considered it more

surety bond

A written instrument filed with a court in which one promises to be liable up to the amount stated in the bond in the event of negligence or failure to perform.

original jurisdiction

The authority an appellate court has to hear a case directly, before the case proceeds through the trial court and then is appealed.

significant that he was conducting the seminars at the behest of the lawyer for whom he worked. He also was handing out law firm brochures, which cloaked his seminars in the unauthorized practice of law. *Id.* at 882. As for the client interviews, the court summarily concluded that answering a client's legal questions was the unauthorized practice of law. *Id.* at 883.

Other jurisdictions, conversely, have taken a different view on paralegals conducting estate-planning seminars. In *In re Conduct of Morin*, 878 P.2d 393 (Or. 1994), the Oregon Supreme Court found that a paralegal who, by himself and at the direction of his supervising lawyer, conducted estate-planning seminars that focused on living trusts, was not committing the unauthorized practice of law. Summarily, the Court believed that providing information to the general public, as opposed to a specific person, was not a practice of law. But the Court concluded that the paralegal committed the unauthorized practice of law *after the seminars*, when he assisted the seminar attendees with choice of trust decisions and when he, back at the office, gave legal advice about specific estate-planning questions and executed wills, all at the behest of his supervising attorney who notarized hundreds of them. *Id.* at 401. It is no surprise that the attorney, before his disbarment, ineffectively claimed that it was not his fault his paralegal broke the law. *Id.* The difficulty that paralegal—and his inattentive boss—evidently had in drawing the line between the allowable dissemination of legal information and the inappropriate provision of legal advice and services seems to be reason enough for the majority of jurisdictions to conclude that paralegals should not give estate-planning or similar legal seminars.

Real Estate Closings

▦ **real estate closing**
The formal consummation of a sale of real estate, which usually involves the signing of many documents, payment of the real estate, and delivery of the deed or title.

Generally, paralegals may not attend and be responsible for any **real estate closing** without attorney supervision, because closings are formal, legal transactions. *See* State Bar of Georgia, Formal Advisory Op. 86–5 (1986), and State Bar of Georgia, Formal Advisory Op. 00–3 (2000) (this opinion specifically says that an attorney may not supervise the paralegal by telephone at the closing; the lawyer must physically be there); Illinois State Bar Association, Real Estate Section Council and Unauthorized Practice of Law Committee, Position Paper (1984) (which was a reaffirmation of earlier guidelines adopted by the Illinois Bar Association); North Carolina Bar Association, Formal Ethics Op. 13 (2000) (this opinion disapproves of a paralegal attending a real estate closing without the attendance of the supervising lawyer, but it does approve of a paralegal overseeing the execution of the closing documents without the attorney's presence in the room, so long as the attorney is present at the closing conference); Virginia Unauthorized Practice of Law Committee, Op. 183 (1999). (The original conclusion, reached in 1999, that non-lawyers may not conduct real estate closings, was revisited in 2002 and applied to out-of-state transactions with Virginia closings, but not vice versa.)

Some jurisdictions, however, do approve of a paralegal attending real estate closings on behalf of a client, provided the supervising lawyer has reviewed the closing documents, the paralegal is properly trained for real estate closings, the client consents, and the paralegal does not give legal advice. *See* Wisconsin State Bar Association, Formal Ethics Op. 95–3 (1995); New York State Bar Association Committee on Professional Ethics, Op. 677 (a paralegal may attend a real estate closing if the supervising attorney is available by telephone). And Guideline 2 of the Connecticut Bar Association's Guidelines for Paralegals specifically allows a paralegal to attend real estate closings even if no lawyer from the paralegal's firm is in attendance. However, Guideline 2 also states that the paralegal may only act as a messenger and should not give any opinion about the execution of the documents.

A unique exception can be found in the state of Washington, which has a rule of court that allows for the limited practice of real estate closing officers. Found in the Washington Rules on Admission to Practice, Rule 12 permits non-lawyers to apply for board certification as closing officers; it also authorizes such persons to prepare and complete real estate closing documents. But, the rule specifically states that closing officers may not give legal advice. It is important to understand that this type of court rule would not necessarily affect the role of a paralegal because even if a Washington State paralegal applied for and received the certification, the right to give legal advice would not be granted and the paralegal's supervising lawyer would still be responsible for the paralegal's performance as a closing officer.

Representation Before Administrative Agencies

While it is clear that paralegals may not represent someone in court, it is not so clear that they may not represent someone before an administrative agency. Administrative agencies, such as a worker's compensation hearing board, are considered quasi-judicial. Their decisions can be binding and are appealable, but the strict rules of evidence generally do not apply, and agency hearings are conducted less formally than are trials. When one person represents another person before an administrative agency, advocacy is taking place, and advocacy is prohibited for non-lawyers. Later in the chapter, rules that allow non-lawyer representation before administrative agencies will be discussed. At this point, however, it is important to realize that those allowances are jurisdiction-specific, and not all administrative agencies allow non-lawyer representation.

Signing Pleadings

Paralegals may draft pleadings but may not be responsible for the pleadings. Pleadings, such as the complaint and the answer, are the initial documents filed in litigation, and lawyers must be legally responsible for all pleadings, as well as motions, filed on behalf of clients. A signature demonstrates such responsibility, and according to Rule 11 of the Federal Rules of Civil Procedure, an attorney representing a party in a lawsuit must sign all pleadings and motions. Likewise, all states have a similar version of Rule 11, and if a paralegal were to sign a pleading or draft and file one that was unsigned by a representing attorney, that would constitute the unauthorized practice of law.

A Florida ethics opinion discussed the propriety of lawyers who are out of their offices and have their secretaries or paralegals sign notices of hearings and discovery notices in their own names, followed by the lawyers' initials. The Opinion stated that under no circumstances could paralegals sign those documents on behalf of their lawyers. Florida Bar Association, Ethics Op. 87–11 (1988). Vermont also reached the same conclusion, stating that even when there was a time crunch (which might necessitate the compulsion to sign the attorney's name on the pleading, followed by the paralegal's initials), the most a non-lawyer employee could do was to contact the court and ask for an emergency time extension. Vermont Bar Association, Advisory Ethics Op. 01–05 (2001). A federal bankruptcy court dealt with this dilemma quite succinctly when, faced with pleadings signed by a lawyer's secretary, it said, "It is simply inexcusable for any attorney to delegate a nonlawyer the task of drafting and signing a court pleading on behalf of the attorney, especially when the attorney never even reviews the pleading that the nonlawyer has drawn up." *Lynch v. Cannatella*, 122 F. R.D. 195, 199 (E.D.La. 1987). See Exhibit 3–6 on miscellaneous paralegal prohibitions.

Inherent in this analysis of the propriety of paralegals signing pleadings is the presumption that those signers are actually paralegals, and not those who simply refer to themselves as paralegals. Later in the chapter, the topic of independent-contracting paralegals is tackled, but at this point it is important to stress (as was discussed in Chapter 2) that those who do not work for lawyers, or whose work lawyers do not directly supervise, are not paralegals or legal assistants. Therefore, they may not even draft pleadings, much less sign them, for anyone but themselves in *pro se* matters. The case law is full of unauthorized practice cases brought against untrained and unsupervised persons who draft and sign pleadings for the bamboozled public.

EXHIBIT 3–6   MISCELLANEOUS UPL PROHIBITIONS

1. Representing someone in Court

2. Taking a deposition

3. Engaging in ADR (under certain circumstances)

4. Executing wills and other legal documents

5. Executing real estate closings (in many jurisdictions)

6. Representing someone before an administrative agency (unless specifically allowed)

7. Signing pleadings

WHAT ACTIVITIES ARE PARALEGALS PERMITTED TO PERFORM?

Having taken into consideration all the activities that paralegals are not allowed to do, a question occurs: Is there anything left for a paralegal to do besides answering the phone? Yes, there is. Remember, though, the key to what a paralegal may do is whether it is generally authorized or, alternatively, whether it has not been specifically prohibited by rules of legal ethics, statutes, or case law.

What Do the Paralegal Ethics Rules Authorize?

The non-lawyer ethics codes affirmatively authorize paralegals to engage in substantive legal work, but the language in the ethics codes ranges from a general affirmation to specific instances of authorized conduct.

The ABA Model Guidelines for the Utilization of Paralegal Services

Guideline 2 authorizes an attorney to delegate to a paralegal any task not otherwise prohibited by law as long as the attorney maintains responsibility for the work product of the paralegal. The Comment to Guideline 2 quotes from an ABA Ethics Opinion concerning the role of the non-lawyer, noting that an attorney "... may employ nonlawyers to do any tasks for him except counsel clients about law matters, engage directly in the practice of law, appear in court . . . so long as it is he who takes the work and vouches for it to the client and becomes responsible for it to the client." ABA Commission on Professional Ethics, Formal Op. 316 (1967). Some of the authorized tasks listed in Comment 2 include legal research, factual investigation, preparation of legal documents, and maintaining **trust accounts**. See Exhibit 3–7 on what the national paralegal ethics code authorizes paralegals to do.

■ **trust accounts**
A special bank account where the property of the client is held and maintained by the attorney.

EXHIBIT 3–7   WHAT DO THE PARALEGAL ETHICS CODES AUTHORIZE?

1. Interviewing prospective clients, current clients, and witnesses

2. Engaging in legal research

3. Drafting (but not executing) legal documents

4. Drafting (and on occasion signing) legal correspondence

5. Drafting (but not signing) pleadings

6. Assisting with discovery

The NFPA Model Disciplinary Rules and Ethical Considerations

The NFPA Model Disciplinary Rules and Ethical Considerations is the first part of the NFPA Model Code of Ethics and Professional Responsibility and Guidelines for Enforcement. There is no specific rule in the NFPA Model Disciplinary Rules and Ethical Considerations that addresses what a paralegal is entitled to do. However, some of the Ethical Considerations mention or imply a variety of authorized tasks. The prohibition on communication with parties represented by counsel, found in EC–1.2(b), implies that paralegals would have direct involvement in litigation support, and contact with witnesses. EC–2.3 and 2.4 concern paralegal access to billing records and client assets. EC–1.5 requires paralegals to keep their supervising attorney informed of any confidential information the paralegal may have in connection with the client's case. If the paralegal would have a duty to inform the supervising lawyer of certain facts of which the latter may not be aware, that would imply that a paralegal could do semi-independent legal tasks for the client. Also, EC–1.7 concerns disclosure of the paralegal's title on professional communication, letterhead, and advertisements. That would presume substantive legal work is being conducted by paralegals. By contrast, secretaries do not "author" professional communication and are not listed in promotional materials.

The NALA Model Standards and Guidelines for Utilization of Legal Assistants

The Preamble to the NALA Model Standards and Guidelines acknowledges that one of the three most commonly raised questions about legal assistants is what duties a paralegal may perform. Guideline 3 states that legal assistants may perform client representation services as long as: the legal assistant does not exercise independent legal judgment; the attorney maintains direct supervision over the legal assistant's work; and the legal assistant's work product merges into the attorney's work product. *Merge*, in this context, means that by the time the client becomes the recipient of the firm's legal services, the substantive work performed by the legal assistant has lost its non-lawyer fingerprints and has taken the identity of the lawyer or firm.

Guideline 5 of the NALA Model Standards and Guidelines is the most succinct source in any rules of legal ethics for the kinds of substantive activities that paralegals can perform. Although nine distinct tasks are listed, not all of them will be discussed here. (Please see Appendix C for Guideline 5 of the NALA Model Standards and Guidelines for Utilization of Legal Assistants.)

- *Paralegals can conduct client interviews.* While not being allowed to establish the attorney-client relationship, it is still significant that paralegals can interview clients, helping assist in the transformation of clients' personal problems into legal problems, as well as conveying the empathy that is associated with trained, active-listening skills.

- *Paralegals can engage in legal research.* A paralegal who has been through a qualified legal education program should be able to do almost all of the legal research that an attorney would regularly do. Using annotated codes, finding and reading case law, understanding the relationship between digests and headnotes, researching legal encyclopedias, flipping through loose-leaf services, and using Westlaw®, Lexis®, or other electronic legal research services are all activities that a competent paralegal should be capable of doing. In fact, a Virginia ethics opinion acknowledged that paralegals may conduct legal research for lawyers, *or for members of the public* who have provided specific citations that need to be found. Virginia State Bar Association Unauthorized Practice of Law Committee, Op. 127 (1989). (Emphasis added.)

- *Paralegals can draft legal documents.* This activity is closely related to legal research and is also authorized by Guideline 5. Law clerks write rough drafts for judges; associates in firms write rough drafts for partners. Likewise, a paralegal who shows exemplary writing skills should be used to write the same kinds of rough drafts, including settlement documents, **memorandum of law**, and trial and appellate briefs.

- *Paralegals can draft legal correspondence.* Many kinds of letters are generated in a law office; all of them can be drafted by paralegals, but not all can be signed by paralegals. Some letters, such as a client engagement letter, can be drafted by a paralegal but must become the official letter of the attorney (including being signed by him), because such a letter would constitute the practice of law. Other letters, such as perfunctory requests for information or documents, can be drafted and signed by a legal assistant.

- *Paralegals can draft pleadings.* These kinds of litigation documents must be signed by the attorney of record, as required by Rule 11 of the Federal Rules of Civil Procedure. However, nothing prevents paralegals from drafting them. In fact, due to the availability of legal forms books and practice manuals, litigation paralegals might be more adept at drafting pleadings than the average lawyer.

- *Paralegals can assist with discovery.* Paralegals can summarize discovery devices, such as depositions or interrogatories. In fact, briefing cases involves honing the types of skills that can also be valuable in litigation, such as analysis and summarization skills. Depositions and interrogatories can amount to hundreds of pages, and trial preparation can include summarizing those voluminous documents in order to assist in case management.

■ **memorandum of law**

An internal memorandum of law is legal analysis on the merits of a client's case. An external memorandum of law is an advocacy document, similar to a trial or appellate brief, presented to a court.

The NALA Code of Ethics and Professional Responsibility

The nine Canons in the NALA Code of Ethics do not specifically list authorized paralegal activities. Canon 2 states what is found in other codes of ethics: a legal assistant may do only what is authorized, delegated, and properly supervised by an attorney. Likewise, Canon 3 restates the familiar refrain that a legal assistant must not engage in UPL, represent a client in court, establish the attorney-client relationship, establish fees, or give legal advice.

Paralegals and the Representation of Others Before Administrative Agencies

An administrative agency, be it federal or state, is often part of the executive branch of government. Government by bureaucracy occurs when the legislature creates an agency and then empowers it to oversee certain aspects of American life that require expertise or constant involvement. For instance, the Internal Revenue Code is the source for federal tax laws passed by Congress, while the Internal Revenue Service is the federal agency that oversees the administration of those tax laws. Administrative agencies have two primary attributes of power: they make administrative regulations; and they adjudicate disputes associated with those regulations. Those adjudications are very much like judicial proceedings. The decisions of a worker's compensation board, for instance, have the effect of law, and can be appealed, but usually only through all administrative channels before entering the courts. Unlike trial courts, the strict rules of courtroom evidence do not always apply in administrative hearings and, on occasion, non-lawyers are allowed to represent others before administrative agencies. Hence, the term quasi-judicial is often used in reference to administrative agency adjudications.

Earlier in the chapter, it was stated that representation of others before administrative agencies is generally considered the practice of law because it involves advocating a legal position on behalf of another person. That would lead to an initial presumption that non-lawyers who represent others before administrative agencies are engaging in the unauthorized practice of law. But specific statutes and administrative rules that allow for non-lawyer representation trump that presumption, and *where specifically allowed, such non-lawyer representation is not the unauthorized practice of law.* Nevertheless, even if a federal, state, or local agency approves of non-lawyer representation, appellate courts can still conclude that it is still the unauthorized practice of law. This can get quite confusing.

Representation Before Federal Agencies

The federal government does allow non-lawyers to appear on behalf of others in front of its administrative agencies. Section 555(b) of the Administrative Procedures Act states in part:

A person compelled to appear in person before an agency or representative thereof is entitled to be accompanied, represented, and advised by counsel or, if permitted by the agency, by other qualified representative. A party is entitled to appear in person or by or with counsel or other duly qualified representative in an agency proceeding. 5 U.S.C. § 555(b).

At least 20 agencies allow non-lawyer representation, from the Consumer Product Safety Commission to the Small Business Administration. But, as the statute states, each agency controls the eligibility prerequisites for non-lawyer representatives. Some agencies require proven expertise before someone may serve as a representative. For instance, the United States Patent Office requires that before patent attorneys or non-lawyer patent agents can practice before the Patent Office, they must be of good moral character and pass the Patent Registration Examination. 37 C.F.R. § 11.7 (2006). The Internal Revenue Service is authorized in 31 U.S.C. § 330 to allow non-lawyer representation, and that is done in 31 C.F.R. § 10.3 (2000) and also in 31 C.F.R. § 10.7(c) (2004), which allows immediate family members to represent each other before the IRS. The Interstate Commerce Commission allows non-lawyers to practice before it, as long as they meet the Commission's requirements, which include meeting certain educational or experiential prerequisites and passing the practitioner's examination (and paying the examination fee). 49 C.F.R. § 1103.3(a), (b) (2001).

Other federal agencies have a more liberal allowance for non-lawyer representation. The Social Security Administration allows a non-lawyer to act as a representative if that person is competent, which means that the representative knows the significant issues in a claim and has a working knowledge of the key provisions of the Social Security Act, regulations, and rulings. *See* 20 C.F.R. § 404.1705(b), § 404.1740(b)(3)(i), and § 416.1505(b) (2001). The Department of Labor allows non-lawyers to represent parties before the Benefits Review Board, as long as they submit their request in writing to the Board and state their education, experience, and relationship to the parties being represented. But the Board has the authority to deny a non-lawyer's application because of that person's lack of qualifications. 20 C.F.R. § 802.202 (2005). And, the Immigration and Naturalization Service/Department of Homeland Security allows four groups of non-lawyers to represent others: law students (under certain circumstances); accredited representatives (who meet INS accreditation requirements); accredited officials (who are appearing in their official capacity); and "reputable individuals" (who can be anyone appearing at the request of the immigrant, and who are not compensated for their appearance). 8 C.F.R. § 292.1 (a) (2005). An interesting case involving the unauthorized representation by a non-lawyer before the Immigration and Naturalization Services (INS) is *In re Disciplinary Action against Tatone*, 456 N.W.2d 717 (Minn.1990), where a lawyer was reprimanded because, for four years, he submitted notices of appearance before the INS, when in reality a non-lawyer, with whom the lawyer shared office space, was representing the clients before the organization. While reprimanding the lawyer, the court noted that the non-lawyer who represented the clients was not authorized as a non-lawyer, under the INS rules, to represent others. *Id.* And because that person was a non-lawyer (therefore, not subject to professional discipline), the court had nothing to say about his conduct. See Exhibit 3–8 for an example of non-lawyer representation before a federal agency.

Representation Before State Agencies

At the state level, the right of a non-lawyer to represent a party in an administrative adjudication is largely determined by state Supreme Court approval because, even if a state statute authorizes non-lawyers to appear in administrative hearings, the state bar association might argue that such activity is the unauthorized practice of law, thus necessitating court intervention. An often considered rubric in the state cases deciding whether non-lawyer assistance in administrative agencies is the (unauthorized) practice of law is the following: (1) does non-lawyer assistance require the application of legal skills or legal knowledge beyond what the average person possesses; (2) is the making of legal judgments needed to order to represent someone; (3) will the assistance occur in an adversarial proceeding in which

---

**An Example of Non-lawyer Representation
in a Federal Agency (INS/DHS)**

5 U.S.C. § 555(b) authorizes federal agencies to permit non-lawyer
  representation

8 C.F.R. § 292.1(a) authorizes four types of non-lawyer
  representation before the Immigration and Naturalization
  Service/Department of Homeland Security

✓ Law students (under certain circumstances)
✓ Accredited representatives (who meet INS accreditation requirements)
✓ Accredited officials (appearing in their official capacity)
✓ Reputable individuals (appearing at the request of the immigrant and
  without compensation)

EXHIBIT 3–8   An Example of Nonlawyer Representation in a Federal Agency

NOT QUITE LINCOLN

What Is Spanish for "Rip-Off"?

How does one lawyer handle over 2,700 immigration cases in over two years? Easy—by not actually doing anything. That's good work, if you can find it. For James Valinoti of Los Angeles, such was the result of the labor of many notarios publicos, the Spanish translation of the words notaries public. These non-lawyer assistants had almost all the contact with the clients: immigrants who were the focus of deportation actions by the Immigration and Naturalization Service (INS). But to many clients from Spanish-speaking countries, the word notario meant that the service provider was a lawyer with immigration expertise. By the time Valinoti met his clients for the first time, at their deportation hearings, the notarios with whom he associated had done all the background work, including completing and filing the asylum applications, and also filing the

pleadings and other court documents. In fact, these non-lawyer, immigration service providers would often pay the filing fees of Valinoti's putative clients, which the disciplinary court later concluded impaired Valinoti's legal judgment. So substandard was Valinoti's representation of those thousands who were officially his clients, that he often was scheduled to appear in different INS hearings at the same time. One of his clients, a 70-year-old woman who had lived in the United States for 17 years, was ordered deported to Syria. Valinoti was paid from $50 to $350 dollars for each court appearance, and according to conservative estimates, he earned about $500,000 dollars during this two-year period. As a result of his assistance in the unauthorized practice of law and his astonishingly neglectful representation, in 2003 he was suspended from the practice of law for three years.

advocacy will take place and a judge or judge-like body will hear evidence; or (4) does the non-lawyer representation occur early in the adjudication, as opposed to a point where appeal rights are limited or nonexistent?

What rarely matters is the forum where the representation will occur or what label is attached to the proceeding. Calling something a "court" or a "hearing board" or a "commission" is not conclusive. Realizing this many decades ago, the Pennsylvania Supreme Court, resolving a claim that non-lawyer representation before the state worker's compensation board was the unauthorized practice of law, stated, "In considering the scope of the practice of law *mere nomenclature is unimportant…It is the character of the act, and not the place where it is performed, which is the decisive factor." Shortz v. Farrell*, 193 A. 20, 21 (Pa. 1937). (Emphasis added.)

Modern courts tend to follow that line of thinking (although not with uniformity) when determining if paralegals or other non-lawyers may be allowed to represent persons in state administrative agencies. After Kentucky amended its workers compensation statute in 1996 to allow non-lawyer representation of injured workers, the Kentucky Bar Association's Unauthorized Practice of Law Committee issued an opinion that determined that non-lawyers may not represent others before the Kentucky Department of Workers' Claims, and then the Department asked the Kentucky Supreme Court, in *Turner v. Kentucky Bar Association*, 980 S.W.2d 560 (Ky. 1998) to review the statute, in light of the ethics opinion. And, in that case, the court found that the statute violated the separation of powers doctrine (remember *Marbury v. Madison*, from Chapter 1) and was an unconstitutional usurpation of the judiciary's absolute power to make rules relating to the practice of law. It then ruled that non-lawyers may not represent workers before any adjudicative tribunal. *Turner* at 565. However, the court did rule in favor of paralegals at the Department advising claimants about their rights in the administrative proceedings and stated the paralegals could even assist claimants at informal arbitrations, provided the paralegals' work was supervised by a Department attorney. *Turner* at 564, 565.

Another contentious example of the administrative agency representation controversy occurred in Indiana. There, the state Attorney General sued to restrain what he considered to be the unauthorized practice of law occurring due to a statute that allowed non-lawyers to appear on behalf of claimants before the state employees appeals commission. The Indiana Supreme Court ruled that such actions were not the practice of law (and therefore, not UPL), basing its decision in part on the facts that: the state employees appeals commission members were not required to possess law degrees; the potential for public detriment was limited because the commission only heard cases from state employees and not the public at large; and the decision of the commission was not the final decision that could be made. *State ex rel. Pearson v. Gould*, 437 N.E.2d 41 (Ind. 1981).

The District of Columbia has an exception in its unauthorized practice of law rule that allows a non-lawyer, referred to as a "District of Columbia Practitioner," to practice before District of Columbia agencies, where those agencies specifically allow it and as long as the practitioner discloses in any advertisements that his practice is limited to specifically named agencies. D.C. Court of Appeals Rules of Court, Rule 49(c)(5). California, by statute, allows non-lawyers to represent others before the State Worker's Compensation Appeals Board (Cal. Bus. & Prof. Code §§ 5501, and 5700), as well as the State Unemployment Insurance Appeals Board (Cal. Unemp. Ins. Code § 1957). A California ethics opinion authorizes law firms to assign their paralegals to represent clients before the Worker's Compensation Appeals Board, provided clients give their consent to the representation and the paralegals' work is adequately supervised. State Bar of California Committee on Professional Responsibility, Formal Op. 1988–103 (1988). Likewise, Michigan has a statute that allows non-lawyers to represent others before the state Unemployment Commission (Mich. Comp. Laws § 421.31), and a Michigan ethics opinion authorizes an employed paralegal to represent others at all administrative hearings where it would not be unlawful for other non-lawyers to do the same, so long as the client consents and the paralegal's supervising attorney is responsible for the paralegal's behavior. Michigan Bar Association, Ethics Op. RI–125 (1992). Illinois unemployment compensation laws allow any individual who is in an administrative proceeding to be represented by a non-lawyer (80 Ill. Comp. Stat. § 405/806), while its Administrative Code only allows non-lawyers to appear in routine matters, such as agreed continuances (Ill. Admin. Code tit. 50, § 720.40(b) (2001)). And New York's statute on non-lawyer representation is quite broad, stating that, "[n]othing herein shall be construed either to grant or to deny to any person who is not a lawyer the right to appear for or represent others before any agency." N.Y. A. P.A. § 501.

Not all bar associations are in favor of even a limited allowance of non-lawyer representation in administrative agencies. For instance, a Delaware ethics opinion states that it would be unethical for a lawyer to delegate to a paralegal the duty to appear before the state industrial accident board to conduct a pretrial conference in a worker's compensation claim. Delaware State Bar Association Committee on Professional Ethics, Op. 1985–3 (1985). Specifically, the Committee on Professional Ethics considered such administrative practice to be adversarial in nature, requiring an understanding of applicable legal principles, as well as the ability to judge the strengths and weaknesses of the client's case.

As the following case shows, one of the key factors to whether a non-lawyer—paralegal or otherwise—can represent someone else before an administrative agency is the level of legal skill considered necessary to adequately represent someone's interest in *that kind of agency*.

CASE LAW *The Florida Bar re Advisory Opinion on Nonlawyer Representation in Securities Arbitration*

696 So.2d 1178 (Fla. 1997)

PER CURIAM.

Pursuant to rule 10–7.1(1) of the Rules Regulating the Florida Bar, Robert Pearce, a Florida attorney, petitioned the Florida Bar Standing Committee on the Unlicensed Practice of Law (the Committee), for an advisory opinion on the following question: Whether non-attorney companies or individuals who offer advice on securities related matters and represent the public before, during or after any National Association of Securities Dealers (NASD), New York Stock Exchange (N.Y.SE), American Stock Exchange (AMEX), or other stock exchange arbitration proceedings for compensation are engaged in the unauthorized practice of law....

The Committee held a public hearing on the matter in June 1996, where both oral and written testimony was received. Following the hearing, the Committee voted to issue a proposed opinion which finds that non-lawyer representatives in securities arbitration who

(continues)

CASE LAW *The Florida Bar re Advisory Opinion on Nonlawyer Representation in Securities Arbitration* (continued)

accept compensation for their services are engaged in the unlicensed and unauthorized practice of law, and that the public is actually being harmed and has the potential for being harmed in the future by this practice. Several non-lawyer securities arbitration representatives filed comments as interested parties in opposition to the proposed opinion. The Standing Committee's proposed opinion is expressly limited to the narrow circumstances in which a securities investor with a claim or claims against a broker is represented before, during or after a securities arbitration to resolve the claim by a non-lawyer retained for compensation. . . .

The Committee is of the opinion that a non-lawyer who is retained to represent an investor in securities arbitration for compensation is engaged in the unauthorized practice at each of the three stages of representation. Specifically, the Committee finds that the advice given and services rendered before the arbitration affects an investor's legal rights because the representative must determine: (1) whether the investor is compelled to arbitrate under any investor-broker agreement; (2) the effect of eligibility rules and statutes of limitations; (3) the scope of the arbitrator's authority; (4) whether to arbitrate or settle the dispute before filing a claim; (5) the merits of specific claims or defenses; (6) whether attorneys or expert witnesses should be hired to assist in the arbitration; (7) whether the investor should file a petition to stay the arbitration; and (8) the possibility of related or alternative civil actions. The proposed opinion further details that a non-lawyer representative also is engaged in the unlicensed practice of law during the course of the arbitration proceeding because the representation requires, among other things: (1) conducting discovery and any related depositions; (2) presenting evidence, raising objections, examinations of witnesses and voir dire of experts, and opening and closing arguments; and (3) preparing and filing the initial written statements of claims, answers, and counterclaims, as well as written and oral motions and legal memoranda concerning the claims at issue.

As to the third stage of representation, the proposed opinion notes that non-lawyer representatives in securities arbitration are engaged in the unlicensed practice of law even after the arbitration proceeding has concluded because any arbitration award or judgment can be confirmed, vacated, or collected only through an action at law and not through further arbitration or some alternative proceeding. Finally, the Committee notes that the non-lawyer representative in a securities arbitration has overstepped proper bounds

(continues)

CASE LAW *The Florida Bar re Advisory Opinion on Nonlawyer Representation in Securities Arbitration* (continued)

because at each of these stages, and throughout the entirety of the representation, the investor places great reliance on the representative to properly prepare and present his or her case.

LACK OF FEDERAL OR STATE REGULATION

The proposed opinion asserts that this Court may—and should—enjoin the activities of non-lawyer securities arbitration representatives because no federal or state rules or regulations specifically authorize these non-lawyer representatives to engage in such activities. The proposed opinion explains that securities arbitration is conducted before self-regulatory organizations (SROs), which are private bodies and not federal offices or agencies. The rules governing the SROs at issue here, namely the National Association of Securities Dealers (NASD), the New York Stock Exchange (N.Y.SE), and the American Stock Exchange (AMEX), are approved by the Securities and Exchange Commission (SEC).

The Committee acknowledges, however, that the rules governing the SROs do not expressly prohibit non-lawyer representation, and that the Arbitrator's Manual published jointly by the SRO's and the Securities Industry Association indicates that parties in securities arbitration "may choose to appear pro se (on their own) or be represented by a person who is not an attorney, such as a business associate, friend, or relative." Nevertheless, the Committee maintains first that neither the rules provision, nor the Manual, constitutes federal legislation preempting this Court's regulatory authority, and, second, that these very general, permissive guidelines do not condone the non-lawyer representation for compensation at issue here. Rather, the Committee maintains in its proposed opinion that these provisions merely recognize, in an informal manner, the right of an investor to appear pro se either by representing himself or with the uncompensated help of a business associate, relative or friend.

Lastly the proposed opinion points to several ways in which the public is harmed by the activities of non-lawyer representatives in securities arbitration. Most importantly, the Committee notes that because the stock brokerage industry arbitration forums have no qualification procedures, and non-lawyer representatives—unlike attorneys—are not supervised or subject to discipline by a state bar or any other regulatory body, instances of misleading advertising, ineffective representation and the unethical conduct of non-lawyer representatives are prevalent but unsanctionable. Specifically, non-lawyers who have been disciplined or suspended by the securities industry or from the practice of law can represent investors in arbitration forums and are not required to meet any ethical standards in their practice. Settlement negotiations and the handling of client's money on deposit goes unregulated.

(continues)

CASE LAW *The Florida Bar re Advisory Opinion on Nonlawyer Representation in Securities Arbitration* (continued)

Testimony before the Committee indicated that non-lawyer representatives are sometimes improperly motivated to settle claims rather than arbitrate because he is unable to go to court to confirm or collect an arbitration award on behalf of his client or defend against a broker's attempt to have the award vacated. Moreover, where claims are not settled and litigation does occur, the investor represented by a non-lawyer is sorely disadvantaged because, at least in the securities setting, the defendant broker or firm is always represented by well-resourced attorneys. And, to make matters worse, investors have no recourse against their compensated representatives for the ineffective representation

. . . . [W]e are persuaded of the need for some regulation of these compensated representatives and approve the UPL Standing Committee's proposed opinion. We conclude that compensated non-lawyer representatives in securities arbitration are engaged in the unauthorized practice of law and pose a sufficient threat of harm to the public to justify our protection. In *State ex rel. Florida Bar v. Sperry*, 140 So.2d 587 (Fla. 1962), this Court set out the framework for determining whether specific activities constitute the practice of law, which bears repeating here. We explained: [I]t is not the nature of the agency or body before which the acts are done, or even whether they are done before a tribunal of any sort or in the private office of an individual, that determines whether that which is done constitutes the practice of law. The best test, it seems to us, is what is done, not where, for the safest measure is the character of the acts themselves. If they constitute the practice of law the fact that they are done in the private office of the one who performs them or before a nonjudicial body in no way changes their character.

It is generally understood that the performance of services in representing another before the courts is the practice of law. But the practice of law also includes the giving of legal advice and counsel to others as to their rights and obligations under the law and the preparation of legal instruments, including contracts, by which legal rights are either obtained, secured or given away, although such matters may not then or ever be the subject of proceedings in a court.

We think that in determining whether the giving of advice and counsel and the performance of services in legal matters for compensation constitute the practice of law it is safe to follow the rule that if the giving of such advice and performance of such services affect important rights of a person under the law, and if the reasonable protection of the rights and property of those advised and served requires that the persons giving such advice possess legal skill and a knowledge of the law greater than that possessed by the average citizen, then the giving of such advice and the performance of such services by one for

(continues)

CASE LAW *The Florida Bar re Advisory Opinion on Nonlawyer Representation in Securities Arbitration* (continued)

another as a course of conduct constitute the practice of law. 140 So.2d at 591. . . . For instance, in *Florida Bar v. Brumbaugh*, 355 So.2d 1186 (Fla. 1978), The Florida Bar filed a complaint against Brumbaugh, a self-employed secretary who advertised typing services for "Do-It-Yourself " divorces, wills, resumes, and bankruptcies, alleging that Brumbaugh was practicing law without a license. Id. at 1189. For a fee, Brumbaugh prepared the necessary documents for pleading, filing, and securing a dissolution of marriage, as well as "detailed instructions as to how the suit should be filed, notice served, hearings set, trial conducted, and the final decree secured." Id. at 1100. . . . Additionally, had Brumbaugh typed forms for her clients, provided she copy only the information given to her in writing by her clients, this too would have been acceptable. However, we ultimately concluded that Brumbaugh's activities constituted the unlicensed practice of law because (1) her customers relied on her to properly prepare the necessary forms for the legal proceeding of a marriage dissolution; (2) she advised clients as to various remedies available to them, or otherwise assisted them in preparing the necessary forms; (3) she inquired into or answered questions of her clients to determine which forms would be necessary, how best to fill out these forms, and how to present the necessary information in court. Id. at 1193–94.

More recently, we addressed the issue of the unlicensed practice of law in the preparation and sales of living trusts in *Florida Bar re Advisory Opinion—Nonlawyer Preparation of Living Trusts*, 613 So.2d 426 (Fla. 1992). In that case, American Family Living Trust petitioned the Florida Bar Standing Committee on the Unlicensed Practice of Law for an advisory opinion concerning: Whether it constitutes the unlicensed practice of law for a corporation or other non-lawyer to draft living trusts and related documents for another where the information to be included in the living trust is gathered by nonlawyer agents of the corporation or by the non-lawyer and the completed documents are reviewed by a member of The Florida Bar prior to execution. Id. at 426. Upon reviewing similar requests from other parties, the Standing Committee held hearings, gathered both oral and written testimony, and subsequently proposed that this Court issue an opinion finding that non-lawyer companies which sell living trusts are engaged in the unlicensed practice of law and the public is or could be harmed by this practice. Id. at 427. . . . Nevertheless, we found that because the "gathering of the necessary information for a living trust" did not constitute the unlicensed practice of law, non-lawyers may properly perform this activity. Id. 680 So.2d at 258-59 (Fla. 1997).

Although we recognize that arbitration was set up to be a nonjudicial alternative for dispute resolution, it is clear that, in light of our caselaw thoroughly discussing the activities that constitute the practice of law, the services provided by non-lawyer representatives in

(continues)

CASE LAW *The Florida Bar re Advisory Opinion on Nonlawyer Representation in Securities Arbitration* (continued)

the alternative but still adversarial context of securities arbitration constitutes the practice of law. As the Committee pointedly and accurately notes in its proposed opinion, non-lawyer representatives give specific legal advice and perform the traditional tasks of the lawyer at every stage of the arbitration proceeding in an effort to protect the investor's important legal and financial interests. We cannot ignore such a situation. Because such activities—when performed by non-lawyers—are wholly unregulated and unsanctionable, we further agree with the proposed opinion that these activities must be enjoined. In these circumstances, the public faces a potential for harm from incompetent and unethical representation by compensated non-lawyers that cannot otherwise be remedied. . . .

Finally, we also must reject the position of the interested parties that this Court has been preempted from regulating the unlicensed practice of law in this instance. Specifically, the interested parties maintain that we are precluded from regulating the activities at issue here because the general rules governing the SROs do not prohibit non-lawyer representation and the Arbitrator's Manual, which serves as a handbook for the arbitration process, expressly authorizes lay representation. . . . We agree with the proposed opinion that neither the SRO rules nor the language in the Arbitrator's Manual constitutes federal or state legislative displacement of our authority to protect the public from harm by regulating the unauthorized practice of law.

We do acknowledge that the Securities and Exchange Commission, the federal agency responsible for oversight of securities arbitration, easily could—and may very well choose—to preempt us in enjoining non-lawyer representation by authorizing or regulating the activities of these professionals. Nevertheless, we think that compensated non-lawyer representatives in securities arbitration are engaged in the unauthorized practice of law and the protection of the public requires us to step in where there is no such legislation or regulation. Accordingly, we enjoin non-lawyers from representing investors in securities arbitration proceedings for compensation from the date this opinion becomes final and we approve the Committee's proposed opinion. It is so ordered.

Case Questions

1. How did this case originate?

2. Why did the court find that non-lawyers could not represent someone in securities arbitration?

3. How does compensation of the non-lawyer representative affect the court's decision?

Local Rules of Court

As discussed in Chapter 1, codes of professional ethics are part of what are called *rules of court*, the kinds of rules affecting lawyers and the litigation that is adopted by a jurisdiction's highest appellate court. Trial courts are local courts, often organized by counties, and those counties, in conjunction with their own judicial authority structure, are allowed to supplement their state's rules of trial procedure with certain local rules of trial procedure that apply within the county's legal system. Such rules might include special rules on filing documents, making appearances, discovery, and pretrial settlements.

The Seattle–King County Bar Association, for instance, has a Legal Assistant Registration Program in its Bar Association Rules. To be eligible to register, legal assistants must meet certain educational and experiential prerequisites. Once registered, legal assistants are entitled, under the bar association's authority, to do certain acts in accordance with the King County local court rules, including checking out files, using the county law library, and presenting agreed orders.

Likewise, some local jurisdictions list specific actions that paralegals are authorized to do, including semi-independent actions. For example, the local rules for the Superior and Circuit Courts of Allen County, Indiana, have a rule that concerns the authority of attorneys' employee, Rule 00-4. Section A of that rule states, "'legal assistants' . . . shall be limited to the performance of tasks which do not require the exercise of legal discretion or judgment that affects the legal rights of any person." Section D lists four activities that legal assistants (as they are referred to in the rule) are allowed to do: (1) filing and obtaining orders on motions; (2) setting pre-trial conferences and other hearing dates, except trials; (3) examining pleadings and chronological case summary sheets; and (4) with the discretion of the court, obtaining approval of orders from the judge's law clerk for notices of hearings, orders to appear and answer interrogatories, stipulations signed and approved by the parties of record, and motions to withdraw appearances.

INDEPENDENT PARALEGAL SERVICES AND THE UNAUTHORIZED PRACTICE OF LAW

As discussed in Chapter 2, lack of paralegal licensure, while perhaps appropriate, has some pitfalls. One of the pitfalls of this unlicensed profession is the lack of clear boundaries on how independent a paralegal may be. To say that a legal assistant must work under the supervision of an attorney presupposes conduct that would clearly be the practice of law if done by the attorney, rather than being supervised by him. However, between representing one's self pro se—which all citizens have the right to do—and representing others in litigation and giving legal advice—which only lawyers have the right to do—there lies a gray area of quasi-legal practice. As an example, if someone is allowed to write his own will, can someone else provide him the will kit or type it for him? Or, if one can help a friend find a statute at the county courthouse and not be guilty of the unauthorized practice of law, may one also charge a fee for finding that statute? Or, may a bank have its loan officers assist home purchasers in completing the mortgage, or other loan documents?

The answers to the preceding questions vary according to state regulations and are inconsistent within the case law. The starting point for any answer is to first examine your state's definition of the practice of law (if there is one), as well as the definition of a paralegal, as found in your state code or rules of professional responsibility. Next, one must examine the state's statutes to see if any specific law allows non-lawyers to engage in certain, quasi-legal activity, such as a state law that allows non-lawyer service providers to assist parties in obtaining uncontested divorces. Then, legal research must be done to analyze the state Supreme Court's view on the matter, as well as any relevant ethics opinions issued by the state disciplinary commission or bar association.

Legal Services Rendered by Non-Lawyers Serving the Public: Treading on Thin Ice

Marilyn Arons, founder of the Parent Information Center, found herself the target of the Delaware State Bar Association because she advised parents of children with special needs about their rights and represented them at school board meetings. In 1997, the Delaware Bar sued Ms. Arons, accusing her of practicing law without a license. She considered herself to be rightfully helping people with public school issues in which lawyers rarely get involved. Ms. Arons is not alone. In recent years, bar associations have sued a variety of service providers under theories of unauthorized practice of law: Banks have been sued in Michigan for charging fees for completing legal documents for loans. A funeral home in Alabama was sued because it charged fees for preparing documents, such as death certificates.

No person or entity draws the ire of the legal community as does Nolo (formerly Nolo Press), the publisher of legal self-help guides, which was the subject of an unauthorized practice of law investigation in 1997 by the Texas State Bar Association for selling its do-it-yourself legal books and computer software. The investigation resulted in skyrocketing sales for the Berkeley, California company, which was founded in the 1970s by two Bay Area legal aid lawyers who grew weary of turning away those who needed legal help. Some people couldn't qualify for legal aid because they were too wealthy, yet they couldn't get a lawyer because they were too poor. When Nolo published its first self-help book on how to get a do-it-yourself divorce in California, the Sacramento Bar Association complained so loudly the self-help guide became a huge hit. So, when Texas considered bringing UPL charges against the company, Nolo struck back, seeking a **declaratory judgment** that its products were legal. After the Texas legislature began drafting a bill (which became law) that expressly legalized the sale of legal self-help books, the state UPL committee dropped its investigation.

It is bar associations, and not dissatisfied clients, who have most often brought the increasing number of UPL cases across the country, raising the question of whether such bar association–prompted lawsuits are consumer protection or turf protection? The American Bar Association appointed a commission in 1992, known as the ABA Commission on Nonlawyer Practice, to study and evaluate the implications of non-lawyer practice to society and the legal profession. In 1995, the commission issued its report to the ABA, which included, among other things: recommending increasing the scope of allowable activities for traditional paralegals; considering the possibility of non-lawyer representation in state administrative hearings; examining the ethics rules so as to promote affordable legal services; and promoting non-lawyer assistance as long as it is subject to review. However, the commission's recommendations went nowhere, and were not even presented to the ABA House of Delegates. For those interested in reading a lengthy essay arguing for the repeal of unauthorized practice of law statutes, in part to lower the high cost of legal fees by allowing non-lawyers to provide legal services, go to the following link for the libertarian think tank, the Cato Institute, and then use the search feature: http://www.cato.org/pubs/regulation.

On occasion, state legislation has been introduced that would allow paralegals to directly serve the public by engaging in limited legal activities without attorney supervision. States, such as California, Illinois, Oregon, Rhode Island, and Washington, have contemplated legislation that would allow independent paralegals to draft and execute wills, represent parties at real estate closings, or represent parties in uncontested divorces. (Remember that the Washington statute on real estate closing officers, discussed earlier in the chapter, does not involve independent paralegals.) All of those bills, however, died in committee or otherwise failed in the legislative process.

That leaves us where we started, treading carefully on the line of demarcation between that which is allowed and that which is unauthorized. A generality that can be applied to this quagmire is that those who offer typing document preparation services directly to the public may do nothing that would involve helping their clientele choose what forms are needed or choose what information should be used to complete the forms. For example, if one were to purchase a will kit from an individual or entity that sells them, the seller of the kit would be engaging in the unauthorized practice of law if the seller decided, or helped the purchaser decide, what kind of will the purchaser needed, and also if the seller executed the will. Selling documents—or even filling in their blanks—is generally legal, but it often provides a too-easy opportunity to commit UPL when the seller does anything more than just that.

declaratory judgment

A judgment granted by the court that, without ordering any performance or determining damages, is close to an "advisory opinion" (which courts do not issue). A declaratory judgment is designed to allow a party to ask a court to resolve a controversy before it becomes a full-blown case.

We The People, a document preparer service with franchises throughout the country, has been accused of committing UPL in a variety of instances. Unlike Nolo, We The People has personal contact with the customers who purchase its documents, and that has led some to believe that the company does more than just sell documents. In 2005, We The People agreed to mediation with the U.S. Bankruptcy Trustee in New York, as a result of a restraining order the U.S. Trustee sought against the company for alleged instances of giving legal advice in bankruptcy cases to its customers (wrong advice in some instances). Part of the agreement to mediate included a public pledge by We The People not to engage in the unauthorized practice of law.

Other bankruptcy courts have found non-lawyers to have committed UPL by crossing the line from document provider to advice giver. Some of those acts include the following:

- Portraying one's services as more than just typing (*In re Calzadilla*, 151 B. R. 622 (Bankr. S.D. Fla. 1993))

- Giving advice on the option of voluntarily repaying one's debts (*In re Herren*, 138 B.R. 989 (Bankr. D. Wyo. 1992))

- Explaining the terms on bankruptcy forms (*In re Skobinsky*, 167 B.R. 45 (E.D. Pa. 1994))

- Explaining the significance of the various bankruptcy chapters as part of advice on which chapter to file (*In re Skobinsky*, 167 B.R. 45 (E.D. Pa. 1994))

- Answering bankruptcy questions by showing the debtor legal reference materials (*Matter of Bright*, 171 B.R. 799 (Bankr. E.D. Mich. 1994))

- Using terms such as "paralegal" or "legal technician" to describe one's bankruptcy assistance services (*In re Robinson*, 162 B.R. 319 (Bankr. D. Kan. 1993))

The following case from Florida shows the kinds of specific conduct committed by non-lawyer, legal services providers that cause courts to be perplexed when they consider whether such activity is crossing the line into the unauthorized practice of law.

CASE LAW   *Florida Bar v. Catarcio*

709 So.2d 96 (Fla. 1998)

PER CURIAM.

We have for review the referee's report regarding the unlicensed practice of law by respondent, Richard Catarcio. We have jurisdiction. Art. V, §15 Fla. Const. On August 28, 1996, the Florida Bar filed a two-count petition against Catarcio, alleging that he had engaged

(continues)

CASE LAW *Florida Bar v. Catarcio* (continued)

in the unlicensed practice of law in relation to his preparation of a bankruptcy petition and the manner in which he advertised his legal forms preparation service. Catarcio filed an answer and moved to dismiss the petition, arguing that the Bar's attempt to regulate his conduct was preempted by 11 U.S.C. §110 (1994), which generally regulates the conduct of a "bankruptcy petition preparer," and that the relief sought in the petition would violate the First Amendment of the United States Constitution as it would unlawfully infringe on his commercial speech. We denied Catarcio's motion and a hearing was held before a referee on September 15, 1997. After conducting the hearing, the referee made the findings of fact set forth below.

Catarcio was not and is not a member of the Florida Bar and is therefore not licensed to practice law in Florida. He operates a paralegal service business under the name "American Paralegal Center, Inc.," a Florida corporation, of which he is the sole officer, director, and owner, and his business card shows the Scales of Justice and identifies him as "Richard T. Catarcio, J.D." Catarcio advertises his business in *The Flyer*, a weekly advertising publication, under the heading "Professional Services" and the subheading "Legal," and the advertisement provides a list of available services, including simple divorce and bankruptcy. The advertisement also contains an offer of "Free Consultation."

In May 1994, Robert Cooper contacted Catarcio for assistance in filing for personal bankruptcy. Cooper met with Catarcio at Catarcio's office, seeking advice as to the appropriateness of filing for bankruptcy, and Catarcio told him that filing for bankruptcy would be proper. Catarcio advised Cooper that he was eligible to file for bankruptcy and that he should file under Chapter 7 of the Bankruptcy Code; Cooper wanted Catarcio to file the bankruptcy petition for him because he thought Catarcio knew what he was doing. Thereafter, Catarcio advised Cooper and Cooper's ex-wife, Michele Caron, to file for joint bankruptcy, advising Caron that if she did not file for joint bankruptcy, the bankruptcy trustee would "come after" her once Cooper's bankruptcy was completed. Catarcio then orally communicated with Cooper concerning the information to be placed in the bankruptcy petition and what to write in filling out the petition. Catarcio decided where to file the petition and what boxes to check on the bankruptcy forms indicating under which statutes Cooper's property should be exempted, as Cooper did not know what placing check marks in the boxes meant. Catarcio also advised Cooper about what qualified as joint property for the purposes of bankruptcy, selected the legal citations to be placed in the petition to indicate the statutory exemptions claimed, and explained the value of Cooper's personal property which could be claimed as exempt. In addition, Catarcio advised Caron to sign her name as "Cooper" on the joint bankruptcy petition even though she told him that she was divorced and that her legal name at the time was Caron.

(continues)

CASE LAW *Florida Bar v. Catarcio* (continued)

Subsequently, when two omissions in the bankruptcy petition were discovered, Cooper again contacted Catarcio. Catarcio advised him to file an amendment to add an omitted creditor, Sears, and to add his vehicle, a van, to the bankruptcy petition. Catarcio informed Cooper that Catarcio would prepare the amendment to the petition and that Cooper "should not worry about it," adding that the effect of the amendment would be that the bankruptcy trustee would be unable to take the van. Catarcio then took the information from Cooper orally to prepare the amendment. Cooper testified that he went to Catarcio to have him properly and competently fill out his bankruptcy forms and that, in preparing the bankruptcy petition and amendment, Catarcio held himself out in such a way that Cooper assumed he was an attorney because of "the way he [Catarcio] talked the law to me [Cooper] about the bankruptcy . . . all these articles and stuff like that." As a result of filing for joint bankruptcy, neither Cooper nor Caron can obtain credit.

Based on the above findings of fact, the referee concluded that Catarcio had engaged in the unlicensed practice of law by (1) advising Cooper and Caron as to various legal remedies available to them and possible courses of action; (2) taking information from Cooper orally to complete the bankruptcy petition and amendment when the forms being completed were not forms approved by this Court; (3) having direct contact with Cooper and Caron in the nature of consultation, explanation, recommendations, advice and assistance in the provision, selection, and completion of legal forms; (4) inducing Cooper to place reliance upon him in the preparation of his bankruptcy forms; (5) advising Cooper and Caron to file a joint bankruptcy petition when they were not married in contravention of 11 U.S.C. §302 (a), which states that joint bankruptcy petitions are filed by a debtor and the debtor's spouse, and by advising Caron to fraudulently sign her name as "Cooper" even though she told him that she was divorced from Cooper and that her legal name at the time was Caron; (6) offering "Free Consultation" in advertising his legal forms preparation service in that it holds him out as able to provide legal services in the nature of consultation and because it goes beyond the limitations placed on non-lawyer advertising by offering more than secretarial and notary services and selling legal forms and general printed materials; and (7) by using the designation "J.D." on his business card in conjunction with his offer of the preparation of legal forms and the depiction of the Scales of Justice.

After arriving at the above conclusions, the referee recommended that this Court find that Catarcio engaged in the unlicensed practice of law based on his conduct in the preparation of Cooper and Caron's joint bankruptcy petition, as well as the manner in which Catarcio advertised his legal forms preparation service. The referee then recommended that Catarcio be enjoined from the unlicensed practice of law and taxed for

(continues)

CASE LAW *Florida Bar v. Catarcio* (continued)

the costs of these proceedings. Catarcio filed objections to the referee's report, essentially raising the same arguments that he raised in his initial motion to dismiss, and the Bar filed a response. We approve the report of the referee. . . .

We also approve the referee's conclusions and recommendations. This Court has issued numerous decisions proscribing the type of conduct engaged in by Catarcio. See *Florida Bar v. Davide*, 702 So.2d 184 (Fla. 1997) (adopting uncontested referee's report finding non-lawyers engaged in unlicensed practice of law by, among other things, advising persons regarding bankruptcy exemptions); *Florida Bar v. Warren*, 655 So.2d 1131, 1132–32 (Fla. 1995) (enjoining non-lawyer from, among other things, counseling persons as to "the advisability of their filing for protection under the United States bankruptcy laws"); *Florida Bar v. Schramek*, 616 So.2d 979, 984 (Fla.1993) (finding non-lawyer engaged in unlicensed practice of law in many areas, including bankruptcy, by providing services "which require[d] a knowledge of the law greater than that possessed by the average citizen"); *Florida Bar v. King*, 468 So.2d 982. 983 (Fla.1985) (adopting uncontested referee's report finding non-lawyer engaged in unlicensed practice of law by, among other things, having "direct contact in the nature of consultation, explanation, recommendations, advice and assistance in the provision, selection and completion of forms"); *Florida Bar v. Martin*, 432 So.2d 54 (Fla. 1983) (approving referee's report finding non-lawyer's use of designation "J.D." in conjunction with his name constituted unlicensed practice of law); *Brumbaugh*, 355 So.2d at 1194 (enjoining non-lawyer from advising clients as to various available remedies, making inquiries or answering questions as to particular forms which might be necessary, how best to fill out such forms, and where to properly file such forms).

This Court has also adopted rules regulating the unlicensed practice of law which proscribe the type of conduct engaged in by Catarcio. See R. Regulating Fla. Bar 10–2.1(a) (1997) (restricting non-lawyer oral communications solely to those eliciting factual information for the completion of forms approved by this Court); see also *Florida Bar Re Approval of Forms Pursuant to Rule 10–1.1(b) of the Rules Regulating The Florida Bar*, 591 So.2d 594, 595 (Fla. 1991) (approving "fill-in-the-blank" forms developed by the Bar for use in "areas amenable to a forms practice").

Federal bankruptcy courts sitting in Florida have found similar conduct constituted the unlicensed practice of law. See *In re Samuels*, 176 B.R. 616, 621–22 (Bankr.M.D.Fla. 1994) (providing exhaustive list of activities constituting the unlicensed practice of law in bankruptcy context in Florida and other jurisdictions, and stating that "[t]he Florida Supreme Court and Florida bankruptcy courts have made it clear that persons wanting to provide services in the bankruptcy area are limited to typing or transcribing written information provided to them by a consumer onto pre-prepared forms"); *In re Calzadilla*,

(continues)

CASE LAW *Florida Bar v. Catarcio* (continued)

151 B.R. 622 625–626 (Bankr.S.D.Fla. 1993) (providing what bankruptcy services a non-lawyer may and may not provide); *In re Bachman*, B.R. at 773–775 (applying this Court's Brumbaugh decision in bankruptcy context).

We agree with the referee that Catarcio has engaged in the unlicensed practice of law, and we enjoin Richard Catarcio individually, his agents and employees, and any other business entities in which he holds an interest, from engaging in the following activities: (1) advising customers of their rights, duties and responsibilities under Florida or federal law, (2) making inquiries and answering questions as to the particular bankruptcy forms that might be necessary, how best to fill out the forms, the information necessary to complete the forms, and where to properly file such forms, (3) giving advice and making decisions on behalf of others that require legal skill and a knowledge of the law greater than that possessed by the average citizen, (4) advising about or explaining legal remedies and possible courses of action that affect the procedural or substantive legal rights, duties and privileges of persons, (5) counseling customers as to the advisability of filing for protection under United States bankruptcy laws, (6) allowing members of the public to rely on Catarcio to properly prepare legal forms or legal documents affecting individuals' legal rights, (7) using the phrase "Free Consultation" in advertising his legal form preparation service, and from advertising any legal form preparation services beyond the business activities of providing secretarial and notary services, and selling legal forms and general printed information, and (8) using the designation "J.D." following his name in the context of print advertisements, business cards, or other offerings of his legal form preparation services, or in any other manner which could mislead the public into believing Catarcio can assist the public in legal matters. Judgment for costs is entered in favor of The Florida Bar and against Richard Catarcio in the amount of $1,182.44, for which sum let execution issue.

It is so ordered.

Case Questions

1. In what conduct did Mr. Catarcio engage that qualified as the unauthorized practice of law?

2. Why was he being sued if he had a J.D., as listed on his business card?

3. What conduct did the court state would be permissible for Catarcio in his bankruptcy petition preparation service?

4. Has the court's ruling effectively put Catarcio out of business? Why do you think the court prohibited Catarcio from using the phrase "free consultation" in his advertisement?

5. Do you think it is likely that Catarcio was aware that his conduct was unauthorized?

6. Do you think this case is an example of turf protection or consumer protection?

In April 2002, the Florida Supreme Court adopted changes to Rule 4–5.3 of the Florida Rules of Professional Conduct, which is the rule that governs the use of non-lawyer assistants. It is surprising that the new rule 4–5.3(a) seems to approve of paralegals directly serving the public, because it says, "A person who uses the title of paralegal, legal assistant, or other similar term *when offering or providing services to the public* must work for or under the direction or supervision of a lawyer or an authorized business entity as defined elsewhere in these Rules Regulating The Florida Bar." (Emphasis added). And new Comments to the rule state:

> If an activity requires the independent judgment and participation of the lawyer, it cannot be properly delegated to a nonlawyer employee. . . . Additionally, this rule would not permit a lawyer to accept employment by a nonlawyer or group of nonlawyers, the purpose of which is to provide the supervision required under this rule.

The changes made to Florida's rule on non-lawyer assistants are quite drastic; however, the rule still requires that lawyers be responsible for the work of paralegals and legal assistants.

The same day Rule 4–5.3 was changed, the Florida Supreme Court also adopted changes to Rule 10–2.1, which governs the unlicensed practice of law. While that rule previously allowed non-lawyers to assist others in filling out legal forms approved by the Florida Supreme Court, a new part of the rule states the following:

"It shall constitute the unlicensed practice of law for a person who does not meet the definition of paralegal or legal assistant as set forth elsewhere in these rules to offer or provide legal services directly to the public or for a person who does not meet the definition of paralegal or legal assistant as set forth elsewhere in these rules to use the title paralegal, legal assistant, or other similar term in providing legal services or legal forms preparation services directly to the public. Florida Rules Governing the Investigation and Prosecution of the Unlicensed Practice of Law, 10–2.1(a)(2)"

And another new part of the rule 10–2.1(b), which concerns paralegals and legal assistants, states, "A non-lawyer or a group of non-lawyers may not offer legal services directly to the public by employing a lawyer to provide the lawyer supervision required under this rule."

Bankruptcy courts have, consistent with the traditional view, refused to allow independent paralegals to assist members of the public in preparing bankruptcy petitions. Those courts have allowed non-lawyers to type information that was provided in writing by bankruptcy customers. However, they stop short when non-lawyers make inquiries of their customers' needs and situations before preparing the bankruptcy petitions. For instance, helping a person fill out schedules of exempt and nonexempt property requires the one doing the assistance to make legal judgments in excess of what is allowed by non-lawyers. *See In re Harris*, 152 B.R. 440 (Bankr. W.D. Pa. 1993). Furthermore, those bankruptcy courts have found that disclaimers signed by customers stating that the assisting independent paralegal has not given legal advice are completely irrelevant to the issue of whether he or she actually crossed the line. In fact, answers given to customers by those paralegals, even when they have sought the advice of lawyers beforehand, constitutes the unauthorized practice of law, and any fees earned must be returned to the bankruptcy customers. *See Matter of Bright*, 171 B.R. 799 (Bankr. E.D. Mich. 1994), where the court provided an extensive analysis on the unauthorized practice of law in bankruptcy settings.

Not every jurisdiction even approves of non-lawyers operating typing services. A Pennsylvania ethics opinion discussed the propriety of a non-lawyer with a paralegal certificate starting a business assisting low-income persons with the completion of bankruptcy and divorce forms. Even though the paralegal claimed that all customers would sign forms stating they had not received any legal advice, the ethics committee found that such a business would violate Pennsylvania's unauthorized practice of law statute. Pennsylvania Unauthorized Practice of Law Committee, Op. 94–102 (1995).

Utah almost became the first state to authorize much of what has traditionally been thought of as the unauthorized practice of law when its statehouse passed legislation in 2003 that was to go into effect in May 2004. Utah Code § 78-9-102(1) defined the practice of law as, "appearing as an advocate in any criminal proceeding or before any court of record in this state in a representative capacity on behalf of another person." Designed specifically to alleviate the problem of those in Utah who make too much to qualify for legal aid but not enough to afford most lawyers, the law, by what it did not say, allowed non-lawyers to provide legal services outside the context of traditional court proceedings. The Utah State Bar Association opposed the legislation, and it may have been that the legislation was a warning to the bar, because it was repealed in 2004 before it could go into effect. Had the legislation survived, it would have unquestionably pushed at the pillars of the legal community. Of course, it also could have been declared unconstitutional by the Utah Supreme Court, which got involved in the controversy by adopting a definition of the practice of law in 2005. This definition is much broader than the short-lived statute, using most of the traditional action verbs (*informing, counseling, advising, assisting, advocating for, drafting*) that, by inference, restrict most legal work to those who are licensed attorneys. Utah Supreme Court Rules of Professional Practice, Special Practice Rule 14–802.

Legal Services Rendered by Non-Lawyers as Independent Contractors to Lawyers

An issue that may be more relevant, at least until the law on independent paralegals changes, is whether a non-lawyer can render legal services to lawyers, on an independent contracting basis, as a freelance paralegal. Such an arrangement would provide the kind of outsourcing benefits that have accrued in other industries and professions during the last economic growth cycle.

(Outsourcing is by no means universally recognized as a win-win situation, but this is not the place for such an analysis.) Law firms and corporate legal departments would still be able to use the services of paralegals to do things from manually preparing documents to case preparation to legal research and writing. However, instead of retaining these legal assistants as employees, the firm would hire them as **independent contractors**, thereby saving overhead costs on employee taxes, benefits, and employee hiring, training, and firing. Such an arrangement has been used for decades with accountants.

Independent-contracting paralegals would then act as entrepreneurs, seeking the immediate legal assistance needs of their clients who would be lawyers or law firms instead of the general public. Ideally, independent-contracting paralegals could work as much—or as little—as they wanted, retaining their autonomy in much the same way that any self-employed individual would. And with the natural selection that occurs in the marketplace, the better paralegals would become more valuable and earn more money.

Do the present rules of professional responsibility allow for such an arrangement? That depends on the set of rules in place. The ABA Model Rules of Professional Conduct seem to allow independent-contracting paralegals. Model Rule 5.3 requires lawyers who have direct supervisory authority over non-lawyer assistants to ensure that those assistants behave compatibly within the Model Rules. The Comment to that rule states in part: "Lawyers generally employ assistants in their practice, including secretaries, investigators, law student interns, and paraprofessionals. Such assistants, *whether employees or independent contractors*, act for the lawyer in rendition of the lawyer's professional services," (Emphasis added.) The Comment to MR 5.5 (which prohibits lawyers from assisting non-lawyers in the unauthorized practice of law) states that such a rule is not intended to prohibit lawyers from employing the services of paraprofessionals, as long as they properly supervise the paraprofessionals and retain responsibility for those services. Likewise, the Ethical Considerations following Canon 5 of the ABA Model Code of Professional Responsibility, discussed earlier in the chapter, imply an approval of independent-contracting paralegals.

Nothing in the ABA Model Guidelines for the Utilization of Paralegal Services prohibits legal assistants from being employed as independent contractors. The emphasis is on supervision of the delegated tasks. Guidelines 1 and 2 make the lawyer responsible for the professional actions of the legal assistant, and their Comments discuss principles of agency law in the context of lawyers delegating legal tasks to, and supervising the legal work of, legal assistants. The only prohibitions mentioned regarding non-lawyer services are the traditional restrictions of unauthorized conduct—giving legal advice, establishing the attorney client relationship, establishing fees, and representing clients in court—not the methods in which non-lawyers may be employed.

A statutorily created definition or description of a paralegal or legal assistant can expressly or impliedly approve of those who are independent contractors. For instance, California's statutory description of a paralegal includes "a person

■ **independent contractors**

One who is self-employed, but hired to do work for others as needed, such as an attorney, an accountant, or a caterer.

who either contracts with or is employed by an attorney, law firm, corporation, governmental agency, or other entity and who performs substantial legal work under the direction and supervision of an active member of the State Bar of California." (Emphasis added.) And a later section states, "[t]he terms 'paralegal,' 'legal assistant,' 'attorney assistant,' 'freelance paralegal,' 'independent paralegal,' and 'contract paralegal' are synonymous for purposes of this chapter." Cal. Bus. & Prof. Code §§ 6450(a), and 6454. And, Maine's statutory definition encompasses freelance paralegals by stating, "'Paralegal' and 'legal assistant' mean a person, qualified by education, training or work experience, *who is employed or retained* by an attorney, law office, corporation, governmental agency or other entity and who performs specifically delegated substantive legal work for which an attorney is responsible." Me. Rev. Stat. Ann. tit. 4, § 921. (Emphasis added.)

Also, the definition of a paralegal adopted by a jurisdiction's rules of court or bar associations can impliedly approve of those who are independent contractors. The American Bar Association's definition of a legal assistant was revised in 1997 and states in part, "A legal assistant or paralegal is a person qualified by education, training or work experience *who is employed or retained* by a lawyer." (Emphasis added.) As was discussed in Chapter 2 on legal assistants joining state bar associations, Article I, Section 6 of the Michigan Bar Association Bylaws describes a legal assistant as "[a]ny person *currently employed or retained* by a lawyer." (Emphasis added.) And, New Hampshire states, in its guidelines on the use of legal assistants, that its definition of a legal assistant "is intended to cover *all lay persons who are employed by or associated with* a member of the Bar but who are not admitted to practice law in the State of New Hampshire." N.H. R. S. Ct., Rule 35 (emphasis added). New Mexico's definition of a legal assistant also incorporates the revised ABA definition of a qualified person who is "*employed or retained* by a lawyer." N.M. Rules Governing Legal Assistant Services, Rule 20–102(A). (Emphasis added.).

Some states have addressed the issue of independent contractors in ethics opinions. For example, South Carolina approved of the use of lawyers employing independent-contract paralegals in a 1996 ethics opinion. Specifically, the question asked was whether a lawyer could use a contract-paralegal service to assist the lawyer in a probate practice, pay the paralegal service, and then bill the client for the paralegal's work. The opinion stated that such an arrangement was allowed, provided the client is aware of the billing arrangement and the lawyer properly supervises and remains responsible for the paralegal's work. South Carolina Bar Association, Ethics Advisory Op. 93–13 (1996). Utah issued an ethics opinion in 2002 that also approves of independent-contracting paralegals, concluding that, "Utah lawyers may hire outside paralegals on an independent-contractor basis, provided the paralegal does not control the lawyer's professional judgment." Utah State Bar Association, Ethics Advisory Committee Op. 02–07 (2002).

New Jersey reversed itself in 1992, when its Supreme Court acknowledged that lawyers were responsible to supervise legal assistants, "whether they are employees of the firm or independent contractors." *In Re Ethics Opinion No. 24 of the Committee on the Unauthorized Practice of Law*, 607 A.2d. 962 (N.J. 1992). Previously, the New Jersey Committee on the Unauthorized Practice of Law had concluded in an ethics opinion that freelance paralegals were engaging in the unauthorized practice of law, due to the intrinsic lack of supervision occurring in such relationships. New Jersey Supreme Court Committee on the Unauthorized Practice, Advisory Op. 24 (1990).

Key parts of the New Jersey Supreme Court's decision approving of independent contracting paralegals are reproduced in the following Case Law section.

CASE LAW *In Re Ethics Opinion No. 24 of the Committee on the Unauthorized Practice of Law*

607 A.2d. 962 (N.J. 1992)

GARIBALDI, J.

The New Jersey Supreme Court Committee on the Unauthorized Practice of Law (the "Committee") concluded in Advisory Opinion No.24, 126 N.J.L.J. 1306, 1338 (1990), that "paralegals functioning outside of the supervision of an attorney-employer are engaged in the unauthorized practice of law." Petitioners are several independent paralegals whom attorneys do not employ but retain on a temporary basis. They ask the Court to disapprove the Advisory Opinion. Like paralegals employed by attorneys, independent paralegals retained by attorneys do not offer their services directly to the public. Nonetheless, the Committee determined that independent paralegals are engaged in the unauthorized practice of law because they are performing legal services without adequate attorney supervision. We agree with the Committee that the resolution of the issue turns on whether independent paralegals are adequately supervised by attorneys. We disagree with the Committee, however, that the evidence supports a categorical ban on all independent paralegals in New Jersey.

I.

The Committee received inquiries from various sources regarding whether independent paralegals were engaged in the unauthorized practice of law. Pursuant to its advisory-opinion powers under Rule 1:22–2, the Committee solicited written comments and information from interested persons and organizations. In response, the Committee received thirty-seven letters from a wide variety of sources. Additionally, the State Bar Association's Subcommittee on Legal Assistants ("Legal Assistant Subcommittee"), the National Association of Legal Assistants ("NALA"), and the National Federation of Paralegal

(continues)

CASE LAW   *In Re Ethics Opinion No. 24 of the Committee on the Unauthorized Practice of Law* (continued)

Associates ("NFPA") provided the Committee with information on regulation, education, certification, and the ethical responsibilities of paralegals. The Committee characterized the information that it received in two ways: first, the material expressed positive views on the value of the work performed by paralegals; second, all of the materials expressly or implicitly recognized that the work of paralegals must be performed under attorney supervision. None distinguished between paralegals employed by law firms and those functioning as independent contractors offering services to attorneys.

...Two attorneys appeared before the Committee. One testified that as long as attorneys supervise independent paralegals, that those paralegals do not work full-time for one attorney or firm does not matter. The second attorney, a sole practitioner, testified that independent paralegals provide many benefits to both small firms and the general public alike. The Committee, he suggested, should focus on others, known as "legal technicians" or "forms practitioners," who offer their services directly to the public, rather than on independent paralegals who do not offer their services directly to the public but who are retained by attorneys.

II.

. . . The Committee summarized its findings as follows:

When the paralegal is employed by the attorney, the nature of the employment relationship makes it possible for the attorney to make the decisions as to which matters are appropriate for handling by the paralegal and which matters require direct hands-on work by the attorney. When the attorney and the paralegal are separated both by distance and the independent nature of the paralegal's relationship with the attorney, the opportunity for the exercise of that most important judgment by the attorney becomes increasingly difficult. This is not to say that there are not matters that could be handled by an independent paralegal with appropriate supervision by the attorney contracting with the paralegal. The problem is that the decisions as to what work may be done by the paralegal should be the attorney's to make but the distance between attorney and paralegal mandated by the independent relationship may result in the making of those decisions by the paralegal or by default. It is the view of the Committee, moreover, that the paralegal practicing in an independent paralegal organization, removed from the attorney both by distance and relationship, presents far too little opportunity for the direct supervision necessary to justify handling those legal issues that might be delegated. Without supervision, the work of the paralegal clearly constitutes the unauthorized practice of law. We found, from the testimony and materials presented to our Committee, that the opportunity for supervision of the independent paralegal diminishes to the point where much of the work of the independent paralegal, is, in fact, unsupervised. That being the case, the independent practice by the

(continues)

paralegal must involve the unauthorized practice of law. The fact that some of the work might actually be directly supervised cannot justify the allowance of a system which permits the independent paralegal to work free of attorney supervision and control for such a large part of the time and for such a large part of the work. [Ibid.] Based on those findings, the Committee concluded that attorneys are currently unable to supervise adequately the performance of independent paralegals, and that by performing legal services without such adequate supervision those paralegals are engaging in the unauthorized practice of law. Ibid.

We granted petitioners' request for review,—N.J.—(1991), and the Chairperson of the Committee granted their motion to stay the enforcement of Opinion No. 24.

III.

. . . The practice of law is not subject to precise definition. It is not confined to litigation but often encompasses "legal activities in many non-litigious fields which entail specialized knowledge and ability." Therefore, the line between permissible business and professional activities and the unauthorized practice of law is often blurred. [Id. at 236, 507A.2d 711 (citations omitted).]

. . . There is no question that paralegals' work constitutes the practice of law. N.J.SA. 2A:170–78 and 79 deem unauthorized the practice of law by a nonlawyer and make such practice a disorderly persons offense. However, N.J.SA. 2A:170–81(f) excepts paralegals from being penalized for engaging in tasks that constitute legal practice if their supervising attorney assumes direct responsibility for the work that the paralegals perform. N.J. SA.2A:170–81(f) states:

Any person or corporation furnishing to any person lawfully engaged in the practice of law such information or such clerical assistance in and about his professional work as, except for the provisions of this article, may be lawful, but the lawyer receiving such information or service shall at all times maintain full professional and direct responsibility to his client for the information and service so rendered.

Consequently, paralegals who are supervised by attorneys do not engage in the unauthorized practice of law.

IV.

. . . New Jersey's Advisory Committee on Professional Ethics also has recognized the value of paralegals to the legal profession:

It cannot be gainsaid that the utilization of paralegals has become, over the last 10 years, accepted, acceptable, important and indeed, necessary to the efficient practice of law. Lawyers, law firms and, more importantly, clients benefit greatly by their work. Those

(continues)

people who perform paraprofessionally are educated to do so. They are trained and truly professional. They are diligent and carry on their functions in a dignified, proper, professional manner. ACPE Op. 647, 126 N.J.L.J. 1525, 1526 (1990).

V.

No judicial, legislative, or other rule-making body excludes independent paralegals from its definition of a paralegal. For example, the ABA defines a paralegal as follows:

A person qualified through education, training or work experience; is employed or retained by a lawyer, law office, government agency, or other entity; works under the ultimate direction and supervision of an attorney; performs specifically delegated legal work, which, for the most part, requires a sufficient knowledge of legal concepts; and performs such duties that, absent such an assistant, the attorney would perform such tasks. (Emphasis added.)

The ABA definition expands the role of a legal assistant to include independent paralegals, recognizing that attorneys can and do retain the services of legal assistants who work outside the law office.

VI.

Under both federal law and New Jersey law, and under both the ABA and New Jersey ethics Rules, attorneys may delegate legal tasks to paralegals if they maintain direct relationships with their clients, supervise the paralegal's work and remain responsible for the work product. Neither case law nor statutes distinguish paralegals employed by an attorney or law firm from independent paralegals retained by an attorney or a law firm. Nor do we. Rather, the important inquiry is whether the paralegal, whether employed or retained, is working directly for the attorney, under that attorney's supervision. Safeguards against the unauthorized practice of law exist through that supervision. Realistically, a paralegal can engage in the unauthorized practice of law whether he or she is an independent paralegal or employed in a law firm. Likewise, regardless of the paralegal's status, an attorney who does not properly supervise a paralegal is in violation of the ethical Rules. Although fulfilling the ethical requirements of RPC 5.3 is primarily the attorney's obligation and responsibility, a paralegal is not relieved from an independent obligation to refrain from illegal conduct and to work directly under the supervision of the attorney. A paralegal who recognizes that the attorney is not directly supervising his or her work or that such supervision is illusory because the attorney knows nothing about the field in which the paralegal is working must understand that he or she is engaged in the unauthorized practice of law. In such a situation an independent paralegal must withdraw from representation of the client. The key is supervision, and that supervision must occur regardless of whether the paralegal is employed by the attorney or retained by the attorney.

(continues)

CASE LAW *In Re Ethics Opinion No. 24 of the Committee on the Unauthorized Practice of Law* (continued)

We were impressed by the professionalism of the paralegals who testified before the Committee. They all understood the need for direct attorney supervision and were sensitive to potential conflict-of-interest problems. Additionally, they all recognized that as the paralegal profession continues to grow, the need to define clearly the limits of the profession's responsibilities increases.

...We recognize that distance between the independent paralegal and the attorney may create less opportunity for efficient, significant, rigorous supervision. Nonetheless, the site at which the paralegal performs services should not be the determinative factor. In large law firms that have satellite offices, an employed paralegal frequently has less face-to-face contact with the supervising attorney than would a retained paralegal. Moreover, in this age of rapidly-expanding instant communications (including fax tele-transmissions, word processing, computer networks, cellular telephone service and other computer-modem communications), out-of-office paralegals can communicate frequently with their supervising attorneys. Indeed, as technology progresses, there will be more communication between employers and employees located at different sites, even different states. That arrangement will be helpful to both the paralegal and the attorney. Parents and disabled people, particularly, may prefer to work from their homes. Sole practitioners and small law firms will be able to obtain the services of paralegals otherwise available only to large firms.

Moreover, nothing in the record before the Committee suggested that attorneys have found it difficult to supervise independent paralegals. Indeed, the paralegals testified that the use of word processing made an attorney's quick review of their work possible. Most of the independent contractors who testified worked under the supervision of attorneys with whom they had regular communication. Although a paralegal's unsupervised work does constitute the unauthorized practice of law, that issue is not unique to independent paralegals. Rather, we emphasize again, it is the lack of educational and regulatory standards to govern their practice that is at the heart of the problem.

VII.

Regulation and guidelines represent the proper course of action to address the problems that the work practices of all paralegals may create. Although the paralegal is directly accountable for engaging in the unauthorized practice of law and also has an obligation to avoid conduct that otherwise violates the Rules of Professional Conduct, the attorney is ultimately accountable. Therefore, with great care, the attorney should ensure that the legal assistant is informed of and abides by the provisions of the Rules of Professional Conduct.

(continues)

CASE LAW   *In Re Ethics Opinion No. 24 of the Committee on the Unauthorized Practice of Law* (continued)

Although an attorney must directly supervise a paralegal, no rational basis exists for the disparate way in which the Committee's opinion treats employed and independent paralegals. The testimony overwhelmingly indicates that the independent paralegals were subject to direct supervision by attorneys and were sensitive to potential conflicts of interest. We conclude that given the appropriate instructions and supervision, paralegals, whether as employees or independent contractors, are valuable and necessary members of an attorney's team in the effective and efficient practice of law.

Subsequent to the issuance of the Committee's decision, the State Bar Association forwarded a resolution to this Court requesting the establishment of a standing committee on paralegal education and regulation. We agree that such a committee is necessary, and will shortly establish it to study the practice of paralegals and make recommendations. The committee may consider guidelines from other states, bar associations, and paralegal associations in formulating regulations for New Jersey paralegals. Any such regulations or guidelines should encourage the use of paralegals while providing both attorneys and paralegals with a set of principles that together with the Rules of Professional Conduct can guide their practices. The guidelines drafted will not be static but subject to modification as new issues arise.

We modify Opinion No. 24 in accordance with this opinion.

Case Questions

1. Why did the Unauthorized Practice Committee decide in 1990 that independent paralegals were engaging in the unauthorized practice of law?

2. Did the court define the practice of law? Why or why not?

3. What reasons did the court give in support of its decision that paralegals in New Jersey could act as independent contractors?

4. Did the court put any limits on the role of independent-contracting paralegals? Whom can independent paralegals serve?

Indiana dealt with a similar quandary. Guideline 9.1 of the Indiana Rules of Professional Conduct specifically states, "Independent legal assistants, to-wit, those not employed by a specific firm or by specific lawyers are prohibited." However, Rule 5.3 of the Indiana Rules of Professional Conduct mirrors the ABA version, and mentions in its Comment the use of "independent contractors." Dealing with the textual inconsistency, the Legal Ethics Committee of the Indiana State Bar Association concluded in 2000 that an attorney could appropriately use the services of an independent-contracting paralegal as long as he or she supervised the work and otherwise complied with the Guidelines in the Indiana Rules that concern the use of paralegals. Indiana State Bar Association, Ethics Op. 3 (2000).

So, can someone truly be an "independent paralegal"? No. As discussed in Chapter 2, a paralegal or legal assistant is someone who performs substantive legal tasks under the direction and supervision of a licensed attorney. Neither title nor certification makes someone a paralegal. Any person who calls himself or herself a paralegal must be someone whose work assignments are generated by an attorney (including a corporate law department or government agency) and whose work product is reviewed by an attorney. Anyone else is not a paralegal, and is either confused about the misuse of the word, or is trying to confuse others about its misuse. Independent-contracting paralegals, however, are not independent of licensed attorneys, so they are not committing the unauthorized practice of law, provided their jurisdictions authorize such an employing relationship, and their conduct is adequately supervised. See Exhibit 3–9 on the differences between independent paralegals and independent-contracting paralegals, and Exhibit 3–10 on quick tips for avoiding UPL.

EXHIBIT 3–9   INDEPENDENT PARALEGALS VERSUS INDEPENDENT-CONTRACTING PARALEGALS

Independent Paralegals	Independent-Contracting Paralegals
✎ Are generally engaged in UPL because paralegals may not be independent of lawyer supervision	✎ Are generally okay, because paralegals can be supervised without being an "employee"
✎ Often masquerade as legal document sellers or preparers	✎ Often engage in discovery, legal research, or other substantive legal tasks
✎ Often advertise to the public, which is highly misleading	✎ Have lawyers, not non-lawyers, as clients

---

EXHIBIT 3–10   QUICK TIPS TO AVOID ENGAGING IN UPL

- Don't answer a fact-specific question with a specific answer.
  ("Do you think my employer had the right to fire me?")

- Don't answer a question about legal fees with a specific answer.
  ("How much will this cost me?")

(continues)

> **EXHIBIT 3–10**   QUICK TIPS TO AVOID ENGAGING IN UPL *(continued)*
>
> • Don't be generous with free legal help to friends and family.
>   *("Can I ask you something about my lease?")*
>
> • Do be careful to check your local rules of court on allowable non-lawyer conduct.
>
> • Do be careful that any independent-contracted work is done for an attorney.
>
> • Do be careful when working if your supervisor is out of the office—even for nondisciplinary reasons.

SUMMARY

The practice of law is allowed only for licensed attorneys not under suspension. What constitutes practicing law is usually defined by case law, although some jurisdictions have statutes or rules of court that define it, and all jurisdictions have statutes that prohibit the unauthorized practice of law, making it a crime. Certain actions are commonly considered the practice of law: representing someone in court; representing someone before an administrative agency in an adjudication; giving legal advice; drafting or completing legal documents; negotiating on behalf of someone where that person's legal rights are involved; and carrying on the business aspects of a law practice.

The unauthorized practice of law is committed when a non-lawyer engages in activities that can only be done by licensed attorneys, when a legal assistant exceeds his authority as defined by the rules of professional conduct, and also when a paralegal engages in otherwise appropriate activities that are unsupervised by the delegating attorney. The rules of ethics list three activities that paralegals are specifically prohibited from performing: giving legal advice; establishing the attorney-client relationship; and establishing fees. The giving of legal advice occurs when one applies legal principles to a specific set of facts. Although paralegals may engage in initial client interviews, they may not say or do anything that gives the impression that a lawyer-client relationship has been established. Paralegals should be careful when answering client questions about fees and be certain that no statements are made that appear to create a fee arrangement.

Additional activities that legal assistants are not allowed to perform include representing others in court, conducting depositions, representing others in legal mediations, executing wills, conducting real estate closings, representing others in administrative proceedings, and signing pleadings and other litigation documents. However, some jurisdictions make limited exceptions to the just-named prohibitions.

All of the national rules of ethics dedicated for the use of paralegals authorize them to perform a variety of substantive, legal functions, as long as those functions are properly delegated and supervised by attorneys who maintain responsibility for the work product. Such activities include client interviewing, trial preparation, case management, and legal research and writing.

Federal law provides that federal agencies may allow non-lawyers, including paralegals, to represent clients in administrative adjudications. At the state level, some administrative practice by non-lawyers is also allowed. Where federal and state laws allow a non-lawyer to represent others before administrative agencies, such representation is conditioned on the non-lawyer representatives meeting certain educational or experiential prerequisites. Local rules of court and local bar association guidelines might also allow paralegals to engage in other court-approved activities.

Independent paralegals may only directly serve the public in ways that are specifically authorized by law, or in ministerial functions such as typing services or document preparation. Some statutes even allow non-lawyers to render certain, law-related services to the public. However, such laws generally prohibit these legal services providers from helping their customers decide what best suits their legal needs. Some jurisdictions, however, allow legal assistants to be employed as independent contractors to law firms as long as there is appropriate lawyer supervision of the contracted work, as well as lawyer responsibility for the work product. And the Ethics 2000 version of Model Rule 5.5 now includes a new Comment that implies an approval of lawyers using the services of independent contracting paralegals, although the ABA House of Delegates made no decision on it.

ETHICS IN ACTION

1. Sarah has been working for about three years for a general practice law firm, which has eight lawyers and four paralegals. Her duties include interviewing prospective clients and working with her firm's clients, which she enjoys. But she has come to realize that frequently people ask her questions to which it is difficult to respond. Occasionally, clients ask her questions, which, if answered, would require her to make a legal judgment of opinion. Just the other day, while talking with one of her firm's clients who was charged with drunk driving, she was asked, "Do you think that Judge Brown will sentence me to jail if I plead guilty to this?" And before getting a chance to respond, the client asked her, "If I'm found guilty, will it be a felony or misdemeanor? I think my last one that happened three years ago was a misdemeanor." Sarah knows Judge Brown's reputation as a "hanging judge" when it

(continues)

ETHICS IN ACTION   *(continued)*

comes to drunk driving, and is aware that Ind. Code § 9–30–5–3 states that operating a vehicle while intoxicated is a Class D felony *if* there is a prior conviction of the same offense within the prior five years.

How should she answer these questions?

2. The chapter opened with a hypothetical scenario about a paralegal named Rachel who was perplexed about her place in the legal system and her desire to help those she knew who seemed unable to afford her law firm. Please reread it before answering the following questions.

    What can Rachel do to assist her friends without crossing the line and engaging in the unauthorized practice of law?

    Say that Rachel does something for a friend that would be considered the unauthorized practice of law, and it is done negligently—such as incorrectly helping a friend execute a will. The friend then sues Rachel and her law firm for negligence, and also contacts her jurisdiction's disciplinary commission to complain about Rachel and her firm. Is anyone in trouble? If yes, who?

3. Melissa is the senior legal assistant for a sole practitioner with a high-volume bankruptcy practice. There are four other legal assistants in the firm who manage the files by keeping track of deadlines, contacting bankruptcy trustees and creditors, and working with the firm's debtor clients. In addition to those tasks, Melissa's duties also involve serving as the liaison between the attorney and the four other legal assistants. After being debriefed from her boss, Sharon, about her new cases, Melissa determines which legal assistants should work on what cases, and conducts initial performance reviews of the other legal assistants for Sharon. Sharon will be taking a three-week cruise to celebrate her 20th wedding anniversary, and has told Melissa to "hold the fort down while I'm at sea." Melissa has been instructed that if prospective clients call, she is to set up appointments for them after Sharon returns from her vacation, but not to interview them. As for current cases, Sharon instructed Melissa to keep things going by having the other legal assistants keep doing what they normally do. Sharon also gives Melissa the cruise ship's phone number, telling her to call if she has any questions. Sharon also tells Melissa, that in the event of an emergency, she should contact the lawyers whose offices are on the floor above Sharon's.

    What can Melissa and the other legal assistants do during Sharon's vacation?

4. Karen is a paralegal in the law department at an Indiana insurance company, which is a division of a financial services conglomerate headquartered in Pennsylvania. She reviews contracts, engages in treasury regulation research, and drafts memoranda

(continues)

ETHICS IN ACTION   *(continued)*

and correspondence. Her attorney-supervisor, Warren, has left the company after serving as the vice president of legal affairs for only three months. Evidently, he had the insurance division president had only one thing in common: they hated each other. The company is searching for a replacement, but in the meantime has asked Karen to temporarily take charge of the law department. When Karen reminded the company that she is not an attorney, the division president, Monica, stated there is no problem for three reasons: (1) the law department doesn't represent anyone other than the company, and the company has no problem with her assuming greater responsibility (and a larger paycheck); (2) because Karen has worked in the law department for eight years, and has always had excellent evaluations, the company believes she knows the department's objectives better than any interim lawyer would; and (3) the company's corporate counsel in Pennsylvania will be supervising her work by e-mail and two-way video conferences, and will be making bi-weekly trips to Indiana to meet with Karen until a new attorney is hired for the law department.

Problem solved?

5. Attorney Tom has recently moved to a new town because his wife's promotion at her company necessitated the address change. Tom knows few people in town, and at the local YMCA he strikes up a conversation with Brad, a recently unemployed financial planner. Brad's position as junior associate in a local financial planning company came to an abrupt conclusion due to the recent lack of interest in financial services products. After talking with Brad a few more times at the Y, Tom decides to offer Brad a job. Because of Brad's background and public speaking confidence, Tom hires Brad to speak on estate planning at area nursing homes and community centers. Tom will place the advertisements, inviting the public to hear Brad the financial expert talking about the consequences of dying without a will, the significance of an estate plan, and how to minimize death taxes. At the seminars, Brad will distribute and outline of his lecture, in the form of a pamphlet that also has Tom's address and phone number on it. If any of the guests want to talk with Brad after the seminar about their wills (or lack thereof), Brad will interview them there and arrange an appointment for them to meet with Tom at Tom's office. During the first seminar, conducted at a nursing home, attorney Greg, who is there visiting his mother-in-law, overhears the commotion in the dining room, and stays long enough to tell Brad that Brad is engaging in the unauthorized practice of law.

Is Brad engaging in the unauthorized practice of law?

(continues)

ETHICS IN ACTION   *(continued)*

6. A father whose 23-year-old daughter will be taking a three-month mission trip to Central America, calls a law firm to ask how much a power of attorney costs and what it would cost to have a will drafted for his daughter. Upon taking the phone call, the receptionist puts the call through to Emily, the attorney's legal assistant. The attorney would take the call, except he is out to lunch (literally only). The father reiterates his questions to Emily. Emily knows that her attorney charges $175 dollars an hour, and that Emily's work is billed at $75 an hour, and she also knows that her firm charges a flat fee of $400 for a simple will.

    How should Emily answer these questions?

7. Gale has worked as a legal assistant for 20 years. After spending many hours sitting on the free-way every morning and evening, fighting traffic, and worrying about being late, she has decided to leave her present position in Tampa Bay and look for a position at a smaller law firm closer to her home. When Gale tells her attorney, Sandy, about her plans, Sandy starts negotiating with Gale. They reach an agreement that would allow Sandy to use Gale's expertise, while Gale avoids having to commute, or even get dressed up: Gale is going to be an independent-contracting legal assistant. Sandy will hire Gale on an as-needed basis, sending her research and writing tasks (pleadings, motions, briefs in support of motions), which Gale will complete and then e-mail to Sandy. When necessary, Gale will work at the firm, but no more than one day a week. The arrangement calls for Gale to be paid hourly for her work, and she expects to work between 15–25 hours a week. Thinking like an entrepreneur, Gale has kicked around the idea of advertising in legal periodicals, such as the *Florida Bar Journal*, if this experiment proves successful.

    Does this arrangement constitute the unauthorized practice of law? May Gale advertise, as she's considering doing?

8. Dawn has been fascinated and encouraged by the role that alternative dispute resolution plays in her legal system. In fact, she used a week's vacation last summer attending the family mediation training, which was offered through her jurisdiction's continuing legal Education forum. She realizes that Rule 2.5(B)(2) of her jurisdiction's Rules for Alternative Dispute Resolution allows a non-lawyer with a bachelor's degree to serve as a registered mediator, and because she has a B.S. in psychology, Dawn has paid her fee to be listed on her jurisdiction's Family Mediation Registry. Dawn is so excited that she talks to the senior partner at the law firm where she works to ask whether she can attempt to get some mediation opportunities. Although he thinks the chances are slim that Dawn will be conducting any domestic relations mediations, he agrees to let her try, provided that she remit

(continues)

> **ETHICS IN ACTION**   *(continued)*
>
> her mediation fee to the firm. When she conducts mediations, she'll be paid her
> salary only, in exchange for being given the chance by her firm to conduct
> mediations, instead of doing her legal work.
>
> *If this arrangement works as Dawn hopes, does it constitute the unauthorized practice*
> *of law?*

■ POINTS TO PONDER_____

1. After examining your jurisdiction's Admission and Discipline Rules, determine if any allowances are made for law students to practice law on a limited basis.

2. What activities are most associated with the practice of law and therefore only allowed to be performed by lawyers?

3. What does it mean to give legal advice?

4. What rules in the ABA Model Rules of Professional Conduct affect the unauthorized practice of law?

5. What attorney rules of ethics in your jurisdiction affect the unauthorized practice of law? Are they different from either the ABA Model Rules or ABA Model Code?

6. Does your jurisdiction incorporate into its set of rules the ABA Model Guidelines for the Utilization of Legal Assistant Services?

7. In what two ways could a paralegal's conduct, even if technically accurate, be considered the unauthorized practice of law?

8. Does your state define the practice of law by statute?

9. Why do you think the ABA did not act on the recommendations of the 1995 committee appointed to examine the changing role of non-lawyer practice?

10. Which ABA version of the practice of law do you think is more effective, the first (and much more comprehensive) version, or the second version?

11. What does it mean to establish the attorney-client relationship or to establish fees?

12. What kinds of activities could a paralegal in a sole practitioner's office do while the attorney is on vacation?

13. Do you think the law should prohibit non-lawyers from assisting others who are representing themselves in court?

14. Why is a paralegal not allowed to take a deposition?

15. Does your jurisdiction allow non-lawyers to conduct real estate closings?

16. Why is it said that what occurs in an administrative agency adjudication is quasi-judicial?

17. What determines whether a non-lawyer is allowed to represent someone before an administrative agency?

18. Does your jurisdiction allow non-lawyers to represent others before any administrative agencies?

19. Does your jurisdiction have any local court rules that authorize paralegals to engage in any legal acts?

20. What kinds of problems can occur when non-lawyers are allowed to provide limited, legal services to the public?

21. What are some advantages to allowing legal assistants to act as independent contractors to lawyers?

22. Does your jurisdiction allow the use of independent contracting paralegals?

■ KEY CONCEPTS

Administrative agency adjudication

Alternative dispute resolution

Arbitration

Establishing fees

Establishing the attorney-client relationship

Giving legal advice

Independent-contracting paralegal/legal assistant

Mediation

Practice of law

Pro se representation

Real estate closing

Unauthorized practice of law (UPL)

Will execution

■ KEY TERMS

adjudication

alternative dispute resolution (adr)

declaratory judgment

independent contractors

mediation

memorandum of law

misdemeanor

motions

original jurisdiction

pleadings

positive law

pro se

real estate closing

status conference

surety bond

trust accounts

Online Companion™
For additional resources, please go to
http://www.paralegal.delmar.cengage.com

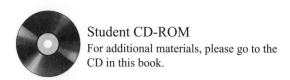

Student CD-ROM
For additional materials, please go to the
CD in this book.

4

Confidentiality

INTRODUCTION

While working on a criminal case, Rachel came across some information that she regretted having found. The firm's client, William, has been accused of sexual assault; the trial is to begin in a few weeks. William is accused of sexually assaulting a woman he met in a hotel bar, while at an out-of-town convention. William claims that they engaged in consensual sex, which makes his testimony critical. While going through William's files, Rachel sees a reference to another file and its file number. Rachel tracks down that file, opens it, and discovers that William has, on two prior occasions within the last eight years, paid large sums of money to women who accused him of "acquaintance rape." Both cases involved William meeting women in a club or a bar while on trips out of the state. Although William was never brought to trial, he was sued each time and reached settlements with both women. Copies of the settlements in the file, which were drafted by Rachel's boss, require each woman not to ever discuss the facts of the dispute or the amount of money she received. Rachel now cannot stand to look at William, believing that he is a serial rapist. She knows the prosecuting attorney will never learn about these two incidents, but she believes if that information came to light, it might help establish a modus operandi (habitual method of procedure). Rachel is considering making an anonymous tip to the prosecuting attorney's office about these other incidents because she fears that William will get away with another assault. Should she do this? If not, is there anything else she can or should do?

One of the hallmarks of the legal profession is its formalized respect for the sanctity of communications between clients and their attorneys. As with doctor-patient and priest-penitent relationships, it is common knowledge that an

> "[F]ew love a spokesman for the despised and the damned."
>
> **CLARENCE DARROW, ONE OF AMERICA'S GREATEST CRIMINAL DEFENSE LAWYERS**

> "Of course people are getting smarter nowadays; they are letting lawyers, instead of their conscience, be their guides."
>
> **WILL ROGERS, HUMORIST**

attorney will not, and indeed may not, disclose to the client's disadvantage what the client tells the attorney. This chapter will explore the concept of lawyer-client confidentiality, which is found in two related bodies of law. First, there will be a discussion of the professional responsibility rules that concern the duty of confidentiality, including when that duty arises, its extension to the paralegal and what exceptions would allow an attorney to disclose confidential information.

Connected to the duty of confidentiality is the attorney-client privilege, which is generally found in statutes on witness competency and prohibits attorneys from testifying against their clients. The attorney client privilege also takes shape in what is known as the work product rule, which is found in the rules of civil procedure and concerns the nondisclosure of certain kinds of **discovery** material. This chapter will also explain the relationship between the attorney-client privilege and the work product rule, and why paralegals need to be aware of its ramifications when working on discovery matters. Finally, this chapter will discuss inadvertent disclosure—what happens when protected attorney-client materials are accidentally turned over to the other party. By the chapter's conclusion, you should be able to differentiate the four siblings that are vital branches of the confidentiality family tree. See Exhibit 4–1 for an initial view.

■ **discovery**

A pre-trial procedure used in litigation where parties gain information from each other. Discovery is designed to promote open disclosure of relevant evidence and is supposed to operate without court involvement.

THE DUTY OF CONFIDENTIALITY

The protection provided by the duty of confidentiality has many facets. First, there is the comfort that comes from knowing that what one says to his or her lawyer is private. That knowledge helps clients overcome some of the fear associated with talking about their problems, embarrassments, or mistakes. Beyond the fear factor, there are practical benefits that accrue when clients fully

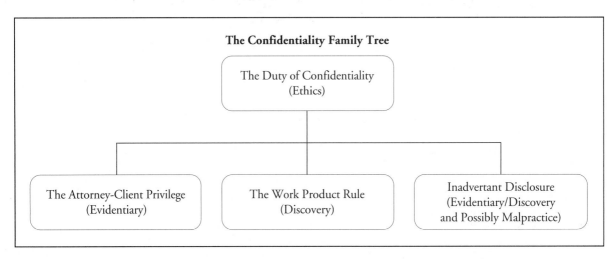

The Confidentiality Family Tree

The Duty of Confidentiality
(Ethics)

The Attorney-Client Privilege
(Evidentiary)

The Work Product Rule
(Discovery)

Inadvertent Disclosure
(Evidentiary/Discovery
and Possibly Malpractice)

EXHIBIT 4–1   The Confidentiality Family Tree

disclose information to their attorneys. As specialists, lawyers need all the facts before them to best assess whether a client's situation is actually a legal problem or, if so, how extensive the legal problem is. If clients only told their attorneys those things the clients thought were relevant or important, then their hired experts would be hindered from working effectively on their behalf. Whether a lawyer's activities fall into the categories of problem avoidance (estate planning or contract drafting) or of problem solving (litigation), both activities require uninhibited fact gathering before proceeding and neither activity can be carried out as anticipated by the client without full disclosure to the attorney.

Distinctions Between the Confidentiality Rules of the Model Rules and Those of the Model Code

The starting point for the duty of confidentiality is the Ethics 2000 version of ABA Model Rule 1.6, wherein, in section (a), it states, "A lawyer shall not reveal information relating to representation of a client unless the client gives informed consent, the disclosure is impliedly authorized in order to carry out the representation or the disclosure is permitted by paragraph (b)." The Model Rule differs from the Model Code's confidentiality rule in that DR 4–101 prohibits the disclosure of only such information as is "gained in" the lawyer-client relationship that the client either has asked be kept confidential or "the disclosure of which would be embarrassing or would be likely to be detrimental to the client." This is a critical distinction because, under MR 1.6, *all information* relating to the representation starts out as being confidential, from whatever the source, and this includes information the lawyer may have acquired from any source, even before having entered into a professional relationship with the client.

The ABA's Ethics 2000 Commission made such significant recommendations regarding MR 1.6 that it was reorganized, although the ABA House of Delegates rejected some of the key proposals. The first change to MR 1.6 is that where the former version allows for disclosure after client consultation and consent, the Ethics 2000 version requires that clients give **informed consent**. The new version gives attorneys broader discretion to disclose confidential information as well. Confidences can now be disclosed to prevent "reasonably certain death or substantial bodily harm," whereas the former exception required first that the lawyer's disclosure would prevent "a crime" involving the risk of death or substantial bodily harm. In addition, the new version expressly allows lawyers to disclose confidences in order to seek legal advice regarding application of the ethics rules, as well as to comply with law or a court order. Two proposed changes that were initially rejected by the ABA House of Delegates, but were then adopted by a close vote in 2003, allow lawyers to disclose confidential information in order to prevent, mitigate, or rectify crimes or frauds committed by the client with the unwitting help of the lawyer's services and which cause substantial financial injury. MR 1.6(b)(2) and (3). See Exhibit 4–2 on the evolving ABA rule on confidentiality.

■ **informed consent**
Giving one's agreement to take a certain action, including doing nothing, after having received a full explanation of the possible ramifications and consequences of taking that action.

EXHIBIT 4–2   THE EVOLVING ABA CONFIDENTIALITY RULE

DR 4-101 (1969)	Model Rule 1.6 (1983)	Ethics 2000 Rule 1.6 (2003)
• Covers the client's confidences and secrets "gained in the lawyer-client relationship" • Generally doesn't cover statements made in the presence of third parties • Allows disclosure to prevent "*any*" client crimes	• Covers all client information, regardless of the source • Generally covers client statements made in the presence of third parties • Allows disclosure to prevent client crimes only if the crime is "*likely to result in imminent death or substantial bodily harm*"	• Also covers all client information • Has broader exceptions than 1983 version • Allows disclosure to "*prevent reasonably certain death or substantial bodily harm*" • Allows disclosure to prevent or rectify fraud or financial harm • Allows disclosure to secure legal advice about the lawyer''s ethics duties

The following case is an example of the broader protection provided to client information in jurisdictions that have adopted either version of Model Rule 1.6.

CASE LAW   *In re Anonymous*

654 N.E.2d 1128 (Ind. 1995)

PER CURIAM.

The respondent has been charged by the Disciplinary Commission in a verified complaint for disciplinary action with violating Rules 1.6 (a), 1.8 (b), and 1.16 (a)(1) of the Rules of Professional Conduct for Attorneys at Law. The Commission and the respondent now tender for this Court's approval a statement of circumstances and conditional agreement for discipline, pursuant to Ind.Admission and Discipline Rule 23, Section 11 (g). In their agreement, the parties agree that the proper sanction for the respondent's misconduct is a private reprimand and that the facts and circumstances of this case should be set forth in an anonymous opinion to educate the Bar. We approve the parties' agreement, and herein more fully set forth the facts and circumstances of this case.

(continues)

CASE LAW *In re Anonymous* (continued)

As stipulated by the parties, the respondent was contacted by an individual (the "mother") in April or May of 1994 about representing her in seeking a child support arrearage due to her from the father ("father") of her minor child. She supplied the respondent with records concerning her support action and her income. Also included in these documents was information regarding the father, including the fact that he was going to receive a substantial inheritance, his salary, his place of employment, and his address. In the course of reviewing the documents supplied by the mother, the respondent discovered that on July 17, 1992, a judgment had been entered against the mother and father, making them jointly liable for almost $4,500 of medical and hospital debt resulting from the birth of their child. The judgment was in favor of the local county welfare department. The respondent was, at all times relevant to this proceeding, the attorney under contract to represent the local county welfare department.

The respondent contacted the mother to determine if the medical debt owed to the welfare department had been paid by either her or the father. It had not. The respondent then informed the mother that he would be unable to represent her in the case because of a conflict of interest, then forwarded her documents, at her request, to another attorney. Thereafter, the respondent received approval from the local county welfare department to file a collection suit against the father, which he did on April 26, 1994. Later, the father's counsel joined the mother as a party defendant in the collection suit. The respondent ultimately obtained a summary judgment against the mother and the father. The respondent did not withdraw from the case after the mother was joined as a party defendant.

We find that, by revealing information relating to the representation of the mother without her consent, the respondent violated Ind.Professional Conduct Rule 1.6(a). By using that information to her disadvantage without her consent, he violated Prof.Cond.R. 1.8(b). By failing to withdraw as counsel for the local welfare department during the collection suit against the mother when such representation violated the *Rules of Professional Conduct,* the respondent violated Prof. Cond.R. 1.16(a)(1).

The respondent and the Commission agree that several factors mitigate the severity of his misconduct. They agree that the information gained by the respondent about the mother's case was readily available from public sources and not confidential in nature. The respondent declined to represent the mother after he learned of her outstanding debt owed to the county welfare department, and advised her to seek other counsel. He did not at any time request that she sign an employment agreement, seek a retainer fee, or otherwise charge her. We see no evidence of selfish motive on the respondent's part.

(continues)

CASE LAW   *In re Anonymous* (continued)

The respondent's use of information gained during consultations with the mother represents misuse of information entrusted to him in his capacity as a lawyer. Such conduct not only threatens harm to the individuals involved, but also erodes the integrity of the profession. At the same time, we note that the respondent appears to have had no sinister motives. For these reasons, we accept the agreed sanction of a private reprimand.

Case Questions

1. What information did the lawyer learn about the mother that the court considered confidential?

2. Why would it have been confidential if it did not relate to the mother's claim against the father for back child support?

3. Notice that this case also involves a conflict of interest, which is the subject of Chapter 5. With that in mind, why do you think the lawyer's conduct implicated a conflict of interest if he ceased representing the mother, never even charging her a fee, before representing the county welfare department against the father?

Other jurisdictions have also concluded that the language of MR 1.6 (or the spirit of other versions of the client confidentiality rule) prohibit a lawyer from releasing or using information of the client that is in the public record, or is obtained from sources other than the client, without client consent. *See* Arizona Ethics Op. 2000–11 (2000). The West Virginia Supreme Court succinctly stated this doctrine in a disciplinary case against the state attorney general, who was found to have violated the duty of confidentiality, by concluding, "[t]he ethical duty of confidentiality is not nullified by the fact that the information is part of the public record or by the fact that someone else is privy to it." *Lawyer Disciplinary Board v. McGraw*, 462 S.E.2d 850, 861 (W. Va. 1995).

MR 1.6 leaves no room for the attorney to speculate as to whether divulging client information would be detrimental or embarrassing to the client. In a Wisconsin case, an attorney working on a corporate acquisition for a client purchased shares in the company his client was going to acquire, and then later sold those shares at a profit. Such an act violated not only laws against insider trading, but also the duty of confidentiality, even though no allegation was made that the corporate client was harmed by the attorney's purchase of the acquiring company's stock. *In re Marick*, 554 N.W.2d 204 (Wis. 1996). A lawyer's duty applies even in the face of danger and applies to information of other clients in the firm. In a tragic case from Indiana, a lawyer's criminal client realized that a witness in his upcoming trial was the husband of a client of the lawyer's partner, and demanded to know the whereabouts of this person in order to kill the witness. After being physically threatened, the lawyer attempted to prove he did not know the other client's address by showing his client an envelope that had been sent to the other client, which had been returned to sender due to "no such street." But, the criminal client wrote down the address, figured out the address's error, and then found and killed the witness. Despite the threat to the lawyer's safety, the lawyer was found to have violated Rule 1.6 by showing what he thought to be the wrong address of someone who was not his client, but was still the firm's client. *In re Goebel,* 703 N.E.2d 1045 (Ind. 1998).

MR 1.6 is also broader than DR 4–101 in that the former gives the attorney implied authority to divulge information that is necessary to the representation, whereas the latter requires that information be divulged only after the client consents. For instance, in a settlement negotiation with an insurance company, a plaintiff's lawyer practicing in a Model Rules–based jurisdiction would not need the client's permission to detail the extent of his or her injuries or complications from those injuries to improve the likelihood of settlement or increase his or her recovery. Another kind of authorized disclosure occurs when an attorney discusses client matters with another member of the firm, unless the client specifically has requested that certain information not be discussed with other members of the firm.

One aspect of client confidentiality that tends to bother the general public is when a lawyer knows facts about a past crime that might bring resolution to the community or the victim's family but fails to disclose that information. Although unjust in the eyes of the public, it is fundamental to the doctrine of confidentiality that attorneys, and their employees, refuse to reveal information relating to their clients' past criminal conduct. Often the stuff of John Grisham novels or other forms of fiction, real-life instances occasionally occur, and they always test an attorney's mettle. In 1973, while preparing an insanity defense for an accused murderer, Francis Belge discovered through interviews with his client and co-counsel that his client had committed three other, unsolved murders. Based on what his client said, Mr. Belge found one of the bodies, a discovery he did not report to the police. But, at the trial, these other murders were disclosed by the client's testimony as part of his insanity defense. When the community realized the secret Mr. Belge had kept since discovering that body, a furor was raised in the community. In response to that furor, the prosecutor empanelled a grand jury, which indicted Mr. Belge for violating a statute that requires anyone who knew of the death of a person lacking medical assistance to report that to the authorities, and violating a statute that requires the proper burial of a dead body. But the court dismissed the indictment and acknowledged that the prosecutor ignored the hard fact that a lawyer has an affirmative duty to refuse to disclose client confidences. The court also acknowledged that Mr. Belge was bound by the ethics Canons of New York and the attorney-client privilege to not report his discovery to the police. *People v. Belge,* 372 N.Y.S.2d 798 (N.Y.Co.Ct. 1975).

NOT QUITE LINCOLN

Good Rule of Thumb: Don't Do Drugs with Your Lawyer

Jason Shwiller of Georgia was an attorney with quite a record—criminal record, that is. In 2005, he wisely surrendered his law license after facing criminal indictments in two different counties. Both indictments involved possession of large amounts of cocaine. His drug use caused him to miss court appearances. And, after one of his arrests, he committed the unpardonable sin of revealing client secrets and confidences to the police. How would his arrest for drug possession lead to disclosing client secrets? Well, with whom might you guess was he using the cocaine? And imagine where he got it?

When Does the Duty of Confidentiality Arise?

retainer

A payment, similar to an advance, made to an attorney, that is made to secure the lawyer's availability. When a retainer is called a general retainer, it is usually nonrefundable because the lawyer has earned the retainer upon payment. When a retainer is called a special retainer, it is usually a refundable payment, much like an advance.

Clearly, the duty of confidentiality attaches to the once-established, attorney-client relationship, but it also applies before a client has signed a fee agreement or paid a **retainer**. See Chapter 7. It would certainly be destructive to the policy behind confidentiality to leave unprotected those statements made by prospective clients in the course of seeking representation, but before a lawyer has agreed to take the case.

But suppose the lawyer does not take the client's case or the client chooses another lawyer? When a prospective client consults an attorney in good faith for the purposes of seeking assistance or representation, the duty of confidentiality may arise even if the attorney declines representation or does nothing on behalf of the would-be client. *See* ABA Commission on Ethics and Professional Responsibility, Formal Op. 90–358 (1990); *Gilmore v. Goedecke*, 954 F. Supp. 187 (E.D. Mo. 1996) (in that case, a firm was disqualified from defending its long-standing client in an age discrimination suit because the plaintiff had called a lawyer in the firm and discussed the matter by phone).

Having noticed the dilemma of what confidentiality duty, if any, is owed someone who, when talking with an attorney is not yet (or perhaps ever) a client, the Ethics 2000 Committee drafted a new rule, 1.18, which was adopted by the ABA House of Delegates. Essentially, Rule 1.18 defines a prospective client as someone who discusses the possibility of hiring the lawyer, and then it establishes what level of protection the lawyer owes the prospective client. The key part of that rule states, "[e]ven when no client-lawyer relationship ensues, a lawyer who has had discussions with a prospective client shall not use information learned in the consultation, except as Rule 1.9 would permit with respect to information of a former client." MR 1.18(b). (The duties owed a former client are discussed in

Chapter Five.) By putting the prospective client in the protective zone with the former client, this new rule guarantees a certain level of confidentiality to someone who contacts an attorney (or his or her paralegal) with the purpose of seeking legal help or hiring the attorney. Granting confidentiality to an initial consultation, for example, is only logical, because without it, prospective clients are caught in a catch-22 where they could only be granted confidentiality if they first hired the lawyers who have yet to hear a word of the clients' problems, some of which will not require a lawyer to be hired.

Although the rule cannot describe every context in which someone might become a prospective client, the rule's second Comment acknowledges that MR 1.18 does not cover someone who unilaterally communicates with a lawyer (e.g., leaving a voice mail or sending an e-mail to a lawyer) without knowing if the lawyer is considering representing the person. At least one ethics opinion has concluded that not only does a lawyer owe no duty of confidentiality to an unsolicited e-mail sent by someone seeking legal help, but the lawyer also may ethically represent the person on the other end of the conflict, *and* may use the information learned from the e-mail. San Diego County Bar Association, Ethics Opinion 2006–1 (2006). And, an earlier ethics opinion from Arizona reached the conclusion that unsolicited e-mails sent to lawyers are not considered confidential (although there was a dissenting opinion). Arizona State Bar Ethics Opinion 02–04 (2004). It did, however, advise Arizona law firms that maintain Web sites with e-mail addresses to publish disclaimers on what protection will be given to unsolicited e-mails. *Id.* Some states, including Indiana and New Hampshire, have adopted some version of MR 1.18. New Hampshire's, for instance, goes beyond the ABA version and uses the phrase, "a lawyer who has *received and reviewed information* from a prospective client..." instead of the original version's focus on a lawyer who has had "discussions" with a prospective client. New Hampshire Rule of Professional Conduct, Rule 1.18(b). The Comment to this new rule, which became effective in 2008, acknowledges that persons who send e-mail or other unilateral communication to lawyers, and who in good faith state confidential information, are intended to be initially protected by 1.18.

Not all ethics advisors subscribe to the notion that unsolicited e-mails are unworthy of confidentiality protection. An opinion from the New York City Bar Association took the alternate position, concluding that a law firm receiving an unsolicited e-mail may not use that information against the sender, even when the law firm already represents the opposing party, particularly when the law firm's Web site has no disclaimer about the status of unsolicited e-mails. The Association of the Bar of the City of New York, Formal Opinion 2001–01 (2001). The opinion acknowledges that its view is contrary to the Ethics 2000 version of 1.18, and those wanting to examine the lengthy opinion in detail can do so by using the search feature on the New York City Bar web site: http://www.nycbar.org. A California ethics opinion from 2005 conflicts to a degree with the San Diego ethics opinion cited in the prior paragraph. It concluded that a law firm that maintains a Web site with a Web page for prospective clients to e-mail legal questions may not discount the confidentiality of those questions by having a small disclaimer at the end of the Web page, acknowledging that no attorney-client confidentiality has attached by virtue of sending the question. If the firm wants to discount the confidential nature of those questions, it has to more clearly show that on its Web site. California State Bar Standing Committee on Professional Responsibility and Conduct, Formal Op. No. 2005–168(2005). The opinion concerned the unfortunate dilemma of a wife seeking representation regarding divorcing her husband, not knowing that the firm already represented the husband and wanted to continue to do so, despite learning what it did about the wife's side of the story in the e-mail she sent it.

But, as will be discussed in Chapter Five, a former client is not owed the same conflicts of interest duty as owed a current client. A later part of MR 1.18 prohibits a lawyer from representing someone opposing the prospective client in the same matter only if what the lawyer learned in the initial discussion with the prospective client would be "significantly harmful to that person...." 1.18(c). One way a lawyer can seek immunization from a future conflict of interest problem is to advise the prospective client that the interview will only go so far as to see if any information elicited gives rise to a conflict of interest with one of the lawyer's (or firms') current (or former) clients. A lawyer can also require that the interview take place only under the condition that whatever the lawyer learns does not prevent him or her from representing someone else, although not every jurisdiction approves of such a forced waiver. N.C. Ethics Op. 244 (1997).

If, however, a prospective client consults an attorney simply for the purpose of disqualifying that attorney (or firm), such shrewdness will not necessarily result in a finding that such a consultation was protected. Suppose that, after the presidential election of 2000 (the one that resulted in litigation and a decision by the United States Supreme Court), former Vice President Al Gore visited Theodore Olson (who would later represent then-Governor George W. Bush before the United States Supreme Court) to discuss retaining Mr. Olson in any future election litigation. If such a visit were made in an effort to disqualify Mr. Olson when Governor Bush retained him, it would be unlikely that a court would find the initial Gore-Olson consultation to be worthy of invoking the confidentiality doctrine. That kind of conflict will be discussed in Chapter 5.

For How Long Does the Duty of Confidentiality Apply?

Near the end of the movie *The Firm*, Tom Cruise's character, Mitch McDeere, uses a brilliant simile to explain to the mafia boss, whom Mitch unwittingly represents, how the ethics rule of confidentiality will protect the mafioso from the Justice Department's prosecution of Mitch's firm, and thereby protect Mitch from the mafioso's inclination to kill him. Mitch compares himself—as long as he is alive—to a ship carrying a cargo that will never reach port.

The attorney's duty of confidentiality is a **fiduciary** duty based on loyalty. It is not simply an obligation based on contract law, in which the obligations contracting parties have toward one another usually end when both parties have performed their part of the bargain. Unless an exception applies, the lawyer's duty of confidentiality survives the representation of the client. As is stated in the **Restatement** (Second) of Agency § 396 (1957), and an often-cited federal case (*States v. Standard Oil Co.*, 136 F. Supp. 345, 355 (S.D.N.Y.1955)): "The confidences communicated by a client to his attorney must remain inviolate for all time if the public is to have reverence for the law and confidence in its guarantees."

This duty generally continues beyond the death of the client, or former client, unless limited exceptions can be found, such as if the information needed is sought in connection with a criminal matter and the party seeking disclosure of the privileged information has met its high burden of showing need for the information. *In re Sealed Case*, 107 F.3d 46 (D.C. Cir. 1997). Occasionally, bearing the burden of confidentiality after a client's death necessitates a lawyer to ask an ethics panel for an oracle. In one instance, a woman hired a divorce attorney and told the attorney she wanted to tell her children about her plans to divorce their father before acting on them, but she died nine days later. When her husband found the check stub for the payment to the attorney, he asked the attorney what his wife had wanted. The lawyer asked the ethics committee for help, and it concluded that if the husband was the estate's executor, the husband was entitled to minimum information about the legal bill, but if the lawyer believed the husband's inquiry was more personal than official, the lawyer could refuse to disclose the reason he was hired. Nassau County Bar Association (NY) Op. 03–04 (2003)

Ken Starr vs. Vince Foster's Lawyer: Confidentiality and the Death of Bill and Hillary Clinton's Close Friend

When the body of Vince Foster was found in Fort Marcy Park, a little known place outside Washington, D.C, in July of 1993, a maelstrom of conspiracy theories descended on the country, perhaps fitting for the highest ranking, current government official to die a violent death since John F. Kennedy's death thirty years earlier. Conspiracy theorists noted that Mr. Foster was the close, personal friend of the Clintons, was a partner in the same Arkansas law firm with Mrs. Clinton, was the Clinton's personal attorney for the White Water investment dealings that eventually formed the foundation of the independent counsel investigations, and had moved with them to Washington six months earlier to become deputy White House Counsel. Ken Starr—by then the independent counsel—concluded the gunshot wound to Mr. Foster's head was self-inflicted. However, Mr. Starr's interest in Vince Foster's possible connection to the White Water investigation was piqued when he realized that nine days before

fiduciary

One who has a legal duty to act in the best interests of another. Lawyers are fiduciaries to their clients, as parents are to their minor children.

restatement

Unified, systematic statements on the common law, created by the American Law Institute. There are many restatements, including the Restatement of Contracts, the Restatement of Agency, and the Restatement of Torts.

committing suicide, Mr. Foster visited with James Hamilton, a Washington, D.C. attorney, who took three pages of notes during the interview. When Mr. Starr sought Mr. Hamilton's notes, Hamilton refused, arguing that his notes were protected by the attorney-client relationship. Starr argued that whatever privilege attached to the notes when taken, Foster's death made it moot because no prosecution could now be brought against Foster, regardless of what the notes detailed. Furthermore, Starr argued that the importance of conducting such a serious criminal investigation mandated an exception to the attorney-client protection. The United States Supreme Court resolved this dispute in 1998 and, in an opinion written by Chief Justice Rehnquist, it held that the attorney-client privilege still attached to the notes, reversing the lower court's decision. *Swidler & Berlin v. U.S.*, 524 U.S. 399. Part of the court's reasoning was that, despite the acknowledged importance of the investigation that led to the subpoena for the attorney's notes, without a posthumous protection, clients might fail to speak frankly with their lawyers, and unintended harm or embarrassment might result to a dead client's friends and family as a consequence of invading the privilege. *Id* at 407.

Do the Principles of Confidentiality Apply to the Lawyer's Employees?

The short answer is yes, the principles of confidentiality do apply. As discussed in Chapter Two, rules of professional responsibility apply to all non-lawyer assistants of the lawyer. Model Rule 5.3(a) requires partners in a law firm to ensure that their non-lawyer employees conduct themselves in conformity with all the obligations of lawyers, and MR 5.3(b) makes those lawyers who supervise non-lawyer employees specifically responsible to ensure that the conduct of all their employees is compatible with the same obligations as those of lawyers. The first paragraph to the official Comment for MR 5.3 specifically mentions that lawyers should warn their non-lawyer employees about their obligation not to breach the duty of confidentiality. The ABA Model Code originally expressed the same idea concerning non-lawyer employees and their duty to keep client confidences, in DR 4–101(D). In a Pennsylvania case, a defendant was convicted of first-degree murder, in part because the district attorney subpoenaed the defense attorney's secretary who received the phone call from the defendant in which the defendant said to the secretary, "I just committed a homicide. I have to talk to Sam [the attorney]." On appeal, the court ruled that the statement to the secretary was privileged communication because it was made for the purposes of seeking legal advice. *Pennsylvania v. Mrozek*, 657 A.2d 997 (Pa. 1995). (There is much more on the attorney-client privilege and how it applies to statements made to paralegals in a later section, "The Attorney-Client Privilege: Related to the Duty of Confidentiality.")

Beyond drawing the logical inference that a lawyer's ethics duty of confidentiality applies to paralegals and legal assistants, one can see that, specifically, the obligation applies. Guideline 6 of the ABA Model Guidelines for the Utilization of Paralegal Services makes lawyers responsible to ensure that legal assistants keep client confidences. The NALA Code of Ethics, Canon 7, requires legal assistants to "protect the confidences of a client," and Rule 1.5 of the NFPA Model Disciplinary Rules and Ethical Considerations states: "A paralegal shall preserve all confidential information provided by the client or acquired from other sources before, during, and after the course of the professional relationship." This standard would require a member of the NFPA to treat as confidential any information relating to a former client that has come to that paralegal's attention after the client has ceased using the services of the paralegal's firm (which will usually mean the information has come from a third party). An interesting example of the tension between lawyer rules of ethics and paralegal association rules of ethics can be found in EC 1.5(d), which establishes the circumstances under which a paralegal may disclose confidential information. Although it closely mirrors the exceptions of the ABA Model Rules, its client-consent exception covers consent made in writing, a standard not used in the Model Rules or the Model Code. See Exhibit 4-3 for how ethics rules apply confidentiality to paralegals.

EXHIBIT 4–3   HOW DO THE ETHICS RULES APPLY CONFIDENTIALITY TO PARALEGALS?

- ABA Model Code DR 4-101(D) applies the duty of confidentiality to the lawyer's employees and associates

- ABA Model Rule 1.6 doesn't discuss the lawyer's employee, *but* a Comment to Model Rule 5.3 (Responsibilities Regarding Non-lawyer Assistants) discusses the legal assistants's duty to not disclose client information

- ABA Model Guideline 6 discusses the lawyer's responsibility to ensure that the paralegal preserve client confidentiality

- NALA Model Standards and Guidelines, Guideline 1.2 requires legal assistants to preserve client confidences and secrets

- NALA Code of Ethics, Canon 7 requires legal assistants to protect client confidences

- NFPA Model Disciplinary Rule 1.5 requires paralegals to preserve all confidential information provided by the client or other sources before, during, and after the course of the professional relationship

How Is Confidentiality Affected When the Client Is an Organization?

constituent

A part of something else that is a distinct entity.

When the client is a person, confidentiality issues are relatively straightforward. However, when the client is an organization, such as a corporation, a discussion about client confidentiality is a bit more layered, and is also affected by conflicts of interest issues, which are the subject of Chapter 5. First, it is important to understand the role of the **constituent**: organizations have constituents, including directors, officers, employees, and shareholders. When a lawyer represents an organization, it is generally the case that the organization is the beneficiary of client confidentiality because the organization itself is the client, rather than the various constituents. Second, because corporations are inanimate creations, they can only act through their authorized agents, usually the board of directors or high-ranking executive officers. See how confidentiality is affected when the client is an organization in Exhibit 4-4.

For instance, if a high-ranking employee told the company's attorney about illegal corporate activities in which the employee had engaged, the attorney would not violate the duty of confidentiality by telling such a secret to the corporation's president or board of directors. *See* D.C. Bar Legal Ethics Comm. Op. 269 (1997). However, if a third party, such as the government, wanted that attorney to divulge what the employee told the attorney, the attorney-client privilege (which is explained later in this chapter) would generally protect

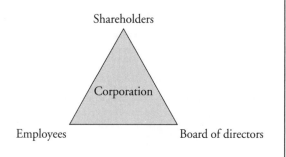

The Organization and Client Confidentiality

- Organizations consist of various constituents.
- For example, corporations consist of shareholders, the board of directors, and employees.
- But, <u>the organization</u>, not the constituents, <u>is the client</u> and is owed the duty of confidentiality.

Shareholders

Corporation

Employees   Board of directors

EXHIBIT 4–4   The Organization and Client Confidentiality

against such disclosure. A leading case in the area of attorney-client privilege in the corporate environment is *Upjohn v. United States*, 449 U.S. 383 (1981), in which the United States Supreme Court held that what a corporation's employee told the corporation's lawyer in connection with a corporation-directed investigation was protected by the attorney-client privilege. Anyone working as a legal assistant at an in-house, corporate legal department must bear in mind that information derived from various constituents is confidential with respect to the organization, but not necessarily confidential with respect to other constituents of the organization, such as corporate officers. In fact, a paralegal at a corporation can even be deposed by the other party to a lawsuit, despite the claim of attorney-client privilege, if the in-house paralegal is not considered to have a rank high enough in the company to warrant the status of "agent" of the client (the corporation). *See Reed Dairy Farm v. Consumers Power Co.*, 576 N.W.2d 709 (Mich. Ct. App. 1998).

Are Certain Kinds of Client Information Considered Not Confidential?

Coming to grips with whether certain client information is not confidential is more difficult than one might think because, for starters, there is a keen distinction about what is considered confidential from an ethics perspective between the ABA Model Code and its replacement, the Model Rules. Under ABA Model Code DR 4–101, information was considered confidential if (a) it was made in the course of the lawyer-client relationship and (b) the client requested that the information be kept confidential or the information if released would be embarrassing or detrimental to the client. That standard places a stronger burden on the client and provides more protection to lawyers and their paralegals accused of violating the rule of confidentiality. Model Rule 1.6, however, is more expansive, neither treating the nature of the client information, its source, nor the date when the lawyer becomes aware of it, as being controlling in determining whether such information must be kept confidential. Because most jurisdictions in the country have ethics rules based on some version of the ABA Model Rules, then some version of 1.6 is likely to be operative. So, for most of the country's lawyers and paralegals, everything a lawyer or paralegal comes to know about the client is protected information.

EXCEPTIONS TO THE DUTY OF CONFIDENTIALITY

Although the duty of confidentiality is one of the sacred principles associated with the practice of law, it is not without its own exceptions. All jurisdictions, whether operating under the Model Code of Professional Responsibility or the Model Rules of Professional Conduct, provide exceptions that allow lawyers to disclose information that would otherwise be considered private. As the following primary exceptions are considered, be aware that the exceptions are discretionary; almost nothing in the ethics rules requires a lawyer to use a confidentiality exception. However, when lawyers make decisions to disclose client information, based upon their jurisdiction's exceptions, they are required to limit their disclosure to only that which is necessary for the purposes of the exception.

Implied Authorizations

As stated earlier in the chapter, lawyers are allowed to divulge such client information as would be required to carry out the representation. Without such an implied authority, a lawyer or a legal assistant could not adequately draft a complaint, because a complaint must allege facts (such as the nature of the client's injuries) that establish a cause of action. Moreover, the Comments to Model Rule 1.6 state that a lawyer has implied authority during litigation to admit to facts that cannot properly be denied. However, this kind of disclosure can sometimes be found to be inappropriate if given without the client's consent. ABA Comm. On Ethics and Professional Responsibility, Formal Op. 93–370 (1993). (An attorney should not reveal to a judge the client's instructions on settlement authority limits or the attorney's opinions on settlement.) In a West Virginia case, a state attorney general was reprimanded for revealing client information without the client's consent. Even though the information was not considered a "client secret," it was still client information. And even though it was information that could have been found in a public document, the Court determined that its disclosure was not impliedly authorized. *Lawyer Disciplinary Bd. v. McGraw*, 461 S.E.2d 850 (W. Va. 1995). The Model Code is stricter with respect to implied authority by requiring that the attorney obtain the client's consent before revealing confidences. DR 4–101(B) and (C).

The sharing of client information among lawyers in a firm (and their employees) is normally considered an acceptable disclosure when other members of the firm are needed to help with the client's case. However, if the client requests that certain information not be disclosed to other members of the firm, then there is no implied authorization exception. Likewise, if a lawyer shares client information or files with lawyers of other firms to get their assistance but does not obtain the client's consent, then that disclosure would be unauthorized. *See In re Mandelman*, 514 N.W.2d 11 (Wis. 1994); ABA Comm. On Ethics and Professional Responsibility, Formal Op. 98–411 (1998).

The Prevention of Client Criminal Conduct or Fraud

If a client tells his or her attorney (or the attorney's paralegal) about crimes that he or she has committed, that information is absolutely protected. Even if its disclosure would help convict an evil person or provide closure to the victim or his or her family, or is done for another good reason, a lawyer would be subject to discipline for doing so.

On the other hand, attorneys are allowed to disclose client information in order to prevent a client from committing a future criminal act. Under the Model Code, the attorney is allowed to disclose information necessary to prevent the client from committing *any crime*, regardless of its severity. DR 4–101(C)(3). Under the current version of Model Rule 1.6(b), preventing a crime the lawyer believes is likely to result in imminent death or substantial bodily harm is no longer the only triggering event that allows this type of exception. The Ethics 2000 version is broader, allowing a lawyer to disclose client information in order to "prevent reasonably certain death or substantial bodily harm." Concerning the kinds of crimes that implicate MR 1.6(b), it is the lawyer's reasonable belief about the likelihood of death or harm that triggers the disclosure. In a Massachusetts case, an apartment building maintenance man who had been fired went to see an attorney at a legal services office. After the discussion, the attorney contacted the police to report that he believed the maintenance man was planning on setting fire to the building. In rendering an opinion concerning the attorney-client privilege as it related to the government's attempt to force the attorney to testify about the conversation, the court found nothing inappropriate about the attorney's initial disclosure to the police. *Purcell v. District Attorney for Suffolk County*, 676 N.E.2d 436 (Mass. 1997). Illinois's confidentiality rule, for instance, is stricter than its ABA counterpart with respect to serious crimes. It requires, rather than allows, a lawyer to disclose client information, "*to the extent it appears necessary* to prevent the client from committing an act that would result in death or serious bodily harm" (emphasis added). Illinois Rules of Professional Conduct 1.6(b).

California, on the other hand, is a jurisdiction where the confidentiality exceptions do not apply as liberally. Until recently, its confidentiality rule, without exception, required attorneys to "maintain inviolate the confidence, and at every peril to himself or herself to preserve the secrets, of his or her client." Cal. Bus. & Prof. Code § 6068(e)(1). But in 2004, the California legislature amended that rule, allowing (but not requiring) an attorney to violate confidentiality based on a reasonable belief that doing so would prevent a crime involving death or serious bodily harm. § 6068(e)(2). This does not mean that a California attorney must refrain from allowing the client to use his or her services to continue ongoing criminal or fraudulent activity, but California's confidentiality requirement is considered to be the strictest in the country because it has no express exceptions. In fact, a local bar association ethics opinion decided that an attorney may not warn a co-defendant or the police even after an attorney's client left the law office waving a gun and threatening to kill the co-defendant. San Diego County Bar Ass'n Legal Ethics and Unlawful Practices Comm., Op. 1990–1 (1990).

Could a lawyer justifiably report a client's impending tax fraud to the Internal Revenue Service, or report a publicly traded corporate client's financial contrivances to the **Securities Exchange Commission (SEC)**, because those crimes are unlikely to result in imminent death or substantial bodily harm? That answer has always been no, until the ABA revised its own version of 1.6 in 2003, narrowly voting to adopt recommended changes it had rejected a few years earlier. These changes, which can be found in the Ethics 2000 version of 1.6(b) (2) and (3), allow an attorney to report his or her client's past or impending crimes or frauds if the client's actions are likely to cause —or already have caused —substantial injury to the financial or property interests of someone else, *and the harm is a result of the client using the lawyer's services.* Not only is it fair to think of Enron and its tale of criminal frauds when analyzing this new and controversial exception, but it is also accurate, because the Enron scandal (and others like it) was a contributing factor to the ABA's narrow passage of the most recent exceptions. Also, there are strong rules, created by virtue of legislation commonly known as the Sarbanes-Oxley Act, which were passed as an attempt to respond to the financial scandals of Enron and other notable corporations and which authorizes the SEC to create strict rules requiring corporate lawyers to disclose their client's financial shenanigans to high-ranking members of the corporation, including the board of directors. 15 U.S.C. § 7245.

Fraud is a word that has different definitions in different legal contexts, but generally it can be thought of as an intentional deception that results in some injury or disadvantage to another person. Before the most recent version of 1.6, if a client used his or her attorney's services to perpetrate or complete a fraud, the attorney, upon recognizing the impending or continuing fraud, had limited rights under a different rule to rectify the situation, including withdrawing from the representation. *See* ABA Model Rule 1.16(b). Furthermore, some courts have held that lawyers may disclose client information in order to extinguish the fraud. For example, in a New Jersey case, a lawyer had prepared mutual wills for a husband and wife (meaning that each spouse's heirs could inherit the estate of the deceased spouse). The firm then discovered that the husband had recently fathered an illegitimate child and had kept that fact from his wife. That could have resulted in the wife's estate passing to this out-of-wedlock child. The law firm sought the court's approval to disclose the confidential information of one co-client to another co-client, and was granted permission under the fraud exception, particularly because New Jersey's version of MR 1.6 was broader than the ABA version, providing more leeway to disclose confidences when fraud is contemplated by the client's use of the lawyer's services. *A. v. B.*, 726 A.2d 924 (N. J. 1999).

securities exchange commission (SEC)

An agency of the U.S. Government, created in 1934 and charged with enforcing federal securities (investments) laws and regulating the securities markets.

fraud

An intentional deception that results in a legal injury to another. Fraud usually involves a material misrepresentation (which can include silence) made to deceive the other party, reliance by the other party on the misrepresentation, and resulting harm.

A related question involves whether a lawyer may warn third parties who might be at risk that the client has a serious disease. A few state ethics opinions have decided that attorneys who are aware of their clients' conditions may not automatically reveal such information to the clients' sexual partners or certain members of the public, such as customers in the restaurant where the client works. Pa. Bar Ass'n Comm. On Legal Ethics and Professional Responsibility, Op. 93–115 (1993);

N.C. State Bar Ethics Comm., Op. 117 (1992); Del. Bar Ass'n Professional Ethics Comm., Op. 1988–2.

NOT QUITE LINCOLN

Maybe They Don't Show The Shawshank Redemption *in Prison*

Marcellius Bradford served six years in prison for a rape and murder he did not commit. Chicago-area lawyer Kathleen Zellner worked heroically for two years to accomplish the most meaningful pursuit in the practice of law—righting a grievous injustice. In so doing, she secured for Mr. Bradford a pardon, filed a claim that could have netted him $120,000 for the six years he was wrongfully imprisoned, and began a civil rights suit against the Chicago Police Department.

Zellner even employed him in her law practice to review pleas for help sent to her by other inmates who also claimed innocence. For her efforts, Ms. Zellner, a former *National Law Journal* Pro Bono Attorney of the Year, was rewarded by her client's attempt to blackmail her. Yes, that's right.

After secretly tape recording one of Ms. Zellner's phone conversations, Bradford and two other clients told her they wanted to fire her and replace her with Johnnie Cochran. Then later they tried to extort $3,000 from her by threatening to release the tape to the media if she didn't pay up.

Evidently, Bradford and the other clients believed that Zellner would be embarrassed by the contents of the tape and would pay to prevent its publication. What they failed to anticipate was that not only might she refuse to pay, but she also might give them a dose of their own medicine.

She provided that dose by going to the district attorney's office. A sting was set up and she wore an undercover wire when meeting with Bradford to exchange money for the tape recording. Before he could say, "three hots and a cot," Bradford was behind bars again, thanks to his own unabated greed.

Some attorneys and legal ethics scholars have opined that it is both unfair and unsettling that a lawyer would breach attorney-client confidentiality in such a manner, even in the circumstances in which Ms. Zellner found herself. But, as she said in response to such sentiment, "I feel I did what I was ethically obligated to do. I'm not going to have a client trying to shake me down."

The Defense of a Claim Against the Lawyer

Self-preservation is an innate response to danger, and when lawyers are the targets of allegations, they are allowed to reveal client information, including confidential information, in order to defend themselves against such allegations. The Model Rules allow a lawyer to: reveal information the lawyer believes necessary to establish a claim or defense on behalf of the lawyer in a controversy between the lawyer and the client; establish a defense to a criminal charge or civil claim against the lawyer based upon conduct in which the client was involved; or respond to allegations in any proceeding concerning the lawyer's representation of the client. MR 1.6(b)(2).

The Model Code similarly states that confidences or secrets can be disclosed as is necessary for a lawyer "to defend himself or his employers or associates against an accusation of wrongful conduct." DR 4–101(C)(4).

Three kinds of situations are applicable to this type of exception. First, there are occasions where clients sue their own attorneys. In a lawsuit alleging legal malpractice, for instance, the attorney would be authorized to disclose client information as necessary to defend the lawsuit. Second, it is possible that an attorney might be charged with a crime with respect to representing a client. In that event, the attorney would be entitled to disclose client information as would be necessary to present a defense. A Pennsylvania ethics opinion addressing that issue decided that when a client who is under investigation for securities violation defends him- or herself on the grounds that it was the lawyer's fault, the lawyer is allowed to contact the Securities and Exchange Commission and disclose client information sufficient to clear him- or herself of wrongdoing. Pa. Bar Ass'n Comm. On Legal Ethics and Professional Responsibility, Op. 96–48. Third, when charged by a disciplinary commission with professional responsibility violations connected to client representation, an attorney would, by necessity, be allowed to disclose client information in order to rebut and defend against the charges. For instance, if a disciplinary commission charges an attorney with failure to use diligence with respect to a client's case, he or she would be allowed to disclose to the disciplinary commission information and materials that would help establish that he or she acted with due diligence when handling the client's matter.

The Collection of Fees

Both the Model Code (by expressly stating it) and the Model Rules (by implication) allow a lawyer to disclose client information necessary to collect an agreed-upon fee. Although it may seem self-serving for the legal profession to grant itself a confidentiality exception to get paid, without such an exception, law firms would be in an unenviable position of trying to prove their right to be paid the agreed fee in cases where the client's refusal to acknowledge the work would be the last word. Even though attorneys are fiduciaries to their clients, clients are not allowed to use such a relationship to their inequitable advantage.

As provided with earlier exceptions, the disclosure can only be what is necessary to collect the fee. There are occasions when law firms hire collection agencies to obtain unpaid client fees. For the collection agency to do its job, it needs certain client information, which begs the question of whether such a disclosure by the firm would be authorized. On the one hand, a collection agency hired by the firm would be an agent of the firm, which would seem to mean that such a disclosure would be authorized similar to the way that disclosures to paralegals working on the client's case are authorized. A few state ethics opinions have authorized attorneys giving client information to collection agencies, but not those collection agencies that keep records for credit report purposes. N.Y. State Bar Ass'n Comm. on Professional Ethics, Op. 684 (1996); S. C. Bar Ethics Advisory Comm., Op. 94–11 (1994); Ohio Sup. Ct. Bd. of Comm'rs on Grievances and Discipline, Op. 91–16 (1991). On the other hand, the use of collection agencies to collect legal fees can be seen as heavy-handed, and not all states allow such disclosure. Texas, for instance, disapproves of lawyers sharing client information with collection agencies without obtaining client consent. State Bar of Texas Professional Ethics Comm., Op. 495 (1994). And Florida allows lawyers to use collection agencies against former clients, but not present clients. Fla. Bar Professional Ethics Comm., Op. 90–2 (1991).

The Order of a Court

Finally, lawyers and paralegals may disclose that which is reasonably necessary to comply with an order of a court or other applicable law. 1.6(b)(5). All court orders can be appealed, but once that process reaches its terminal point, lawyers must obey a court order, even one to disclose client information. Conflicts between professional ethics and legal requirements can occur. Such is the case with a federal law requiring lawyers to report on an IRS form the names of clients and their paid legal bills and when the fees were paid if the clients pay in excess of $10,000 in cash. 26 U.S.C. § 6050. Because this is a federal law, federal courts have not warmed to the argument that this requirement violates lawyer-client confidentiality. *United States v. Sindel*, 53 F.3d 874 (8th Cir. 1995).

Perhaps no conflict is uglier than when divorcing spouses fight for custody of the children. And, unfortunately, sometimes a parent will hide the children from the parent who has been, or will be, awarded custody. If it is thought that the missing spouse's attorney knows where the children are, that attorney will be the focus of the other parent and the court. Does the duty of confidentiality cover such a scenario? Generally, it does not, as was decided by the Connecticut Superior Court when it ordered an attorney to disclose where her client—the mother—had absconded with the children who had been awarded to the father.

Even though the court acknowledged the attorney played no role in the mother's flight from the country with the children, it concluded that the duty of confidentiality did not allow the attorney, through her refusal to disclose where they were, to passively assist in the fraud being perpetrated on the legal process. *Bersani v. Bersani*, 565 A.2d 1368 (Conn. Super. Ct. 1989). See Exhibit 4–5 on the Ethics 2000 exceptions to the confidentiality rule.

EXHIBIT 4–5   ETHICS 2000 EXCEPTIONS TO THE DUTY OF CONFIDENTIALITY

- Implied authorizations needed to carry out the representation
- To prevent reasonably certain death or substantial bodily harm (revised exception)
  - This exception is not limited to preventing the client from committing a predicate crime, unlike the former version.
- To prevent, mitigate, or rectify a financial fraud perpetrated by the assistance of the lawyer's services
- To allow the lawyer to get legal advice regarding his or her duty to follow the ethics rules (new exception)
- To defend claims made against the lawyer
- To collect fees
- To comply with the law or a court order (new exception)

TECHNOLOGY AND CLIENT CONFIDENTIALITY

One of the ironies about the technological age in which we presently live is that all the time-saving devices invented in the last few decades—including microwave ovens, desktop and laptop computers, fax machines, and electronic organizers—give us more time to work. If it now takes 15 minutes to prepare a client's bill (thanks to computerized record-keeping and billing software) where once it took an hour, the remaining 45 minutes are considered anything other than free time. A sad consequence of technological advances is that the more electronic devices benefit our lives, the less our lives have privacy. Increasingly, people are becoming victims of identity theft as more and more professional and personal information is stored and accessed on electronic files, which can be accessed by hackers or destroyed by electronic viruses. As it concerns the law office, three common methods of communication—e-mail, faxes, and mobile phones—have become recent client confidentiality issues needing to be addressed.

E-Mail Messages and Client Confidentiality

E-mail messages, especially those that are unencrypted, are anything but private. Even if deleted, e-mail is still susceptible to being recovered from the e-mail servers that were used in the transmission, as well as from the hard drive on which the e-mail was created. Deleting e-mail messages is akin to how a bachelor cleans his apartment: he puts everything in a closet and hopes no one opens the closet door. Perhaps no better example of the public nature of e-mail can be found than in *United States v. Microsoft*, one of the most significant and expensive legal cases in history, which pitted the United States government against the world's largest computer software company and its co-founder and chief executive officer, Bill Gates, at one time the world's richest man. The case, in which the government successfully accused Microsoft of being a monopoly and violating antitrust laws, took many years to complete and resulted in a verdict against Microsoft in April 2000 (although Microsoft won at the appellate level and the case was eventually settled). It is fascinating that much of the government's ammunition against this computer software giant included hundreds of damaging e-mails sent by Microsoft executives, including Gates himself. The e-mails tended to support the government's theory that Microsoft had engaged in unfair, pillaging business practices with respect to its Internet Explorer Web browser. A thorough and fascinating account of the case and its major players is found in Ken Auletta's book, *World War 3.0: Microsoft and Its Enemies* (Random House, 2001). As reported in the book, David Boies, the lawyer who represented the U.S. government and won the case at the trial level (and later represented Al Gore in the 2000 election litigation) and considered by some to be the best trial lawyer in America, is someone who would not even use e-mail (Auletta, 11).

Is the use of e-mail to communicate with clients, or about client matters, a violation of the professional duty of confidentiality? Is confidentiality lost when a lawyer gives legal advice by way of an e-mail document? The American Bar Association's Ethics Committee considered this controversy when it issued an ethics opinion on the subject in 1999. The ABA's conclusion was that the use of unencrypted e-mail does not violate the doctrine of confidentiality, as expressed in MR 1.6(a), because there is a reasonable expectation of privacy in e-mail. The committee reasoned that just because e-mail is susceptible to interception does not mean it should not automatically be used. The committee considered e-mail no more of a risk to interception than other methods of communication—postal mail, telephone conversations—that can also be intercepted. Furthermore, the reasonable expectation of privacy is bolstered by federal law, which prohibits the interception of electronic communication (wiretapping). 18 U.S.C.A. § 2511. However, the opinion did state that if the nature of an e-mail message to be sent to the client was highly sensitive, then a lawyer should seek the client's preferences on sending the communication through another means. ABA Standing Committee on Ethics and Professional Responsibility, Formal Op. 99–413 (1999).

Some states have also issued ethics opinions regarding e-mail, most of them deciding that confidentiality requirements are not breached by its use. South Carolina originally held that the use of e-mail for client communications was inappropriate unless the client expressly waived the confidentiality protection. S. C. Bar Ethics Advisory Comm. Op. No. 94–27 (1994). Three years later, however, South Carolina reversed itself. S.C. Bar Ethics Advisory Comm. Op. No. 97–08 (1997). Other jurisdictions endorse the use of e-mail: Alaska Bar Ass'n Op. 98–2 (1998); D.C. Bar Op. 281 (1998); Delaware State Bar Ass'n Comm. on Prof. Ethics Op. 2001–2 (2002); Illinois State Bar Ass'n Advisory Op. on Professional Conduct No. 96–10 (1997); Ky. Bar Ass'n Ethics Comm. Advisory Op. E–403 (1998); New York State Bar Ass'n Comm. on Professional Ethics Op. 709 (1998); North Dakota State Bar Ass'n Ethics Comm. Op. 97–09 (1997); Utah State Bar Ethics Advisory Op. 00–01 (2000); Vermont Advisory Ethics Op. 97–5 (1997).

A few ethics opinions have taken a more cautious approach to the use of e-mail. Pennsylvania advises that lawyers get client consent before using e-mail to communicate with them. Pennsylvania Bar Ass'n Comm. on Legal Ethics Op. 97–130 (1997). Arizona advises that lawyers use encrypted e-mail or warn clients about e-mail risks. State Bar of Arizona Advisory Op. 97–04 (1996). And two states have issued ethics opinions advising against the use of e-mail: Iowa Bar Ass'n Op. 1997–1 (1997) and North Carolina State Bar Opinion 215 (1995).

Although the ABA and other ethics bodies have noted that regular mail is susceptible to interception, making the use of e-mail not necessarily more risky, e-mail is actually more capable of protection than the regular mail. Encryption software, spyware, malware, and firewalls can all be used to protect e-mail and other computer-originated information from being seen by unintended eyes. And yet, lawyers are not doing such a great job protecting their electronic information. A survey of 3,904 lawyers, taken by the ABA Legal Technology Resource Center and released in 2003, showed that over 80 percent did not use firewall software on their personal desktop computers. It is amazing that over one-third of the lawyers said that such software was not even available at their law firms. And more than 20 percent of the lawyers acknowledged that, like Luddites, they did not even know if their firms had firewalls. Considering the growth in the use of wireless Internet devices, from laptop computers to Personal Digital Assistants (such as the iPhone and the Blackberry), one would think that law firms would be more mindful of the risks of inadequately guarding client data that travels through the air, so to speak. Those who work online while traveling on public transportation, or who take their laptop to a favorite coffee bar should only do so after imagining their name on the headline of a news article or in the text of a disciplinary case discussing the ramifications of the failure to protect private information in public areas.

There is at least one lawyer who knows a bit about Internet security. Unfortunately, Kristine Katherine Trudeau's knowledge was, like Darth Vader's powers, used for the dark side. She was suspended indefinitely in 2005 for, among other things, illegally installing a spyware program on someone's computer. The *other things* included violating restraining orders issued against her, interfering with a 911 call, lying to the police while intoxicated, and filing frivolous litigation against someone she was harassing. It is no surprise that part of her disciplinary agreement included psychiatric counseling and addiction treatment. *In re Disciplinary Action against Trudeau*, 705 N.W.2d 409 (Minn.2005).

For those who, like some of the lawyers in the ABA survey, could benefit from a tutorial on computer firewalls and their significance, a lot can be learned by using the search feature from the aptly titled Web site, How Stuff Works: http://www.howstuffworks.com. Free firewall software is available on the Internet and many options are provided at the following link from the technology Web site CNET.com: http://www.download.com.

Fax Machines and Client Confidentiality

Facsimile (fax) machines are usually kept in a central location in an office, which makes their use to transmit client information slightly more risky than e-mail, because anyone in an office can intercept a fax as it comes from the fax machine. Fax numbers can also be dialed incorrectly, resulting in the wrong fax machine receiving what should have been received elsewhere. But the same ABA ethics opinion that discussed the appropriateness of e-mail also made reference to faxes and, while failing to expressly declare fax use ethical, found that the use of faxes has become so commonplace that courts take for granted that it is an appropriate method of communicating that does not violate the duty of confidentiality. ABA Standing Comm. on Ethics and Professional Responsibility, Formal Op. 99–413 (1999). And an earlier opinion considered the attorney-client privilege would not be ruined in the event a fax was accidentally sent to the wrong place. ABA Standing Comm. on Ethics and Professional Responsibility, Formal Op. 94–382 (1994).

Mobile Phones and Client Confidentiality

Like e-mail, mobile phone usage is susceptible to eavesdropping, unintentional or otherwise. During his meteoric rise and fall as Speaker of the United States House of Representatives, Newt Gingrich found himself the subject of ongoing controversy. Another controversy was added when a phone conversation he was having in 1996 with another Republican congressman was taped. Gingrich, who was on a mobile phone (discussing how to handle ethics charges made against him), was secretly tape-recorded by an elderly couple. The couple claimed that they just happened to pick up the conversation on a scanner in their car while Christmas shopping for their grandchild. They then gave the recording to Democratic congressman Jim McDermott, who was a member of the House Ethics Committee. Eventually, the tape recording ended up in the hands of the national press, which released its contents. Because it is illegal to intentionally intercept someone's phone conversation, the couple was prosecuted, pleaded guilty to violating 18 U.S.C. § 2511, and were fined $500. The congressman whose mobile phone conversation was illegally tape-recorded then sued congressman McDermott, claiming he illegally gave the tape to the news media. In May 2002, McDermott acknowledged in court filings that he did leak the tape recording to the press, but claimed that it was within his free speech rights. What followed was a long and winding road of litigation and appeals, with McDermott challenging the original decision a federal judge made that McDermott violated federal law, resulting in an order to pay a tab of over $600,000. McDermott got another shot at defending his actions, but a second federal court (as well as the appellate court) ruled against him. Undeterred, he sought the U.S. Supreme Court's review, which was denied in 2007. And, the House Ethics Committee concluded over a decade after the original dustup that congressman McDermott's actions violated House ethics rules.

More than a few bar associations have weighed in on the use of cordless or mobile phones, expressing cautious approval. New Hampshire and Massachusetts have issued ethics opinions cautioning lawyers against using cordless or mobile phones, stating that before talking about sensitive matters with their clients on mobile phones, lawyers should explain to their clients the risks of talking on unprotected lines and the implications that such a phone conversation might be seen as a waiver of attorney-client privilege and then get their clients' consent before continuing. N.H Bar Ass'n Ethics Comm. Opinion 1991–92/6; Mass. Bar Ass'n, Ethics Comm. Opinion No. 1994–5 (1994). Iowa, North Carolina, and Washington have issued similar opinions that obligate attorneys, when talking on mobile or cordless or portable phones (or when they believe their clients are using such phones) to inform their clients about the likelihood of loss of confidentiality. Iowa State Bar Ass'n Opinion 90–44 (1990); N.C. State Bar Ass'n, Ethics Comm. Opinion 251 (1995); Washington State Bar Ass'n Informal Ethics Op. 91–1 (1991). Arizona advises its attorneys to use caution when talking about client matters on mobile phones, but refrains from stating that all client discussions on mobile phones are automatically unethical. State Bar of Ariz. Comm. on Rules of Professional Conduct Opinion 95–11 (1995). And the Delaware ethics opinion (cited earlier) that approved of the use of e-mail also discussed the use of mobile phones, concluding that such use is not a violation of Delaware's confidentiality rule. This decision was reached in part because of the federal statutes that prohibit mobile phone interception and disclosure. Delaware State Bar Ass'n Comm. on Prof. Ethics Op. 2001–2 (2002).

THE ATTORNEY-CLIENT PRIVILEGE: RELATED TO THE DUTY OF CONFIDENTIALITY

There is a slight misunderstanding concerning the duty of confidentiality and the attorney-client privilege in that the two ideas are sometimes discussed as if they were identical. They actually are two branches of the same tree. Although *attorney-client privilege* is a phrase that might be used in cases dealing with confidentiality, the duty of confidentiality is a professional responsibility doctrine that obligates attorneys and their agents to keep client information and communication confidential.

The attorney-client privilege, on the other hand, is not an ethics doctrine but rather a discovery or evidentiary doctrine. The attorney-client privilege prevents lawyers from being forced to testify against their clients, and is usually formalized in legislation that concerns the competency of witnesses, rather than in the rules of court that govern trial procedure or the professional responsibilities of attorneys. For instance, Indiana's attorney-client privilege is found in the statute that also includes the doctor-patient privilege, the clergy-parishioner privilege, and the husband-wife privilege. It simply states, "Except as otherwise provided by statute, the following persons shall not be required to testify regarding the following communications: (1) Attorneys, as to confidential communications made to them in the course of their professional business, and as to advice given in such cases." Ind. Code § 34–46–3–1(1). Oklahoma's attorney-client privilege is a separate statute that includes definitions for key words in the statute, as well as conditions for the application of, and exemption from, the privilege. Oklahoma's attorney-client privilege statute also encompasses paralegals because it covers confidential communication between the client and "his attorney's representative." Okla. Stat. tit. 12, § 2502(B)(1). An attorney's representative is defined as "one employed by the attorney to assist the attorney in the rendition of professional legal services." § 2502(A)(3). See the outline of attorney-client privilege in Exhibit 4-6.

Connected to the attorney-client privilege is the work product rule, which will be discussed in detail later in the chapter. However, at this point, one should recognize that there are three related concepts in this area, each with their own primary authority source: the duty of confidentiality (found in the professional

---

EXHIBIT 4–6   THE ATTORNEY-CLIENT PRIVILEGE

- Is related to the ethics duty of confidentiality

- Is found in witness competency statutes

- Is an evidentiary rule, not an ethics doctrine

- Protects against the compelled disclosure of *confidential communication*

responsibility rules); the attorney-client privilege (usually found in the statutes on witness competency, although there are exceptions: for instance, Delaware's attorney-client privilege is found in Rule 502 of the Delaware Rules of Evidence); and the work product rule (found in the rules of civil procedure). In most instances, attorneys cannot be forced to give testimony that concerns their clients because the attorney-client privilege protects that kind of confidential information. The attorney-client privilege can also shield the attorney from being forced to testify about conversations the attorney had with the client before the lawyer-client relationship began. See Exhibit 4-7 for examples of the relationships between confidentially doctrines.

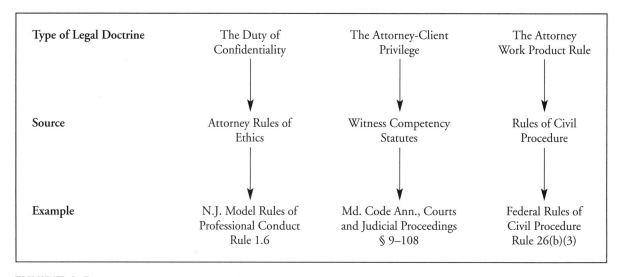

Type of Legal Doctrine	The Duty of Confidentiality	The Attorney-Client Privilege	The Attorney Work Product Rule
Source	Attorney Rules of Ethics	Witness Competency Statutes	Rules of Civil Procedure
Example	N.J. Model Rules of Professional Conduct Rule 1.6	Md. Code Ann., Courts and Judicial Proceedings § 9–108	Federal Rules of Civil Procedure Rule 26(b)(3)

EXHIBIT 4–7 The Relationship among the Confidentiality Doctrines

As the following tragic case shows, conversations between prospective clients and paralegals can be covered by the attorney-client privilege as well.

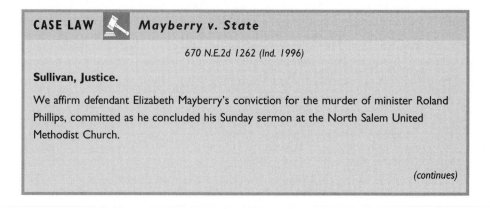

CASE LAW   *Mayberry v. State*

670 N.E.2d 1262 (Ind. 1996)

Sullivan, Justice.

We affirm defendant Elizabeth Mayberry's conviction for the murder of minister Roland Phillips, committed as he concluded his Sunday sermon at the North Salem United Methodist Church.

(continues)

CASE LAW   *Mayberry v. State* (continued)

In May, 1992, defendant met Phillips, a student pastor at the North Salem United Methodist Church, at a singles retreat sponsored by the United Methodist Church. Defendant and Phillips dated for several months after the retreat. During the course of their relationship, defendant, then 35 years old, claims that Phillips encouraged her to allow him to kiss her using his tongue, engage in consensual, mutual, oral sex with him, fondle and kiss her breasts, and digitally penetrate her vagina. Defendant had never before had intimate physical contact with a man. Phillips would later deny to church officials that he had ever engaged in oral sex with defendant. Defendant's relationship with Phillips took a turn for the worse in August of 1992. In an attempt to salvage the relationship, defendant wrote Phillips letters inquiring into the status of their relationship. In one of these letters, she asked Phillips to attend counseling with her. In November, 1992, defendant received a letter from Phillips in which he stated that their relationship was over. This letter deeply hurt defendant and made her angry.

In December, 1992, defendant filed a complaint with the United Methodist Church (UMC) in which she alleged that Phillips had engaged in sexual misconduct. When speaking about her relationship with Phillips to Reverend Harry Coleman, defendant stated: "My concern is for the next woman with whom he chooses to have a relationship. What kind of damage will he do to her life? He says his behavior is a pattern. I believe it is one which must be broken." After several hearings on defendant's complaint, the UMC Committee on Ordained Ministry determined, in May, 1993, that Phillips was to retain his position as a student pastor. Upon learning the result of her complaint, the defendant became extremely distraught.

Despite the fact that defendant sought counseling, in June, 1993, she started having thoughts about killing herself. . . . On August 2, 1993, defendant purchased a handgun and box of ammunition in Bloomington. On August 19, 1993, a firearms expert and trainer spent two hours with defendant at her house showing her how to use and care for the gun. On September 18, 1993, defendant loaded the gun with five cartridges. On Sunday morning September 19, defendant, with the gun concealed in her purse, drove to North Salem United Methodist Church. Defendant arrived in front of the church at about 11:00 A.M. and parked her car across the street. Upon entering the sanctuary, defendant never took her eyes off of Phillips, who was delivering a sermon from the pulpit. Defendant walked down the center aisle toward the pulpit. As she approached the pulpit, Phillips turned and looked at her and told her that he would speak with her after the service concluded. Defendant stood silently at the left side of the pulpit and watched Phillips finish his sermon. Phillips finished his sermon, asked the congregation to stand, and announced the last hymn. Defendant pulled the gun out of her purse, aimed it directly at Phillips and fired twice. Phillips's knees buckled and he fell to the floor. Defendant exclaimed: "You raped me! You

(continues)

CASE LAW *Mayberry v. State* (continued)

raped me!" Phillips responded: "No I didn't. No I didn't." Defendant walked closer to Phillips and fired the gun two more times. . . . The paramedics arrived shortly thereafter and took Phillips to the hospital where he died due to loss of blood from gunshot wounds to the neck, chest, wrist, and leg.

On September 20, 1993, the State filed an information charging defendant with Murder. On October 11, 1993, defendant filed a notice of insanity pursuant to Indiana Code § 35–36–2–1 (1993). Defendant's jury trial commenced on June 13, 1994. The jury found defendant guilty but mentally ill of Murder on June 22, 1994. The trial court sentenced defendant to a term of sixty years on July 20, 1994.

In a hearing outside the presence of the jury, defense witness Jennie Maretto, a friend of Phillips and a paralegal for a law firm in Fishers, Indiana, testified that Phillips contacted her at work to obtain legal advice regarding a letter he wrote to the UMC in response to the complaint that defendant had filed. Maretto testified that she felt that she was not legally able to give Phillips legal advice but would have to consult with an attorney. Maretto stated that Phillips asked her to consult an attorney. Maretto also testified that she gave a statement regarding her conversations with Phillips to Officer Danny Williams. When defense counsel inquired about the letter Phillips asked Maretto to look over, the State asserted the attorney-client privilege on Maretto's behalf as to any communication between Maretto and the victim. The trial court sustained the State's objection to the admission of Maretto's testimony.

In an offer to prove, the defense introduced into evidence a police report prepared by Officer Williams. In the report, Officer Williams states that when he spoke with Maretto she informed him that Phillips had contacted her to obtain legal advice. The report also states that Maretto advised the officer that Phillips stated that Phillips and defendant had engaged in consensual, mutual oral sex.

Defendant contends that the trial court erroneously determined that the attorney-client privilege attached to comments Phillips made to Maretto because Maretto did not adequately establish that Phillips contacted her in an effort to employ an attorney for professional advice or aid. *In Colman v. Heidenreich*, 269 Ind. 419, 381 N.E.2d 866 (1978), this court made the following observations:

The attorney-client privilege is a very important provision in our law for the protection of persons in need of professional legal help. It makes provision for a person to give complete and confidential information of an attorney, so that the attorney may be fully advised in his services to the client. At the same time, it assures the client that these confidences will not be violated. *Colman*, 269 Ind. at 421, 381 N.E.2d at 868.

(continues)

CASE LAW *Mayberry v. State* (continued)

Indiana Code §34–1–14–5 (1993) provides that attorneys shall not be competent witnesses "as to confidential communications made to them in the course of their professional business, and as to advice given in such cases." This "attorney-client privilege not only plays a role in our law of evidence but is also fundamental to our rules of professional conduct which forbid attorneys from revealing 'information relating to representation of a client unless the client consents after consultation.' See Ind.Professional Conduct Rule 1.6." *Corll v. Edward D. Jones & Co.*, 646 N.E.2d 721, 724 (Ind. Ct. App. 1995). As long as an attorney is consulted on business within the scope of the attorney's profession, "it is of no moment to the privilege's application that there is no pendency or expectation of litigation. Neither is it of any moment that no fee has been paid." *Colman*, 269 Ind. at 423, 381 N.E.2d at 869 (citations omitted). Rather, the essential prerequisites to invocation of the privilege are to establish by a preponderance of the evidence (i) the existence of an attorney-client relationship and (ii) that a confidential communication was involved. See *Colman*, 269 Ind. at 423, 381 N.E.2d at 869. To meet the burden of showing that an attorney client relationship existed, the State had to, at the very least, establish that the communication at issue occurred in the course of an effort to obtain legal advice or aid, on the subject of the client's rights or liabilities, from a professional legal advisor acting in his or her capacity as such. *Id.*; *United States v. Demauro*, 581 F.2d 50, 55 (2nd Cir. 1978).

Defendant suggests that Phillips's communications with his friend Maretto are privileged "only if his asking her to have an attorney look over his papers can be construed to be an attempt by Phillips to employ legal counsel." Defendant also states that the State failed to meet its burden of establishing that Maretto's communications with Phillips were privileged because she did not testify that Phillips intended to or sought to employ her firm to represent him concerning his difficulties with the complaint defendant filed with the church. Defendant misstates the State's burden. Although Maretto and Phillips were social friends, the record reveals that Phillips approached Maretto at the law firm where she worked as a paralegal/office manager and asked her to consult an attorney regarding his legal concerns. We believe these facts can be read to establish that the communications at issue occurred in the course of an effort to obtain legal advice or aid from a professional legal advisor in his capacity as such. *Colman*, 269 Ind. at 423, 381 N.E.2d at 869; *Demauro*, 581 F.2d at 55. Therefore, we cannot say that the trial court erred in determining that the State met its burden of showing the existence of an attorney-client relationship. And if the communications at issue occurred during an attempt to procure professional legal aid, confidential communications were involved here. See *Colman*, 269 Ind. at 423, 381 N.E.2d at 869. Therefore, the trial court did not abuse its discretion in determining that the communications between Maretto and Phillips were subject to the attorney-client privilege.

(continues)

Are Certain Types of Information Not Covered by the Attorney-Client Privilege?

At this point, the confidentiality family tree analogy is being stretched to the point of becoming the Jeff Foxworthy joke about a redneck's family tree having no branches, because here is where the ethics duty of confidentiality and the evidentiary doctrine of attorney-client privilege seem to coalesce. So easy is it to consider the two concepts as one that, occasionally, courts do so. As stated earlier, what paralegals come to learn about their clients (information which is broader than just what clients tell their lawyers and paralegals) is considered confidential from an ethics perspective in most jurisdictions. But a smaller scope of coverage is intended for the attorney-client privilege, in part because courts disfavor evidentiary privileges because they obviously prevent what would otherwise be relevant evidence from being admissible. There is no denying that privileges like attorney-client, priest-penitent, and the spousal privilege, hide the truth.

The key to understanding the attorney-client privilege's smaller application is to focus on what it is meant to cover: a) communication (statements or something similar); b) intended by the client to be confidential when made to the attorney or paralegal (secrets, intimate details, information harmful to the client); and c) made in the context of an attorney-client relationship (which includes a prospective client attempting to create that relationship). As a result, clients are sometimes gravely disappointed to learn that not as much as they hoped would be blanketed by the attorney-client privilege. Earlier in the text, a case was cited involving a paralegal at a corporation who was ordered to appear at a deposition—even though the corporation for whom she worked claimed attorney-client privilege—because she did not qualify as an agent of the client (her employer). *Reed Dairy Farm v. Consumers Power Co.*, 576 N.W.2d 709 (Mich. Ct. App. 1998). That court also concluded that, regardless of the paralegal's position in the company, what she possessed were "facts," not confidential communications, and what the corporate defendant was simply trying to do was shield one of its employees from having to give evidence. *Id.* at 712.

NOT QUITE LINCOLN

Is Serving as the Secret Voice of a Silenced Terrorist Protected by Attorney-Client Privilege?

Is there something Orwellian about the press referring to an American lawyer as a "civil rights lawyer," when she is on the record as saying in an interview, "I don't have any problem with Mao or Stalin or the Vietnamese leaders or certainly Fidel [Castro] locking up people they see as dangerous."? It is ironic that this attorney, who thinks Mao Tse Tung and Joseph Stalin (who together killed over 60 million people) should be able to lock up *dangerous* people, defended and sought the release from prison of a man convicted in the first World Trade Center bombing. That bombing killed six people and injured hundreds in 1993. Ms. Stewart's representation of that defendant, Omar Abdel Rahman, commonly known as the "blind sheikh," eventually resulted in her being charged and convicted of aiding terrorism. Ms. Stewart's allies and defenders believe that her being charged and convicted was a grotesque attack by the Justice Department on the attorney-client privilege.

In 1996, when the blind sheikh was convicted for masterminding the first World Trade Center bombing and attempting to do the same at other New York sites, he was sentenced to life in prison. Because the sheikh was still advising his terrorist networks from behind bars, special administrative actions were instituted to limit his external communication.

Those limitations included restricting Ms. Stewart from transmitting any messages made by the terrorist to her, by phone, letter, or in-person, to third parties on the outside world. Ms. Stewart agreed in writing to those terms. However, in 2002 she was accused of violating that agreement by passing along the sheikh's messages to an Egyptian terrorist group. Charged with materially aiding terrorist organizations and lying to the government, Ms. Stewart strenuously defended her actions on the grounds that she had a constitutional right to free speech. She also claimed that the evidence against her was gathered in violation of the attorney-client relationship and the related attorney-client privilege between her and the sheikh. She was supported by various legal groups, including the National Association of Criminal Defense Lawyers. After a seven-month trial, followed by 12 days of deliberation, Ms. Stewart was convicted of all five charges.

Although she was facing up to 30 years in prison, Ms. Stewart was sentenced to only 28 months and was automatically disbarred in New York because of her felony convictions.

Statements Made in the Presence of Third Parties

One of the more puzzling aspects of confidentiality concerns the situation where a client (or prospective client) says something that would be thought of as confidential, but it is said in the presence of someone else—someone not covered by this duty. For instance, if a prospective client brings a friend to the lawyer's office as an emotional support, it is possible that what the prospective client tells the lawyer will not be covered by the attorney-client privilege. This is because a court could consider that the statements were never originally confidential because the speaker made them in the presence of the third party. Although the lawyer would still be subject to discipline for voluntarily repeating the statements, he or she could be subpoenaed to testify about what was said. For example, in a Minnesota case, a divorce lawyer met with a husband and wife to discuss the financial ramifications of their divorce. Later, when the husband was tried for his wife's murder, the lawyer was called as a witness to testify about what was said in that discussion. On appeal, the husband argued that his lawyer's testimony was a violation of the attorney-client privilege. However, the court disagreed, finding that, because only the husband was the lawyer's client, what was said in the office that day was not protected by attorney-client privilege because of the presence of the wife. *State v. Rhodes*, 627 N.W.2d 24 (Minn. 2001). Beyond the scope of this tragic example, someone who qualifies as a third-party listener would obviously not be affected by either the duty of confidentiality or the attorney-client privilege, and could likely testify about what he or she heard.

The following concerns a famous celebrity murder case. Jean Harris was accused of murdering her boyfriend, Dr. Herman Tarnower, the author of the national bestseller *The Scarsdale Diet*. The case created many national headlines, and the appeal concerned, in part, the problem with talking to one's lawyer but doing so in a public way.

CASE LAW *People v. Harris*

442 N.E.2d 1205 (N.Y. 1982)

GABRIELLI, J.

Defendant, Jean Harris, was convicted, following a jury trial, of murder in the second degree and criminal possession of a weapon in the second and third degrees. This appeal presents for our consideration several purported errors occurring during the course of that trial, which defendant urges mandate reversal of the judgment of conviction. Inasmuch as our resolution of these issues leads us to the conclusion that reversible error was not committed, there should be an affirmance.

Defendant's trial for murder arose out of the shooting death of Dr. Herman Tarnower in his home on March 10, 1980. The People's case proceeded on the theory that Mrs. Harris, who had been Dr. Tarnower's paramour and companion for nearly 14 years, went to his home on the evening of the shooting and, acting out of jealous rage over the doctor's relationship with a younger woman, deliberately shot and killed him. One of the prosecution's witnesses, Dr. Tarnower's house manager, testified to the difficulties that had resulted from the doctor's relationships with the two women. Mrs. Harris's oral statements, testified to by the police officers who were investigating the shooting, were also relied upon as evidence of her motivation in going to the Tarnower estate on the evening of the shooting. The prosecution also utilized the so-called "Scarsdale letter," written by Mrs. Harris to the doctor over the weekend prior to his death, as strong evidence of Mrs. Harris's state of mind. In this letter, which contained several unflattering references to the younger woman in Dr. Tarnower's life, Mrs. Harris described her feelings of anguish and rejection over the doctor's apparent preference for this younger woman.

The defense theory was that Mrs. Harris, physically agitated by the lack of medication she had been taking for some time and suffering from recent failures and disappointments in her professional life, had determined that she wanted to end her life. Intending to see Dr. Tarnower once more before she died, Mrs. Harris drove to his home on March 10, hoping only to speak with him for a few moments. She entered the doctor's home and went into his bedroom, where she found him sleeping. Mrs. Harris was unable to rouse the doctor in order to have a conversation with him. Apparently upset by his lack of responsiveness and the presence of the belongings of the other woman in the bathroom, Mrs. Harris decided to kill herself there in the doctor's bedroom. According to Mrs. Harris, as she attempted to carry out her desire, the doctor, who had by now awakened, tried to prevent her from shooting herself. Several struggles ensued, during which Mrs. Harris's gun discharged, shooting Dr. Tarnower and inflicting four gunshot wounds from which he died. Evidence concerning Mrs. Harris's version of these events and her state of mind on the night of the shooting and previously thereto was presented largely through the testimony of Mrs. Harris

(continues)

CASE LAW   *People v. Harris* (continued)

herself. The defense also relied upon a will and certain letters, written by Mrs. Harris just prior to her departure for the Tarnower estate on March 10, to demonstrate her belief that she would never return to her home, because she intended to end her life. In addition, the defense offered a number of witnesses who testified that Mrs. Harris had indeed been distraught over recent events occurring in connection with her position as headmistress of the Madeira School. . . .

I

On the night of her arrest at the Tarnower residence, defendant made a statement over the telephone to her attorney. She contends that the introduction into evidence of that statement, testified to by a police officer who overheard it, violated her right to counsel under the Constitution of this State. It appears that Mrs. Harris, having been read her Miranda rights several times, having waived those rights and made statements to the police officers who were investigating the shooting, was thereafter asked if she would like to make a telephone call. Mrs. Harris responded that she would like to call a lawyer friend. After an attempt to make this call at a nearby telephone was unsuccessful, one of the officers, Lieutenant Flick, went into the house manager's bedroom to place the call for Mrs. Harris. When the lieutenant reached Mrs. Harris's party, he left the bedroom to so inform her. Officer Tamilio, at Lieutenant Flick's request, assisted Mrs. Harris to the bedroom. When they entered the room, the house manager's husband was already there, standing a few feet from the telephone. Immediately upon picking up the telephone, Mrs. Harris made the statement: "Oh, my God, I think I've killed Hy." Its admission into evidence is now challenged.

It is clear that, at the time Mrs. Harris made this statement, her right to counsel had attached by virtue of her request to speak with an attorney (*People v. Cunningham*, 49 N.Y.2d 203). Once the right to counsel had been invoked, no further questioning of Mrs. Harris would have been per missible, unless she had affirmatively waived her rights in the presence of her attorney (*People v. Rogers*, 48 N.Y.2d 167; *People v. Hobson*, 39 N.Y.2d 479). Notwithstanding this rule, statements made by a defendant who has invoked the right to counsel may nevertheless be admissible at trial if they were made spontaneously. In order for such statements to be characterized as spontaneous, it must "be shown that they were in no way the product of an 'interrogation environment,' the result of 'express questioning or its functional equivalent'" (*People v. Stoesser*, 53 N.Y.2d 648, 650). . . .

Although we hold today that a statement properly characterized as spontaneous is no less so simply because it was made to an attorney, a further aspect of the admissibility of such statements should be considered. Given that the communication received in evidence was made to an attorney, the attorney-client privilege is implicated, in addition to the right to counsel. This privilege protects those communications made by a defendant to an

(continues)

CASE LAW   *People v. Harris* (continued)

attorney that are intended to be confidential (*People v. Buchanan*, 145 N.Y. 1; *Baumann v. Steingester*, 213 N.Y. 328). It cannot be said, on the facts of this case, that Mrs. Harris, in speaking over the telephone to a lawyer in the known presence of both a police officer and the house manager's husband, intended this communication to be confidential. Generally, communications made in the presence of third parties, whose presence is known to the defendant, are not privileged from disclosure (see Richardson, Evidence [10th ed], § 413; 8 Wigmore, Evidence [McNaughton rev], § 2311). We see no reason to depart from this general rule simply because one of those parties present was a police officer, who, as has been noted, did nothing to purposely overhear the conversation or conceal his presence from defendant. Thus, we conclude that defendant's attorney-client privilege was not violated by the officer testimony regarding this communication and that the testimony was properly admitted by the trial court. . . .

Case Questions

1. For what reason was the statement that Ms. Harris clearly made to her lawyer not covered by the attorney-client privilege?

2. Do you think Ms. Harris was aware that she was waiving the attorney-client privilege by talking on the phone to her lawyer in the presence of others?

3. Is it unfair to say that there was no cloak of confidentiality surrounding her statement because she was in police custody and had invoked her right to counsel, and because she knew she was talking to her lawyer?

The doctrine of third-party presence breaking the attorney-client privilege still holds in New York. *See Delta Financial Corp. v. Morrison*, 820 N.Y.S.2d 745 (N.Y. Sup. Ct. 2006). An even more famous murder trial than that of Jean Harris involved a similar situation with a different result. After O.J. Simpson was arrested for the murders of his ex-wife, Nicole, and Ron Goldman, retired football great turned-actor-turned-minister Rosey Greer visited Mr. Simpson in jail. During the course of their conversation, a sheriff's deputy was reported to have overheard Simpson loudly admit the murders to Greer. But, ruling against the prosecution, Judge Ito concluded that, regardless of Simpson's volume, which allowed the guard to overhear what was said, the guard could not testify.

In the following case, the court takes the view that there are occasions where statements made by third parties to lawyers can be considered as confidential statements, and thus protected by the attorney-client privilege.

CASE LAW *Palomba v. Sullivan*

1998 WL 928392 (Conn. Super. Ct. 1998)

PELLEGRINO, J.

The Plaintiff's decedent, Carla Palomba (hereinafter Plaintiff), a passenger in an automobile, died as result of injuries sustained in an accident when the automobile she was riding in collided with another automobile. The instant action was instituted against both the drivers and the owners of the vehicles involved in the accident. This motion for protective order follows a deposition of Candice Palomba, a non-party who is the sister of the Plaintiff.

At the deposition, Candice Palomba was asked by counsel for one of the Defendants about conversations at a meeting attended by herself, attorney Bruce Diamond, her mother Judith Palomba and her sister Crystal Palomba. The meeting was held prior to the commencement of this action. Mr. Diamond represents that he acted as legal counsel for the entire Palomba family, including Candice Palomba, during the meeting. Candice Palomba has invoked the attorney-client privilege in refusing to answer questions, at the deposition, as to whether attorney Diamond had given her any information about the accident during the meeting.

"The attorney-client privilege protects communications between client and attorney when made in confidence for the purpose of seeking or giving legal advice." *Ullmann v. State*, 230 Conn. 698, 711, 647 A.2d 324 (1994). "Whether a communication is privileged is a question of law for the trial court." *Miller v. Anderson*, 30 Conn. Sup. 501, 505, 294 A.2d 344 (App. Div. 1972). "[An] . . . initial consultation between the defendant and his trial counsel . . . [may fall] within the scope of the privileged communication. *The client may not be required to divulge the advice which his attorney gave him*" (Emphasis added.) (*Id.*, 505).

"When two or more people consult an attorney together on a matter of joint interest, these competing considerations are normally resolved by allowing their communications to be privileged as to the outside world, though not as to each other in a later controversy between themselves." *State v. Cascone*, 195 Conn. 183, 186–87, 487 A.2d 186 (1985).

". . . [A] direct communication from a client to his attorney either made in or sent to the attorney's office; in such a case, relatively little factual foundation would ordinarily be required to establish the privilege and, so, the inadmissibility of any question concerning the subject matter of the communication." *State v. Hanna*, 150 Conn. 457, 467, 191 A.2d 124 (1963). "[E]ven if [an attorney] never communicated specific legal opinions . . . that fact would not change the nature of the attorney-client relationship. . . . It is not the rendering of legal advice that establishes the attorney-client relationship. If that were the case, the initial communications between the client and attorney, those that are often the most sensitive and most in need of confidentiality, would be unprotected. Rather it is the client's seeking of legal advice . . . that establishes the relationship. . . ." *Shew v. Freedom of Information Comm.*, Superior Court, judicial district of Hartford/New Britain at Hartford, Docket No. 539639, 15 CONN. L. RPTR. 309 (September 19, 1995) (Maloney, J.), affirmed on other grounds, 245 Conn. 149, (1998).

(continues)

CASE LAW   *Palomba v. Sullivan* (continued)

Connecticut's courts have addressed similar factual circumstances as the one presented in the instant case in terms of the presence of a third party during an attorney-client conversation. In *Grodovich v. Immediate Medical Care, CTR*, Superior Court, judicial district of Hartford/New Britain at Hartford, Docket No. 515617, 12 CONN. L. RPTR. 234 (August 4, 1994) (Wagner, J.), the court addressed an issue wherein "the plaintiff now moves to compel [the defendant] to disclose matters he discussed with his insurance representative in the presence of his attorney, the defendants objecting to that motion on the basis of attorney-client privileges." (*Id.*) The court held that

[i]n the present case, the expectation of privacy continues. . . . The legal and economic interests of the defendants and the insurance company are so thoroughly intertwined, that the mere presence of the insurance agent does not cause the privilege to be waived, but the privilege continues to protect the confidentiality of the communications.

In this case, the members of the Palomba family sought legal advice from Attorney Diamond concerning the death of their sister, the Plaintiff in this action. Those communications are privileged and therefore the court will grant the Plaintiff 's motion for protective order.

Case Questions

1. On what legal theory does the court find that the statements the sister of the decedent made to the attorney were confidential and, therefore, covered by the attorney-client privilege?

2. Who is the client in this case?

3. Based on the court's reasoning, and assuming the sister had a boyfriend, would the result be the same if the sister had brought her boyfriend to the initial meeting? If the sister had told her boyfriend about what happened that day in the lawyer's office, could the boyfriend be deposed about what the sister told him?

The Client's Identity

The client's identity can be considered information that is not confidential, but not without exception. Generally, the client's identity is a fact that, in and of itself, does not qualify as protected information. See *In re Subpoena to Testify before Grand Jury*, 39 F.3d 973 (9th Cir. 1994), a case where a lawyer was required to divulge the identity of a client who happened to give the attorney a counterfeit $100 bill. In circumstances where revealing the client's identity can convey information that is privileged, such as acknowledging guilt that would have led the client to seek legal advice, this can serve as the basis for rightfully withholding the client's identity. *In re Grand Jury Subpoena*, 976 F.2d 1314, 1317 (9th Cir.

1992). In a Delaware case, a client accusing her lawyer of wrongful sexual advances was denied, on the grounds of confidentiality, the right to access the lawyer's client list. *Brett v. Barques*, 706 A.2d 509 (Del. 1998).

The Client's Location

Where a client is located can also be desired information, particularly if he or she is a parent in a custody dispute and has gone into hiding with the children who are the subject of the dispute. A client's location is information that is received in the course of representation, so it is, **prima facie**, protected information. However, lawyers must abide by the final orders of a court, and if, for instance, a court orders a lawyer to divulge the location of the client—and the lawyer has exhausted all available appeals—the lawyer is then required to disclose the otherwise confidential information, but on as limited a basis as possible. *See* ABA Comm. On Ethics and Professional Responsibility, Formal Op. 94–385 (1994).

Fee Arrangements

Fee arrangements made between clients and their lawyers are usually not considered to be confidential information. One exception to that is the doctrine of "last link," which also applies to client identity controversies. This doctrine stems from a famous case, *Baird v. Koerner*, 279 F.2d 623 (9th Cir. 1960), and holds that if otherwise unprotected information would, if disclosed, serve as the last link to implicate the client in criminal activity, then that information is protected. When insurance companies are third-party payers of the client's legal bill, they often want the legal fees audited. Many state ethics committees are opposed to such transfer of billing information without client consent, on the grounds that such disclosure would compromise attorney-client confidentiality and could disclose legal strategies. Alaska Bar Ethics Commission, Op. 99–1 (1999); D.C. Bar Legal Ethics Comm., Op. 290 (1999); Md. State Bar Ass'n Comm. On Ethics, Op. 99–7 (1998).

Disclosures After the Client Waives the Privilege

The attorney-client privilege is the client's privilege and the attorney exercises the privilege on behalf of the client. Unless authorized, the attorney usually may not waive the privilege because only the client has the right to waive it. However, if the client waives the privilege, the attorney's duty with respect to what has been waived ends. For example, as Timothy McVeigh's execution was drawing near, he granted interviews and wrote many letters to two journalists, who then, based on the correspondence, published a book titled *American Terrorist: Timothy McVeigh and the Oklahoma City Bombing* (Regan Books, 2001). Renowned defense attorney Stephen Jones, who represented McVeigh at the trial, granted interviews contemporaneous with the scheduled execution date and challenged some of the statements made by McVeigh, particularly his

---

■ **prima facie**

On its face, or on the surface.

assertion that he acted alone. Jones's statements to the press would not qualify as violating the doctrine of client confidentiality because McVeigh went public first with his assertions, some of which were highly critical of Jones's representation.

Martha Stewart, an E-Mail, and the Possible Waiver of Attorney-Client Privilege

If the client waives the privilege, particularly in a criminal matter, then the question becomes whether the other side may use what has been waived, which in itself is a conundrum. Such was the question needing to be answered during the pre-trial maneuverings of the Martha Stewart criminal case. Although not criminally charged with insider trading, Ms. Stewart's legal troubles stemmed from a sale of stock, ImClone, in December of 2001. The government believed the stock sale was made because of an illegal tip given to Stewart by Sam Waksal. Waksal, ImClone's founder and one of Ms. Stewart's best friends, pled guilty to the insider trading of ImClone's stock and was sentenced to seven years in prison. During their review of documents, government lawyers discovered an e-mail Ms. Stewart had sent to one of her lawyers in June of 2002, and then the next day to her daughter Alexis. The e-mail allegedly explained her reason for selling the stock that led to charges that Ms. Stewart lied to federal investigators when asked about why she sold it. So, the federal prosecutors sought to use the e-mail on the grounds that once she forwarded the message to her daughter, Ms. Stewart had waived the attorney-client privilege. To support her claim that she had not waived the privilege, Ms. Stewart put forth an affidavit, calling her daughter, "the closest person in the world to me....She is a valued confidante and counselor to me" In a 20-page opinion, federal judge Miriam Goldman Cederbaum ruled that neither the attorney-client privilege nor the attorney work product doctrine (to be discussed later in the chapter) were waived, citing Ms. Stewart's affidavit in her opinion. Of course, the victory in that battle did not change the outcome of the war, which resulted in a five-month prison term.

For a thorough and quite interesting article, written by CNN's chief legal analyst Jeffrey Toobin, on the Martha Stewart criminal case, including personal insights into the key participants, search for it on the web page of the New Yorker magazine: http://www.newyorker.com.

Paralegals should be extremely cautious with regard to the previously noted kinds of information that might not be considered confidential. Even if a paralegal could, after conducting legal research in his or her jurisdiction, feel confident that a client's identity would not be confidential information, it is best to treat it as confidential and not disclose it unless specifically authorized by a supervising attorney. Ultimately, whether information is or is not confidential can be up to a court to decide, and any error of disclosure could place the paralegal's attorney at risk of being accused of failing to properly supervise non-lawyer employees. Also, one could argue that determining whether a client's identity is or is not confidential information constitutes making a legal judgment, which would make it something only lawyers are authorized to do.

The Basics of Discovery

Although television shows about lawyers often save the key witness or piece of evidence as a surprise for the thrilling ending, the reality of litigation is that the rules of discovery are designed to avoid surprises at trial by allowing each side to have access to the other side's case. This information gathering is done through **interrogatories** of the parties, depositions of parties and witnesses, examination of the parties' documents or other things, entry on the parties' land or other property for the purposes of inspection, physical and mental examinations, and requests for admissions. Federal Rules of Civil Procedure, Rule 26(a)(5) (2006). The attorney-client privilege is implicated when lawyers, upon being asked for certain discovery items, claim that such information is protected against disclosure by the attorney-client privilege. Though this is not a civil procedure or evidence book, a limited discussion of the basic operation of discovery will help put the attorney-client privilege in context.

What can generally be discovered is governed by Civil Procedure Rule 26(b), which states in part:

(b) Discovery Scope and Limits. Unless otherwise limited by order of the court in accordance with these rules, the scope of discovery is as follows:

(1) Parties may obtain discovery regarding any matter, not privileged which is relevant to the subject-matter involved in the pending action, whether it relates to the claim or defense of the party seeking discovery or the claim or defense of any other party. . . . Relevant information need not be admissible at the trial if the discovery appears reasonably calculated to lead to the discovery of admissible evidence. Fed. R. Civ. P. 26(B).

What can be obtained in discovery is much broader than what can be presented as evidence in the event of a trial, because the preceding rule allows a party to seek discovery of any information if that information could reasonably lead to the discovery of other information that would be admissible at trial. For example, a party's offer to settle a lawsuit is generally inadmissible at trial, but interrogatories and depositions can be used to find out if a party made an offer to settle the case.

The Basics of the Work Product Rule

Because client information is to be protected by the duty of confidentiality and the attorney-client privilege, discovery requests could seemingly always be thwarted by the other side simply by claiming that the information being sought is confidential, end of story. That is where Rule 26(b)(3) comes to the rescue, by

■ **interrogatories**

A discovery device that involves one party sending to the other party a set, or sets, of questions that are to be answered under oath and in writing.

distinguishing among kinds of attorney-client information and then determining if and when the attorney-client privilege protects against the disclosure of that information to the other side. Rule 26(B)(3) states, in part:

> (3) *Trial preparations: Materials.* Subject to the provisions of subdivision (b)(4) or this rule, a party may obtain discovery of documents and tangible things otherwise discoverable under subdivision (b)(1) of this rule and prepared in anticipation of litigation or for trial by or for another party or by or for that other party's representative (including his attorney, consultant, surety, indemnitor, insurer, or agent) only upon a showing that the party seeking discovery has substantial need of the materials in the preparation of his case and that he is unable without undue hardship to obtain the substantial equivalent of the materials by other means. In ordering discovery of such materials when the required showing has been made, the court shall protect against disclosure of the mental impressions, conclusions, opinions, or legal theories of an attorney or other representative of a party concerning the litigation.

The preceding section is commonly referred to as the *work product rule.* The first part of the rule allows one side in litigation to compel the other side to disclose tangible information that was prepared in anticipation or connection with litigation by the other side, provided: (a) the side desiring the tangible information demonstrates a substantial need of it; and (b) the side desiring the tangible information demonstrates that they would be unable to obtain the same information on their own without incurring extreme hardship. For example, imagine that a plaintiff sues a defendant over a car accident and, before the defendant has an opportunity to examine and photograph the plaintiff's car, it is mistakenly crushed at the junkyard. Under the work product rule, the defendant would be able to have access to the photographs taken by the plaintiff's lawyer (or the lawyer's agents, such as investigators) because they were taken by the plaintiff in connection with the litigation and because there would be no way for the defendant to make his or her own examination of the car.

The second part of the rule is sometimes referred to as the *attorney-opinion work product rule;* it serves as an exception to the exception that certain kinds of client information must be disclosed to the other side. This part of the rule absolutely protects from disclosure any otherwise discoverable client information if what is sought would reveal the attorney's legal strategies, theories, or opinions about the case. To continue the preceding example, the attorney-opinion aspect of the work product rule would protect the plaintiff from being compelled to turn over to the defendant any and all notes written by the plaintiff's lawyer that would show the plaintiff's game plan at trial (perhaps demonstrating that the defendant was negligently driving the car). The attorney-client privilege would also prevent the plaintiff, in an attempt to find out if the defendant stated or implied he or she might be at fault, from compelling his or her attorney to turn over notes of interviews with him or her. The defendant's attorney would be prohibited from disclosing that information because of the ethical duty of confidentiality (the first branch of the confidentiality tree), and in this instance, such discussions would be protected from discovery by the attorney-client privilege (the second branch). See Exhibit 4-8 for the two parts of the work product rule.

EXHIBIT 4–8   THE TWO PARTS OF THE WORK PRODUCT RULE

The Work Product Rule	The Attorney Opinion Work Product Rule
Documents and other tangible things created in connection to litigation are discoverable *only if:*	*Even if* work product materials are discoverable under the work product rule...
a) it is shown that there is substantial need of the materials *and* b) there is no substantial equivalent	*the attorney's (or the party's other representatives') mental impressions, theories, or legal strategies are not discoverable*

Attorney-Client Privilege, the White House, and the First Lady

A controversial example of the relationship of the attorney-client privilege and attorney notes involved the Whitewater Investigation and then–first lady Hillary Clinton. Long before the country ever heard of an intern named Monica Lewinsky and a former **solicitor general** named Kenneth Starr, the **Office of Independent Counsel (OIC)**, originally headed by Robert B. Fiske, Jr., was appointed to investigate the possible crimes committed in Arkansas by the Clintons and their Whitewater land investment partners, James and Susan McDougal. As part of that investigation, the OIC issued a grand jury subpoena to the White House, directing it to turn over to the grand jury any and all notes taken by two White House lawyers during meetings held in the White House that included the presence of Mrs. Clinton and her personal lawyer. The White House Counsel's Office and Mrs. Clinton argued in response that the notes were protected by the attorney-client privilege. However, the Eighth Circuit Court of Appeals disagreed, in *In re Grand Jury Subpoena Duces Tecum*, 112 F.3d 910 (8th Cir. 1997). The Court ruled that the White House Counsel represents the public's interests, not the interests of the first lady. Therefore, because the White House Counsel's client is the United States and the OIC is a part of the U.S. government, White House lawyers cannot assert the attorney-client privilege against their own client, particularly when the OIC's investigation concerned the affairs of the Clintons before Mr. Clinton was elected president.

The Eighth Circuit Court of Appeals also found unpersuasive the argument that the attorney-client privilege applied to the conversations and the notes the White House lawyers took of those conversations because Mrs. Clinton believed

solicitor general

The third ranking member of the U.S. Justice Department. The solicitor general represents the federal government before the U.S. Supreme Court.

office of independent counsel (OIC)

A statutorily created special legal office, empowered to investigate and prosecute misconduct by members of the executive branch of government and other high-ranking government officials.

the attorney-client privilege applied, since she and her personal lawyer also attended those meetings in the White House. Instead, the court found that argument irrelevant because Mrs. Clinton correctly did not assert that she believed that the White House lawyers were representing her personally. Also, the White House claimed the notes were protected by the work product doctrine, because the notes were prepared in anticipation of the OIC's investigation of Mrs. Clinton, which was something akin to litigation. To that argument, the court reiterated that because the OIC was not investigating the White House, but rather was investigating its occupants for activities occurring in Arkansas, the work product doctrine did not apply. The Supreme Court refused to review the decision, so it became the final word on the matter. Some critics argue the decision will cause a chill in the communication lines between public officials and government lawyers and that it chips away at the attorney-client privilege. Others, however, contend the decision may be politically controversial but is not legally controversial because it restates a common notion, which is that government lawyers take as their client the government, that is, the public.

Inadvertent Disclosure: What to Do When Mistakes Occur

As has been discussed, though the rules of discovery are meant to facilitate the sharing of information between parties, there are certain kinds of information that do not have to be disclosed to the other side. But mistakes happen. Suppose at a poker game, a player holds his or her cards so lazily that the nearest player can see them. Would anyone expect the beneficiary of such sloppiness to pretend that nothing was seen, and not take advantage of such good luck? Of course not. Opponents in all endeavors look for each other's mental errors precisely to take full advantage, and almost no one would expect anything different. Before the battle of Antietam, the single bloodiest day of the Civil War, Union soldiers found the mislaid battle plans of Robert E. Lee, the Confederate commander and most romanticized figure of the war. A copy of his September 9, 1862 plans, known as Special Orders No. 191, were wrapped around three cigars and carelessly discarded by a Confederate officer, only to be found by a Union private and given to General George McClellan, who was reported to have said, "Here is a paper with which if I cannot whip Bobby Lee I will be willing to go home." Home is where General McClellan did go before the war's end after being relieved of command by President Lincoln, but not because he refused to read what serendipitously dropped into his lap in 1862.

Litigation can be different, however. During the paper-burying process of discovery, a law firm might, on occasion, unintentionally send to the other firm documents or other tangible items that should not have been sent because they were protected work product material. When either firm horrifyingly or pleasantly discovers the error, what happens next can depend on the jurisdiction.

Material Inadvertently Disclosed Retains Its Privileged Status

The ABA Ethics Commission issued an opinion concerning inadvertent disclosure in 1992. Specifically, the question addressed concerned a lawyer who received privileged information by a fax that was erroneously sent. The ABA reached the conclusion that if a lawyer receives information from the opposing party that the lawyer believes to be confidential or protected, the lawyer should: (a) refrain from further examining the materials; (b) inform the lawyer who sent the materials; and (c) abide by the wishes of the sending lawyer. ABA Comm. on Ethics and Professional Responsibility, Formal Op. 92–368 (1992). Some state ethics opinions adhere to that advice and require attorneys who are erroneously sent confidential or protected materials to return those materials to opposing counsel without further examining them. Oregon State Bar Legal Ethics Comm., Op. 1998–150 (1998); Standing Comm. on Legal Ethics of Virginia State Bar, Op. 1702 (1997).

Then in 2002, the ABA adopted a new rule pertaining to inadvertent disclosure, when Rule 4.4 was amended by the addition of a new part. 4.4(b) states, "A lawyer who receives a document relating to the representation of the lawyer's client and knows or reasonably should know that the document was inadvertently sent shall promptly notify the sender." The official Comment acknowledges that the rule does not govern what the receiving lawyer should do with the document (for example, stop reading it, send it back), or if it has lost its privileged status, leaving those questions to the jurisdictions. A later Comment shows the rule's coverage includes e-mail and other electronic information capable of being put in readable form. A few Model Rules jurisdictions have adopted 4.4(b), including Arizona, Indiana, Louisiana, and New Jersey. Furthermore, Louisiana's and New Jersey's versions adopt the stricter line found in the 1992 ABA ethics opinion, because they require a lawyer who receives inadvertently sent documents to not only stop reading them and notify the sender, but to also return them.

In 2005, the ABA issued Formal Ethics Opinion 05–437, which is significant because in it the ABA formally withdrew a key part of its 1992 ethics opinion on inadvertent disclosure. In the 2005 opinion, the ABA recognized that the 1992 opinion instructed a lawyer to not read inadvertently sent, privileged materials, while Rule 4.4(b), adopted in 2002, does not prohibit reading what was inadvertently sent. It simply requires the receiving lawyer to notify the sending lawyer about the disclosure.

The following case, involving a divorce client suing her law firm for malpractice, illustrates the view that inadvertent disclosure does not result in an effective waiver of the attorney-client privilege. The parts of the court's decision addressing the law of attorney malpractice are redacted from the version presented. While reading the case, notice how the Court adopts the ABA's traditional position that inadvertent disclosure does not result in the waiver of attorney-client privilege.

CASE LAW *Corey v. Norman, Hanson & DeTroy*

742 A.2d 933 (Maine 1999)

CLIFFORD, J.

Susan W. Corey appeals from a summary judgment (Cumberland County, Cole J.) entered in favor of the defendants. The court concluded that Susan failed to establish the necessary elements to establish malpractice in her action brought against the law firm of Norman, Hanson & DeTroy and the accounting firm of Dawson, Smith, Purvis & Bassett, P.A. (referred to collectively as NH&D). Susan contends that the trial court erred in basing its decision to grant a summary judgment on what it concluded was an insufficient statement of material facts filed by Susan pursuant to M.R. Civ. P. 7(d)(2). Susan also appeals from an order (Saufley, J.) requiring her attorney to return to the attorney for NH&D a document that the trial court found to be privileged. She contends that the court erred in finding that an inadvertent disclosure of a privileged document does not constitute a waiver of the attorney-client privilege. We affirm both the summary judgment and the court's order regarding the privileged document.

In the spring of 1995, Susan retained attorney Peter DeTroy of NH&D to represent her in divorce proceedings against her then husband John B. Corey, a dentist specializing in periodontics. DeTroy hired Dawson, Smith, Purvis & Bassett, P.A., certified public accountants, to value assets of the marital estate and to assist in distinguishing between marital and nonmarital property for purposes of the divorce. The parties agreed that John Corey's dental practice was marital property. DeTroy stipulated to the $37,700 valuation of the dental practice proposed by John's attorney. No formal appraisal of the dental practice was conducted by DeTroy or the accountants he hired. The divorce was finalized in March of 1996. In the divorce judgment, the stipulated value of the dental practice was accepted by the court and the practice was set aside to John. More than $1.6 million in marital property was awarded to Susan. In addition, John was ordered to pay his former wife alimony in excess of $300,000 over ten years.

In January of 1997, Susan filed a complaint in the Superior Court charging NH&D with professional negligence. Susan alleged that . . . NH&D breached that duty by failing to obtain an independent valuation and by stipulating to the $37,700 valuation of the dental practice. This breach, Susan alleges, "caused the dental practice, a valuable marital asset, to be seriously undervalued," thereby resulting in a property distribution to Susan "of substantially less value than that to which she was entitled." The $37,700 figure to which NH&D stipulated was the value of the dental and business equipment less debt, and did not account for the good will of the dental practice, which, Susan contends, has a substantial value. . . .

(continues)

The Superior Court entered a summary judgment in favor of NH&D based on Susan's failure to present sufficient evidence of any loss that was proximately caused by negligence on the part of NH&D. Therefore, the court concluded, her claim for damages was overly speculative. Susan has appealed from that judgment. . . .

II. ATTORNEY-CLIENT PRIVILEGE

On February 4, 1997, Michael Waxman, Susan's attorney, went to the office of Harrison L. Richardson, the attorney for NH&D, to view NH&D's file regarding the Corey divorce. Richardson was not in his office, but he had told his secretary to photocopy any documents Waxman wished to have. Inadvertently placed in the boxes of documents available for Waxman's review was a memorandum with the phrase "CONFIDENTIAL AND LEGALLY PRIVILEGED" written at the top of the page. The memorandum is a summary of a telephone conference between Richardson and DeTroy, the attorney who represented Susan in her divorce. Waxman requested and received a copy of the document from a firm secretary without the knowledge of Richardson. The secretary contacted Waxman later that day to request the return of the copy of the document. Waxman refused that request, believing that he did not have an obligation to return the document because the attorney-client privilege was waived by the inadvertent disclosure of the document. He then informed Richardson, in writing, of his receipt of the document.

The Superior Court granted NH&D's motion for a protective order and required Waxman to return his copy of the memorandum to Richardson and to make no further use of it. An appeal of that ruling is now before us. . . .

The purpose of the attorney-client privilege "is to encourage clients to make full disclosure to their attorneys," see *Fisher v. United States*, 425 U.S. 391, 403 (1976), and "to protect not only the giving of professional advice to those who can act on it but also the giving of information to the lawyer to enable him to give sound and informed advice," see *Upjohn Co. v. United States*, 449 U.S. 383, 390 (1981). Any rule regarding inadvertent disclosures must uphold this underlying purpose.

In ordering the return of the inadvertently disclosed privileged document, the trial court, adopting the rule first established in *Mendenhall v. Barber-Greene Co.*, 531 F. Supp. 951 (N.D. Ill. 1982), concluded: A truly inadvertent disclosure cannot and does not constitute a waiver of the attorney-client privilege. The issue for counsel and the court upon a claim of inadvertent disclosure must be whether the disclosure was actually inadvertent, that is, whether there was intent and authority for the disclosure. . . . If receiving counsel understands the disclosure to have been inadvertent, no waiver will have occurred. Unless receiving counsel has a reasonable belief that the disclosure was authorized by the client and intended by the attorney, the receiving attorney should return the document and make no further use of it. See id. at 954-55. We agree with the Superior Court and its adoption of the

(continues)

CASE LAW   *Corey v. Norman, Hanson & DeTroy* (continued)

common sense rule set out in Mendenhall. . . . Underlying this rule is the notion that the client holds the privilege, and that only the client, or the client's attorney acting with the client's express authority, can waive the privilege. . . .

The rule adopted by the Superior Court, which we now adopt, is consistent with the rule adopted by the American Bar Association's committee on Ethics and Professional Responsibility: A lawyer who receives materials that on their face appear to be subject to the attorney-client privilege or otherwise confidential, under circumstances where it is clear they were not intended for the receiving lawyer, should refrain from examining the materials, notify the sending lawyer and abide the instructions of the lawyer who sent them. ABA Comm. on Ethics and Professional Responsibility, Formal Op. 92–368 (1992); see also ABA Comm. on Ethics and Professional Responsibility, Formal Op. 94–382 (1994).

We agree with the Superior Court's rejection of the alternate approaches followed by other courts. In one line of cases, an inadvertent disclosure of a privileged document can amount to a waiver of the privilege if the client and the client's attorney did not take adequate steps to prevent the disclosure. See *Gray v. Bicknell*, 86 F.3d 1472, 1483-84 (8th Cir. 1996); *see also Hartford Fire Ins. Co. v. Garrey*, 109 F.R.D. 323, 331-32 (N.D. Cal. 1985). The Gray approach has been criticized as creating an uncertain, unpredictable privilege, dependent on the proof of too many factors concerning the adequacy of the steps taken to prevent disclosure. *See Berg Elecs., Inc. v. Molex, Inc.*, 875 F. Supp. 261, 262-63 (D. Del. 1995). Another line of cases concludes that all inadvertent disclosures of documents constitute a waiver of the privilege because the information is no longer confidential. *See International Digital Sys. Corp. v. Digital Equip. Corp.*, 120 F.R.D. 445, 449-50 (D. Mass. 1988); John Henry Wigmore, Evidence in Trials at Common Law § 2325(3) (John T. McNaughton ed., 1961). Although this approach has been adopted by the United States District Court for the District of Maine, *see Federal Deposit Ins. Corp. v. Singh*, 140 F.R.D. 252, 253 (D. Me. 1992), it takes away from the client the ability to control when the privilege is waived and discourages communication between attorneys and clients.

The Superior Court was correct in concluding that there was no waiver of the privilege, and in ordering the return of the document and prohibiting the disclosure of its contents.

The entry is: Order regarding the privileged document is affirmed; judgment affirmed.

Case Questions

1. Do you think the receiving attorney did anything wrong by examining the letter he was given by the secretary for the opposing lawyer?

2. Why did the court state that the attorney-client privilege had not been waived despite a clear occurrence of inadvertent disclosure?

3. Based on this decision, under what circumstances would the attorney-client privilege be waived?

In 1994 the ABA dealt with a slightly different question, which concerned what to do when a lawyer receives privileged materials from a third party (such as a disgruntled former employee of the opposing party or law firm), instead of erroneously from the opposing lawyer. Similar to the 1992 opinion, the ABA decided that the lawyer, once discovering the privileged materials, should contact the opposing party to inform them of the situation and then follow their instructions. ABA Comm. on Ethics and Professional Responsibility, Formal Op. 94–382. Some states have expressed similar sentiment to the effect that lawyers should not take advantage of the situation when a third party sends them privileged information. North Carolina State Bar Ethics Comm., 252 (1997); Standing Comm. on Legal Ethics of Virginia State Bar, Op. 1702 (1997). Other states, however, consider such a fortuitous finding to incur no duty by the receiving lawyer to rectify the situation. Maryland State Bar Ass'n Comm. on Ethics Op. 96–38 (1996) (Maryland said there was no duty to inform the opposing counsel when a third party gave to the lawyer's client documents pulled out of a dumpster); Ohio Sup. Ct. Bd. of Comm'rs on Grievances and Discipline Op. 93–11 (1993).

But, for similar reasons that the 1992 ABA Formal Opinion was withdrawn by the 2005 Opinion mentioned earlier, the 1994 ABA Formal Opinion was withdrawn by a 2006 Formal Opinion, 06-442. This ethics opinion deals with "metadata," which is geek-talk for information that is embedded in electronic documents, something most of us do not think about when we create a document on a computer, but which can be unearthed like a latent fingerprint with the right technology. For example, if one lawyer sends to another lawyer an e-mail and attachment, it is possible for the receiving lawyer or paralegal to discover the dates and times when the documents were created and last worked on, to learn how many revisions were made and what person or persons worked on the documents, and even to see formerly deleted materials in the document. Much of this metadata can be eliminated ("scrubbed" as it called), but how many lawyers, paralegals, legal assistants, secretaries, interns, and clerks (not to mention everybody else with computers) scrub their electronic documents before sending them?

So, the question facing the ABA in 2006 was, *is it unethical for a lawyer to read the metadata on electronic documents, regardless of how the documents ended up in the lawyer's possession?* While recognizing that some legal authorities consider the practice unethical and dishonest, the ABA opined that, because Model Rule 4.4 (b) only requires a lawyer who receives inadvertent disclosure to notify the sender, there is nothing unethical in examining the metadata of any electronic document, regardless if it is inadvertent and who sent it. Not all jurisdictions subscribe to this view. Five years before the ABA's opinion on the subject, the New York State Bar Association concluded that it was unethical and wrong for an attorney to use software to plumb the depths of electronic documents sent by the opposing party or counsel, in search of metadata. N.Y. State Ethics Op. 749 (2001). Three years later, the same committee concluded that a lawyer had a duty to use "reasonable care" to prevent e-mailed documents from being transmitted with metadata "containing client confidences and secrets." N.Y. State Ethics Op. 782 (2004). And in 2006, a Florida ethics opinion concluded that it was unethical for a lawyer to attempt to retrieve metadata from electronic documents received from another lawyer, and that a lawyer who receives unintended metadata has a duty to notify the sending lawyer. Florida Bar Professional Ethics Opinion 06–02.

For information on how to handle the problem of metadata in Microsoft Word documents, search two of Microsoft's Web sites: htttp://support.microsoft.com; and http://office.microsoft.com.

The following case involves a curious form of inadvertent disclosure by a third party: the third party is the plaintiff, who also happens to be her attorney's paralegal.

CASE LAW *Lipin v. Bender*

193 A.D.2d 424 (N.Y. App. Div. 1, 1993)

Appeal from the Supreme Court, New York County (Karla Moskowitz, J.).

This is seemingly a matter of first impression, the issue being whether, under the unique circumstances presented, dismissal of the complaint is an appropriate sanction for plaintiff's surreptitious removal and use of confidential documents constituting privileged material and defense counsel's attorney's work product. The underlying facts are not in dispute. Plaintiff, a former high ranking employee of defendant American Red Cross in Greater New York (NYRC), brought this action for sexual harassment and discrimination pursuant to New York's Human Rights Law and 42 U.S.C. § 1983 and 1985.

On June 28, 1991, the parties appeared before Special Referee Birnbaum in a hearing room on the second floor of the New York County Courthouse at 60 Centre Street to argue certain discovery matters. Plaintiff, who since her termination by NYRC had been working as a paralegal for her attorney in this matter, found immediately in front of her at her "customary" location at the counsel table, a stack of documents of some 200 pages. It is unclear why and by whom the documents were placed in that precise location and not otherwise safeguarded, but counsel for defendants were sitting directly across the 12 by 6 foot counsel table.

Typed on the top page of the stack of documents was the heading:

"Weil, Gotshal & Manges MEMORANDUM
Two Files From Lawrence J. Baer
Re: Joan Lipin v American Red Cross"

(continues)

CASE LAW *Lipin v. Bender* (continued)

The documents contained a series of internal memoranda prepared by counsel containing notes of various interviews with defendant Bender and other individuals employed or associated with NYRC concerning this action. The documents also included digests of depositions which had previously been taken in this action.

As counsel were engaged in argument concerning certain discovery matters, plaintiff slipped these documents off the table, placed them on her lap, and began to read them. As plaintiff read through the documents, she recognized that they were interviews with various witnesses relevant to this action. According to the hearing testimony, "I decided that I was going to obtain possession of these papers for my own protection." When argument before the Special Referee had ended, plaintiff informed her attorney that she had just read various inflammatory statements taken in interviews concerning her, and that she was "horrified." Counsel stated that he would not read the documents until he had obtained a "second opinion." During the luncheon recess, plaintiff went to counsel's office and copied the documents.

Counsel examined the documents on Sunday, June 30, 1991. According to him, the documents contained inflammatory references to plaintiff, as well as evidence of a "conspiracy to ruin her career." After conferring with the attorney who had originally referred the matter to him, both attorneys formed the opinion that they were entitled to retain the documents under a claim of right, and that any claim of confidentiality had been waived in view of the circumstances of the discovery of the documents—that they had been left unsecured, directly in front of the plaintiff, in a public area, such that plaintiff had been "invited" to read the documents.

Thereupon, plaintiff's counsel requested that opposing counsel attend a "settlement" conference at his offices at 2:00 P.M. on Tuesday, July 2, 1991. At that time, plaintiff's counsel made various demands, including (1) that Weil, Gotshal & Manges withdraw as counsel based upon a conflict of interest in representing both defendants Bender and NYRC, (2) a monetary settlement, and (3) "suitable action" to withdraw, with an apology for false information allegedly disseminated concerning plaintiff. In response to these demands, defense counsel demanded return of the documents and an explanation as to the manner in which plaintiff had obtained them. Plaintiff's counsel refused to reveal how the documents had been obtained, and also refused to return the copies which had been made, asserting that in any event he had no control over his client, who could conceivably give the documents to the mass media.

(continues)

CASE LAW *Lipin v. Bender* (continued)

Defendants immediately sought, by order to show cause, an order pursuant to CPLR 3103 N.Y.C.P.L.R. suppressing the privileged documents, disqualifying plaintiff's attorney, and imposing sanctions. Pending a hearing, the IAS Court directed that no use be made of the documents and that any and all copies made of the documents be secured.

An evidentiary hearing was held, at which plaintiff revealed the manner in which she had removed the documents. Plaintiff admitted that in her employment as a paralegal, she was aware of the nature of the attorney-client privilege. Plaintiff further revealed that counsel had advised her, on the day the documents were obtained, that "you can't lie so you have to say yes, you by mistake picked up his documents." The plaintiff insisted, however, that the documents were not taken by mistake, but rather, "it was my own recognizance and my own protection." Following the hearing, defendants moved to amend their motion to seek dismissal of the complaint, based upon the hearing testimony given by plaintiff.

In a decision read into the record, the court found that the documents were on their face clearly attorney's work product, and that plaintiff, as an employee of her counsel, had an obligation to return those documents to opposing counsel. Instead, copies of the documents were made, for which there was "no justification." The court stated, "I have to conclude that the actions of the plaintiff and her attorney were so egregious in taking this material * * * so heinous that the only remedy, as much as I dislike to do this, is to dismiss the lawsuit."

In Matter of Beiny (129 A.D.2d 126), counsel for petitioner in a trust accounting proceeding clandestinely obtained, by means of an improperly issued subpoena, discovery of confidential and privileged material from the adverse party's former law firm without notifying that party. This Court, in modifying the order of the Surrogate so as to disqualify petitioner's counsel in addition to the previously ordered suppression of the 107 improperly obtained documents, found that the sanction of disqualification, while regrettable, in that it deprived petitioner of his chosen counsel, was necessary

"not only to sanitize the proceeding but to prevent the offending lawyer or firm from deriving any further benefit from information obtained and used in violation of basic ethical precepts and statutory obligations * * * [T]o impose a sanction short of disqualification would be to treat the conduct at issue with a degree of lenity practically inviting its recurrence. Our principal concern under the circumstances must be to preserve the integrity of the process by which rights are vindicated. (Supra, at 143–144.)

Under the circumstances of this case, although there is not the premeditation found in Beiny (supra, at 133), plaintiff's initial conduct is equally or even more egregious in terms of an appropriate sanction inasmuch as it was plaintiff herself who seized the opportunity presented to obtain an unfair advantage over her

(continues)

CASE LAW *Lipin v. Bender* (continued)

adversaries in this litigation. Her improper conduct was then compounded by counsel, who could have readily returned the documents or sought further direction from the court, rather than permitting his client to return this office and make copies of the disputed documents and then sought to take advantage of such improper conduct by scheduling a "settlement conference."

Although plaintiff's contention that CPLR 3103 N.Y.C.P.L.R. does not authorize a court to dismiss a complaint for discovery abuses has some facial appeal, as noted by Professor Siegel in his Practice Commentaries to the section, the factual variations that arise from case to case are limitless and a detailed listing of all possible abuses and remedies would be impractical and unwise. "If, for any reason sufficient to invoke that undefinable commodity known as judicial 'discretion,' an adjustment in the use of disclosure is called for by the facts of any case, CPLR 3103.

N.Y.C.P.L.R. is at hand to confer the discretion." (Siegel, Practice Commentaries, McKinney's Cons Laws of NY, Book 7B, CPLR C3103:1, at 356.)

Thus, although the statute does not list dismissal as a remedy for a discovery abuse, it does not purport to set forth an exhaustive list of remedies, leaving the court the wide discretion to make "an appropriate order" to prevent the abuse of disclosure devices, including but not limited to suppression of information improperly obtained. Under the unique circumstances presented, particularly the sort of willful misbehavior engaged in by plaintiff and her attorney, we conclude that the IAS Court did not improvidently exercise its discretion in invoking the drastic sanction of dismissal of the complaint.

We have considered plaintiff's other points and find them without merit. Her attempt to portray the defendants as having engaged in dilatory and sharp practices appears to have but one purpose—to obscure the issue of her own misconduct. Moreover, there is no support for her claim that defendants waived any attorney-client privilege and, regardless of whether the documents were privileged, the highly improper manner in which they were obtained, combined with their subsequent use by plaintiff's counsel to defendants' detriment, constitutes a sufficient basis for the court's action (*see, Matter of Beiny, supra,* at 136). "[I]t is not unduly harsh to expect and indeed to require that civil litigants gather the information needed to prosecute or defend their actions in conformity with the applicable CPLR provisions." (*Supra,* at 137.)

Concur—Sullivan, J.P., Rosenberger, Kupferman and Asch, JJ.

Case Questions

1. How did the controversial materials end up in the plaintiff's hands?

2. Did the plaintiff know that the materials were covered by the attorney-client privilege?

(continues)

> **CASE LAW** *Lipin v. Bender* (continued)
>
> 3. Why did the plaintiff's attorney allow the materials to be copied?
>
> 4. Why did the defendant amend its motion, requesting the complaint be dismissed?
>
> 5. Is it fair that the plaintiff's serious claims be dismissed as a sanction for the misbehavior of her and her attorney?

Inadvertent Disclosure Results in Waiver

Another response to the inadvertent disclosure of privileged materials is to declare that the privilege has been **waived**, and the other side has the right to use the materials. Even though the attorney-client privilege belongs to the client, and even though the attorney may have committed the error, the privilege can be waived without the client's express consent because the client acts through his or her appointed agent, the attorney. Some state ethics opinions expressly disagree with the 1992 ABA ethics opinion mentioned earlier (which requires the receiving lawyer to take no advantage of the mistakenly sent privileged materials), arguing that the ABA's position is too idealistic. Comm. on Professional Ethics of Illinois State Bar Ass'n Op. 98–4 (1999); D.C. Bar Legal Ethics Commission Op. 256 (1995). These jurisdictions distinguish between two situations. In the first situation, the receiving lawyer is aware of the other lawyer's mistake, and then proceeds to examine the materials. That would be considered unethical. In the second situation, the receiving lawyer is unaware of the mistaken disclosure before examining the protected materials. Here, these opinions state that there is no ethics violation if the receiving lawyer uses those materials because a lawyer's ethical duty to zealously represent the client (Model Rule 1.3 and Model Code Canon 7) should take priority over helping the other, careless lawyer correct his or her mistake.

In a Texas case, a lawyer representing a plaintiff in an employment discrimination case was the object of an attorney disqualification motion by the opposing attorney because one of the plaintiff's coworkers (who later became a client with the plaintiff in the same matter) gave the lawyer privileged materials of the defendant. While refusing to disqualify the attorney, the Texas Supreme Court steered away from the bright-line requirements of the ABA's ethics opinion on inadvertent disclosure by a third party. The court stated that a lawyer who has received materials inadvertently disclosed by the other side has no duty to inform the other side about the disclosure, or to return the materials. *In re Meador*, 968 S.W.2d 346, 352 (Tex. 1998).

The view that inadvertent disclosure results in waiver is followed in certain federal jurisdictions. One of the more famous cases, *In re Grand Jury Investigation of Ocean Transportation*, 604 F.2d 672 (D.C. Cir. 1979), involved a subpoena that the Anti-Trust Division of the U. S. Government issued to a company. Although

■ **waived**
To waive a right or prerogative is to give it up. A waiver can be implied.

the company instructed its lawyer not to disclose any materials covered by the attorney-client privilege, the lawyer turned over two sets of documents that the company, after firing its first lawyer and retaining a different lawyer, later claimed were protected. The Court of Appeals ruled that the company absolutely waived the privilege with respect to the first set of documents because the original lawyer did not even mark those documents as protected or privileged. Therefore, it could not later be claimed by the second lawyer that the materials were privileged when sent to the government. The second set of documents, however, was marked with a "P." Regarding those documents, the court found that the privilege was also waived because the government, upon discovering the materials, contacted the original counsel inquiring whether the materials were, in fact, protected. The original counsel inexplicably stated they were not, and it was not until over a year had passed that the original counsel claimed those materials were privileged (the second lawyer being the one who issued the formal demand that the materials be returned). Because the government acted appropriately upon its discovery of the materials, and because so much time had passed during the interim—which time included the government's use of the materials—it was too late to try to close the Pandora's box.

Other federal courts hold a similar view that inadvertent disclosure results in a waiver of the privilege. *See Weil v. Investment/Indicators, Research & Management, Inc.,* 647 F.2d 18 (9th Cir 1981); *Liggett Group v. Brown & Williamson Tobacco Corp.,* 116 FRD 205, (M.D. N.C. 1986); *International Digital Systems Corp. v. Digital Equipment Corp.,* 120 FRD 445 (D. Mass. 1988).

Some state courts also hold that inadvertent disclosure can result in waiver of the attorney-client privilege, as the following case from Oregon shows.

CASE LAW   *Goldsborough v. Eagle Crest Partners, Ltd.*

848 P.2d 1049 (Oregon 1992)

VAN HOOMISSEN, J.

The sole question in this case is whether defendant waived its lawyer-client privilege as to a letter that defendant wrote to its lawyer and that defendant's lawyer voluntarily gave plaintiff in response to plaintiff's pretrial request for production of documents. The trial court ruled that defendant waived its privilege, and the Court of Appeals affirmed. *Goldsborough v. Eagle Crest Partners, Ltd.,* 105 Or. App. 499, 805 P.2d 723 (1991). We also affirm. Plaintiff sued her employer for statutory remedies pursuant to ORS 659.121 (1) and for common law wrongful discharge, alleging that defendant had fired her in violation of ORS 659.030 as retaliation for her filing an administrative claim of sex discrimination. Before trial, plaintiff served on defendant a request for production of documents, ORCP 43, seeking: "3. Any and all correspondence between defendants and any other entity other than defense counsel regarding plaintiff." (Emphasis added.) In response, defendant's lawyer voluntarily gave

(continues)

plaintiff a letter written by defendant's personnel director to defendant's lawyer concerning plaintiff's employment. [The letter stated in part: "In reviewing my notes on Vicki's interview of October 27th, she made the following statement, 'Yes, a lot of guys come on to me, I try and support four kids.' There has to be a reason guy's [sic] 'come on' to her. . . . At present, Vicki's performance has been 'Excellent,' so I'll just have to wait."]

At trial, plaintiff offered the letter in evidence. Defendant's lawyer objected, arguing for the first time that the letter was privileged and that defendant did not intend to waive its lawyer-client privilege when the letter was given to plaintiff. Defendant offered no evidence, and did not argue, that the disclosure was inadvertent, mistaken, or not authorized by the client. In response, plaintiff conceded that the letter was a confidential communication, but argued that, because of the voluntary disclosure during discovery, defendant had waived its privilege. Defendant's lawyer acknowledged that he had voluntarily disclosed the letter, but argued that, notwithstanding, defendant did not intend to waive its privilege and, further, that the burden was on plaintiff to show that the client specifically consented to a waiver. The trial court ruled that the privilege had been waived and admitted the letter in evidence. The jury later found for plaintiff and awarded her damages.

On appeal, defendant contended that the trial court erred in admitting the letter into evidence and requested a new trial. ORCP 64B(6). Finding no Oregon cases directly on point, and relying primarily on federal cases, the Court of Appeals affirmed, stating: "Defendant has the burden to show that the letter was privileged and that it did not waive the privilege. Defendant concedes that it voluntarily disclosed the document. . . ." The Court of Appeals rejected defendant's argument that there must be "specific evidence of authorization" by the client in order to find that a lawyer's disclosure of a privileged document is a waiver. . . .

On review, defendant argues, as it did in the Court of Appeals, that its lawyer's voluntary disclosure of the letter during discovery did not waive its privilege and that it had no such intent here. Defendant reasons that, because the lawyer-client privilege belongs to the client (and not to the lawyer) and because a waiver is an intentional relinquishment of a known right, its lawyer's voluntary disclosure was not an intentional relinquishment of a known right by the client. Defendant argues further that there can be no waiver found without specific evidence of the client's consent, and that the burden is on plaintiff to show that the client specifically consented to a waiver.

OEC 503(2)(a) provides in part: "A client has a privilege to refuse to disclose and to prevent any other person from disclosing confidential communications made for the purpose of facilitating the rendition of professional legal services to the client." OEC 511 provides in part: "A person upon whom [OEC 503 to 514] confer a privilege against disclosure of the confidential matter or communication waives the privilege if the person ✳ ✳ ✳

(continues)

CASE LAW   *Goldsborough v. Eagle Crest Partners, Ltd.* *(continued)*

voluntarily discloses or consents to disclosure of any significant part of the matter or communication. This [rule] does not apply if the disclosure is itself a privileged communication." . . .

By traditional doctrine, waiver is the intentional relinquishment of a known right. *Johnson v. Zerbst,* 304 U.S. 458, 464, 58 S Ct 1019, 82 L Ed 1461 (1938). However, in the confidential privilege situations, once confidentiality is destroyed through voluntary disclosure, no subsequent claim of privilege can restore it, and knowledge or lack of knowledge of the existence of the privilege appears to be irrelevant. California Evidence Code § 912; 8 Wigmore § 2327. Kirkpatrick, Oregon Evidence 282-83 (2d ed 1989).

See Smith v. Aleyska Pipeline Service Co., 538 F. Supp. 977, 980-82 (D Del 1982), *aff'd* 758 F.2d 668 (1st Cir 1984), *cert den* 471 U.S. 1066 (1985) (lawyer-client privilege waived when the lawyer, acting on behalf of the client, voluntarily sent to the opposing party a copy of an opinion letter addressed to the client concerning the litigation).

Defendant relies primarily on *Bryant v. Dukehart,* 106 Or. 359, 210 P. 454 (1923), a pre-Oregon Evidence Code case. In *Bryant,* there was no showing that the party claiming the privilege had turned over the privileged material. Indeed, it was not known how the privileged material reached the opposing party. Here, defendant admits that its lawyer voluntarily gave the letter to plaintiff during pretrial discovery. . . .

It is common practice for clients to authorize their lawyers to respond to discovery requests. In the absence of evidence to the contrary, an inference may be drawn that a lawyer who voluntarily turns over privileged material during discovery acts within the scope of the lawyer's authority from the client and with the client's consent. The lawyer's action in voluntarily giving privileged material in response to a demand for discovery is at least an implicit representation by the lawyer that the lawyer has the client's consent to do so, *i.e.,* that the client has waived the privilege. A voluntary disclosure by a client's lawyer under facts such as those present here is, accordingly, sufficient to permit a trial court to find a waiver.

A court need not necessarily conclude that the lawyer-client privilege has been waived when a document has been produced during discovery. Factors to be considered by the court may be whether the disclosure was inadvertent, whether any attempt was made to remedy any error promptly, and whether preservation of the privilege will occasion unfairness to the opponent.

McCormick, Evidence 342-43, ¤§93 (4th ed 1992). As noted above, defendant conceded that its lawyer voluntarily gave the letter to plaintiff in response to plaintiff's discovery request. Plaintiff had not requested the letter. Defendant offered no evidence, and did not argue, that the disclosure was mistaken, inadvertent, or unauthorized by the client. Defendant argued only that it did not intend to waive its privilege when its lawyer voluntarily

(continues)

gave plaintiff the letter and that proof of the client's specific consent is necessary to find a waiver. There was no evidence or argument that the disclosure was mistaken or inadvertent or that defendant's lawyer was acting outside the scope of his authority. There is no general legal requirement that a client have specifically consented to the release of a particular document in order for a waiver to be established.

We conclude that there was sufficient evidence to support the trial court's ruling under OEC 104(1) that defendant waived its privilege. We therefore hold that the trial court did not err in admitting the letter in evidence.

The decision of the Court of Appeals and the judgment of the circuit court are affirmed.

Case Questions

1. Why does this court disagree with the premise that the attorney-client privilege is not waived unless the client affirmatively waives it?

2. What factors in the court's reasoning helped it reach the conclusion that the privilege had been lost?

3. Do you agree with this court's view on inadvertent disclosure, or do you agree with the ABA's position on inadvertent disclosure?

THE LEGAL ASSISTANT AND CONFIDENTIALITY

It is critical that the non-lawyer employee understand the ramifications of violating the duty of confidentiality, which begins with learning what kind of confidentiality rule is in place in his or her jurisdiction. If the paralegal is working in a state that follows the ABA Model Rules, as most do, then more than just client "secrets" are confidential; all client information, from whatever the source, is considered confidential and must be held sacred. Examining one's jurisdiction's confidentiality rule will allow the legal assistant to see if the rule has broader exceptions than the Model Code or Model Rules (as does New Jersey's), more stringent exceptions (as does Illinois's), or almost no exceptions (as does California's).

How Does the Attorney-Client Privilege Cover the Paralegal?

As stated earlier in the chapter, if a client or prospective client contacts a paralegal for the purposes of seeking legal advice from the lawyer, the statement made to the paralegal can be considered protected by the attorney-client privilege, provided it meets the requirements of the privilege, which are strict. That the statement was made to a non-lawyer does not ruin the attorney-client privilege because the more important consideration concerns the type of statement and the manner in which it was made: the statement was the kind the attorney-client privilege covers (seeking legal advice, and "confidential"), and was made to an authorized agent of the lawyer who received the statement within the scope of employment (the paralegal).

A more difficult question involves whether the attorney-client privilege applies to the paralegal's work, performed at the direction of the supervising attorney on behalf of a client matter. If, for example, the information gathered during litigation by an attorney's paralegal was outside the scope of the attorney-client privilege, the paralegal's role would then be relegated to that of a secretary and would include no substantive work assignments.

Fortunately, that is not how courts apply the attorney-client privilege. One of the more famous cases in this area is *Samaritan Foundation v. Superior Court*, 844 P. 2d 593 (Ariz. App. Div. 1 1992). In this case, parents of a baby who had a cardiac arrest during surgery sued the hospital and two doctors. Following the cardiac arrest, the hospital's legal department assigned a nurse-paralegal to interview three nurses and a scrub technician who witnessed the surgery. During the litigation, the plaintiffs deposed those four witnesses, who then claimed they could not remember what had happened in the operating room. When the plaintiffs learned that the witnesses had been interviewed soon after the surgery, they petitioned the trial court to order disclosure of the summaries of the interviews taken by the paralegal, arguing that because she was not an attorney, her notes were not covered by the attorney-client privilege statute, which did not include paralegals (although the statute did include an attorney's secretary, stenographer, or clerk). The court of appeals concluded, however, that since the law has recognized that lawyers may appropriately and efficiently act through their paralegals, lawyers should not have to stop assigning litigation tasks to paralegals just to maintain the privilege. Therefore, it held that, "a lawyer does not forfeit the attorney-client privilege by receiving otherwise privileged client communications through the conduit of a properly supervised paralegal employee." *Id* at 599–600. Nevertheless, the court concluded that the paralegal's summaries were discoverable by the plaintiff, under the first part of the work product rule. (This case was later vacated in part by *Samaritan Foundation v. Goodfarb*, 862 P.2d 870 (Ariz. 1993), on grounds unrelated to the paralegal's role in the interviews.)

Other courts have also held that the attorney-client privilege and the work-product rule can apply to the work of the paralegal, or some other agent of the attorney. *See State v. Post*, 513 N.E.2d 754 (Ohio 1987). In a Kentucky case involving a plaintiff suing Wal-Mart over a purse snatching in its parking lot, Wal-Mart's tactics included delaying its responses for discovery materials. When pressed again for the materials, someone from the defense, later identified as a paralegal for Wal-Mart's in-house counsel, responded in writing that the materials did not exist. The plaintiff then sought to depose the paralegal (which was agreed to by the defense), resulting in Wal-Mart firing its defense counsel and hiring new counsel who moved to prohibit the deposition. In ruling that the paralegal could be deposed on a limited basis not involving privileged information, the Kentucky Supreme Court concluded that, as a matter of law, the attorney-client privilege and the work product rule apply with equal force to a properly supervised paralegal. *Wal-Mart Stores v. Dickinson*, 29 S.W.3d 796 (Ky. 2000).

But it is not true that everything a paralegal does during litigation is protected by the attorney-client privilege or covered by the work product rule. Courts usually hold that for a non-lawyer's work to be covered by the attorney-client privilege, the work must be of such a nature that the performance of it required professional skill. If the non-lawyer's work required no particular expertise and could have been done by a layperson, the argument could be made that the work should not be protected by the privilege. In fact, in *Samaritan Foundation v. Superior Court*, discussed earlier, the court made sure to emphasize that it was not creating a paralegal-client privilege. It was only applying the attorney-client privilege where the paralegal's work was of such a substantive nature that it warranted being covered by the attorney-client privilege. *Samaritan Foundation v. Superior Court* at 600.

Determining exactly what types of litigation-related work require professional skill is not as easy as it seems. That documents might take more than a few hours to prepare does not necessarily mean that professional skill was required to prepare them. In a New York case, plaintiffs sued a car company for injuries sustained in a car accident. During discovery, the plaintiffs' attorney traveled to the defendant's offices in Dearborn, Michigan, to examine boxes of documents concerning the design and development of the automobile plaintiff was driving at the time of the accident. About 30 of the 76 boxes were not available because, according to the defendant's attorneys, they were protected and confidential materials. Upon learning that one of the defendant's attorneys and two paralegals had reviewed all the boxes and prepared indexes describing the contents of the boxes, the plaintiff sought the indexes, and the defendant claimed the indexes were also privileged. The court found that indexes were not protected by the work product rule because the defendant presented no evidence that the indexes were created by using "any particular legal skills." *Bloss v. Ford Motor Co.*, 126 A.D.2d 804, 805 (N.Y. App. Div. 1987). See Exhibit 4–9 on how the paralegal's work is covered by the attorney-client privilege, which includes the work product rule.

EXHIBIT 4–9   THE PARALEGAL'S WORK PRODUCT AND THE ATTORNEY-CLIENT PRIVILEGE

- Statements made to the Paralegal in an attempt to seek legal assistance are covered by the attorney-client privilege, even where the jurisdiction's attorney-client privilege statute doesn't mention paralegals

- But, for the paralegal's work product—created during the course of litigation—to be covered by the attorney-client privilege, the *work must have required professional skill* (i.e. attorney skill)

The Attorney Work Product Rule and Dr. Phil

Before he began delivering psychological advice to the maladjusted guests on his television show, Dr. Phil McGraw was a therapist and jury consultant. Dr. Phil's fame was birthed by Oprah Winfrey after he advised her during the libel trial she won in 1998, a case where Texas cattlemen sued her for a disparaging comment she made about hamburger during one of her shows. And in 2003, Dr. Phil's consultation services in a federal class action lawsuit were the subject of an appeal resolving how a non-lawyer consultant's advice falls under the work product rule. When the accounting giant Ernst & Young was sued for accounting fraud (along with its client Cendant Corp.), it retained Dr. Phil to, among other things, help its witnesses prepare to testify. But that case was settled, and the two defendants then turned on each other. During the second case's discovery, Cendant Corp. sought what advice Dr. Phil had given to Ernst & Young employees expected to testify in the first case. Ernst & Young argued that Dr. Phil's work qualified for attorney work product rule protection, even though Dr. Phil was not an attorney, nor was he an employee of an attorney representing someone in the case, nor was he expected to offer expert testimony (that type of expert is covered by another procedural rule). Overruling the district court, the 3rd Circuit Court of Appeals concluded that Dr. Phil's advice and notes were covered by the work product rule, despite his status as a non-lawyer consultant, because he was hired at the behest of Ernst & Young's defense counsel as part of its defense. And because Dr. Phil's advice was sought for the confidential purpose of trial strategy and was given in the presence of Ernst & Young's attorneys, the Court of Appeals ruled that Dr. Phil's advice and notes were also covered by the more stringent, "attorney-opinion work product" rule. *In re Cendant Corp. Securities Litigation*, 343 F.3d 658 (3rd Cir. 2003). Dr. Phil himself is no stranger to ethical scrapes, including being reprimanded by the Texas State Board of

Examiners of Psychologists, being accused of not paying his business expenses, and agreeing to a $10.5 million settlement with plaintiffs who sued him over his promotion of diet supplements.

Tips to Protect Confidentiality and the Attorney-Client Privilege

Certain practices can be deployed to minimize unintended breaches of confidentiality. First, lawyers and paralegals need to be vigilant about discussing client matters outside the office, especially in public places such as the hallways of the courthouse or in restaurants. The word *overheard* is in the dictionary for a reason. Client matters should also not be discussed at home with family members or with personal acquaintances for this simple reason: what is the guarantee that the person to whom you tell client matters will not violate a promise to you to keep things confidential when he or she knows that you are already broke your promise to the client?

At the office, a few extra steps to ensure protection of client information can be taken. Although e-mail can be sent unencrypted without violating the duty of confidentiality, it should be encrypted because encryption is relatively easy to accomplish. Having on file the client's permission to communicate by e-mail can protect against later malpractice charges. Paralegals should also change their computer passwords regularly to make it more difficult for others to access e-mail accounts and computer files. Files should never be left in the open, or even given to unauthorized personnel in the firm, because there is no such thing as an absolute, implied authorization that covers all employees of a law firm. Phone conversations with clients or about client matters should not occur within earshot of others. Mobile phones should not be used to discuss client matters. And those legal assistants who work for lawyers who share common office space (such as waiting or conference rooms) with other lawyers who are not in a partnership must be especially careful. Because what a client says in public areas can be considered unprotected by the attorney-client privilege, then receptionists, secretaries, and legal assistants should do their best to prevent clients—and prospective clients—from discussing their situation in common areas. And if an occasion occurs where the client tells the paralegal something, but requests that the paralegal not pass that information on to the lawyer (a minor subplot in the comedy *Legally Blonde*), the paralegal needs to tactfully explain to the client that the duty of confidentiality starts with the attorney. Paralegals may withhold no client information from their supervising attorneys, regardless of any client requests to the contrary. See Exhibit 4-10 on tips to avoid breaching client confidentiality.

EXHIBIT 4–10 PROTECTING AGAINST BREACHES OF CONFIDENTIALITY

- Use encrypted e-mail.
- Get client permission to communicate by email.
- Change computer passwords frequently.
- Be careful on the phone.
- Be careful in common office space.
- Protect files and other client documents from the eyes of others.
- Remember the WWII phrase, "loose lips sink ships".

Because paralegals do considerable amounts of discovery work, it is critical that they never send discovery materials to the opposing party's counsel without making sure the materials can be sent. Although many jurisdictions refuse to consider that the attorney-client privilege has been waived by inadvertent disclosure, there is no guarantee that harm will not come to the client (or paralegal) due to the error. Asking a supervising lawyer whether certain documents should be sent, even if the original instructions by the attorney were that the documents should be sent, can prevent the paralegal from being wrongfully blamed for sending protected materials. Because lawyers balance many cases at the same time, good legal assistants should take it upon themselves to be a bit paranoid and, if in doubt, ask their supervising lawyers for confirmation that what was instructed to be sent should in fact be sent.

When marking discovery materials as protected, paralegals should mark them in a permanent way, because Post-it® notes and other labels can fall off privileged materials. If inadequately labeled privileged materials are mistakenly sent to the opposing party's counsel and the receiving counsel is initially unaware of the mistake, the attorney-client privilege can be considered waived in certain jurisdictions. Even if a court were to find that the privilege has not been lost by inadvertent disclosure, that in no way protects the firm if and when the disgruntled client files a grievance with the disciplinary commission or a malpractice action against the firm. See Exhibit 4–11 on how to protect against inadvertent disclosure, and Exhibit 4–12 on the confidentiality family tree.

EXHIBIT 4–11   QUICK TIPS TO PROTECT AGAINST INADVERTENT DISCLOSURE

1. Mark privileged or permanent documents in a permanent way.

2. When in doubt whether certain discovery materials should be sent to the other side, confirm with your lawyer.

3. If you think you may have inadvertently sent privileged materials, or have received privileged materials, tell someone quickly!

EXHIBIT 4–12   SUMMARIZING THE CONFIDENTIALITY FAMILY TREE

1. The Duty of Confidentiality (ethics rules: MR 1.6 or DR 4-101; MR 1.18)
   • prohibits the voluntary disclosure of client information

2. The Attorney-Client Privilege (witness competency statutes)
   • prevents the compelled disclosure of confidential information

3. The Work Product Doctrine (civ. pro. rule 26(b)(3))
   • presides over the discoverability of lawyer and paralegal-created materials, prepared in the course of litigation

4. Inadvertent Disclosure (MR 4.4(b))
   • provides the opportunity to cry foul after fouling up

SUMMARY

The doctrine of confidentiality is one of the foremost ethical considerations in the law, and it takes shape in three interrelated concepts: the duty of confidentiality; the attorney-client privilege; and the work product rule. The duty of confidentiality is found in the rules of professional responsibility, while the attorney-client privilege is located in the litigation-related rules of discovery and evidence.

Jurisdictions that apply the Model Rules consider client information, from whatever the source, protected as confidential. However, jurisdictions that apply the Model Code consider client confidences and secrets protected. The American Bar Association's Ethics 2000 proposal for Model Rule 1.6 was significantly different from its prior version. The most recent version allows the disclosure of client confidences to prevent reasonably certain death or substantial bodily harm, as well as to seek legal advice. In 2003 the ABA approved an earlier-rejected proposal allowing for disclosures necessary to prevent a crime or fraud caused by the client's use of the lawyer's services.

Client confidentiality attaches before the client has retained the lawyer's services and survives the lawyer-client relationship. A new Model Rule, 1.18, addresses what confidentiality is owed a prospective client. If the client is an organization, the organization, and not its constituents, is the recipient of the duty of confidentiality. Agents of the lawyer, such as the lawyer's paralegal, are also covered by the duty of confidentiality and are expected to treat client information in the same manner as is expected of the lawyer. Lawyers have implied authorization to disclose client information that is necessary to proceed with the representation, such as in settlement negotiations.

Both the Model Rules and the Model Code allow a lawyer to disclose client information, even sensitive information, under certain, exceptional circumstances. The duty of confidentiality can be breached to prevent the client from committing serious crimes or fraud or to defend against criminal charges or charges made by the client or collect fees. When the law allows an attorney to disclose client information, the attorney may only disclose that which is essential for the purpose of the exception.

Although there are risks involved in using certain technology to conduct client business or to communicate with clients, many jurisdictions do not prohibit attorneys from using e-mail, fax machines, mobile phones, or wireless Internet when engaged in client business. Some jurisdictions advise obtaining client consent before using e-mail or mobile phones, and a few jurisdictions caution against using either technology. The ABA issued a recent ethics opinion on the propriety of attorneys searching for metadata (the data embedded in electronic documents) when receiving electronic documents in e-mails, and the conclusion reached was that such investigation did not violate the Model Rules.

The attorney-client privilege is a concept derived from the rules of discovery and evidence. It generally protects against lawyers being compelled to testify against their clients or to disclose otherwise confidential client communication, and is usually found in statutes on witness competency rather than in the rules of ethics. If the client makes statements to his or her lawyer in a context that can reasonably be construed as not made in confidence, those statements can be obtained if a court considers that the context effected a waiver of the attorney-client privilege. As well, certain kinds of information, such as fees or the client's identity, can be considered not covered by the duty of confidentiality.

The work product rule, as found in federal and state versions of civil procedure rule 26(b)(3), does allow a limited exception for client information that was prepared in anticipation of litigation to be turned over to the other party under extreme circumstances. However, even within that exception, parties are not allowed access to materials that express the legal strategies or theories of the other parties' attorneys. The attorney-client privilege covers employees of the attorney, including legal assistants who are the recipients of information made by clients or prospective clients. If, during the course of discovery, lawyers inadvertently disclose privileged materials to the other party, that mistake can result in a waiver of the attorney-client privilege. However, many jurisdictions consider inadvertently disclosed materials to remain covered by the privilege.

Paralegals and legal assistants are expressly authorized to deal in client matters and can have access to client information. While working on client matters, they should take precautions to prevent unauthorized persons from having access to client information, and should refrain from discussing client matters with those not covered by attorney-client confidentiality. Moreover, while working on discovery matters, paralegals and legal assistants should exercise great caution when marking materials as protected materials and also when turning discovery materials over to the other parties' attorneys, because it is possible that inadvertent disclosure can result in a waiver of the attorney-client privilege, if not a malpractice claim. For a paralegal's work to be covered by the attorney-client privilege or the work product rule, it must be the kind of work that requires some level of professional skill.

ETHICS IN ACTION

1. Kennedy was quite surprised to see Robert come through the doors of her law firm. Robert was a family friend whom she had known for decades, because Kennedy's and Robert's mothers had become friends at college. And just last month, Kennedy attended Robert's mother's funeral. Kennedy worked for a lawyer in the firm's tax department, and when she saw Robert meeting with an attorney who did estate planning, she thought Robert was there to have an estate plan created, as a result of his mother's death. She exchanged pleasantries with him as he was getting ready to leave the office, but didn't ask him about why he was there. Later in the afternoon, she stopped by the office of Kathleen, the attorney Robert had seen, and mentioned that she was a friend of Robert. In response, Kathleen told Kennedy that Robert was planning on suing to set aside his mother's will on the grounds that Robert's mother lacked the capacity to make a will. Evidently, Robert had heard from his sister Caroline, whom he despised and was the estate's executor, that their mother had given almost nothing to him. After hearing Kathleen exclaim about what a loyal and good son Robert had been to his mother, Kennedy remarked, "That's not really true. He pretty much ignored her in the last few years." Kennedy then shared some juicy stories about Robert's relationship with his mother and sister that Kennedy had heard from her mother.

   Did Kathleen violate the duty of confidentiality by discussing Robert's case with Kennedy? Did Kennedy violate the duty of confidentiality by discussing Robert's family history with Kathleen?

(continues)

ETHICS IN ACTION   *(continued)*

2. Sarah works for an attorney who uses her in a variety of substantive capacities, and one of the things she really enjoys is interviewing clients. Just yesterday, she got another opportunity when Frank came to the firm. Sarah's boss introduced himself and Sarah to Frank, and then left to attend an emergency hearing on another matter. Sarah and Frank engaged in some small talk and then got down to business. Frank was there because he had been injured at Disney World and was considering suing. During the course of the interview, Sarah learned the facts of the incident and Frank's injuries. She also learned that Frank was so angry at how Disney employees treated him after he fell out of the "It's a Small World" ride (he reached to touch one of the singing characters), that he vandalized a men's bathroom and stole about $50 worth of merchandise from a Disney store in the German part of Epcot. Frank said it in passing, almost as if he didn't realize he was talking out loud. Frank never hired Sarah's boss to represent him because the day after the interview Frank saw a television commercial by a lawyer who said, "Big corporations fold like cheap suitcases when they see my name on a lawsuit!"

    Does the duty of confidentiality protect Frank's criminal actions from being disclosed by Sarah or her boss because Frank never was their client? Would your answer change if either Sarah or her boss were Disney Corporation shareholders?

3. Dan has been accused of hit and run. The evidence at the accident scene led investigators to his house. Inside Dan's garage was his pick-up truck. Paint from the victim's car was on the front fender of Dan's truck. Dan hired Mario to represent him and is planning to plead guilty, hoping for a light sentence because no alcohol was involved and because Dan has a clean driving record. Mario's paralegal Rick had been discussing plea bargain options with the prosecuting attorney's office and asked Dan to come to the office to discuss them. While talking with Dan, Rick blurted out something that had been weighing on him. Rick said that it didn't make sense that Dan would have been out late at night when the accident occurred, particularly because Dan is raising his teenage grandson, who would have been home alone when Dan caused the accident. Having watched one too many *CSI* episodes, Rick told Dan that he wondered if maybe Dan's grandson was driving the car that night. Dan paused for a few seconds, and then acknowledged that Rick's hunch was right: Dan was in bed sleeping that night and his grandson, who took the keys without permission, was the one who caused the accident. Dan said he couldn't bear the thought of his grandson, who has already had a few minor brushes with the law,

(continues)

ETHICS IN ACTION *(continued)*

having to go to a juvenile facility or even to jail, so he took the blame. After telling Rick the real story about the accident, Dan became quite agitated when he insisted that Rick keep this secret to himself and not tell Mario.

Does the duty of confidentiality require that Rick abide by Dan's request?

4. Nadia is an attorney hired by an automobile company to internally investigate whether the company covered up safety issues on its largest and biggest selling line of SUVs. A consumer watchdog group has made these charges in the press, and the company is quietly investigating the allegations, while publicly denying the charges. Nadia has begun interviewing employees in the engineering division and yesterday met with Erin, a secretary to one of the engineers. She seemed almost relieved to talk to Nadia. Erin began to tell Nadia that her boss Russell told her last year to lose the original safety test results on those SUVs because the company didn't like the results and was going to put a different-sized tire on the test vehicle and re-run the tests. Erin knows that the tires used in the first round of tests were the tires put on the SUVs at the factory for the first six months of production. She also knows that the safety results the company touts come from the second set of tests done with the tires now put on the SUVs. She did destroy the original test results, but not before making a copy to take home, which violates company policy. In fact, Erin is the anonymous source who caused the consumer group to raise the charges when they did. After telling Nadia what has been burdening her for the past few months, she exclaimed, "I'm so glad the company hired an outside attorney because I know I can trust you to keep this confidential. I'll lose my job if they find out what I did, and I'm a single mother of two. But, I just had to get this off my chest."

Is Nadia bound by the duty of confidentiality to keep Erin's secret? Does Nadia have a duty to report what she knows to the proper government authority?

5. Darrin is a college professor being sued for sexual harassment by Elizabeth, a colleague who claims that Darrin repeatedly made unwanted and untoward comments to her, leered at her while she was in her office, and touched her inappropriately in an elevator. Darrin denied making any inappropriate comments to Elizabeth, claimed he has no idea how anyone could judge what constitutes a leer, and says he touched her in the elevator because he was pushed up against her by the rush of people crammed into it during finals week. Lauren is defending Darrin, and Colin is Lauren's paralegal. Colin has been helping Darrin with discovery tasks and has quite a cordial relationship with him. One Saturday while Colin was grocery shopping, he saw Darrin in the bakery. They were chatting while others were placing their bread orders and Darrin made a comment about Elizabeth that Colin didn't hear. Out of habit, Colin said, "What did you say?" and Darrin repeated even louder

(continues)

ETHICS IN ACTION   *(continued)*

an ugly comparison between a sourdough loaf and a part of Elizabeth's anatomy. Even worse, a friend of Elizabeth's overheard Darrin crassly mention Elizabeth's name and then start laughing. So, the friend told Elizabeth, who then told her lawyer, who then sought to depose Colin about what Darrin told him at the grocery store that day.

In your jurisdiction, is Colin covered generally by the attorney-client privilege? If so, do you think the attorney-client privilege shields Colin from being deposed?

6. Two computer companies are engaged in copyright infringement litigation over software that company A claims it now owns after purchasing the small company that created it. Company B claims it has a valid licensing agreement that predates the sale of the small company to A. During discovery, company A asks company B for any correspondence between it and its legal counsel regarding the viability of continuing the licensing agreement if the company were ever sold. Although company B's lawyers in this present suit were getting ready to refuse that request, claiming it was protected by attorney-client privilege, copies of some letters and e-mails between company B and its legal counsel were inadvertently sent to company A. During the firestorm that followed the inadvertent disclosure, company A learned that one of company B's paralegals summarized every correspondence and e-mail that had been inadvertently been sent, as well as other correspondence and e-mail that hadn't been sent. The trial court ruled that the privilege still attached to those correspondences and e-mail, so company A's counsel then requested that company B send the paralegal's summaries.

Are those summaries covered by the work product rule or the attorney-client privilege?

■ POINTS TO PONDER

1. What are the reasons the duty of confidentiality is such a hallowed principle?

2. How does the Model Rules version on confidentiality differ from the Model Code version?

3. What is the difference between client information and client confidences?

4. How does the Ethics 2000 version of MR 1.6 differ from its prior version?

5. Using your jurisdiction's rules, determine whether your jurisdiction's confidentiality rule is based on the Model Code or the Model Rules and whether your jurisdiction's rule is different from its ABA counterpart.

6. When would an attorney have an implied authorization to disclose client information?

7. Are there any kinds of information that can generally be considered as not confidential?

8. What is the ABA's position on what confidentiality duty is owed a prospective client? Does your jurisdiction have any official position on confidentiality and the prospective client?

9. How do the confidentiality rules affect paralegals and legal assistants?

10. What makes the doctrine of confidentiality more difficult to grasp in cases where the client is an organization, such as a corporation?

11. Going back to the scenario at the beginning of the chapter, what advice would you give Rachel about her dilemma concerning whether to do anything about the information that the client, William, has settled with other women who accused him of sexual assault?

12. What are the basic exceptions to the requirement that client information be kept confidential?

13. What policy concern is consistent behind all of the exceptions identified in question 12?

14. Do you think a lawyer should be allowed to tell a grieving family where their child is buried if he or she knows where the client buried the body and the client has already been found not guilty? What if the client has been found guilty? If the lawyer discloses the information, should he or she be disbarred for breaching one of the duties of professional responsibility?

15. What limitations apply when a lawyer is considering disclosing client information to prevent a crime or fraud?

16. Do you think a lawyer should be obligated to disclose to a client's sexual partner that the client has an infectious disease?

17. What is the attorney-client privilege? How is it different from the duty of confidentiality?

18. When would a paralegal be covered by the attorney-client privilege?

19. What is the work product rule?

20. Is the paralegal covered by the work product rule?

21. What distinguishes the two kinds of work product?

22. Why do jurisdictions consider that the attorney-client privilege has not been waived in cases where privileged materials have been inadvertently disclosed to the other party?

23. What is the criticism of the ABA ethics opinion stating that when lawyers are in receipt of protected materials mistakenly sent to them that they should not examine them and instead should follow the other lawyer's wishes about returning the materials?

24. Do you think a lawyer should be allowed to take advantage of the opposing party's otherwise protected material when it is erroneously sent to him or her?

25. Do you think it is fair for an attorney or paralegal to search for metadata when in receipt of the opposing counsel's electronic documents? What can be done to prevent the release of metadata?

26. In addition to techniques mentioned in the chapter, are there other techniques paralegals can use to help ensure client confidentiality?

27. In addition to techniques mentioned in the chapter, are there other techniques legal assistants can use to help ensure that they are not involved in inadvertent disclosure?

■ KEY CONCEPTS

Attorney-client privilege	Implied authorizations
Attorney-opinion work product rule	Inadvertent disclosure
Confidentiality exceptions	Informed consent
Corporate constituents	Last link doctrine
Discovery	Privileged materials
Duty of confidentiality	Witness competency statutes
Encrypted e-mail	Work product rule
Fiduciary	

■ KEY TERMS

constituent	interrogatories	securities exchange commission
discovery	office of independent counsel (OIC)	(SEC)
fiduciary	prima facie	solicitor general
fraud	restatement	waived
informed consent	retainer	

Online Companion™
For additional resources, please go to
http://www.paralegal.delmar.cengage.com

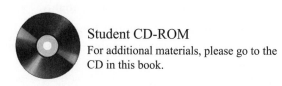

Student CD-ROM
For additional materials, please go to the
CD in this book.

CHAPTER 5

Conflicts of Interest

INTRODUCTION

If a hall of fame for great American lawyers were to be built, the first inductee might be John Adams. Although one of the most significant founding fathers and early presidents (see Chapter 1), Adams's austere personality was less memorable than those of colonial icons Benjamin Franklin and Patrick Henry. And Adam's presidency was sandwiched between two historical giants, George Washington and Thomas Jefferson. Like Jefferson, Adams was a lawyer.

In fact, as a Boston-area resident, Adams was involved in one of the most wrenching legal cases of the colonial period. On March 5, 1770, British soldiers in Boston fired on an angry crowd that had begun throwing rock-filled snowballs and sticks at a British sentry. Five people were killed in what became known as the Boston Massacre. Among those killed was Crispus Attucks, a free black man who has been called America's first casualty of the fight for independence. The British soldiers were charged with murder and in desperate need of a capable lawyer, because most people in Boston thought the trial would be a formality to the soldiers' execution.

Although he was an area resident with ties to the local protest movement, John Adams agreed to serve as the soldiers' lead defense counsel, all other local lawyers having turned down the defendants' requests. His task was to convince the jury that in response to the activities of the mob in the street that day, the soldiers had fired in self-defense. So successful was Adams in the six-day trial (the first trial in Massachusetts to last longer than a day) that all but two of the defendants were acquitted. Moreover, the two convictions were for manslaughter, rather than murder, and the punishment was thumb branding rather than death.

"No man is above the law and no man is below it; nor do we ask any man's permission when we ask him to obey it."

PRESIDENT THEODORE ROOSEVELT

"When the President does it, that means it is not illegal."

PRESIDENT RICHARD NIXON

235

How was John Adams treated during this ordeal? He was reviled by his fellow townspeople and patriots for his lack of loyalty to their cause. Those fellow townspeople included John Adams's cousin, Samuel Adams, believed by some to have been the instigator behind the mob gathering that day. (Samuel Adams would later achieve immortality for instigating the Boston Tea Party and having a beer named after him.) John Adams's wife and children were also treated maliciously. Adams, however, believed that every accused person had a right to a fair trial. So great was the tension over the conflict between Adams's political and personal beliefs as a New England colonial and his professional obligations as a lawyer that he wrote in his diary that during that time period, that he was "never in more misery my whole life." However, John Adams's duty to the law was so strong that he later wrote of his defense of the Boston Massacre defendants, "It was, however, one of the most gallant, generous, manly and disinterested Actions of my whole Life, and one of the best Pieces of Service I ever rendered my Country." L. H. Butterfield, ed. *The Diary and Autobiography of John Adams.* Boston: Harvard University Press, 1961. Such a wonderful testament to professionalism in the face of a conflict of interest is even more impressive in light of the fact that Adams reported that he was never even thanked by the highest-ranking British officer for whom Adams had obtained an acquittal.

When a lawyer undertakes to represent a client, he or she not only pledges confidentiality to the client but also pledges, in a more general sense, loyalty to the client. Loyalty is the starting point for conflicts of interest rules. Because lawyers are fiduciaries, they are bound to put their clients' interests ahead of their own. Although it may have been advantageous for the cause of the New England protestors—a group to whom John Adams belonged—that the British soldiers be found guilty of the Boston Massacre, upon agreeing to take the case, John Adams's loyalties to his friends and fellow citizens took a backseat to the loyalty to his clients. If the same situation were to occur today, would the conflicts of interest rules even allow a lawyer such as John Adams to undertake such a representation? We will see.

The duty of loyalty takes effect most directly in the rules of professional responsibility that concern conflicts of interest: ABA Model Rules 1.7 through 1.11, and 1.13; and DR 5–101 through 107, DR 7–106, and DR 9–101 of the ABA Model Code. Because paralegals are obligated to comport themselves in the same professional manner as lawyers, they also need to be concerned with the various conflicts that can occur in the lawyer-client relationship. However, because paralegals do not directly advocate on the client's behalf, the conflicts rules may not always be directly applicable to them. This chapter's discussion will include an examination of conflicts of interest that arise in the following situations: when two present clients of the lawyer are in conflict with one another; when a present client is in conflict with a former client; when two present clients are seeking joint representation; and when a client's interest may be in conflict with the lawyer's interests. We will also analyze certain kinds of transactions between lawyers and clients that are either prohibited or severely

---

EXHIBIT 5–1   WHAT MAKES CONFLICTS OF INTEREST SO SIGNIFICANT?

- The fiduciary duty of **client confidentiality**
- The danger of **divided loyalties**

---

limited. Finally, we will examine the difficulties that occur when lawyers and legal assistants move from one firm to another and then represent clients whose interests are in opposition to a party represented by the firm where the lawyers or legal assistants used to work. This is known as imputed disqualification, and here, the law generally provides more leeway to paralegals than it does to lawyers. Bear in mind, as the conflicts rules are examined, that the lawyer's and the paralegal's right to earn a living and the general public's freedom to have the lawyer of their choice will occasionally allow for exceptions to the conflicts rules. Exhibit 5–1 shows why conflicts of interest are such a big deal for law firm employees.

The Model Rules' Starting Point for Conflicts of Interest

The source for many jurisdictions' general rule on conflicts of interest states the following:

(a) A lawyer shall not represent a client if the representation of that client will be directly adverse to another client, unless:
(1) the lawyer reasonably believes the representation will not adversely affect the relationship with the other client; and
(2) each client consents after consultation.

(b) A lawyer shall not represent a client if the representation of that client may be materially limited by the lawyer's responsibilities to another client or to a third person, or by the lawyer's own interests, unless:
(1) the lawyer reasonably believes the representation will not be adversely affected; and
(2) the client consents after consultation. When representation of multiple clients in a single matter is undertaken, the consultation shall include explanation of the implications of the common representation and the advantages and risks involved. ABA Model Rule 1.7.

Section (a) of the rule concerns actual conflicts of interest between different clients, while section (b) concerns possible conflicts between different clients, between the client and a third party, and between the client and the lawyer's own interests. This rule, as with many rules, has exceptions, but in this case do the exceptions overshadow the rule? If a client can consent to the representation notwithstanding the conflict, as is the case in both sections of MR 1.7, then is anything prohibited by the rule? Yes, there are some absolutes. The Comment to MR 1.7 states that clients may not be given the opportunity to give consent to continued representation involving directly adverse conflicts when "a disinterested lawyer would conclude that a client should not agree to the representation." While what is direct or material may not always be clear, it is clear that in such situations, the client cannot consent to the lawyer's continuing representation.

Ethics 2000 and Conflicts of Interest

There have been more than a few changes made to the conflicts of interest rules by the Ethics 2000 Commission, which will be summarized throughout the chapter. At this point, an overview of the changes to MR 1.7 is necessary.

The newer version of MR 1.7 is structurally different; the rule is entirely rewritten. See Exhibit 5–2 for the Ethics 2000 version of MR 1.7. The emphasis now is on what is referred to as a "concurrent conflict of interests." There is a single paragraph that defines concurrent conflict of interest to mean either directly adverse conflicts between current clients or conflicts occurring when there is a "significant risk that the representation of one or more clients will be materially limited by the lawyer's responsibility to another client, a former client, or a third person or by a personal interest of the lawyer."

The new version also makes it explicitly clear that the lawyer may not seek client waiver in certain kinds of conflicts, such as when two clients of the same lawyer are suing each other. (That issue will be discussed in a later section of the chapter.) The proposal requires "informed consent" (as opposed to the words "consent after consultation," as used in the 1983 version) and also requires that for the lawyer to establish that the client has given informed consent, the consent must be given in writing. Informed consent is a fuller concept than consent; it is defined in Ethics 2000 Rule 1.0(e) to include the lawyer "communicat[ing] adequate information and explanation about the material risks of and reasonably available alternatives to the proposed course of conduct."

The Model Code and General Conflicts of Interest

The Model Code of Professional Responsibility has a rule that is similar to the 1983 version of MR 1.7. DR 5–101(A) states, "Except with the consent of his client after full disclosure, a lawyer shall not accept employment if the exercise of his professional judgment on behalf of the client will be or reasonably may be affected by his own financial, business, property, or personal interests." DR 5–105 (A) states that a lawyer shall decline proffered employment if the exercise of his independent professional judgment in behalf of a client will be or is likely to be

EXHIBIT 5–2 ABA MODEL RULE 1.7 – THE ETHICS 2000 VERSION

Present and Possible Conflicts	The Exceptions
1.7(a) Except as provided in paragraph (b), a lawyer shall not represent a client if the representation involves a concurrent conflict of interest. A concurrent conflict of interest exists if: (1) the representation of one client will be directly adverse to another client; or (2) there is a significant risk that the representation of one or more clients will be materially limited by the lawyer's responsibilities to another client, a former client or a third person or by a personal interest of the lawyer.	**1.7(b)** Notwithstanding the existence of a concurrent conflict of interest under paragraph (a), a lawyer may represent a client if: (1) the lawyer reasonably believes that the lawyer will be able to provide competent and diligent representation to each affected client; (2) the representation is not prohibited by law; (3) the representation does not involve the assertion of a claim by one client against another client represented by the lawyer in the same litigation or other proceeding before a tribunal; and (4) each affected client gives informed consent, confirmed in writing.

adversely affected by the acceptance of the proffered employment, or if it would be likely to involve him in representing differing interests, except to the extent permitted under DR 5–105(C).

Section (C) states: a lawyer may represent multiple clients if it is obvious that he can adequately represent the interest of each and if each consents to the representation after full disclosure of the possible effect of such representation on the exercise of his independent professional judgment of behalf of each.

COMMON CONFLICTS OF INTEREST

Because there is more than one conflicts of interest rule, the possibilities of conflicts that face attorneys and their non-lawyer employees are many (see Exhibit 5–3). An analysis of all the conflicts of interests envisioned by the rules is beyond the scope of this text. But there are some conflicts of interest that are more likely than others to occur, six of which will be explained below.

Double Representation: One Lawyer Representing the Plaintiff and the Defendant

A lawyer cannot represent the plaintiff and the defendant in the same lawsuit because there is no more direct conflict that can occur between parties than when they are on opposite sides of litigation. Suppose someone who is sued for negligence stemming from an automobile accident tries to retain a lawyer to represent them, only to find out that lawyer is already representing the plaintiff.

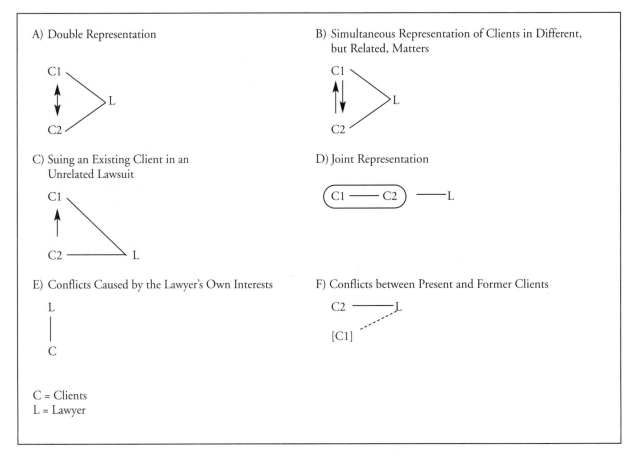

A) Double Representation

B) Simultaneous Representation of Clients in Different, but Related, Matters

C) Suing an Existing Client in an Unrelated Lawsuit

D) Joint Representation

E) Conflicts Caused by the Lawyer's Own Interests

F) Conflicts between Present and Former Clients

C = Clients
L = Lawyer

EXHIBIT 5–3 Common Conflicts of Interest

Unlike a character from a television comedy who has accidentally booked two dates in the same restaurant at the same time, the lawyer can have no loyalty to either client if representing both of them at the same time, against one another. As a California court put it neatly, "[an] attorney's duty of loyalty to a client is not one that is capable of being divided." *Flatt v. Superior* Court, 885 P.2d 950, 953 (Cal. 1994). *See also Alex Munoz Gen. Contractor, Inc. v. MC3D, Inc.*, 1998 WL 831806 (N.D. Ill. Nov. 25, 1998) (a law firm that represents a corporation cannot also represent the shareholders of the corporation in a lawsuit against the corporation); *In re Cendant Corp. Securities Litigation*, 124 F.Supp.2d 235 (D.N.J. 2000) (a law firm may not represent a corporate defendant in litigation when it also represents a former high-ranking employee of the opposing party in the same case).

As mentioned earlier, the Ethics 2000 version of MR 1.7 specifically addresses this conflict. MR 1.7(b)(3) prohibits a lawyer from representing one client asserting a claim against another client who is represented in that case by the same lawyer. Some states, such as Texas, expressly prohibited lawyers from representing opposing parties in the same litigation before the ABA did. Texas Disciplinary Rules of Professional Conduct, Rule 1.06(a) (1999). But since the Ethics 2000 revisions, many states have adopted the current version of 1.7—which prohibits a lawyer from this most direct conflict of interest. Those states include Arizona, Arkansas, Colorado, Delaware, Indiana, Louisiana, Minnesota, Nebraska, Nevada, Rhode Island, South Carolina, Utah, and Vermont.

Can Divorcing Spouses Share the Same Lawyer?

Perhaps you have heard about divorcing couples who have used the same lawyer because the breakup was amicable and both spouses agreed to all the terms of the divorce. While it is possible that such a non-confrontational divorce could be obtained (with both spouses satisfied in the cost savings that come from sharing one lawyer), it is important to remember that spouses getting divorced are officially antagonists to each other, so sharing the same lawyer is like playing with matches. An Ohio case shows the conscience-straining conflict that is attendant when one lawyer crosses the fence separating warring spouses. In it, a lawyer was suspended indefinitely for, among other violations, representing men accused of domestic violence, while, at the same time, representing their wives, who invoked their Fifth Amendment rights so they would not have to testify against their husbands. Although not divorcing spouses, at least not yet, the husbands were the accused attackers and the wives were the alleged victims and, therefore, the court found such dual representations to be impermissible, even though agreed to. *Office of Disciplinary Counsel v. Brown*, 737 N.E.2d 516 (Ohio 2000).

Some jurisdictions expressly prohibit a lawyer from representing both spouses in a divorce, regardless of the circumstances. Iowa, for instance, not only has the current version of 1.7, but it has an additional sentence, 1.7(c), which states, "In no event shall a lawyer represent both parties in dissolution of marriage proceedings." Utah has an ethics opinion that prohibits it. Utah Bar Ethics Op. 116 (1992). Wisconsin has expressly held that lawyers may not represent both spouses seeking a divorce. *In re Whitnall*, 619 N.W.2d 926 (Wis. 2000). Two West Virginia cases show the evolution of such a prohibition. In the first one, the West Virginia Supreme Court held that an attorney may not represent both spouses in any stage of a separation or divorce. *Walden v. Hoke*, 429 S.E.2d 504 (W.Va.1993). Three years later, an attorney was sanctioned because, while representing the husband in an amicable divorce, he also prepared the response to the divorce complaint for the wife, who was representing herself, pro se. Although the lawyer prepared the wife's answer at the request of the husband, that did not alter the court's view that the lawyer violated his duty of loyalty to the husband. *Lawyer Disciplinary Bd. v. Frame*, 479 S.

E.2d 676 (W.Va. 1996). And in a more egregious Georgia case, an appellate court upheld a jury's finding of punitive damages against a lawyer who initially represented a husband in a divorce, but later switched sides to represent the wife, and eventually the lawyer and her paralegal forged the husband's signature. *Peters v. Hyatt Legal Services*, 469 S.E.2d 481 (Ga. Ct. App. 1996).

There are, however, some jurisdictions that have given limited approval to divorcing spouses sharing their lawyer. An Oregon ethics opinion initially states that such a representation is inappropriate, but it then lists 10 divorce-related factors and states that if all 10 are present, then dual representation may be appropriate. Oregon Formal Op. 1991–86 (1991). Some of those factors include there being no minor children, the wife not being pregnant at the time of the divorce, and the couple having no substantial assets or liabilities. And in an Indiana case where a lawyer was charged with violating Ind. Rule 1.7 for representing both spouses in a divorce and later representing the husband against the wife's suit for nonpayment of a loan, the court concluded that defending the husband violated the conflict of interest rule, but that the evidence was inconclusive about whom the lawyer represented in the divorce. Nonetheless, it stated that, "[r]egardless, the evidence does establish that the [lawyer's] actions were taken with the full knowledge and consent of the husband and the wife." *Matter of Lively*, 658 N.E.2d 903, 905 (Ind. 1995).

Which Client Gets the Lawyer?

Whom should the lawyer represent if the plaintiff and the defendant are current clients? The Comments to MR 1.7 state that when such conflicts of interest arise, whether at the beginning, or during the course, of representation, the lawyer is obligated to withdraw from the representation. MR 1.16(a)(1) also requires that a lawyer withdraw from representing a client if "the representation will result in violation of the rules of professional conduct." Therefore, if an attorney is requested by two current clients to represent them in litigation against each other, he or she must decline both requests. And if, during the course of representing a client, the attorney becomes aware that the representation will cause a direct conflict with another client, he or she must withdraw. Direct conflicts can also occur when another client is not an opposing party but might be involved as a witness on the opposing side. A 1992 ABA ethics opinion even stated that a lawyer may not represent a client in litigation if he or she would be required, in the course of the litigation, to cross-examine another of his or her own clients. ABA Comm. on Ethics and Professional Responsibility, Formal Op. 92–367 (1992).

A slightly different problem occurs when a lawyer represents two current clients in a matter that has not yet reached the situation where one client is suing the other. Imagine, for instance, an attorney acting as an advisory intermediary between two clients discussing the terms for the sale of a piece of real estate. If the performance of the contract terms is thought to be insufficient by one of the parties, such conflict could lead to litigation. Although the exception to the earlier-cited rule requires client consent, a client can only be given the option to consent after the lawyer determines that the conflict is not a direct conflict. See *Florida Bar v. Sofo*, 673 So. 2d 1 (Fla. 1996), in which a lawyer was disciplined for representing different corporations in the same matter, which eventually became contentious.

Simultaneous Representation of Clients in Different, but Related, Matters

A lawyer cannot properly represent both the plaintiff and the defendant in the same lawsuit; that much is clear. But a similar conflict can arise when a lawyer represents two clients who are in different lawsuits that involve a related issue or antagonist positions. For example, imagine an attorney representing a defendant in a tort case that results in settlement following mediation. Following the mediation, however, the defendant refuses to honor the settlement agreement and the plaintiff seeks the representation of the defendant's lawyer who helped negotiate the settlement. Even though attempting to enforce a settlement agreement is distinct from the original cause of action, the defendant's lawyer cannot represent the plaintiff because the connection between the two matters is too close.

For example, in a Florida case, a lawyer was reprimanded for the following reasons: she represented an employee in a successful unemployment compensation case; the employer then brought a suit against the employee, which was dismissed. Then, when the employee brought a malicious prosecution suit against the employer, the lawyer represented the employer. *Florida Bar v. Milin*, 502 So.2d 900 (Fla. 1986). Similarly, a Colorado ethics case involved one bad accident and one close call. A lawyer was hired to represent an uninsured driver charged with crimes in connection to a car accident, one in which his passenger was injured so badly he was put into a medically induced coma, suffered memory loss, and endured two months of convalescence. After the passenger made contact with the lawyer to help his driver-friend, the passenger began to complain about his medical treatment and his own insurance company's response to his situation. The lawyer then entered into a contingent fee arrangement to represent the passenger, but quickly withdrew upon realizing the danger zone he had entered. That quick u-turn helped the lawyer prevent his own accident. *People v. Mercer*, 35 P.3d 598 (Colo. O.P.D.J. 2001).

This kind of conflict of interest can also occur in settings other than litigation. In an Indiana case, a lawyer who was representing a bankruptcy client proceeded to sell a car to that client that the lawyer was leasing from another client (but was authorized to sell). The lawyer never informed the client who purchased the car that he was selling it on behalf of another client. In reprimanding the lawyer, the court mentioned that both clients' interests were clearly antagonistic because a buyer and seller have opposite aims, with the seller wanting the highest price possible and the buyer wanting the lowest price possible. Therefore, the lawyer should have informed the purchasing client about the conflict of interest and given that client an opportunity to seek independent representation for the purchase of the car, or to consent to the lawyer's continued representation. *In re Horine*, 661 N.E.2d 1206 (Ind. 1996). Other jurisdictions have formally expressed disapproval of lawyers representing both buyers and sellers in the same transaction: *In re Wagner*, 599 N.W.2d 721 (Iowa 1999); *In re Ford*, 732 N.Y.S.2d 115 (App. Div. 2001). But other jurisdictions' ethics opinions allow for such a dual representation, provided the clients are made aware of the potential for problems and give their informed consent to continue: S.C. Ethics Op. 00-17 (2000); Mass. Ethics Op. 90-3 (1990).

Suing an Existing Client in an Unrelated Suit

In *The Godfather*, Vito Corleone is the only client of his lawyer, who also happens to be one of Corleone's sons, albeit an adopted son. Such is not the case for most real-life lawyers, who have many clients. And, as law firms get bigger and establish offices in different cities or even countries, it is possible that lawyers from one office of the same firm might be asked to be involved in litigation against another party who is a client from another office of the same firm. Although the firm could not represent both sides to the same litigation, it is possible that it could be involved in the unrelated suit against another client, if both clients give their consent. This would require one of the clients using a different firm for their representation, or else the matter would no longer be "unrelated." The Comments to MR 1.7 acknowledge such a representation by saying that a corporate or government lawyer may serve as an advocate against the corporate enterprise or government in unrelated matters if doing so would not adversely affect the lawyer's relationship with the main client, and if both parties consent after consultation. Not only is a conflict of loyalties a pitfall in such a representation, but there is also a danger of a breach of the duty of confidentiality. These possibilities must be discussed with both clients as part of the consent consultation.

Conflicts issues of this type can be difficult to grasp because, outside the clearly prohibited representations, whether consent can be given or whether the representation is appropriate is extremely fact-sensitive and depends on whether there is a "directly adverse" conflict. A Nebraska lawyer was publicly reprimanded for a violation of this sort. The Nebraska lawyer had assisted an Iowa lawyer in representing a plaintiff attempting to sue an insurance carrier on a worker's compensation claim. However, at the same time the former lawyer was the insurance carrier's lawyer in different matters. Reprimand was the chosen sanction because, rather than being an intentional violation, the lawyer negligently failed to discover the conflict. *State ex rel. Nebraska Bar Ass'n v. Frank*, 631 N.W.2d 485 (Neb. 2001). In an older case, a lawyer was sanctioned for representing a husband in a worker's compensation claim while at the same time representing the man's wife in the couple's divorce. The court called the unrelated representations "decidedly antagonistic." *Memphis & Shelby County Bar Ass'n v. Sanderson*, 52 Tenn. App. 684, at 707 (Tenn. App. 1963). In another case, a law firm represented a bank in a matter and then was disqualified from representing a defendant who was being sued by the bank in an unrelated matter involving a **trust**. *Harrison v. Fisons Corp.*, 819 F. Supp. 1039 (M.D. Fla. 1993). And in a complex Florida case, a law firm was disqualified from representing the trust of a man who died **intestate** (because his will was improperly executed), where the trustee was trying to move the dead man's assets into the trust, while the law firm already represented an heir of the dead man (on similar but directly unrelated matters) who hoped to inherit whatever was available. *Morse v. Clark*, 890 So.2d 496 (Fla. App. 2004).

The American Bar Association, as well as state and local bar associations, have issued ethics opinions in this area of conflicts of interest. The ABA issued an opinion in 2004 involving a dicey quandary where a client asked a lawyer to draft a new will disinheriting the testator's son, a child who was the lawyer's client on another matter. May the lawyer do such a thing? Generally yes, because drafting a will for a father is not "directly adverse" to the son, at least not in the sense conveyed by conflicts of interest doctrines. ABA Comm. on Ethics and Professional Responsibility, Formal Op 05–434 (2004).

In 1995, an ABA ethics opinion concluded that a lawyer who represents a corporate entity is not *per se* disqualified from representing a client in an unrelated matter that is adverse to an affiliate of the corporate entity. However, the corporate entity must give its consent to the representation. ABA Comm. on Ethics and Professional Responsibility, Formal Op. 95–390 (1995). And in 1991, the ABA cautioned against lawyers simultaneously representing individual partners of a partnership and the partnership on unrelated matters. The caution was because of the chance that the lawyer will come into confidential information that he or she would not be allowed to convey to the other client and that might require him or her to withdraw from representing both clients. ABA Comm. on Ethics and Professional Responsibility, Formal Op. 91–361 (1991). The Illinois ethics committee found that it is not automatically inappropriate for a lawyer to represent a city government that is a defendant in a personal injury suit and also represent a party suing the same city in a zoning case, as long as both clients consent following consultation. Ill. State Bar Ass'n Comm. on Professional Ethics, Op. 94–21 (1995). And a Philadelphia ethics opinion said that a law firm may represent unrelated clients in unrelated matters and advocate antagonistic positions. But if both cases result in appeals to the same appellate court, then the firm must obtain both clients' consent to continue the representation. Philadelphia Bar Ass'n Professional Guidance Comm., Op. 89–27 (1990).

■ **trust**
A legal mechanism where property is held by one party for the benefit of another. A trust is created when the Donor transfers the property into the trust, where the Trustee holds the legal title to the property, while the Beneficiary of the trust has the equitable title in the property, which means the benefits (income) of the trust are provided to the beneficiary.

■ **intestate**
The legal status of someone who dies without having left a will, which includes having a will that is later deemed invalid.

Issue Conflicts

Issue conflicts, rather than actual, positional conflicts, can arise in this area as well. An issue conflict occurs when a lawyer makes a legal argument on behalf of one client that, if successful, could be detrimental to the situation of another of the lawyer's clients. Suppose that in 1995, the Los Angeles Police Department tried to hire Johnnie Cochran to defend it against charges stemming from the formal investigation, following the Rodney King riots, of allegations that it had historically conspired against minorities and occasionally planted evidence against suspects. Even though Johnnie Cochran was a more than capable defense attorney, he was, at that time, advocating an argument on behalf of his client, O. J. Simpson, which included specifically arguing that the Los Angeles Police Department did conspire against a minority and planted evidence. Even though the two, separate lawsuits do not involve the same parties (the state of California, not the police department, was prosecuting O. J. Simpson), there is a clear issue conflict here. It would be unlikely, therefore, that O. J. Simpson could consent (assuming he wished to) to such a dual representation involving antagonistic issues. A 1993 ABA ethics opinion, speaking to the problem of issue conflicts, makes it more likely that issue conflicts can be overcome with client consent if the two matters are pending in different jurisdictions. ABA Comm. on Ethics and Professional Responsibility, Formal Op. 93–377 (1993).

Joint Representation: Two Clients with the Same Lawyer

When two clients seek joint representation by the same lawyer, they appear to have interests that are aligned. Unlike two parties on opposite sides of the lawyer's conference table, being on the same side does not present the kind of problem the conflicts of interest rules directly address. But what starts out on friendly terms can eventually take a turn for the worse, and the Ethics 2000 version of Model Rule 1.7(a)(2) addresses this type of risk. Bear in mind, though, that 1.7(b) provides the triggers that allow two or more clients to consent to sharing the same lawyer, despite the potential for it resulting in headaches or fireworks. Three areas of joint representation will be discussed: joint representation in criminal cases; joint representation in civil cases; and joint representation in non-litigation settings.

Joint Representation in Criminal Cases

Should an attorney represent co-defendants in a criminal case? According to the official Comment for MR 1.7, "The potential for conflict of interest in representing multiple defendants in a criminal case is so grave that ordinarily a lawyer should decline to represent more than one codefendant." For example, when the infamous tandem of Lyle and Erik Menendez were charged with murdering their parents in 1989, each brother had his own defense lawyer, even though the brothers' defense was aligned (both claimed parental abuse and self-defense). Because a criminal defendant's liberty is at stake, the possibility that one co-defendant's defense could be at odds with that of another is so grave that many legal scholars believe joint representation should not be undertaken.

On the other hand, criminal defendants do have a constitutional right to defense counsel, a choice that could include a co-defendant's counsel. But a defendant's desire to have the same lawyer as a co-defendant's can be trumped by the conflict of interest dangers. The United States Supreme Court has issued several cases on joint representation of co-defendants in criminal cases. In *Wheat v. United States*, 486 U.S. 153 (1986), the Court upheld a district court's refusal to allow a defendant in a drug conspiracy case to use the lawyer of two fellow defendants (both of whom had consented to the joint representation and one of whom had pled guilty to a lesser charge). Even though the Court acknowledged a defendant's generalized right to choose his or her own lawyer, it stated that a defendant's Sixth Amendment rights are not violated when a trial court sees an actual conflict of interest and refuses to allow the joint representation. *Id.* at 162. Two other Supreme Court cases, *Holloway v. Arkansas*, 435 U.S. 475 (1978), and *Glasser v. United States*, 315 U.S. 60 (1942), show the Court's contrary view on joint representation in criminal cases. One state even took the position that convictions will be reversed when there is joint representation of co-defendants unless the trial record shows that the defendants made a written request for joint representation and then clearly waived the possibility of conflicts of interest. *Shongutsie v. State*, 701 P.2d 361 (Wyo. 1992).

The U.S. Supreme Court continued to shape the conflict of interest doctrine in a case in 2002 that, although not involving co-defendants, concerned a curious possible conflict in a criminal case. In *Mickens v. Taylor*, 535 U.S. 162, a defendant who was sentenced to death for a heinous sexual assault and murder argued that his Sixth Amendment right to counsel was in effect denied. He argued this because one of his court-appointed lawyers was representing the murder victim on unrelated criminal charges at the time of the murder, a fact the lawyer did not acknowledge to the trial court or the defendant. But the court concluded that such a *possible* conflict of interest, without any evidence that that the representation was affected by an *actual* conflict that affected the outcome of the trial, does not equal ineffective assistance of counsel.

Joint Representation in Civil Cases

Clients who seek joint representation in civil litigation must still be consulted as to the ramifications that their joint interests might diverge. The likelihood that the representation of one client will adversely affect the lawyer's relationship with the other client is increased in a corporate setting if the lawyer represents both a corporation and members of its board of directors. If, for instance, the corporation and the board members are sued for misconduct in a **shareholder's derivative lawsuit**, the lawyer who represents the corporation and the board will be in a bind and may have to **recuse** himself or herself from either representation, as will be discussed later in the chapter.

■ **shareholder's derivative lawsuit**

A lawsuit in which a shareholder of a corporation, on behalf of the corporation, sues the corporation's board of directors, alleging that their actions have harmed the corporation. Any benefits from the derivative lawsuit flow to the corporation, not personally to the shareholder.

■ **recuse**

When someone, such as a judge or other person of influence, removes him or herself from participation in a matter, because of a conflict of interest.

When co-plaintiffs are considering settling, conflicts can arise if some plaintiffs want to settle but others do not. The ABA has stated that when there is disagreement about settlement among co-plaintiffs in a mass tort case, the lawyer must first obtain a waiver of conflicts from the co-plaintiffs who do not want to settle, or else obtain independent counsel for them before proceeding further on behalf of the plaintiffs who want to settle. ABA Comm. on Ethics and Professional Responsibility, Formal Op. 371 (1993). In an Arizona case, an attorney represented co-defendants being sued for breach of contract and fraud. In the course of the litigation, it became clear that the co-defendants had inconsistent positions, but rather than informing them about the conflict, the attorney continued to represent both clients. He then showed his divided loyalty in a letter to one client when, in reference to the defense of the other client, he wrote, "It is to *our obvious advantage* to assure that [the other client] is as friendly as possible to us." *In re Shannon*, 876 P.2d 548, 557 (Ariz. 1994). Needless to say, the attorney was severely disciplined. *Id.* at 577.

As litigation progresses, specific theories of liability can evolve as investigation and discovery take place. Although joint defendants and joint plaintiffs might seem to have identical claims or objectives, the attorney representing the simultaneous parties may come to realize that the parties have conflicting interests, despite the similar objectives. This can occur in the insurance field, where the lawyer who is employed as in-house counsel for the insurance company (who might want to settle the case or bring it to an end quickly) to represent or defend the insured party (who might not want to settle the case at all) finds himself or herself on the horns of a dilemma: the employer or the client? The ABA issued an ethics opinion on that subject in 2003, concluding that insurance staff counsel may represent the insurance company's clients, provided they acknowledge their employment status with their clients and exercise independent judgment for their clients. ABA Comm. on Ethics and Professional Responsibility, Formal Op. 03-430 (2003).

The following case from Florida shows, almost comically, how extreme conflicts can arise when an attorney represents two plaintiffs in the same litigation.

CASE LAW   *Florida Bar v. Mastrilli*

614 So.2d 1081 (Fla. 1993)

PER CURIAM.

This cause is before the Court on complaint of The Florida Bar for review of the referee's recommendation that Kenneth W. Mastrilli, an attorney, be disciplined for ethical violations. We have jurisdiction. Art. V, § 15, Fla. Const.

(continues)

CASE LAW *Florida Bar v. Mastrilli* (continued)

The referee's findings of fact are supported by substantial competent evidence and thus are accepted by this Court. In 1989, Mastrilli undertook representation of two women allegedly injured in an accident while one was the driver and one was the passenger in the same vehicle. Mastrilli issued demand letters on behalf of the passenger against the insurance carrier of the driver on grounds the latter had been negligent, resulting in alleged injuries to the passenger totalling $100,000.00. The driver's insurance policy would cover only $50,000.00 of any loss.

When the insurance company denied payment, Mastrilli then filed suit in 1990 against the driver on behalf of the passenger. In effect, he filed suit against his own client in the same matter for which he had been retained. The driver terminated Mastrilli's employment when she received the complaint and learned she had been sued by her own attorney. The passenger's lawsuit eventually was settled for $20,000.00, within the limits of liability.

The referee concluded that Mastrilli had violated Rules of Professional Conduct 4–1.7 (a) and 4–1.7(b) and noted that Mastrilli has shown no remorse for his actions. The referee then recommended discipline of six months' suspension.

Mastrilli now argues that he was merely negligent in failing to discover a conflict of interest and that, in any event, no harm has come to either client. We do not agree with Mastrilli's representation that he was merely negligent. Mastrilli undertook representation of both the passenger and driver, and he either knew or should have known that their interests were adverse when he sued one on behalf of the other. The Florida Standard for Imposing Lawyer Sanctions 4.32 states:

> Suspension is appropriate when a lawyer knows of a conflict of interest and does not fully disclose to a client the possible effect of that conflict, and causes injury or potential injury to a client.

Here, Mastrilli either knew or should have known of the conflict; and there was a potential that his actions would expose his client, the driver, to a personal liability of up to $50,000.00. Accordingly, suspension is warranted. Accordingly, we adopt the referee's findings of fact and findings that Mastrilli violated the rules of conduct noted above. We suspend Mastrilli from the practice of law for a period of six months. The suspension will be effective thirty days from the filing of this opinion so that Mastrilli can close out his practice and protect the interests of existing clients. If Mastrilli notifies this Court in writing that he is no longer practicing and does not need the thirty days to protect existing clients, this Court will enter an order making the suspension effective immediately. Mastrilli shall accept no new business from the date this opinion is filed. Costs in the amount of $2,451.12 are hereby assessed against Mastrilli, for which sum let execution issue.

(continues)

CASE LAW   *Florida Bar v. Mastrilli* (continued)

Case Questions

1. Reread your state's version of MR 1.7 and then decide whether Mr. Mastrilli was capable of joint representation of both plaintiffs in the first place.

2. Do you think that the plaintiff/driver was likely to be aware of the theory her lawyer had in mind for her fellow plaintiff/passenger?

3. Why could it be said, despite Mastrilli's defense argument, that it is worse to be negligent in failing to see the conflict of interest in this joint representation than to proceed despite the observable conflict?

Joint Representation in Nonlitigation Settings

Two spouses getting divorced clearly should have independent representation. But should two spouses seek independent representation when having a will drafted? Probably they should not: most marital wills will rarely involve the kinds of conflicts of interest envisioned by the conflicts rules because most spouses likely share the same wishes about passing on their assets. However, when an engaged couple enters into a **prenuptial agreement**, should each party have independent representation? Although a prenuptial agreement is a transactional document made between two people whose personal interests are so aligned that they want to get married, the possibility of a conflict still exists because a prenuptial agreement is like a **liquidated damages clause** in a contract: it concerns breach of the relationship. Courts have voided prenuptial agreements due to conflicts problems in cases where one lawyer seemed to represent both parties, but was really representing one to the disadvantage of the other. *See Rowland v. Rowland*, 599 N.E.2d 315 (Ohio Ct. App. 1991). Conflicts can also arise when divorcing couples have other legal matters pending in which they are joint parties. For instance, suppose a husband and wife are divorcing. The husband has a divorce attorney, while the wife does not. At the same time, the couple is in bankruptcy proceedings and the husband's divorce attorney represents both spouses in that matter. Is this an impermissible conflict? An ethics opinion says yes, because the lawyer's interest in advocating for his client in the divorce is sufficiently threatened by representing the wife and the husband in the bankruptcy. Ill. State Bar Ass'n Comm. on Professional Ethics, Op. 98–06 (1998). Or suppose that two spouses are sharing the same lawyer in an uncontested divorce while the attorney is representing the husband against charges that he sexually assaulted the couple's seven-year-old daughter, among other things. Does that sound too unreasonable to be true? Unfortunately, it is true, and the court that suspended that attorney for 18 months (although the suspension was deferred) told him that it was unreasonable for him to think he could engage in such co-representation. *In re Houston*, 985 P.2d 752 (N.M. 1999).

■ **prenuptial agreement**

A contract entered into by two people intending to marry each other, in which the people agree in writing to their respective property rights in the event of divorce or death.

■ **liquidated damages clause**

A part of a contract that predetermines the monetary damages one party would owe the other in the event of breach of contract. Liquidated damages need to be a reasonable estimate of the damages suffered in order to be valid.

Similar conflicts can arise when buyers and sellers of real estate share the same lawyer. Because the buyer wants to pay as little as possible and the seller want to sell for as much as possible, the lawyer representing them both faces the risk that buyer's remorse, seller's remorse, or other problems are likely to be directed at the lawyer who, one party may feel, did not adequately look out for him or her. Some states, such as New Jersey, prohibit buyers and sellers in complex real estate transactions from sharing the same lawyer. *Baldasarre v. Butler*, 625 A.2d 458 (N.J. 1993). However, other states, such as New York, Florida, and Massachusetts, allow lawyers to represent sellers and buyers (or lenders and buyers) if the parties consent and the lawyer clearly explains the terms to all parties. *In re Pohlman*, 604 N.Y.S.2d 636 (App. Div. 1993); *Florida Bar v. Belleville*, 591 So. 2d 170 (Fla. 1991); Mass. Bar Ass'n Ethics Comm., Op. 90–3 (1990).

The following case from Florida shows what can happen when one lawyer represents both parties to a real estate transaction and one of the parties is underrepresented.

CASE LAW *Florida Bar v. Clark*

513 So.2d 1052 (Fla.1987)

PER CURIAM

This disciplinary proceeding is before the Court for consideration of the referee's report. The referee found the respondent attorney, Frank Clark, III, guilty of professional misconduct and recommended disbarment. The respondent has not filed a petition for review. As provided by Rule 3–7.6 of the Rules Regulating The Florida Bar, this Court must review the referee's report and render an appropriate judgment.

The referee found that Lois Resch agreed to purchase a condominium from Ronald A. and Angela Kenney. Ms. Resch agreed to assume the obligations of first and second mortgages on the property. The parties to the sale met at respondent's office for the closing. Ms. Resch had the impression that respondent as attorney was advising both the Kenneys and herself. Respondent, the referee found, did nothing to discourage this impression. The closing statement reflected that the two parties to the sale were each charged half of the attorney's fee exacted for the transaction. Ms. Resch executed documents assuming responsibility for the two existing mortgages. She was provided payment coupon books and was instructed to make payments without contacting the mortgagees.

Later Ms. Resch discovered that the mortgagees were under no obligation to allow her to assume the mortgages and that neither the sellers nor respondent had sought consent for the assumption of the mortgages. As a result the mortgagees declared the loans due and Ms.

(continues)

CASE LAW   *Florida Bar v. Clark* (continued)

Resch was forced to refinance the indebtedness in order to retire the preexisting mortgages. She obtained a less favorable interest rate and had to pay arrearages that had accrued before her purchase.

Although not recited by the referee, record testimony also showed that in addition to assuming the two mortgages, Ms. Resch also signed a promissory note in favor of the sellers, Mr. and Mrs. Kenney. They sold the note to a third party. When Ms. Resch discovered the nonassumable nature of the mortgages, she suspended payment on the note. The purchaser of the note filed a legal action to collect the amount due. The purchaser was represented in that legal action by the respondent.

The referee found that respondent had violated the following Disciplinary Rules of the former Florida Bar Code of Professional Responsibility: D.R. 5–105(A), for accepting employment when it was likely to affect the representation given to another client; D.R. 5–105 (B), for continuing multiple employment when his independent professional judgment was likely to be adversely affected; D.R. 6–101(A)(2), for handling a matter without adequate preparation; and D.R. 6-101(A)(3), for neglecting a legal matter entrusted to him. . . .

We approve the referee's report. Frank Clark, III, is hereby disbarred. As it appears that he is presently under suspension for nonpayment of bar dues, this disbarment shall take effect immediately.

Case Questions

1. Was Clark the attorney for Ms. Resch? Why or why not?

2. What legal misunderstandings caused Ms. Resch so many problems?

3. In addition to his underrepresentation of Ms. Resch, what else did Clark do that may have contributed to his disbarment?

Conflicts of interest are at stake when the same lawyer in a private adoption represents the adoptive and biological parents. For instance, if the biological mother would like some periodic visitation rights or information about the child's well being, but the adoptive parents are opposed, each side will need independent representation. Two New York cases involving joint representation of biological and adoptive parents have shown the courts' disapproval. *In re Michelman*, 616 N.Y.S.2d 409 (App. Div. 1994); *In re Adoption of Vincent*, 602 N.Y. S.2d 303 (Fam. Ct. 1993). Furthermore, the ABA has opposed joint representation of biological and adoptive parents in private adoptions. ABA Comm. on Ethics and Professional Responsibility, Informal Op. 87–1523 (1987).

Conflicts Caused by the Lawyer's Own Interests

Could John Adams adequately represent the Boston Massacre defendants under today's rules on conflicts of interest? Clearly, a lawyer in favor of independence, with friends and family members involved in the same cause, has to have a considerable internal conflict when faced with the prospect of representing British soldiers accused of murdering that lawyer's fellow colonials. While Model Rule 1.7(a) (or Ethics 2000 1.7(a)(1)) concerns representations that involve conflicts between clients of the lawyer, MR 1.7(b) (or Ethics 2000 1.7 (a)(2)) concerns how the lawyer's ability to represent the client is affected by the lawyer's responsibilities to a third person, as well as the lawyer's own interests. It prohibits a lawyer from taking a case if the representation of the client, "may be materially limited by the lawyer's responsibilities to another client or to a third person, or by the lawyer's own interests." But if the lawyer believes that this type of conflict of interest will not adversely affect his or her representation of the client, he or she can continue the representation after seeking the client's consent. Had this type of rule existed in 1770, John Adams could have ethically represented the British soldiers, because they obviously would have consented to Adams's representation, considering no other lawyers would take their case. The kinds of personal interests that may materially limit the lawyer's representation of the client include financial, business, or personal interests. Certain, specific kinds of interests are covered later in this chapter, in the section titled "Special Circumstances: Prohibited Transactions."

Financial Interests

Although a lawyer may refuse a case because of financial concerns, it is unethical to base representation decisions on his or her own financial interests. The United States Supreme Court, when dealing with a case involving the propriety of a civil rights case settlement being conditioned on the plaintiffs waiving their right to have the defendant pay the plaintiffs' legal fees, not only stated that such fees waivers can be accomplished, but also found that there is really no ethical dilemma for the plaintiffs' attorney because the attorney's duty to advise the plaintiffs about the decision to settle should be made only with respect to the clients' interests, without any consideration of the lawyer's financial interests. *Evans v. Jeff D.*, 476 U.S. 717, at 728 (1986).

Business Interests

If a lawyer has a business interest connected to representation of the client, it may cloud his or her advice. Such a business interest is not an automatic impediment, but the lawyer needs to make the client aware of the possible conflict and seek his or her consent to continue the representation. For example, in a Wisconsin case, an attorney represented a restaurant corporation in which he was also a shareholder and director. When another client later asked the attorney to represent him in some business dealings with the restaurant corporation, this client was aware that the attorney represented the restaurant corporation but unaware that the attorney had a personal, business interest in the restaurant corporation. The attorney never advised the client about his own business interest in the corporation nor how it might be affected by the actions desired by the client. The lawyer was disbarred for this and other conflicts of interest violations. *In re Charlton*, 498 N.W.2d 380 (Wis. 1993).

Conflicts of Interest and America's Best Trial Lawyer

One of the legal community's superstars is David Boies, previously mentioned in Chapter 4. He has been called America's best trial lawyer, a worthy title for a man whose persuasive skills won him a professor's wife while attending his first law school, requiring that he attend a second law school. One of the country's most sought after—and highest paid—attorneys, with a client list of the powerful and influential, Mr. Boies is not without his share of conflicts of interest entanglements. He founded his law firm, Boies, Schiller & Flexner LLP, after leaving the mega-firm of Cravath, Swain, & Moore over a conflict of interest in 1997. At the time, he was representing George Steinbrenner, mercurial owner of the New York Yankees, who was suing Major League Baseball. Suing the league, in actuality, involved suing all the other owners, one of whom is Ted Turner, mercurial owner of the Atlanta Braves and also a client of Cravath, Swaine & Moore. Forty-Eight hours after being informed of the conflict, Boies left and formed his current firm. A more recent conflict of interest involved the intertwining of professional, personal, and business relationships. Many of Boies's clients need documents to be accessed, organized, stored, and copied for discovery purposes, and for the corporate clients, that can involve millions of pieces of paper. What those clients did not know was that the company Boies's law firm used for document-management services was Amici, a company owned in part by David Boies's children and founded by a Yale classmate who was convicted of felonies, including overbilling his clients. In one bankruptcy case, lawyers from Boies's former law firm, Cravath & Swaine, who were representing an accounting firm involved in that case, alleged it was forced to use Amici's services, and asked the bankruptcy judge to force Boise's current firm to resign from representing the bankruptcy client (cable company Adelphia). Boise Schiller did step down—after Adelphia requested it do so. Other bankruptcy clients, including Tyco International and Qwest Communications, have made similar claims that they were steered to use Amici's services, paying millions of dollars in fees, without knowing that, at least indirectly, this was benefiting Boies's children, who also owned a stake in a document-copying company, Echelon, which also provided services to Boies Schiller clients. In 2006, Amici was purchased by Xerox for $174 million, netting Mr. Boies's children $26 million.

Personal Interests

Although lawyers engage in advocacy for their clients, most clients do not expect that their lawyers personally agree with them or their beliefs. A prosecutor might be personally opposed to the death penalty, yet still argue for its imposition on behalf of the state; a defense lawyer might have no antipathy for capital punishment but argue that it is unconstitutional. A medical malpractice defense lawyer might never want to be anywhere near his or her client's stethoscope, but that need not prevent the lawyer from defending the doctor. These types of personal interest conflicts are accounted for by the Ethics 2000 version of MR 1.7(a)(2), but are not impediments to representation, provided the lawyer, "reasonably believes that the lawyer will be able to provide competent and diligent representation...." MR 1.7(b)(1).

Occasionally, lawyers fail the personal-interest-test not because of their personal beliefs, but because of their personal relationships. A New York ethics opinion concluded it was improper for a lawyer to send his real estate clients to a title company that was partially owned by his wife (N.Y. State Ethics Op. 738 (2001)). Another ethics opinion stated that no lawyer in a firm may represent a criminal defendant when the prosecution attorney is a sibling or spouse of one of the firm's lawyers (N.Y. State Ethics Op. 654 (1993).

Sexual Relationships with Clients

Strangely enough, the dating and intimate relationships between lawyers and their clients depicted in television and film might be the most accurate portrayal of all that passes for the practice of law, because there is plenty of case law concerning such relationships. However, usually left out of the fictionalized stories are the charges the clients will eventually bring against their paramours. Nevertheless, neither the Model Code nor the Model Rules had an express prohibition on such relationships, that is, until Ethics 2000 added a new part to Rule 1.8. Now, 1.8(j) forbids a lawyer-client sexual relationship, unless it predated the lawyer-client relationship. And not just "clients" are forbidden fruit: a prosecuting attorney was suspended for having a sexual relationship with her chief witness in a sexual assault case (*In re Joslin*, 13 P.3d 1286 (Kan. 2000)); a lawyer was reprimanded for having an affair with his client's spouse (*In re Munden*, 559 S.E.2d 589 (S.C. 2002)).

The dangers associated with lawyers engaged in intimate relationships with their clients are primarily two-fold. First, there is the problem of coercion or duress. The lawyer-client relationship is not an equal relationship (remember that lawyers are fiduciaries to their clients) and, on many occasions, clients are in varying states of vulnerability. That combination can lead to clients succumbing to pressure for sex because they feel they must comply with their lawyers' wishes. Even before Ethics 2000 expressly prohibited sexual relationships between lawyers and their clients, courts were quick to find violations of the former MR 1.7(b) and other rules, when lawyers engaged in such coercion. An Illinois case illustrates the coercion problem. A lawyer was suspended from the practice of law for three years because he had engaged in sexual relations with four clients, all encounters occurring at least seven years before the charges were brought. The clients were female divorce clients who claimed a similar pattern of sexual contact: the lawyer approached them in a sexual way in his office upon the first or second meeting and then had sex with them on later occasions. He also took nude pictures of some of them. All the clients claimed they felt they had to have sex with the lawyer because they feared that if they did not, their cases would be harmed or they would lose the retainer money they had paid him. Despite the lawyer's denial that any sexual relations occurred with these clients while he or his firm were representing them, he also argued that he could not be sanctioned because there was no express rule in Illinois forbidding lawyer-client sexual contact. The court found the argument unpersuasive, stating that the ethics rules are not manuals intended to govern a lawyer's conduct only when specifically covering every conceivable situation. *In re Rinnella*, 677 N.E.2d 909, 914 (Ill. 1997). And in a Kansas case, a lawyer was disbarred for having sexual relations with what the court termed "vulnerable divorce clients," even though there was no specific rule forbidding it. *In re Berg*, 955 P.2d 1240 (Kans. 1998).

The other danger involves the loss of objectivity that can accompany even those lawyer-client sexual relationships that are not a result of coercion or intimidation. Even if such intimacies would reasonably be considered mutual and not the product of coercion, such mixing of personal and professional relationships can cause the lawyer to represent the client in a way that is advantageous to the lawyer's personal interest. The ABA issued a formal opinion on this topic in 1992 and, while not expressly opposing all lawyer-client sexual involvement, it did advise lawyers against such behavior and stated that if such sexual relationships lead to impaired representation, "the lawyer will have violated the ethical obligations to the client." ABA Comm. on Ethics and Professional Responsibility, Formal Op. 92–364 (1992).

Some states have issued stronger statements than the ABA opinion, including Alaska (Alaska State Bar Gen. Counsel. Op. 92–6), Pennsylvania (Pa. Bar Ass'n Comm. on Legal Ethics and Professional Responsibility, Op. 97–100), and Maryland (which changed its Comment to MR 1.7 to discuss the matter). Some jurisdictions, such as Washington State, have modified their conflicts of interest rules by expressly prohibiting lawyers from having sexual relationships with their *current* clients. Wash. R.P.C., Rule 1.8(k). Even before doing so, the Washington Supreme Court suspended its former state bar president for having consensual sexual relationships with six of his former divorce clients, the last of which resulted in an ethics complaint. *In re Disciplinary Proceedings Against Halverson*, 998 P.2d 833 (Wash. 2000). And some jurisdictions, such as California, have modified their conflicts of interest rules to include sexual relationships with clients but have framed the rules in terms of whether the representation is conditioned on sexual relations, whether the client is coerced into sexual relations, or whether the representation will be adversely affected by such relations. Cal. Bus. & Prof. Code § 6106.9; Cal. R.P.C. 3-120.

How does this controversial subject apply to the paralegal? On the one hand, the stakes would be different if paralegals and clients were to become romantically involved because the dangers of coercion seem to be nonexistent. This is because the paralegal does not represent the client and is in no position to threaten him or her with limited or no representation. Also, because legal assistants do not actively represent the client and are prohibited from giving legal advice, the dangers of impaired representation due to such personal relationships seem not to apply. For example, Washington State's prohibition on lawyers having sexual relationships with their clients defines, for the purpose of the prohibition, a lawyer as "any lawyer who assists in the representation of the client, but does not include other firm members who provide no such assistance." Wash. R.P.C. 1.8(k)(3).

NOT QUITE LINCOLN

I Thought Only the Lawyers on on the TV show The Practice *Called Sex with a Client "A Hug Gone Bad"*

Sebastian Burns was in a Seattle jail in 2002 awaiting the beginning of the trial that would determine his fate and that of his best friend Atif Rafay. Rafay stood accused of bludgeoning Rafay's parents and sister to death in 1994. Burns and Rafay would eventually be convicted of murder and sentenced to three consecutive life sentences in 2004.

However, in 2002 Burns had been represented for two years by the capable public defender Theresa Olson. For reasons known only to them (but which can be surmised, as it concerns the 26-year-old, triple murder defendant sitting in jail for two years), their relationship evolved from professional to personal. This was evidenced in part by a three-page, sexual-innuendo-filled letter the married Ms. Olson sent to her 17-year-younger client at the King County Jail.

The other evidence was deduced by jail guards who, upon walking in on a meeting between lawyer and client in a conference room, observed Burns and Olson partially unclothed and using the conference table in what might be described as having sex. However, Ms. Olson provided the best description. In Clintonian fashion at the disciplinary proceeding that ensued, she refused to acknowledge what the guard claimed to have seen, and instead referred to the sexual congress as, "A hug gone bad." That depends on whom you ask.

Ms. Olson was removed from the case, and in 2005 was suspended from the practice of law for two years. Intentionally reminiscent of the former president's linguistic defense to similar accusations, two justices from the Washington State Supreme Court dissented from the suspension decision. They concluded that the discipline was too harsh because no witness testified to seeing the "act" of sex between Olson and her client.

Are paralegals and legal assistants immune to the chemical forces or temptations that have ensnared more than a few lawyers? No, and in a Missouri case, a legal assistant was accused of not only having an affair with the husband of a divorce client—during the divorce proceedings—but also disclosing client information and strategy to the husband. When the wife discovered the affair, she sued the law firm under the theory of employer-employee liability. *Logan v. Hyatt Legal Plans, Inc.*, 874 S.W.2d 548 (Mo.App. 1994).

There is another facet to consider, which is that relationships can dissolve, and when they do, both sides can have hurt feelings. That can lead a client, even long after the breakup, to bring charges against the lawyer or sue him or her for malpractice. Even if such charges would not lead to a judgment against the lawyer, the legal costs alone, as well as the embarrassment, should be enough to cause legal assistants to avoid romantic relationships with their firms' clients.

Although the following **companion cases** do not involve a paralegal, notice that these are the kinds of cases that could involve a paralegal. The first case involves a disciplinary process against an attorney for having a sexual relationship with his client. The second case concerns the malpractice case against the same attorney. As you read excerpts from the first case, notice the court's analysis of the nature of the relationship between the lawyer and his client. Then, while reading excerpts from the second case, notice the different version of the personal history as the client presented it against her former lawyer at trial, and also try to determine why the client sued her lawyer.

■ **companion cases**

Two or more appellate cases that are connected because they involve the same parties in similar legal situations, or different parties with the same legal issue.

CASE LAW   *In re DiSandro*

680 A.2d 73 (R.I. 1996)

PER CURIAM

This matter is before the court pursuant to a decision and recommendation of the Supreme Court Disciplinary Board (board) that the respondent, Edmond A. DiSandro, be publicly censured. The facts giving rise to these proceedings are as follows. In 1977 Maria del Rosario Vallinoto (Vallinoto) married Dennis Ledo. In 1987 the husband filed an action for divorce against Vallinoto in the Family Court. Among the issues involved in the divorce case were

(continues)

CASE LAW *In re DiSandro* (continued)

custody of a minor child of the marriage and distribution of the marital assets. Vallinoto retained the services of an attorney to represent her in the divorce filed by her husband. She quickly became dissatisfied with the quality of that attorney's representation and discharged him approximately one month later. She retained a second attorney but discharged that attorney after approximately two months. In May of 1987 she retained the services of respondent, who represented her to the conclusion of the divorce proceedings. The record discloses that Vallinoto received custody of the minor child of the marriage and was awarded approximately 60 percent of the marital assets.

In January of 1991 Vallinoto filed a multicount civil action in the Superior Court against respondent and his firm, alleging, inter alia, legal malpractice, battery, deceit, negligence, and the intentional infliction of emotional distress. A disciplinary complaint was also filed on her behalf with the Supreme Court Disciplinary Counsel. The civil action resulted in a jury verdict in favor of Vallinoto in the amount of $225,000. *Vallinoto v. DiSandro*, C.A. 91–390. These disciplinary proceedings commenced upon the conclusion of the civil action before the Superior Court. The board concluded that the sexual relations between respondent and Vallinoto were consensual. In reaching this conclusion, the board heard the testimony of Vallinoto and of respondent and had the opportunity to observe their demeanor and to assess their credibility. Vallinoto testified that she and respondent acted as boyfriend and girlfriend in front of others and that she was cordial to respondent's office staff. A friend of Vallinoto's testified at the disciplinary hearing that Vallinoto had told her that she was dating respondent. Vallinoto presented respondent with gifts, including a Christmas gift and a tape of love songs. The documentary exhibits before the board included a birthday card from Vallinoto to respondent with the written notation, "Love, Rosario," and another card with the printed notation, "You've got me right where I want me."

Rule 1.7 (b) of the Rules of Professional Conduct is substantially similar to Disciplinary Rule 5–101 (A). Rule 1.7 (b) provides, in pertinent part:

A lawyer shall not represent a client if the representation of that client may be materially limited . . . by the lawyer's own interests, unless:

(1) the lawyer reasonably believes the representation will not be adversely affected; and
(2) the client consents after consultation.

As we noted in *In the Matter of Robert F. Dipippo*, No. 96–235–M.P. (R.I., filed July 10, 1996), there is no specific prohibition contained within the Rules of Professional Conduct (or the Code of Professional Responsibility) regarding sexual activity between attorneys and their clients. However, any attorney who practices in the area of domestic relations must be aware that the conduct of the divorcing parties, even in a divorce based on irreconcilable

CASE LAW *In re DiSandro* (continued)

differences (a so-called no-fault divorce) may have a significant impact on that client's ability to secure child custody and/or may materially affect the client's rights regarding distribution of marital assets. An attorney who engages in sexual relations with his or her divorce client places that client's rights in jeopardy. The lawyer's own interest in maintaining the sexual relationship creates an inherent conflict with the obligation to represent the client properly. When an attorney represents a divorce client in a case in which child custody, support, and distribution of marital assets are at issue, the attorney must refrain from engaging in sexual relations with the client or must withdraw from the case.

We note that although the respondent's conduct may have placed his client's case in jeopardy, no actual adverse effect on the outcome of the client's case resulted. Accordingly we accept the recommendation of the board and impose the sanction of public censure upon the respondent. Had the client's case actually been prejudiced by the respondent's conduct, a more serious sanction may have been appropriate.

Vallinoto v. DiSandro, 688 A.2d 830 (R.I. 1997)

Bourcier, Justice

This case comes before us on appeal from a final judgment entered in the Superior Court following a jury's verdict in favor of the plaintiff, Maria Del Rosario Vallinoto (Vallinoto), and against the defendant, Edmond A. DiSandro (DiSandro). . . .

In May 1987, Vallinoto retained DiSandro to represent her in a divorce action brought against her by her former husband, Dennis Ledo (Ledo). Vallinoto, a citizen of Spain, married Ledo while living in Spain in 1977. They thereafter moved to this country. Ledo was an American citizen, but Vallinoto was not and was here on a so-called "green card." The marriage produced one child, Christina, who was also an American citizen. Vallinoto's marriage was by no means a tranquil or a happy one. She testified that during the course of her marriage to Ledo she had been restricted to the marital home, verbally abused, badgered, and belittled. She claims to have suffered severe mental depression and stress, to have entertained suicidal thoughts, and to have been "isolated" and "victimized" by Ledo throughout the course of their ten-year marriage. It was Ledo, however, who commenced the fateful divorce proceedings, with Vallinoto later counterclaiming for divorce.

After having retained and then dismissing two other attorneys with whom she had become dissatisfied in the course of the divorce proceedings, Vallinoto retained DiSandro in May of 1987. DiSandro's legal efforts on her behalf appear to have been both well performed and successful. DiSandro was able to obtain for her an increase in the weekly child support payments previously ordered for her daughter, Christina, from $15 to $30 per week to $150 to $200 per week. Moreover, at the time that her divorce became final on April 25, 1989, Vallinoto was awarded custody of Christina, 60 percent of the marital assets, several priceless paintings and heirlooms, and attorney's fees. Vallinoto, by her own account,

(continues)

CASE LAW *In re DiSandro* (continued)

acknowledged receiving excellent legal representation from DiSandro in her divorce proceedings as well as successful final results, all clearly evidenced in her final judgment of divorce. Unfortunately, however, DiSandro's relationship with Vallinoto extended far beyond his legal representation of her.

In August of 1987, some three months after having been retained to represent Vallinoto in her divorce action, DiSandro and Vallinoto became involved in an intimate physical relationship. That relationship continued until Vallinoto's last hearing on her divorce petition in December of 1988. DiSandro viewed the relationship as consensual. Vallinoto, on the other hand, alleged that she was compelled to perform sexual acts with DiSandro in part because of an alleged threat that DiSandro had once made to her, stating that if he discontinued his representation of her, she would be deported and lose custody of her child. She also alleged, in like vein, that DiSandro told her that he had undertaken to represent her only because she had been referred to him by a mutual friend and that good lawyers like himself usually did not take cases that other lawyers had started, which she interpreted to mean that if he withdrew as her counsel in her case, other good attorneys would not undertake to represent her. Vallinoto asserted that as a result of those implied threats, she felt compelled to comply with DiSandro's sexual demands, fearing that he would terminate his representation of her and that she would not thereafter be able to engage another competent attorney. Over the course of their approximately eighteen-month relationship, Vallinoto estimated that she and DiSandro were actively intimate almost 200 times, all without her consent. She later testified at disciplinary board hearings that the 200 number was really a guess on her part. In any event, the occurrence rather than the number is the significant factor.

During the jury trial below, DiSandro's law partner, Z. Hershel Smith (Smith), was called as a witness by Vallinoto to testify with regard to the nature of the relationship that existed between Vallinoto and DiSandro. Smith testified that contrary to Vallinoto's view of her relationship with DiSandro, he considered Vallinoto to be DiSandro's girlfriend. He recalled that at Christmas time, Vallinoto cheerfully came to DiSandro's law office and gave gifts to the office personnel, including DiSandro. Vallinoto herself testified that in the course of the relationship she frequently sent different greeting cards to DiSandro, many of which ended with an expression of "love" obviously intending to convey that emotion to DiSandro. Among the many trial exhibits was a greeting card containing the phrase "you got me right where I want me." By the time Vallinoto's divorce became final in early 1989, the affairs, both legal and nonlegal, between her and DiSandro had ended. She returned, however, to DiSandro some eight months later, seeking legal assistance on another matter

(continues)

CASE LAW *In re DiSandro* (continued)

in which she was being sued by her former husband, Ledo. She and DiSandro did not renew their sexual intimacy during that particular attorney-client relationship, and Vallinoto has never complained of DiSandro's handling of that matter for her.

The record also reveals that Vallinoto's extramarital interests, however, were not restricted to her attorney's participation. She admitted that during her ongoing sexual relationship with DiSandro and prior to the time of concluding her divorce petition hearings and continuing on thereafter into late 1989, she was dating someone other than DiSandro. In the summer of 1989 she traveled to Hawaii with that other person and shared the same hotel room with him for some two weeks. Later, in early 1990, she then began dating a new and different man. It was while planning with this latest man to purchase a larger house in which to live together that she decided to tell him of her previous sexual relationship with DiSandro. She eventually married that man in December 1990. It was some three weeks later, in January 1991, that she decided, with the encouragement of her new husband, to commence her litigation seeking monetary damages from DiSandro.

In her civil action . . . [s]he sought compensatory as well as punitive damages ...and the jury returned a general verdict for Vallinoto, covering all claims, for $25,000 in compensatory damages and $200,000 in punitive damages. DiSandro appealed. . . .

The case before us involves ...a negligence-based legal malpractice claim as opposed to a legal malpractice claim based on a breach of fiduciary duty. However, under either theory, plaintiff's claim for legal malpractice would fail. There is no relevant probative evidence in the trial record that suggests to us that the legal services rendered by DiSandro were made contingent on sexual involvement with Vallinoto. She clearly had the ability and the knowledge to discharge and leave DiSandro at any time if she was ever dissatisfied with his legal representation in her divorce case. She had earlier, prior to retaining DiSandro, discharged two previous attorneys with whom she had been dissatisfied. Moreover, according to her testimony, there were more than 200 incidents of sexual encounters between her and DiSandro, some taking place after romantic dinners at intimate restaurants and others during sleepovers at DiSandro's house. The numerous greeting cards she sent to DiSandro over the many months of the relationship, all expressing her love and affection for him, seem to indicate that it was a two-way affair. Additionally, she returned to DiSandro for legal representation long after the incidents of the alleged forced sexual relations concerned in her civil action had terminated and at a time when she was dating at least two other men, one of whom she married just before filing her action against DiSandro.

All those facts suggest to us that DiSandro's legal representation was kept separate and apart from the personal relationship that he embarked upon with Vallinoto. Accordingly, even though we certainly cannot and do not condone or excuse DiSandro's actions involving his extralegal relationship with his client, there is an absence of evidence in the

(continues)

CASE LAW *In re DiSandro* (continued)

record before us that would support Vallinoto's contention that DiSandro's legal services departed from the standard of due care required of DiSandro in his handling of her divorce case litigation by the attorney-client relationship.

We note additionally that even if a factfinder were to find that the legal services by DiSandro were a quid pro quo for sexual favors, Vallinoto's claim would still fail because of the complete absence of any competent and relevant probative evidence of damages that resulted to her legal position, or to her legal detriment personally, as a result of DiSandro's inappropriate sexual activities. She testified that DiSandro did an "excellent" job in representing her in her divorce action. She in fact received more than she had ever anticipated at the conclusion of her divorce proceeding. She was awarded custody of her child, an increase in support payments, 60 percent of the marital assets and several priceless paintings and heirlooms, as well as her attorney's fees. Her divorce action by all accounts, including hers, was certainly settled satisfactorily, and that result reflects the competency of DiSandro's legal representation. The complete absence of any evidence of damages resulting to her from his legal efforts on her behalf prevents any recovery on a negligence-based legal malpractice claim such as the one Vallinoto asserts in her complaint.

Accordingly, we conclude . . . the trial justice erred in not granting DiSandro's motion for a directed verdict on the malpractice count. . . .

Flanders, Justice, dissenting

I respectfully dissent because I believe that the defendant Edmond A. DiSandro's sexual depredation of the plaintiff while serving as her divorce attorney constituted a flagrant breach of the fiduciary duties he owed to his client and that this breach constituted legal malpractice. When, as here, a lawyer handling a divorce for a client enters into a sexual relationship with that client, I believe that lawyer has committed legal malpractice, regardless of the legal results obtained and how well the lawyer has performed the necessary legal services. Such misconduct is "a wrong that is distinct and independent from professional negligence *but still is legal malpractice*." (Emphasis added.) 2 Ronald E. Mallen & Jeffrey M. Smith, *Legal Malpractice* ¤ 14.1 at 229 (4th ed. 1996). . .

[The majority and dissenting opinions were quite long, dealing with five separate issues. Ultimately, the majority reversed the jury's verdict, and remanded the case for a new trial, while the dissent wrote that the jury's verdict was sustainable.]

Case Questions

1. Bearing in mind that the same court issued both of the preceding opinions— although the first opinion dealt with the disciplinary charges, while the second opinion concerned the civil lawsuit—what differences are noticeable in the presentation of the facts against the attorney?

(continues)

2. What did the client accuse her lawyer of doing to her? Why did the court refuse to agree with the jury's finding that her charges were valid?

3. Why did the court only reprimand the lawyer in the disciplinary case?

4. Why do you think the client filed a lawsuit against the attorney years after the representation ceased?

5. Based on both of the court's opinions, do you think a lawyer who does not have divorce clients (or who has divorce clients without any children or property disputes) may have sexual relationships with clients?

6. Do you think the court unfairly painted the amorous character of the client with too broad a brush in order to justify its decision, or do you think she got what she deserved for concocting a convoluted tale of woe? (One of the footnotes from the disciplinary case *In re DiSandro*, read in part: "The evidence presented to the Superior Court, tried before a jury, and that presented to the disciplinary board was significantly different. At the civil trial Vallinoto testified that she had been 'raped' 200 times by respondent. In the disciplinary proceeding, however, she acknowledged that there were far fewer incidences of sexual contact between her and respondent.")

Conflicts Between Present and Former Clients

As discussed in Chapter 4, lawyers continue to owe certain fiduciary duties to former clients, even those clients who fired their lawyers. Model Rule 1.9 concerns the duty of loyalty to former clients by establishing grounds whereby a lawyer would be prohibited from representing a present client because of the lawyer's prior-established duty to a former client. The Ethics 2000 version of Model Rule 1.9(a) states the following:

"A lawyer who has formerly represented a client in a matter shall not thereafter represent another person in the same or a substantially related matter in which that person's interests are materially adverse to the interests of the former client unless the former client gives informed consent, confirmed in writing."

The Model Code of Professional Responsibility had no disciplinary rule counterpart to MR 1.9, but Canon 9, which said, "A lawyer should avoid even the appearance of impropriety," was thought to cover former client conflicts, including those conflicts occurring when lawyers move to different firms. Because impropriety was undefined in the Model Code, little guidance was given by such a Canon.

MR 1.9(a) provides more leeway to the lawyer than does MR 1.7(a). Notice that under MR 1.7(a), the lawyer could seek both clients' consent to continue representing them when a conflict was discovered *only if* the lawyer concluded that the continued representation of one client would *not be directly adverse* to the other client. But MR 1.9(a) allows the lawyer to seek the consent of the former client *even if the representation of the present client involves the same or a substantially related matter that is materially adverse to the former client.* Therefore, if the lawyer concludes that a present client's case is not the same or substantially related to a former client's case, the lawyer need not seek the former client's consent to continue representing the present client. If the former client believes that his or her lawyer should not be representing parties who have adverse interests to the former client and sues the lawyer for malpractice or seeks to enjoin the lawyer's continued representation, the correct presumption (usually unstated in the case law) is that the lawyer did not seek the former client's consent before embarking upon the present client's representation. *See Hyman Cos., v. Brozost*, 964 F. Supp. 168 (E.D. Pa. 1997); *see also Damron v. Herzog*, 67 F.3d 211 (9th Cir. 1995).

Three important determinations must be made for this kind of conflict of interest analysis: when is a client a former client; when is the lawyer-client relationship created for the new client; and what makes a legal matter substantially related?

When Is a Client a Former Client?

If a client fires his or her lawyer, then clearly the client is a former client. When a client hires a lawyer to draft a will, then it is logical to presume that once the will's execution is complete and the client pays the fee, the lawyer-client relationship is complete. But identifying the end of every lawyer-client relationship is not always easy. Because there is no concrete standard on when a present client becomes a former client, sometimes it is to the law firm's advantage to consider the client as being a former client, because the conflicts rule of MR 1.9 is more lenient than MR 1.7. This can lead to the problem of the "hot-potato" client, who is dropped (and then becomes the former client) in favor of a new client with interests that are conflicting, but more lucrative, to the recently dropped client.

Law firms have, on a few occasions, been found to have wrongfully dropped current clients in favor of new clients with opposing interests. A federal judge in New Jersey ordered a law firm to be disqualified from representing the estate of an extremely wealthy man being sued by the dead man's live-in girlfriend who was conspicuously left out of the will. While alive, the man had been a long-standing client of the firm in question and had asked it to represent his much-younger girlfriend in a variety of legal matters. After the man died, his executor asked the firm to represent the estate in any future litigation. After the woman indicated her intent on suing the estate, the law firm sent a letter to the woman firing her as its client, demanding she pay her $8,000 legal bill, and then began to represent the estate—that is, until the girlfriend cried foul. *Santacroce v. Neff*, 134

F. Supp.2d 366 (D. N.J. 2001). In another federal case involving the former client conflict, the court stated that law firms may not drop clients like hot potatoes in favor of newer, more profitable clients. *Munoz Gen. Contractor, Inc., v. MC3d, Inc.,* 1998 WL 831806 (N.D. Ill, Nov. 25, 1998). And at least one state ethics committee has stated that lawyers may not drop a client so as to reap the benefits of the more lenient standard associated with former client conflicts. State Bar of Mich. Comm. on Professional and Judicial Ethics, Op. RI–139 (1992).

When Is the Lawyer-Client Relationship Created?

The second component also has its fuzzy aspects. On the clear side, the lawyer-client relationship is obviously created when a lawyer accepts the client's case and sends the client an **engagement letter**, or when the client pays a retainer to the lawyer. But the fuzzy part is trying to determine if the lawyer-client relationship is created even if the lawyer engages in no representation of the prospective client. The answer to that question usually revolves around whether the lawyer became aware of confidential information in the initial consultation with the prospective client or whether he or she rendered any advice to the prospective client. In a Nebraska case, the disgruntled buyer of a house costing over $200,000 called an attorney at his home to discuss her situation. Almost two years later, the buyer (represented by a different firm) sued the seller of the house to rescind the real estate contract, and the seller retained a different lawyer at the same firm of the attorney who had the phone conversation with the buyer many months earlier. Even though the buyer of the house was never billed by the attorney for the at-home phone call (in fact, the attorney claimed to not remember talking with the buyer on the phone), she was able to disqualify the firm representing the seller due to the theory that she was a former client of the firm and the firm was wrongfully representing the seller in the same matter. *Richardson v. Griffiths,* 560 N.W.2d 430 (Neb. 1997). See "Imputed Disqualification: Effects on the Firm of One Lawyer's Conflict" later in this chapter.

Intentionally Creating a Lawyer-Client Conflict

Connected to the problem of prospective clients being considered former clients for the purposes of conflicts in substantially related legal matters is the situation where clients might intentionally try to create a conflict of interest. As was mentioned in Chapter 4, a client could try to retain a particular lawyer solely for the purpose of preventing that lawyer (and his or her firm) from being used in future litigation by an opposing party to the client. Such a practice is the inverse of the hot-potato trick that lawyers have been known to play. The idea of retaining a lawyer just to make him or her a victim of the conflicts rules is frowned upon by some authorities. An Indiana ethics opinion, dealing with lawyers sending their divorce clients to other lawyers for the purpose of preventing them from representing the divorce clients' spouses, found that,

■ engagement letter
A letter from a lawyer to a client that formally acknowledges that the firm has accepted the client's case and sets forth the terms of the representation.

although the rules do not expressly prohibit such activities, such behavior violates the spirit of the ethics rules. Indiana State Bar Association Ethics Opinion no. 2 (2000).

A curious Maryland case illustrates such a maneuver almost perfectly. A lawyer was teaching a continuing legal education seminar, and during the seminar, an attorney in attendance asked the teacher for advice about one of her current cases. Later, the teacher represented an opponent of this former student's client, whereupon the former student sought to disqualify the teacher on the theory that he had become her lawyer by answering her legal question at the seminar. The court disagreed, finding that no lawyer-client relationship was created simply because the lawyer teaching the seminar answered the student's question. *Davis v. York International Corp.* 1993 WL 180224 (D.C. Md. 1993)

When Is a Legal Matter Substantially Related?

A new paragraph was added to the official comments by the Ethics 2000 revisions of MR 1.9, explaining what makes a legal matter substantially related. Part of that comment states that legal matters between present and former clients are substantially related if, "they involve the same transaction or legal dispute or if there otherwise is a substantial risk that confidential factual information as would normally have been obtained in the prior representation would materially advance the client's position in the subsequent matter." For example, if a lawyer represents two spouses in a bankruptcy case, may the lawyer later represent the wife in the divorce? Probably not, unless the husband was to consent in writing to this new representation, because one could safely presume that, during the bankruptcy representation, the lawyer learned confidential information about the husband that might be used against him in the divorce.

Model Rule 1.9(b) concerns conflicts that can occur when lawyers move to different firms, as does MR 1.10; that kind of conflict and its resolution will be discussed in the section on imputed disqualification. MR 1.9(c) is similar to MR 1.6 in that it prohibits lawyers from using the confidential information of their former clients in any way that is detrimental to them except for disclosures that are authorized. (See Chapter 4.)

SPECIAL CIRCUMSTANCES: PROHIBITED TRANSACTIONS

The conflicts rules examined so far can be difficult to grasp because they are general rules whose application is broad. Determining whether a client's case will be adversely affected because of a conflict is not subject to a mathematical analysis. But there are some specific behaviors of lawyers that are forbidden or carefully limited. Those prohibited transactions are covered in ABA Model Rule 1.8, which complements Model Rule 1.7. Not only does MR 1.8 cover certain transactions whose conflict relates generally to MR 1.7, it also covers certain transactions that are not implicated by MR 1.7 but are prohibited due to the risk of attorneys taking unfair advantage in certain situations.

The Ethics 2000 Commission made certain stylistic and substantive changes to MR 1.8, including retitling it to make it more compatible with the new MR 1.7. Included in these parallel changes is continuing the requirement of *informed consent* being given by the client in writing in places where the 1983 version of MR 1.8 simply required *consent after consultation*. MR 1.8(k) now adds an imputation rule—specifically covering what MR 1.10 generally covers—that prohibits all lawyers associated in a firm from engaging in any of the proscriptions of MR 1.8 if any lawyer is so prohibited, except for the sexual relationship prohibition. The concept of *imputed disqualification* will be tackled later in the chapter. See Exhibit 5–4 for key types of specific prohibitions, as listed in ABA Model Rule 1.8.

EXHIBIT 5–4   A FEW SPECIFIC PROHIBITIONS UNDER MR 1.8 (EITHER VERSION)

- <u>Business with clients</u> (If done, the terms must be fair to the client, put in writing, and signed by the client.)

- <u>Gifts from clients</u> (Don't solicit any substantial gifts, including in an instrument drafted by lawyer.)

- <u>Media rights to the client's story</u> (Not before the representation ends.)

- <u>Gifts to clients</u> (Not allowed, except for litigation costs.)

- <u>Third-party payments</u> (The client, not the third party paying the bill, is owed the fiduciary duties.)

- <u>Settling combined claims</u> (All clients must consent to the settlement of a combined claim.)

- <u>Limiting malpractice liability</u> (Unless the client is represented by another lawyer during the process.)

- <u>Owning the client's case</u> (Except for contingency fees and using a lien against the client to get paid.)

- <u>Sexual relationships with the client</u> (Unless that relationship predates the lawyer-client relationship.)

Business Transactions with Clients

Model Rule 1.8(a) prohibits lawyers from entering into a business transaction with a client unless: (1) the terms are fair and presented to the client in straightforward, written language; (2) the client is given a fair chance to seek another lawyer's advice concerning the pending business transaction; and (3) the client consents to the transaction in writing. (*See* ABA Comm. on Ethics and Professional Responsibility, Formal Op. 00–416 (2000), and Formal Op. 00–418 (2000) for more on business transactions with clients.) This rule does not apply to former or prospective clients, only present clients. And unlike almost every other contract, whose agreement is a result of the dog-eat-dog world of negotiations, this rule requires that the terms are fair to the client.

This rule also applies to the lawyer obtaining a possessory interest or **security interest** that is adverse to the client, such as the following: if the lawyer were purchasing an apartment complex where a client was a tenant; if planning on purchasing a client's real estate at a foreclosure sale; or if the client were to execute a promissory note to him or her as part of a fee arrangement. And, certainly, the rule would apply to lawyers borrowing money from, or lending money to, their clients. The Comments to this rule make clear that it does not apply to common commercial transactions between a lawyer and client for products (for example, the client is the Dell Computer Co. and the lawyer buys Dell computers for the firm) or services (the client is The Charles Schwab Co. and the lawyer has a Schwab brokerage account) that the client sells to others.

Even if the business arrangement has terms that are fair to the client, a violation will still be found if the terms are not adequately disclosed to the client or if the client is not given the requisite triggers for consent. This restriction has also been found to apply even when the client is extremely sophisticated in business matters. *See In re Ober*, 714 A.2d 856 (Md. 1998). But some transactions are considered improper, regardless of client consent. For instance, Rhode Island prohibits attorneys from selling insurance products to their estate-planning clients and prohibits attorneys who sell insurance from selling estate-planning legal services to their insurance clients. R.I. Sup. Ct. Ethics Advisory Panel, Op. 96–26 (1996).

One of the problematic transactions in this type of conflict occurs when lawyers sell property to or buy it from their clients. Lawyers not only occupy a superior bargaining position because of the trust their clients place in them, but they also tend to be quite a shrewd group of people. These advantages can lead to **undue influence**. In an illustrative New Jersey case, a divorce client moving out of state asked her lawyer to find a buyer for her house, hoping to get $95,000. Another of the lawyer's clients was interested in buying the house for that price, but after the lawyer received the signed contract from the seller, he never contacted the other client to tell him to sign the contract. Both clients never knew that the other was willing to complete the sale. Then, a few months later, the lawyer bought the house from the seller for $85,000, and within 10 days he then resold the house to another buyer for $150,000. The court suspended the lawyer for one year, noting, in part, that the lawyer never properly informed the seller of the true value of her home nor kept either client informed of their respective rights to seek independent representation in their dealings with him. *In re Dalto*, 614 A.2d 1344 (N.J. 1992).

▧ **security interest**

Where a creditor secures the repayment of a loan by taking legal title to certain property of the debtor, known as collateral. In the event of default, the creditor has rights to the collateral. A mortgage is an example of a security interest.

▧ **undue influence**

Where one party, in a position of strength over another party who is in a position of weakness, causes that party to enter into a contractual relationship with the superior party, or causes that party to give a gift to the superior party. Undue influence takes away the free will of the weaker party because of the unfair influence of the superior party.

Using Client Information to the Client's Detriment

Model Rule 1.8(b) prohibits lawyers from using information—not just confidential information—gained in the lawyer-client relationship to the disadvantage of the client, with limited exception (including client consent). This prohibition is connected to other conflicts already covered by other rules. First, this rule has been applied to situations where lawyers have engaged in business transactions disadvantageous to the client, based upon information learned during the representation. Second, this rule has also been applied to situations where lawyers have begun sexual relationships with their clients after learning, during the course of the representation, of their emotional or sexual vulnerability.

Gifts from Clients

Model Rule 1.8(c) expressly prohibits a lawyer from drafting any instrument (such as a will or trust) that gives any substantial gift to the lawyer unless he or she is related to the party making the gift. Self-dealing and undue influence are the obvious concerns here; notice that there is no client consent exception. There is an exception, however, for lawyers' relatives, such that a lawyer could draft a will for his or her parents that included bequests to the lawyer himself or herself. Just what makes a gift a "substantial gift" is not monetarily defined, but the Comments say that an appropriate gift "meets a general standard of fairness." The Ethics 2000 version of 1.8(c) has now been modified to include a prohibition on lawyers soliciting substantial gifts from their clients. The exception for when the lawyer drafts a gift instrument for a related person who gives a gift to the lawyer now defines related persons, and includes in that definition, an "individual with whom the lawyer or client maintains a close, familial relationship."

States that operate under the Model Code of Professional Responsibility might allow for gifts to lawyers in wills drafted by those lawyers, because there is no Model Code counterpart to MR 1.8(c). In an interesting Washington State case, a lawyer was found not to have violated the ethics rules by drafting a will for a client in which the lawyer himself was named as a 10 percent beneficiary under the will because, when the will was drafted, the Model Code's disciplinary rules were in effect. However, the lawyer was disciplined for not deleting himself from the will when he revised it a few years later (he actually increased his share to 20 percent), which was after the Model Rules had been adopted. *In re Gillinghamn,* 896 P.2d 656 (Wash. 1995). Inexplicably, the lawyer defended himself by blaming his paralegal for the second will, claiming the paralegal drafted it. The court considered that argument groundless—regardless of its truthfulness—because lawyers are obviously responsible for the acts of their paralegals.

Other than gifts presented in an instrument, nothing in MR 1.8(c) prevents lawyers from accepting gifts from clients. But courts and commentators have considered the substantial gift language as it relates to instruments as applicable to gifts to lawyers in general. The Comments to MR 1.8 mention as appropriate gifts of appreciation, token gifts, and holiday gifts made by clients to their lawyers.

In 2003, the Maryland State Bar Association's Ethics Committee dealt with a question involving what might be considered an indirect gift, and answered it through interpreting MR 1.7. A lawyer who was active in his church was the chair of a church committee that encouraged the parishioners to include the church in their wills or estate plans. Specifically, the lawyer's question was could he ethically write the wills—on a pro bono basis—for those who wanted to leave a financial legacy to the church. The Maryland opinion concluded that, despite the lawyer's "laudable interest" in helping his church, it would be an incurable conflict of interest for him to serve as an objective estate-planning advisor to those clients for whom he had already advocated a particular method of giving. Maryland State Bar Association Ethics Committee Opinion 2003–08 (2003).

Gifts to Legal Assistants

A legal assistant can also be the object of a client's affection and generosity. Although nothing in the language of the rule makes it applicable to client gifts to the lawyer's employees, such gifts are not without similar appearances of undue influence or impropriety. If the firm has no policy that prohibits employees from accepting client gifts, then the legal assistant is wise to seek the permission of the firm before accepting anything other than minor tokens of appreciation. And if it is too late to seek permission, seek ratification instead.

Even though the legal assistant is not the client's advocate, that does not prevent a disgruntled party from suing him or her in the belief that he or she overreached in a personal relationship with a client. An Illinois case that displays an ever-increasing friendship between a lawyer's paralegal and the lawyer's client should serve as a caution to all legal assistants. In that case, a paralegal became friends with an elderly client following the death of the client's wife. The paralegal would visit the widower at his apartment, helping him with household duties and getting his groceries. Eventually, the paralegal suggested that the widower move to a safer apartment, which just happened to be in a building owned by the lawyer. The widower also gave his checkbook to the paralegal so she could pay his bills. Although she was not paid for her assistance, the widower gave her gifts in return. Finally, the widower called the lawyer to the apartment with a request to transfer ownership of his bank accounts to his "sweetheart" (the paralegal) and also to draft a will giving the lawyer and the paralegal $3,000 each. Following the widower's death, the paralegal withdrew all the money out of the bank accounts, and the widower's relatives sued after they discovered that the bank accounts held over $165,000! Their lawsuit was based on a legal theory that attempted to hold the paralegal liable as a fiduciary to the widower because she was an employee of the lawyer, who was a fiduciary to the widower/client. The relatives, however, never sued the attorney. Although the court refused to hold that paralegals are liable as fiduciaries to their lawyers' clients and never found that the paralegal acted improperly, the mess could have been avoided if the paralegal had initially told her lawyer about the relationship and also if the lawyer had formulated a policy on gifts from clients to his staff, as well as himself. *In re Estate of Divine*, 635 N.E.2d 581 (Ill. App. 1 Dist. 1994).

Media Rights in the Client's Story

Model Rule 1.8(d) prohibits a lawyer from acquiring the media rights related to a client's case while he or she still represents the client. Even if the client's limited payment options would make exchanging the literary or media rights of his or her case for representation a financially feasible option, it may not be done before or during the course of the representation. This rule is designed to prevent lawyers, especially in celebrity or controversial cases, from altering their representation of their clients in order to make the "story" more interesting or scandalous instead of doing what would be in their clients' best interest.

One of the most famous celebrity cases in U.S. history involved the 1974 kidnapping of Patty Hearst, granddaughter of William Randolph Hearst, the publishing tycoon and loosely drawn subject of the movie *Citizen Kane*, starring Orson Welles. While with the terrorists who kidnapped her, Patty Hearst was caught on tape robbing a bank and was later prosecuted for the robbery. F. Lee Bailey, perhaps the most famous criminal defense lawyer of the last 50 years, represented her, arguing that she was brainwashed by the terrorists and not responsible for her actions. Hearst was convicted and, after firing Bailey, argued on appeal that Bailey's representation of her was detrimentally affected because he wrongfully acquired the publication rights to her story while he was still her lawyer. Their agreement required Hearst to fully cooperate with Bailey's account of her story and to not publish her own version of her story within 18 months of the publication of Bailey's version. Despite Bailey's argument that the agreement was made after the trial and was necessary to pay for his fees, the court found it to be an impermissible conflict of interest and a violation of the ABA Model Code of Professional Responsibility. *United States v. Hearst*, 638 F.2d 1190 (9th Cir. 1980). (See Chapter 7 for more on F. Lee Bailey's legal ethics scrapes.)

Helping the Client Financially

Although bar associations encourage **pro bono** activities, lawyers are generally prohibited by Model Rule 1.8(e) from giving financial assistance to their clients. Two exceptions are granted in that rule. First, lawyers may pay a client's litigation costs and expenses in advance. Such an exception would allow the lawyer to make the client's obligation to repay those costs dependent upon a favorable outcome (the contingency fee, for example). And second, the rule also allows lawyers to pay, without the need for reimbursement, the litigation costs of their **indigent** clients.

Outside the preceding exceptions, lawyers may not provide a direct financial benefit to their clients. Paying a client's living expenses is not allowed, nor is lending the money, instead; only the advancing of litigation expenses is allowed.

■ **pro bono**

Legal services provided to a client free of charge, or at a reduced rate. The original Latin form was pro bono publico, which means for the public good or welfare.

■ **indigent**

Poor, determined to be incapable of paying for a lawyer's services.

Although such a rule might seem cold-hearted, it is predicated on a prior stated concern that lawyers would acquire a financial stake in the litigation and base their legal advice on factors other than professional objectivity. Such a rule can, however, lead to ironic outcomes. For example, in a Mississippi case, a personal injury lawyer helped pay the living expenses of a client whose leg was amputated in a motorcycle accident, including giving the client's girlfriend money to purchase Christmas gifts for her children, paying the client's child support to his ex-wife, and loaning the client money to pay for his prosthetic leg. However, the client brought charges against the lawyer for these actions two years later, and the court disciplined him for his generosity with a private reprimand. *Mississippi Bar v. Attorney HH*, 671 So.2d 1293 (Miss. 1996). As odd an outcome as this might seem, it is supported by a 1954 ABA opinion that prohibits lawyers from advancing living expenses to their clients (ABA Comm. on Ethics and Professional Responsibility, Formal Op. 288—1954), as well as state ethics opinions (State Bar of Ariz. Comm. on Rules of Professional Conduct, Op. 95–01). Lawyers have been sanctioned for helping their clients pay their electric bills (*In re Strait*, 540 S.E.2d 460 (S.C. 2000)) and providing interest-free loans to their disabled clients to help them pay their living expenses (*State ex rel. Oklahoma Bar Ass'n v. Smolen*, 17 P.3d 456 (Okla. 2000)).

Other jurisdictions, however, take a more charitable view toward lawyers who have done the same, particularly when their clients are in dire need of basic living expenses. In a Florida case, a lawyer was charged with violating this rule when he provided $200 in living expenses to his indigent, medical malpractice client and gave used clothing to her child. The Florida Supreme Court upheld the referee's finding of no violation, concluding that the lawyer's actions were a case of humanitarianism. *The Florida Bar v. Taylor*, 648 So.2d 1190, 1192 (Fla. 1994). Likewise, the Mississippi Supreme Court refused to sanction a lawyer who helped his client pay medical insurance premiums, despite the presence of Rule 1.8(e), which was slightly more liberal than the ABA version. *In re G.M.*, 797 So.2d 931 (Miss. 2001).

Someone Other than the Client Paying the Legal Expenses

If someone is sued for automobile negligence, the benefits of car insurance become immediately cognizable because many policies provide legal coverage. As a result, the client does not have to pay legal fees—at least up to the amounts of the legal expenses coverage. Model Rule 1.8(f) is designed to protect the client in the situation where a third party is paying the legal costs by requiring that: (1) the client must give informed consent to such an arrangement; (2) the lawyer's judgment must in no way be affected by the payment arrangement; and (3) the lawyer must maintain client confidentiality. The pitfall that can occur when someone other than the client pays his or her legal fees is that the person paying the bill could possibly have interests that are adverse to the client's interests, which could affect the lawyer's loyalty to the client. The rules make clear that, regardless of who pays the bill, the client's interests must prevail.

Although third-party payers can come in a variety of forms, the insurance company is of principal concern here. Clearly, there are occasions where the insurance company's interests can be adverse to the interests of the insured (client), such as if the insurance company wants the case settled but the client does not want to settle. Many ethics opinions have been issued that state that the lawyer must act in conformity with the client's wishes. ABA Comm. on Ethics and Professional Responsibility, Formal Op. 01–412 (2001) (the lawyer may not reveal to the insurance company confidential information that is materially adverse to the client's interest unless the client consents); Florida Bar Professional Ethics Comm., Op. 98–2 (1998) (the lawyer may not allow his or her independent judgment to be affected when accepting set fees for representing the insurance company's customers); Pennsylvania Bar Ass'n Comm. on Legal Ethics and Professional Responsibility, Op. 97–119 (1997) (a law firm may not release confidential information or "work product" to the insurance company's auditing agency in order to support the legal fees being billed to the insurance company).

Settlement of Combined Claims

■ **aggregate settlement**

A settlement made by all parties on the same side of a case. Sometimes called a joint settlement.

When a lawyer represents joint clients, including class action plaintiffs, and a settlement of claims is being considered, Model Rule 1.8(g) requires that *all* clients give their consent to the settlement before the lawyer accepts any settlement on their behalf. The rule predicates the clients' consent on a consultation that would explain the meaning of the settlement to the respective joint clients. When a lawyer makes an **aggregate settlement** on behalf of all the lawyer's clients but without all the clients having been consulted, much less given the opportunity to refuse consent, the lawyer can end up paying for that error figuratively (being professionally disciplined) and literally (having to reimburse the clients who were not consulted). *See State ex rel. Oklahoma Bar Ass'n v. Watson*, 897 P.2d 246 (Okla. 1994). In 2006, the ABA issued a formal opinion on this rule, wherein it concluded that before reaching an aggregate settlement, a lawyer must explain to each client the total amount or result of the settlement or agreement, the amount and nature of every client's participation in the settlement or agreement, the fees and costs to be paid to the lawyer from the proceeds or by an opposing party or parties, and the method by which the litigation costs are going to be split by each client.

Agreements Limiting the Lawyer's Liability

Model Rule 1.8(h) is really two rules rolled into one, both of which concern the propriety of lawyers limiting their liability with clients. The first part of the 1983 version of the rule puts limits on a lawyer's ability to prospectively limit his or her liability with the client at the outset of the representation by allowing it only if (a) it is permitted in the lawyer's jurisdiction and (b) the client is independently represented. Some states, such as Ohio, believe it is unsettling to the public to have lawyers tell their new clients that they should go see another lawyer to get advice about agreeing to limit the first lawyer's liability for future negligence, and so have expressed opposition to these type of agreements. S.Ct. Ohio Board of Commissioners on Grievances and Discipline Op. No. 96–9 (1996). The Ethics 2000 version of MR 1.8 now places no prohibition on lawyers making agreements with their clients that limit the lawyer's malpractice liability, but it still requires that the client have independent representation when considering whether to limit the lawyer's liability.

Sometimes, lawyers insert **arbitration** clauses in their retainer agreements, and ethics commissions and courts generally do not oppose such clauses because arbitration agreements do not limit the lawyer's liability but, instead, choose a method for resolving liability claims. Virginia Ethics Op. 1707 (1998); State Bar of California Committee on Professional Responsibility and Conduct, Formal Op. 1989–116 (1989).

The other part of MR 1.8(h) involves a lawyer settling an existing malpractice claim with a present or former client. For a lawyer to settle such a dispute with a client or former client, he or she must first advise the client in writing of the client's right to seek another lawyer's advice concerning any settlement. Under Ethics 2000, this part of the rule now includes "potential claims," such as if the client signs a release of liability as part of the resolution over contested legal fees.

Although adults are generally free to make any contract they desire, the rules presume that disgruntled clients are in a disadvantageous bargaining position with their (former) lawyers when negotiating such financial settlements. For example, in a Florida case, a lawyer hired a second lawyer to file an appearance on behalf of the first lawyer's client. The second lawyer negligently failed to timely file the appearance, so the client's case was dismissed. Even though the client was already represented by the original lawyer, the second lawyer was disciplined for settling the malpractice claim with the client without first advising the client of the need to seek independent representation. *Florida Bar v. Jordan*, 705 So.2d 1387 (Fla. 1998).

Related Lawyers Opposing Each Other

The 1983 version of Model Rule 1.8(i) was designed to protect clients where the family relationships of the lawyers might affect their representation. The rule states that lawyers who are related as either parents, children, siblings, or spouses may not oppose each other in litigation unless each client consents, after being made aware of the family relationships involved. This rule only requires client consent if the related lawyers are directly opposing each other. But under Ethics 2000, this rule has been deleted. The commission believed the rule was both under and over inclusive, so instead it added a Comment to MR 1.7 that concerns conflicts of interest growing out of a lawyer's family relationships.

■ **arbitration**

An alternative dispute resolution mechanism where parties agree to submit their dispute to a neutral third party, called an arbitrator, who renders a decision, which is usually binding. Arbitration, usually a creature of contract, is quicker and, therefore, less expensive than traditional litigation.

The Lawyer's Ownership of the Client's Case

barratry

Historically, barratry was the crime of stirring up frivolous, or groundless, litigation.

champerty

An agreement between the lawyer and client where the lawyer agrees to pay the costs of the litigation in exchange for the client transferring to the lawyer the client's ownership in any future judgment. The historical prohibition of champerty has been relaxed by the allowances of contingency fees.

The former Model Rule 1.8(j), now 1.8(i) under Ethics 2000, is a hybrid of two common law crimes: **barratry** and **champerty**. Barratry involved someone stirring up groundless litigation (today sometimes called ambulance chasing), and champerty involved a lawyer making an agreement to pay the client's litigation expenses in exchange for owning part of the client's eventual damages award. This rule makes it unlawful for a lawyer to have an ownership interest in the client's cause of action, with two exceptions. First, the lawyer can, in an attempt to get paid, obtain a lien against the client, which ultimately allows the lawyer to have the client's assets seized in order to pay the legal fees. Second, the lawyer can make a contingency fee arrangement with the client that is "reasonable" and in civil cases only. (See the discussion on contingency fees in Chapter 7.)

The difference between a contingency fee, which is allowed, and an ownership stake, which is not, can be difficult to distinguish. Summarily, contingency fees are payable to the lawyer from a recovery the plaintiff gets following the conclusion of a claim made against the defendant. For example, in a Hawaii case, a lawyer represented the male half of an unmarried couple fighting over a jointly owned house. The couple was close to agreeing that the man would sell his interest in the house to the woman for $25,000, a sum the man's lawyer called ridiculous. But later, the lawyer purchased the man's interest in the house for the same amount (this purchase ended the client's financial obligation to the lawyer) and executed a contract that stated that the male client understood he was waiving the lawyer's conflict of interest (something the lawyer never explained to the client). The court considered the lawyer's purchase to be an impermissible ownership interest in the subject matter of the cause of action. *Lee v. Aiu*, 936 P.2d 655. (Haw. 1997).

Sexual Relationships with Clients

As has been mentioned earlier in the chapter, there is a new rule in Ethics 2000, MR 1.8(j), which expressly prohibits sexual relationships between lawyers and their clients, with the only exception being if there was a consensual sexual relationship existing between the parties at the time the lawyer-client relationship began. Although some jurisdictions had already prohibited such controversial sexual relationships when they involved coercion (such as a means to reduce or forgive one's legal fees), the commission believed a total ban alerts both lawyers and clients to the severity of the conflict. Because the relationship between a lawyer and client is "almost always unequal," it can involve unfair exploitation. Furthermore, the commission took the view that the lawyer's objectivity is sacrificed when there is such a sexual relationship. Almost all of the country's jurisdictions have added this express prohibition to their versions of

1.8, or have a similarly written rule. And a few jurisdictions, such as California, provide a definition for " sexual relationship." Cal. Rule of Professional Conduct 3–120(A).

The Model Code and Prohibited Transactions

Many of the listed prohibitions in MR 1.8 are found in the Model Code of Professional Responsibility's Disciplinary Rules (DR 5–104, DR 4–101, DR 5–103, DR 5–105, DR 5–106, and DR 6–102) and Ethical Considerations (EC 5–3 and EC 5–5). But the Model Code has no rules that allow lawyers to pay the litigation costs of their indigent clients, concern settling malpractice claims with former clients, or prohibit related lawyers from opposing each other.

CONFLICTS WHEN THE CLIENT IS A CORPORATION OR OTHER ORGANIZATION

ABA Model Rule 1.13 addresses conflicts that can arise when the client is an entity, such as a corporation or a partnership. Although the text of the rule is voluminous, covering many issues, two of those issues will be discussed: determining who the client is in a corporate setting and learning how conflicts of interest are affected by corporate criminal activity. The Ethics 2000 Commission recommended only minor grammatical changes to this rule, and the House of Delegates adopted those changes.

Who Is the Client?

MR 1.13(a) makes it clear that the organization is the client, and not the persons who control, work at, or own the organization, all of whom are known as the organization's constituents. What is not clear is how this works in reality. Imagine that a lawyer represents Martha Stewart Living Omnimedia, Inc., the publicly traded company founded by Martha Stewart to run her television and radio show, produce her publications, and sell her products. Clearly, Martha Stewart is the boss at the company, regardless of the formalities that required her to step down from certain official posts following her conviction in 2004 for lying to federal investigators and the civil settlement she reached with the Securities and Exchange Commission in 2006. (Formerly, she was its chief executive officer as well as the chair of the board of directors.) But the company, not Martha, is the client. This means that the lawyer's duty of loyalty is owed to the company. But as, or formerly as, the boss, Martha is the company's head and, therefore, has the right to direct the lawyer's activities on behalf of the company. (See the Comments to MR 1.13 for more explanation on the corporate client and those who control it.)

Employees and shareholders are also constituents. And as the rule and its Comments make clear, when the interests of the constituents and the organization are in conflict, the lawyer must protect the interests of the organization. In fact, MR 1.13(d) says that in such situations, the lawyer must explain to the constituents that the organization is the client, and not they. But such conflicting interests can occur after the fact. In a federal case, a school principal who lost her job filed a wrongful termination suit against her school district. Part of her legal strategy included attempting to disqualify the school district's lawyer on the theory that the lawyer advised her on matters relating to her decision to fire several employees during her tenure as principal. Therefore, she argued, she was the lawyer's client. However, the court disagreed, finding that the lawyer-client relationship never attached because she sought the lawyer's advice on official matters, not personal matters. He was the lawyer for the school (the entity), not for the principal (the constituent). *Cole v. Ruidoso Mun. Schools,* 43 F.3d 1373 (10th Cir. 1994) See Exhibit 5–5 on how to visualize an intangible thing: a corporation.

What If the Organization Is Engaging in Illegal Activity?

How does an organization engage in illegal activity? Because it is inanimate, it acts through its authorized representatives. For example, when the Ford Motor Co. was tried for criminal homicide in 1980 in connection with the deaths of three women caused by the Ford Pinto, and when the accounting firm of Arthur Anderson was convicted in 2002 of obstruction of justice in connection with the shredding of Enron financial documents, both sets of charges were made under a legal theory that the companies were criminally liable for acts committed or ratified by their high-ranking employees.

If a corporate lawyer believes that representatives of the organization are acting illegally, it is his or her responsibility to inform the highest executive of the organization about the misdeeds. *See* ABA Comm. on Professional Ethics, Formal Op. 93–375 (1993). But, anyone who has ever read or seen a movie version of conspiracy thrillers such as *All the President's Men, The Pelican Brief,* or *The Insider* knows that telling the powers that be that someone in the organization is dirty is often career suicide, nay homicide. And yet, as anyone who has seen *Erin Brockovich* can attest, being a whistle-blower can make all the difference in the world. Can the corporate lawyer be a whistle-blower and inform outsiders about the illegal activities of his or her employer? Traditionally, no, because such disclosure would violate the duty of confidentiality and would obviously harm the corporation/client. If the chief executive officer refuses to rectify the illegal activities, the lawyer could resign from the representation, assuming no confidences would be revealed by the method in which this is done.

Some courts consider the duty of confidentiality so important that they do not allow in-house corporate lawyers to sue their former employers for retaliatory discharge after having been fired for being seen as irksome meddlers for trying to mitigate or rectify the corporate transgressions or for blowing the whistle on those responsible for the illegalities. A leading case on this issue comes from Illinois, where a corporation's in–house attorney was fired for threatening to report that the corporation was planning on selling defective dialysis machines. The day after being fired, the attorney blew the whistle on his former employer, and the Food and Drug Administration eventually seized dangerous machines. But when the lawyer sued for "retaliatory discharge" (being wrongfully and vengefully fired), courts repeatedly concluded that his duty not to disclose client information outweighed his desire to protect the public, and prevented his use of confidential information in his suit. *Balla v. Gambro, Inc.*, 584 N.E.2d 104 (Ill. 1991). Thirteen years later, the Appellate Court of Illinois refused to allow a former in-house attorney for Arthur Anderson LLC, the mega-accounting firm, to sue the accounting firm for wrongfully firing her after she opposed certain business activities she believed violated internal policies. *Ausman v. Arthur Anderson, LLP*, 810 N.E.2d 566 (Ill.App. 2004). It followed the *Balla* decision, concluding that allowing such lawsuits would unfairly chill the communications and relationship between those attorneys and their client, and its decision was not reviewed by the Illinois Supreme Court. 823 N.E.2d 962.

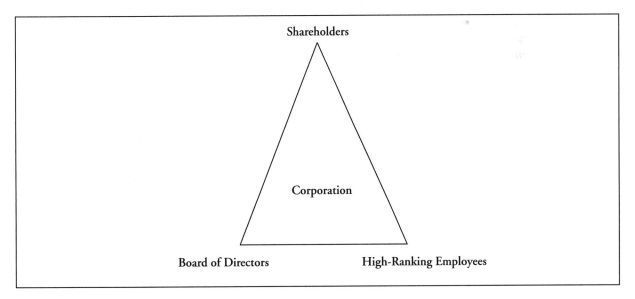

EXHIBIT 5–5 Corporations and Their Constituents

A few jurisdictions give fired corporate counsel a limited right to sue their former employer, assuming the allegations can be proved without disclosing confidential information. *See also General Dynamics Corporation v. Superior Court*, 32 Cal. Rptr. 2d 1 (Cal. 1994); *Fox Searchlight Pictures v. Paladino, Inc.*, 106 Cal. Rptr. 2d 906 (Cal. Ct. App. 2001). And New Jersey allows attorneys to sue for retaliatory discharge, in light of a state whistle-blower protection statute, but permits employers to file ethics complaints based on the disclosure of confidential information used in those disclosures. *Parker v. M & T Chemicals, Inc.*, 566 A.2d 215 (N.J. Super. Ct. App. Div. 1989).

Other jurisdictions allow in-house counsel not only to sue for wrongful discharge but also to use confidential information while doing so. The Montana Supreme Court decided in 2000 that Montana's Rules of Professional Conduct do not prevent in-house counsel from suing his or her employer for wrongful termination and using confidential information to establish the claim. *Burkhart v. Semitool, Inc.*, 5 P.3d 1031 (Mont. 2000). And the ABA issued a trailblazing ethics opinion in September 2001 declaring that the ABA Model Rules do not prohibit a lawyer from suing his or her former client and employer for wrongful termination, even if the suit involved disclosing confidential information. ABA Commission on Professional Ethics, Formal Op.01–424 (2001). The ABA did state, however, that only the amount of confidential information necessary to establish the lawyer's claim for wrongful discharge could be disclosed. One year later, the Tennessee Supreme Court decided that in-house counsel has the right to sue his or her corporate employer for wrongful termination and may also use confidential information to establish the claim. *Crews v. Buckman Laboratories Intern., Inc.*, 2002 78 S.W.3d 852 (Tenn. 2002). But the court limited a lawyer's right to disclose client confidences and secrets to only that which is necessary and to those who need to know. *Id* at 866. And in 2003, the Utah Supreme Court ruled that an in-house attorney for State Farm Insurance could bring a wrongful discharge suit and could use any confidential information that would be necessary to establish his claim. *Spratley v. State Farm Mutual Auto Ins. Co.*, 78 P.3d 603 (Utah 2003).

The Paralegal as a Corporate Employee

The paralegal working in a corporate law department might become aware of information that implicates the company in inappropriate or illegal activities. This puts him or her in a difficult position because the employer is his or her client. Generally, employees have no inherent duty to protect their employer's discriminatory or illegal activities. On many occasions, corporate criminal activity is only established with the help of the whistle-blower. Certain whistle-blowers become famous for exposing their employers' fraudulent and illegal activities, such as Sherron Watkins who worked at Enron, and Cynthia Cooper, who worked at WorldCom. Their activities resulted in them being put on *Time* magazine's "People of the Year" list for 2002. And some, like Frank Serpico, who exposed police corruption in New York City in the 1970s, or "Deep Throat," who was Woodward and Bernstein's slightly embellished secret, government source for much of their Watergate reporting (and who was a lawyer, by the way), reach infamy for their disclosures. For more on Sherron Watkins and Cynthia Cooper, one should be able to find by using the search feature on Time Magazine's Web site, http://www.time.com, the 2002 article extolling their courageous actions.

Beyond being protected by whistle-blower statutes, some who disclose the misdeeds of others are rewarded. For instance, the IRS has the authority to reward those who report on the tax fraud of others—including their employers— by giving the whistle-blower a percentage of whatever the IRS recovers from the tax cheat. For more information, search for IRS Publication no. 733, on the IRS Web site, http://www.irs.gov.

For paralegals or other non-lawyer employees working in corrupt corporations, a sense of justice or moral outrage might compel them to report the misdeeds of their employers. That may be done to insiders within the company. But any whistle-blowing done outside the company (to the government or the press) is likely to be an unprotected disclosure, because paralegals are bound by the same rules of confidentiality as lawyers and must protect their clients' confidences, even harmful confidences. One might presume that in jurisdictions which allow corporate attorneys to sue for wrongful discharge (Montana, New Jersey, Tennessee, and Utah, for instance) corporate paralegals would have the same prerogative, but as stated earlier, many jurisdictions do not allow whistle-blowing lawyers to cry foul after being fired. See Exhibit 5–6 on the dilemma corporate paralegals face.

EXHIBIT 5–6   THE PARALEGAL IN THE CORPORATE LAW DEPARTMENT

- The paralegal's employer is also his or her client.

- Occasionally, that employer could be engaging in inappropriate activity (or worse).

- Historically, corporate lawyers couldn't be whistle-blowers, because of the duty of confidentiality and the conflicts of interest problem.

- Corporate paralegals have a similar duty of confidentiality and loyalty, but they can't be sanctioned, like lawyers can, for violating a duty of confidentiality when reporting corporate misbehavior to outsiders.

The Model Code and the Corporate Entity

The Disciplinary Rules of the Model Code of Professional Responsibility had no singular rule that was equivalent to MR 1.13. However, DR 5–107(B) required a lawyer who was employed by someone to render legal services for another to refuse to allow the employing person to affect his or her judgment. And EC 5–18 provided that a "lawyer employed or retained by a corporation or similar entity owes his allegiance to the entity and not to a stockholder, director, officer, employee, representative, or other person connected with the entity."

IMPUTED DISQUALIFICATION: ONE LAWYER'S CONFLICT AFFECTING THE FIRM

So far, the kinds of conflicts of interests that have been discussed required a determination of whether the lawyer may continue to represent his or her client despite a conflict of interest the lawyer does, or might, have. If the lawyer cannot obtain the client's consent for those conflicts that allow for client consent, the lawyer must withdraw. Likewise, the lawyer must withdraw from those direct, or materially adverse, conflicts, for which the rules do not allow client consent. This seems simple enough. But can another lawyer in the same firm take a case that the conflicted lawyer either may not take or may not continue? Or is the whole firm disqualified if one of its lawyers is disqualified?

The General Policy: Disqualification

In the days of Alexander the Great, it was considered smart practice for a new leader to kill all the possible family heirs of the former—or dead—leader in order to prevent a "Who's in charge around here?" controversy. And during the plagues of the Middle Ages, children of those infected with the deadly disease were often banished—including being denied food—because of the fear that the contagion might have spread to them. Such is the nature of relationship liability.

The legal system has its own, less deadly, form of shunning: imputed disqualification. This doctrine generally holds that when a lawyer is prevented from representing a client because of the application of certain conflicts of interest rules, no one else at the law firm may represent the client. Imputed disqualification is based on the doctrine of shared confidences; the idea that all lawyers in the firm have access to and share in the confidential information of all the clients.

ABA Model Rule 1.10(a) covers the kinds of situations where the disqualification of one lawyer in the firm will be imputed to the entire firm. The gist of the Ethics 2000 version of MR 1.10(a) is that *all lawyers in a firm* are disqualified from representing a client *if any lawyer in the firm* would be disqualified due to the application of two situations: (1) the general conflicts found in MR 1.7; and (2) the former client conflicts found in MR 1.9. The imputed disqualification situations are quite broad because, as an example, the general lawyer conflicts encompassed by MR 1.7 are broad. The former version of MR 1.10(a) also included two more rules under its coverage, 2.2 and 1.8(c)).

MR 1.10 is a strict rule that makes an entire law firm bear the responsibility for the conflict of one of their lawyers because of the overriding concern for loyalty to the client. But a new exception provided by the current version is that imputed disqualification is not required when a lawyer in the firm would be prohibited due to a "personal interest" conflict, as long as there is no significant risk that the representation will be materially limited by the continued representation. This exception would allow, for instance, one lawyer in a firm to represent a born-again Christian seeking to have a Bible-study class allowed at the public college he or she attends, even though another lawyer in the firm is an atheist and would refuse such a case due to a personal conflict of interest with the client's objective.

Imputed disqualification might be called "lawyer leprosy," because it quarantines all the lawyers in the firm because one of them is "infected." This harsh rule is based on a presumption that all lawyers in the firm have access to, and share in, all of the firm's clients' confidential information. For example, in a New Jersey case, a local police officer who was also licensed to practice law wrote the state ethics committee for advice about any limitations that might apply to a law firm he was considering joining on a part-time basis. The committee decided —and the New Jersey Supreme Court affirmed—that the law firm would be able to represent no private defendants in criminal matters arising in the municipality where the police officer was employed if he joined the law firm. Such imputed disqualification was based, in part, on the **appearance of impropriety** standard being applied to MR 1.10(a), because clearly the lawyer/police officer could not represent any clients accused of crimes in the township where he was employed as a police officer. *In re Advisory Committee*, 616 A.2d 1290 (N.J. 1992). The Model Code applied a tougher standard than does the Model Rules in that DR 5–105 (D) required that if a lawyer was disqualified from representing the client for any reason under the Model Code, then no lawyer associated with the first lawyer was able to take the case.

Imputed Disqualification: Formerly Associated Lawyers

Imputed disqualification gets uglier when a lawyer switches employers, ending up at the law firm of an opponent of a former client of the attorney's former law firm. The Comments to MR 1.10 make clear that section (a) concerns lawyers who are currently associated with each other. MR 1.10(b), however, applies to situations where conflicts are imputed to a law firm because of a conflict-affected lawyer who used to work at the firm. This section does allow a law firm to represent a client whose interests are adverse—even materially adverse—to another client who was represented by a lawyer when that lawyer used to work at that firm, provided two conditions exist. First, the matter cannot be the same or substantially related to the matter with which the formerly associated lawyer was connected. And second, if the matter is the same or

▧ **appearance of impropriety**

A standard of ethical conduct, found in the Model Code of Professional Responsibility, in which lawyers are advised to avoid certain activities because those activities look bad, rather than actually being bad.

substantially related, there can be no remaining lawyer in the firm who has any confidential information about the matter in question. As an example, suppose that attorney A at law firm 1 represented a plaintiff in a sexual harassment case against the plaintiff's former employer. Then, attorney A leaves that law firm and moves to law firm 2, taking that plaintiff with her. Later, the employer from the sexual harassment case comes to law firm 1, seeking representation on a zoning matter. Can law firm 1 represent the employer? Yes, because the matter is not the same, which means there is no need to consider whether any lawyer possesses confidential information about the sexual harassment plaintiff.

Now, suppose that attorney A at law firm 1 represented the employer against a charge of sexual harassment by one of its employees. Then, attorney A leaves that law firm and moves to law firm 2, taking the employer/client with her. Later, another employee of that company comes to law firm 1, seeking representation in a claim of sexual harassment against that employer/former client. Can law firm 1 represent that employee? Probably not, because the matter (a sexual harassment allegation) is substantially related to the kind of case lawyer A worked on for the employer/client when she worked at law firm 1. There is a strong presumption that other lawyers in law firm 1 had access to confidential information of the employer/client when lawyer A was associated with that firm.

The Presumption of Shared Confidences

The presumption that other remaining lawyers in the firm had access to confidential information is rebuttable, as presumptions in the law tend to be. Therefore, if courts are willing to consider the argument that the remaining lawyers in the firm had no access to the confidential information of the aggrieved former client, imputed disqualification might not be required. In a Missouri case, a husband and wife were divorcing. The husband tried to disqualify the law firm that represented the wife because that firm recently hired a lawyer who, at one time, was employed by the law firm representing the husband. The court, in denying the husband's motion, found that imputed disqualification was inappropriate in light of these facts: the lawyer in question never represented the husband at the former law firm; nor was she representing the wife at the present law firm; and the husband never alleged that the lawyer in question ever learned any of his case's information, confidential or otherwise, while working at the law firm that had represented him. *In re Marriage of Carter*, 862 S.W.2d 461 (Mo. Ct. App. 1993). Even if a lawyer at the former firm performed legal research for the client before moving to the firm representing the client's opponent, that might not necessarily require the new firm to be disqualified from representing the client's opponent if there is no evidence that the lawyer acquired confidential information while working at the first firm. *See Pacific Employers Ins. Co. v. P.B. Hoidale Co.*, 804 F. Supp. 137 (D. Kan. 1992); *Lansing-Delaware Water Dist. v. Oak Lane Park, Inc.*, 808 P.2d 1369 (Kan.1991).

Some jurisdictions do not accept the doctrine that the presumption of shared confidential information is rebuttable. Instead, these courts draw a strict line that requires disqualification of a law firm that employs a lawyer who used to work at the firm whose client is involved in the same, or substantially the same, matter as a client of the new firm. *See State ex rel. FirsTIER Bank v. Buckley*, 503 N. W.2d 838 (Neb. 1993); *Elan Transdermal Ltd. v. Cygnus Therapeutic Sys.*, 809 F. Supp. 1383 (N.D. Cal. 1992).

Imputed Disqualification and Client Consent

MR 1.10(c) does allow imputed disqualification obstacles to be overcome by client consent, but only the kind of client consent allowed under MR 1.7, the general conflict of interest rule. That rule allows clients to give their consent to their lawyers' continued representation, despite the presence of a conflict of interest, but not in all situations. (Remember, client consent would not cure the conflict of two clients suing each other and wanting to share the same lawyer.)

Consent can sometimes be found to have occurred passively if the affected client waits too long to oppose the disputed representation. Occasionally, courts have found that, by delaying for too long, clients have waived the right to oppose their former lawyer's representation of a client affected by MR 1.10. For instance, in a federal case in California, a former client was found to have waived the right to object to his former lawyer's representation of an adverse party because he did not formally object to the representation until over a year after becoming aware of the adverse representation. *Employers Ins. of Wausau v. Albert D. Seeno Const. Co.*, 692 F. Supp. 1150 (N.D. Cal. 1988).

IMPUTED DISQUALIFICATION: THE USE OF SCREENS FOR THE TAINTED EMPLOYEE

So far, we have learned that, generally, in cases where a lawyer would be disqualified from representing a client because of what we could call "an incurable conflict of interest," the entire firm would be disqualified (unless the client consents), due to the presumption that all lawyers in the firm have access in, and share, the confidential knowledge of all the firm's clients. That presumption, however, can be overcome by evidence that the affected (or "tainted") lawyer possessed no confidential information because the lawyer only worked at the former law firm but did no work on behalf of the client at the former firm who is attempting to disqualify the lawyer's present firm.

But what if the lawyer did work on a matter for client A before moving to a new firm, which is representing client B with a position adverse to client A? This would require disqualification of the new firm, because the affected lawyer actually possesses confidential information of client A, unless the tainted lawyer can be effectively "screened" from the other lawyers in the firm.

The Use of Screens for Tainted Lawyers

What if, rather than treating an entire firm as tainted because of one of its lawyer's incurable conflicts, that lawyer were quarantined? An iron lung is a bit over-the-top and a Hawaiian vacation will instill grievous jealously among the other lawyers, so why not screen the affected lawyer? A screen is also known by other names, including a "Chinese wall" (a bad analogy since the Great Wall of China was breached without great difficulty by the Mongol conqueror Genghis Khan), an "ethical wall," or a "cone of silence." Nothing in MR 1.10 or its Comments mentions lawyer screening as a technique to avoid disqualification. Although the Ethics 2000 Commission did include lawyer screening as an alternative to imputed disqualification in its proposed version of that rule, the ABA House of Delegates rejected that proposal.

Screening, however, is specifically mentioned in the Ethics 2000 version of Model Rule 1.11(b)(1), as allowable for former government lawyers working in private practice. (Formerly, this provision was in MR 1.11(a)(1).), and it is defined in the terminology section of the Ethics 2000 version of ABA Model Rules, Rule 1.0(k). Screening allows, for instance, a lawyer working for the federal government in the Securities and Exchange Commission (SEC) and involved in investigating and prosecuting **insider trading** to move to a private firm where lawyers in the firm represent those targeted by the SEC. The policy behind allowing former government lawyers to be screened is that, by allowing screening, the government can attract highly competent attorneys (who will earn much less than if they were in private practice), because those lawyers need not fear that their future employability will be at risk when they leave government service to practice the same type of law, except on the other side.

Many changes were made to the Ethics 2000 version of MR 1.11, including a re-titling, designed to include not only former government lawyers, but also lawyers who move between government agencies. One of the changes is an addition to the rule that makes government lawyers subject to rule MR 1.9 (concerning duties to former clients), as are other lawyers. Some terms (such as "consent after consultation") are changed (to "informed consent"), and others (such as "confidential government information") are defined. There are also new Comments that explain the relationship between MR 1.9 and MR 1.11.

In light of the ABA's disapproval of screens for private practice lawyers, many jurisdictions have followed suit. But some courts have expanded the concept of screening for former government lawyers to lawyers not in government

■ **insider trading**
The buying or selling of a company's stock, by the company's insiders, based on information the insiders know, and before that information is released to the public. Insiders are usually defined as executive officers, directors, or shareholders of a corporation owning at least 10 percent of the corporation's stock.

employment. The first significant case in which screening for private practice lawyers switching firms was approved was *Schiessle v. Stephens*, 717 F.2d 417 (Seventh Cir. 1983). Courts that break rank with the ABA and acknowledge the viability of screens must still be convinced that these screens were actually used. The following internal mechanisms, put in place by the firm with the tainted lawyer, can help to show that he or she has been effectively screened: (1) the lawyer is prevented from having any involvement in the controversial case; (2) the lawyer is prevented from having any access to the files of the case; (3) the lawyer declares under oath that he or she did not, nor will not, disclose any information of the former client to any other lawyer in the firm; and (4) the lawyer is prevented from sharing in the fees from the case. *See* D.C. Bar Comm. on Legal Ethics, Op. 279 (1998). (This opinion discusses the appropriate measures taken to screen an infected government lawyer, as well as non-lawyer employees, including paralegals, and cites many cases where screens have been approved.) See Exhibit 5–7 on the internal mechanisms for an effective lawyer screen.

EXHIBIT 5–7   INTERNAL MECHANISMS FOR AN EFFECTIVE LAWYER SCREEN

- The tainted lawyer is prevented from having any involvement in the controversial case.

- The lawyer is prevented from having any access to the files of the case.

- The lawyer signs an affidavit declaring that he or she did not, nor will not, disclose any information of the former client to any lawyer in the present firm.

- The lawyer is prevented from sharing in the fees from the case for which the screen is created.

A few jurisdictions have amended their rules of professional conduct to expressly allow screening for private practice lawyers, thereby avoiding the dilemma of their own trial judges having to refuse a solution that might make sense to them, because trial courts lack the power to make precedent. For instance, Indiana, Michigan, Pennsylvania, and Oregon have amended their imputed disqualification rules and now allow such lawyers to be screened. *See* Ind. Rules of Professional Conduct, Rule 1.10(c); Mich. Rules of Professional Conduct, Rule 1.10(b); Pa. Rules of Prof. Conduct, Rule 1.10(b); Or. Rules of Professional Conduct, Rule 1.10(c).

More than a few jurisdictions, however, do not approve of screens for lawyers in private practice, finding that the interest of protecting the former client's confidential information is paramount to the lawyer's economic interest in seeking new employment at a firm that might put that former client's interest at risk. Arizona, Georgia, New Jersey, and Kansas are some of the states that prohibit the screening of private practice lawyers moving to other firms. A California case discussing the Chinese wall doctrine specifically limited it to former government lawyers and stated that California law was clear that screens could not be used to overcome imputed disqualification caused by lawyers switching firms. *Henriksen v. Great American Savings & Loan*, 14 Cal. Rptr. 2d 184 (Ct. App. 1992). That stance, which prohibits private practice lawyers from being screened, has occasionally been criticized by later California appellate decisions, but it is yet to be overturned. *See Hitachi, Ltd. v. Tatung Co.* 419 F.Supp.2d 1158 (N.D.Cal. 2006).

Screens for Non-lawyer Employees: The News Is Quite Good

There are two ways of viewing a lawyer as tainted: either the lawyer simply worked at another firm (firm 1) where there was a client (client A) with a matter adverse to a client (client B) at the lawyer's present firm (firm 2). The second scenario might be that the lawyer actually worked on the former client's (client A) case and then moved to the present firm (firm 2), which represents a client (client B) with a matter adverse to client 1. Both situations could require firm 2 to be disqualified from representing client B (assuming client A moves to have the firm disqualified). Likewise, both types of imputed disqualification could be avoided by screening the tainted lawyer, assuming the jurisdiction allows for such screens.

Both these situations are just as likely to occur where paralegals and legal assistants are involved and, logically, the use of screens for lawyers has been extended to non-lawyer employees. In fact, the use of screens for non-lawyer employees is better received across the country than the use of screens for lawyers. The American Bar Association issued an ethics opinion in 1988 that approved the use of screens for non-lawyer employees (such as paralegals and investigators) moving between firms who are representing opposing clients, as long as the non-lawyer employees did not work on both sides of the same matter. The concern expressed by the ABA opinion was two-fold: to protect client confidences and to protect the employability of highly skilled non-lawyer employees, who would otherwise lose their chance of being hired at other firms if they were held to the same imputed disqualification standards as lawyers. ABA Comm. on Ethics and Professional Responsibility, Informal Op. 88–1526 (1988). And one of the Ethics 2000 additions to MR 1.10 is the fourth paragraph in the Comments, which acknowledges that, as it concerns its paralegals and secretaries, a law firm can avoid disqualification by the use of a screen. Thus, in 2002 the ABA granted to paralegals, in a Comment, what it would not to lawyers, in a rule. See a summary on paralegal screening in Exhibit 5–8.

EXHIBIT 5–8   SCREENS FOR PARALEGALS?

- In 1988, the ABA gave its approval to screens for non-lawyer employees.

- The ABA's concern, besides protecting client confidentiality, was to help ensure non-lawyer employment mobility.

- Many ethics opinions and case law approve of paralegal screening, even if the tainted paralegal possesses confidential information.

- Some jurisdictions have begun amending their rules to allow for lawyer screening —which is also good news for paralegals.

- However, other jurisdictions still disapprove of paralegal screening.

Many jurisdictions have issued their own ethics opinions approving of screens for paralegals or legal assistants, as well as secretaries: Ala. Office of General Counsel, Op. 02–01 (2002); Ala. Office of General Counsel, Op. 91–02 (1991); Conn. Bar Assoc. Committee on Prof. Ethics, Op. 00-23 (2000); Maine Professional Ethics Commission of the Board of Overseers of the Bar, Opinion 186 (2004); State Bar of Mich. Comm. on Professional and Judicial Ethics, Op. RI–285 (1996); State Bar of Mich. Comm. on Professional and Judicial Ethics, Op. R–115 (1992); Mo. Office of the Chief Disc. Counsel, Op. 980149 (1998); Neb. St. Bar Assoc. Advisory Comm. Op. 94–4 (1994); N.J. Sup. Ct. Advisory Comm. on Professional Ethics, Op. 665 (1992); N.C. State Bar Ethics Comm. Op. 176 (1994); Ethics Comm. of State Bar Ass'n of N.D., Op. 98–1 (1998); Pa. Bar Assoc. Formal Op. 98–75 (1998); Board of Prof. Resp. of the S. Ct. of Tenn., Formal Ethics Opinion No. 2003-F–147 (2003); Vt. Bar Assoc. Advisory Ethics Op. 97–9 (1997).

A citation to a favorable ethics opinion is not necessarily a blank check for paralegals switching sides. The Alabama ethics opinions cited earlier illustrate this, because the 2002 opinion restricts the meaning of the 1991 opinion. In the 2002 opinion, the Alabama Office of General Counsel, upon reflecting on the discontent some jurisdictions experienced after allowing non-lawyer employees to be screened, concluded that paralegals must be held to the same screening standard of lawyers. Therefore, the opinion refused to allow a screen to prevent imputed disqualification when firm-switching paralegals possess confidential information of their former clients.

Many Courts Approve of Screens for Paralegals and Legal Assistants

There is much case law showing approval of screens as a way of avoiding the disqualification of the paralegal's and legal assistant's new firm. Some of the factors that tend to be significant for law firms trying to avoid vicarious disqualification include the following:

- <u>The size of the firm.</u> The larger the firm, the better the chances that the screen will prevent the disqualified, or tainted, employee from having contact with the members of the firm working on the matter that is the subject of the opposing law firm's disqualification motion. This is especially if the tainted employee works at a different office of the firm than the office of the lawyers who are working on the disputed matter.

- <u>The level of departmentalization at the firm.</u> The clearer the lines of distinction between different departments of the firm, the more believable it is that the screen being employed will prevent the tainted employee from having contact with the members of the department working on the matter.

- <u>The methods employed in creating the screen.</u> What can be done to establish that the new law firm actually screened the paralegal from the former law firm? A memo to the firm's employees informing them of the screening measure in place for the affected employee is helpful, as would be a letter to the former law firm of the affected paralegal that informs it of the screening measures that were taken. And, an affidavit, signed by the affected employee in which he or she affirms under oath to abide by the screen and keep confidential all information of the former client, is also a helpful device.

See Exhibits 5-9 and 5-10 for more on paralegal screening.

EXHIBIT 5–9   ELEMENTS OF AN EFFECTIVE PARALEGAL SCREEN

1. The screen is put in place at the time the tainted legal assistant moves to the new firm.

2. The legal assistant signs an affidavit declaring that he or she will have no involvement in the case that is the subject of the conflict controversy and that no information from the former firm's client has been, or will be, disclosed to anyone at the new firm.

3. The new firm physically separates the legal assistant from the lawyer or lawyers working on the affected case.

4. The new firm instructs all members, particularly those working on the case, not to discuss the affected case with the legal assistant.

5. A memo is sent to all members of the firm confirming the screening instructions.

6. A letter is sent to the legal assistant's former firm, informing it of the screening measures that are in place to protect against any breach of confidentiality.

EXHIBIT 5–10 PARALEGAL SCREENING CONSIDERATIONS

1. **The Size of the Firm**
   Larger firms = better chance for more effective screen

2. **The Level of Departmentalization**
   Firms with different departments = better for paralegal to be placed when being screened

3. **The Screening Methods Employed**
   Showing how the paralegal was screened = better chance that a court will believe it took place

---

A few recent cases show the trend of appellate courts approving of paralegal screens, or reversing earlier decisions prohibiting them. In *Hayes v. Central States Orthopedic Specialists, Inc.*, 5 P.3d 562 (Okla. 2002), the Oklahoma Supreme Court dealt with an appeal involving a plaintiff who disqualified the defendant's law firm because a secretary who worked at the plaintiff's law firm left her employment there and went to work for the defendant's law firm. Reversing the decision of the trial court, the supreme court concluded two things: (1) the plaintiff waived the right to disqualify the defendant's firm because of waiting over eight months before objecting to the secretary's employment change; and (2) the use of a "Chinese wall" screening device can be an effective device to prevent a law firm from being disqualified after it has hired a non-lawyer employee who used to work at the opposing party's law firm. Specifically, the court applied the logic of screens for government lawyers in allowing screens for non-lawyer assistants at private law firms, finding that—like government lawyers —non-lawyer assistants do not have a financial stake in the outcome of the cases on which they work, and they cannot choose their clients. To its credit, the Oklahoma Supreme Court acknowledged that, in reaching its decision, it considered the **amicus curiae** brief filed by the National Association of Legal Assistants, arguing in support of screens for non-lawyer assistants. *Id.*, at 564.

In 2003, a New York court dealing with imputed disqualification due to a secretary-conflict disagreed with—although it did not overrule—an earlier decision from the New York Court Supreme Court, Appellate Division, which had disqualified a law firm because it hired a paralegal who previously worked on the same case for the opposing side's firm. In *Mulhern v. Calder*, 763 N.Y.S2d 741 (Sup. Ct. 2003), the court concluded that the earlier decision in *Glover Bottled Gas Corp. v. Circle M. Beverage Barn, Inc.*, 514 N.Y.S.2d 440 (App. Div. 1987), disapproving of paralegal screening for reasons similar to those disapproving of lawyer screening, was no longer relevant since the harsh position in New York on lawyer screening had been tempered in later cases. *Mulhern* then found the screening measures placed around the secretary prevented the disqualification of her present law firm. *Id* at 745).

▨ **amicus curiae**

A Latin phrase that means "friend of the court." An amicus curiae brief is a brief filed by one who is not a party to the lawsuit, but who believes the court needs to read the legal perspective presented in the amicus brief in order to make a correct decision.

That jurisdictions are on record as approving of a non-lawyer screen as a way to avoid imputed disqualification does not mean that courts will not disqualify a firm that claims to have had a screen in place. The following case is famous in the area of non-lawyer screening, with a deceitful paralegal at the center of the controversy.

CASE LAW *In Re Complex Asbestos Litigation*

283 Cal. Rptr. 732 (Cal. App. 1991)

Chin, J.

Attorney Jeffrey B. Harrison, his law firm, and their affected clients appeal from an order disqualifying the Harrison firm in nine asbestos-related personal injury actions. The appeal presents the difficult issue of whether a law firm should be disqualified because an employee of the firm possessed attorney-client confidences from previous employment by opposing counsel in pending litigation. We hold that disqualification is appropriate unless there is written consent or the law firm has effectively screened the employee from involvement with the litigation to which the information relates.

FACTS

Michael Vogel worked as a paralegal for the law firm of Brobeck, Phleger & Harrison (Brobeck) from October 28, 1985, to November 30, 1988. Vogel came to Brobeck with experience working for a law firm that represented defendants in asbestos litigation. Brobeck also represented asbestos litigation defendants, including respondents. At Brobeck, Vogel worked exclusively on asbestos litigation. During most of the period Brobeck employed Vogel, he worked on settlement evaluations. He extracted information from medical reports, discovery responses, and plaintiffs' depositions for entry on "Settlement Evaluation and Authority Request" (SEAR) forms. The SEAR forms were brief summaries of the information and issues used by the defense attorneys and their clients to evaluate each plaintiff 's case. The SEAR forms were sent to the clients.

Vogel attended many defense attorney meetings where the attorneys discussed the strengths and weaknesses of cases to reach consensus settlement recommendations for each case. The SEAR forms were the primary informational materials the attorneys used at the meetings. Vogel's responsibility at these meetings was to record the amounts agreed on for settlement recommendations to the clients. Vogel sent the settlement authority requests and SEAR forms to the clients. He also attended meetings and telephone conferences where attorneys discussed the recommendations with clients and settlement authority was granted. Vogel recorded on the SEAR forms the amount of settlement authority granted and distributed the information to the defense attorneys. The SEAR form information was included in Brobeck's computer record on each asbestos case. The SEAR forms contained

(continues)

CASE LAW *In Re Complex Asbestos Litigation* (continued)

the plaintiff 's name and family information, capsule summaries of medical reports, the plaintiff 's work history, asbestos products identified at the plaintiff 's work sites, and any special considerations that might affect the jury's response to the plaintiff 's case. . . .

In 1988, Vogel's duties changed when he was assigned to work for a trial team. With that change, Vogel no longer was involved with the settlement evaluation meetings and reports. Instead, he helped prepare specific cases assigned to the team. Vogel did not work on any cases in which the Harrison firm represented the plaintiffs. . . . [In October 1988] Brobeck gave Vogel two weeks' notice of his termination, though his termination date was later extended to the end of November. Vogel contacted a number of firms about employment, and learned that the Harrison firm was looking for paralegals. The Harrison firm recently had opened a Northern California office and filed a number of asbestos cases against respondents. Sometime in the second half of November 1988, Vogel called Harrison to ask him for a job with his firm. In that first telephone conversation, Harrison learned that Vogel had worked for Brobeck on asbestos litigation settlements. Harrison testified that he did not then offer Vogel a job for two reasons. First, Harrison did not think he would need a new paralegal until February or March of 1989. Second, Harrison was concerned about the appearance of a conflict of interest in his firm's hiring a paralegal from Brobeck. Harrison discussed the conflict problem with other attorneys, and told Vogel that he could be hired only if Vogel got a waiver from the senior asbestos litigation partner at Brobeck. Vogel testified that he spoke with Stephen Snyder, the Brobeck partner in charge of managing the Northern California asbestos litigation. Vogel claimed he told Snyder of the possible job with the Harrison firm, and that Snyder later told him the clients had approved and that Snyder would provide a written waiver if Vogel wanted. In his testimony, Snyder firmly denied having any such conversations or giving Vogel any conflicts waiver to work for Harrison. The trial court resolved this credibility dispute in favor of Snyder. . . . Harrison did not contact Brobeck to confirm Vogel's claim that he made a full disclosure and obtained Brobeck's consent. Nor did Harrison tell Vogel that he needed a waiver from Bjork [another firm doing asbestos-related work, where Vogel was employed immediately before his employment with Harrison].

[A]t the end of February 1989, Vogel was asked to finish another paralegal's job of contacting asbestos plaintiffs to complete client questionnaires. The questionnaire answers provided information for discovery requests by the defendants. Vogel contacted Bjork and others to request copies of discovery materials for the Harrison firm. Vogel also assisted when the Harrison firm's asbestos trial teams needed extra help. In March 1989, Snyder learned from a Brobeck trial attorney that Vogel was involved in asbestos litigation. In a March 31 letter, Snyder asked Harrison if Vogel's duties included asbestos litigation. Harrison responded to Snyder by letter on April 6. In the letter, Harrison stated Vogel told

(continues)

CASE LAW *In Re Complex Asbestos Litigation* (continued)

Snyder his work for the Harrison firm would include periodic work on asbestos cases, and that Harrison assumed there was no conflict of interest. Harrison also asked Snyder to provide details of the basis for any claimed conflict. There were no other communications between Brobeck and the Harrison firm concerning Vogel before the disqualification motion was filed.

In June, a Harrison firm attorney asked Vogel to call respondent Fibreboard Corporation to see if it would accept service of a subpoena for its corporate minutes. Vogel called the company and spoke to a person he knew from working for Brobeck. Vogel asked who should be served with the subpoena in place of the company's retired general counsel. Vogel's call prompted renewed concern among respondents' counsel over Vogel's involvement with asbestos litigation for a plaintiff 's firm. On July 31, counsel for three respondents demanded that the Harrison firm disqualify itself from cases against those respondents. Three days later, the motion to disqualify the Harrison firm was filed; it was subsequently joined by all respondents.

The trial court held a total of 21 hearing sessions on the motion, including 16 sessions of testimony. During the hearing, several witnesses testified that Vogel liked to talk, and the record indicates that he would volunteer information in an effort to be helpful. A critical incident involving Vogel's activities at Brobeck first came to light during the hearing. Brobeck's computer system access log showed that on November 17, 1988, Vogel accessed the computer records for 20 cases filed by the Harrison firm. On the witness stand, Vogel at first flatly denied having looked at these case records, but when confronted with the access log, he admitted reviewing the records "to see what kind of cases [the Harrison firm] had filed." At the time, Vogel had no responsibilities for any Harrison firm cases at Brobeck. The date Vogel reviewed those computer records was very close to the time Vogel and Harrison first spoke. The access log documented that Vogel opened each record long enough to view and print copies of all the information on the case in the computer system. . . . Vogel denied recalling what information for the Harrison firm's cases he saw on the computer, and Brobeck's witness could not tell what specific information was on the computer that day.

Vogel, Harrison, and the other two witnesses from the Harrison firm denied that Vogel ever disclosed any client confidences obtained while he worked for Brobeck. However, Harrison never instructed Vogel not to discuss any confidential information obtained at Brobeck. Vogel did discuss with Harrison firm attorneys his impressions of several Brobeck attorneys. After the disqualification motion was filed, Harrison and his office manager debriefed Vogel, not to obtain any confidences but to discuss his duties at Brobeck in detail and to assess respondents' factual allegations. During the course of the hearing, the Harrison firm terminated Vogel on August 25, 1989.

(continues)

The trial court found that Vogel's work for Brobeck and the Harrison firm was substantially related, and that there was no express or implied waiver by Brobeck or its clients. The court believed there was a substantial likelihood that the Harrison firm's hiring of Vogel, without first building "an ethical wall" or having a waiver, would affect the outcome in asbestos cases. The court also found that Vogel obtained confidential information when he accessed Brobeck's computer records on the Harrison firm's cases, and that there was a reasonable probability Vogel used that information or disclosed it to other members of the Harrison firm's staff. The court refused to extend the disqualification beyond those cases where there was tangible evidence of interference by Vogel, stating that on the rest of the cases it would require the court to speculate. The trial court initially disqualified the Harrison firm in all 20 cases Vogel accessed on November 17, 1988, which included 11 cases pending in Contra Costa County. However, on further consideration, the trial court restricted its disqualification order to the nine cases pending in San Francisco. The Harrison firm timely noticed an appeal from the disqualification order, and respondents cross-appealed from the denial of disqualification in the Contra Costa County cases and all asbestos litigation.

DISCUSSION

The courts have discussed extensively the remedies for the ethical problems created by attorneys changing their employment from a law firm representing one party in litigation to a firm representing an adverse party. Considerably less attention has been given to the problems posed by nonlawyer employees of law firms who do the same. The issue this appeal presents is one of first impression for California courts. While several Courts of Appeal have considered factual situations raising many of the same concerns, as will be discussed below, the decisions in those cases hinged on factors not present here. In short, this case is yet another square peg that does not fit the round holes of attorney disqualification rules. . . .

The Harrison firm argues that conflict of interest disqualification rules governing attorneys should not apply to the acts of nonlawyers, citing *Maruman Integrated Circuits, Inc. v. Consortium Co.* (1985) 166 Cal.App.3d 443, [212 Cal.Rptr. 497] and *Cooke v. Superior Court* (1978) 83 Cal.App.3d 582 [147 Cal.Rptr. 915]. The courts in both cases refused to disqualify attorneys who possessed an adverse party's confidences when no attorney-client relationship ever existed between the party and the attorney sought to be disqualified. . . .

A law firm that hires a nonlawyer who possesses an adversary's confidences creates a situation, similar to hiring an adversary's attorney, which suggests that confidential information is at risk. We adapt our approach, then, from cases that discuss whether an entire firm is subject to vicarious disqualification because one attorney changed sides. (See, e.g., *Klein v. Superior Court, supra,* 198 Cal.App.3d at pp. 908–914; *Chambers v. Superior Court*

(continues)

CASE LAW *In Re Complex Asbestos Litigation* (continued)

(1981) 121 Cal.App.3d 893 [175 Cal.Rptr. 575].) The courts disagree on whether vicarious disqualification should be automatic in attorney conflict of interest cases, or whether a presumption of shared confidences should be rebuttable. (See *Klein, supra*, at pp. 910–913.) An inflexible presumption of shared confidences would not be appropriate for nonlawyers, though, whatever its merits when applied to attorneys. There are obvious differences between lawyers and their nonlawyer employees in training, responsibilities, and acquisition and use of confidential information. These differences satisfy us that a rebuttable presumption of shared confidences provides a just balance between protecting confidentiality and the right to chosen counsel.

The most likely means of rebutting the presumption is to implement a procedure, before the employee is hired, which effectively screens the employee from any involvement with the litigation, a procedure one court aptly described as a "'cone of silence.'" (See *Nemours Foundation v. Gilbane, Aetna, Federal Ins.* (D.Del. 1986) 632 F. Supp. 418, 428.) Whether a potential employee will require a cone of silence should be determined as a matter of routine during the hiring process. It is reasonable to ask potential employees about the nature of their prior legal work; prudence alone would dictate such inquiries. Here, Harrison's first conversation with Vogel revealed a potential problem—Vogel's work for Brobeck on asbestos litigation settlements.

The leading treatise on legal malpractice also discusses screening procedures and case law. (1 Mallen & Smith, Legal Malpractice (3d ed. 1989) §§ 13.18–13.19, pp. 792–797.) We find several points to be persuasive when adapted to the context of employee conflicts. "Screening is a prophylactic, affirmative measure to avoid both the reality and appearance of impropriety. It is a means, but not the means, of rebutting the presumption of shared confidences." (Id., § 13.19, at p. 794, original italics, fn. omitted.) Two objectives must be achieved. First, screening should be implemented before undertaking the challenged representation or hiring the tainted individual. Screening must take place at the outset to prevent any confidences from being disclosed. Second, the tainted individual should be precluded from any involvement in or communication about the challenged representation. To avoid inadvertent disclosures and to establish an evidentiary record, a memorandum should be circulated warning the legal staff to isolate the individual from communications on the matter and to prevent access to the relevant files. (Id., at pp. 795–796.) . . .

Respondents' alternative formulation, that a substantial relationship between the type of work done for the former and present employers requires disqualification, presents unnecessary barriers to employment mobility. Such a rule sweeps more widely than needed to protect client confidences. We share the concerns expressed by the American Bar Association's Standing Committee on Ethics and Professional Responsibility:

(continues)

CASE LAW *In Re Complex Asbestos Litigation* (continued)

It is important that nonlawyer employees have as much mobility in employment opportunity as possible consistent with the protection of clients' interests. To so limit employment opportunities that some nonlawyers trained to work with law firms might be required to leave the careers for which they are trained would disserve clients as well as the legal profession. Accordingly, any restrictions on the non-lawyer's employment should be held to the minimum necessary to protect confidentiality of client information. (Imputed Disqualification Arising from Change in Employment by Nonlawyer Employee, ABA Standing Com. on Ethics & Prof. Responsibility, Informal Opn. No. 88–1526 (1988) p. 3.)

Respondents' suggested rule could easily result in nonlawyer employees becoming "Typhoid Marys," unemployable by firms practicing in specialized areas of the law where the employees are most skilled and experienced. . . .

Absent written consent, the proper rule and its application for disqualification based on nonlawyer employee conflicts of interest should be as follows. The party seeking disqualification must show that its present or past attorney's former employee possesses confidential attorney-client information materially related to the proceedings before the court. The party should not be required to disclose the actual information contended to be confidential. However, the court should be provided with the nature of the information and its material relationship to the proceeding. (See *Elliott v. McFarland Unified School Dist., supra,* 165 Cal.App.3d at p. 572.) Once this showing has been made, a rebuttable presumption arises that the information has been used or disclosed in the current employment. . . . To rebut the presumption, the challenged attorney has the burden of showing that the practical effect of formal screening has been achieved. The showing must satisfy the trial court that the employee has not had and will not have any involvement with the litigation, or any communication with attorneys or coemployees concerning the litigation that would support a reasonable inference that the information has been used or disclosed. If the challenged attorney fails to make this showing, then the court may disqualify the attorney and law firm. . . .

There can be no question that Vogel obtained confidential attorney-client information when he accessed the Harrison firm's case files on Brobeck's computer. Respondents need not show the specific confidences Vogel obtained; such a showing would serve only to exacerbate the damage to the confidentiality of the attorney-client relationship. As discussed above, respondents had to show only the nature of the information and its material relationship to the present proceedings. They have done so. To blunt the impact of Vogel's misconduct, the Harrison firm argues that the cases on the computer were newly filed and that no evidence showed the computer information to be more than appeared on the face of the complaints, which are public records. The argument is wrong on both points. While many of the cases were entered on the computer little more than a week earlier, others

(continues)

were entered weeks or months before Vogel looked at them. Moreover, the fact that some of the same information may appear in the public domain does not affect the privileged status of the information when it is distilled for an attorney-client communication. . . .

CONCLUSION

We realize the serious consequences of disqualifying attorneys and depriving clients of representation by their chosen counsel. However, we must balance the important right to counsel of one's choice against the competing fundamental interest in preserving confidences of the attorney-client relationship. . . . Attorneys must respect the confidentiality of attorney-client information and recognize that protecting confidentiality is an imperative to be obeyed in both form and substance. A requisite corollary to these principles is that attorneys must prohibit their employees from violating confidences of former employers as well as confidences of present clients. Until the Legislature or the State Bar chooses to disseminate a different standard, attorneys must be held accountable for their employees' conduct, particularly when that conduct poses a clear threat to attorney-client confidentiality and the integrity of our judicial process.

The order of the trial court is affirmed. Each party shall bear its own costs.

Case Questions

1. What specific facts indicate the deceitfulness of Vogel, the paralegal?

2. What standard for imputed disqualification did the Brobeck firm want the court to apply? Why did the court apply a more lenient standard?

3. Notice that, even though the court disqualified the Harrison firm from nine asbestos cases, the court approved of screens for paralegals, despite that screens are not allowed for California lawyers (as discussed earlier in the Chapter). That having been said, what screening mechanism did the court adopt?

4. Why did the court believe that the Harrison firm was in possession of Brobeck's confidential client information?

5. How did Harrison's own conduct contribute to the court's decision to affirm his firm's disqualification?

Not All Courts Approve of Screens for Paralegals and Legal Assistants

When courts approve of legal assistant screening, they usually do so in one of three possible stances (Exhibit 5–11): (a) the screening is approved, despite the fact that lawyer screening is not approved; (b) the screening is approved because lawyer screening is already approved; or (c) the screening is approved at a level beyond that allowed for lawyer screening (such is the standard in *In re Complex Asbestos Litigation,* noted earlier). And, as the previous case shows, just because a

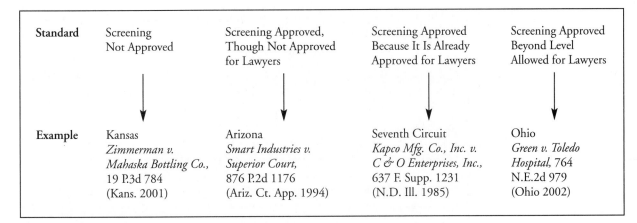

Standard	Screening Not Approved	Screening Approved, Though Not Approved for Lawyers	Screening Approved Because It Is Already Approved for Lawyers	Screening Approved Beyond Level Allowed for Lawyers
Example	Kansas *Zimmerman v. Mahaska Bottling Co.,* 19 P.3d 784 (Kans. 2001)	Arizona *Smart Industries v. Superior Court,* 876 P.2d 1176 (Ariz. Ct. App. 1994)	Seventh Circuit *Kapco Mfg. Co., Inc. v. C & O Enterprises, Inc.,* 637 F. Supp. 1231 (N.D. Ill. 1985)	Ohio *Green v. Toledo Hospital,* 764 N.E.2d 979 (Ohio 2002)

EXHIBIT 5–11   The Shifting Screening Standards for Paralegals Switching Firms

jurisdiction approves of non-lawyer screening does not mean it will refuse to disqualify a law firm that has hired a legal assistant from the opposing party's firm. The screen must be real—and not simply claimed—and in effect at the time the legal assistant is hired; moreover, its effects must be demonstrable to the opposing firm, as well as the trial court at the disqualification hearing.

But not all jurisdictions approve of non-lawyer screening measures as a way of a firm avoiding disqualification when the firm has hired a non-lawyer employee who was formerly employed at the opposing party's firm. Some ethics opinions expressly reject the screening of tainted non-lawyer employees. Kansas Bar Association Professional Ethics Advisory Comm. Op. 90–05 (1990). And, by judicial decision, certain jurisdictions disapprove of non-lawyer screening. *See Owens v. First Family Financial Services, Inc.,* 379 F. Supp.2d 840 (S.D.Miss. 2005); *Zimmerman v. Mahaska Bottling Co.,* 19 P.3d 784 (Kans. 2001); *Koulisis v. Rivers,* 730 So.2d 289 (Fla. Dist. Ct. App. (1999); *Glover Bottled Gas Corp. v. Circle M. Beverage Barn, Inc.,* 514 N.Y.S.2d 440 (N.Y. Sup. Ct.1987); *Williams v. Trans World Airlines,* 588 F.Supp. 1037 (W.D. Mo. 1984). These jurisdictions apply a disconcerting logic, which is: (a) if legal assistants work on behalf of lawyers; and (b) if the professional responsibility rules make the lawyer responsible for ensuring that the conduct of non-lawyer employees is compatible with the professional obligations of the lawyer (MR 5.3 and also, in a way, DR 4–101[D]); then (c) if the jurisdiction does not approve of screens for lawyers, it could not approve of screens for non-lawyers even under some general theory of leniency or employability. The incongruity in the conclusion is that equating non-lawyer employees to lawyers in an area such as imputed disqualification, while professionally laudable, places equal employability limitations on non-lawyer employees who are paid considerably less than their lawyer counterparts, whose considerably higher pay is due in part to the theory that they might be disqualified from future, lucrative work because of past client conflicts.

The following case was a benchmark for the alternate view that non-lawyer screening should not be allowed.

CASE LAW *Ciaffone v. District Court*

945 P.2d 950 (Nev. 1997)

PER CURIAM

On May 27, 1993, petitioners Linda Ciaffone, Joseph Ciaffone, and Carla Ciaffone, individually, and Kathleen Hornbrook as Special Administratrix, on behalf of the estate of Joseph Ronald Ciaffone, the deceased, ("Ciaffones") filed a wrongful death action against Skyline Restaurant & Casino ("Skyline") for the shooting of Joseph Ciaffone. The law firm of Gillock, Koning, Markley & Killebrew, P.C. ("Gillock firm") represented the Ciaffones while Skyline retained the law firm of Thorndal, Backus, Armstrong & Balkenbush ("Thorndal firm"). The case was scheduled for trial in April 1996, but was continued until December 30, 1996.

On February 11, 1995, Ingrid Decker ("Decker") was employed by the Thorndal firm through a "temp" agency and worked in the word processing unit. On March 25, 1995, Decker was hired directly by the Thorndal firm to serve as a legal secretary to attorney David Clark ("Clark"). Although Clark was not assigned to the Ciaffone v. Skyline Restaurant & Casino ("Ciaffone v. Skyline") litigation, Decker admits that she performed some work on Ciaffone v. Skyline in a limited "overflow" secretarial capacity.

After Clark left the Thorndal firm, Decker remained for several months. Decker sat from March 18, 1996, to March 25, 1996, as a floating secretary to attorney of record in Ciaffone v. Skyline, Janiece Marshall ("Marshall"). Although Decker claims she did not do any work on Ciaffone v. Skyline while working for Marshall, she does admit that she may have done some work in Ciaffone v. Skyline in her brief duties as a word processor at the Thorndal firm.

On September 9, 1996, Decker began her employment at the Gillock firm as a secretary to Julie A. Mersch ("Mersch"), attorney of record in Ciaffone v. Skyline. The Gillock firm made efforts to screen Decker from any involvement in the Ciaffone v. Skyline case; the trial court found these efforts sufficient, despite some minor involvement by Decker with the case.

On November 25, 1996, the Thorndal firm moved to disqualify the Gillock firm based on Decker's involvement in Ciaffone v. Skyline and the absence of any authority in Nevada recognizing nonlawyer screening. Judge Sobel, based on written motions, affidavits, and an informal hearing, ruled as follows:

The Motion to Disqualify poses at least two significant issues.

(continues)

CASE LAW   *Ciaffone v. District Court* (continued)

First, should "screening" be allowed where a non-lawyer is involved? I think it should be permitted, but there is a complete absence, as far as I can tell, of applicable Nevada law permitting it. . . .

Second, was the screening effective with respect to Ingrid Decker? I believe that the screening was effective in this case, and that Decker did not, after taking her new employment, have the significant participation in the case that the nonlawyer had in [Smart Industries Corp. v. Superior Court, 876 P.2d 1176 (Ariz. Ct. App. 1994)].

However, I feel constrained as a trial judge to find that neither by rule or case has our state yet recognized screening. . . .

I believe if screening is to take place with respect to nonlawyers in Nevada, in the face of rules that apparently do not permit it, it should be the Supreme Court, the maker of Supreme Court rules, and not me, who gives permission for screening.

The Motion to Disqualify is therefore granted reluctantly.

Ciaffones then petitioned this court for a writ of mandamus ordering the district court to reinstate the Gillock firm as attorneys of record. . . .

Skyline argues that regardless of the efforts taken by the Gillock firm to screen Decker from participation in Ciaffone v. Skyline, no statute or case law exists in Nevada permitting nonlawyer screening. Skyline further contends that because Nevada law does not authorize screening when lawyers move from one private firm to another, nonlawyers should be held to the same standard. We conclude that Skyline's argument correctly states Nevada law.

Although Nevada has not addressed the problem of nonlawyer screening, this court has taken the position in SCR 160(2) that lawyer screening is prohibited. In part, SCR 160(2) provides:

When a lawyer becomes associated with a firm, the firm may not knowingly represent a person in the same or a substantially related matter in which that lawyer, or a firm with which the lawyer was associated, had previously represented a client whose interests are materially adverse to that person and about whom the lawyer had acquired information protected by Rules 156 and 159(2) that is material to the matter.

SCR 156 and 159(2) address the disclosure of confidential and privileged information between the attorney and client. Additionally, SCR 187 requires lawyers to hold nonlawyer employees to the same professional standards. In relevant part, SCR 187 states:

With respect to a nonlawyer employed or retained by or associated with a lawyer:

1. A partner in a law firm shall make reasonable efforts to ensure that the firm has in effect measures giving reasonable assurance that the person's conduct is compatible with the professional obligations of the lawyer;

(continues)

CASE LAW *Ciaffone v. District Court* (continued)

2. A lawyer having direct supervisory authority over the nonlawyer shall make
   reasonable efforts to ensure that the person's conduct is compatible with the
   professional obligations of the lawyer. . . .

When SCR 187 is read in conjunction with SCR 160(2), nonlawyer employees become
subject to the same rules governing imputed disqualification. To hold otherwise would grant
less protection to the confidential and privileged information obtained by a nonlawyer than
that obtained by a lawyer. No rationale is offered by Ciaffones which justifies a lesser degree
of protection for confidential information simply because it was obtained by a non-lawyer as
opposed to a lawyer. Therefore, we conclude that the policy of protecting the attorney-
client privilege must be preserved through imputed disqualification when a nonlawyer
employee, in possession of privileged information, accepts employment with a firm who
represents a client with materially adverse interests. . . . Therefore, we decline to carve out
an exception allowing screening of nonlawyers in situations where lawyers would be
similarly disqualified.

In contrast, Ciaffones cite *Smart Industries Corp. v. Superior Court*, 876 P.2d 1176 (Ariz.
Ct. App. 1994), for the proposition that jurisdictions may expressly prohibit lawyer
screening while allowing nonlawyer screening. In justifying this seemingly contradictory
position, the Smart Industries court adopted the rationale of ABA Informal Opinion 88–
1526 (June 22, 1988): Imputed Disqualification Arising From Change in Employment by
Nonlawyers Employees.

It is important that nonlawyer employees have as much mobility in employment
opportunity as possible consistent with the protection of clients' interest. To so limit
employment opportunities that some nonlawyers trained to work with law firms might be
required to leave the careers for which they are trained would disserve clients as well as the
legal profession. *Smart Industries*, 876 P.2d at 1183.

The reasoning of Smart Industries implicitly recognizes that a nonlawyer's employment
opportunities or mobility must be weighed against client confidentiality before disqualification occurs. While this approach may appear fairer to the paralegal/secretary, it has been
roundly criticized for ignoring the realities of effective screening and litigating that issue
should it ever arise. For example, one commentator explained that a majority of courts have
rejected screening because of the uncertainty regarding the effectiveness of the screen, the
monetary incentive involved in breaching the screen, the fear of disclosing privileged
information in the course of proving an effective screen, and the possibility of accidental
disclosures. M. Peter Moser, Chinese Walls: A Means of Avoiding Law Firm Disqualification
When a Personally Disqualified Lawyer Joins the Firm, 3 Geo. J. Legal Ethics 399, 403, 407

(continues)

> **CASE LAW** *Ciaffone v. District Court* (continued)
>
> (1990). Accordingly, we conclude that adherence to the existing SCR scheme is the better rule. We, therefore, refrain from creating an exception to the imputed disqualification rule embodied in SCR 160. Thus, we conclude a writ of mandamus is not warranted.
>
> **Case Questions**
>
> 1. Is Ms. Decker's previous employment at the Thorndal firm what caused the disqualification of the Gillock firm?
>
> 2. What evidence is there that Ms. Decker was in possession of confidential information?
>
> 3. Why does the court criticize the ABA opinion approving of non-lawyer screens and the line of cases that follow such a theory?
>
> 4. What is the policy behind the strict rule laid down by the court?
>
> 5. What could legal assistants, such as Ms. Decker, do to avoid a future disqualification?

The British dramatist and novelist W. Somerset Maugham wrote in 1915 what might apply to some courts today, "Like all weak men he laid an exaggerated stress on not changing one's mind." For those who opposed paralegal screening, *Ciaffone v. District Court* was a beacon. But exhibiting strength, the Nevada Supreme Court overruled its earlier and often-cited decision six years later in *Leibowitz v. The Eighth Judicial District Court of the State of Nevada,* 78 P.3d 515 (Nev. 2003).

In *Leibowitz,* a case where both the paralegal of the firm representing a divorcing husband, and the paralegal of the firm representing the wife switched sides, the court concluded that automatically applying the imputed disqualification standard for lawyers to legal assistants was too harsh. Instead, the use of a screen was mandated when a firm discovers that its newly hired paralegal had access to confidential information while at the opposing party's law firm. Furthermore, the court concluded that evidence of the effectiveness of the screen could then be used to rebut a motion to disqualify that law firm. *Leibowitz,* at 522.

Final Thoughts on Imputed Disqualification and Paralegal Screening

Even in jurisdictions where paralegal screening is not allowed, there are two ways to avoid lawyer or law firm disqualification when a paralegal switches sides. First, if the paralegal acquired no confidential information at his or her former law firm, then whether the jurisdiction approves of screens is usually moot, because screens are necessary if the paralegal has acquired confidential information. The presumption of shared confidences—which applies to lawyers switching firms—does not necessarily apply to non-lawyer employees simply because they worked at a firm that had a client in opposition to a client at the non-lawyer employee's new firm. Notice that even in the *Ciaffone* case, which took a strict position on paralegal screening, although the court refused to allow for Ms. Decker to be screened, it mentioned that disqualification was necessary because she was "in possession of privileged information." And in *Owens v. First Family Financial Services, Inc.*, cited earlier, the district court's refusal to allow a screen to save a firm from being disqualified because its supervising paralegal used to work for the opposing party's firm was predicated, in part, because screens could only apply if the person to be screened did not possess confidential information.

Second, even if the paralegal acquired confidential information, the paralegal's new firm does not have to be disqualified if the former client consents to waive the disqualification. Just because a jurisdiction does not allow for the unilaterally imposed screening of a paralegal does not prevent a screen from being employed in cases where both sides agree to it. Such consent would obviously be contingent on demonstrable measures that show the effective screening of the paralegal. See Exhibit 5–12 for considerations on how to avoid paralegal-caused, law firm disqualification.

EXHIBIT 5–12   ALTERNATIVES TO AVOIDING PARALEGAL-CAUSED IMPUTED DISQUALIFICATION

- If the paralegal does not possess confidential information of the former firm's client, then a screen might be unnecessary.

- If the former firm's client consents to waive the conflict—in jurisdiction where there would be imputed disqualification—then a screen could be used by agreement.

Finally, those paralegals and other non-lawyer employees who work for government agencies need not worry whether their jurisdiction approves of lawyer screening and, by extension, non-lawyer screening. The lawyer screening controversy involves lawyers moving between private firms. But screening is explicitly accepted in the ethics rules as a failsafe device for lawyers—and, by extension, non-lawyers—moving from government work to private employment.

THE PARALEGAL AND CONFLICTS OF INTEREST RULES

All three of the major sets of ethics rules designed to apply specifically to non-lawyer employees have rules concerning conflicts of interest. Guideline 7 of the ABA Model Guidelines for the Utilization of Paralegal Services states that a lawyer should have measures in place that prevent the paralegal from having the kinds of conflicts of interest that apply to the lawyer.

The NALA Code of Ethics and Professional Responsibility has a recently added Canon that specifically discusses conflicts of interest. The new Canon 8 requires a paralegal to, "disclose to his or her employer or prospective employer any pre-existing client or personal relationship that may conflict with the interests of the employer or prospective employer and/or their clients." Guideline 1, Section 3, of the NALA Model Standards and Guidelines for Utilization of Legal Assistants warns legal assistants to "avoid any action which would involve the attorney in a violation of the Rules [of Professional Responsibility], or give the appearance of professional impropriety." The Comment to Guideline 1 discusses conflicts of interest.

Rule 1.6 of the NFPA Model Disciplinary Rules and Ethical Considerations states, "A paralegal shall avoid conflicts of interest and shall disclose any possible conflict to the employer or client, as well as to the prospective employers or clients." There are seven Ethical Considerations that follow the rule, many of which concern the conflicts that can arise when a paralegal changes employment. EC–1.6(d) requires a paralegal to maintain a "record keeping system that identifies clients, matters, and parties with which the paralegal has worked, to be able to determine whether an actual or potential conflict of interest exists." EC-1.6(e) mandates that a paralegal reveal "non-confidential" information about current or former clients in order to conclude if a conflict of interest exists. And EC-1.6(g) requires a paralegal to, "comply fully with the implementation and maintenance of an ethical wall" when the former client has consented to it.

TIPS ON AVOIDING CONFLICTS OF INTEREST

What follows are a few strategies for minimizing the traditional conflicts of interest problems between clients, and also between employers.

Protecting the Interests of Present and Former Clients

While working at the law firm, the paralegal can do a few things to help limit conflicts of interest problems. The client intake form needs to include questions concerning other lawsuits in which the prospective client may have been involved. Then, conflict-checking systems should be in place to allow the paralegal to find categories of the firm's former and present clients, including protected persons connected to the clients, such as spouses, or business partners, to see if any adverse representation conflicts are involved. The conflict-checking system should also include information about the lawyers and paralegals in the firm, because they may have formerly worked at firms that represented parties in matters adverse to the prospective client, which would necessitate the implementation of a screening device.

Protecting Oneself When Seeking Different Employment

When seeking other legal employment, the paralegal needs to walk a fine line between protecting the client confidences of former clients and alerting prospective employers to potential conflicts of interest. Because screening is acceptable in all jurisdictions for legal employees moving from government employment to private employment, the former government paralegal need not fear losing a job opportunity because of a dilemma involving a potential conflict with a former client. And because paralegal screening is approved in many jurisdictions for paralegals moving between private firms, the job-changing legal assistant can alert the interviewer to possible conflicts without risk that such a contingency would thwart a job offer. Remember, for screening to be effective, it must be put in place at the time the firm becomes aware of an imputed disqualification problem. If a law firm is unaware of potential conflicts when it hires a legal assistant and an opposing firm seeks to disqualify the paralegal's new firm, the fact that the jurisdiction may provide greater screening leeway to non-lawyer employees than it does to lawyers will be of little benefit to the firm or its soon-to-be-unemployed paralegal. However, the paralegal must be extremely careful not to disclose former client confidences when alerting a prospective employer about potential former client conflicts.

SUMMARY

Lawyers and their non-lawyer employees are advised to avoid conflicts of interest with their clients. As with the rules that concern confidentiality, rules concerning conflicts of interest are grounded in the fiduciary obligation of loyalty. There are more than a few conflicts of interest rules in the ABA Model Rules of Professional Conduct, but MR 1.7 is the general conflicts of interest rule. It prohibits lawyers from representing a client if that representation will be directly adverse to another of the lawyer's clients. Exceptions are provided for client consent, but only if the lawyer first believes that the representation will not adversely affect the other client.

MR 1.7 also prohibits a lawyer from representing a client if that representation might be materially limited by the lawyer's duty to another client or other person or by the lawyer's own interests. Again, exceptions are provided that allow for client consent, but only after the lawyer reaches the conclusion that the representation will not be adversely affected. An example of the kind of conflict of interest that would not allow the lawyer to seek client consent is where the plaintiff and defendant are seeking the representation of the same lawyer. The kinds of common conflicts that can occur include clients suing each other in unrelated matters, joint representation, and client conflicts caused by the lawyer's own personal interests, such as a business interest.

Specific transactions between lawyers and their clients are either expressly prohibited or severely limited. Such transactions include lawyers entering into business transactions with their clients, lawyers receiving gifts from their clients, lawyers negotiating for the media rights to a client's story, lawyers giving financial assistance to their clients, lawyers accepting payments for a client's bill from a third party, and lawyers making malpractice limitation agreements with their clients. Where such transactions are allowed, the acceptable procedure includes the lawyer consulting with the client about the ramifications of a proposed transaction and advising the client of the opportunity to seek the advice of another lawyer. Occasionally, the client's consent to such transactions must be made in writing.

Lawyers and paralegals working for corporate legal departments (or other kinds of entities) need to be aware that the client is the entity, and not its constituents. Conflicts of interest can occur when those individuals who employ the legal department are acting in a way that is detrimental to the entity. If the corporation or certain employees within it are violating the law, the corporate legal team owes its allegiance to the entity, which means that the legal department may not violate the duty of confidentiality and report such illegal activity, although recent corporate scandals and ensuing federal legislation have impacted the traditional view.

When certain kinds of conflicts of interest prevent a lawyer from representing a client, then, as a general rule, every other lawyer in the firm is also prevented from representing the client. Such a policy, known as imputed disqualification, is predicated on the assumption that all members of the firm have access to, and share in, the confidential information of all the clients in the firm. Imputed disqualification can also occur when lawyers move from government service to private employment and when lawyers move between law firms. Following such job switches, imputed disqualification is required if the lawyer's new firm represents a client in a matter that is adverse and substantially related to the former client. Imputed disqualification can be avoided if the former client consents by waiving the imputed disqualification.

Former government lawyers are expressly allowed to be screened and thereby avoid the harshness of imputed disqualification. Although the ethics rules do not provide for screening for lawyers moving between firms, some jurisdictions allow for it in their case law. To be effective, a screen must be put in place at the time the firm becomes aware of the imputed disqualification conflict. The mechanisms of an effective screen include separating the tainted lawyer from the case and its files, informing the other lawyers and support staff to refrain from discussing the case with the tainted lawyer, and preventing the tainted lawyer from sharing in the fees from the case.

When legal assistants move to another firm, they are faced with same realities of imputed disqualification. The American Bar Association expressly approves of paralegal screening, and many jurisdictions allow paralegals and legal assistants to be screened. Some jurisdictions even allow paralegals to be screened in situations where lawyers cannot. However, some jurisdictions do not allow paralegals to be screened, finding that the interests of client confidentiality outweigh the employability options of paralegals and holding paralegals to the same imputed disqualification standards as lawyers. All the major ethics codes drafted by or for paralegals and legal assistants have rules or ethical considerations that advise non-lawyer employees to avoid conflicts of interest, including conflicts of a personal nature.

Conflicts checking systems can be used with new or prospective clients as a means to detect possible conflicts with the firm's present or former clients. Such systems can be computerized, or they can be maintained by file cards. When legal assistants take positions with other firms, they need to be careful to disclose any possible former client conflicts without violating any confidences of the former clients.

Quite a few changes were made to the Ethics 2000 version of the conflicts of interest rules. Some of these changes include making it clear where client consent may not be sought, and replacing the phrase "consents after consultation" with "informed consent." MR 1.8 has been changed to require clients to give their written consent where consent is needed for certain lawyer-client transactions; it prohibits lawyers from soliciting substantial gifts from their clients; and it prohibits lawyers from having sexual relationships with their clients. MR 1.10's changes include an imputed disqualification exception that concerns conflicts caused by the lawyer's personal interests, but the proposal to expressly provide for screening where lawyers move between private firms was rejected by the House of Delegates. Fortunately, the Comment approving of paralegal screening was accepted.

ETHICS IN ACTION

1. Bill and Laura have been married for 20 years, but won't be much longer. They have decided to divorce, after realizing that for the past three or four years they have led two singularly distinct lives. This was clear to them when their daughter graduated from college and moved out of the house. The husband makes considerably more money than the wife, and although they have no prenuptial agreement and do not

(continues)

ETHICS IN ACTION   *(continued)*

live in a community property state, the husband has agreed to split their assets, including retirement packages, right down the middle. Because they believe in remaining the best of friends after the divorce, and feel they have nothing to fight over, they want to use one lawyer to help them file the documents required to end their marriage. They make an appointment to see their good friend Nancy, who drafted their will and helped them sell a second home.

Can Nancy represent them? If she does, what attendant problems might arise for all three of them?

2. Henry is suing Havel over an easement dispute. Henry bought a small piece of lakefront property that has a small, brick house he and his girlfriend plan to inhabit on a few summer weekends every year. Between Henry's property and the property on the left is a grassy area on which sits a pier that is owned by Havel, who lives a block away. Havel's property has a deeded easement 10 feet in width at the water's edge. Henry, being a rich snob, doesn't want to have Havel as his waterfront neighbor, so he has brought a claim before the state's department of natural resources that Havel's pier interferes with his riparian rights as a waterfront landowner. Havel goes to see David, an attorney known for fighting for the little guy. After Havel gives David some background on the situation, David agrees that these types of suits are ridiculous and that he hopes to help Havel. But David mentions that about five years ago, he represented Henry when Henry sued his former medical partnership to be released from a noncompete agreement.

Can David represent Havel against Henry?

3. Mary is looking for a new car, or, at least, a car new to her. What she wants is a used BMW 3-Series sedan, preferably a 5-speed with heated seats. But what she is looking for costs about $2,000 more than she can afford, and good deals are hard to find, because many BMW owners know the existing demand for their cars. As an estate-planning paralegal, she has considerable client contact, and often helps executors with the minutia of settling an estate. This week, Mary was talking on the phone with one of the firm's new clients, Evelyn, a widow in her early 50s whose husband died of cancer. Evelyn's husband was wise enough to title as much property jointly as he could in order to minimize probate, but one of the pieces of property that Evelyn now owns outright, which she doesn't want, is a red, six-year-old BMW 328i with only 40,000 miles on it. Evelyn can't drive a stick shift and cares little about cars. She mentions in passing that she is thinking about placing an ad for the car in the local paper, but doesn't even know what to ask for the car. Mary can't believe her good fortune.

(continues)

ETHICS IN ACTION *(continued)*

Can Mary ethically purchase Evelyn's car? If so, how would she have to go about doing so?

4. Working in a family law clinic, Gretchen sees many sad situations, some of which are made worse by the legal system. Whether it's abusive spouses, or custody battles, or children scarred by battles waged between parents, Gretchen has seen it all, and sometimes wonders whether she is making a real difference in the world. Even though the family law clinic's attorneys make salaries that are much smaller than what their traditional firm counterparts make, too many of Gretchen's clients are in extreme financial distress. When Gretchen saw in a case file last week that one of her clients is about to be evicted from her apartment because her ex-husband has not paid any child support in a year, Gretchen decides she has to put her intentions into action. She is planning on withdrawing from her savings and writing a check to the client for her unpaid rent.

    May Gretchen do this? If she can't, what rule would prevent her from doing so? Are there any other options Gretchen might choose to help that client other than writing a check to her?

5. Martha worked for five years as a paralegal at the prosecuting attorney's office. After being denied a promotion, she decided to investigate her options, and had a job interview with Andy, a criminal defense attorney who was a sole practitioner. During the interview, Andy told her about his caseload, including a case involving a client accused of selling marijuana to an undercover police officer. Martha asked about the specifics of the case, and realized that she was familiar with the facts of the case since she had made a few phone calls for the prosecuting attorney to whom it had been assigned a few months earlier. Andy said, "Well, what can you tell me about the case? I need to know if there is a going to be a problem." After telling him what she knew about the arrest and the officers with whom she spoke, Andy said, "I guess I should call the prosecutor, but I would like to hire you." Martha accepted the offer.

    Is imputed disqualification required?

6. Karen worked as a paralegal in a law firm that did a lot of estate-planning work. Her duties included working with clients, preparing financial documents, and assisting her boss in drafting and executing wills, living wills, and other related documents. After her boss retired, Karen found another position at a firm across town. Naturally, they assigned her to the estate-planning department. About three months into her new job, she was assigned to a case involving a son suing the estate of his dead father because the father had disinherited him. Karen was shocked to realize that she had worked on the father's will, and had talked with him and heard him discussing why

(continues)

ETHICS IN ACTION   *(continued)*

he wanted to disinherit his son (it involved marrying outside the family's wishes). Karen talked with her boss Susan about this situation, and Susan contacted the lawyer representing the estate, who demanded that Karen's firm cease working for the son. Susan protested, stating that Karen was an honest paralegal and would never violate the estate's confidences, and would continue to work on the case. After two weeks of nasty letter games, Susan decided that she would pull Karen from the case, and sent a letter to the other lawyer telling him that Karen would no longer work on the case, and that she had been instructed not to discuss the case with anyone at the firm.

Is imputed disqualification required?

7. Jenna worked in the medical malpractice defense side of a law firm with about 16 attorneys, half of whom worked in the corporate division, and half of whom worked in the medical malpractice division. She was assigned to a lawyer whose caseload included defending a plastic surgeon sued by a man who claimed his nose whistled when breathing, thanks to a botched nose job. The doctor claimed the nose job didn't cause the problem, but that it was caused by years of snorting cocaine while playing in a rock band. When Jenna looked at the file, she chuckled to her boss Patti that she remembered that guy because he was a client at her former firm. Jenna hadn't done any substantive work on the case, but had done some clerical tasks for it and had heard about the client's strange situation from others in that firm. Jenna's former firm became that client's former firm because he eventually fired his lawyer and went somewhere else, and the second law firm was representing him now. Patti figured there was no conflicts-of-interest problem and Jenna began working on the case. About two months later, the other side realized that Jenna was working for the defense. They claimed they smelled a conspiracy and moved to disqualify Jenna's firm.

Is imputed disqualification required?

■ POINTS TO PONDER

1. Could John Adams have represented the Boston Massacre defendants if the Model Rules of Professional Conduct or the Model Code of Professional Responsibility were in effect then?

2. Why do the rules of ethics take conflicts of interest so seriously?

3. How does the general conflicts of interest rule work? What determines if the lawyer cannot seek the client's consent to continue the representation when a conflict is discovered?

4. How is Model Rule 1.7(a) different from MR 1.7(b)?

5. When, if at all, could a firm represent one client who has sued another client?

6. What risks are involved when a lawyer simultaneously represents two or more clients on the same side of litigation?

7. What risks are involved when a lawyer simultaneously represents two clients in a non-litigation matter, such as when one client sells property to another client?

8. What kinds of client conflicts can be caused by the lawyer's own interests?

9. Does your jurisdiction expressly prohibit lawyers from being sexually involved with their clients? Do you think paralegals should be held to the same standard as lawyers with respect to romantic relationships with clients?

10. How does the rule related to a lawyer's obligation to former clients differ from the general conflicts of interest rule?

11. What is the hot-potato client?

12. For the purposes of the former-client conflict of interest, when has someone become a client (and, therefore, deserving of the former-client protection)?

13. Under what conditions can a lawyer enter into a business relationship with a client?

14. Why does the law presume that lawyers and clients cannot negotiate from a position of equal strength, as is the case with most other business negotiations?

15. Under what conditions can a lawyer accept a gift from a client?

16. Do you think it should be permissible for a legal assistant to be included in a client's will?

17. What is the policy behind prohibiting lawyers from rendering financial aid to their clients in almost all situations?

18. Can a third party pay a client's legal expenses? If not, why not? If so, what possible conflicts can occur?

19. Does your jurisdiction allow lawyers to limit their malpractice liability with their clients?

20. Situations such as lawyers engaging in business transactions with their lawyers or limiting their liability with their clients call for the lawyer to advise the client about the propriety of seeking independent representation before moving forward. Why is it, however, that such advice could be of little value?

21. How are the conflicts of interest dynamics different when the client is a corporation or other entity?

22. When working in the legal department of a corporation, what steps should the paralegal take, upon discovering illegal behavior, to protect the client as well as the paralegal's employment?

23. Does your jurisdiction now allow corporate lawyers to sue their former employers for wrongful termination? Do you think paralegals working in corporate law departments should be held to the traditional standard applied to lawyers, prohibiting them from suing their former employers for wrongful or retaliatory termination?

24. What is imputed disqualification? What policy is promoted by imputed disqualification?

25. For what kinds of job switches do the rules specifically allow lawyers to be screened?

26. Where jurisdictions allow tainted lawyers to be screened and thereby avoiding imputed disqualification for the firm, what kinds of evidence show that the screen is effective?

27. Why does the ABA take a more lenient position on legal assistant screening than it does on lawyer screening?

28. On what basis do certain jurisdictions forbid legal assistant screening?

29. Does your jurisdiction allow for legal assistant screening?

30. How can the paralegal help assess possible conflicts of interest with prospective or new clients?

31. When a paralegal is seeking different legal employment, what can be done to avoid future conflicts problems at the prospective employer?

32. What significant differences are there between the conflicts of interest rules in the ABA Model Rules and the ABA Model Code?

33. What, if any, significant changes to the conflicts of interest rules were made by the Ethics 2000 revisions?

▓ KEY CONCEPTS

Appearance of impropriety	Issue conflict
Barratry	Joint representation
Champerty	Presumption of shared confidences
Conflict of interest	Screen (or ethical wall or cone of silence)
Former client conflict	Simultaneous representation
Hot-potato client	Tainted employee
Imputed disqualification	Undue influence

▓ KEY TERMS

aggregate settlement	engagement letter	recuse
amicus curiae	indigent	security interest
appearance of impropriety	insider trading	shareholder's derivative lawsuit
arbitration	intestate	trust
barratry	liquidated damages clause	undue influence
champerty	prenuptial agreement	
companion cases	pro bono	

Online Companion™
For additional resources, please go to
http://www.paralegal.delmar.cengage.com

Student CD-ROM
For additional materials, please go to the
CD in this book.

Advertising and Solicitation

INTRODUCTION

The subjects of advertising and solicitation sit at the intersection of commerce and profession. While the marketing of sneakers, sandwiches, and sink cleansers is commonplace and acceptable, the marketing of legal services is commonplace but not fully acceptable. Many lawyers and consumers bemoan the television commercials that tell daytime viewers that if they have been injured, for instance, they should call the 800 number on the screen to talk to lawyers who "have graduated with honors," "have years of experience fighting big insurance companies," or "grew up in the same community where they work." For example, an eruption overflowed in Chicago in 2007 when Fetman, Garland & Associates, a small law firm, put up a billboard advertisement that provided all the profundity of a fortune cookie: "Life's Short. Get a Divorce." Less than a month after the odd proverb was placed 20 feet in the air in a part of Chicago some call the "Viagra Triangle," and put between the sculpted torsos of a man and a woman who might be found on the covers of Men's Health or Maxim magazines, the city tore it and another one down. But not only did that short-lived ad campaign spike the divorce business of Fetman, Garland & Associates, it provided a second source of revenue: T-shirts.

For a look at the billboards, a little more information on this agitation, and its resulting capitalism, see the naturally titled, following Web link: http://www. lifeshortgetadivorce.com/.

Beyond the general marketing of legal services is the solicitation of legal services, which involves personally seeking legal business through the direct contact of prospective clients. This chapter will examine the controversial subject of lawyer advertising and solicitation, including an analysis of the rules and significant cases that control the marketing of legal services and the solicitation of legal services. Technological changes have expanded the lawyer's ability to advertise and solicit, and this chapter will also examine what newer rules or guidance concern the marketing of legal services on the Internet.

A SHORT HISTORY OF LAWYER ADVERTISING

Today we accept as commonplace the practice of lawyer advertising. From television to radio commercials and from the Yellow Pages to the foldout advertisements in the front of the phone book, the fact that lawyer advertising is prevalent would lead one to safely conclude that is a lawful practice. But a quick history lesson will show that lawyer advertising was once considered unlawful, and before that it was just considered in poor taste. Eventually, the U.S. Supreme Court changed its own view on the subject, over the disagreement of some justices and to the disappointment of many bar associations. Exhibit 6–1 summarizes a quick trip through the history of legal advertising.

From the Nineteenth Century to the 1950s

As was mentioned in Chapter 1, the American Bar Association's first rules of ethics, the 1908 Canons of Professional Ethics, were based on the Alabama Code of Ethics of 1887, which was the first formal set of lawyer ethics rules in the United

EXHIBIT 6–1   A SHORT HISTORY OF LEGAL ADVERTISING

Professional tradition dictated that lawyers not advertise.

1887: Alabama Code of Ethics allowed for restrained advertising in newspapers.

1908: ABA Canons of Professional Ethics stated that advertising not warranted by personal relations is unprofessional.

1951: ABA Canons of Professional Ethics were modified to allow advertising in phone books and legal directories.

1977: *Bates v. State Bar of Arizona* changed the law, holding that states may not constitutionally prohibit truthful advertising that states the costs of routine legal services.

1985: *Zauderer v. Office of Disciplinary Counsel* held that drawings in ads aren't misleading per se.

1999: *Peel v. Attorney Registration and Disciplinary Commission* held that lawyers have a right, under certain circumstances, to advertise a specialty.

States. Prior to the creation of those rules of conduct, lawyers regulated themselves similarly to the way English lawyers did, simply through tradition and the following of professional etiquette. Nothing prohibited lawyers from advertising, and lawyers, from President Abraham Lincoln to Supreme Court Justice Howell Jackson, advertised their services. (Exhibit 6–2). The Alabama Code of Ethics also did not prohibit lawyer advertising; Canon 16 of the Alabama Code allowed for lawyer advertising in newspapers (calling for restraint in the method of presentation), but prohibited solicitation. Other states, however, began to conclude that advertising was inappropriate. For instance, in 1893, the Colorado Supreme Court suspended an attorney who placed an advertisement in a newspaper for his divorce practice, stating, "The ethics of the legal profession forbid that an attorney should advertise his talent or skill, as a shopkeeper advertises his wares." *People ex rel. Attorney General v. MacCabe,* 32 P. 280 (Col. 1893).

That first ABA Canons of Professional Ethics altered the Alabama Code's view on advertising by stating in Canon 27 that that "solicitation of business by **circulars** or advertisement, or by personal communications, or interviews, not warranted by personal relations, is unprofessional." An early ABA ethics opinion that concerned Canon 27 found that "[a]ny conduct that tends to commercialize or bring 'bargain counter' methods into the practice of law, lowers the profession in public confidence and lessens its ability to render efficiently that high character of service to which the members of the profession are called." ABA Comm. on Professional Ethics and Grievances, Formal Op. 1 (1924). By 1951, the ABA had modified Canon 27 to allow lawyers to list themselves in telephone books and legal directories, a modification many lawyers opposed.

The Supreme Court's View Shifts from the 1940s Through the 1970s

Regardless of whether one considers lawyer advertising distasteful, it seems that lawyers would have the freedom of speech right to advertise their services, or even solicit clients. But the First Amendment's protections are greatest in the areas of religious speech and political speech; **commercial speech**—communication connected to business or capitalism—is not on that level, and

■ **circulars**

Notices or advertisements sent to certain groups of people.

■ **commercial speech**

Communications made for business purposes. Speech made in the pursuit of capitalism is commercial speech, and it is less protected under free speech doctrines than religious or political speech.

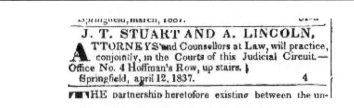

EXHIBIT 6–2   1837 Advertisement of Abraham Lincoln and His Law Partner

can easily be restricted. Therefore, when states began to prohibit certain kinds of commercial advertising beyond telephone book listings, courts, including the Supreme Court, upheld the states' prerogative to restrict such forms of commercial speech. *See Valentine v. Chrestensen*, 316 U.S. 52 (1942). The law on lawyer advertising was clear: it was prohibited. But, by 1976, the U.S. Supreme Court, in *Virginia State Board of Pharmacy v. Virginia Citizens Consumer Council*, 425 U.S. 748 (1976), overturned a statute that prohibited drug price advertisements by pharmacies, finding that the benefits of such price advertising outweighed the state's interests in regulating such business practices. However, the decision's effect was limited to pharmacies.

The seminal case for attorney advertising occurred one year later, in *Bates v. State Bar of Arizona*, 433 U.S. 350 (1977). In *Bates*, two lawyers who advertised their legal clinic's services were found to be in violation of the Arizona disciplinary rules against advertising. The U.S. Supreme Court took the appeal and forever changed the restrictions on lawyer advertising.

Before reading *Bates*, look at the advertisement which was the subject of the controversy (Exhibit 6–3). Then, while reading the case, pay attention to the arguments the state of Arizona put forward in support of its prohibition of lawyer advertising, as well as the Court's response to those arguments.

EXHIBIT 6–3   Appendix to the Opinion of the Court

CASE LAW Bates v. State Bar of Arizona

433 U.S. 350 (1977)

Mr. Justice BLACKMUN delivered the opinion of the Court.

As part of its regulation of the Arizona Bar, the Supreme Court of that State has imposed and enforces a disciplinary rule that restricts advertising by attorneys. This case presents two issues: whether §§1 and 2 of the Sherman Act, 15 U.S.C. §§1 and 2, forbid such state regulation, and whether the operation of the rule violates the First Amendment, made applicable to the State through the Fourteenth. [The part of the opinion dealing with the Sherman Act has not been included.]

Appellants John R. Bates and Van O'Steen are attorneys licensed to practice law in the State of Arizona. As such, they are members of the appellee, the State Bar of Arizona. After admission to the bar in 1972, appellants worked as attorneys with the Maricopa County Legal Aid Society. In March 1974, appellants left the Society and opened a law office, which they call a "legal clinic," in Phoenix. Their aim was to provide legal services at modest fees to persons of moderate income who did not qualify for governmental legal aid. In order to achieve this end, they would accept only routine matters, such as uncontested divorces, uncontested adoptions, simple personal bankruptcies, and changes of name, for which costs could be kept down by extensive use of paralegals, automatic typewriting equipment, and standardized forms and office procedures. More complicated cases, such as contested divorces, would not be accepted. Because appellants set their prices so as to have a relatively low return on each case they handled, they depended on substantial volume. After conducting their practice in this manner for two years, appellants concluded that their practice and clinical concept could not survive unless the availability of legal services at low cost was advertised and in particular, fees were advertised. Consequently, in order to generate the necessary flow of business, that is, "to attract clients," appellants on February 22, 1976, placed an advertisement in the Arizona Republic, a daily newspaper of general circulation in the Phoenix metropolitan area. As may be seen, the advertisement stated that appellants were offering "legal services at very reasonable fees," and listed their fees for certain services.

Appellants concede that the advertisement constituted a clear violation of Disciplinary Rule 2–101(B), incorporated in Rule 29(a) of the Supreme Court of Arizona, 17A Ariz.Rev. Stat., p. 26 (Supp. 1976). . . . In the instant case we are confronted with the arguments directed explicitly toward the regulation of advertising by licensed attorneys.

The issue presently before us is a narrow one. First, we need not address the peculiar problems associated with advertising claims relating to the quality of legal services. Such claims probably are not susceptible of precise measurement or verification and, under some circumstances, might well be deceptive or misleading to the public, or even false. Appellee does not suggest, nor do we perceive, that appellants' advertisement contained claims,

(continues)

extravagant or otherwise, as to the quality of services. Accordingly, we leave that issue for another day. Second, we also need not resolve the problems associated with in-person solicitation of clients at the hospital room or the accident site, or in any other situation that breeds undue influence by attorneys or their agents or "runners." . . .

The heart of the dispute before us today is whether lawyers also may constitutionally advertise the prices at which certain routine services will be performed. Numerous justifications are proffered for the restriction of such price advertising. We consider each in turn:

1. The Adverse Effect on Professionalism. Appellee places particular emphasis on the adverse effects that it feels price advertising will have on the legal profession. The key to professionalism, it is argued, is the sense of pride that involvement in the discipline generates. It is claimed that price advertising will bring about commercialization, which will undermine the attorney's sense of dignity and self-worth. The hustle of the marketplace will adversely affect the profession's service orientation, and irreparably damage the delicate balance between the lawyer's need to earn and his obligation selflessly to serve. Advertising is also said to erode the client's trust in his attorney: Once the client perceives that the lawyer is motivated by profit, his confidence that the attorney is acting out of a commitment to the client's welfare is jeopardized. And advertising is said to tarnish the dignified public image of the profession.

We recognize, of course, and commend the spirit of public service with which the profession of law is practiced and to which it is dedicated. The present Members of this Court, licensed attorneys all, could not feel otherwise. And we would have reason to pause if we felt that our decision today would under-cut that spirit. But we find the postulated connection between advertising and the erosion of true professionalism to be severely strained. At its core, the argument presumes that attorneys must conceal from themselves and from their clients the real-life fact that lawyers earn their livelihood at the bar. We suspect that few attorneys engage in such self-deception. And rare is the client, moreover, even one of the modest means, who enlists the aid of an attorney with the expectation that his services will be rendered free of charge. . . . In fact, the American Bar Association advises that an attorney should reach "a clear agreement with his client as to the basis of the fee charges to be made," and that this is to be done "[a]s soon as feasible after a lawyer has been employed." . . . If the commercial basis of the relationship is to be promptly disclosed on ethical grounds, once the client is in the office, it seems inconsistent to condemn the candid revelation of the same information before he arrives at that office.

Moreover, the assertion that advertising will diminish the attorney's reputation in the community is open to question. Bankers and engineers advertise, and yet these professions are not regarded as undignified. In fact, it has been suggested that the failure of lawyers to

(continues)

CASE LAW *Bates v. State Bar of Arizona* (continued)

advertise creates public disillusionment with the profession. The absence of advertising may be seen to reflect the profession's failure to reach out and serve the community: Studies reveal that many persons do not obtain counsel even when they perceive a need because of the feared price of services or because of an inability to locate a competent attorney. Indeed, cynicism with regard to the profession may be created by the fact that it long has publicly eschewed advertising, while condoning the actions of the attorney who structures his social or civic associations so as to provide contacts with potential clients.

It appears that the ban on advertising originated as a rule of etiquette and not as a rule of ethics. Early lawyers in Great Britain viewed the law as a form of public service, rather than as a means of earning a living, and they looked down on "trade" as unseemly. . . . Eventually, the attitude toward advertising fostered by this view evolved into an aspect of the ethics of the profession. But habit and tradition are not in themselves an adequate answer to a constitutional challenge. In this day, we do not belittle the person who earns his living by the strength of his arm or the force of his mind. Since the belief that lawyers are somehow "above" trade has become an anachronism, the historical foundation for the advertising restraint has crumbled.

2. The Inherently Misleading Nature of Attorney Advertising. It is argued that advertising of legal services inevitably will be misleading (a) because such services are so individualized with regard to content and quality as to prevent informed comparison on the basis of an advertisement, (b) because the consumer of legal services is unable to determine in advance just what services he needs, and (c) because advertising by attorneys will highlight irrelevant factors and fail to show the relevant factor of skill.

We are not persuaded that restrained professional advertising by lawyers inevitably will be misleading. Although many services performed by attorneys are indeed unique, it is doubtful that any attorney would or could advertise fixed prices for services of that type. The only services that lend themselves to advertising are the routine ones: the uncontested divorce, the simple adoption, the uncontested personal bankruptcy, the change of name, and the like: the very services advertised by appellants. Although the precise service demanded in each task may vary slightly, and although legal services are not fungible, these facts do not make advertising misleading so long as the attorney does the necessary work at the advertised price. The argument that legal services are so unique that fixed rates cannot meaningfully be established is refuted by the record in this case: The appellee, State Bar itself sponsors a Legal Services Program in which the participating attorneys agree to perform services like those advertised by the appellants at standardized rates.

The second component of the argument—that advertising ignores the diagnostic role— fares little better. It is unlikely that many people go to an attorney merely to ascertain if they have a clean bill of legal health. Rather, attorneys are likely to be employed to perform

(continues)

CASE LAW *Bates v. State Bar of Arizona* (continued)

specific tasks. Although the client may not know the detail involved in performing the task, he no doubt is able to identify the service he desires at the level of generality to which advertising lends itself.

The third component is not without merit: Advertising does not provide a complete foundation on which to select an attorney. But it seems peculiar to deny the consumer, on the ground that the information is incomplete, at least some of the relevant information needed to reach an informed decision. The alternative—the prohibition of advertising— serves only to restrict the information that flows to consumers. Moreover, the argument assumes that the public is not sophisticated enough to realize the limitations of advertising, and that the public is better kept in ignorance than trusted with correct but incomplete information. We suspect the argument rests on an underestimation of the public. In any event, we view as dubious any justification that is based on the benefits of public ignorance. . . .

3. The Adverse Effect on the Administration of Justice. Advertising is said to have the undesirable effect of stirring up litigation. The judicial machinery is designed to serve those who feel sufficiently aggrieved to bring forward their claims. Advertising, it is argued, serves to encourage the assertion of legal rights in the courts, thereby undesirably unsettling societal repose. There is even a suggestion of barratry.

But advertising by attorneys is not an unmitigated source of harm to the administration of justice. It may offer great benefits. Although advertising might increase the use of the judicial machinery, we cannot accept the notion that it is always better for a person to suffer a wrong silently than to redress it by legal action. As the bar acknowledges, "the middle 70% of our population is not being reached or served adequately by the legal profession." ABA, Revised Handbook on Prepaid Legal Services 2 (1972). Among the reasons for this underutilization is fear of the cost, and an inability to locate a suitable lawyer. Advertising can help to solve this acknowledged problem: Advertising is the traditional mechanism in a free-market economy for a supplier to inform a potential purchaser of the availability and terms of exchange. The disciplinary rule at issue likely has served to burden access to legal services, particularly for the not-quite-poor and the unknowledgeable. A rule allowing restrained advertising would be in accord with the bar's obligation to "facilitate the process of intelligent selection of lawyers, and to assist in making legal services fully available." ABA Code of Professional Responsibility EC 2–1 (1976).

4. The Undesirable Economic Effects of Advertising. It is claimed that advertising will increase the overhead costs of the profession, and that these costs then will be passed along to consumers in the form of increased fees. Moreover, it is claimed that the additional cost of practice will create a substantial entry barrier, deterring or preventing young attorneys from penetrating the market and entrenching the position of the bar's established members.

(continues)

CASE LAW *Bates v. State Bar of Arizona* (continued)

These two arguments seem dubious at best. Neither distinguishes lawyers from others . . . and neither appears relevant to the First Amendment. The ban on advertising serves to increase the difficulty of discovering the lowest cost seller of acceptable ability. As a result, to this extent attorneys are isolated from competition, and the incentive to price competitively is reduced. Although it is true that the effect of advertising on the price of services has not been demonstrated, there is revealing evidence with regard to products; where consumers have the benefit of price advertising, retail prices often are dramatically lower than they would be without advertising. It is entirely possible that advertising will serve to reduce, not advance, the cost of legal services to the consumer.

The entry-barrier argument is equally unpersuasive. In the absence of advertising, an attorney must rely on his contacts with the community to generate a flow of business. In view of the time necessary to develop such contacts, the ban in fact serves to perpetuate the market position of established attorneys. Consideration of entry-barrier problems would urge that advertising be allowed so as to aid the new competitor in penetrating the market.

5. The Adverse Effect of Advertising on the Quality of Service. It is argued that the attorney may advertise a given "package" of service at a set price, and will be inclined to provide, by indiscriminate use, the standard package regardless of whether it fits the client's needs. Restraints on advertising, however, are an ineffective way of deterring shoddy work. An attorney who is inclined to cut quality will do so regardless of the rule on advertising. And the advertisement of a standardized fee does not necessarily mean that the services offered are undesirably standardized. Indeed, the assertion that an attorney who advertises a standard fee will cut quality is substantially undermined by the fixed-fee schedule of appellee's own prepaid Legal Services Program. Even if advertising leads to the creation of "legal clinics" like that of appellants' clinics that emphasize standardized procedures for routine problems it is possible that such clinics will improve service by reducing the likelihood of error.

6. The Difficulties of Enforcement. Finally, it is argued that the wholesale restriction is justified by the problems of enforcement if any other course is taken. Because the public lacks sophistication in legal matters, it may be particularly susceptible to misleading or deceptive advertising by lawyers. After-the-fact action by the consumer lured by such advertising may not provide a realistic restraint because of the inability of the layman to assess whether the service he has received meets professional standards. Thus, the vigilance of a regulatory agency will be required. But because of the numerous purveyors of services, the overseeing of advertising will be burdensome.

It is at least somewhat incongruous for the opponents of advertising to extol the virtues and altruism of the legal profession at one point, and, at another, to assert that its members will seize the opportunity to mislead and distort. We suspect that, with advertising, most

(continues)

CASE LAW   *Bates v. State Bar of Arizona* (continued)

lawyers will behave as they always have: They will abide by their solemn oaths to uphold the integrity and honor of their profession and of the legal system. For every attorney who over-reaches through advertising, there will be thousands of others who will be candid and honest and straightforward. And, of course, it will be in the latter's interest, as in other cases of misconduct at the bar, to assist in weeding out those few who abuse their trust.

In sum, we are not persuaded that any of the proffered justifications rise to the level of an acceptable reason for the suppression of all advertising by attorneys. . . .

In holding that advertising by attorneys may not be subjected to blanket suppression, and that the advertisement at issue is protected, we, of course, do not hold that advertising by attorneys may not be regulated in any way. We mention some of the clearly permissible limitations on advertising not foreclosed by our holding.

Advertising that is false, deceptive, or misleading of course is subject to restraint. See Virginia Pharmacy Board v. Virginia Citizens Consumer Council, 425 U.S., at 771–772, and n. 24, 96 S.Ct., at 1830–1831. . . . In fact, because the public lacks sophistication concerning legal services, misstatements that might be overlooked or deemed unimportant in other advertising may be found quite inappropriate in legal advertising. For example, advertising claims as to the quality of services a matter we do not address today are not susceptible of measurement or verification; accordingly, such claims may be so likely to be misleading as to warrant restriction. Similar objections might justify restraints on in-person solicitation. We do not foreclose the possibility that some limited supplementation, by way of warning or disclaimer or the like, might be required of even an advertisement of the kind ruled upon today so as to assure that the consumer is not misled. In sum, we recognize that many of the problems in defining the boundary between deceptive and nondeceptive advertising remain to be resolved, and we expect that the bar will have a special role to play in assuring that advertising by attorneys flows both freely and cleanly.

As with other varieties of speech, it follows as well that there may be reasonable restrictions on the time, place, and manner of advertising. . . . And the special problems of advertising on the electronic broadcast media will warrant special consideration.

The constitutional issue in this case is only whether the State may prevent the publication in a newspaper of appellants' truthful advertisement concerning the availability and terms of routine legal services. We rule simply that the flow of such information may not be restrained, and we therefore hold the present application of the disciplinary rule against appellants to be violative of the First Amendment.

The judgment of the Supreme Court of Arizona is therefore affirmed in part and reversed in part.

It is so ordered.

(continues)

AN OVERVIEW OF THE RULES ON ADVERTISING

Unlike the principles of client confidentiality, whose consequences may be controversial to the public but are not necessarily to the legal profession, the rules allowing advertising can raise the hackles of those within the legal profession, as well as those outside of it. Many lawyers, including past presidents of the American Bar Association, still believe that lawyer advertising is unseemly and should be prohibited. Because lawyers are regulated at the state level, it is important that one become familiar with one's own jurisdiction's rules on lawyer advertising. Those rules may differ significantly from the general rules created by the ABA.

Information About Legal Services Shall Not Be False or Misleading

ABA Model Rule 7.1 states, "A lawyer shall not make a false or misleading communication about the lawyer or the lawyer's services." This rule is broader than just advertising and encompasses any communication lawyers (or their employees) would make about their legal services, whether made to the public or to an individual. All communications made by the law firm, from a television commercial to a holiday greeting card, need to occur within the bounds of the governing ethics rules. The ABA Model Code stated that a "lawyer shall not . . . use . . . any form of public communication containing a false, fraudulent, misleading, deceptive, self-laudatory or unfair statement or claim." DR 2–101. It also allowed a lawyer to list certain kinds of information, such as memberships in bar associations or foreign language fluency, and it allowed lawyers to publish such information in the geographic areas in which "the lawyer resides or maintains offices or in which a significant part of the lawyer's clientele resides." DR 2–101(B). That rule also required that such information be "*presented in a dignified manner.*" (Emphasis added)

The 1983 version of ABA Model Rule 7.1 categorized three kinds of information that qualify as false or misleading: (a) fraudulent information: material misrepresentations of fact or law or equivalent omissions of fact; (b) inappropriate implications, which are statements that are likely to create unjustified expectations of success or that give the impression the lawyer can succeed by sidestepping the law; or (c) inappropriate comparisons, which are unsubstantiated statements that compare one lawyer's services to another's (See Exhibit 6–4). The newer version of MR 7.1 eliminates sections (b) and (c) because they were thought to be overly broad. However, the message of those two sections has been turned into two Comments. One Comment explains how truthful statements can still be misleading if there is a "substantial likelihood that it will lead a reasonable person to formulate a specific conclusion about the lawyer or the lawyer's services for which there is no reasonable factual foundation." The other former part of the rule is now a Comment concerning lawyers who create unjustified expectations based on unsubstantiated comparisons to other lawyers' services. That Comment also states that "the inclusion of appropriate disclaimer or qualifying language may preclude a finding that a statement is likely to create unjustified expectations. . . ."

Fraudulent Information

Generally, fraud involves some material misrepresentation of fact designed to induce someone to act in reliance on the misrepresentation, as well as the resulting harm to the person whose reliance was miscast. Misrepresentations of fact can also be made through silence, in a situation where one would have a duty to speak. For instance, if a statute requires car dealers to inform their customers about the dealers' cars that contain engines that have been rebuilt, a car dealer could commit fraud two ways: lying about whether a car's engine was rebuilt, or simply saying nothing about a car containing a rebuilt engine.

Determining what makes a statement fraudulent is not always easy. In a Minnesota case, a lawyer placed an advertisement in the Yellow Pages that said, "we have an office near you" and then listed nine cities. Of those nine locations, seven of them were simply office buildings where the lawyer rented space on an

---

EXHIBIT 6–4   THREE KINDS OF MISLEADING COMMUNICATION

1. **Fraudulent Information**

   Material misrepresentations of fact: *"no recovery, no fees."*

   Omissions can also be fraudulent: *"Our clients got 5 million last year"* might actually mean, *"one client settled for 4.9 million and the others lost at trial."*

2. **Inappropriate Implications**

   Unjustified expectations, sidestepping the law: *"All of our clients became millionaires."*

3. **Inappropriate Comparisons**

   Comparisons that are unverifiable: *"Everyone knows that Yale lawyers are better than Penn lawyers."*

---

hourly basis whenever he would meet with clients in those areas. The state ethics committee concluded that such an advertisement was false and misleading and that it warranted discipline. The lawyer argued that his clients never complained about the advertisement and that some were grateful he made spaces available for them far from his primary office. The Minneapolis Supreme Court reversed the decision of the ethics committee, finding that, although the lawyer's advertisement was vague and not forthcoming, it was not a material misrepresentation as a matter of law. *In re Charges of Unprofessional Conduct against 95–30,* 550 N.W.2d 616 (Minn. 1996). However, when a lawyer advertised by using his name and the phrase "and Affiliates," he was reprimanded because there were, in fact, no affiliates. Instead, the attorney was a sole practitioner who had occasionally shared office space with other lawyers. *Medina County Bar Assn v. Grieselhuber,* 678 N.E.2d 535 (Ohio 1997).

Statements made about a lawyer's fees can be found to be material misrepresentations. Although Chapter 7 discusses legal fees, at this point is important to recognize that a prospective client's misunderstanding about what constitutes "fees" can be exacerbated by deceitful statements or advertisements made by lawyers. (Remember, because paralegals are prohibited from establishing fees because that would constitute the unauthorized practice of law, misunderstandings about fees should rarely occur because of the legal assistant's misstatements.) A United States Supreme Court case is illustrative in that it involved a lawyer who was sanctioned for a variety of advertising violations, including an advertisement that included the statement, "If there is no recovery, no legal fees are owed by our clients." That statement was found to be misleading

NOT QUITE LINCOLN

Perhaps He Should Have Argued That It Was the Medication Talking

Colorado attorney Kallman Elinoff was in court attending a hearing the day after injuring his arm in a snowboarding accident, and was taking pain medication. The judge, aware of Mr. Elinoff's condition, inquired whether the hearing should be continued and received Elinoff's assurances that he was fully capable of representing his client.

At the hearing's conclusion, Elinoff's client was ordered to jail, and became frantic that he couldn't say goodbye to his girlfriend, who herself would be going to jail the next day. His pleading with the detectives who placed him in handcuffs after the hearing, that he be released so he could see his girlfriend one more time, was to no avail.

So, Elinoff approached the officers in the presence of his client, pulled out hundreds of dollars of cash, and offered it to them as a bribe to allow his client to be free for one day.

The officers didn't take the bait, and the next day Elinoff apologized to them for his bribe. Although he wasn't arrested or charged with bribery, Elinoff was charged with professional misconduct. Elinoff's mind-boggling motivation in the bribe attempt was to show his client that nothing more could be done to effect his release.

The Hearing Board saw no wit or humor in the joke-bribe, and disbarred him, concluding that whatever Elinoff's motive was, he had clearly shown the intent to offer a bribe to two police officers. However, at a rehearing on the matter, the Board reduced the sanction to a three-year suspension, taking into consideration Elinoff's deep remorse for his ill-advised tactic. The Colorado Supreme Court upheld the reduced sanction.

because it did not include any mention that the client would be liable for the costs and expenses of litigation. *Zauderer v. Office of Disciplinary Counsel*, 471 U.S. 626 (1985). In a California case, an attorney was disciplined for communication violations, including mailing letters to prospective bankruptcy clients that mentioned that only $60 in cash was needed to apply for debt relief, but failed to mention that legal fees would reach 10 times as much. *Leoni v. State Bar*, 704 P.2d 183 (Cal. 1985). Other courts have found that incomplete statements about fees or advertised fees that are lower than the charged fees are examples of misleading statements. *See People v. Roehl*, 655 P.2d 1381 (Colo. 1983); *Florida Bar v. Gudish*, 421 So. 2d 501 (Fla. 1982).

Not saying something crucial can be as misleading as falsely saying something. So, the ethics rules and the case law hold lawyers responsible for omissions that leave the wrong impression. A Kentucky case serves as a good (or, perhaps, bad) example. When a lawyer learned through some friends about the death of a hospital patient, she wrote a syrupy and mournful letter to the former patient's widow. Besides writing five spelling or punctuation errors ("truely," "solicite," "husbands"), the lawyer told the widow, who already had an attorney, "I am a strong Christian. I believe that God has reasons for everything and if it is in his perfect plan that I represent you, then he will provide the means. If someone else is to represent you, then he will insure that my information reaches that person." (If that quotation is hard to follow, it is because the pronouns "his" and "he" should be "His" and "He" in reference to God.) The lawyer also wrote in the letter, "that my background provides me with a strong basis of knowledge with which to protect your interests...." That phrase caught the attention of the Kentucky Supreme Court, which considered it a misleading statement because the letter omitted to mention that the lawyer had only been practicing law for two years and had never taken a medical malpractice case. She was suspended for six months. *Kentucky Bar Ass'n v. Mandello*, 32 S.W.3d 763 (Ky. 2000).

Inappropriate Implications

No lawyer in his or her right mind would say to a prospective client, "Choose me, but be advised that your chances of getting what you want are no greater than if you choose a lawyer by throwing a dart at the phone book." All marketing is designed to get the public to want the products or services being advertised. But statements made in connection with legal services, whether made for the mass media or communicated in person by the paralegal, must avoid creating an unjustified expectation of success or giving the impression that success can be obtained through flouting the law.

UNJUSTIFIED EXPECTATIONS. Unjustified expectations are created when the client is led to believe that a favorable outcome is assured or that because of the lawyer's past performance, similar results will occur. As to the former, lawyers are generally not allowed to engage in a selling technique known as **puffing**, which involves making grand statements about a product or service but does not qualify as a **warranty**. For instance, the seller of a house can say, without getting in trouble, "This is the best house on the block," because no prospective buyer should expect to win a lawsuit arguing that the seller lied and that, in fact, the house was only the second best on the block. But lawyers and their employees may make no such grand statements. In an Arizona case, a lawyer was suspended for 30 days for, **inter alia**, running a television advertisement that showed a car accident, a couple in a hospital waiting room, the husband/father kissing his daughter goodbye for the last time, and then the lawyer arguing before a jury in a courtroom. Because the lawyer never took cases to trial as a matter of law firm policy and had never tried a personal injury case, the court found the commercial to be misleading. *Matter of Zang*, 741 P.2d 267 (Ariz. 1987).

▨ **puffing**

A real word, used in sales contexts to mean an opinion or belief that is not meant to be taken as a statement of fact or warranty.

▨ **warranty**

A statement that amounts to a promise of quality or the assurance of certain facts.

▨ **inter alia**

A Latin phrase that means "among other things."

Promoting one's track record can also create unjustified expectations. Such was the problem in an Indiana case where an attorney was disciplined for sending an improper solicitation letter to prospective clients that included detailing the attorney's track record in successfully **plea bargaining** drunk driving cases. *In re Frank*, 440 N.E.2d 676 (Ind. 1982). The problem associated with statements about a lawyer's track record is that, even if unstated, an implication might be inferred that future clients can expect the lawyer to achieve the same results. Statements of fact, however, are not always held to be misleading, including stating that "thousands of successful claims have been brought against this particular manufacturer." D.C. Bar Comm. on Legal Ethics, Op. 188 (1987).

Testimonials can also lead to unjustified expectations. The Comment to MR 7.1 mentions advertisements containing client endorsements as something that would ordinarily be prohibited if they create unjustified expectations. Some states, including Arkansas, Connecticut, Florida, Indiana, Nevada, and Pennsylvania take a conservative approach to client testimonials or endorsements and expressly ban them. Other states, such as California and New York, allow limited use of testimonials. California requires the disclosure of impersonators and dramatizations in advertisements (Cal. Bus. & Prof. Code § 6157.2), and New York allows the use of client testimonials as long as the testimonials do not come from currently pending cases and as long as they include a disclaimer stating that past results cannot guarantee or predict similar future outcomes (NY DR 2-101 (c)(1); N.Y. State Bar Ass'n Comm. on Professional Ethics, Op. 614 [1990]).

Inconspicuous disclaimers are often an obligatory part of advertising, from the "Don't try this at home" statement placed on the screen of a television commercial right before a weekend jock engages in a Herculean feat of strength after chugging a sports drink, to the barely noticeable "Past performance is no indication of future results" line. That line is usually at the bottom of the magazine ad for a financial services conglomerate, telling you in much larger print that it has a proven track record of astounding investment success. Well, one state, Missouri, has put quite the buzzkill on its lawyer advertisements by requiring that those ads—which by their very existence imply "I'm a good lawyer"—include the following conspicuous disclaimer: "The choice of a lawyer is an important decision and should not be based solely on advertisements." Missouri Rules of Prof. Conduct, Rule 4–7.3(f).

SIDESTEPPING THE LAW. Although it almost goes without saying, lawyers and their paralegals are not allowed to make any statements in connection with legal services that give the impression that favorable results can be obtained through means that are outside the scope of applicable ethics rules or other laws. Certain lawyers carry more influence than others, and many clients are more than willing to pay for such influence, but lawyers may not imply that they can represent legal matters through the use of impermissible influence. Suppose that a criminal defense lawyer states to a client that she (the lawyer) is a friend of the district attorney and so the chances of a favorable plea bargain are good. That kind of statement would violate MR 7.1(b). In a South Carolina case, a lawyer

> **plea bargaining**
> Negotiating in a criminal case, resulting in the prosecutor and the defendant agreeing to dispose of the charges through a settlement in which the defendant pleads guilty to a lesser charge.

aired two television commercials involving automobile accidents. In one of the commercials, an actor playing a police officer called the lawyer to the accident scene to get the lawyer's opinion about who was at fault; in the other commercial, the lawyer was directing the police officer's on-scene activities. Both commercials were found to be in violation of South Carolina's version of MR 7.1(b), because they implied that the lawyer had influence over the police. *Matter of Pavilick*, 488 S.E.2d 309 (S.C.1997).

Inappropriate Comparisons

The third kind of misleading statements prohibited by MR 7.1 involve unsubstantiated comparisons of one lawyer's services to another. MR 7.1(c). Again, the distinction between lawyer advertising and other forms of business advertising needs to be made. While no legitimate advertising can be **libelous**, sellers of products and services are allowed to say, "You'll like ours better than theirs." Lawyers, on the other hand, are prohibited from making comparisons to other lawyers unless those comparisons are factually substantiated. Some bar associations have issued ethics opinions that provide specificity to this general prohibition. Alabama prohibited the use of a commercial that suggested viewers call a lawyer referral service, rather than "take a chance" on the phone book (Ala. State Bar Gen. Counsel, Op. 89–18 [1989]); Philadelphia prohibited the advertising phrase, "Big city experience, small town service," because it subjectively implied that the advertising lawyer's services were better than other lawyers' services (Philadelphia Bar Association Guidance Comm.; Op. 94–12 [1995]); and Virginia prohibited the use of an advertising letter to criminal defendants in which the lawyer stated that his fees were lower than others in the community (Va. State Bar Comm. on Legal Ethics, Informal Op. 862 [1986]).

Grand statements and superlatives are not the only kind of inappropriate comparisons; any comparison that is unverified is inappropriate. Even words such as "experienced" and phrases such as "quickly becoming recognized as a premier personal injury law firm" have been found to be inappropriate because of the difficulty in verifying them. *See Spencer v. Honorable Justices of Superior Court*, 579 F. Supp. 880 (E.D. Pa. 1984); *In re Anonymous*, 637 N.E.2d 131 (Ind. 1994).

Lawyer Advertising: The Nuts and Bolts

Although lawyers were allowed to advertise in phone books before *Bates*, that decision resulted in the expansion of lawyer advertising into other media. The 1983 version of Model Rule 7.2(a) expressly allows lawyers to advertise their "services through public media, such as a . . . newspaper or other periodical, outdoor advertising, radio or television, or through written or recorded communication." The Ethics 2000 version MR 7.2(a) eliminates the specific

---

■ libelous

Libel is a false written statement that is published and made in order to harm the reputation of another. Slander is the spoken form of libel. Libel and slander are different forms of defamation.

NOT QUITE LINCOLN

If **The Most Petulant Lawyers In America** *Book Is Ever Published, Virginia Will Have a Few Inductees*

The Richmond law firm of Allen, Allen, Allen, & Allen wasn't too shy about crowing that the 2002 edition of *The Best Lawyers in America* listed three of its lawyers. While one might debate the merits of how anyone can conclude each year who the best lawyers are, out of the hundreds of thousands across the country, that book has been doing so since 1983.

As part of promoting itself, the Allen, etc. law firm included in one of its television advertisements the statement that of the four Richmond lawyers who practice personal injury law listed in *The Best Lawyers in America*, three of them were from Allen, Allen, Allen, & Allen.

Mortally afflicted by one of the seven deadly sins, envy, other Richmond lawyers raised such a ruckus that the Virginia Bar Council issued an ethics opinion stating that a law firm that touted its inclusion in *The Best Lawyers in America* was making extravagantly self-laudatory statements in violation of Virginia's ethics rules. This ethics opinion was a response to complaints made by other obviously excluded lawyers. The excluded lawyers complained about the methods used and the fees required to be included in the book.

Allen, Allen, Allen, & Allen sued the Virginia Bar in federal court, claiming that its ethics opinion violated free speech. The federal judge involved agreed with that view. He expressed in harsh terms his thoughts on the matter when, during a hearing, he stated "I have been a member of the Virginia State Bar for 52 years, and I have never thought the Virginia State Bar would let itself be used as a stalking-horse to accommodate competitors who are trying to get a drop on a law firm. And this is exactly what this case is all about... and why [the Virginia State Bar] were simple-minded enough to accept this assignment is a total mystery to me."

Getting the message loud and clear, the Virginia Bar Council reversed itself in a second ethics opinion, concluding that although a lawyer may not call himself or herself "the best" or "the greatest," it may advertise that it is listed in a publication that does so.

To see similar statements that led to the original controversy, check out the law firm's Web site: http://www.allenandallen.com/.

examples of advertising in favor of the phrase, "recorded or electronic communication, including public media." Such a broader phrase allows the rule to keep pace with current technology.

The 1983 version of Model Rule 7.2(b) requires lawyers to keep a copy of every recording of an advertisement or communication for two years, as well as a record of its use, while the current version eliminates that requirement because the Committee found that it was too burdensome. The former MR 7.2(c) (now 7.2(b)) prohibits lawyers from paying anyone for recommending the lawyer's services, with three exceptions: (1) lawyers may pay for the costs associated with permissible advertising; (2) lawyers may make contributions to a not-for-profit legal lawyer referral service or legal service organization; and (3) lawyers may purchase a law firm (provided it comports with the rule on sales of law firms, MR 1.17). The current version of MR 7.2(b) also includes a fourth exception, namely that lawyers may form nonexclusive agreements to refer clients to one another, provided the clients being referred are made aware of the arrangements.

Finally, the 1983 version of MR .2 requires any lawyer advertisement to "include the name of at least one lawyer responsible for its content," while the current version allows a law firm also to be responsible for an advertisement's content. An addition to one of the Comments now discusses the Internet and mentions e-mail as permissible advertising. The Model Code's provision on advertising, DR 2–101, is quite similar to the 1983 Model Rules provisions, except the Model Code did not require that advertisements include the name of a lawyer responsible for the ad.

After Bates: Can States Still Restrict Lawyer Advertising?

The short answer is yes, state ethics rules can place certain restrictions on the methods by which lawyers advertise or promote their services. The restrictions can vary from jurisdiction to jurisdiction. For instance, South Carolina issued an ethics opinion authorizing lawyers to offer discount coupons for their services as part of the "Welcome Wagon" program for new community residents (S.C. Bar Ethics Advisory Comm.; Op. 96–27 [1997]); Alabama, however, does not, believing that participation in the Welcome Wagon gives the misleading impression that a third party is endorsing the lawyer's services (Ala. State Bar General Counsel, Op. 91–17 [1991]).

Whatever the limits placed on lawyer advertising, all restrictions must be constitutionally legitimate, which means that if commercial speech is to be restricted, it must be tied to a legitimate state interest. Two U.S. Supreme Court cases that followed *Bates* are instructive.

In re R.M.J. In *In re R.M.J.*, 455 U.S. 191 (1982), Missouri's Supreme Court Advisory Committee moved to disbar a lawyer because he advertised in ways other than those listed as permissible in the Missouri rules. Two of his violations included the fact that he listed his areas of practice using words other than those allowed in the rules (he used "personal injury" and "real estate" instead of "tort law" and "property law") and he had sent announcement cards to persons other than lawyers, clients, former clients, personal friends, and relatives (as limited in the rules). The Missouri Supreme Court reprimanded him instead, and he appealed. The United States Supreme Court reversed, finding that because the attorney's advertisements were not misleading, they could not be prohibited because the state had failed to show any substantial interest in restricting the use of the words the lawyer had chosen to describe his areas of practice. Moreover, the Court ruled that the state had shown no evidence that it was necessary to place an absolute ban on mailing announcement cards to anyone other than allowed in the state's rule.

Zauderer v. Office of Disciplinary Counsel The Supreme Court dealt with the restrictions on illustrations used in lawyer advertising in *Zauderer v. Office of Disciplinary Counsel*, 471 U.S. 626 (1985). That case involved an Ohio lawyer who was reprimanded by the Ohio Supreme Court for placing an advertisement in 36 newspapers that sought clients who may have been harmed by an intrauterine contraceptive device (IUD) known as the Dalkon Shield. The advertisement included a line drawing of the Dalkon Shield, as well as the question, "Did you use this IUD?" The ad then proceeded to inform readers how they could contact the lawyer and included information on fees that said: "The cases are handled on a contingent fee basis of the amount recovered. If there is no recovery, no legal fees are owed by our clients." Over 200 women contacted the lawyer after seeing the advertisement. The Ohio Supreme Court found that the ad violated the advertising rules because those rules prohibited drawings or illustrations, required ads to be dignified, and required any mention of contingency fees to also disclose the distinction between fees and costs.

While acknowledging that jurisdictions have the authority to limit lawyer advertising, the U.S. Supreme Court focused its analysis on misleading or false advertising. The Court found that Ohio could not prohibit the advertisement under the general theory that it was seeking a particular class of client because the advertisement was not deceptive and did not amount to illegal solicitation.

Furthermore, the Court found that it was an unconstitutional infringement of free speech to prohibit drawings or illustrations in lawyer advertisements because of an assumed danger of viewer confusion when, as was the case here, the illustration of the Dalkon Shield was accurate. Concerning the state's interest in promoting dignified advertising, the Court noted that Ohio made no suggestion that the ad was undignified. And (more fundamentally) even if such a danger of undignified ads was palpable, that would still be insufficient to trigger an outright ban on ads with illustrations. The Court also decided that a general interest in promoting dignified communication does not allow for an abridgement of First Amendment rights. However, the Court did agree with the Ohio Supreme Court that the advertisement warranted a reprimand because the statements in the advertisement concerning fees were misleading: the ad failed to alert the viewer to the difference between contingency fees and litigation costs.

A Few More Generalities About Lawyer Advertising

Beyond the larger concepts of the constitutionality and free speech aspects of lawyer advertising, there remain the specifics of such advertising. What follows are some explanations on a few advertising guidelines found in the ABA Model Rules and Model Code and their effects in certain jurisdictions. For more basic rules on lawyer advertising, see Exhibit 6–5.

EXHIBIT 6–5   GENERALITIES ABOUT LAWYER ADVERTISING

- Lawyers are allowed to advertise in print, on radio, on TV, and on the Internet.

- Many jurisdictions require lawyers to retain a copy of an advertisement for a year or more.

- Lawyers may not pay finder's fees to those, *including paralegals*, who would recommend a lawyer's services.

- Lawyers must usually refrain from referring to themselves as specialists in an area of the law, unless they have met the specialization requirements of their jurisdiction.

- Some jurisdictions prohibit lawyers from using testimonials or dramatic action in their advertisements.

- A few jurisdictions still retain the curious requirement that advertisements be "dignified."

TYPES OF TRUTHFUL INFORMATION THAT CAN BE INCLUDED IN AN ADVERTISEMENT. The ABA Model Rules and Model Code provide a framework on advertising that the jurisdictions that regulate lawyers put in effect by specifying the kinds of information that are appropriate to be communicated in an advertisement. And, as previously stated, those rules vary considerably. Pennsylvania, for instance, prohibits the use of advertisements containing the endorsements of a celebrity or public figure. Pennsylvania Rules of Professional Conduct, 7.2(d). Some states, including Indiana, advise as to what factual information is appropriate in legal advertisements. The following excerpt from New York's ethics rules is an example of the kinds of information that can be communicated:

It is proper to include information, provided its dissemination does not violate the provisions of DR 2-101 [1200.6] (A), as to:

1. legal and nonlegal education, degrees and other scholastic distinctions, dates of admission to any bar; areas of the law in which the lawyer or law firm practices, as authorized by the Code of Professional Responsibility; public offices and teaching positions

held; memberships in bar associations or other professional societies or organizations, including offices and committee assignments therein; foreign language fluency;

2. names of clients regularly represented, provided that the client has given prior written consent;

3. bank references; credit arrangements accepted; prepaid or group legal services programs in which the attorney or firm participates; and

4. legal fees for initial consultation; contingent fee rates in civil matters when accompanied by a statement disclosing the information required by DR 2–101 [1200.6] (L); range of fees for services, provided that there be available to the public free of charge a written statement clearly describing the scope of each advertised service; hourly rates; and fixed fees for specified legal services. New York Code of Professional Responsibility DR 2–101(C).

RECORD KEEPING. As stated earlier in the chapter, the 1983 version of the Model Rules required that lawyers retain a copy of any advertisement for two years, while the Ethics 2000 version eliminated the retention requirement, because The Ethics 2000 Commission believed it was too burdensome a requirement. Nevertheless, many jurisdictions, including those that have become Ethics 2000 jurisdictions, still retain the requirement that lawyers keep copies of their advertisements for specified periods of time. Those jurisdictions include: Alabama (six years); Alaska (two years); Arkansas (five years); California (two years); Florida (three years); Illinois (three years); Indiana (six years); Kansas (two years); Louisiana (three years); Mississippi (three years); Nevada (four years); New Mexico (five years); New York (one year for computer-accessed ads, three years for all others); Oklahoma (three years); Pennsylvania (two years); South Carolina (two years); Texas (four years); Virginia (one year); Wisconsin (two years).

Some states include Internet advertising in their rules. New York and Utah modified their requirements on retaining advertisements to cover Internet advertising and mandate that firms retain every Web page from their Web sites. In New York's case, the Web site's current version must be saved every 90 days. Alternatively, Iowa exempts from its advertising rules information available from a lawyer's Web site hyperlink. Iowa Rule of Professional Conduct, Rule 32:7.2(a)(3).

Although the ABA rules do not require that advertisements be approved before dissemination, a few states require lawyers to submit a copy of their advertisements to the appropriate regulatory authority, sometimes before the ad is to be placed: Florida (Florida Rules of Prof. Conduct, Rule 4–7.7(a–c); Kentucky (Rules of the Supreme Court of Kentucky, Rule 3.130); Mississippi

(Mississippi Rules of Prof. Conduct, Rule 7.5); South Dakota (S.D. Rules of Prof. Conduct, Rule 7.3). In Florida's case, there was much rancor expressed by some lawyers when the new rules were proposed, not only because of having to fulfill the requirements of sending in all ads (including radio and television) for preapproval, but also because of the belief that these rules were unconstitutional restraints on free speech.

■ **patent**

The grant of ownership in an invention, giving the owner exclusive rights over the invention for a certain number of years.

■ **admiralty**

Admiralty law involves the traditional rules and practices associated with the navigation of the sea or commercial transaction conducted on navigable waterways. Admiralty law is also known as maritime law.

ADVERTISING A SPECIALTY. ABA Model Rule 7.4 has guidelines under which lawyers may advertise that they specialize in a particular area of the law. The general rule in the 1983 version of 7.4 is that lawyers may not state or imply that they specialize in a field of practice unless one of three exceptions apply: (a) lawyers may list themselves as a **patent** attorney (or something similar) if they have been admitted to practice before the United States Patent and Trademark Office; (b) lawyers who practice **admiralty** law may designate that fact; and (c) lawyers may advertise that they have been certified as a specialist if the certification was granted by an approved certification agency or, if the agency is not approved by the jurisdictions where the lawyers practice, that fact is listed in the advertisement. As shown by the case *In re Anonymous*, used in the Chapter 1 "How to Brief a Case" section, lawyers can even be sanctioned if they use an advertisement that implies they are specialized, if they have not been certified according to their jurisdiction's certification prerequisites.

The Ethics 2000 version of 7.4 has a revised title, "Communication of Fields of Practice *and Specialization*." (Emphasis added.) The rule has been effectively rewritten such that the parts concerning specialization are in a section distinct from the parts on patent attorneys and admiralty practice. Another change prohibits lawyers from claiming or implying certification if the certifying organization is not approved by an appropriate state authority, or accredited by the ABA, while requiring that when lawyers are allowed to claim a certification, the certifying organization be "clearly identified" in the advertisement. This allows the prospective client to investigate the claim of certification. Finally, the Comments that allowed for non-approved, certifying organizations have been eliminated.

The Model Code had a stricter rule on specializations, as did the original version of the Model Rules, but the ABA amended Model Rule 7.4 after the Supreme Court's decision in *Peel v. Attorney Registration and Disciplinary Commission*, 496 U.S. 91 (1990). In *Peel*, the Court overturned an Illinois rule that prohibited all specialization listings except admiralty, patent, and trademark. Although Illinois argued that, because it had no certification or specialization programs of its own, it had the right to protect the public from misleading designations, the Court found that such a blanket prohibition was too broad. Therefore, Illinois could not prohibit Peel from identifying himself as "Certified Trial Specialist by the National Board of Trial Advocacy."

In light of *Peel*, many states have amended their specialization allowances, but Kansas has removed its prerequisites on specialization altogether. Its specialization rule simply says, "A lawyer may communicate the fact that the lawyer does or does not practice in particular fields of law." Kansas Rules of Professional Conduct, Rule 7.4. Regardless of a jurisdiction's specialization or certification rules, lawyers in that jurisdiction may always advertise that their practice is limited to certain areas of practice (for instance, personal injury law). Such a statement is not the same as a statement concerning a specialization.

Many jurisdictions have modified the exact language of MR 7.4. Some, like Oregon and the District of Columbia, have no 7.4, but have prohibitions on misleading statements of specialization in other advertising rules. And others—including Colorado, Missouri, South Dakota, and Wyoming—require lawyers claiming a special certification to provide a disclaimer in their advertisements to the effect that those jurisdictions' Supreme Courts do not grant them.

PAYING FOR ADVERTISEMENTS. Obviously, lawyers have an obligation to pay for their advertisements. MR 7.2(c)(1). But both the Model Rules and the Model Code prohibit lawyers from giving anything of value to someone in exchange for a recommendation of the lawyer's services. This means that a lawyer may not pay someone a "finder's fee" for steering business their way. Lawyers have been sanctioned for paying money—or giving free legal services—to everyone, from other lawyers to business associates and even prison inmates, as a way to get more clients. Giving something of value to someone or some entity as part of a referral arrangement can also occur indirectly. For instance, lawyers can have business relationships that can lead to payments that ethics commissions view as referral fees. It has been found to be improper for a real estate company to market a lawyer's services to its clients and then charge a fee to the lawyer for such promotion. Ill. State Bar Association Comm. on Professional Ethics, Op. 96–04 (1996). It has also been found to be improper for a lawyer to speak at an estate-planning seminar if the financial planner conducting the seminar recommends the lawyer's services to the attendees. Cincinnati Bar Association Ethics Comm., Op. 95–05. The ABA has even taken the position that a law firm may not make a loan to another law firm when the method of repaying the loan is the debtor firm making referrals to the creditor firm. ABA Comm. on Ethics and Professional Responsibility, Formal Op. 94–388 (1995).

One of the exceptions to the general prohibition of paying for referrals is that lawyers may pay the usual charges of a not-for-profit lawyer referral service or legal services organization. MR 7.2(C)(2). Some examples of the kinds of organizations that would qualify are a public defender's office, a military legal assistance office, a legal aid society, and a referral agency sponsored by a bar association. A few states list the kinds of organizations that qualify. As an example, Indiana categorizes in its advertising rules the four kinds of qualified lawyer referral services that a lawyer may compensate. Indiana Rules of Professional Conduct, Rule 7.3(e)(1–4).

Often it is non-lawyers—including paralegals and legal assistants—who are the payees of money courts later conclude was wrongful. And because it is not always the payment itself, but rather the context or arrangement behind making the payment, which determines if it was an illegal finder's fee, one can be left grasping at straws trying to understand when a payment would be wrongful. A few examples of when those payments have resulted in disciplinary cases might be helpful to gain context. A Colorado lawyer was suspended for paying his incarcerated clients 10 percent of his retainer fees for referring any other inmates' cases to him. *Colorado v. Shipp,* 793 P.2d 574 (Colo. 1990). A Georgia lawyer made an agreement to pay what he thought was a legitimate referral service, not knowing that it used **accident runners** to find clients. When the lawyer realized how this business operated, he refused to pay the referral fees, but was still suspended. *In re Maniscalco,* 564 S.E.2d 186 (Ga. 2002). An Ohio lawyer concocted a scheme with a shady entrepreneur and a chiropractor, in which the first associate would form a business to call accident victims, informing them of their rights and recommending the lawyer for their legal needs and the chiropractor for their spinal needs. Another person was hired to listen for accident reports on a police scanner so he could get to the accident scenes (sometimes before the police arrived) and recommend the lawyer's services. For this, the lawyer paid his business associate over $1,000 a month, which he might have been able to afford had his law license not been suspended indefinitely because of the scheme. *Cincinnati Bar Assn. v. Rinderknecht,* 679 N.E.2d 669 (Ohio 1997).

Payments made to paralegals and legal assistants can also violate the rules against finder's fees. But, similar to what occurs in Washington when lobbyists and government officials cross paths, it can be quite difficult to distinguish a bribe from a that's-the-way-things-work-around-here payment. In a fascinating case that illustrates this type of uncertainty, a Washington, D.C., area lawyer was accused of unlawfully paying someone to refer his services after he hired another firm's paralegal and paid her a salary of $80,000 a year. The paralegal had formerly worked at a high-volume personal injury firm and became disgruntled because the firm was going to drastically reduce her salary, so she contacted another lawyer whose practice rarely included personal injury law. As a result of the paralegal's boasts about the number of her "contacts and friends" and her prediction of helping the lawyer build his practice, the lawyer hired her. Before starting employment at the new firm, she showed her new employer copies of many client information cards that she had accumulated while working at her former firm. (Keeping copies of those cards violated her former firm's employee policies.) Her new employment with the second firm was conditioned on that firm obtaining 100 personal injury files within a year of hiring her. Later, the lawyer who hired her sent cards announcing the opening of his new office to about 100 of his paralegal's former clients. Eventually and naturally, the paralegal's former firm accused the lawyer of paying the paralegal to refer clients to him, and the disciplinary tribunal agreed. However, the Maryland Court of Appeals dismissed the disciplinary charges, finding there was no evidence that the salary to the paralegal constituted an inappropriate payment, particularly in light of the fact that the paralegal's compensation package at her former firm included a salary of $87,000, a car lease, and a gasoline credit card! *Attorney Grievance Commission of Maryland v. Wills,* 705 A.2d 1121 (Md. 1998).

▨ **accident runners**
Persons hired by lawyers to find personal injury clients, usually by going to the scene of accidents or disasters. Accident runners are respected even less than ambulance chasers.

Lawyer Advertising Beyond the Printed Page

Nothing in the U.S. Supreme Court's decisions on lawyer advertising prohibits lawyers from advertising on the radio or television; likewise, nothing in the Model Rules or Model Code prohibits such advertising. Many states allow such advertising, finding that if lawyer advertising were restricted to just the printed page, such a restriction would unconstitutionally deny information about legal services to those who are illiterate, handicapped, or financially disadvantaged—the kinds of people who would need such advertising. *See Grievance Comm. for Hartford–New Britain Judicial Dist. v. Trantolo*, 470 A.2d 228 (Conn. 1984); *In re Petition for Rule of Court Governing Lawyer Advertising*, 564 S.W.2d 638 (Tenn. 1978). (However, in the Tennessee case, the Court banned the use of billboard advertising.)

A few states do place strict limitations on the use of television advertisements. Florida prohibits lawyer advertisements on radio and television from having "any spokesperson's voice or image that is recognizable to the public." Florida Rules of Prof. Conduct, Rule 4–7.5(b)(1)(B). Iowa's rule on advertising lists 19 kinds of information that may be communicated and, as concerns television advertisements, states:

> The same information, in words and numbers only, articulated by a single non-dramatic voice, not that of the lawyer, and with no other background sound, may be communicated on television. No visual display shall be allowed except that allowed in print as articulated by the announcer. Iowa Rules of Professional Conduct, Rule 32:7.2(e).

A challenge was brought to that rule but the Iowa Supreme Court upheld it, and the U.S. Supreme Court refused to hear the case. *Committee on Professional Ethics and Conduct v. Humphrey*, 377 N.W.2d 565 (Iowa 1985), appeal dismissed, 475 U.S. 1114, reh'g denied, 476 U.S. 1165 (1986). New Jersey modified its rule on advertising (N.J. Rules of Professional Conduct 7.2[a]) following a decision by the New Jersey Supreme Court that prohibited drawings, animations, dramatizations, music, or lyrics used in connection with televised advertising. *Petition of Felmeister and Isaacs*, 518 A.2d 188 (N.J. 1986).

One step beyond radio and television advertising is prerecorded telephone advertising. This kind of advertising involves a computer-generated phone call, placed to recipients (not necessarily seeking specific legal help) who, upon answering the phone, have the opportunity to listen to a taped lawyer advertisement. This kind of advertisement became allowed under the ABA Model Rules in 1989, after MR 7.2 was changed, adding "recorded" communication to the list of permissible communication.

Although this kind of communication is commonly called telephone solicitation—and rarely well received, for that matter—it is actually considered advertising and not solicitation, because the receiver of the phone simply needs to hang up to end the phone call. However, if the lawyer knows that the recipient does not want such phone calls, then placing a prerecorded phone call constitutes impermissible solicitation. More than a few state ethics opinions authorize the prerecorded telephone advertisement. Ill. State Bar Ass'n Comm. on Professional Ethics, Op. 97–6 (1988); Ind. State Bar Ass'n Legal Ethics Comm., Op. 3 of 1996; Iowa State Bar Ass'n Comm. on Professional Ethics and Conduct, Op. 86–6 (1986); Md. State Bar Ass'n Comm. on Ethics, Op. 88–61. However, Alabama does not allow such advertising (Ala. State Bar Gen. Counsel, Op. 87–43 [1987]); and neither does Ohio, a state whose rules are based on the ABA Model Code (Ohio Sup. Ct. Bd. of Comm'rs on Grievances and Discipline, Op. 90–2 [1990]). Exhibit 6–6 highlights advertising beyond print ads.

EXHIBIT 6–6   ADVERTISING BEYOND THE PRINTED PAGE

Advertising may occur on the radio, on TV, and on the Internet.

Some jurisdictions place limits on what may presented in a televised commercial, such as prohibiting testimonials, actors, or music.

A few jurisdictions (Florida, Kentucky) require review and preapproval of TV ads.

Prerecorded, computer-generated telephone ads are generally allowed, unless the lawyer knows of the recipient's opposition to such a call.

Law firm Web sites are generally permitted, but might be required to be saved for record keeping purposes.

Some jurisdictions prohibit law firms from linking with third-party referral, Web sites.

Advertising on the Internet

Doing business on the Internet was thought to be, during the late 1990s, the ticket to immense wealth. Then the Internet bubble burst in 2000. (Anybody remember furniture.com or pets.com?) Much of that downturn was in the area of pure business-to-consumer Internet businesses, where profit margins were thin or nonexistent, except to giants like Amazon and Ebay.

But as technology has advanced, the ability to advertise has expanded. As early as 1995, bar associations and legal scholars were considering the propriety of lawyer advertising on the Internet, with the consensus being that lawyers can do so as long as their advertising complies with applicable ethics rules.

A law firm Web page is a common form of advertising that is considered in the same category as telephone directory advertising, and is allowable. For instance, Florida expressly allows Internet advertising in its ethics rules and declares that "computer-accessed communications" are a permissible form of advertising. Florida Rules of Professional Conduct, Rule 4–7.1(a). Specific rules governing Internet advertising are also in place (Rule 4–7.6) and include allowing the sending of unsolicited e-mail advertisements to prospective clients within certain guidelines, such as requiring that all subject lines in e-mail advertising have the statement "legal advertising" (Rule 4–7.6[c][3]). New York allows a lawyer to maintain a Web site that has a domain names different than the lawyer's name, provided the lawyer's name is conspicuously on all Web site's pages. New York Lawyer's Code of Professional Responsibility, DR2-102(E). And New York's proposed ethics rules based on the ABA Model Rules severely restricts a lawyer's use of Internet pop-up ads, as well as meta-tags and hidden codes. Rule 7.1(g). Texas requires that a hard copy of the opening screen of a firm's Web site be sent to the Texas Advertising Review Committee, in compliance with the Texas Disciplinary Rules of Professional Conduct, Rule 7.07. Other states' ethics opinions have given approval to legal advertising on the Internet, subject to applicable advertising rules. State Bar of Ariz. Comm. on Rules of Professional Ethics and Conduct, Op. 96–1 (1996); Iowa State Bar Ass'n Comm. on Professional Ethics, Op. 96–10 (1997); State Bar of Mich. Comm. on Professional and Judicial Ethics, Op. RI–276 (1997); Tenn. Sup. Ct. Bd. of Professional Responsibility Ethics Comm., Op. 95–A–570 (1995).

Allowing law firms to advertise on the Internet does not mean a jurisdiction will give the firms carte blanche. For instance, New York allows Internet advertising, but prohibits the type of ads we all have come to hate: pop-up ads. New York Code of Professional Responsibility, DR 2–101(G)(1).

Baker & McKenzie is reputed to be America's largest law firm, with over 3,400 lawyers, 70 offices in 38 countries, and annual revenues of over $1.5 billion. It maintains an extensive Web site, which includes links on how paralegals can apply for employment: http://www.bakerinfo.com/BakerNet/default.htm.

Some law-related Web sites allow users to be linked to law firm Web sites. Once they are accessed by a prospective client seeking general legal information, these third-party Web sites categorize law firms and provide direct links to the firms' home pages. Some jurisdictions do not allow law firms to participate in such linked Internet advertising if the firm must pay a fee to a for-profit Web site in order to provide such a link (see the previous section on referral fees). Arizona Ethics Op. 05–08 (2005); Ohio Supreme Court Board of Commissioners on Grievances and Discipline, Op. 2001–2 (2001); Ohio Supreme Court Board of Commissioners on Grievances and Discipline, 2000–5 (2000); Nebraska State Bar Association Adv. Op. 95–3 (1995). Iowa makes no distinction between for-profit and not-for-profit linked Web sites, and it prohibits its attorneys from using such on-line referral services. Iowa State Ass'n Comm. on Professional Ethics and Conduct, Op. 00–07 (2000). A recent Texas ethics opinion concluded that its lawyers may not subscribe to for-profit referral services that collect information over the Internet from prospective clients about their legal problems and then forward that information to subscribing lawyers. Texas Prof. Ethics Opinion 561 9(2005).

Other jurisdictions do allow attorneys to associate with for-profit Web sites in order to access clients, including class-action plaintiffs. Some of those jurisdictions who have issued favorable ethics opinions include: District of Columbia Bar Legal

Ethics Committee, Op. 302 (2000); Maine Board of Bar Overseers Professional Ethics Comm., Op. 174 (2000); Bar Association of Nassau County Committee on Professional Ethics, Op. 01–4 (2001); S.C. Ethics Advisory Op. 01–03 (2001).

The legal search engine Findlaw.com provides third-party referrals, as can be found on its home page: http://www.findlaw.com/.

Finally, it should be advised that the issues concerning legal advertising on the Internet are distinct from issues concerning practicing law on the Internet. Because a jurisdiction allows its lawyers to advertise on the Internet does not mean it also allows lawyers to practice law through such electronic means of communication.

Should Advertising Be Dignified?

At a speech in 1995, former U.S. Supreme Court Chief Justice Warren Burger referred to "huckster-shyster" advertising lawyers, who bring shame to the profession by the methods in which they advertise. He further stated the following:

> Unfortunately, the shyster conduct in solicitation and advertising is no longer limited to the "ambulance chasers." Today we see television ads, Yellow Pages ads, and (believe it or not) ads on billboards 40 feet wide and 15 feet high, touting a lawyer or law firm reaching out for clients. With such ads, lawyers usually emphasize that the "First Conference Is Free." Doesn't this have the ring of "Come into my parlor, said the spider to the fly?" It is sheer nonsense to say that the public needs lawyer advertising for people to have effective access to the judicial system. 63 Fordham Law Review 949 (1995).

The ABA Model Code of Professional Responsibility required that advertisements be presented in a "dignified manner." DR 2–101 (B). Even though the ABA Model Rules do not require dignified ads, an ABA Commission on Advertising put forward some nonbinding, aspirational goals, adopted in 1988, which included calling for dignified lawyer advertising. And some states, such as Indiana and Iowa, which have adopted the ABA Model Rules, still retain a requirement that advertising be done in a "dignified manner." Ind. Rules of Prof. Conduct, Rule 7.2(b); Iowa Rules of Professional Conduct, Rule 32:7.2(g). Other states, such as New Jersey, removed the dignity requirement from their rules. *Petition of Felmeister and Isaacs*, 518 A.2d 188 (N.J. 1986).

PROVOCATIVE ADVERTISEMENTS: ARE THERE ANY LIMITS? New York (whose state bar in 2007 proposed switching to ethics rules based on the ABA Model Rules, but who still follows the ABA Model Code until the Appellate Division of its Supreme Court adopts the recommendation) also removed the dignity requirement from its advertising rule. One wonders, had New York not removed the dignity requirement, what it would have done with the case of Rosalie Osias, a real estate lawyer from Long Island who uses sexually suggestive poses and double entendre to advertise her legal services. Some of her ads, placed in banking trade magazines, have shown her sitting atop a Harley-Davidson motorcycle, in high heels, wearing a short leather skirt and a low-cut jacket, with the caption, "We will ride anything . . . to get to your closing on time." In other ads, she is similarly dressed and sprawled across a desk or is wearing only lingerie. One ad shows her in high heels, wearing a short skirt, with her leg propped up on a stack of law books with the attached caption, "Anywhere . . . Anytime . . . Anyhow . . . Anybody . . . ANY POSITION . . . We are Ready . . . [then, in a smaller type size] to close your loan."

It is no surprise that other lawyers were less than thrilled with her methods of advertising. In fact, her county's bar association contemplated bringing charges against her, believing her ads were a disgrace, but eventually decided against it. Ms. Osias claimed victory—she said her practice increased 800 percent—and argued that her ads were a necessary means to help her break into the New York real estate market, something she says is run by an "old-boys network." She was even quoted in an *ABA Journal* article as saying, "I think female attorneys should market themselves visually. . . . They're not going to make money just being smart and having a J.D. in hand. It's OK as long as they deliver serious and good legal work." 83 A.B.A. Journal, at 14 (1997). However, one male lawyer, in the spirit of "if you can't beat them, join them," decided to compete with her by running an advertisement that showed him topless behind a shower curtain, with the caption, "I might not look as good in a bikini as other attorneys, but I do good loans."

Ms. Osias runs a self-titled foundation, whose stated mission is "to explore the dynamics of the feminist movement and, through an aggressive and innovative public information program, champion femininity in the workplace as a means of achieving meaningful career advancement." With more than a few provocative pictures of its founder on its Web site, the foundation offers the chance to book the legal gadfly for a personal appearance, provides her personal biography (including her aforementioned triumph against the bar association), and also posts her unique essays on feminism and the workplace. It also offers an "Ally McBeal Law School Scholarship" for women who, in addition to providing photographs, compete for $25,000 by writing an essay on how they have embraced the philosophy of the lead character from the 1990s television show, *Ally McBeal.* This can be done by explaining how the "use of femininity and their application of sexual tension has aided the applicant in cracking the glass ceiling that has impeded their professional career or academic growth." Interested applicants, or the just plain curious, can find Ms. Osias's Web site at: http://www.osiasfoundation.org/. "Rosalie Osias has a kindred spirit in Corri Fetman, the lead partner in Fetman, Garland, and Associates, the law firm that placed the "Life's Short. Get a Divorce." billboards, discussed in the Chapter's introduction. In addition to practicing law, Ms. Fetman writes "The Lawyer of Love" column for Playboy's Web site, where she answers readers' legal questions and provides a few not-safe-for-court pictures of herself."

ADVERTISING AND THE PARALEGAL

Whenever paralegals and legal assistants speak about their firms' legal services, they need to be especially careful that whatever they say could not reasonably be construed to be false or misleading. Because paralegals need to follow their jurisdictions' lawyer conduct rules, they should likewise be careful about statements that compare one lawyer's services to another or create unjustified expectations.

Those paralegals and legal assistants who perform administrative tasks in smaller firms should be extra careful that, before placing any advertisement for the firm, the advertisement does not violate some of the more esoteric parts of the various advertising rules in their jurisdiction. For instance, although ABA Model Rule 7.5(a) (including the current version) does not prohibit law firms using trade names that do not imply a government or charitable connection, more than a few jurisdictions prohibit or heavily restrict the use of law firm trade names ("Divorce Deliverance, P.C."), including Arizona, Indiana, Mississippi, New York, and Ohio. And some jurisdictions prohibit the use of advertisements with dramatizations, testimonials, or endorsements, including California, Louisiana, Oregon, Virginia, Wisconsin, and Wyoming. And, as has been discussed earlier, jurisdictions are parsimonious about allowing their lawyers to call themselves *specialists*, or anything resembling that word.

For illustration on the types of advertisements that can and, more importantly, cannot be placed, examine the following advertisements in Exhibit 6–7, which come from the Web site of the Florida Bar. Some of advertisements comply with Florida's advertising rules, and some do not. Notice the comments on why certain advertisements violate Florida's advertising rules.

The Paralegal as Part of the Law Firm's Advertising

Many jurisdictions have adopted an addition to Model Rule 7.5 (or another advertising rule) and allow paralegals to be listed on the firm's letterhead and other stationery, as well as to be included in the firm's advertising. Alternatively, jurisdictions that have adopted some form of the ABA Model Guidelines on the Utilization of Paralegal Services are likely to expressly allow paralegals and legal assistants to be listed on letterhead, as well as have their own business cards, because Guideline 5 authorizes that. Whether paralegals would be listed on letterhead is another matter: professional letterhead can be quite expensive, and because paralegals are not part of the more permanent structure of the firm (i.e., the partners), firms may decide to limit their letterhead listings. Similarly, paralegals and legal assistants may have law firm business cards that list them as such, including their educational degrees or certifications. This realization should come as no surprise because such listings, if true and clearly delineated, do not violate the principles against false or misleading communication.

EXAMPLES OF COMPLYING AND NONCOMPLYING ADS

A. PRINT ADVERTISEMENTS

1. PRINT ADVERTISEMENT THAT *COMPLIES* WITH APPLICABLE BAR RULES

[THIS AD IS *EXEMPT* FROM THE FILING REQUIREMENT, UNDER RULE 4-7.8(a).]

PERSONAL INJURY and WRONGFUL DEATH

No Recovery, No Fees or Costs
Office Hours: 9 a.m. to 6 p.m. M-F
Weekend and evening appointments available.

John Smith, P.A.
Attorney at Law

Board Certified civil trial specialist by The Florida Bar.
Also licensed as M.D. in Florida.

(407) 555-7890
123 Main Street
Orlando

–1–

EXHIBIT 6–7a   Samples of Complying/Noncomplying FL Ads—Print Advertisements

2. PRINT ADVERTISEMENT THAT *COMPLIES* WITH APPLICABLE BAR RULES (*NOT EXEMPT FROM FILING*)

34   ATTORNEYS   Centel Directory Co.

PERSONAL INJURY AND DEATH CASES

FREE FIRST VISIT

LAW OFFICES OF
JONES & BROWN, P.A.
TRIAL ATTORNEYS
SINCE 1971

MR. JONES RECEIVED A DEGREE IN PHARMACY. THAT MEDICAL AND SCIENTIFIC KNOWLEDGE HELPS HIM UNDERSTAND MEDICAL AND SCIENTIFIC LITIGATION. MR. BROWN HAS 24 YEARS EXPERIENCE AS A PERSONAL INJURY TRIAL LAWYER.

- ☒ Auto & Truck Accidents
- ☒ Birth Related Injuries
- ☒ Defective Products
- ☒ Medical Negligence
- ☒ Workers Compensation
- ☒ Insurance Company Disputes
- ☒ Dog Bites

NO FEE IF NO RECOVERY*
***EXCLUDES COSTS**

555-7890
432 Main Street, Tampa

Jones & Brown, P.A. Office Building

–2–

EXHIBIT 6–7b   Samples of Complying/Noncomplying FL Ads—Print Advertisements

Reprinted with Permission of the Florida Bar

3. PRINT ADVERTISEMENT THAT *COMPLIES* WITH APPLICABLE BAR RULES
(*NOT EXEMPT FROM FILING*)

DIVORCE?

**Caring Representation in Family Law Matters.
I Want to Help You Through this Difficult Time.**

SUSAN JONES, P.A.

Serving St. Pete Residents Since 1975	111 Main Street St. Petersburg 555-1234	Payment Plans Available

Susan Jones is Board Certified in Marital and Family Law by The Florida Bar

–3–

EXHIBIT 6–7c Samples of Complying/Noncomplying FL Ads—Print Advertisements

Reprinted with Permission of the Florida Bar

4. PRINT ADVERTISEMENT THAT *COMPLIES* WITH APPLICABLE BAR RULES
(*NOT EXEMPT FROM FILING*)

FAMILY LAW

An Attorney Who Cares For Your Rights!

BILL BROWN
Attorney-at-Law
Orlando

Se Habla Español   **555-1234**   **Free Consultation**

—4—

EXHIBIT 6–7d Samples of Complying/Noncomplying FL Ads—Print Advertisements
Reprinted with Permission of the Florida Bar

5. PRINT ADVERTISEMENT THAT DOES *NOT COMPLY*

INJURED?

Then you need
an attorney. ❷

❶

We Will Recover $ for You! ❸

❸

Call Us Today at
555-1234

SMITH, JONES & JONES, P.A.
Tampa & Orlando

❶ - Illustration is a visual portrayal that is deceptive, misleading or manipulative in violation of Rule 4-7.2(c)(3).

❷ - Misleading in violation of Rule 4-7.2(c)(1)(B) because an attorney is not always required.

❸ - Statement and illustration promise results in violation of Rule 4-7.2(c)(1)(G).

–5–

EXHIBIT 6–7e   Samples of Complying/Noncomplying FL Ads—Print Advertisements
Reprinted with Permission of the Florida Bar

6. PRINT ADVERTISEMENT THAT DOES **_NOT_ COMPLY**

**Is Your Money
All Tied Up
By Creditors?** ❶

Then You Want to
Consider the Benefits of

BANKRUPTCY:

* **Stop Creditor Calls** ❷
* **Stop Foreclosures** ❷
* **Discharge Debts** ❷

Best Bankruptcy Law Firm ❸

222 Main Street
Tallahassee
555-1234

❹

Chapter 7 - $499❺

❶ - Illustration is a visual portrayal that is deceptive, misleading or manipulative in violation of Rule 4-7.2(c)(3).

❷ - Promises Results in violation of Rule 4-7.2(c)(1)(G) because it promises relief that is sometimes available when bankruptcy is filed but fails to disclose that such results may be only temporary or that such results are not always obtainable.

❸ - Trade Name characterizes the quality of the lawyer's services in violation of Rule 4-7.2(c)(2).

❹ - Does not disclose the name of the attorney responsible for the ad. Rule 4-7.2(a)(1).

❺ - Fails to disclose whether client will be liable for costs in addition to the fee. Rule 4-7.2(c)(7).

–6–

EXHIBIT 6–7f Samples of Complying/Noncomplying FL Ads—Print Advertisements

7. PRINT ADVERTISEMENT THAT DOES *NOT COMPLY*

❶TOPFLIGHT ATTORNEYS

MAIN OFFICE:
Jacksonville Address
111 South 32nd Boulevard
Suite 1000
Jacksonville, Florida 32201

1-800-TOP-ATTY❷
or
1-800-539-5050

Top Flight Attorneys is a law firm of ❷ top-rated trial lawyers. The firm limits its practice to personal injury and wrongful death. We have helped hundreds of people who have suffered injury due to someone else's negligence. Top Flight Attorneys will ensure that you recover the full financial compensation you deserve. ❸

EXPERIENCE MAKES THE DIFFERENCE! ❹

❺

❶ Trade name that characterizes the quality of legal services violate Rule 4-7.2(c)(2).
❷ Use of the term "top-rated" & TOP-ATTY characterizes the quality of legal services and, therefore violates Rule 4-7.2(c)(2).
❸ This sentence promises results, in violation of Rule 4-7.2(c)(1)(G).
❹ Because experience of the attorneys may not effect the outcome of a particular case, this sentence violates Rule 4-7.2(c)(1)(B) which prohibits misleading communications.
❺ Fails to include the name of at least one attorney responsible for the ad's content, as required by Rule 4-7.2(a)(1).

–7–

EXHIBIT 6–7g   Samples of Complying/Noncomplying FL Ads—Print Advertisements
Reprinted with Permission of the Florida Bar

In 1989, the ABA issued Informal Ethics Opinion 1527, in which the ABA expressly approved of paralegals and legal assistants being listed on letterhead and having their own business cards. Likewise, state ethics opinions give such approval, sometimes overturning prior ethics opinions that prohibited the practices. For example, New Jersey and Texas issued ethics opinions expressly allowing paralegals to be listed on law firm letterhead, thus rescinding prior opinions that prohibited it. (New Jersey State Bar Committee on Attorney Advertising, Op. 16 (1994)); (Professional Ethics Committee of the Supreme Court of Texas, Op. 436 (1986)). The following is a nonexclusive list of other jurisdictions that have issued ethics opinions or rules of court permitting the listing of paralegals on firm letterhead and/or on business cards: Alabama (1986); Cleveland, OH (1989); Colorado (1990); Connecticut (1985); Florida (1986); Hawaii (1984); Illinois (1989); Indiana (1984, and in the Guidelines for the Use of Legal Assistants, 1994); Kansas (1992); Massachusetts (1983); Michigan (1991, and in the Guidelines for the Utilization of Legal Assistants, 1993); Minnesota (1980); Mississippi (1984); Missouri (in the Guidelines for Practicing with Paralegals, 1987); New Hampshire (business cards only, 1987); New Mexico (business cards only, 1986); New York (1997, although in 1992 it prohibited the use of "paralegal coordinator" or any title that includes the word "advocate"); North Dakota (1997); Oregon (1977); Rhode Island (business cards only, 1993); South Carolina (1988); South Dakota (in the Guidelines for the Utilization of Legal Assistants, 1992); Vermont (1999, but independent contracting paralegals may not be listed on letterhead); Virginia (1989); Washington (in the Guidelines for the Utilization of Legal Assistant Services, 1994); and Wisconsin (1985).

Where paralegals and legal assistants are allowed to be listed on firm publications or to have their own business cards, the delineation as a non-lawyer needs to be clearly shown, or else the risk of a misleading communication might come to fruition. A Michigan ethics opinion spoke to that issue when, in answering the question put to it by a law firm, it concluded that putting a non-lawyer on the firm's letterhead without clearly identifying that person as a non-lawyer would violate Michigan's advertising rules. The employee in question was someone with an MBA degree who worked extensively in the estate-planning department of the firm, and who the firm wanted to put on its letterhead, with the title "Estate Administrator" along with "MBA." Although nothing in Michigan expressly prohibits non-lawyer employees from being listed on firm letterhead, the reason for the opinion's conclusion was that, without affirmatively stating that the employee was not a lawyer, such an omission was misleading. Mich. Ethics Op. RI–323 (2001). Exhibit 6–8 summarizes some important guidelines about paralegals and legal advertising.

EXHIBIT 6–8 THE PARALEGAL AND ADVERTISING

- ABA Model Guideline for the Utilization of Paralegal Services, Guideline 5, states: *A lawyer may identify paralegals by name and title on the lawyer's letterhead and on business cards identifying the lawyer's firm.*

- Many jurisdictions have followed suit, authorizing in their rules of court, or ethics opinions, that paralegals and legal assistants may be listed on firm letterhead and may have their own business cards.

- Independent-contracting paralegals could only advertise to lawyers, not the general public, as that would be the unauthorized practice of law.

Direct Advertising by Independent Contracting Paralegals: Be Careful

As was discussed in Chapters 2 and 3, some jurisdictions allow paralegals to operate as independent contractors. As entrepreneurs, those paralegals have a keen interest in getting the message out that they can provide legal assistant services. Then, for them, advertising becomes a means to an end. Although there is almost no direct authority on the subject, entrepreneurial paralegals should safely be able to advertise their services as long as they remember one important fact: because only lawyers or law firms can hire a freelance paralegal, the advertising can only be directed toward lawyers. Advertising that is directed toward the public is illegal, because only lawyers can represent the public. Advertisements placed by an independent-contracting paralegal in the Yellow Pages, for instance, which give the impression that anyone in need of legal services should contact the paralegal, are the kinds of misleading communications that can result in legal action against the paralegal.

A case discussed in Chapter 2, *State v. Robinson*, 468 S.E.2d 290 (S.C. 1996), is instructive on this point. There, a paralegal advertised his services in the Yellow Pages quite dramatically with the statement, "If your rights have been violated—call me," in an attempt to get prospective litigants as customers. He also distributed a business card that referred to him as a "paralegal consultant." In fact, he represented others in court 16 times. It is no surprise that the South Carolina Supreme Court issued an **injunction** against him, denying his claim that he had a First Amendment right of free speech to advertise the way he did. As to his business card, the phrase *paralegal consultant* should be avoided by all independent-contracting paralegals because it is a misleading title.

injunction
A court order forbidding a party to do something or ordering them to start doing something.

SOLICITATION

Although advertising and solicitation have the same objective—getting clients—the rules that govern solicitation are the inverse of the rules that govern advertising. The ethics rules generally allow lawyers to advertise and then present exceptions that limit or prohibit certain kinds of advertising. But the ethics rules generally prohibit lawyers from soliciting and then present limited exceptions that allow certain kinds of solicitation.

So strict are the solicitation rules that some states actually make illegal solicitation a crime, usually under the label of barratry: Georgia, in Ga. Code Ann. § 16–10–95[b], made barratry a felony punishable by up to five years in prison until the law was repealed in 2006; New Mexico, in N.M.Stat. Ann. § 30–27–3(C), makes barratry a misdemeanor; Texas has a barratry statute, Tex. Pen. Code § 38.12(a)(b), which specifically applies to lawyers in subsection d, and in a 2005 barratry case, part of the evidence against the convicted attorney was his paralegal's testimony, who had been given immunity even though she was an accomplice who admitted at trial that she lied when testifying to the grand jury. *State v. Mercier*, 164 S.W.3d 799 (Tex. Ct. App. 2005). Although one could argue that criminalizing barratry—which is a form of speech—is unconstitutional, those statutes are almost always upheld. *See State v. Sullivan*, 19 P.3d 1012 (Wash. 2001).

What makes solicitation of prospective clients so different from advertising to them? The answer lies in the means to achieve the objective. Advertising is intended toward no one specifically; it is directed toward the masses. Solicitation is more personal, occurring very often in face-to-face situations or toward targeted groups. Although one of the funniest scenes in the movie version of *The Rainmaker* involves Danny DeVito's character scrounging for clients in the rooms of the local hospital and signing up a patient in traction who is unable to sign the retainer agreement, his behavior is clearly unethical and, in some jurisdictions, illegal. Because it is quite difficult for courts to regulate such personal contact between lawyers and prospective clients, and because of the belief that solicitation is highly susceptible to abuse, the U.S. Supreme Court has approved the banning of certain forms of solicitation (Exhibit 6–9).

Advertising	Solicitation
• is generally allowed, but has limitations and some restrictions	• is generally prohibited, but has limited exceptions
• is directed to the masses	• is targeted to individuals
• is passive, requiring the recipient to do nothing	• is confrontational, requiring the recipient to respond
• is considered less susceptible to abuse	• is considered highly susceptible to abuse

EXHIBIT 6–9   Advertising vs. Solicitation

There is an alternative view to the strict approach to solicitation taken by the U.S. Supreme Court and the states. A few legal ethics scholars believe that the abuses associated with client solicitation are overblown and that by continuing to prohibit or severely restrict solicitation, the bar perpetuates the unfortunate notion of lawyers as predators hunting financial gain. Furthermore, these scholars argue that the more information consumers have about legal services, the better off they are, particularly those in the general public who need low-cost legal services.

The Rules Against Direct Contact with Prospective Clients

The Ethics 2000 version of ABA Model Rule 7.3(a) provides,

"A lawyer shall not by in-person, live telephone, or real-time electronic contact solicit professional employment from a prospective client when a significant motive for the lawyer's doing so is the lawyer's **pecuniary** gain, unless the person contacted:

1. is a lawyer; or

2. has a family, close personal, or prior professional relationship with the lawyer."

> ■ **pecuniary**
> That which concerns money.

The former version of 7.3(a) did not include "electronic real-time," and did not include an exception for soliciting close personal friends. An Internet chat room is an example of a real-time electronic contact under this rule. ABA Model Code DR 2–104(A) forbade a lawyer from accepting employment that came as a result of unsolicited legal advice to a layperson who was not a "close friend, relative, former client (if the advice is germane to the former employment), or one whom the lawyer reasonably believes to be a client." Notice that the current version of 7.3 is more in line with the Model Code's version because they both allow the solicitation of close friends.

In-Person Solicitation

While the exceptions will be discussed in the following paragraphs, it is important to bear in mind that the strictest application of the anti-solicitation rules is in the area of direct contact: in-person or live telephone solicitation. The U.S. Supreme Court gave its express approval of such a prohibition in *Ohralik v. Ohio State Bar Association*, 436 U.S. 447 (1978).

While reading *Ohralik*, pay attention to the reasons given by the Court for allowing the ban on in-person solicitation.

Some jurisdictions have made the text of the ABA's anti-solicitation rule even stricter. The state of Washington's version prohibits lawyers from using "a third person" to solicit prospective clients. More than a few jurisdictions prohibit lawyers from soliciting other lawyers, including: Alabama (which also forbids

CASE LAW   *Ohralik v. Ohio State Bar Association*

436 U.S. 447 (1978)

Mr. Justice POWELL delivered the opinion of the Court.

In Bates v. State Bar of Arizona, 433 U.S. 350, 97 S.Ct. 2691, 53 L.Ed.2d 810 (1977), this Court held that truthful advertising of "routine" legal services is protected by the First and Fourteenth Amendments against blanket prohibition by a State. The Court expressly reserved the question of the permissible scope of regulation of "in-person solicitation of clients—at the hospital room or the accident site, or in any other situation that breeds undue influence—by attorneys or their agents or 'runners.'" Id., at 366, 97 S.Ct., at 2700. Today we answer part of the question so reserved, and hold that the State—or the Bar acting with state authorization—constitutionally may discipline a lawyer for soliciting clients in person, for pecuniary gain, under circumstances likely to pose dangers that the State has a right to prevent.

Appellant, a member of the Ohio Bar, lives in Montville, Ohio. Until recently he practiced law in Montville and Cleveland. On February 13, 1974, while picking up his mail at the Montville Post Office, appellant learned from the postmaster's brother about an automobile accident that had taken place on February 2 in which Carol McClintock, a young woman with whom appellant was casually acquainted, had been injured. Appellant made a telephone call to Ms. McClintock's parents, who informed him that their daughter was in the hospital. Appellant suggested that he might visit Carol in the hospital. Mrs. McClintock assented to the idea, but requested that appellant first stop by at her home. During appellant's visit with the McClintocks, they explained that their daughter had been driving the family automobile on a local road when she was hit by an uninsured motorist. Both Carol and her passenger, Wanda Lou Holbert, were injured and hospitalized. In response to the McClintocks' expression of apprehension that they might be sued by Holbert, appellant explained that Ohio's guest statute would preclude such a suit. When appellant suggested to the McClintocks that they hire a lawyer, Mrs. McClintock retorted that such a decision would be up to Carol, who was 18 years old and would be the beneficiary of a successful claim.

Appellant proceeded to the hospital, where he found Carol lying in traction in her room. After a brief conversation about her condition, appellant told Carol he would represent her and asked her to sign an agreement. Carol said she would have to discuss the matter with her parents. She did not sign the agreement, but asked appellant to have her parents come to see her. Appellant also attempted to see Wanda Lou Holbert, but learned that she had just been released from the hospital. He then departed for another visit with the McClintocks.

(continues)

CASE LAW *Ohralik v. Ohio State Bar Association* (continued)

On his way appellant detoured to the scene of the accident, where he took a set of photographs. He also picked up a tape recorder, which he concealed under his raincoat before arriving at the McClintocks' residence. Once there, he re-examined their automobile insurance policy, discussed with them the law applicable to passengers, and explained the consequences of the fact that the driver who struck Carol's car was an uninsured motorist. Appellant discovered that the McClintocks' insurance policy would provide benefits of up to $12,500 each for Carol and Wanda Lou under an uninsured-motorist clause. Mrs. McClintock acknowledged that both Carol and Wanda Lou could sue for their injuries, but recounted to appellant that "Wanda swore up and down she would not do it." Ibid. The McClintocks also told appellant that Carol had phoned to say that appellant could "go ahead" with her representation. Two days later appellant returned to Carol's hospital room to have her sign a contract, which provided that he would receive one-third of her recovery.

In the meantime, appellant obtained Wanda Lou's name and address from the McClintocks after telling them he wanted to ask her some questions about the accident. He then visited Wanda Lou at her home, without having been invited. He again concealed his tape recorder and recorded most of the conversation with Wanda Lou. After a brief, unproductive inquiry about the facts of the accident, appellant told Wanda Lou that he was representing Carol and that he had a "little tip" for Wanda Lou: the McClintocks' insurance policy contained an uninsured-motorist clause which might provide her with a recovery of up to $12,500. The young woman, who was 18 years of age and not a high school graduate at the time, replied to appellant's query about whether she was going to file a claim by stating that she really did not understand what was going on. Appellant offered to represent her, also, for a contingent fee of one-third of any recovery, and Wanda Lou stated "O.K."

Wanda's mother attempted to repudiate her daughter's oral assent the following day, when appellant called on the telephone to speak to Wanda. Mrs. Holbert informed appellant that she and her daughter did not want to sue anyone or to have appellant represent them, and that if they decided to sue they would consult their own lawyer. Appellant insisted that Wanda had entered into a binding agreement. A month later Wanda confirmed in writing that she wanted neither to sue nor to be represented by appellant. She requested that appellant notify the insurance company that he was not her lawyer, as the company would not release a check to her until he did so. Carol also eventually discharged appellant. Although another lawyer represented her in concluding a settlement with the insurance company, she paid appellant one-third of her recovery in settlement of his lawsuit against her for breach of contract.

Both Carol McClintock and Wanda Lou Holbert filed complaints against appellant with the Grievance Committee of the Geauga County Bar Association. The County Bar Association referred the grievance to appellee, which filed a formal complaint with the

(continues)

CASE LAW *Ohralik v. Ohio State Bar Association* (continued)

Board of Commissioners on Grievances and Discipline of the Supreme Court of Ohio. After a hearing, the Board found that appellant had violated Disciplinary Rules (DR) 2–103(A) and 2–104(A) of the Ohio Code of Professional Responsibility. The Board rejected appellant's defense that his conduct was protected under the First and Fourteenth Amendments. The Supreme Court of Ohio adopted the findings of the Board, reiterated that appellant's conduct was not constitutionally protected, and increased the sanction of a public reprimand recommended by the Board to indefinite suspension. . . . We now affirm the judgment of the Supreme Court of Ohio.

The solicitation of business by a lawyer through direct, in-person communication with the prospective client has long been viewed as inconsistent with the profession's ideal of the attorney-client relationship and as posing a significant potential for harm to the prospective client. It has been proscribed by the organized Bar for many years. Last Term the Court ruled that the justifications for prohibiting truthful, "restrained" advertising concerning "the availability and terms of routine legal services" are insufficient to override society's interest, safeguarded by the First and Fourteenth Amendments, in assuring the free flow of commercial information. Bates, 433 U.S., at 384, 97 S.Ct., at 2709. The balance struck in Bates does not predetermine the outcome in this case. The entitlement of in-person solicitation of clients to the protection of the First Amendment differs from that of the kind of advertising approved in Bates, as does the strength of the State's countervailing interest in prohibition.

A

Appellant contends that his solicitation of the two young women as clients is indistinguishable, for purposes of constitutional analysis, from the advertisement in Bates. Like that advertisement, his meetings with the prospective clients apprised them of their legal rights and of the availability of a lawyer to pursue their claims. . . .

[T]he State does not lose its power to regulate commercial activity deemed harmful to the public whenever speech is a component of that activity. . . . In-person solicitation by a lawyer of remunerative employment is a business transaction in which speech is an essential but subordinate component. While this does not remove the speech from the protection of the First Amendment, as was held in Bates and Virginia Pharmacy, it lowers the level of appropriate judicial scrutiny. Unlike a public advertisement, which simply provides information and leaves the recipient free to act upon it or not, in-person solicitation may exert pressure and often demands an immediate response, without providing an opportunity for comparison or reflection. The aim and effect of in-person solicitation may be to provide a one-sided presentation and to encourage speedy and perhaps uninformed decisionmaking; there is no opportunity for intervention or counter-education by agencies of the Bar, supervisory authorities, or persons close to the solicited individual. . . .

(continues)

CASE LAW   *Ohralik v. Ohio State Bar Association* (continued)

It also is argued that in-person solicitation may provide the solicited individual with information about his or her legal rights and remedies. In this case, appellant gave Wanda Lou a "tip" about the prospect of recovery based on the uninsured-motorist clause in the McClintocks' insurance policy, and he explained that clause and Ohio's guest statute to Carol McClintock's parents. But neither of the Disciplinary Rules here at issue prohibited appellant from communicating information to these young women about their legal rights and the prospects of obtaining a monetary recovery, or from recommending that they obtain counsel. DR 2–104(A) merely prohibited him from using the information as bait with which to obtain an agreement to represent them for a fee. The Rule does not prohibit a lawyer from giving unsolicited legal advice; it proscribes the acceptance of employment resulting from such advice. . . .

B

The state interests implicated in this case are particularly strong. In addition to its general interest in protecting consumers and regulating commercial transactions, the State bears a special responsibility for maintaining standards among members of the licensed professions. . . . The substantive evils of solicitation have been stated over the years in sweeping terms: stirring up litigation, assertion of fraudulent claims, debasing the legal profession, and potential harm to the solicited client in the form of overreaching, overcharging, underrepresentation, and misrepresentation. The American Bar Association, as *amicus curiae,* defends the rule against solicitation primarily on three broad grounds: It is said that the prohibitions embodied in DR2–103(A) and 2–104(A) serve to reduce the likelihood of overreaching and the exertion of undue influence on lay persons, to protect the privacy of individuals, and to avoid situations where the lawyer's exercise of judgment on behalf of the client will be clouded by his own pecuniary self-interest. We need not discuss or evaluate each of these interests in detail as appellant has conceded that the State has a legitimate and indeed "compelling" interest in preventing those aspects of solicitation that involve fraud, undue influence, intimidation, overreaching, and other forms of "vexatious conduct." Brief for Appellant 25. We agree that protection of the public from these aspects of solicitation is a legitimate and important state interest.

We agree that the appropriate focus is on appellant's conduct. And, as appellant urges, we must undertake an independent review of the record to determine whether that conduct was constitutionally protected. *Edwards v. South Carolina,* 372 U.S. 229, 235, 83 S.Ct. 680, 683, 9 L.Ed.2d 697 (1963). But appellant errs in assuming that the constitutional validity of the judgment below depends on proof that his conduct constituted actual overreaching or inflicted some specific injury on Wanda Holbert or Carol McClintock. His assumption flows from the premise that nothing less than actual proved harm to the solicited individual would be a sufficiently important state interest to justify disciplining the attorney who

(continues)

> ### CASE LAW *Ohralik v. Ohio State Bar Association* (continued)
>
> solicits employment in person for pecuniary gain. Appellant's argument misconceives the nature of the State's interest. The Rules prohibiting solicitation are prophylactic measures whose objective is the prevention of harm before it occurs. The Rules were applied in this case to discipline a lawyer for soliciting employment for pecuniary gain under circumstances likely to result in the adverse consequences the State seeks to avert. . . .
>
> On the basis of the undisputed facts of record, we conclude that the Disciplinary Rules constitutionally could be applied to appellant. . . . The facts in this case present a striking example of the potential for overreaching that is inherent in a lawyer's in-person solicitation of professional employment. They also demonstrate the need for prophylactic regulation in furtherance of the State's interest in protecting the lay public. We hold that the application of DR2-103(A) and 2-104(A) to appellant does not offend the Constitution.
>
> Accordingly, the judgment of the Supreme Court of Ohio is affirmed.
>
> **Case Questions**
>
> 1. Attorney Ohralik argued that there was no evidence that anyone suffered harm as a result of his solicitation activities. Is that accurate?
>
> 2. What did you think was the key general distinction the Court made between advertising and solicitation?
>
> 3. What exactly did the Court decide with respect to solicitation?
>
> 4. Why was this case not decided simply on the basis of Ohralik's free-speech rights?
>
> 5. What arguments were put forth by the Court that supported its decision?
>
> 6. Ohralik did more than engage in improper solicitation. Reexamine the facts and find other ethics violations in Ohralik's activities.

lawyers from permitting their employees to do that), Alaska, Arkansas, California, Colorado, Florida (which also forbids the lawyer's employees), Illinois, Kentucky, Maine, New Hampshire, New Jersey, Oklahoma, Tennessee, Texas, Virginia, and Wisconsin. And some of the same jurisdictions still prohibit the solicitation of personal friends of former clients: Maine, New Jersey, Virginia.

Solicitation Other Than in Person

Although it is seems obvious to think of solicitation as a face-to-face endeavor, other forms of direct contact with prospective clients are also viewed as solicitation, rather than advertising. Three forms will be discussed: written solicitation, telephone solicitation, and Internet solicitation.

NOT QUITE LINCOLN

Talk About a Rainmaker – This Lawyer Created His Own Cloud Cover

In a law firm, being good at serving client needs is often less important to one's career than being skilled at getting clients. While some associates become partners through the brilliance of their legal skills, nothing helps to ensure rising from the ranks of the worker bees like being known for bringing in the clients and their fees.

The client cultivation methods employed by Mason Pimsler of Queens, New York, might have gotten the young lawyer a partnership share if he hadn't been convicted and disbarred in the process. While working for the firm of Mallilo & Grossman in 1998 and 1999, every weekend Pimsler would call the answering service for the law firm of Rosenberg, Minc, Falkoff & Wolff, a Manhattan personal injury firm, pretending to be partner Daniel Minc. Pimsler then asked for the recent prospective client messages. Pimsler's next step was to hustle off to those persons and sign them up as clients of his firm before Rosenberg Minc lawyers could get to them after receiving the message list prepared by the answering service.

One could question which is more startling: that it took Rosenberg Minc quite some time to start to wonder if it had been infiltrated by an imposter, or that Mallilo & Grossman didn't stop to wonder how a lawyer fresh out of law school could have brought in over 100 personal injury cases in about a year?

However, retaining personal injury clients with high-profile and valuable cases can cause a firm to look the other way. Rosenberg Minc began to realize they were victims of fraud when a disgruntled client, who thought she was a Rosenberg Minc client, called to complain about the promised limousine that never arrived.

Soon, the cops were involved, a sting was set up, and Pimsler was arrested for criminal impersonation, which led to his disbarment and guilty plea. At his disbarment proceedings, he begged for leniency, claiming the source for his actions was his inexperience and the pressure he was under at his firm.

Rosenberg Minc then sued Pimsler for fraud, and Mallilo & Grossman for, among other things, unjust enrichment. The law firm pled ignorance to no avail, and in 2004 a jury awarded Rosenberg Minc $1.4 million. Since his disbarment, Pimsler is reported to have attended medical school in a foreign country. He should have gone to business school instead.

WRITTEN SOLICITATION. When does a written advertisement become a written solicitation? It does so when it is a targeted mailing. Although many jurisdictions had for some time prohibited mailed solicitations, the U.S. Supreme Court ruled in a few cases that a total ban on such solicitation was unconstitutional. In *In re R.M.J.*, 455 U.S. 191 (1982) (previously discussed in this chapter), the Supreme Court ruled that Missouri could not prohibit lawyers from mailing announcement cards to classes of persons not listed in Missouri's rules (clients, former clients, lawyers, personal friends, and relatives). Although the Court recognized the state's interest in regulating commercial speech (solicitation), it found that such a broad prohibition was too restrictive.

Then, in *Shapero v. Kentucky Bar Association*, 486 U.S. 466 (1988), the Court reversed Kentucky's decision that prohibited a lawyer from sending advertisement letters to any prospective client whose home was subject to **foreclosure**. Even though the letters were targeted solicitations made for pecuniary gain, the Court found that such a total ban on targeted mailings was unconstitutional in light of the fact that the mailings were truthful. The Court distinguished written solicitation from in-person solicitation, finding less danger of coercion in solicitation letters.

In 1995, however, the U.S. Supreme Court upheld Florida's 30-day time restriction on certain targeted, direct-mail solicitations in *Florida Bar v. Went For It, Inc.*, 515 U.S. 618. As you read the case, notice the Court's emphasis on the balance between free speech and the negative perception of lawyers.

■ **foreclosure**

The act of a creditor to take ownership and control of property that was used as collateral by the debtor.

CASE LAW   *Florida Bar v. Went For It, Inc.*

515 U.S. 618 (1995)

Justice O'CONNOR delivered the opinion of the Court.

Rules of the Florida Bar prohibit personal injury lawyers from sending targeted direct-mail solicitations to victims and their relatives for 30 days following an accident or disaster. This case asks us to consider whether such Rules violate the First and Fourteenth Amendments of the Constitution. We hold that in the circumstances presented here, they do not. In 1989, the Florida Bar (Bar) completed a 2-year study of the effects of lawyer advertising on public opinion. After conducting hearings, commissioning surveys, and reviewing extensive public commentary, the Bar determined that several changes to its advertising rules were in order. In late 1990, the Florida Supreme Court adopted the Bar's proposed amendments with some modifications. The Florida Bar: Petition to Amend the Rules Regulating the Florida Bar—Advertising Issues, 571 So.2d 451 (Fla.1990). Two of these amendments are at issue in this case. Rule 4–7.4(b)(1) provides that

> [a] lawyer shall not send, or knowingly permit to be sent, . . . a written communication to a prospective client for the purpose of obtaining professional employment if: (A) the written communication concerns an action for personal injury or wrongful death or otherwise relates to an accident or disaster involving

(continues)

CASE LAW *Florida Bar v. Went For It, Inc. (continued)*

the person to whom the communication is addressed or a relative of that person, unless the accident or disaster occurred more than 30 days prior to the mailing of the communication.

Rule 4–7.8(a) states that

[a] lawyer shall not accept referrals from a lawyer referral service unless the service: (1) engages in no communication with the public and in no direct contact with prospective clients in a manner that would violate the Rules of Professional Conduct if the communication or contact were made by the lawyer.

Together, these Rules create a brief 30-day black-out period after an accident during which lawyers may not, directly or indirectly, single out accident victims or their relatives in order to solicit their business.

In March 1992, G. Stewart McHenry and his wholly owned lawyer referral service, Went For It, Inc., filed this action for declaratory and injunctive relief in the United States District Court for the Middle District of Florida challenging Rules 4–7.4(b)(1) and 4–7.8(a) as violative of the First and Fourteenth Amendments to the Constitution. McHenry alleged that he routinely sent targeted solicitations to accident victims or their survivors within 30 days after accidents and that he wished to continue doing so in the future. Went For It, Inc., represented that it wished to contact accident victims or their survivors within 30 days of accidents and to refer potential clients to participating Florida lawyers. In October 1992, McHenry was disbarred for reasons unrelated to this suit, Florida Bar v. McHenry, 605 So.2d 459 (Fla.1992). Another Florida lawyer, John T. Blakely, was substituted in his stead.

Constitutional protection for attorney advertising, and for commercial speech generally, is of recent vintage. . . . In Bates v. State Bar of Arizona, supra, the Court struck a ban on price advertising for what it deemed "routine" legal services. . . . Nearly two decades of cases have built upon the foundation laid by Bates. It is now well established that lawyer advertising is commercial speech and, as such, is accorded a measure of First Amendment protection. (Citations omitted.) Such First Amendment protection, of course, is not absolute. . . . Mindful of these concerns, we engage in "intermediate" scrutiny of restrictions on commercial speech, analyzing them under the framework set forth in Central Hudson Gas & Elec. Corp. v. Public Serv. Comm'n of N.Y., 447 U.S. 557, 100 S.Ct. 2343, 65 L.Ed.2d 341 (1980). Under Central Hudson, the government may freely regulate commercial speech that concerns unlawful activity or is misleading. Id., at 563–564, 100 S.Ct., at 2350. Commercial speech that falls into neither of those categories, like the advertising at issue here, may be regulated if the government satisfies a test consisting of three related prongs:

(continues)

CASE LAW *Florida Bar v. Went For It, Inc.* *(continued)*

First, the government must assert a substantial interest in support of its regulation; second, the government must demonstrate that the restriction on commercial speech directly and materially advances that interest; and third, the regulation must be "'narrowly drawn.'"

We have little trouble crediting the Bar's interest as substantial. On various occasions we have accepted the proposition that

"States have a compelling interest in the practice of professions within their boundaries, and . . . as part of their power to protect the public health, safety, and other valid interests they have broad power to establish standards for licensing practitioners and regulating the practice of professions. Goldfarb v. Virginia State Bar, 421 U.S. 773 (1975)

. . . . Under Central Hudson's second prong, the State must demonstrate that the challenged regulation "advances the Government's interest 'in a direct and material way.'". . . The Bar submitted a 106-page summary of its 2-year study of lawyer advertising and solicitation to the District Court. That summary contains data—both statistical and anecdotal—supporting the Bar's contentions that the Florida public views direct-mail solicitations in the immediate wake of accidents as an intrusion on privacy that reflects poorly upon the profession. As of June 1989, lawyers mailed 700,000 direct solicitations in Florida annually, 40% of which were aimed at accident victims or their survivors. Summary of the Record in No. 74,987 (Fla.) on Petition to Amend the Rules Regulating Lawyer Advertising (hereinafter Summary of Record), App. H, p. 2. A survey of Florida adults commissioned by the Bar indicated that Floridians "have negative feelings about those attorneys who use direct mail advertising." Magid Associates, Attitudes & Opinions Toward Direct Mail Advertising by Attorneys (Dec. 1987), Summary of Record, App. C(4), p. 6. Fifty-four percent of the general population surveyed said that contacting persons concerning accidents or similar events is a violation of privacy. Id., at 7. A random sampling of persons who received direct-mail advertising from lawyers in 1987 revealed that 45% believed that direct-mail solicitation is "designed to take advantage of gullible or unstable people"; 34% found such tactics "annoying or irritating"; 26% found it "an invasion of your privacy"; and 24% reported that it "made you angry." Ibid. Significantly, 27% of direct-mail recipients reported that their regard for the legal profession and for the judicial process as a whole was "lower" as a result of receiving the direct mail. Ibid. The anecdotal record mustered by the Bar is noteworthy for its breadth and detail. With titles like "Scavenger Lawyers" (The Miami Herald, Sept. 29, 1987) and "Solicitors Out of Bounds" (St. Petersburg Times, Oct. 26, 1987), newspaper editorial pages in Florida have burgeoned with criticism of Florida lawyers who send targeted direct mail to victims shortly after accidents. See Summary of Record, App. B, pp. 1-8. . . .

(continues)

CASE LAW *Florida Bar v. Went For It, Inc.* *(continued)*

The study summary also includes page upon page of excerpts from complaints of direct-mail recipients. For example, a Florida citizen described how he was "'appalled and angered by the brazen attempt'" of a law firm to solicit him by letter shortly after he was injured and his fiancee was killed in an auto accident. Summary of Record, App. I(1), p. 2. Another found it "'despicable and inexcusable'" that a Pensacola lawyer wrote to his mother three days after his father's funeral. Ibid. Another described how she was "'astounded'" and then "'very angry'" when she received a solicitation following a minor accident. Id., at 3. Still another described as "'beyond comprehension'" a letter his nephew's family received the day of the nephew's funeral. Ibid. One citizen wrote, "'I consider the unsolicited contact from you after my child's accident to be of the rankest form of ambulance chasing and in incredibly poor taste. . . . I cannot begin to express with my limited vocabulary the utter contempt in which I hold you and your kind.'" Ibid.

In light of this showing—which respondents at no time refuted, save by the conclusory assertion that the Rule lacked "any factual basis," . . . we conclude that the Bar has satisfied the second prong of the Central Hudson test.

Passing to Central Hudson's third prong, we examine the relationship between the Bar's interests and the means chosen to serve them. . . . "What our decisions require," . . . "is a 'fit' between the legislature's ends and the means chosen to accomplish those ends," a fit that is not necessarily perfect, but reasonable; that represents not necessarily the single best disposition but one whose scope is 'in proportion to the interest served,' that employs not necessarily the least restrictive means but . . . a means narrowly tailored to achieve the desired objective." Ibid. [citations omitted]. . . . We are not persuaded by respondents' allegations of constitutional infirmity. We find little deficiency in the ban's failure to distinguish among injured Floridians by the severity of their pain or the intensity of their grief. Indeed, it is hard to imagine the contours of a regulation that might satisfy respondents on this score. Rather than drawing difficult lines on the basis that some injuries are "severe" and some situations appropriate (and others, presumably, inappropriate) for grief, anger, or emotion, the Bar has crafted a ban applicable to all postaccident or disaster solicitations for a brief 30-day period. . . . The Bar's rule is reasonably well tailored to its stated objective of eliminating targeted mailings whose type and timing are a source of distress to Floridians, distress that has caused many of them to lose respect for the legal profession. . . .

We believe that the Bar's 30-day restriction on targeted direct-mail solicitation of accident victims and their relatives withstands scrutiny under the three-pronged *Central Hudson* test that we have devised for this context. The Bar has substantial interest both in protecting injured Floridians from invasive conduct by lawyers and in preventing the erosion of confidence in the profession that such repeated invasions have engendered. The Bar's proffered study, unrebutted by respondents below, provides evidence indicating that the

(continues)

harms it targets are far from illusory. The palliative devised by the Bar to address these harms is narrow both in scope and in duration. The Constitution, in our view, requires nothing more.

The judgment of the Court of Appeals, accordingly, is *Reversed.*

Case Questions

1. What exactly was the solicitation restriction that Florida instituted that precipitated this case?

2. What is the *Central Hudson* test for regulating commercial speech?

3. The Court categorized three kinds of information gathered by the Florida Bar Association that helped convince the Court that Florida's regulation advanced the "Government's interest in a direct and material way." What were those three categories of information?

4. Do you think this case would have been decided differently had not the Florida Bar collected such scathing rebukes from the public concerning accident victim solicitations?

5. Can you think of any reasons the Court's decision could be considered wrong or too restrictive?

Florida is not alone in putting a time distance between accidents and the lawyer-solicitation of accident victims. Arizona, Arkansas, Colorado, Connecticut, Georgia, Kentucky, Louisiana, Missouri, New Mexico, New York, Maryland, and Tennessee are some of the other jurisdictions which also require lawyers to wait 30 days after an accident or disaster before soliciting the victims or family members of those who may have a personal injury of wrongful death lawsuit. Maryland's original, 30-day ban (Md. Code Ann., Bus. Occup. & Prof. § 10–605.1) also applied to the solicitation of criminal or traffic defendants, but a federal court found that part of the statute to be unconstitutional. *Ficker v. Curran*, 119 F.3d 1150 (Fourth Cir. 1997).

Model Rule 7.3(c) also adds a condition to allowing written solicitations, requiring that the words "Advertising Material" be placed on the outside of the envelope. A few jurisdictions put additional requirements in their targeted mailings rules: Arizona requires that "Advertisement" be in a font size on the outside of the envelope at least twice that of the font used on the body of the letter (Arizona Rules of Prof. Conduct, Rule 7.3(c)); California requires that mailed advertisements be labeled "Advertisement" or "Newsletter" in at least 12-point typeface on the first page (Ca. Prof. Conduct Rule 1–400(E), Standard 5); Iowa requires that the phrase, "Advertisement Only" be placed on the written solicitation in at least 9-point type (Iowa Rules of Prof. Conduct, Rule 32:7.3(d)). Other jurisdictions require lawyers who send written solicitations to also send a copy to the appropriate regulatory body, including Arizona, Florida, Indiana (which also requires a $50 filing fee every time), Iowa, New York, South Carolina (also requires a $50 filing fee), Texas, and Wisconsin.

TELEPHONE SOLICITATION. According to MR 7.3(a), live telephone contact made to a prospective client is prohibited if a significant motive for such contact is pecuniary gain. As was previously discussed in the section on advertising, pre-recorded telephone advertising is allowed in many jurisdictions, but when the lawyer knows that the recipient does not want to receive such an advertising phone call, then to do so would be constitute unlawful solicitation. And, according to the Comments in MR 7.3, because the contents of live telephone conversations between a lawyer and a prospective client are not subject to third-party scrutiny, the danger of misleading communication is heightened.

INTERNET SOLICITATION. While many jurisdictions have drawn the parallel between Yellow Pages advertising and Internet advertising, they have also consistently drawn a parallel between in-person solicitation and Internet chat room solicitation. Internet chat rooms, where people can gather (almost anonymously) and talk to each other in real-time, would generally be considered off-limits for lawyers to use as an alternative to the in-person solicitation prohibition. A few jurisdictions have issued ethics opinions forbidding lawyer solicitation in such chat rooms: Florida Bar Standing Committee on Advertising, Ethics Op. A–00–1 (2000); Illinois State Bar Association, Ethics Op. 96–10 (1996); Michigan State Bar Association, Ethics Op. RI–276 (1996); Philadelphia Bar Association, Ethics Op. 98–6 (1998); Utah State Bar Ethics Advisory Commission, Op. 97–10 (1997); Virginia State Bar Advertising Committee's Op. A–0110 (1998); West Virginia Lawyer Disciplinary Board Op. 98–03 (1998).

The sending of e-mails to prospective clients does not fall within the above-mentioned prohibition, but could still be unlawful if done outside the scope of the controlling jurisdiction's rules. The ABA authorizes the use of e-mail solicitations in the Ethics 2000 version of Model Rule 7.3(c) and requires that such solicitation have the words "Advertising Material" at the beginning and end of every e-mail, referred to as an "electronic communication" in the rule. One could logically liken e-mail solicitations to written solicitations—targeted mailings that also require the label "Advertising Material" on the envelope and/or front page. If so, then it would seem that if a jurisdiction requires lawyers to file with the appropriate regulatory body copies of written solicitations, then copies of e-mail solicitations would also have to be forwarded, which could be cumbersome for lawyers and regulatory agencies alike. Anyone who has had an e-mail account for more than 30 minutes comes to realize that spam doesn't just come in those cute little cans. In 2004, Ohio issued an ethics opinion on lawyer-sent spam and cautioned against it, but did not conclusively oppose it. The Ohio Board of Commissioners on Grievances and Discipline, Opinion No. 2004-1.

An important quandary raised by Internet solicitation is that the lawyer may be in violation of the solicitation rules of jurisdictions to which the lawyer's Internet communications are sent, if those jurisdictions have rules that differ from the jurisdiction where the lawyer is licensed. Moreover, discussions with prospective clients in chat rooms where the lawyer is not the initiating party would be, by definition, viewed as something other than prohibited solicitation. *See* Illinois State Bar Association, Ethics Op. 96–10 (1996). See Exhibit 6–10 for a summary of the rules on solicitation when not occurring face-to-face.

EXHIBIT 6–10   SOLICITATION OTHER THAN IN PERSON

Written Solicitation	Telephone Solicitation	Internet Solicitation
• Targeted mailings are allowed, but usually must be labeled as such. • Some jurisdictions prohibit such mailings from being immediately sent to accident victims or family members.	• Like face-to-face solicitation, phone solicitation is similarly prohibited. • Pre-recorded telephone solicitation is regulated as advertising (and generally allowed).	• Using an Internet chat room to solicit is generally prohibited, because it is direct and occurs in real-time. • Responding in a chat room, however, to another's question is generally not solicitation. • E-mail solicitation is generally allowed, much like targeted mailings.

Beyond providing samples of complying and noncomplying lawyer advertisements on its Web site, the Florida Bar also provides samples of written solicitation letters that comply or do not comply with Florida's solicitation rules. See Exhibit 6–11 for these samples.

Permissible Solicitation

As a general principle, lawyers are prohibited from soliciting prospective clients in face-to-face situations or real-time electronic situations when the primary motive is financial gain. Lawyers are allowed to solicit prospective clients through written mailings or prerecorded telephone calls. Even where the

B. DIRECT MAIL COMMUNICATIONS

(ALL DIRECT MAIL ADS MUST BE FILED FOR REVIEW)

1. DIRECT MAIL THAT *COMPLIES* WITH APPLICABLE BAR RULES

Law Offices of

Elizabeth Smith, P.A.

111 First Street
Anytown, Florida 98765
(904) 555-1234

April 30, 2002

Ms. Edwina Johnston
Post Office Box 111
Anytown, Florida 98765

Dear Ms. Johnston:

If you have already retained a lawyer for this matter, please disregard this letter.

I obtained your name from a list of investors who purchased a limited partnership in ABC Company from a nationally known brokerage firm. The list was provided to me by ABC. If you invested in ABC based upon representations made by the firm that the ABC limited partnership investment was "safe" and that it could be sold to provide you with income if needed, you may be entitled to recover money damages from the brokerage firm.

Choosing a law firm to represent you in this matter is an important decision. I limit my practice to representing people in securities matters and have done so for the past two years. Prior to opening my own firm, I was an associate at a Miami firm which handled similar cases. To date, I have personally tried 15 cases against brokerage firms and their agents. I graduated from the Florida State University College of Law in 1991 and became a member of The Florida Bar that same year. Before attending law school, I was a certified public accountant and, therefore, have some working knowledge of financial matters that may be useful to your case.

I look forward to hearing from you soon.

Sincerely,

Elizabeth Smith

ADVERTISEMENT (In red ink)

–8–

EXHIBIT 6 – 11a   Samples of Complying and Noncomplying FL Solicitations—Direct Mail
Communications

Reprinted with Permission of the Florida Bar

2. DIRECT MAIL THAT *COMPLIES* WITH APPLICABLE BAR RULES

Joseph Smith, P.A.
Attorney at Law
123 Main Street
Anytown, Florida 98765

April 30, 2002

Mr. Jerry Johnson
444 Vine Street
Anytown, FL 98765

Dear Mr. Johnson:

If you have already retained a lawyer for this matter, please disregard this letter.

My review of public records at the Orange County Clerk's Office indicates that a foreclosure suit was recently filed against you. My knowledge about the specifics of your case is limited to the information in the public record. Because a foreclosure action could have serious ramifications, it may be in your best interest to consult with an attorney.

I was admitted to The Florida Bar in 1987 after graduating from Florida State University in 1986. I worked as an assistant county attorney in the Orange County Attorney's Office for two years, then opened my own law practice. I have worked exclusively on real property matters for the past five years and have handled over 100 foreclosures. I am also a member of the Orange County Bar Association. I invite you to compare my qualifications and experience to those of other attorneys you might be considering.

I offer a free initial consultation, and weekend and evening appointments are available for your convenience.

Sincerely,

Joseph Smith

ADVERTISEMENT
(In red ink)

–9–

EXHIBIT 6–11b   Samples of Complying and Noncomplying FL Solicitations—Direct Mail Communications

Reprinted with Permission of the Florida Bar

3. DIRECT MAIL THAT *COMPLIES* WITH APPLICABLE BAR RULES

JOHN DAVIS, P.A.
1001 Tenth Avenue, Suite A
Anytown, Florida 98765
(305) 555-1234

ADVERTISEMENT
(In red ink)

April 30, 2002

Mr. Robert James
Rt. 1, Box 333
Anytown, Florida 98765

If you have already retained a lawyer for this matter, please disregard this letter. I read in the October 29th edition of the *Anytown Herald* that you were recently arrested.

It's a good idea to hire an experienced attorney when you are facing criminal charges. After you examine my qualifications, I think you will want to call me for help.

. I graduated from the University of Florida Law School, with high honors, in 1970.

• I have been a member of The Florida Bar since 1970.

• I have practiced criminal law for 30 years -- 5 years as a public defender and 25 years in private practice.

• I have handled hundreds of jury trials, ranging from misdemeanors to capital felonies.

• I am board certified in criminal trial law by The Florida Bar.

• I am also a member of the Federal Bar and admitted to practice in the U.S. District Court for the Southern District of Florida.

There is no charge for an initial consultation, and I offer payment plans to suit any budget. Please call my office for an appointment.

Sincerely,

John Davis

JD/dh

–10–

EXHIBIT 6–11c   Samples of Complying and Noncomplying FL Solicitations—Direct Mail Communications

Reprinted with Permission of the Florida Bar

4. DIRECT MAIL THAT DOES *NOT COMPLY*

(123) 555-7890
Main Street

Anytown, FL 98765

JOHN JONES & ASSOCIATES   23

April 30, 2002

Ms. Jane Smith
111 First Street
Anytown, Florida 98765

Dear Ms. Smith:

Thank you for taking the time to review this letter.❶ It has come to our attention that you were recently injured in a car accident.❷ Because this firm specializes in personal injury matters, we would like the opportunity to consult with you about your accident.❸ It may interest you to know that our firm has had many past successes in handling cases similar to yours.❹

You probably have many questions that you would like answered by a qualified attorney.❺ I will be glad to discuss your case at no charge. If you choose to hire this firm, the fee will be based upon a percentage of the total recovery we may obtain. This means you will pay us no fees unless we recover money.❻

Please call our office at your convenience. I look forward to meeting with you in the near future.

Very truly yours,

John Jones, Esquire

JJ/dh

❼

❶ The first sentence of the communication involving a specific matter is not: "If you have already retained a lawyer for this matter, please disregard this letter." Rule 4-7.4(b)(2)(F).

❷ Communication prompted by a specific occurrence involving the recipient fails to disclose how the lawyer obtained the information prompting the communication. Rule 4-7.4(b)(2)IJ).

❸ Uses the term "specializes" when the attorney is not board certified. Rule 4-7.2(c)(6). Also, "personal injury" is not an area of Florida Bar certification, and a law firm cannot be certified.

❹ Refers to past results in violation of Rule 4-7.2(c)(1)(F) and Comment.

❺ Communication fails to contain a statement of the lawyer's or law firm's qualifications and experience. Rule 4-7.4(b)(2)(D).

❻ Fails to disclose whether the client will be liable for costs in the absence of a recovery. Rule 4-7.2(c)(7).

❼ 1st page is not plainly marked "Advertisement" in red ink. Rule 4-7.4(b)(2)(B).

–11–

EXHIBIT 6–11d   Samples of Complying and Noncomplying FL Solicitations—Direct Mail Communications

prospective client can be solicited, lawyers may not engage in any solicitation where the prospective client communicates that he or she does not want to be solicited; nor may lawyers use solicitation that involves harassment or duress. MR 7.3(b)(1), (2).

Other kinds of solicitation are permitted, however, either because they are expressly allowed by the rules or are not covered in the rules.

Prior Relationships

All sets of rules allow a lawyer to solicit those with whom the lawyer has had a professional or family relationship. The Model Code also allowed lawyers to solicit close friends, which the Ethics 2000 version of 7.3(a)(1) also does. The allowance for lawyers to solicit present or former clients, as well as family members (and friends), demonstrates that there is less a threat of abuse—which is at the heart of the strict solicitation rules—when those being solicited already know the lawyer.

Class Actions

The Comments to MR 7.2 state that "[n]either this Rule nor Rule 7.3 prohibits communications authorized by law, such as notice to members of a class in **class action** litigation." Moreover, in *Gulf Oil Co. v. Bernard*, 452 U.S. 89 (1981), the Supreme Court held that the Federal Rules of Civil Procedure allow for direct contact with those who may be potential plaintiffs in a class action lawsuit. That decision does not mean that such solicitation is automatically allowed in class actions brought in state courts, but some jurisdictions do allow the solicitation of members of a class, either by court decisions, ethics opinions, or through their advertising and solicitation rules. *See Kittler v. Eckberg, Lammers*, 535 N.W.2d 653 (Minn. Ct. App. 1995); Mass. Bar Association Committee on Prof. Ethics, Op. 93–5 (1993).

class action
A lawsuit brought by a representative of a large group of plaintiffs (or prospective plaintiffs) on behalf of the group. Rule 23 of the Federal Rules of Civil Procedure governs class actions.

Not-for-Profit Solicitation

The same day the Supreme Court upheld the ban on in-person solicitation in *Ohralik v. Ohio State Bar Association*, 436 U.S. 447 (1978), it reached a different conclusion in *In re Primus*, 436 U.S. 412 (1978). There, the Court affirmed the right of a lawyer associated with the American Civil Liberties Union to send a solicitation letter to women who might have been harmed in connection with government-provided medical services, informing the women that free legal services were available. The Court distinguished *Primus* from *Ohralik* on the grounds that not-for-profit solicitation was a form of political expression and, therefore, protected under the First Amendment. Traditionally, solicitation is a commercial endeavor, which is why the solicitation restriction in MR 7.3(a) concerns solicitation, "when a significant motive for the lawyer's doing so is the lawyer's pecuniary gain." Such a different view toward not-for-profit solicitation can even be traced back to an ABA ethics opinion from 1935 that stated the anti-solicitation Canon was not aimed at lawyers who were willing to devote some of their time to representing indigent citizens whose constitutional rights may have been violated. ABA Comm. on Professional Ethics and Grievances, Formal Op. 148 (1935). Exhibit 6–12 summarizes key exceptions to the anti-solicitation rules.

EXHIBIT 6–12 COMMON PERMISSIBLE SOLICITATIONS

1. Solicitations based upon prior relationships
   - This could include family members, close friends, former clients.
   - Not all jurisdictions have this exception.

2. Soliciting other lawyers
   - New exception in Ethics 2000 MR 7.3(a)(1).

3. Soliciting for a class action
   - The Comments to ABA MR 7.2 discusses this, as does a U.S. Supreme Court case dealing with the Federal Rules of Civil Procedure.

4. Not-for-profit solicitations
   - Confirmed by the U.S. Supreme Court in 1978.

5. Soliciting those to be part of a prepaid legal insurance plan
   - This exception applies when the insurance program, not the lawyer, is soliciting memberships.

Solicitation and the Paralegal

Consistent with the theme of this text, paralegals and legal assistants can do nothing that lawyers cannot do. Therefore, all non-lawyer employees must be acquainted with their jurisdictions' solicitation rules and follow them accordingly. Because lawyers pay the price for the misconduct of their employees, paralegals who demonstrate their knowledge of the nuances of the applicable solicitation rules can save their firms from unintended sanctions. Knowing whether one's jurisdiction allows for the solicitation of class action members, or puts a time buffer between accidents and the contacting of prospective clients, is as important as knowing what the unauthorized practice of law is.

By way of example, Washington, D.C., has more than one solicitation prohibition in its version of Model Rule 7.1. The first prohibition states the traditional position of soliciting non-lawyers for pecuniary gain. District of Columbia Rules of Professional Conduct, Rule 7.1(b)(1). A second prohibition, which expressly applies to "...any person acting on behalf of a lawyer," concerns soliciting non-pro bono civil and criminal clients, and prohibits any solicitation, "in the District of Columbia Courthouse, on the sidewalks on the north, south, and west sides of the courthouse, or within 50 feet of the building on the east side." 7.1(d).

Furthermore, ABA Model Rule 8.4(a) states that it is professional misconduct for a lawyer to knowingly assist or induce someone else to violate the Rules of Professional Conduct, or use someone else to violate the Rules. While the scope of that rule is broad, it has been specifically applied in situations where lawyers have employed accident runners, or have paid fees to marketing firms that solicit business in ways that violate the rules. As well, there is too much case law involving lawyers who were caught using their non-lawyer employees—from their paralegals to their secretaries and investigators—to illegally solicit legal business. See Exhibit 6–13 for key principles governing solicitation and paralegals.

EXHIBIT 6–13 SOLICITATION AND THE PARALEGAL

- The lawyer solicitation rules apply equally to paralegals and legal assistants.

- The solicitation rules vary jurisdictionally, so paralegals and legal assistants must learn their jurisdictions' solicitation rules.

- Finder's fees and accident running are unethical and, in some circumstances, illegal.

A Case Study in Illegal Solicitation

In 1996, the *Wall Street Journal* wrote a blistering expose on one very rich lawyer and the gritty tactics he used to find lucrative clients. Did you ever wonder how the fox got in the hen house? In John O'Quinn's case, he hired a chicken to let him in the front door. Mr. O'Quinn, of Houston, Texas, is a renowned tort lawyer and car collector (more on the cars later), who has won millions in breast implant litigation and who has had a few ethics scrapes in his considerably successful career. In 1987, the State Bar of Texas sought his disbarment because of his use of "accident runners" to solicit clients following a plane crash. Pleading no contest to the charges helped him retain his law license. *Forbes* magazine estimated he made 40 million dollars in 1995, and *Fortune* magazine once put him on its cover with the heading, "Lawyers from Hell."

On July 2, 1994, USAir Flight 1016 went down not far from Charlotte, North Carolina, killing 37 passengers and wounding 14. As sad as that tragedy was, it presented a ripe, but short-lived opportunity for plaintiffs' lawyers to secure clients. Because the solicitation rules are clear that face-to-face solicitation of prospective clients, particularly lucrative ones, is prohibited, lawyers who choose to subvert the rules might do so through an intermediary. Mr. O'Quinn used two. The first was Benton Musslewhite, a Houston lawyer who had in the past worked as Mr. O'Quinn's accident-running middleman, which earned him a three-year suspension in the 1987 case involving O'Quinn. The second intermediary was accident runner Betty Edward, an energetic former client of Musslewhite's, 49-years-old, unemployed and surviving on Medicaid and Supplemental Social Security Income. Who could resist the offer Musslewhite made to Betty—even though it was illegal for her to work while on Medicaid? In return for her flying to South Carolina, where many of the crash victims lived, and signing up those surviving victims or family members for Mr. O'Quinn, she would be paid $1,000 a day, plus expenses, and a bonus every time one "her" clients' cases settled.

Why would a disabled woman from Houston, without any legal or investigative experience, who has never worked in a law firm, much less as a paralegal, be sent to South Carolina to fish for clients for a lawyer she didn't know? Two reasons: she was black, as were most of the South Carolina crash victims; and, it was presumed she likely would not realize how illegal her activities were, nor would she seem to care, at least not after getting paid. So off to South Carolina she went, carrying a list of the all the accident victims (printed on O'Quinn's letterhead), her luggage stuffed full of O'Quinn's resumes, favorable press clippings, a video by O'Quinn, and preprinted forms authorizing O'Quinn's firm to represent the "undersigned" clients for a contingency fee.

Aiding Ms. Edward in her efforts at finding these prospective clients and gaining entry to them at funeral parlors and churches was The Rev. Charles Williams, Jr., a former sheriff's deputy. Proving that Musslewhite's belief in Betty's people-skills was correct (under the arrangement, he would get some of the clients, too), after some weeks living out of a hotel, Betty had signed up seven clients from the crash, worth millions of settlement dollars. In fact, she was so dedicated while working in South Carolina with one of Mr. O'Quinn's lawyers, she ran out of O'Quinn's resumes and press clippings and needed more sent to her by FedEx. She also earned about $39,000.

So how did this illegal scheme fall in on itself? Betty Edward told on everybody. Why, you ask, would she do that? It wasn't that she got religion; it was that she didn't get fully paid, the very thing that ensnared O'Quinn in the 1987 solicitation ruckus. As is said, there is no honor among thieves. Helping to prove her allegations, she saved receipts and even tape-recorded phone conversations, including one with the Rev. Williams, where Betty said to him, "We could go to the penitentiary for them and they got money like that, millions of dollars, and us thinking we just working innocently, uh, honestly, y'know. Pitiful." To which, Rev. Williams replied, "That's right."

By the time the Texas Bar got involved in the matter, Mr. Musslewhite had filed bankruptcy, and Mr. O'Quinn—through his own lawyer Thomas McDade—claimed "there was never any relationship between Mr. O'Quinn and Betty Edward ....She was retained by Mr. Musslewhite and worked solely for him." Adding to the confusion was the question of which state, Texas or South Carolina, had jurisdiction over the matter. Texas had nothing to do with the illegal solicitation and South Carolina had nothing to do with the licenses of the lawyers in question.

In April 1997, John O'Quinn, Charles Benton Musslewhite, and two other lawyers were indicted by the South Carolina attorney general and accused of conspiracy, the unauthorized practice of law, illegal solicitation of clients, and illegal fee splitting. The two other attorneys charged in the matter were Carl Shaw, a lawyer in O'Quinn's office who worked with Ms. Edward in South Carolina, and Charles Benton Musslewhite, Jr. The South Carolina Attorney General chose to bring criminal charges because the South Carolina bar had no authority to bring disciplinary charges against out-of-state attorneys. O'Quinn's attorney responded by describing the South Carolina anti-solicitation statute as archaic and unconstitutional. Continuing to rely on the argument that Musslewhite and others committed the transgressions, O'Quinn was quoted as saying: "I have done nothing wrong and am innocent of these charges. There are rules about soliciting clients, as there should be, and we followed every one of them."

By July 1997, South Carolina adopted a rule requiring out-of-state lawyers who promote their services or advertise in South Carolina to comply with its rules regarding solicitation and advertising. Failure to comply would subject out-of-state lawyers to a variety of sanctions, including having to refund all legal fees gained through the unlawful tactics. And as for John O'Quinn, his legal troubles in South Carolina came to a close when he agreed to plead guilty to practicing law without a license in South Carolina. Part of his plea bargain included the irony of paying a fine of approximately $300,000 to fund legal ethics programs.

Mr. O'Quinn is unlikely to believe in *karma*, because he professes conservative religious beliefs that are no where close to Hinduism or Buddhism. But he might accept *kismet*. Whatever one calls it, it came back to Mr. O'Quinn in the form of a paroled convict he hired as a personal assistant who succeeded (until getting caught) in defrauding O'Quinn to the tune of about $3 million. Zev Isgur, the employee who would eventually put in charge of O'Quinn's $100 million car collection (ever wonder who owns Pope John Paul's pope-mobile?), devised an elaborate ruse to overpay for additions to the collection, pocketing the difference. In some instances, Isgur created purchases for cars that were never sold. Spending his ill-gotten gain on all the typicals (women, clothing, gambling) Isgur's scam was eventually discovered and back to prison he went, being sentenced to 25 years.

SUMMARY

Although nothing explicitly prohibited lawyers from advertising before the first rules of ethics were created, most lawyers refrained from advertising their services because of the tradition against it. The first ABA set of ethics rules frowned on lawyer advertising. But by the 1950s, the ABA modified its rules to allow lawyers to advertise in phone books and legal directories.

Because advertising and solicitation qualify as commercial speech, they can be regulated more strictly than religious or political speech. And for much of the twentieth century, the U.S. Supreme Court upheld state laws that severely restricted lawyer advertising. The Supreme Court then changed its position in *Bates v. State Bar of Arizona*, finding that lawyers had a First Amendment right to truthfully advertise certain kinds of standardized information about their legal services. Following that decision, states could not prohibit all forms of advertising.

The rules on communication about a lawyer's services prohibit lawyers from making any false or misleading statements. Three types of information are usually considered false or misleading statements: fraudulent statements, or material misrepresentations of fact or law; statements that are likely to create unjustified expectations about the likelihood of success; and unsubstantiated comparisons of one lawyer's services to another's. Statements that concern legal fees have been found to be misleading when they do not accurately represent that the client will have to pay certain fees or costs. Some rules also prohibit statements that are self-laudatory, and a few require that advertisements be dignified.

The current version of the ABA's rules on lawyer advertising allows lawyers to advertise in print, on radio, on television, and on the Internet. However, lawyers must often retain copies of their advertisements, and in some jurisdictions, must obtain prior approval before placing advertisements. The Supreme Court struck down restrictions on the types of words used to describe a lawyer's practice, and prohibitions on illustrations in advertisements in decisions that followed *Bates.* Although lawyer advertising is allowed, the bar can still restrict certain types or methods of advertising, including prohibiting the use of celebrity endorsements or testimonials. All jurisdictions can require that advertisements be kept for a certain number of years, and can prescribe the manner in which lawyers advertise themselves to be specialists. While a lawyer is allowed to pay for lawful advertisements, the rules prohibit a lawyer from paying someone to recommend the lawyer's services. Such referral, or finder's, fees are allowed when the referral service is a not-for-profit service or legal aid society.

Although radio and televised advertisements are allowed, restrictions on such advertising can include prohibiting dramatizations, music, or testimonials. Some jurisdictions allow the use of prerecorded telephone advertisements, unless the sending lawyer knows that the recipient does not want such phone calls. The newest form of lawyer advertising is Internet advertising. Most jurisdictions allow lawyers to advertise on the Internet, including maintaining a law firm Web site, but the rules on record keeping still apply.

The Model Code originally required that advertising be dignified, but eventually that requirement was removed. The Model Rules have no rule regarding dignified ads. Although this is an amorphous concept to enforce, some jurisdictions still maintain the dignified presentation requirement.

When communicating to prospective clients, paralegals and legal assistants must be careful not to make false or misleading statements about their firm's services because, as agents of the firm, they can implicate their supervising lawyers in violation of the communication and advertising rules. Many jurisdictions allow paralegals to have their own business cards, and to be listed on firm letterhead. Paralegals who are self-employed as independent contractors can advertise in order to get business, but only to lawyers or law firms. A paralegal who advertises to the general public is engaging in the unauthorized practice of law.

Solicitation is a much different activity than advertising because solicitation is targeted toward individuals or specific groups. As opposed to advertising, solicitation is considered a suspect activity because of its susceptibility to abuse, and is only allowed under certain conditions. But a few legal scholars argue that the restrictions on solicitation are too severe and prevent the public from learning more information about their legal options. Both the Model Rules and Model Code prohibit face-to-face solicitation of prospective clients with whom the lawyer has no prior relationship and when financial gain is the primary reason for the solicitation. The Supreme Court affirmed the right of a state to prohibit in-person solicitation in *Ohralik v. Ohio State Bar Association*, finding that the potential for coercion and other forms of abuse allow for such a strict restriction.

Solicitation other than in-person solicitation, such as written solicitation, is also highly regulated, but not as strictly as the former. In a few Supreme Court cases, the Court ruled that states could not institute outright bans on mailed solicitations when those solicitations are truthful, but in *Florida Bar v. Went For It, Inc.,* the Supreme Court upheld the right of states to institute time restraints on the mailing of written solicitations. Many jurisdictions have followed suit, and limit when a lawyer may send a targeted mailing to an accident victim or family member. Telephone and Internet solicitation are also restricted, with some jurisdictions prohibiting lawyers from using Internet chat rooms for solicitation purposes.

Certain kinds of solicitation are allowed, however. Lawyers can solicit their relatives, and their present and former clients. The Model Code's solicitation rule also allows lawyers to solicit their friends, and, in similar fashion, the Ethics 2000 version of the solicitation rules allows lawyers to solicit those with whom they have a close personal relationship. Lawyers can also solicit prospective clients to find members for a class action suit. Another exception to the anti-solicitation rules is not-for-profit solicitation, such as solicitation made to help prospective clients assert political, or other constitutional, rights.

Paralegals need to know the specific solicitation rules governing the jurisdiction where they work, because the solicitation rules vary from jurisdiction to jurisdiction. Beyond the need to protect the firm against unintended solicitation violations, paralegals also need to protect against engaging in the kind of unlawful solicitation known as accident running. Although paralegals could not be sanctioned by the bar for engaging in unlawful solicitation or for taking inappropriate fees for finding clients, such behavior reflects poorly on the paralegal profession.

The Ethics 2000 version of the advertising rules includes a few other changes, including dropping the part of the rule that requires lawyers to keep copies of their advertisements for stated periods of time, as well as expressly allowing the use of e-mail advertisements. The solicitation rules have also been updated to include real-time electronic contact as impermissible solicitation. The specialization rules have been tightened to prohibit a lawyer from advertising a legal certification that does not come from an ABA- or state-approved certifying organization.

ETHICS IN ACTION

1. Franklin has been asked by his boss Edward to put a radio advertisement on the local talk radio station. Edward practices employment and discrimination law. Although he hasn't ever taken a certification course in employment law, Edward spends a lot of his time representing employees and former employees who believe they were mistreated at work, or were discriminated against, or were terminated because of their political views. Edward believes that talk radio is on in many offices and factories in his and the surrounding counties, and thinks that advertising to those who are keen to the national policy disputes, local strife and gossip, and the occasional pettiness, would be an effective way to find more clients. Franklin meets with the advertising department from the talk radio station, to devise a catchy spot. At the conclusion of the meeting, the ad that is created says in part, "Have you been screwed at work?? Been given the shaft by your boss?? Well, then you have to call Edward Scissorhands today, because he specializes in employment law and will cut your employer into little ribbons."

   Would that ad be allowed in your jurisdiction? If not, who would be in trouble?

2. Actor George Clooney was injured on a film set when he choked on a crudit, which is a snobby Hollywood word for a cut, raw vegetable. It seems Mr. Clooney took a big bite of a carrot stick covered in an organic, tahini-based vegetable dip while walking out of his makeup trailer and, whoops, down he went. The ensuing choking and Heimlich maneuvers left him with a broken sternum and a voice too hoarse for acting. The production of the film was delayed three weeks and, to make matters worse, a paparazzo took a devilishly funny picture of the world's sexiest man being bear hugged from behind while spewing forth a carrot projectile. Mr. Clooney sued the caterer who served those carrot sticks, the hairdresser who saved his life, and the photographer who took and sold the photograph to *US Weekly*. Attorney Deborah represented George Clooney in those lawsuits and all she wanted in return was an autograph and George's face on a Yellow Pages ad which said, "Deborah didn't choke after I did, and she got me five million dollars!"

   Is that an allowed advertisement in your jurisdiction?

3. To appear more worthy of charging at a minimum a 40 percent contingent fee in his personal injury cases, sole practitioner Olbermann films a television commercial of himself getting up from his cherry-finished desk, behind his oak-paneled bookshelf

   (continues)

ETHICS IN ACTION   *(continued)*

and, while walking over to a painting of Abraham Lincoln hanging on his office wall, earnestly saying to the camera, "At my firm, we don't give your cases to paralegals, like most of the other firms in this town do. While those lawyers find it suits their profit margins to employ many paralegals to run their caseloads and handle most of the client contact, I think lawyers, who are trained to represent injured people, should be responsible to make sure that those who are injured by the negligence of others get the most careful and professional representation available. So, at Olbermann and Associates, all of our clients work with lawyers and only lawyers."

Is this advertisement in violation of any of your jurisdiction's advertising rules?

4. After church one Sunday morning, Greta sees Christine coming out of the restroom and stops to say hello. Greta recently came to know Christine when they both attended a women's retreat the prior month. While chatting, Christine mentions that her husband has been working in his basement workshop on a no-drip paint brush, and that they are really excited about the prospects of contacting Wal-Mart, Lowes, and Home Depot to try and get this new product on those retailers' shelves. Greta asks Christine if her husband has gotten a patent for his invention, and Christine responds that they had thought about it and visited the U.S. Patent Office Web site, but that's about it. Thinking of her boss's recent foray into intellectual property law, Greta tells Christine about her boss Randy, a patent attorney, and suggests that Christine or her husband call Greta the next day to set up an appointment for them to talk to Randy about protecting the paint brush from being stolen by a competitive interest.

Do Greta's actions violate any of your jurisdiction's ethics rules, or any of NALA's or NFPA's ethics rules?

5. Having been a paralegal before going to law school, Johanna is eager to promote the use of her own paralegals. So when her senior paralegal Ashton succeeds in passing the NFPA's Paralegal Advanced Competency Exam (PACE), Johanna takes Ashton out to a celebration dinner and gives Ashton a raise—albeit a small one. In addition, Johanna provides Ashton with a new business card, and puts Ashton on the firm's letterhead. Both the business card and the letterhead list Ashton as "Ashton Campbell, R-P."

Would both of these actions be allowed in your jurisdiction? Regardless, can you think of any way to improve Ashton's designation on her business card or the letterhead?

6. Ed is representing two families who believe they have been afflicted with various illnesses, including cancer, because they were poisoned by radiation leaking from a power plant that is about one mile from where Ed's plaintiffs have lived for many

(continues)

ETHICS IN ACTION   *(continued)*

years. Due to the population explosion in that part of the state, and the attendant subdivisions, there are approximately 10,000 people within a five-mile radius of the power plant. Rather than blow a figurative foghorn by mailing flyers to those residents to inquire about their health, thus alerting the nuclear plant to an impending battle before the complaints are filed, Ed comes up with an alternate plan. He sends his paralegal Erin out on foot to go door-to-door, to inquire whether any of the residents: A) have the types of afflictions Ed's clients have; and, B) have any interest in joining the upcoming litigation. If Erin finds sufficient interest and can sign enough clients, Ed is planning on seeking to turn this case into a class action litigation.

In your jurisdiction, can Erin do what Ed has proposed?

7. Kirsten was in a car accident a week ago when a drunk driver on a suspended license hit her as she was braking in order to pull into a left-turn lane. The drunk driver was following too closely and failed to notice her applying the brakes. His pick-up truck slammed into the back of her Toyota Prius, knocking it into oncoming traffic, where it was also hit by another car. Kirsten suffered a broken back, a punctured lung, a fractured skull, and many abrasions. Worse, her daughter, sitting in her car seat, has been in a coma since the accident. Yesterday, Kirsten's mother brought Kirsten's mail to the hospital, and included in the pile of envelopes was a letter from an area law firm bearing the words, "Advertising Material" on the face of the letter. The letter told Kirsten what she already knew: namely, that she and her daughter had been in a horrific car accident caused by a drunk driver, and that she and her daughter had suffered excruciating injuries. The letter then told Kirsten that she needs to protect her legal rights, and that the lawyers at that firm are specialists in seeking just compensation for those who have been injured through the actions of drunk drivers. Kirsten is mortified and furious to have received such a letter, and can't believe that lawyers are allowed to hound people like her and her daughter.

Are lawyers or paralegals in your jurisdiction allowed to send such a letter to Kirsten?

▓ POINTS TO PONDER_____

1. Why did lawyers originally refrain from advertising?

2. On what basis did the American Bar Association begin to prohibit lawyer advertising?

3. Advertising is considered commercial speech and, as such, is relatively easy to regulate. Why?

4. On what basis did the Supreme Court decide in *Bates* that the bar could not prohibit lawyer advertising?

5. How do the ABA rules on communication of a lawyer's services differ (slightly) from the rules on advertising?

6. What kinds of statements about the lawyer's services are prohibited?

7. What three kinds of information fall under those prohibitions?

8. When could a lawyer or his or her legal assistant make a comparative statement about another lawyer's services?

9. Does your jurisdiction's communication or advertising rules prohibit other categories of statements not mentioned in the ABA's rules?

10. What is the difference between lawfully paying for advertisements and unlawfully paying someone to refer clients to the firm?

11. Does your jurisdiction have any particular restrictions on the use of radio or television advertisements?

12. Does your jurisdiction have any rules that apply to Internet advertising?

13. Do you think lawyer advertising should be dignified? What would make an advertisement undignified? What do you think of Rosalie Osias's view on seductively applying femininity to get ahead in the legal profession, or of Corri Fetman's involvement with the Playboy company? Are they hindering the cause of women in the legal profession, or is it being prude to criticize them?

14. Regardless of whether it is specifically allowed, why could it be said there is nothing wrong with a law firm letterhead that lists paralegals or business cards that list paralegals?

15. Does your jurisdiction have a legal assistant rule or guideline that allows legal assistants to be listed on letterheads or have their own business cards?

16. Can an independent-contracting paralegal advertise?

17. How is solicitation distinguished from advertising?

18. Why is solicitation more strictly regulated than advertising?

19. What kind of solicitation is the most restricted?

20. What kind of solicitation is the least restricted?

21. Do you think the rules on solicitation are too severe? Why or why not?

22. Does your jurisdiction have any limitations on authorized solicitation, such as instituting a blackout period for solicitation following accidents or disasters?

23. Do your jurisdiction's solicitation rules apply geographical limitations as does the District of Columbia's?

24. What is the difference between telephone advertising and telephone solicitation?

25. What kind of activity on the Internet is generally considered to be impermissible solicitation? How is e-mailing prospective clients different from contacting them in chat rooms?

26. Under what circumstances is solicitation not restricted?

27. What kinds of solicitation could qualify as not-for-profit solicitation?

28. Why is it critical that paralegals know their jurisdiction's solicitation rules?

29. Why is accident running considered to be so sleazy? Is it really as bad is the press makes it out to be?

30. Are there any rules of thumb a paralegal or legal assistant should keep in mind that can help prevent engaging in impermissible solicitation?

31. What noticeable changes did the Ethics 2000 Commission make to the ABA Model Rules on advertising and solicitation? Has your jurisdiction adopted those changes?

■ KEY CONCEPTS

Accident runner

Advertising

Commercial speech

Finder's fee

Inappropriate implications

Internet advertising

Internet solicitation

Material misrepresentation

Not-for-profit solicitation

Referral service

Solicitation

Third-party advertising Web sites

Unjustified expectations

Written solicitation

■ KEY TERMS

accident runners

admiralty

circulars

class action

commercial speech

foreclosure

injunction

inter alia

libelous

patent

pecuniary

plea bargaining

puffing

warranty

Online Companion™
For additional resources, please go to
http://www.paralegal.delmar.cengage.com

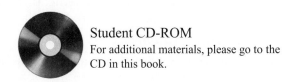
Student CD-ROM
For additional materials, please go to the
CD in this book.

Fees and Fee Sharing

INTRODUCTION

As the cliché says, you get what you pay for. Yet, when many clients pay for legal services, they get something else—heartburn. Lawyers are not cheap unless they are free, in which case the client is most likely an indigent person accused of a crime. But why should lawyers be inexpensive? They go to college with one goal in mind: to get good enough grades to get into law school. Those who succeed make it to law school, which is both extremely expensive and arduous. After a few years of the terror and tedium of law school, graduates spend additional money applying for and studying to pass the bar exam, which is also, once again, expensive and arduous. Failure means they must try again or seek other employment. After giving up at least seven income-producing years, new attorneys then must seek their way in an ever-more-crowded and specialized field. With experience and success come the fruits of their labors: wealth. That is the American way. Those lawyers wise enough to hire and use paralegals and legal assistants can earn more income while their clients receive less heartburn.

This chapter will examine the rules governing legal fees. Included in this chapter will be a discussion of the types of legal fees and the principles that help determine whether a legal fee is unreasonable, as well as the distinction between fees and expenses. Also, ethics considerations concerning fees and the paralegal will be discussed, including the rules that prohibit the splitting of legal fees between lawyers and non-lawyer employees. Finally, there will be an examination of the rules and case law that allow paralegal and legal assistant fees to be recovered from the opposing party in jurisdictions where the law already authorizes the recovery of lawyers' fees.

> "A lawyer's opinion is worth nothing unless paid for."
>
> **ENGLISH PROVERB**

> "A lawyer with his briefcase can steal more than a hundred men with guns."
>
> **DON CORLEONE, FROM *THE GODFATHER*, BY MARIO PUZO**

TYPES OF LEGAL FEES

Despite what people may conclude from lawyer jokes, the principal options for paying a legal bill are not the client's future inheritance, firstborn child, or soul. The common methods for paying for legal services are the hourly rate, the contingent fee, and the fixed fee. See Exhibit 7-1 for types of legal fees.

Hourly Rate

Although rarely used before the 1950s as a method to calculate a fee, lawyers often bill their clients based on an hourly rate, which is then measured for billing purposes in fractions, such as one-tenth or one-sixth of an hour. Hourly rates can fluctuate drastically, with variables ranging from the experience and reputation of the lawyer to the type of practice and the lawyer's location. Lawyers in larger metropolitan areas generally charge more than their counterparts in smaller cities. When the *National Law Journal* surveyed America's 250 largest law firms in 2006 (with 116 firms responding), asking for hourly rate information, responses showed the highest hourly rate was charged by Benjamin Civiletti, former U.S. attorney under Jimmy Carter and the chair of the Baltimore law firm, Venable LLP. His hourly rate can go up to $1000 an hour, and is thought to be the first ever four-figure hourly rate. The lowest average hourly rates from the surveyed firms were at the Philadelphia firm of Marshall, Dennehey, Warner, Coleman &

EXHIBIT 7–1   TYPES OF LEGAL FEES

Hourly Rate	Blended Rate	Contingent Fee	Fixed Fee
• Measured in fractions and based on specific record keeping • Hourly rates are higher for partners than associates, and higher for senior paralegals than other paralegals and legal assistants	• An hourly rate that is the average of the higher and lower hourly rates at the firm • For instance, dividing in half the total of a partner's and an associate's hourly rates (225 + 150) ÷ 2 = $187.50), and applying that rate to all clients • Some think this method of billing is a bad idea	• A percentage of the client's recovery • Increases as the lawyer's efforts for recovery increase (settlement vs. trial vs. appeal) • Only valid if the outcome is unknown • Often associated with personal injury cases	• Also known as a flat fee, or a unit fee • Based on all legal work needing to be done • Thought to be consumer friendly

Goggin, where associates bill between $130 to $275 an hour, and where partners bill between $145 to $350 an hour. According to the 2006 Survey of Law Firm Economics (surveying 285 U.S. law firms), conducted by the law firm-consulting group Altman Weil, Inc., the average hourly rate for an **equity partner** in a law firm with over 150 lawyers was $350; and the average hourly rate for an associate lawyer in firms that size was between $220 and $325. Partners with at least 21 years of experience had an average hourly rate of $305, while associates with four to five years of experience had an average hourly rate of $195. Partners with at least 21 years of experience averaged 1,640 billable hours per year, while associates with four to five years of experience averaged 1,939 billable hours per year, which is considerably larger than the 1,300 hours per year for associates, proposed by the ABA in a 1958 pamphlet.

equity partner
A partner in a law firm who is a shareholder, having voting rights.

According to the 2006 Annual Compensation Survey for Paralegals/Legal Assistants and Managers, conducted by Altman Weil, Inc., (which surveyed 261 law firms), the average paralegal hourly rate was $95 for paralegal clerks, $150 for paralegals, and $210 for paralegal case managers. (Remember, the hourly rate is what the client is charged, not what the paralegal is paid.) According to the 2007 Altman Weil survey, the median billable hours reported for paralegals was 1,490 hours per year, with litigation paralegals having a median of 1,562 billable hours per year, and insurance paralegals employed at law firms having a median of 1,638 billable hours per year.

NFPA's 2006 Compensation and Benefits Report showed that slightly less than 70 percent of the respondents had a billable rate, of which the mean was $111 an hour and the median was $106 an hour. For those who reported having annual billable hours requirements, the mean was 1,479 hours a year and the median was 1,500 hours a year. The NFPA's 2006 Compensation and Benefits Study Report can be purchased, but the executive summary of it can be accessed as a PDF file on the NFPA Web site, http://www.paralegals.org. Just use the search feature.

NALA's 2008 National Utilization and Compensation Survey Report showed that the average hourly rate of a NALA member was $102 an hour, while the average hourly rate for a respondent working in a law firm with at least 100 lawyers (the highest size category) was $123 an hour. Sixty-two percent of the respondents of the 2002 survey reported being expected to bill between 26–35 hours per week, which equals between 1,300 and 1,750 hours per year (based on a year with a two-week vacation). The following link is to NALA's 2008 National Utilization and Compensation Survey Report: http://www.nala.org/Survey_Table.htm. Table 3 from the Survey concerns billable rates.

For more information on lawyer salaries and billable hours, as well as pro bono hours, go to the career center on Findlaw's Web site: http://www.careers.findlaw.com/. From there, click the "Salary Charts" link, which will put you on a Web page for information.com, from which you can pick your state, and then your city, or one nearest yours.

A more recent variation of the hourly rate is the "blended rate." Under this approach, one hourly rate is charged to all clients, and this number is reached by averaging the partners' higher hourly rates with the associates' lower hourly rates. Theoretically, clients will be charged a lower rate when partners work on their cases, and vice versa. Some argue that this is a viable, value-billing alternative to the traditional hourly rate, while others believe that emphasizing the discount nature of this rate minimizes the inefficiency of associates who, because of their lack of experience, will be billing more hours at a rate higher than their actual associate rates. At least one ethics opinion has approved of a blended rate for all work done by lawyers or paralegals at a firm, based on the average of those different rates, provided the client agrees. New York County Ethics Op. 695 (1993).

It is an easy claim, and one often made, that lawyers charge too much. But no one is forced to hire any particular lawyer, and regardless of a lawyer's hourly rate, lawyers earn less than their stated rate because the overhead, or expenses, of running a law firm (from the office rent to the coffee filters) are paid from that hourly rate. One method gaining in popularity for defraying the out-of-pocket costs for hiring a lawyer is the use of prepaid legal insurance. Prepaid legal insurance operates similarly to other forms of insurance: the consumer pays a premium, sometimes called a membership fee, and is then entitled to either fully covered or discounted legal services in certain specified instances. Although prepaid legal services cannot cover a defendant accused of a crime such as murder, more standardized legal needs, such as wills or real estate matters, are provided by lawyers within the legal service providers network. The ABA promotes the use of prepaid legal insurance plans, and is closely affiliated with the American Prepaid Legal Services Institute, which provides lawyers and consumers with information on those organizations or companies that offer group or prepaid legal services plans.

For more information on prepaid legal insurance, use the search feature on the ABA's Web site, http://www.abanet.org. From there, you should find a link to the web page for the ABA Standing Committee on Group and Prepaid Legal Services.

Contingent Fee

■ **contingent fee**

A fee paid to a lawyer that is paid only if the lawyer succeeds in recovering a settlement or judgment for the client. The contingent fee is a percentage of what the client obtains.

A **contingent fee**, also called a contingency fee, is a method of payment in which the lawyer's fee is dependent on a recovery for the client and is a percentage of that recovery. The United States Supreme Court first recognized the legitimacy of the contingent fee contract in 1853, in *Wylie v. Coxe,* 56 U.S. 415, a case in which a plaintiff's attorney was to be paid 5 percent of whatever was recovered for the plaintiff in a claim against a foreign government. Usually, the lawyer's percentage of the client's recovery increases as the lawyer's efforts to obtain success increase. For instance, contingent fee percentages can range from

25 to 35 percent if the case settles to 35 to 40 percent if the case is won at trial, and an even higher percentage if the judgment is successfully kept on appeal. Lawyers can also arrange to charge an hourly or flat fee, which is then translated into a contingent fee if they succeed in recovering a settlement or judgment. Lawyers who charge a contingent fee obviously have a financial stake in the outcome of the case, but a contingent fee is an American exception to laws against champerty. (Contingent fees that are a percentage of the judgment are prohibited in Great Britain and much of Canada because of their laws against champerty and barratry.)

Although the contingent fee is most often associated with personal injury cases, it can be used in a variety of cases, including civil rights actions and real estate tax appeals. However, for a contingent fee to be legitimate, the outcome must be unknown. For instance, a lawyer could not charge a contingency fee for drafting someone's will and take 30 percent of whatever the testator's property he successfully brings under the will, because the property already belonged to the client. And although plaintiffs' lawyers most often use contingent fee arrangements, defense attorneys can use them as well. Such an arrangement, called a **reverse contingent fee**, involves the lawyer being paid a percentage of what he saves the client from losing.

The contingent fee has been historically promoted as a method to provide a low-income person access to justice, because the cash-poor client owes the lawyer no fee unless he succeeds. Three problems are associated with that premise. First, it may be inaccurate (see the section, "Fees in Excess of Statutory Allowances"). Second, some clients would prefer to pay a fixed fee rather than a contingent fee. Although the lawyer is obligated to offer the client reasonable alternatives to a contingency fee, some critics argue that the contingent fee is overused. In his book *Litigation Explosion* (Truman Talley Books–Dutton, 1991), scholar and litigation-reform advocate Walter K. Olson discusses contingent fees and states that a Federal Trade Commission report found that 97 percent of personal injury lawyers took cases only on a contingent basis, refusing to be paid on an hourly basis (Olson, 47). Third, regardless of the client's wealth or lack thereof, contingent fees can be enormous, resulting in claims that lawyers are siphoning from the public welfare. For instance, the United States Chamber of Commerce was so irritated by the $11 billion in legal fees awarded to the plaintiffs' attorneys as a result of the 1998 class-action settlement involving 21 states and the tobacco industry that it called on the U.S. Congress to investigate the fees award. And *Time* magazine published a cover story in July 2000 on class actions and legal fees that asked the question, "Are lawyers running America?"

It is no surprise that Joe Jamail, regarded as America's richest lawyer, is a tort lawyer whose income is mostly derived from contingency agreements. Mr. Jamail was prominently featured in the mid-1990s on a thought-provoking television show hosted by John Stossel, "The Trouble with Lawyers," which can be found by using the search feature on this link at ABC's Web site: http://www.abcnewsstore.com.

■ **reverse contingent fee**

A type of contingent fee arrangement that involves the lawyer being paid a percentage of what the lawyer saves the client from losing, as opposed to a percentage of what the lawyer obtains for the client.

Anyone who saw that show, or has seen Mr. Jamail in action, knows why jurors repeatedly fall in love with this salty, charismatic Texan. How wealthy is he? For starters, the University of Texas football stadium bears his name. And in 2006, *Forbes* magazine put him—once again—on their "America's 400 Richest Americans" list at number 278, with a net worth of $1.4 billion. His *Forbes* profile can be found by using the search feature, or by clicking on "The World's Billionaires," at this link: http://www.forbes.com/lists/.

Mr. Jamail has his own Web site, where one can learn about his many career highlights and see the cover of his autobiography, *Lawyer*: http://www.joejamail.com/.

Fixed Fee

fixed fee

A predetermined fee that covers all of the lawyer's efforts in services rendered for a particular client matter. A fixed fee is distinguished from an hourly rate.

A **fixed fee**, also called a flat fee, involves the lawyer charging a predetermined amount for the legal services the client desires. The ABA has defined a fixed fee as a fee that "embraces all work to be done, whether it be relatively simple and of short duration, or complex and protracted." ABA Commission on Ethics and Professional Responsibility, Informal Op. 1389 (1977). Fixed fees can be commonplace for fairly routine and standardized legal services, such as drafting a simple will or a real estate document, representing a party in an uncontested divorce, or representing a debtor in a straightforward, Chapter 7 bankruptcy petition. Fixed fees are viewed as being consumer-friendly, because the client knows when hiring the lawyer just how much he will cost. And because the process of finding a lawyer is a consumer activity, the use of fixed fees for certain services allows the consumer to comparison shop.

The following link is to The Devil's Advocate®, a legal fees analysis and consulting firm, which has links to summaries on types of legal fees, provides what it calls "A Client's Bill of Rights," and has a whistleblower page, where law firm personnel can anonymously and confidentially get advice when they believe they are being asked to engage in unethical billing practices: http://www.devilsadvocate.com/Default.htm.

THE RULES ON LEGAL FEES

There are at least three sources of rules that concern the lawyer's relationship to the client's money. First, there are the rules that directly concern legal fees, which are found in ABA Model Rule 1.5 and ABA Model Code DR 2–106. There are also rules concerning the safekeeping of the client's property, which includes the client's money, that are found in MR 1.15, and DR 9–102. And there are rules concerning the lawyer's duty to return the client's property, including unearned fees, when the lawyer and client relationship is terminated, that are found in MR 1.16 and DR 2–109.

A Lawyer's Fee Shall Not Be Unreasonable

The Ethics 2000 version of Model Rule 1.5(a) states that "A lawyer shall not make an agreement for, charge, or collect an unreasonable fee," whereas the prior version of MR 1.5(a) stated, "A lawyer's fee shall be reasonable." This change from requiring a reasonable fee to prohibiting an unreasonable fee is similar to the Model Code's version, DR 2–106(A), which states that a lawyer "shall not enter into an agreement for, charge, or collect an illegal or clearly excessive fee." The new MR 1.5(a) also now prohibits a lawyer from charging "an unreasonable amount for expenses." This change incorporates what is expressed in ethics opinions: excessive expenses are as bad as excessive fees. See Exhibit 7-2 for the evolution of legal fees, and Exhibit 7-3 for the ethics of legal fees.

Nothing in the Model Rules or Model Code explicitly defines an unreasonable or clearly excessive fee, and that has caused some consternation from those who wish there were more specific guidelines on fees. (DR 2–106(B) states, "A fee is excessive when, after a review of the facts, a lawyer of ordinary prudence would be left with a definite and firm conviction that the fee is in excess of a reasonable fee.") Both versions, however, provide a nonexclusive list

---

EXHIBIT 7–2   THE EVOLUTION OF THE ABA'S RULES ON LEGAL FEES

- **ABA Model Code DR 2-106(a)**: "A lawyer shall not enter into an agreement for, charge, or collect an illegal or excessive fee."

- **ABA Model Rule 1.5 (1983 version)**: "A lawyer's fee shall be reasonable."

- **ABA Model Rule 1.5 (Ethics 2000 version)**: "A lawyer shall not make an agreement for charge, or collect an unreasonable fee or an unreasonable amount for expenses."

- **All three versions list factors that help determine what makes a fee reasonable:**
  - The time, labor, and skill required, as well as the difficulty of the case
  - The chance that taking the client's case will prevent taking another case
  - The customary fee charged in the community
  - The results obtained
  - The time limits imposed by the client or the circumstances
  - The nature and length of the relationship with the client
  - The experience, reputation, and ability of the lawyer
  - Whether the fee is fixed or contingent

> **EXHIBIT 7–3** KEY CHANGES TO THE ETHICS 2000 RULE ON LEGAL FEES
>
> - There is now a prohibition on charging an unreasonable amount for expenses.
> - The basis for the expenses of the case must be explained to the client.
> - Contingent fee agreements must be in writing and signed by the client.
> - Contingent fee agreements must clearly state if the client is liable for expenses if the client loses.

of factors to be taken into consideration when determining whether a fee is reasonable or excessive. Some of those factors include the following: the time and labor involved; the level of skill required to perform the services; the chance that other legal employment will be precluded by taking the client's case; the nature and length of the professional relationship with the client; the fee customarily charged in the locality for similar legal services; the experience and reputation of the lawyer performing the services; and whether the fee is fixed or contingent. MR 1.5(a); DR 2–106(B). See Exhibit 7-4 for examples of excessive fees.

Certain Activities Are Nonbillable

Not everything lawyers or their non-lawyer employees do can be billed. Some activities are considered nonbillable, which makes the act of billing the client, not the size of the bill, unreasonable. That means if a lawyer bills 40 hours a week, he must work anywhere from 5 to 15 percent more than 40 hours a week to account for activities that are not billable. And the same goes for the paralegal whose time is billable. Although it might seem too obvious for mention, some lawyers have still needed express confirmation that a lawyer may not bill a client for the time it takes him to respond to ethics charges made by that client. *In re Lawyers Responsibility Board Panel No. 94–17*, 546 N.W.2d 744 (Minn. 1996). And although proofreading one's work is a necessary activity, a court refused to honor

> **EXHIBIT 7–4** WHAT CAN MAKE A LEGAL FEE UNREASONABLE?
>
> - Certain activities are nonbillable: *overhead*
> - Fee limits sometimes apply: *28 U.S.C. § 2678*
> - Fees occasionally need to be reduced: *lawyers are fiduciaries to their clients*
> - Lawyers and paralegals may not be inefficient or deceitful: *bill padding or overbilling*
> - Lawyers and paralegals may not be overly efficient: *double billing*

a bill that included the time a lawyer spent proofreading an internal memorandum. *Wright v. U-Let-Us Skycap Services, Inc.*, 648 F.Supp. 1216 (D. Colo. 1986). Likewise, a court suspended an attorney for 30 days because, after being hired to collect a debt, the lawyer billed his client almost $1000 for writing two letters: one to the client telling him how a debt could be collected ($583), and a second letter demanding payment for having written the first letter ($360). *In re Schneider*, 710 N.E.2d 178 (Ind. 1999).

Generally, overhead costs are not billable to the client because they are recouped through the lawyer's fee. Overhead, sometimes called "housekeeping," is that which is needed to keep the legal ship afloat, from coffee filters to toilet paper, and billing the client for those consumables is thought inappropriate. See ABA Commission on Ethics and Professional Responsibility, Formal Op. 93–379 (1993), which opposes the separate billing of office overhead and wherein it states, "The lawyer's stock in trade is the sale of legal services, not photocopy paper, tuna fish sandwiches, computer time, or messenger services."

A new Comment to the Ethics 2000 version of Model Rule 1.5 states that a lawyer may bill a client for overhead costs *if the client agrees in advance* or the lawyer may seek reimbursement of those costs, such as copying and phone calls. *Connecticut* issued an ethics opinion that considered it inappropriate for a law firm to add to its clients' bills a flat "administrative expense" that covered expenses such as long-distance phone calls, photocopying, and postage. Connecticut State Bar Association Commission on Professional Ethics, Op. 94–24 (1994). Courts have also found that the typical office housekeeping activities associated with litigation may not be billed separately to the client. In a federal case where the plaintiff's attorney fees were recoverable under a federal statute, the court refused to award fees for over 102 hours claimed by the plaintiff's attorneys, paralegals, and secretaries for such things as copying and distributing memos, tagging exhibits, reviewing and organizing files, and reproducing documents. The court declared such clerical activity to be the kind of housekeeping expenses that the firm's hourly rate was meant to cover. *Keith v. Volpe*, 644 F. Supp. 1317 (C.D. Cal. 1986). And in a considerably lengthy bankruptcy court opinion involving the fees requested by the attorney, the court reaffirmed that neither paralegals nor lawyers may charge for clerical work. *In re Castorena*, 270 B.R. 504 (D. Idaho 2001).

Fees in Excess of Statutory Allowances

Although the ethics rules place no limit on the percentage of a contingent fee, some statutes put limits on certain kinds of fees. For instance, the Federal Tort Claims Act puts a cap on contingency fees at 25 percent and provides for fines and imprisonment for lawyers who violate the contingency fee limit. 28 U.S.C. § 2678. Many jurisdictions have a cap on legal fees in worker's compensation cases. New York has a contingency fee cap for medical, dental, and podiatric malpractice cases; it starts at 30 percent of the first $250,000 recovered. As the recovery increases, the contingency percentage decreases, capping out at 10 percent of any amount over $1,250,000 of the sum recovered. N.Y. Jud. Law § 474–a(2). California has a cap on contingency fees for medical malpractice cases that ranges from 40 percent on the first $50,000 recovered, and de-escalates to 15 percent on any recovery over $600,000. Cal. Bus. and Prof. Code § 6146.

Florida has a similar sliding scale for contingency fees in personal injury actions, which can be found in the state's professional responsibility rule on legal fees. Fla. State Bar Rule 4–1.5(f)(4). It is significant that the enmity between doctors in Florida and the lawyers who sue them reached critical mass in 2004, when the doctors—collectively yelling, "I'm mad as hell and I'm not going to take it anymore"—succeeded in getting citizens to vote to change the Florida Constitution and limit legal fees in medical malpractice cases. Article I, Section 26, known as "Claimant's right to fair compensation," caps legal fees at 30

NOT QUITE LINCOLN

These Bills Might Cause Everyone to Choose to Represent Themselves Pro Se

When the ABA asked readers of its *ABA Journal eReport* to send in some the strangest billing tactics or stories they had seen, it received more than a dozen doozies. Here are a few of them. Let's hope the people reporting these fee fiascos aren't the source of them.

After being fired by his clients for doing nothing on their medical malpractice claim, an attorney demanded part of the fee the second attorney earned for obtaining a sizable settlement. In support of his claim, he presented a bill to the second attorney showing the work he performed on the case, and included on that bill were the following items:

"Open & read holiday card from client, 25 minutes...$150."

"Open & read birthday card from client...30 minutes...$170."

A summer intern at a law firm described on his time sheet the following activity for his 0.4 hours of billing time: "doing stuff."

When the in-house attorney for a large company received a bill from outside counsel that the corporate attorney thought was too high, he complained to the outside counsel and negotiated a lower bill. Upon receiving the revised bill, he noticed that the new bill included a fee for the time the outside counsel took to investigate and correct his original, faulty bill.

An attorney in a large metropolitan area billed his clients for the five hours he spent golfing with them. That might not be too unusual, but it was that he billed them for the golf balls he lost during the afternoon.

And the king of all galling bills has to be the one sent by a divorce lawyer to the client with whom he had an affair. The disciplinary commission caught the lawyer after his client lost that loving feeling, right around the time she received a bill for the time he spent with her...*in discovery*.

percent of the first $250,000 recovered, and at 10 percent for any exceeding amount (excluding litigation costs), regardless of the number of defendants. Although this provision was opposed by the Academy of Florida Trial Lawyers, as well as the ABA Task Force on Contingent Fees, enough Floridians believed— rightly or wrongly—that a root source of the towering medical and health insurance costs was the connection between medical malpractice settlements and awards and the attendant contingent fees.

When lawyers charge fees in violation of authorized caps, courts not only will reject the petitioned fees, but may also issue sanctions for violating the limitations. In a West Virginia case, a lawyer who represented worker's compensation claimants violated the state statute that capped attorneys' fees in permanent disability claims at 20 percent of the benefits to be received. He instead charged some clients upward of 40 percent. During the disciplinary proceeding, the lawyer claimed that the clients had waived their rights to hold the lawyer within the statutory limits. However, the court decided that such a waiver may not be made under the statute's clear language. It suspended the lawyer for 91 days and required him to pay restitution to his clients. *Committee on Legal Ethics of West Virginia State Bar v. Burdette*, 445 S.E.2d 733 (W. Va. 1994). And in a Colorado case, a lawyer charged the statutorily required 20 percent contingent fee in a worker's compensation case, but also charged his client a separate fee of $1000 after thinking the 20 percent fee would not make his efforts worthwhile. As a result, the lawyer was censured and ordered to return the $1000 to his client. *In re Wimmershoff*, 3 P.3d 417 (Colo.2000).

Can a Fee Be Unreasonable Because It Is too High?

One of the many ingenious aspects of a free-market economy is that the prices of goods and services are what they should be because the law of supply and demand sets the price. A car, whether a Saturn or a BMW, costs what it should—whatever the marketplace will bear. Absent fraud, no one purchasing a car would likely then sue the dealer by claiming the price was too high, because he agreed to the price in the first place. Such is not the case with purchasing legal services because legal fees can be too high, despite the client's original agreement to pay the fee. The lawyer-client relationship imposes fiduciary obligations on the lawyer, so charging the client a fee is an act that is different from other commercial endeavors, such as selling someone a car. Even where there is a written fee agreement, courts always retain the power to review a legal fee for reasonableness. In a case that serves as a reminder of why the public likes car dealers better than it likes lawyers, a lawyer represented a client in a personal injury action, resulting in a settlement of $1000. After the case was settled, the client got to keep only $45. When the matter came to the attention of the court, the lawyer argued that the fee agreement and the final bill were detailed in writing to the client and the client agreed to the charges. Nevertheless, the court found that the attorney had taken advantage of a client "with very limited understanding," and the lawyer was disbarred. *State ex rel. Oklahoma Bar Ass'n v. Hatcher*, 452 P.2d 150 (Okla. 1969).

A lawyer's fee can also be considered unreasonable or excessive when it is not earned. If the lawyer does very little work to earn a sizable fee, the fact that the client agreed to the fee is secondary to the question of whether the fee should have been reduced. For example, in an Illinois case, an elderly woman in the hospital, who believed that some of her financial assets, such as **certificates of deposits (CDs)**, had been stolen, contacted a lawyer for help. The lawyer told her he would charge her $175 an hour, or a contingency fee of one-third of whatever he recovered for her. She opted for the contingency fee. The lawyer's work involved him discovering that her 23 CDs were safe and sound at the various banks where she had purchased them, a fact that the woman had, in the interim, discovered on her own. Then the lawyer registered the CDs in the name of a trust he created for the client and charged her a fee of $160,000, amounting to one-third of the value of her CDs. Not only did the court find that the lawyer wrongly used a contingency fee because he actually "recovered" nothing for the client, it also found that the fee was excessive in light of the minimal work required to do what the client needed. *In re Gerard*, 548 N.E.2d 1051 (Ill. 1989). (And because the attorney was also licensed in Indiana, Missouri, and Wisconsin, those jurisdictions suspended him too.)

Fees can also be considered unreasonable when a lawyer is inefficient. Because the rules require lawyers to act competently (MR 1.1; DR 6–101(A)), a lawyer who is inexperienced should not charge the client for the time it takes him to become competent to handle the client's case. *In re Estate of Larson*, 694 P.2d 1051 (Wash. 1985). A lawyer who worked on a constitutional matter for a client billed 19 hours for research on the Eleventh Amendment, and also billed for 49 discussions with co-counsel. The excessive hours showed the lawyer's inexperience on the matter, making the bill unreasonable. The bill was reduced by half, including the paralegal's portion. *Heavener v. Meyers*, 158 F.Supp.2d 1278 (E.D. Okla. 2001). When a lawyer who charges an hourly rate works really slowly, especially intentionally, a court can order him to reduce or return the fee. An Indiana lawyer was suspended for 30 days for billing a client for, among other things, the 6 hours it took him to drive to a law library, when there was one 15 minutes away. *In the Matter of Comstock*, 664 N.E.2d 1165 (Ind. 1996).

Topping even that, an Iowa lawyer sought payment for his own plagiarism. Representing a client in a federal discrimination suit, the lawyer applied to the court for his legal fees (under a fee-shifting provision, which will be discussed later in the chapter). He requested over $100,000 in fees and over $13,000 in expenses. Included in his fees were $16,000 dollars for 80 hours of time spent writing a post-trial brief. But it seemed from the footnotes that the brief he submitted belonged to another author. The U.S. magistrate gave the lawyer 10 days to identify his source. After that deadline passed, a fire destroyed the attorney's files in the matter. Finally, it came to light that 18 pages of the legal

---

certificates of deposits (CDs)

A type of conservative investment wherein someone gives money to a bank or other financial institution in exchange for promissory notes from the institutions detailing the interest to be paid on the money and the date on which the principal and interest will be paid to the investor.

arguments in the brief were word-for-word pulled right from a **legal treatise**. However, when the attorney submitted his sources for the brief, he slid the treatise's title into the list of 200 sources on which he claimed to rely in his research and writing. He was suspended for six months. *Iowa Supreme Court Board of Professional Ethics and Conduct v. Lane*, 642 N.W.2d 296 (Iowa 2002).

The ABA has stated that a lawyer may not bill for being "doubly efficient"— billing one client for working on a matter while at the same time billing another client for traveling on a different matter. ABA Commission on Ethics and

> ■ **legal treatise.**
> A form of secondary authority, much like a legal textbook, but which is often accorded higher status because of its longstanding reputation in the legal community.

NOT QUITE LINCOLN

And You Thought Your Long Distance Plan Was Steep

David Brite of California began receiving calls from heir locater services telling him that his step-grandmother, Mary Kay Brite of South Pasadena, Florida, had died and that he might be the only heir of her estate. A long time had passed since David had any contact with his step-grandmother and he knew little about her estate, including if she had a will. To help with the search, he got a copy of his long-deceased grandfather's will. When he couldn't tell from examining it if his step grandmother had a will and, if she did, where it was, he contacted St. Petersburg attorney Ed Jagger for help. For a fee of 25 percent of Mrs. Brite's estate, Jagger agreed to investigate if Mrs. Brite left any valid will at the time of her death, try to find it, and probate it if it was found. David Brite didn't notice the small typeface of the preparing law firm on his grandfather's will, but Jagger did. After one phone call to one of that firm's partners, Jagger located Mrs. Brite's will. According to David Brite, Jagger's one phone call resulted in Brite receiving a legal bill of $350,000. Thanks to smart investing, the aptly named Mrs. Brite died a millionaire at the age of 86. After getting what he thought was the world's biggest phone bill, David Brite went to court in 2002, asking that Jagger's fee be reduced as excessive. By Jagger's account, he did much more than make one now-infamous phone call: After the call, he found the lawyer who drafted her will, and then he and his son examined 12 cartons of Mrs. Brite's personal effects looking for a copy of that will. Jagger and his son then created a litigation strategy in the event someone contested the will. Jagger defended against the accusation that he overcharged by saying he didn't know if he would have to work for untold hours trying to find the will of a woman of unknown but substantial wealth. By doing so, he took the risk that he might earn 25 percent of next to nothing. Jagger also pointed out that had he not found the will, his client might have gotten 100 percent of nothing. Although no newspaper reported the resolution of this fee dispute, attorney Jagger has since become Judge Jagger.

▨ **double billing**

A dishonest billing practice that involves billing two clients at the same time.

▨ **bill padding**

A dishonest billing practice that involves one exaggerating the time spent working on a client's case.

Professional Responsibility, Formal Op. 94–389 (1994). **Double billing** (billing two clients at the same time) is different from **bill padding** (inflating one's billable hours for a particular client), but both are deceitful practices.

A lawyer also may not bill the client at the lawyer's hourly rate for work that he did that could have been done by the legal assistant or other support staff and then would have been billed at their lower hourly rate. *Davis v. City and County of San Francisco*, 976 F.2d 1536 (9th Cir. 1992). When qualified paralegals are part of a practice, it is required that they be used cost-effectively for clients.

No Honor Among Thieves or Legal Staff

Who is likely to expose a lawyer, or testify against him, when the bills are fraudulent? Right—the paralegals and secretaries. Such was the case with a Washington lawyer involved in brazenly deceitful billing tactics. While representing several insurance companies, the attorney repeatedly billed his clients at his higher rate for work that was done by his associates and staff. He accomplished this by putting his initials next to the work done by others on the "rough draft" versions of his bills, and then had his staff re-create the bills. He also flew first-class, even though his clients told him they were only going to pay for coach tickets. That ruse was effected by having his travel agency create two invoices for tickets—one for coach (which was sent to the clients) and one for first-class. And while having a cabin built, the attorney also instructed his paralegal and secretary to "bury" various phone calls to contractors and charges for blueprints in the bills of his clients—something his staff should not have done. Perhaps they purged their guilt by testifying against their former boss at the disciplinary hearing. He, of course, claimed not to know about the deceitful bills and that his paralegal and secretary had devious motives and were lying. When the dust settled, he was suspended for two years. *Matter of Disciplinary Proceeding Against Haskell*, 962 P.2d 813 (Wash. 1998).

Legal Fees Must Be Clearly Explained to the Client

The new version of Model Rule 1.5(b) requires that the lawyer communicate to the client the scope of the representation, the basis for the fee, and expenses the client will have to pay, preferably in writing. It also requires that changes in the calculation of fees or expenses be explained to the client. The former version of that rule was not explicit concerning explaining the expenses a client will have to pay or if changes in the fees and expenses needed to be communicated. This change is designed to promote the client's understanding of any future obligations to the lawyer.

The ABA Model Code had no similar rule, but an Ethical Consideration did state that it is "usually beneficial to reduce to writing the understanding of the parties regarding the fee, particularly when it is contingent." EC 2–19. The Comments to MR 1.5 declare that a lawyer does not have to set forth all the factors that contribute to the fee; rather, stating whether the rate is an hourly charge, a fixed fee, or an estimated fee is sufficient. Confusion can occur due to the lawyer's inadequate explanation of the fee or the client's failure to understand the arrangement, the latter case still being the lawyer's responsibility. Although neither the Model Rules nor the Model Code require written fee arrangements for all representations, the Ethics 2000 proposal for 1.5(b) included requiring all fee agreements to be in writing, but that was rejected. Three areas of fees explanation will be discussed in the following sections: the explanation the initial client should receive; the difference between fees and costs; and the difference between an advance and a retainer.

Explanation for the New Client

The first Comment to Model Rule 1.5 provides that when the lawyer is hired by a new client, "an understanding as to the fee should be promptly established." Again, such a maxim falls short of requiring that a written fee agreement be established for the new client, but there is a greater emphasis on the lawyer's responsibility to attend to the understanding of the new client. The rules are more relaxed when it comes to a client with whom the lawyer has a continuing professional relationship. However, the new client might have never before retained any lawyer—not just the lawyer about to be retained—and might have no idea how the overall legal fee system works. Here, a careful initial interview of the prospective client, by the lawyer or the lawyer's paralegal, can alert the lawyer to the need to clearly explain the fee agreement. A few jurisdictions have altered the "preferably in writing" language from MR 1.5(b) and require that the fee agreement be put in writing if the lawyer has not regularly represented the client. *See* Conn. R.P.C. 1.5(b); D.C.

R.P.C. 1.5(b); N.J. R.P.C. 1.5(b); Pa. R.P.C. 1.5(b). The ABA has, on a few occasions, issued ethics opinions that concern the need for the lawyer to fully explain the fee arrangement with a prospective client. *See* ABA Commission on Ethics and Professional Responsibility, Formal Op. 94–389 (1994); Formal Op. 93–379 (1993); Informal Op. 86–1521 (1986).

What Should the Fee Agreement for the New Client Contain? Although most jurisdictions do not require every fee agreement to be in writing, fee agreements—like other contracts—benefit those involved if they are put on paper. The fee or retainer agreement should explain what the lawyer was hired to do and the extent of his services to the client. It should explain how the lawyer's fee is going to be calculated, including how any legal assistant time will be billed to the client; how certain items, such as travel time and expenses, will be billed; how often the client is going to be billed; and how the client is to pay the lawyer. Concerning methods of payment, the American Bar Association issued an ethics opinion in 2000 that approved of lawyers accepting credit card payments as a method for clients to pay their legal bills. ABA Commission on Ethics and Professional Responsibility, Formal Op. 00–419 (2000). That opinion invalidated prior opinions from the 1960s and 1970s that had opposed credit card payments for legal fees. Not all jurisdictions allow lawyers to accept credit card payments from clients, and some put limitations on their use. A majority decision by Texas's Committee on Professional Ethics, for instance, allowed lawyers to accept credit card payments, although the committee acknowledged the minority's dissent. But the committee unanimously opposed the advertisement of credit card emblems or decals in law offices, believing that such use would constitute unlawful solicitation. Texas State Bar Association Committee on Professional Ethics, Op. 349 (1969). Montana allows lawyers to accept credit card payments in all but bankruptcy cases. State Bar of Montana Ethics Committee, Op. 000003 (2000).

If there is a contingent fee arrangement, the agreement should cover how the lawyer's percentage will be calculated, including whether the contingent fee will be taken from the recovery before or after litigation expenses have been paid. Regardless of the type of fee arrangement, the agreement should also clearly provide procedures concerning how any future fee dispute will be handled, such as whether the agreement calls for mediation or arbitration mechanisms. Giving up the right to resolve a dispute in the traditional forum of the legal system is no small waiver (e.g., there is almost no right to appeal an arbitrator's decision), so the ABA, in an ethics opinion in 2002, stated that when a lawyer inserts a binding arbitration clause in a retainer agreement, the lawyer should first inform the client of the advantages and disadvantages of that resolution mechanism and get the client's informed consent. See Exhibit 7-5 for a client fee explanation.

EXHIBIT 7–5   FEES EXPLANATIONS FOR THE CLIENT

- ABA Model Rule 1.5(b) (Ethics 2000) requires that a clear explanation on fees and expenses be given to the new client, *preferably in writing*, and include when the fees or expenses are going to change.

- What could be in a written fee agreement?
  - The scope of the representation
  - The type of fee to be charged
  - The method used to calculate the fee
  - How expenses will be charged
  - Whether paralegal fees will be charged separately and how much those fees will be
  - How fee disputes will be resolved

The following samples of client retention letters in Exhibit 7-6, courtesy of the Indiana Continuing Legal Education Forum, show the types of issues and details that can be covered in basic fee agreements.

PERSONAL AND CONFIDENTIAL

[Date]

Name and address

In re: _____

Dear _____ :

    Per our recent communications, this letter serves to confirm the retention by _____ ("Corporation") of _____ (the "Firm") in the above-referenced bankruptcy case and related proceedings (the "Proceedings"), currently pending in the United States Bankruptcy Court, District of _____. This letter also serves to advise the Corporation of the fee rates charged by the Firm in connection with this matter, and our general billing practices.

    It is my understanding that the Corporation has agreed to retain the Firm for purposes of representing the Corporation in the Proceedings and matters incidental thereto. Because of the relative uncertainty of what action the Firm will be required to take in the course of this representation, I am unable to give you a firm estimate of what services, and accordingly, what fees, will be incurred by the Firm on the Corporation's behalf during our representation. In the meantime, I will confirm that the Firm generally determines its fees on the basis of time spent by our attorneys and paralegals on a particular matter. Each attorney in the Firm has a separate billing rate, ranging from $_____ to $_____ per hour for associates, and $_____ to $_____ per hour for partners. As the partner responsible for this matter, you should note that my billing rate is $_____ per hour. I also expect that my partner_____, will regularly assist me in this matter. His/her billing rate is $_____ per hour. I also expect to use the services of my associate _____ ($_____ per hour) and, on occasion, paralegal services ($_____ per hour).

    Because the nature of these proceedings, the Firm will require an initial retainer in the amount of $_____. This sum, which is payable towards the Firm's fees and expenses, will be placed in an interest bearing account and will be returned at the conclusion of our representation if all outstanding bills have been paid. During the course of the matter, depending on the level of activity and the timeliness of payment of invoices, it may become necessary that we ask for an additional retainer prior to the Firm providing additional services. In order to process your check for deposit into an interest bearing account, the Firm's accounting department requests that the Corporation provide the Firm with a Federal W-9 Form signed by a duly authorized representative.

EXHIBIT 7–6a   Sample Client Retention Letters – Example #1

In determining the amount of the fee to be charged in a matter, it may be necessary, on occasion, to deviate from the standard hourly rates set forth above due to factors, including the novelty and difficulty of the issues presented, and time limitations imposed by circumstances related to the matter. At this time, it is not possible to determine if any of these factors will apply in this particular case.

The Firm's policy is to bill for services rendered and disbursement on a monthly basis, having learned that most clients appreciate receiving invoices every month. Such statements will itemize the rates and services charged by each attorney. We expect our statements to be paid promptly upon their presentation. In the event that a statement is not paid within 30 days of receipt, the Firm reserves the right to charge interest on the outstanding balance at an annual rate of five percent (5%) for the period which the statement remains unpaid after the initial 30 days.

The Firm reserves the right to withdrawal from this representation should the Corporation fail to honor the terms of this engagement letter, fail to follow the Firm's advise on material matters, fail to be honest or forthright in any material matter, or if, for any other reason, in the Firm's judgment, the Firm's ability to continue an attorney/client relationship with the Corporation in a lawful and ethical manner is impaired. Such withdrawal will not relieve the Corporation of its obligation to pay for all services rendered and costs or disbursements incurred up to the date which representation is terminated.

As with any professional relationship, close cooperation and frequent communication will improve our ability to serve the Corporation's legal needs in an efficient and effective manner. If you have questions about the Firm's representations, or services being rendered, please feel free to contact me.

Please confirm the terms of our agreement for representation by co-signing this letter below and returning it to the undersigned with the retainer described above.

On behalf of the Firm, thank you very much for allowing the Firm to represent the Corporation's interests in the Proceedings.

Very truly yours,

AGREED: [Client]

By: _____
Its: _____
Date: _____

316330

EXHIBIT 7–6a   Sample Client Retention Letters – Example #1 *(continued)*

Dear _____ :

Our Firm is pleased to have the opportunity to serve as legal counsel to_____
in connection with _____. Our Firm is committed to providing
you with legal services in an effective and economical manner.

This letter confirms the terms and conditions under which our Firm will undertake to represent
_____. [Unless instructed otherwise, our representation of
_____ shall be limited to the following:
_____.] Our fees for legal services will be billed on an hourly basis
according to the billing rates charged by each lawyer or paralegal of our Firm, which currently
range from $____.00 an hour for paralegals to $____.00 an hour for senior partners. These billing
rates are subject to adjustment without notice from time to time by the Firm.   In certain
instances, other factors may be taken into consideration in determining our fees, including the
responsibility and liability assumed, the novelty and difficulty of the legal problem involved,
whether the Firm is requested to issue its formal legal opinion associated with some facet of its
representation, the benefit resulting to the client and any unforeseen circumstances arising in the
course of our representation.

We will provide you with invoices on a monthly basis. The invoices will describe our services
and itemize our expenses in accordance with our standard Firm policies. A schedule of our
standard charges for these expenses is enclosed for your reference. These expenses include such
items as photocopying, long-distance telephone charges, facsimile charges, travel and related
expenses, computerized legal research, postage and delivery or courier services. If certain major
expenses such as printing or filing fees are anticipated to be incurred, we may request that you
pay these expenses directly at the time they are incurred.

Our Firm's policy is to require a retainer to be paid prior to the rendering of any legal services
for new clients. For this particular matter, our Firm will require a retainer in the amount of
$____.00 before proceeding with any legal work on your behalf. We will charge our initial fees
and expenses against such retainer and credit them on our invoices. The retainer is not an
estimate of the total fees to be incurred or expenses advanced, but is a prepayment of the initial
fees to be incurred with regard to this matter. Once the retainer amount is fully credited towards
fees incurred and expenses advanced, it is essential to our representation that you remain current
in the payment of all invoices for fees and expenses. We reserve the right to require the payment
of subsequent retainers after the initial retainer is depleted.

Payment relating to all invoices will be due within thirty (30) days after such invoices are
mailed. Subject to any limitations imposed by the Indiana Code of Professional Responsibility,
our Firm will be entitled to discontinue work on any aspect of this representation in the event
that any invoices are not paid within thirty (30) days after the invoice is mailed. If we are

EXHIBIT 7–6b   Sample Client Retention Letters – Example #2

required to resort to collection proceedings to recover from you fees incurred and expenses advanced on your behalf, we shall also be entitled to recover all costs incurred in connection with such collection proceedings including reasonable attorneys fees incurred either by us or separate counsel.

You shall have the right at any time to terminate our services and representation upon written notice to the Firm. Such termination shall not, however, relieve you of the obligation to pay for all services rendered and costs or expenses incurred on your behalf prior to the date of such termination. As permitted by law, we reserve the right to retain your files until all invoices have been paid in full.

We reserve the right to withdraw from your representation if, among other things, you fail to honor the terms of this engagement letter, you fail to cooperate or follow our advice on a material matter, or any fact or circumstance would, in our view, render our continuing representation unlawful or unethical. If we elect to withdraw from your representation, you agree to take all steps necessary to free us of any obligation to perform further, including the execution of any documents reasonably necessary to complete our withdrawal, and we will be entitled to be paid for all services rendered and costs and expenses incurred on your behalf through the date of withdrawal.

In the event that we use electronic mail at any time to communicate with each other, or with third parties, you acknowledge that we have advised you that electronic mail may be subject to a greater risk of interception or unauthorized access than wire-line telephone communication. If at any time you desire that we not use electronic mail, you will advise us of such desire and we will act in accordance with your instruction. If you do not so advise us, we will assume that you consent to the use of electronic mail for communications between our attorneys (and staff) and you or other persons with respect to your matters and in particular this transaction.

Payment of each invoice is due upon receipt. Subject to any limitations imposed by the Indiana Rules of Professional Conduct, our firm will be entitled to cease work on any aspect of this representation if any invoices are not paid within thirty (30) days after the invoice is mailed. If we are required to resort to collection proceedings to recover any amounts from you, we will also be entitled to recover all costs incurred concerning such collection proceedings including reasonable attorneys' fees incurred either by us or separate counsel. By signing and returning the additional copy of this letter, you agree that in any such collection proceedings or dispute regarding the attorney-client relationship, venue shall be in the Superior or Circuit Court of Marion County, Indiana, or the United States District Court for the Southern District of Indiana, Indianapolis Division, and you consent to the jurisdiction and venue of such court.

If the foregoing terms and conditions accurately summarize and confirm the understanding of our proposed attorney-client relationship, please indicate your approval and acceptance by dating, signing and returning this letter, together with the retainer check made payable to the

EXHIBIT 7–6b   Sample Client Retention Letters – Example #2 *(continued)*

Firm, in the enclosed self-addressed stamped envelope. An additional copy of this letter is enclosed for your records.

Once again, we appreciate this opportunity to serve _____. Should you have any questions or concerns with regard to the matters discussed in this letter, please do not hesitate to contact me.

Very truly yours,

_____

Agreed to and accepted this ____ day of _____, 200__.

By:_____
Printed:_____
Title:_____

EXHIBIT 7–6b   Sample Client Retention Letters – Example #2 *(continued)*

The Difference Between Fees and Costs

"If you don't recover, we don't take a fee." How many times has that or another similar phrase been stated on radio or television or put into print? More importantly, how many members of the public understand the meaning of such phrases? Part of the lawyer's duty in explaining the fee arrangement is to distinguish fees from costs for the client. Generally, fees are what the lawyer charges for his professional effort, be it hourly or contingent fees. Costs are different. Costs are general expenses, such as court filing fees or litigation expenses, including discovery costs. (Costs, however, are different from administrative overhead expenses, discussed in the section "Certain Activities Are Nonbillable.") That means that even in a contingent fee arrangement in which the plaintiff ultimately does not recover a judgment, the lawyer might still present a bill for the litigation costs. See Exhibit 7-7 for a comparison of fees and costs.

When confusion arises over the meaning of the fee arrangements, courts will favor the client rather than the lawyer. For example, an Illinois lawyer billed a client a fixed fee of $10,000 in a divorce representation. A lawsuit ensued over the fee because the lawyer refused to provide the client an itemized bill. Despite the lawyer's claim that a fixed fee need not be itemized, the court declared that the client is always entitled to an itemized bill, and remanded the case for a determination of whether the fee was reasonable. *In re Marriage of Pitulla*, 491 N. E.2d 90 (Ill. App. Ct. 1986). In a Colorado case, a client hired a lawyer for a matter and agreed to pay a contingent fee under the terms of a written agreement. The terms of the agreement required the client to pay the fee even if

EXHIBIT 7–7   FEES VS. COSTS

Fees	Costs
Fees are what the lawyer's and paralegal's time and efforts are worth.	Costs are expenses associated with the representation.
Fees could be hourly, contingent, or fixed.	Costs could include expert witness fees, medical exams, and other discovery expenses.
Clients intuitively understand that they will owe legal fees.	Clients, especially plaintiffs, might not realize there will be costs.

he fired the lawyer, regardless of success on the merits. During the representation, the lawyer was granted a motion to remove himself from the representation for "an irreconcilable conflict." Then the lawyer billed the client, who refused to pay. The court found in favor of the client because nothing in the fee agreement mentioned whether the client had any financial responsibility to the lawyer under the facts presented in the case: the lawyer, and not the client, terminated the lawyer-client relationship. The court also rejected the lawyer's request for recovery under the theory of **quantum merit**, resolving the ambiguity in the contract in favor of the client. *Elliott v. Joyce,* 889 P.2d 43 (Colo. 1994).

Clearly Explain the Paralegal or Legal Assistant's Contribution to the Bill. Generally, clients are willing to pay fees associated with the time billed by the legal assistant because of the legal assistant's lower hourly rate. The effective use of paralegals and legal assistants allows the firm to be more profitable because the lawyers are able to maintain their own billable hours expectations, while the paralegals and legal assistants are able to separately bill at a lower rate, providing the clients with a lower bill. However, part of the fees explanation to the client should include distinguishing the lawyer's billable time from the legal assistant's billable time. A South Carolina ethics opinion states that a lawyer may charge the client separately for the work of a paralegal or a secretary, provided the client agrees in advance to the arrangement and as long as the work performed by the lawyer's staff is not administrative or secretarial. South Carolina Bar Association, Ethics Op. 94–37 (1995).

In an Ohio case, a lawyer contracted with a client for a contingency fee of 33 percent if the case settled, plus "all necessary filing fees, court costs, and other out-of-pocket expenses incurred in said litigation." The case settled for $30,000. The lawyer took $9,900 as his fee, but also billed the client for $2,982, which consisted of the billable hours of the lawyer's secretary and paralegal. The court ruled that in a contingency fee case, litigation costs do not include the billable hours of the lawyer's employees. *Columbus Bar Association v. Brooks,* 721 N.E.2d 23 (Ohio 1999). More significantly for Ohio lawyers, the court also stated that when a lawyer charges an hourly rate, secretarial costs may not be billed separately

■ quantum merit

A Latin phrase that means "as much as he deserved." Quantum merit is an equitable principle used in contract cases by plaintiffs attempting to recover something for their efforts when courts have already determined that operative legal principles deny the validity of a contract.

because such costs are "overhead" costs, but the court approved of paralegal hours being separately billed if the client agrees to that in writing. *Id.* at 25. Unfortunately, when lawyers engage in deceitful billing practices, they often inflate the time their paralegals worked on projects or their paralegals' hourly rates, or both. *See generally Case of Kalled,* 607 A.2d 613(N.H.1992); *In re Disciplinary Proceedings Against Gilbert,* 595 N.W.2d 715 (Wis. 1999).

The Difference Between an Advance and a Retainer

Lawyers can require that clients pay money up front; the Comments to MR 1.5 acknowledge that. Another reason the fee agreement should be put in writing is to avoid confusion as to whether the money paid up front to the lawyer is in the form of an **advance** or a retainer, because the difference between an advance and a retainer is significant. An advance is a prepayment of legal fees before they have been earned. That makes an advance a payment that is subject to being returned, at least in part, in the event that the lawyer-client relationship terminates before the lawyer's billable time has equaled the advance. Both Model Rule 1.16(d) and DR 2–110(A)(2) and (3) require lawyers to return any unearned portion of an advance payment. If a lawyer fails to return the unearned portion of an advance fee, sanctions can range from suspension to disbarment. See *In re Baltimore,* 522 N.Y.S.2d 563 (N.Y. 1987), where a lawyer was disbarred for repeated violations involving refusing to return unearned portions of advance fees.

A retainer, sometimes called a general retainer, is a payment made to secure the lawyer's availability, not a prepayment of the lawyer's future services. To put a lawyer "on retainer" is to pay the lawyer for the right to use him presently or at a future date or for a future matter, or to pay him so that another prospective client cannot retain the lawyer's services. (Think of a retainer like reserving the presidential suite at a swank hotel. You might not sleep there, but now no one else can, either.) Because of the nature of a retainer, a lawyer actually earns the retainer upon its being paid. This makes the general retainer a nonrefundable payment. *Baranowski v. State Bar,* 593 P.2d 613 (Cal. 1979).

Because nonrefundable retainers are drastic, more and more jurisdictions require such a retainer agreement to be clearly explained to the client, while some jurisdictions are starting to reject them on **public policy** grounds. Alabama takes the position that lawyers may not call fees nonrefundable nor use any language in the fee agreement that suggests that any fee paid to the lawyer is not subject to an adjustment or refund. Alabama State Bar General Counsel, Op. R 93–21 (1993). Wisconsin, however, allows for the use of nonrefundable retainers. State Bar of Wisconsin Commission on Professional Ethics, Op. E–93–4 (1993). Indiana's Supreme Court concluded in 2004 that a lawyer may not characterize a retainer as nonrefundable, because to do so would violate the reasonableness requirement of the rule on legal fees. *In re Kendall,* 804 N.E.2d 1152 (Ind. 2004). See Exhibit 7-8 for the differences of advances and retainers.

■ **advance**
A prepayment for future legal services made to an attorney at the beginning of the representation. As the lawyer works on the case, the advance is being earned.

■ **public policy**
Generalized views about the American culture or ideals upon which specific laws are made.

EXHIBIT 7–8   ADVANCES VS. RETAINERS

Advance	Retainer
A prepayment for future legal services	A payment made to secure a lawyer's availability
Is earned as the lawyer and paralegal work	Is earned upon payment
Is subject to being refunded	A general retainer can be nonrefundable where it is allowed.

Whatever form a retainer takes, it is still subject to the general doctrine of reasonableness. In a New York case, a client seeking a divorce signed a written fee agreement with her lawyer that called for the payment of a $15,000 retainer that was "not to be returned to the client, in whole or in part, under any circumstances." When the client reconciled with her husband, the divorce became unnecessary and she sought the return of her money. Despite the clear language in the agreement concerning the nonrefundability of the fee, the court found that the nonrefundable retainer was unconscionable for a variety of reasons. First, the court considered it grossly excessive and shocking of its conscience because the attorney worked fewer than five hours for the client before she wanted to drop the divorce proceedings. Second, the court considered the retainer agreement to be in the form of an unreasonable liquidated damages provision. Furthermore, the court found that nonrefundable retainer agreements violate what it called "the universal contract principle which requires the non-breaching party to mitigate its damages." *Joel R. Brandes, P.C. v. Zingmond,* 573 N.Y.S.2d 579 (N.Y. Sup. 1991).

Does a million-dollar retainer payment pass the reasonableness test when a lawyer works for 10 weeks, after which the client demands the retainer back? Yes, said the Third Circuit Court of Appeal, in *Ryan v. Butera, Beausang, Cohen & Brennan,* 193 F.3d 210 (1999). In the case, a company heading toward bankruptcy dangled the huge payment in front of the law firm, in the hope of attracting its services, and the law firm took the bait. The retainer agreement clearly referred to the million-dollar payment as a "nonrefundable retainer." Still, the court had to conclude the agreement was reasonable to allow the firm to keep the entire amount. Finding that the client was no novice in legal matters and had offered the massive retainer payment to five other law firms, and that both parties expected the representation to continue for a considerable time, the court found it reasonable that the payment was nonrefundable.

Where Is the Client's Money to Be Kept?

When a client pays a retainer or an advance to a lawyer, that money does not automatically become the property of the lawyer to do with as the lawyer pleases; and ABA Model Rule 1.15 and DR 9-102 concern how the lawyer should keep the client's money. These rules also apply to situations where the lawyer receives funds for the client, such as when an insurance company settles a case with the plaintiff and sends a check to the plaintiff's lawyer.

The Client Trust Account

The client's money must be kept in an account that is separate from the lawyer's personal bank account until the lawyer earns the money. This separate account is known as a client trust account and accurate records must be kept showing when the client's money was deposited in the account, when it was withdrawn, and how it was disbursed, such as to pay experts, court reporters, or legal fees. Although there need not be a separate trust account for every client in the firm, there must be clear records for all the clients' assets kept in the trust account. The Ethics 2000 version of Model Rule 1.15 has two new parts concerning trust accounts. Section 1.15(b) provides that a lawyer may deposit his own money into the trust account where necessary to pay bank charges for maintaining the account. And 1.15(c) expressly requires a lawyer to deposit a client's advance payments into a trust account, "to be withdrawn by the lawyer only as fees are earned or expenses incurred."

The lawyer also may not use the funds as if they were part of the law firm's cash flow. When the client's money and the lawyer's money are in the same account, such **commingling** of funds violates MR 1.15(a) and DR 9–102(A). Commingling can also lead to a more serious transgression, **conversion**, which involves the lawyer using the client's money as if it were his own. To avoid such a violation, a law firm must establish trust accounts, put its clients' money in those accounts, and maintain accurate records. Believe it or not, a lawyer who was given over $34,000 of his estate client's money put the money in a box and stuck it under a floorboard in his attic. Later, when asked about the money, the lawyer claimed it was safe and sound in his mother-in-law's safe deposit box, which, if true, would have still been the wrong place to keep the money. *Cuyahoga County Bar Association v. Petrancek*, 669 N.E.2d 828 (Ohio 1996).

The Paralegal and the Client Trust Account

Paralegals and legal assistants can and do manage client trust accounts, and if they make accidental or fraudulent errors, their supervising lawyers will be called on the carpet. In one instance from Indiana where a lawyer's secretary had such difficulty balancing the trust account, the IRS put two liens on the trust account. The lawyer was unaware of the liens until a client bounced a check

■ **commingling**
The unlawful mixing of one person's money with another person's money in the same account.

■ **conversion**
A tortuous act that involves one exercising authority over another's property, to the deprivation, and without the permission, of the innocent party.

drawn on the account. The Indiana Supreme Court ordered the lawyer to take a trust account management continuing legal education course. *In re Paras*, 742 N. E.2d 924 (Ind.2001). The secretary did not get a second chance.

In the same year, the same court heard a more severe example of paralegal mismanagement of a trust account. This case involved theft by the paralegal while her boss looked the other way. Citing Ind. R.P.C. 5.3, the court suspended the attorney for 30 days, while the paralegal went unnamed. *In re Silverman*, 750 N.E.2d 376 (Ind.2001). Unfortunately, there are too many instances of paralegals and legal assistants stealing from their firms' client trust accounts, and in some instances they get caught:

- *In re Disciplinary Action Against Kaszynski*, 620 N.W.2d 708 (Minn. 2001) (lawyer disbarred for, among other things, allowing his paralegal unfettered access to the trust account, which was pilfered)

NOT QUITE LINCOLN

Maybe He Thought She Wasn't Dead, But Just Really, Really Tired

Richard Bauer was a Colorado lawyer with over 30 years of experience practicing in the areas of probate, estate planning, and real estate. In March of 1998, Mr. Bauer's wife died. At the time of her death, Mrs. Bauer was receiving almost $1100 dollars a month in Social Security payments, which were electronically deposited in her checking account. Although Mr. Bauer was his deceased wife's personal representative and the sole beneficiary in her will, he was not authorized to write checks from her account, which was in overdraft when she passed away. To remedy the overdraft, Mr. Bauer withdrew money from his law office trust account and deposited it in his deceased wife's account. As wrongful as that was, it pales in comparison to what he did next

—or, rather, failed to do next. Instead of informing the Social Security Administration that his wife had died, as required by law, Mr. Bauer kept his wife's checking account open while her Social Security checks continued to be electronically deposited into that account for eight months, until the Social Security Administration learned of her death. In the interim, he wrote nine checks on his dead wife's account, totaling over $7,000 dollars, and made them payable to himself. He also deposited into his trust account the proceeds of the sale of his marital home and sale of an automobile. As a result of his violations of numerous provisions of Colorado's Rules of Professional Conduct, Mr. Bauer was disbarred in 2000.

- *Disciplinary Counsel v. Ball*, 618 N.E.2d 159 (Ohio 1993) (lawyer was suspended for six months because his paralegal stole over $200,000 from the client accounts throughout a decade; she pled guilty to five counts of theft)

- *Louisiana State Bar Ass'n v. Edwins*, 540 So.2d 294 (La. 1989) (lawyer disbarred for, among other things, helping his paralegal to commit UPL and neglect the client trust account)

- *Matter of Stransky*, 612 A.2d 373 (N.J. 1992) (lawyer whose wife was his secretary/bookkeeper was suspended for one year because she "borrowed" over $34,000 from his trust account and bounced 80 checks on the lawyer's personal account, all without his knowledge)

In the following case, one of America's most famous lawyers became one of its most infamous lawyers after being disbarred for mishandling client funds. Pay extra attention to the long-and-winding fact pattern and the novel arguments F. Lee Bailey made defending himself.

CASE LAW **The Florida Bar v. Bailey**

803 So.2d 683 (Fla. 2001)

PER CURIAM.

F. Lee Bailey seeks review of a referee's report finding numerous, serious violations of the Rules Regulating the Florida Bar and recommending permanent disbarment. . . . For the reasons that follow, we approve the referee's findings of guilt and order that F. Lee Bailey be disbarred.

   FACTS

   The Florida Bar filed a complaint against Bailey alleging seven counts of misconduct in violation of various Rules Regulating the Florida Bar in the course of Bailey's representation of his client, Claude Duboc. [1] After a final hearing was held over a number of days in which witnesses testified and exhibits were introduced into evidence, the referee issued a detailed twenty-four page report containing her findings of fact and conclusions of law. The referee began the report with an overview of the factual setting that provided the framework for further findings as to all counts of charged misconduct:

   In 1994, Bailey represented Duboc in a criminal case filed against Duboc by the United States alleging violations of Title 21 of the United States Code, which prohibits drug smuggling. The indictment also included forfeiture claims under Title 18 of the United States Code. Bailey worked out a deal with the United States Attorneys ("U.S. Attorneys") covering Duboc's plea, repatriation of assets, and payment of attorneys' fees. Under the agreement, Duboc would plead guilty and forfeit all of his assets to the United States Government. All of Duboc's cash accounts from around the world would be transferred to

(continues)

CASE LAW   *The Florida Bar v. Bailey* (continued)

an account identified by the U.S. Attorney's Office. To deal with the forfeiture of Duboc's real and personal property, 602,000 shares of Biochem Pharma ("Biochem") stock, valued at $5,891,352.00, would be transferred into Bailey's Swiss account. Bailey would use these funds to market, maintain and liquidate Duboc's French properties and all other assets. In order to put this unusual arrangement in context, we set forth the specific factual findings surrounding this plea agreement and Bailey's role in it:

The ultimate strategy employed by Respondent [Bailey] was that Duboc would plead guilty and forfeit all assets to the United States Government in the hopes of a reduction of sentence based on what [Bailey] described as "extraordinary cooperation." First, Duboc would identify and transfer all cash accounts from around the world into an account identified by the United States Attorney's Office.

The forfeiture of the real and personal properties held in foreign countries presented some nettlesome problems. Duboc owned two large estates in France and valuable car collections, boats, furnishings and art works. Most of these properties were physically located in France. The two estates required substantial infusions of cash for maintenance.

The idea proposed by [Bailey] was to segregate an asset, a particular asset, one that would appreciate in value over time, so that when it came time for Duboc to be sentenced following entry of a plea of guilty, the United States Government would not argue in opposition to a defense claim that part of the appreciation in value was not forfeitable to the United States. Ultimately, the object was to sequester a fund which would not be entirely subject to forfeiture.

The identified asset was 602,000 shares of Biochem Pharma Stock. This would serve as a fund from which [Bailey] could serve as trustee and guardian of Duboc's French properties. Duboc's primary interest was to maximize the amount of forfeitures that would be turned over to the United States. This stock would provide a sufficient fund from which to market, maintain and liquidate the French properties and all other assets. [Bailey] explained that it would be prudent to hold the Biochem stock because the company was conducting promising research on a cure for AIDS, and the loss the government would suffer if large blocks of stock were dumped on the market.

Money was transferred immediately into a covert account identified by the United States Attorney's Office. Duboc provided written instructions to the various financial institutions and the orders were then faxed. On April 26, 1994, the Biochem stock certificates were transferred to [Bailey's] Swiss account at his direction. The Respondent provided the account number. On May 17, 1994, United States District Court Judge Maurice Paul held a pre-plea conference in his chambers. At the conference, the following arrangement as to attorneys' fees, including those for Bailey, was reached: "[T]he remainder value of the stock which was being segregated out would be returned to the court at the

(continues)

CASE LAW *The Florida Bar v. Bailey* *(continued)*

end of the day, and from that asset the Judge would be—a motion would be filed for a reasonable attorney's fee for Mr. Bailey." Later in the day on May 17, Duboc pled guilty to two counts in open court and professed his complete cooperation with the U.S. Attorney's Office. . . .

Count I of the Bar's complaint charged Bailey with commingling. Bailey was entrusted with liquidating stock that belonged to Duboc, referred to as "the Japanese Stock." Upon liquidation, Bailey was then to transmit the proceeds to the United States. Bailey sold the Japanese stock and deposited approximately $730,000 into his Credit Suisse account on or about July 6, 1994. Bailey then transferred the money into his Barnett Bank Money Market Account. The money was paid to the United States Marshal on or about August 15, 1994. The referee found that Bailey admitted that his money market account was not a lawyer's trust account, nor did Bailey create or maintain it as a separate account for the sole purpose of maintaining the stock proceeds. In concluding that Bailey had engaged in commingling, the referee rejected Bailey's claims that there were no personal funds in the Barnett Bank account at the time Bailey transferred the funds from the Japanese Stock into this account, and that Bailey's deposit of the proceeds into a non-trust account was "inadvertent error." The referee concluded that Bailey violated Rule Regulating the Florida Bar 4–1.15(a) by failing to set up a separate account for these funds and also by commingling client funds with his personal funds.

Count II of the Bar's complaint charged Bailey with misappropriating trust funds and commingling. On or about May 9, 1994, the 602,000 shares of Biochem stock were transferred into Bailey's Credit Suisse Investment Account. Bailey sold shares of stock and borrowed against the stock, deriving over $4 million from these activities. Bailey then transferred $3,514,945 of Biochem proceeds from the Credit Suisse account into his Barnett Bank Money Market Account. Bailey had transferred all but $350,000 of these proceeds into his personal checking account by December 1995. From this account, Bailey wrote checks to his private business enterprises totaling $2,297,696 and another $1,277,433 for other personal expenses or purchases. Bailey further paid $138,946 out of his money market account toward the purchase of a residence. The referee rejected Bailey's two defenses to the Bar's charge of misappropriation: (1) he never held the stock in trust for Duboc or the United States; rather, it was transferred to him in fee simple absolute; and (2) this stock was not subject to forfeiture. The referee found Bailey guilty of violating Rules Regulating the Florida Bar 3–4.3 (lawyer shall not commit any act that is contrary to honesty and justice), 4–1.15(a) (commingling funds), 4–8.4(b) (lawyer shall not commit a criminal act that reflects adversely on the lawyer's honesty, trustworthiness, or fitness as a lawyer), 4–8.4(c) (lawyer shall not engage in conduct involving deceit, dishonesty, fraud or misrepresentation), and 5–1.1 (requiring money or other property entrusted to an attorney to be held in trust and applied only for a specific purpose).

(continues)

CASE LAW *The Florida Bar v. Bailey* (continued)

Count III charged Bailey with continuing to expend Biochem funds in contravention of two federal court orders. In January 1996, Judge Paul issued two orders regarding the Duboc criminal case; one on the 12th and the other on the 25th. The January 12 order relieved Bailey as Duboc's counsel, substituting the Coudert Brothers law firm. The order further required Bailey to give within 10 days "a full accounting of the monies and properties held in trust by him for the United States of America." The order froze all of the assets received by Bailey from Duboc and further prohibited their disbursement. The January 25 order directed Bailey to bring to a February 1, 1996, hearing all of the shares of Biochem stock that Duboc had turned over to Bailey. The referee found that Bailey continued to use the Biochem proceeds that he held in trust after service and knowledge of the January 12 and January 25, 1996, orders. . . .

The referee found Bailey guilty of violating Rules Regulating the Florida Bar 3–4.3 (lawyer shall not commit an act that is contrary to honesty and justice), rule 4–8.4(b) (lawyer shall not commit a criminal act that reflects adversely on the lawyer's honesty, trustworthiness, or fitness as a lawyer), rule 4-8.4(c) (lawyer shall not engage in conduct involving deceit, dishonesty, fraud or misrepresentation). . . .

Count IV of the Bar's complaint charged Bailey with giving false testimony. The referee found that Bailey testified falsely before Judge Paul and the U.S. Attorneys that he did not see the January 12 or January 25 orders until the morning of a civil contempt hearing held on February 2, 1996. The referee further found that Bailey was not being truthful when: (1) in his answer to the Bar's complaint, Bailey denied that he had received the orders and that he had testified falsely before Judge Paul; and (2) Bailey testified before the referee at the final hearing.

Specifically, the referee found numerous reasons why this testimony was false. First, Bailey had a conversation with the Assistant U.S. Attorney about the terms of the January 12 order following its entry. Indeed, on January 19, when Bailey met with the Assistant U.S. Attorneys, he accused them of obtaining the order from the judge ex parte. In addition, when Bailey returned to his Palm Beach office on January 18, he marshaled documents in support of the accounting that the January 12 order required him to provide. In the letter to Judge Paul dated January 21, 1996, Bailey "plainly concedes that he knew of the terms of the order as early as January 16, 1996." In that letter, he referred to the manner, mode and method by which Judge Paul entered the order. He complained in the letter that "Your Honor was persuaded to act on representations which are at a minimum subject to sharp challenge." As the referee notes, "these assertions could not have been made unless [Bailey] had seen the January 12 order." Further, as to the January 25, 1996, order, it was served upon Bailey by "fax transmission, United States mail, and personally by the U.S. Marshal's Service pursuant to the very terms of the order." Based on these factual findings, the referee

(continues)

found Bailey guilty of violating Rules Regulating the Florida Bar 3–4.3, 4–8.4(b), 4–8.4(c), and 4–3.3(a)(1) (lawyer shall not knowingly make a false statement of material fact or law to a tribunal).

Count V of the Bar's complaint charged Bailey with self-dealing in the course of his representation of Duboc. [The gist of this complaint was that, since Bailey argued he owned the Biochem stock outright, the more of the gains from the stock he kept, the less his client, Duboc, would be able to turn over to the government in an attempt to reduce his sentence, which obviously created a conflict of interest between Bailey and his client. Also, the referee concluded that Bailey procrastinated in selling one of Duboc's French estates, and that he did so for his own personal benefit. The referee concluded that these acts violated Florida's version of ABA Model Rule 1.7(b), 1.8(a), and 1.8(b).]

Count VII of the Bar's complaint charged Bailey with ex parte communications, self-dealing, and disclosure of confidential information. In connection with this count, the referee found that on May 17, 1994, Duboc appeared before Judge Paul and entered a plea and cooperation agreement. Duboc pled guilty to counts II and III of the indictment. The referee found that the only way Duboc would get a reduced sentence was if Judge Paul was convinced that Duboc had completely and totally cooperated and had forfeited all of his assets to the United States. On January 4, 1996, Bailey wrote a letter to Judge Paul stating, "I have sent no copies of this letter to anyone, since I believe its distribution is within Your Honor's sound discretion." (Emphasis added.) This letter contains an express admission that it was ex parte. In this ex parte letter to Judge Paul, Bailey stated that: (1) Duboc pled guilty because he had no defense due to the strength of the case, (2) Duboc chose this course because it was his only option, not in a spirit of remorse or cooperation, (3) Duboc was a "multimillionaire druggie," (4) by consulting with other counsel, Duboc was no longer acting in the spirit of cooperation, and (5) Duboc's new defense team had interests contrary to those of his client and the court. Bailey sent a second letter to Judge Paul on January 21, 1996, a copy of which was sent to the U.S. Attorney's Office, threatening to seek an order to invade the attorney-client privilege in an attempt to defeat Duboc's position that the stock was held in trust.

The referee found that both of Bailey's letters were sent to compromise Duboc before the sentencing judge and to protect Bailey's interest and control of Duboc's and the U.S. Government's money. The referee recommended that Bailey be found guilty of violating Rules Regulating the Florida Bar 4–1.6(a) (lawyer shall not reveal information relating to representation of a client), 4–1.8(a), 4–1.8(b), 4–3.5(a) (lawyer shall not seek to influence a judge), 4–3 .5(b) (in an adversary proceeding, lawyer shall not communicate as to the merits of the cause with a judge).

(continues)

CASE LAW *The Florida Bar v. Bailey (continued)*

Having made the above findings of fact and recommendations as to guilt, the referee considered the appropriate discipline for Bailey's misconduct: . . .

Prior to considering any aggravating or mitigating factors, the referee stated that "any of the violations of the rules regulating the Florida Bar which have been proven by the Bar as set forth above, would singularly warrant [disbarment]. . . ." The referee then listed the following aggravating factors: dishonest or selfish motive, a pattern of misconduct, multiple offenses, submission of false statements, refusal to acknowledge the wrongful nature of the conduct, and substantial experience in the practice of law. Further, the referee considered that a federal judge recently found Bailey to be in civil contempt in another case. The referee noted that Bailey has two prior disciplinary actions; a censure in Massachusetts in 1970 and a suspension for one year of the privilege of applying for permission to appear pro hac vice in New Jersey in 1971; however, these incidents were too remote in time to be considered in aggravation. The referee did not find any mitigation.

ANALYSIS . . .

Having reviewed the extensive record before us, we conclude that there is competent substantial evidence to support the referee's findings of fact and conclusions of guilt as to each count of misconduct. Although each of the rule violations is extremely serious, ranging from trust account violations to misappropriation of funds, lying to a federal judge, self-dealing and compromising the position of a client, we focus on Bailey's actions regarding the Biochem stock (count II) because the gist of his defense in this case was that the Bar never established the stock was to be held by Bailey in trust. In connection with this, we also review whether, regardless of Bailey's claim that the stock had been transferred to him in "fee simple," this claimed right to the stock would permit him to act in disregard of the judge's orders (count III).

The Biochem Pharma Stock (Count II)—The most contested issue in this case is whether a trust was created with the transfer of the Biochem stock from Duboc to Bailey. The Bar argued that the plea agreement with the U.S. Government provided that Bailey was to hold the stock in trust for the benefit of the U.S. Government. Bailey would use the stock to maintain and liquidate Duboc's properties. After this was accomplished, the stock or its replacement assets would be forfeited to the United States in order to maximize any benefit to Bailey's client for his cooperation. However, Bailey argued that the stock was transferred to him in fee simple. He agreed that he was required to utilize the Biochem stock to derive the funds necessary to maintain and liquidate the French properties. However, Bailey asserted that after the properties were sold, he was only accountable to the United States for the value of the stock on the date that Duboc transferred it to Bailey's Swiss account (which was approximately $6 million), and not for any appreciation—which, as of January 1996, amounted to over $10 million. In other words, Bailey claims that he was entitled to all

(continues)

of the Biochem stock and proceeds from the sale of the stock, minus the approximate $6 million for which he was accountable to the U.S. Government. As he wrote Judge Paul in his letter of January 21, 1996:

I viewed [the value of the stock of $5,891,352.00 on May 9, 1994] as an account in which the United States had an interest to this extent: after the payment of costs associated with the case and fees approved by Your Honor, any balance of the $5,891,352.00 remaining would revert to the United States. Because of this view, I did not declare the funds to be income to myself. (Emphasis omitted.)

We conclude that regardless of the manner in which he was to hold the stock, Bailey is guilty of the most serious and basic trust account violations. The stock, by his own admission, was given to Bailey by his client neither as a gift, nor as an earned fee. Rather, the stock was given to Bailey to be used for the benefit of Duboc, and ultimately the U.S. Government. Bailey was required to use the stock to maximize Duboc's forfeitures to the U.S. Government in the hope that Duboc would receive a reduction of sentence for his cooperation. In his January 21, 1996, letter to Judge Paul, even Bailey recognized that the U.S. Government had an interest in the transfer value of the Biochem stock. Nevertheless, from the day it was transferred to him, Bailey treated the money as his own. . . .

A lawyer shall hold in trust, separate from the lawyer's own property, funds and property of clients or third persons that are in a lawyer's possession in connection with a representation. . . . In no event may the lawyer commingle the client's funds with those of the lawyer or those of the lawyer's law firm. . . .

Further and importantly, Bailey admits that Judge Paul would approve the amount of Bailey's fee for representing Duboc, and that his fee would be taken from the approximate $6 million value of the Biochem proceeds. Therefore, even if some of the initial $6 million corpus was to be used for payment of an attorneys' fee, Bailey was not entitled to the fee until it was approved by Judge Paul—a fact that Bailey admits in his January 21 letter to Judge Paul, and that he admits in this case. Indeed, in a letter written to his own client, Duboc, before a falling out occurred, Bailey explained that:

You do not face the dilemma since I will be paid with Chief Judge Paul's approval—only that amount which is commensurate with the result achieved in your case, and the amount of work that went into it. Our interests are therefore in perfect alignment. . . .

Therefore, under Rule Regulating the Florida Bar 5-1.1, Bailey had a duty to safekeep this property and use it only for the aforementioned purposes. The transfer value of this stock or its proceeds could neither be commingled nor could it be withdrawn. The fact that a portion of this fund was to be used for payment of any attorneys' fees only serves to highlight this fact—that the monies were to be held in trust for a specific purpose. . . .

(continues)

CASE LAW   *The Florida Bar v. Bailey* *(continued)*

The January 12 and January 25 orders (Count III)—Judge Paul's January 12, 1996, order provides that "[a]ll monies, real and personal property and other assets received by Bailey from or on behalf of Duboc, including the aforementioned Biochem Pharma stock shall be frozen as of the date of this order and no further disbursement of any of these funds shall be made unless authorized by this Court." The January 25 order required Bailey to "bring with him all shares of stock of Biochem Pharma, Inc. held by him, or by others, which represent the stock turned over to him by the Defendant, Claude Duboc, or Duboc's representatives. If the Biochem Pharma, Inc. stock has been replaced by any other form of asset while in the possession of Mr. Bailey, then the replacement stock will be brought to this Court at the time of the above hearing." . . .

Even if Bailey felt that he was entitled to the stock proceeds in his personal account, this does not permit him to act in contravention of two federal court orders. . . . Therefore, we conclude that Bailey violated rules 3–4.3, 4–3.4(c), 4–8.4(a) and 4–8.4(d) by acting in contravention of Judge Paul's orders.

DISCIPLINE

Bailey has committed multiple counts of egregious misconduct, including offering false testimony, engaging in ex parte communications, violating a client's confidences, violating two federal court orders, and trust account violations, including commingling and misappropriation. Disbarment is the presumed discipline for many of these acts of misconduct. For example, as to Bailey's mishandling of the Biochem stock, Standard 4.11 of the Florida Standards for Imposing Lawyer Sanctions provides: "Disbarment is appropriate when a lawyer intentionally or knowingly converts client property regardless of injury or potential injury." As to Bailey's violation of the January 12 and 25 orders, Standard 6.21 provides that "[d]isbarment is appropriate when a lawyer knowingly violates a court order or rule with the intent to obtain a benefit for the lawyer or another, and causes . . . potentially serious interference with a legal proceeding." Regarding Bailey's ex parte communication with Judge Paul, Standard 6.31 provides that "[d]isbarment is appropriate when a lawyer: . . . (b) makes an unauthorized ex parte communication with a judge or juror with intent to affect the outcome of the proceeding."

Case law also supports disbarment for the types of misconduct committed by Bailey. . . . Bailey has committed some of the most egregious rules violations possible, evidencing a complete disregard for the rules governing attorneys. "[M]isuse of client funds is one of the most serious offenses a lawyer can commit. Upon a finding of misuse or misappropriation, there is a presumption that disbarment is the appropriate punishment." [*Florida Bar v.*] *Tillman,* 682 So.2d at 543.

(continues)

CASE LAW *The Florida Bar v. Bailey* (continued)

Bailey's false testimony and disregard of Judge Paul's orders demonstrate a disturbing lack of respect for the justice system and how it operates. Bailey's self-dealing and willingness to compromise client confidences are especially disturbing. Not only did Bailey use assets that his client intended to forfeit to the U.S. Government for Bailey's own purposes, but Bailey also attempted to further his own interests by disparaging his client in an ex parte letter to the judge who would sentence his client. Bailey's self-dealing constitutes a complete abdication of his duty of loyalty to his client. His willingness to compromise his client for personal gain shows an open disregard for the relationship that must be maintained between attorney and client: one of trust, and one where both individuals work in the client's best interest. Such misconduct strikes at the very center of the professional ethic of an attorney and cannot be tolerated.

By this disbarment, Bailey's status as a member of The Florida Bar shall be terminated and he may not reapply for readmission for a period of five years, and then he may "only be admitted again upon full compliance with the rules and regulations governing admission to the bar." R. Regulating Fla. Bar 3-5.1(f). This includes retaking the Florida bar examination, complying with the rigorous background and character examination, and demonstrating knowledge of the rules of professional conduct required of all new admittees. [4]

CONCLUSION

Accordingly, F. Lee Bailey is hereby disbarred from the practice of law in the State of Florida. . . .

WELLS, C.J., and SHAW, HARDING, ANSTEAD, PARIENTE, LEWIS, and QUINCE, JJ., concur.

[In March 2002, Mr. Bailey was suspended from the U.S. Supreme Court, and then in April 2002, he was disbarred by the Massachusetts Supreme Judicial Court. In 2005, Mr. Bailey attempted to get his law license back by arguing in federal court that new evidence in his case made his disbarment a "grave injustice," but was denied. He then appealed to the First Circuit Court of Appeal, but lost again in 2006.].

The following case footnotes correspond to the portions of the case that are printed in the textbook. Although it may seem that other footnotes are missing, they are not presented because their corresponding portions of the court's opinion have been redacted.

[1] Count number six of the Bar's complaint was dismissed and is therefore not discussed further.

[4] Although we regard these rule violations as extremely serious and warranting disbarment, we do not accept the referee's recommendation of permanent disbarment. Under the rules, the minimum period of disbarment is for five years (and thereafter until the attorney is readmitted to the practice of law). See R. Regulating Fla. Bar 3-5.1(f). In 1998, the Court amended the Rules Regulating the Florida Bar to specifically provide for permanent

(continues)

CASE LAW   *The Florida Bar v. Bailey* (continued)

disbarment. See In re Amendments to Rules Regulating The Florida Bar, 718 So.2d 1179, 1181 (Fla.1998) (amending rule 3-5.1(f) "to authorize permanent disbarment as a disciplinary sanction").

Case Questions

1. Why did Mr. Bailey have possession of his client's stock?

2. How did the court conclude that Mr. Bailey went beyond commingling his client's property to converting his client's property?

3. What exactly was Mr. Bailey's defense to the charge that he misappropriated his client's property?

4. What facts caused the court to also conclude that Mr. Bailey engaged in acts that damaged his client's interests? What were his client's interests?

5. If Mr. Bailey's acts were so egregious (including lying to a federal judge) and there were no mitigating factors, why did the court refuse to uphold the referee's recommendation of permanent disbarment?

■ **subrogation**

When someone who has made a payment on another's behalf has the legal or equitable right to be paid back from the party who was originally liable for the payment. Subrogation often occurs when an insurance company pays its insured party under the terms of the insurance contract, and then is subrogated in the insured party's lawsuit against the defendant.

There is a wrinkle to the separate accounts situation, which involves retainers. If a retainer is viewed as a payment to secure the lawyer's availability (called a general or nonrefundable retainer), then it is earned upon receipt, which would seem to make it the lawyer's money. However, not only are there some jurisdictions that refuse to accept the notion of the nonrefundable retainer, but there are some that require all advance payments, be they "advances" or "retainers," be placed in trust accounts. *See Iowa Supreme Court Bd. of Professional Ethics and Conduct v. Apland,* 577 N.W.2d 50 (Iowa 1998); Oklahoma Bar Association Legal Ethics Committee, Ethics Op. 317 (2002); *but see State ex rel. Special Counsel for Discipline, Nebraska Supreme Court v. Fellman,* 678 N.W.2d 491, 497 (Neb. 2004).

When the lawyer receives money on behalf of the client, such as a settlement check, the lawyer must notify the client promptly, and deliver the money promptly to the client. Ethics 2000 version of Model Rule 1.15(d); DR 9-102(B). This also applies where a third party has an interest in the money, such as a case in which the plaintiff 's insurance company has the right to **subrogation** for its costs in covering the plaintiff 's medical bills. And if, at the end of the representation, the client disputes the lawyer's fee, the Ethics 2000 version of MR 1.15(e) and DR 9–102(A) require that the funds that are the subject of the dispute remain in the trust account until the dispute is resolved.

Interest on Lawyers' Trust Accounts (IOLTA)

When client funds are placed in a bank account, does the client get any interest earned on those deposited funds or does the lawyer get to keep the money for setting up and administering the account? Neither, because every state and the District of Columbia have in place an Interest on Lawyers' Trust Account (IOLTA) program. Such a program requires that any interest earned on client trust accounts that are nominal or of a short duration be turned over to the state bar association to promote charitable services, such as low-cost legal aid offices. Florida created the first IOLTA program in 1981, and the ABA issued an ethics opinion in 1982, finding it permissible for a lawyer to participate in an IOLTA program. ABA Commission on Ethics and Professional Responsibility, Formal Op. 348 (1982). Such programs are possible due to a 1980 change in the federal banking laws that allows banks to pay interest on any demand deposit accounts (sometimes called a **NOW account**. 12 U.S.C. § 1832.

States differ on how IOLTA programs are administered. For instance, the Virginia Legal Services Corporation has administered Virginia's IOLTA program since 1995, and uses those funds to support its 10 local Legal Services organizations, which help provide legal services to the poor. North Carolina's IOLTA program, in operation since 1984, provides grants in four categories: providing civil legal aid to indigents; enhancement and improvement of grievance and disciplinary procedures for lawyers; development and maintenance of a fund for student loans for legal education on the basis of need; and such other programs designed to improve the administration of justice as may be proposed by the IOLTA Board of Trustees and approved by the North Carolina Supreme Court. North Carolina claims that less than 10 percent of the IOLTA funds are used to administer the program, which leaves quite an impressive payout ratio.

IS AN IOLTA PROGRAM CONSTITUTIONAL? The United States Supreme Court rendered a controversial decision concerning IOLTA programs in 1998, in *Phillips v. Washington Legal Foundation*, 524 U.S. 156 (1998). In this case, a public interest group, an attorney, and a businessman who regularly used attorneys sued the Texas Supreme Court, arguing that Texas's IOLTA program (under the authority of the Texas Supreme Court) violated the Fifth Amendment's Takings Clause. The plaintiffs' theory was that the interest remitted for IOLTA purposes was client property because it was earned from money that belonged to the client, and therefore, the property could not be taken without "just compensation." The Supreme Court framed the issue on appeal as "whether the interest on an IOLTA account is 'private property' of the client for whom the principal is being held." And in a five-to-four decision written by Chief Justice William Rehnquist, the Court ruled that the interest earned in IOLTA accounts was the private property of the

■ **now account**
Negotiable order of withdrawal account. A NOW account is an account that allows the depositor to withdraw sums of money from the account at will. NOW accounts are also called demand deposit accounts.

owner of the principal (i.e., the client). However, the Court did not express any opinion on whether IOLTA programs constituted a "taking" under the Fifth Amendment's Takings Clause. The Court then remanded the case back to the lower court to determine whether Texas's IOLTA program constituted a taking, in violation of the Fifth Amendment.

To the dismay of the American Bar Association and the Texas Supreme Court, in October 2001, the Fifth Circuit Court of Appeal reversed the district court and ruled that the Texas IOLTA program violated the Fifth Amendment. *Washington Legal Foundation v. Texas Equal Access to Justice Foundation*, 270 F.3d 180 (Fifth Cir. 2001).

A similar decision was reached in January 2001, when the Ninth Circuit Court of Appeal found that the state of Washington's IOLTA program constituted a taking of private property and remanded the case to the district court to determine whether any just compensation was due. *Washington Legal Foundation v. Legal Foundation of Washington*, 236 F.3rd 1097 (9th Cir. 2001). But in November 2001, on appeal from the remand to the District Court, the Ninth Circuit Court of Appeal took a different view and ruled that Washington's IOLTA program does not violate the Fifth Amendment. 271 F.3d 835 (9th Cir. 2001).

Then, in June 2002, the U.S. Supreme Court agreed to take the appeal from the Ninth Circuit's most recent decision on IOLTA. 122 S.Ct. 2355 (2002). And in 2003, the U.S. Supreme Court rendered what seems to be the final word on the constitutionality of IOLTA programs, when it ruled in a 5–4 decision that the interest earned in IOLTA accounts may be used to fund charitable legal services. B*rown v. Legal Foundation of Washington*, 538 U.S. 213. Essentially, the court ruled there was no Fifth Amendment "takings" problem, concluding that clients suffer no real loss when interest earned in their trust accounts is used to fund legal services programs. Therefore, no "just compensation" was required.

Special Rules Regarding Contingent Fees

Because of the nature of a contingent fee arrangement and its susceptibility to misunderstanding by the client or overreaching by the lawyer, there are a few rules that apply specifically to contingent fees.

Contingent Fees Must Be in Writing

As stated earlier in the chapter, neither the ABA Model Rules nor the ABA Model Code require that all fees arrangements be put in writing for the client. However, ABA Model Rule 1.5(c) does require that a contingent fee agreement shall be in writing and shall state the method by which the fee is to be determined, including: the percentage or percentages that shall accrue to the lawyer in the event of settlement, trial, or appeal; litigation expenses to be deducted from the recovery; and whether such expenses are to be deducted before or after the contingent fee is calculated. This type of language requires not only a declaratory written fee agreement, but also an explanatory written fee agreement. For instance, which is the higher fee: (a) 25 percent of the net recovery at settlement; or (b) 20 percent of the gross recovery at settlement? Even though that answer cannot be made unless one knows the settlement amount and the litigation costs, that the Model Rules require a delineation of how the contingent fee will be determined helps clients—especially new clients —get a better handle on what their lawyers expect to be paid.

The Ethics 2000 version of Model Rule 1.5(c) has two noticeable changes. First, it requires that the client sign the contingent fee agreement (instead of simply being in writing). Second, it requires that the contingent fee agreement "clearly notify the client of any expenses for which the client will be liable whether or not the client is the prevailing party." This change is in concert with MR 1.8(e), which allows a lawyer to advance litigation expenses, but the client may eventually have to pay those expenses. There are also new Comments to the amended rule that discuss the reasonableness of legal expenses, as well as the reasonableness of contingent fees.

The ABA Model Code, however, does not require contingent fees to be in writing (DR 2–106), although the Ethical Consideration that expressed the preference that fee agreements be in writing particularly mentioned the contingent fee (EC 2–19). Of those states that follow (or followed) the Model Code format on legal fees, some states, such as New York, require a written contingency agreement, including requiring the signature of the client and the lawyer on the agreement. N.Y. C.P.R DR 2–106(C). Other states, such as Nebraska, Ohio, and Oregon, did not require written contingent fee agreements when they were Model Code jurisdictions. Neb. C.P.R. DR 2–106(C); Oh. C.P.R. DR 2–106(C); Or. C.P.R. DR 2–106(C).

Lawyers in Model Rules jurisdictions are subject to discipline, not only for failing to put a contingent fee agreement in writing, but also for collecting fees that exceed the contingent fee agreement. In an Indiana case, a lawyer contracted with a client to take 33 1/3 percent of any amount recovered in a personal injury suit against a nursing home. The case was settled for $27,500. The attorney kept $9,516.16 of the settlement, which was $300 more than 33 1/3 percent. In addition to being sanctioned for taking more than provided in the fee agreement, the lawyer was also sanctioned for violating another aspect of MR 1.5(c), the requirement that at the conclusion of the matter, the lawyer provide the client with a written statement that details how the contingent fee came to be what the lawyer kept. *Matter of Brown*, 669 N.E.2d 989 (Ind. 1996). See Exhibit 7-9 for a summary of the ABA's rule on contingency fees.

Certain Kinds of Cases May Not Be Taken on a Contingent Basis

There are two prohibitions on contingent fees. First, both the Model Rules and the Model Code prohibit contingent fees in criminal cases. MR 1.5(d)(2); DR 2–106(C). Second, the Model Rules prohibit a lawyer from taking a contingent fee in a domestic relations case in which the lawyer's payment "is contingent upon the securing of a divorce or upon the amount of **alimony** or

alimony
Payments made by one spouse to another spouse, following a divorce, that are made to support the other spouse. Some states have eliminated alimony as a general requirement in divorce.

> **EXHIBIT 7–9** CONTINGENT FEES
>
> - ABA Model Rule 1.5(c) (Ethics 200) says contingent fees must be in writing and signed by the client.
> - Contingent fee agreements must state whether the percentage taken will be based on the net or the gross.
> - Contingent fee agreements must state how litigation costs and expenses will be calculated and if the client must pay them in the event of a loss.
> - Contingent fee agreements are not allowed in criminal cases in all jurisdictions.
> - Contingent fee agreements are not allowed in divorce cases in Model Rules' jurisdictions.

support, or property settlement." MR 1.5(d)(1). The Model Code has no similar prohibition, but it does have an Ethical Consideration that declares, "[c]ontingent fee arrangements in domestic relation cases are rarely justified." EC 2–20. However, some states, such as Iowa, New York, and Oregon, added the domestic relations contingent-fee prohibition to their versions of the Model Code. Ia. C.P.R. DR 2–106(C); N.Y. C.P.R. DR 2–106(C)(1); Or. C.P.R. DR 2–106 (C)(1).

As to the former, a contingent fee arrangement in a criminal case is considered to be an incurable conflict of interest for the lawyer under MR 1.7 and DR 5–101. Also, the Ethics 2000 version of Model Rule 1.8(i)(2) provides for an allowance of contingent fees only in civil cases (formerly, that was 1.8(j)). Because of the high stakes for the defendant accused of a crime, it is believed to be too dangerous a risk that the lawyer's judgment might be affected by having a financial stake in the outcome of a criminal case. As to the latter, domestic relations cases—divorce, property settlement, child support, paternity, and so on —can be highly emotional matters, and courts have taken the view that when a lawyer takes a contingency fee in a divorce case, for instance, such an arrangement goes against public policy. Not only does it hinder chances of reconciliation, but as one court put it many years ago:

"The sanctity of the marriage relation, the welfare of children, the good order of society, the regard for virtue, all of which the law seeks to foster and protect are ample reasons why such [a contingent fee] contract should be held to be contrary to public policy." *Opperud v. Bussey*, 46 P.2d 319 (Okla. 1935).

A new Comment added to the Ethics 2000 version of 1.5 approves of using a contingency fee in a post-divorce action, such as collecting on a property distribution or alimony award. Some jurisdictions do allow lawyers to take contingency fees in post-divorce or domestic relations matters where an attempt is made to collect property that was supposed to be transferred as part of the property distribution arrangement, or to collect back child support. *See Doe v. Doe*, 24 P.3d 1059 (Haw. Ct. App. 2001); *Eastmond v. Earl, 912 P.2d 994 (Utah App. 1996)*. Illinois State Bar Association Commission on Professional Ethics, Op. 96–16 (1996); Kansas Bar Association Professional Ethics Commission, Op. 97–4 (1997).

Fee Sharing Between Lawyers of Different Firms

While there is no restriction on how lawyers within a firm share their fees, there are restrictions on how lawyers of different firms may share fees. The Ethics 2000 version of ABA Model Rule 1.5(e) states that lawyers from different firms who are working on the same case may share fees only if:

1. the division is in proportion to the services performed by each lawyer or each lawyer assumes joint responsibility for the representation;

2. the client agrees to the arrangement, including the share each lawyer will receive, and the agreement is confirmed in writing; and

3. the total fee is reasonable.

The Model Code also allows for an almost-identical type of fee sharing. DR 2–107(A). The key difference between the two versions is that the Model Code requires the shared fee to be proportionate to the work done by each lawyer, while the Model Rules allow for disproportionate sharing, provided that all involved lawyers assume joint responsibility for the work. Both schemes require the client's consent to the fee-sharing arrangement, while the most current version of 1.5(e), in keeping with earlier parts of the rule, requires the client's agreement to be shown in writing.

PROHIBITION AGAINST FEE SHARING BETWEEN LAWYERS AND NON-LAWYERS

Both the Model Rules and Model Code allow lawyers in different firms to share a fee, provided the client consents to the fee sharing, but there is no similar allowance for the sharing of fees between a lawyer and a non-lawyer. In fact, the legal assistant exceptions to the fee-sharing prohibition seem more like exemptions, because they do not allow the sharing of client fees so much as they allow for the sharing of the lawyer's (or law firm's) income under certain circumstances.

Why Is Sharing Fees with a Non-lawyer Prohibited?

One of the strongest arguments in support of the increased use of paralegals is that clients get a smaller bill. Because a paralegal can do many tasks in place of a lawyer and because a paralegal's billing rate is considerably less than an associate's or partner's rate, the client gets high-quality legal services at a lesser cost. Therefore, assuming that a paralegal, on behalf of the attorney and in support of the client's case, engages in substantive legal work but does not engage in the unauthorized practice of law, what would be wrong with allowing him to share in the fee? The answer lies in the title of ABA Model Rule 5.4, "Professional Independence of a Lawyer." 5.4(a) states that lawyers and law firms may not share legal fees with a non-lawyer. The Model Code has the same prohibition in DR 3–102(A). The interest promoted by such a prohibition is that the professional judgment of the lawyer—that for which the client is paying—could be at risk if a non-lawyer has direct rights to share in the fee.

Fee Sharing and Independent Contractors

The reasoning behind prohibiting fee sharing between lawyers and their independent contractors has been expressed in a number of national ethics opinions, one of which found that the prohibition protects against the unauthorized practice of law and the chance that the lawyer's independence

NOT QUITE LINCOLN

Stranger Than Fiction

Guess which of the following are true stories and which are plot lines from a lawyer novel: (A) A woman in Cleveland calls 911, claiming that her married, lawyer-boyfriend beat her up. After the police arrive, she tells them her boyfriend was part of a conspiracy to help a Los Angeles eye doctor commit insurance fraud by having another lawyer steal a Picasso and a Monet from the doctor's house. This leads to a multi-billion-dollar, federal fraud case against a law firm that didn't even employ the Cleveland lawyer.

(B) A gigantic law firm that specializes in representing the little guy against big corporations—Enron, for instance—is the subject of accusations by a business-favorable U.S. Justice Department. The Department said the law firm engaged in the same kind of dirty tricks the law firm accused the big corporations of committing in the past four decades. The Department said the law firm squeezed over 40 billion dollars from those "little-guy" defendants.

(C) A mega-lawyer has earned tens of millions in fees by, in large measure, threatening defendants to settle with him or face his wrath. The same lawyer spent a night in the Lincoln Bedroom at the White House thanks to his generous political contributions to a particular political party. He also was a fundraiser for a lawyer running for that party's presidential nomination. The mega-lawyer is sent to prison for illegally paying millions of dollars to his clients, all class-action plaintiffs.

Have you decided which cases are fact and which are fiction? Although the first backstory could come from Turrow, the second from Grisham, and the third from Martini, they are all true and all about the same law firm. The firm is Milberg Weiss, the country's biggest class-action firm, and once referred to by *Fortune* magazine as "America's meanest law firm." Proving once again that fiction is often spun from the threads of real life, the mighty firm of Milberg Weiss would likely never have been brought low had it not been for that fateful 911 call. The curious allegations made on the night of August 22, 1996, by Pamela Davis against her beau James Little were just the beginning. What does art insurance fraud in Los Angeles have to do with a dishonest lawyer in Cleveland and the New York-based Milberg Weiss? Without a score card, a flow chart, and CliffsNotes, it is almost too much to explain, but most of it concerns class action suits and illegal fees. A class action case is premised on the idea that it is more practicable and equitable that many plaintiffs, who claim to have experienced common injuries, officially band together to sue large defendants, rather than bring hundreds or thousands of individual suits.

Plaintiffs in class actions often get very little for their trouble, but that's not true for their lawyers. And, for a law firm to make the astronomical fees that Milberg Weiss did, it has to be first to file the class action. It also must have its client serve as lead plaintiff, a title that provides almost no benefit to the one who seeks to have the class certified. To guarantee primacy, a firm could "plant" plaintiffs by having willing persons buy a few shares in companies that are ripe for a class action suit (and extortion-based settlement, as some have called it) and then pay the planted plaintiffs a percentage, usually 10 percent, of future contingency fees. This type of arrangement makes perfect sense, except that it is completely illegal for the client and firm. So, when the stolen paintings were found in a warehouse in Cleveland, a mystery of fictional proportions began unraveling, leading years later to numerous federal indictments. The charges ranged from fraud to bribery to obstruction of justice to racketeering. The defendants included some of the planted class action plaintiffs, lawyers of other firms who served as the fraudulent conduits of the illegal client compensation, Milberg Weiss (which earned over $200 million in class action fees during its existence and which actually sued Enron), and a few of its key or former partners. Among those partners were William Lerach, who agreed to plead guilty to some of the charges and was sentenced in March 2008 to two years in prison, David Bershad, Steven Schulman, and Bob Sugarman, who was given immunity in exchange for testifying against Milberg Weiss.

Melvyn Weiss, the 72-year-old founding partner of this ignominious law firm, and the lawyer who is thought to be the mastermind behind it all, fought his indictment until March 2008 when he agreed to plead guilty to racketeering and conspiracy, and face up to 33 months in prison.

NOT QUITE LINCOLN

Stranger Than Fiction, the Sequel

At some point, we might just stop buying legal fiction and instead read the news. The real thing is as full of the drama and duplicity, the highbrow and the high jinks, as almost any tale about torts, even the tall ones. Take for instance, Dickie Scruggs, a lawyer whose name not only sounds like it could be found in a John Grisham novel about southern lawyers, but who is thought to have been the model for *The King of Torts*, one of many Grisham best-sellers. Dickie Scruggs is a Mississippi lawyer—as is Mr. Grisham—whose life and career include being a navy fighter pilot, a life-long democrat whose brother-in-law is the powerful and retired Republican senator from Mississippi, Trent Lott, a benefactor of the University of Mississippi, and maybe the most renowned tort lawyer of them all. Included on his career biography is being the lead litigator against the tobacco industry, which resulted in a 1998 settlement of over 240 billion dollars and legal fees of over 1.4 billion dollars. That case got him characterized in the Russell Crowe film *The Insider*, which chronicled a controversial "60 Minutes" story on a tobacco scientist who perilously turned on his industry by providing damaging evidence to CBS News. Recently, Mr. Scruggs was leading a class action suit against State Farm Insurance related to Hurricane Katrina. And it is during that case where the super-rich-lawyer-for-the-little-guy was indicted in 2007 for attempting to offer a $50,000 bribe to a Mississippi judge over the splitting of a 26 million dollar legal fee. Part of the prosecution's evidence included wiretaps in which one of Mr. Scruggs's co-defendants is heard referring to the bribe money as "sweet potatoes." In March 2008, Mr. Scruggs agreed to plead guilty to bribery and conspiracy, and will face up to 5 years in prison, which is about 70 years less than he would have faced had he been convicted. Also agreeing to plead guilty to lesser charges were other lawyers, including Dickie Scruggs's son David Zachary Scruggs. Sadly for Mr. Grisham, when he first heard of the indictment against Dickie Scruggs, Grisham said he didn't "believe it." Wouldn't you know that bribing judges is the plot to a Scott Turow novel, *Personal Injuries*. Of course you would – by now.

will be at risk. ABA Commission on Ethics and Professional Responsibility, Formal Op. 86–1519 (1986). *See also* ABA Commission on Ethics and Professional Responsibility, Formal Op. 87–355 (1987). In a New Jersey case, a lawyer made an agreement with an investigator specializing in workers' compensation and personal injury litigation that stated: "I will give you 50 percent of everything you bring in. If you go into business with me, we will draw the same money. I consider us full and equal partners." However, not only did the court refuse to honor the contract, declaring it void as a matter of law because it violated the fee-sharing prohibition, but under the theory of quantum merit, it also refused to award the investigator any award for his efforts. *Infante v. Gottesman*, 558 A.2d 1338 (N.J. Super. 1989).

In a Colorado case involving this prohibition, a lawyer representing sexual harassment plaintiffs was disciplined for attempting to make a contingent fee with a private investigator and a counselor working on the case for him. Rather than pay the investigator and the counselor an hourly fee for their services with respect to the sexual harassment cases, the lawyer wanted to pay them a percentage of whatever he recovered. *People v. Easley*, 956 P.2d 1257 (Colo. 1998).

In an Arizona case, a lawyer was disciplined for a fee arrangement he made with a debt-collection agency that hired him, which involved him remitting his entire fee to the collection agency, whereupon the agency would pay him his share of the fee. *In re Struthers*, 877 P.2d 789 (Ariz. 1994). This prohibition has been found to apply even where a lawyer shares a fee with a suspended lawyer. *Attorney Grievance Commission of Maryland v. Brennan*, 714 A.2d 157 (Md. 1998).

Fee Sharing and Law Firm Employees

Despite the clear language of MR 5.4(a), lawyers are occasionally disciplined for sharing fees with their non-lawyer employees. Occasionally, these arrangements violate not only the fee-sharing prohibition, but also the prohibition of paying someone a finder's fee. A New Jersey case illustrates this kind of double-sided arrangement. In *Gallagher v. Weiner*, 1993 WL 460101 (U.S. Dist. N.J., 1993), Gallagher was hired as the office manager of Weiner's firm under a contract that called for him to be paid $15,000 of every $250,000 collected by the firm from clients he brought with him. Although the contractual arrangement was clear, the court found it to be unenforceable because it violated a New Jersey law that prohibited fee splitting and finder's fees.

In a South Carolina case, a lawyer used private investigators in his civil and criminal practice, and beyond their salary and mileage reimbursements, they were paid bimonthly bonuses of between 6–8 percent of the fees generated during those time periods by their investigations. Four years later, the lawyer consulted another lawyer about this, after which he stopped paying them bonuses tied to their investigation. The South Carolina Supreme Court found those earlier bonuses violated the fee-sharing prohibition because they were inextricably linked to the lawyer's fees. *Matter of Anonymous Member of South Carolina Bar*, 367 S.E.2d 17 (S.C. 1988).

Fee Sharing and Paralegals

How does this apply to the paralegal? If the danger of a lawyer sharing a fee with a non-lawyer is that the lawyer's professional independent judgment could be hindered when a non-lawyer has a financial stake in the case, does that danger apply to the paralegal? Assuming other applicable ethics rules are being followed —unauthorized practice of law and illegal solicitation, for instance—will the lawyer's professional judgment be at risk by rewarding the paralegal directly from the lawyer's fee? Usually, employees have no ability to control the professional actions of their employers. It is interesting that the originally proposed version of MR 5.4 (1983 version) would have allowed a lawyer to share a legal fee with a non-lawyer if the compensation was reasonable and the non-lawyer used no solicitation to receive the compensation. That version, however, never made it out of the ABA House of Delegates.

Thus, we return to the original premise: a paralegal or legal assistant may not directly share in the legal fees earned by a lawyer. That notion is also supported by paralegal and legal ethics guidelines. Guideline 9 of the ABA Model Guidelines on the Utilization of Paralegal Services prohibits fee splitting or tying compensation to the paralegal's referral of cases; Guideline 7 of the Connecticut Bar Association for Legal Assistants; Rule 1.5(g) of the North Dakota Rules of Professional Conduct; Guideline 8 of the North Carolina State Bar Guidelines for Use of Non-Lawyers in Rendering Legal Services; Guideline VII of the PA Keystone Alliance of Paralegal Associations, Guidelines for Paralegals in the Commonwealth of Pennsylvania.

Despite the general (and occasionally specific) prohibition on fee sharing, lawyers will occasionally attempt to skirt the rules. In an Iowa fee-sharing case, a lawyer retained the services of a paralegal recently released from prison, and the paralegal provided the lawyer with a client still behind bars. Upon taking the case, the lawyer required the client to pay a retainer to the lawyer and a retainer to the paralegal (who then proceeded to do unsupervised legal work for the client). The court found that such an arrangement was a violation of the prohibition of fee sharing and suspended the lawyer indefinitely. By the time the disciplinary case made its way to the Iowa Supreme Court, the paralegal had made his way back to prison. *Committee on Professional Ethics and Conduct of Iowa State Bar Association v. Lawler*, 342 N.W.2d 486 (Iowa 1984). Other jurisdictions have disciplined attorneys who have shared their fees with their non-lawyer staff, including paralegals and legal assistants:

- *In re Trauffer*, 532 S.E.2d 96 (Ga.2000) (debt collection fees shared);

- *Attorney AAA v. Mississippi Bar*, 735 So.2d 294 (Miss. 1999) (lawyer wrote check to paralegal for half of lawyer's legal fee on the same day attorney received the fee);

- *Gassman v. State Bar*, 553 P.2d 1147 (Cal. 1976) (paralegal's compensation was 20 percent of his lawyer's fees in cases in which the paralegal worked, and paralegal drafted his own paychecks, signing the lawyer's name)

- *State Bar of Texas v. Faubion*, 821 S.W.2d 203 (Tex. Ct. App. 1991) (lawyer paid paralegal/investigator 20-33 1/3 percent of the legal fees for cases on which the paralegal worked).

Tying a paralegal's or legal assistant's compensation to the number of cases filed is also a violation of the fee-sharing rules. In a Michigan case, a firm that specialized in bankruptcy cases paid a base salary to its legal assistants who conducted initial interviews with prospective clients if the firm filed a minimum of 15 bankruptcy cases per week. If the firm filed more than 15 cases per week, those legal assistants would receive more pay, in increments that leveled off at $1,150 per week. Although the firm said that the lawyers and their clients, and not the legal assistants, made the decisions whether to file bankruptcy petitions, the court found that the compensation scheme created a vested financial interest in the legal assistants, which encouraged them to present their consultation information to the lawyers in ways that would promote the filing of bankruptcies. *In re Bass,* 227 B.R. 103 (E.D.Mich. 1998). A much more miserly bankruptcy attorney got caught in a similar scheme. Without the slightest sense of irony, he paid his paralegals $5 "motivational bonuses" when their clients paid a $300 retainer payment, or when their clients completed their bankruptcy question-naire, or when they signed and executed living wills/durable powers of attorney. The bankruptcy trustee opposed the 36 instances of these bonus payments—most of which went unreported, in violation of a federal statute and a bankruptcy rule requiring full disclosure when seeking compensation from a debtor's estate. The court concluded that the payments violated the bankruptcy rules and the applicable state's ethics rules on fee sharing with non-lawyer employees. *In re Holmes* 304 B.R. 292 (N.D.Miss. 2004).

A variety of ethics opinions share the view that the compensation of paralegals and legal assistants may not be directly tied to their work product. Maryland held that a lawyer may not pay non-lawyer employees compensation based on a percentage of the client's total recovery. Maryland State Bar Association Commission on Ethics, Op. 94–103 (1984). Ohio declared that a law firm may not pay non-lawyer employees compensation calculated as a percentage of their billable hours for work performed on behalf of a client. Ohio State Bar Association Ethics Op. 97–4 (1997). New York City's Bar Association also decided that firms may not pay commissions or bonuses to non-lawyer employees that are directly tied to specific fees, or for cases brought to the firm by those employees. New York City Bar Association, Ethics Op. 95–11 (1995). *See also* Pennsylvania Bar Association Formal Op. 98–75 (1998); Illinois State Bar Association Advisory Opinion on Professional Conduct, Op. 94–8 (1994); Dallas, Texas, Bar Association Ethics Op. 1991–03 (1991); Colorado State Bar Association Ethics Op. 97 (1991); Georgia Bar Association Advisory Op. 21 (1977).

Getting What Was Promised: Breach of Contract and Illegal Fee Sharing

Can paralegals recover their promised compensation even if the arrange-ments violate the fee-sharing rules? Generally, the answer is no, because contracts that violate the law are usually considered to be void and, therefore, ineligible for breach of contract consideration. For instance, courts do not hear breach of contract suits over illegal gambling contracts.

An Indiana case, *Trotter v. Nelson,* 684 N.E 2d 1150 (Ind. 1997), serves as a blueprint demonstrating the way many courts treat suits over illegal fee-sharing agreements. In the case, a non-lawyer employee (who was something short of a legal assistant) sued her former employer, an attorney, over an alleged compensation promise. She claimed that the attorney promised her 5 percent of any fees from worker's compensation cases that she personally referred to the attorney. The attorney argued the agreement did not exist, and even if it did, it violated the referral fee rules and was unenforceable. The employee argued that the agreement was a permissible profit-sharing arrangement, which made it an enforceable contract. Because the agreement was not in writing, the legal analysis was made under an assumption that the agreement had actually been made. The Indiana Court of Appeals had held that even if the agreement violated the rules of professional conduct, it could still be enforced because a contract that violates the rules of professional responsibility is not the same as a contract that violates a statute. But the Indiana Supreme Court disagreed, declaring that the rules of professional conduct are a declaration of the state's public policy. As to the lawsuit, the court first found that the agreement, if it actually existed, was an impermissible profit-sharing agreement, as argued by the employer. Then, the court found that such an agreement was unenforceable because it violated "public policy." *Trotter*, at 1155.

Such a view is not the case everywhere, or at least not in Texas. In *Atkins v. Tinning*, 865 S.W.2d 533 (Tex. App. 1993), the Texas Court of Appeals reached an opposite conclusion on facts similar to *Trotter v. Nelson*. *Atkins* involved a private investigator who sued an attorney for failure to honor an oral agreement in which the private investigator was to receive one-third of the attorney's contingency fees from cases where he gathered evidence. When the attorney failed to pay the investigator a $300,000 fee, the investigator sued the attorney, whereupon the attorney had the investigator arrested and charged with barratry. Although the Court found that such an alleged contract between a lawyer and non-lawyer was in violation of the disciplinary rules—and could subject the attorney to professional sanction—it specifically refused to find that the disciplinary rules had any application to non-lawyers. Such a view distinguished the disciplinary rules from other kinds of law, such as statutes. Therefore, the Court said the agreement, if made, was not illegal, even though the agreement violated the disciplinary rules. *Atkins*, at 537.

When Is a Compensation Scheme Not Fee Sharing and What Is the Difference?

Model Rule 5.4(a) does have four exceptions, after Ethics 2000. Three do not apply to the paralegal. The first two exceptions allow a lawyer or law firm to pay money to the estate (or other qualified representative) of a dead (or disabled) lawyer that the lawyer was owed in connection with earned fees or the sale of a law practice. MR 5.4(a)(1)and(2). The only Ethics 2000 change to the fee sharing part of Model Rule 5.4 is an allowance for lawyers to share court-awarded fees with a nonprofit organization that was directly involved in the case.

5.4(a)(4). This change is in concert with an ABA ethics opinion (93–374) that found that sharing fees with a nonprofit organization does not threaten the independent judgment of a lawyer, which is the danger that is avoided by prohibiting the sharing of fees between a lawyer and a non-lawyer.

Model Rule 5.4(a)(3) does apply to the paralegal and legal assistant, because it states "A lawyer or law firm may include non-lawyer employees in a compensation or retirement plan, even though the plan is based in whole or in part on a profit-sharing arrangement." This exception allows a lawyer or law firm to fund retirement compensation programs, such as a **401(k) plan**, for their non-lawyer employees. It also allows paralegals to be paid bonuses or be included in profit-sharing plans. The predecessor Model Code has a similar exception in DR 3–102(A)(3).

If legal assistants cannot be paid directly from the legal fees earned by the lawyer or otherwise share in those fees, then how can they be paid bonuses or be part of a profit-sharing plan using contributions from the firm's legal fees? There are two differences between prohibited fee-sharing and allowed-compensation plans.

Extra Compensation Can Come from Net Proceeds

The first difference between prohibited fee-sharing and allowed-compensation plans is that an allowed retirement compensation program or profit-sharing plan is funded from the net proceeds of earned legal fees. Paid legal fees constitute **gross revenue**, which is what may not be shared with a legal assistant or any other non-lawyer. Retirement compensation programs and profit-sharing plans are funded from monies left over after expenses and overhead have been paid. Fee-sharing prohibitions concern gross revenues, but a lawyer or law firm can share whatever they want with whomever they want from what is left over after paying the bills.

Extra Compensation Can Come from General Success Rather Than Specific Success

The second difference is that compensation plans, such as bonuses, may not be made payable to a paralegal or legal assistant contingent on the success of a specific matter. A general bonus, such as a quarterly bonus, may be paid to a paralegal, but if he is paid a specific bonus for work on a particular case, that kind of transaction would be inappropriate because it vests in the paralegal a direct, financial interest in the case and could affect his judgment. Although MR 5.4(a) concerns protecting the professional judgment of lawyers, paralegals (as agents of their lawyers) also need to exercise their duties without having their judgment inappropriately clouded. Furthermore, specific bonuses can masquerade as finder's fees, in violation of the rules that prohibit a lawyer from compensating someone for recommending his services. MR 7.2(c); DR 2–103(B).

■ **401(k) plan**

An employee retirement plan authorized by Section 401 of the Internal Revenue Code, sometimes called a salary reduction plan. In a 401k plan, an employee's pre-tax contributions are matched in some percentage by their employer's contributions.

■ **gross revenue**

Sometimes called gross income, this is the total revenue received before deductions, such as expenses.

The American Bar Association issued an ethics opinion in 1979 that approved of the inclusion of non-lawyer employees in a law firm's profit-sharing plan. Although the opinion specifically concerned a firm's non-lawyer administrator, its reasoning is equally applicable to all non-lawyer employees, in that its approval of non-lawyer participation in profit-sharing plans is contingent on two factors: the profit-sharing method must be based on the firm's net profits; and the profit-sharing is not based on a percentage of specific client fees. ABA Commission on Ethics and Professional Responsibility, Informal Op. 1440 (1979). Some states have followed suit and issued opinions approving of profit-sharing plans. Virginia, for instance, issued three closely related opinions that approve of the following: law firms including non-lawyer employees in profit-sharing plans (Virginia State Bar Standing Comm. on Legal Ethics, Op. 767 (1986)); law firms paying bonuses to secretaries based on profits (Op. 806 (1986)); and collections firms compensating non-lawyer employees on a percentage of collections profits (Op. 885 (1987)). Other jurisdictions have issued ethics opinions approving of bonuses or profit-sharing plans for paralegals and legal assistants, provided the extra compensation is not tied to specific cases: Florida Bar Prof. Ethics Committee, Op. 02-1 (2002); Connecticut State Bar Assoc. Ethics Op. 93-1 (1993); L.A. Cty. Bar Assn. Formal Op. No. 457 (1989).

A few jurisdictions have issued ethics opinion on the fee-sharing exceptions that are different from the traditional view summarized earlier. Concerning the sources of finances that are used to fund extra-compensation plans, Utah has stated that non-lawyer employees may be included in retirement plans, *regardless of whether the payments are based on the firm's gross or net income,* as long as there is nothing in the arrangement that would impair the lawyer's independence and the payment is not tied to a fee from a specific case. Utah State Bar Association, Ethics Advisory Committee Op. 139 (1994). And the same 2002 ethics opinion authorizing independent contracting paralegals (discussed in Chapter 3) prohibits lawyers from sharing fees with their independent contracting paralegals to the extent allowed for paralegals who are firm employees. Utah State Bar Association, Ethics Advisory Committee Op. 02–07 (2002). Although the opinion approves of firms compensating their employed paralegals based on a percentage of the firm's fees, it disapproves of the same compensation for independent contractor-paralegals, reasoning that they are in a "less subordinate role" than their employed counterparts, which implicates the independent judgment policy behind a prohibition on sharing fees with non-lawyers. A South Carolina ethics opinion approved of a lawyer's desire to pay his paralegal a bonus based on the number of hours the paralegal billed clients on cases, provided the amount billed to the clients is "reasonable." South Carolina Bar Ethics Advisory Op. 97-02 (1997). A Mississippi ethics opinion found no problem with a bonus system in which associates and paralegals were paid a bonus based on the number of hours they billed above a stated annual minimum, and where the source of the bonus fund will include a percentage going to partners. Op. No. 154 of the Mississippi State Bar (1988). See Exhibit 7-10 for rules on fee sharing between lawyers and paralegals.

EXHIBIT 7–10   FEE SHARING BETWEEN LAWYERS AND PARALEGALS

- ABA MR 5.4 prohibits lawyers from sharing legal fees with non-lawyers, which includes paralegals and legal assistants.

- For instance, a lawyer may not pay a paralegal or legal assistant based on the number of cases brought in by that employee, or based on a percentage of what the lawyer made on a particular case.

- There are exceptions that allow a lawyer or firm to include a paralegal or legal assistant in a profit-sharing or retirement-compensation plan.

- There are generally two parameters for legitimate fee-sharing plans:
  1. Compensation must come from *net proceeds*, not gross proceeds.
  2. Compensation must come from *general success*, not specific success.

RECOVERY OF LEGAL FEES FROM THE OPPOSING PARTY IN LITIGATION

There are occasions where successful litigants can keep more of their recovery because the other side must pay the legal fees for both sides. Such a system, commonly known as "loser pays," is thought by some legal reformers to be a desirable way to minimize the filing of frivolous or otherwise wasteful litigation. Some statutes authorize trial courts to allow plaintiffs to recover their attorneys' fees in addition to their damages. At the federal level, 42 U.S.C. § 1988 (b) grants trial courts the discretion to award "a reasonable attorney's fee" to successful plaintiffs suing under certain federal civil rights statutes.

Such fee-shifting reform, though, is not without controversy in cases where the public perceives lawyers as acting piggish at the public trough. For example, when Rodney King was severely beaten by Los Angeles police in March 1991—and recorded on one of the most infamous home videos of all time—what followed were two prosecutions against the police officers, a riot that killed 55 people and caused $1 billion in damage, and a lawsuit against the city of Los Angeles. As a result of the civil rights case settled between Mr. King and Los Angeles, Mr. King's legal fees were paid by the city, which is the way it should be. But not the way it should be was that the legal bill his 23 lawyers submitted to the city totaled $4.4 million, $600,000 more than the $3.8 million Mr. King received from the city. Included in the 13,000-hour bill presented to the federal court overseeing the case was time Mr. King's lawyers spent on talk shows, attending his birthday party, and even $3,981 for what they called efforts given to combat the negative publicity against Mr. King when, two months after the beating, he was arrested with a transvestite prostitute and on suspicion of trying to run down the arresting officer. The day the lawyers presented their mammoth bill to him in court, U.S. District Judge John Davies said, "No wonder lawyers have such a bad name."

Separate Recovery of Paralegal Fees in Federal Cases

One of the important moments in the history of legal assisting occurred in 1978, when a federal bankruptcy statute was amended to allow the bankruptcy court the discretion to also award the recovery of the fees of a paralegal (called a "paraprofessional") employed by an attorney. 11 U.S.C. § 330(a)(1)(A). But what if there is no reference to the lawyer's employees in a fee-shifting statute? An important, connected question is whether legal assistant fees also can be recovered where a statute authorizes the recovery of attorney's fees, but does not mention legal assistant fees.

The following case, which serves as a watershed moment in the history of the paralegal profession, answers that question affirmatively, at least where federal, civil rights statutes authorize the recovery of an attorney's fee. While reading the case, notice how the Court gives its approval to the paralegal's role in a law firm. Notice also the focus of the dissenting opinion.

CASE LAW 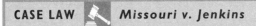 *Missouri v. Jenkins*

491 U.S. 274 (1989)

Justice BRENNAN delivered the opinion of the Court.

This is the attorney's fee aftermath of major school desegregation litigation in Kansas City, Missouri. We granted certiorari, 488 U.S. 888, 109 S.Ct. 218, 102 L.Ed.2d 209 (1988), to resolve two questions relating to fees litigation under 90 Stat. 2641, as amended, 42 U.S.C. § 1988. First, does the Eleventh Amendment prohibit enhancement of a fee award against a State to compensate for delay in payment? Second, should the fee award compensate the work of paralegals and law clerks by applying the market rate for their work?

I

This litigation began in 1977 as a suit by the Kansas City Missouri School District (KCMSD), the school board, and the children of two school board members, against the State of Missouri and other defendants. The plaintiffs alleged that the State, surrounding school districts, and various federal agencies had caused and perpetuated a system of racial segregation in the schools of the Kansas City metropolitan area. They sought various desegregation remedies. KCMSD was subsequently realigned as a nominal defendant, and a class of present and future KCMSD students was certified as plaintiffs. After lengthy proceedings, including a trial that lasted 7 1/2 months during 1983 and 1984, the District Court found the State of Missouri and KCMSD liable, while dismissing the suburban school

(continues)

districts and the federal defendants. It ordered various intradistrict remedies, to be paid for by the State and KCMSD, including $260 million in capital improvements and a magnet-school plan costing over $200 million. . . .

The plaintiff class has been represented, since 1979, by Kansas City lawyer Arthur Benson and, since 1982, by the NAACP Legal Defense and Educational Fund, Inc. (LDF). Benson and the LDF requested attorney's fees under the Civil Rights Attorney's Fees Awards Act of 1976, 42 U.S.C. § 1988. 1 Benson and his associates had devoted 10,875 attorney hours to the litigation, as well as 8,108 hours of paralegal and law clerk time. For the LDF the corresponding figures were 10,854 hours for attorneys and 15,517 hours for paralegals and law clerks. Their fee applications deleted from these totals 3,628 attorney hours and 7,046 paralegal hours allocable to unsuccessful claims against the suburban school districts. With additions for post-judgment monitoring and for preparation of the fee application, the District Court awarded Benson a total of approximately $1.7 million and the LDF $2.3 million.

In calculating the hourly rate for Benson's fees the court noted that the market rate in Kansas City for attorneys of Benson's qualifications was in the range of $125 to $175 per hour, and found that "Mr. Benson's rate would fall at the higher end of this range based upon his expertise in the area of civil rights." It calculated his fees on the basis of an even higher hourly rate of $200, however, because of three additional factors: the preclusion of other employment, the undesirability of the case, and the delay in payment for Benson's services. The court also took account of the delay in payment in setting the rates for several of Benson's associates by using current market rates rather than those applicable at the time the services were rendered. For the same reason, it calculated the fees for the LDF attorneys at current market rates. Both Benson and the LDF employed numerous paralegals, law clerks (generally law students working part time), and recent law graduates in this litigation. The court awarded fees for their work based on Kansas City market rates for those categories. As in the case of the attorneys, it used current rather than historic market rates in order to compensate for the delay in payment. It therefore awarded fees based on hourly rates of $35 for law clerks, $40 for paralegals, and $50 for recent law graduates. The Court of Appeals affirmed in all respects.

II

[Here, the Court resolved the first issue, deciding that the Eleventh Amendment's principle of sovereign immunity does not prohibit an award against a state for attorney's fees to be enhanced because the state delayed in making the required payment to the plaintiff.]

III

Missouri's second contention is that the District Court erred in compensating the work of law clerks and paralegals (hereinafter collectively "paralegals") at the market rates for their services, rather than at their cost to the attorney. While Missouri agrees that compensation for the cost of these personnel should be included in the fee award, it suggests that an hourly rate of $15—which it argued below corresponded to their salaries,

(continues)

CASE LAW *Missouri v. Jenkins* (continued)

benefits, and overhead—would be appropriate, rather than the market rates of $35 to $50. According to Missouri, § 1988 does not authorize billing paralegals' hours at market rates, and doing so produces a "windfall" for the attorney.

We begin with the statutory language, which provides simply for "a reasonable attorney's fee as part of the costs." 42 U.S.C. § 1988. Clearly, a "reasonable attorney's fee" cannot have been meant to compensate only work performed personally by members of the bar. Rather, the term must refer to a reasonable fee for the work product of an attorney. Thus, the fee must take into account the work not only of attorneys, but also of secretaries, messengers, librarians, janitors, and others whose labor contributes to the work product for which an attorney bills her client; and it must also take account of other expenses and profit. The parties have suggested no reason why the work of paralegals should not be similarly compensated, nor can we think of any. We thus take as our starting point the self-evident proposition that the "reasonable attorney's fee" provided for by statute should compensate the work of paralegals, as well as that of attorneys. *The more difficult question is how the work of paralegals is to be valuated in calculating the overall attorney's fee* [emphasis added].

The statute specifies a "reasonable" fee for the attorney's work product. In determining how other elements of the attorney's fee are to be calculated, we have consistently looked to the marketplace as our guide to what is "reasonable." . . . A reasonable attorney's fee under § 1988 is one calculated on the basis of rates and practices prevailing in the relevant market, i.e., "in line with those [rates] prevailing in the community for similar services by lawyers of reasonably comparable skill, experience, and reputation," and one that grants the successful civil rights plaintiff a "fully compensatory fee," Hensley v. Eckerhart, 461 U.S. 424, 435, 103 S.Ct. 1933, 1940, 76 L.Ed.2d 40 (1983), comparable to what "is traditional with attorneys compensated by a fee-paying client."

All else being equal, the hourly fee charged by an attorney whose rates include paralegal work in her hourly fee, or who bills separately for the work of paralegals at cost, will be higher than the hourly fee charged by an attorney competing in the same market who bills separately for the work of paralegals at "market rates." In other words, the prevailing "market rate" for attorney time is not independent of the manner in which paralegal time is accounted for.8 Thus, if the prevailing practice in a given community were to bill paralegal time separately at market rates, fees awarded the attorney at market rates for attorney time would not be fully compensatory if the court refused to compensate hours billed by paralegals or did so only at "cost." Similarly, the fee awarded would be too high if the court accepted separate billing for paralegal hours in a market where that was not the custom.

We reject the argument that compensation for paralegals at rates above "cost" would yield a "windfall" for the prevailing attorney. Neither petitioners nor anyone else, to our knowledge, has ever suggested that the hourly rate applied to the work of an associate

(continues)

CASE LAW *Missouri v. Jenkins* (continued)

attorney in a law firm creates a windfall for the firm's partners or is otherwise improper under § 1988, merely because it exceeds the cost of the attorney's services. If the fees are consistent with market rates and practices, the "windfall" argument has no more force with regard to paralegals than it does for associates. And it would hardly accord with Congress' intent to provide a "fully compensatory fee" if the prevailing plaintiff 's attorney in a civil rights lawsuit were not permitted to bill separately for paralegals, while the defense attorney in the same litigation was able to take advantage of the prevailing practice and obtain market rates for such work. Yet that is precisely the result sought in this case by the State of Missouri, which appears to have paid its own outside counsel for the work of paralegals at the hourly rate of $35.[9]

Nothing in § 1988 requires that the work of paralegals invariably be billed separately. If it is the practice in the relevant market not to do so, or to bill the work of paralegals only at cost, that is all that § 1988 requires. Where, however, the prevailing practice is to bill paralegal work at market rates, treating civil rights lawyers' fee requests in the same way is not only permitted by § 1988, but also makes economic sense. By encouraging the use of lower cost paralegals rather than attorneys wherever possible, permitting market-rate billing of paralegal hours "encourages cost-effective delivery of legal services and, by reducing the spiraling cost of civil rights litigation, furthers the policies underlying civil rights statutes."[10]

Such separate billing appears to be the practice in most communities today.[11] In the present case, Missouri concedes that "the local market typically bills separately for paralegal services," (Tr. of Oral Arg. 14), and the District Court found that the requested hourly rates of $35 for law clerks, $40 for paralegals, and $50 for recent law graduates were the prevailing rates for such services in the Kansas City area. (App. to Pet. for Cert. A29, A31, A34.) Under these circumstances, the court's decision to award separate compensation at these rates was fully in accord with § 1988.

IV

The courts below correctly granted a fee enhancement to compensate for delay in payment and approved compensation of paralegals and law clerks at market rates. The judgment of the Court of Appeals is therefore Affirmed.

Justice MARSHALL took no part in the consideration or decision of this case. . . .

Chief Justice REHNQUIST, dissenting.

I agree with Justice O'CONNOR [who dissented in part] that the Eleventh Amendment does not permit an award of attorney's fees against a State which includes compensation for delay in payment. Unlike Justice O'CONNOR, however, I do not agree with the Court's approval of the award of law clerk and paralegal fees made here.

(continues)

CASE LAW *Missouri v. Jenkins* (continued)

42 U.S.C. § 1988 gives the district courts discretion to allow the prevailing party in an action under 42 U.S.C. § 1983 "a reasonable attorney's fee as part of the costs." The Court reads this language as authorizing recovery of "a 'reasonable' fee for the attorney's work product," which, the Court concludes, may include separate compensation for the services of law clerks and paralegals. But the statute itself simply uses the very familiar term "a reasonable attorney's fee," which to those untutored in the Court's linguistic juggling means a fee charged for services rendered by an individual who has been licensed to practice law. Because law clerks and paralegals have not been licensed to practice law in Missouri, it is difficult to see how charges for their services may be separately billed as part of "attorney's fees." And since a prudent attorney customarily includes compensation for the cost of law clerk and paralegal services, like any other sort of office overhead—from secretarial staff, janitors, and librarians, to telephone service, stationery, and paper clips—in his own hourly billing rate, allowing the prevailing party to recover separate compensation for law clerk and paralegal services may result in "double recovery."

The Court finds justification for its ruling in the fact that the prevailing practice among attorneys in Kansas City is to bill clients separately for the services of law clerks and paralegals. But I do not think Congress intended the meaning of the statutory term "attorney's fee" to expand and contract with each and every vagary of local billing practice. Under the Court's logic, prevailing parties could recover at market rates for the cost of secretaries, private investigators, and other types of lay personnel who assist the attorney in preparing his case, so long as they could show that the prevailing practice in the local market was to bill separately for these services. Such a result would be a sufficiently drastic departure from the traditional concept of "attorney's fees" that I believe new statutory authorization should be required for it. That permitting separate billing of law clerk and paralegal hours at market rates might "'reduc[e] the spiraling cost of civil rights litigation'" by encouraging attorneys to delegate to these individuals tasks which they would otherwise perform themselves at higher cost, may be a persuasive reason for Congress to enact such additional legislation. It is not, however, a persuasive reason for us to rewrite the legislation which Congress has in fact enacted. . . .

I also disagree with the State's suggestion that law clerk and paralegal expenses incurred by a prevailing party, if not recoverable at market rates as "attorney's fees" under § 1988, are nonetheless recoverable at actual cost under that statute. The language of § 1988 expands the traditional definition of "costs" to include "a reasonable attorney's fee," but it cannot fairly be read to authorize the recovery of all other out-of-pocket expenses actually incurred by the prevailing party in the course of litigation. Absent specific statutory authorization for the recovery of such expenses, the prevailing party remains subject to the limitations on cost recovery imposed by Federal Rule of Civil Procedure 54(d) and 28 U.S.C.

(continues)

CASE LAW *Missouri v. Jenkins (continued)*

§ 1920, which govern the taxation of costs in federal litigation where a cost-shifting statute is not applicable. Section 1920 gives the district court discretion to tax certain types of costs against the losing party in any federal litigation. The statute specifically enumerates six categories of expenses which may be taxed as costs: fees of the court clerk and marshal; fees of the court reporter; printing fees and witness fees; copying fees; certain docket fees; and fees of court-appointed experts and interpreters. We have held that this list is exclusive. *Crawford Fitting Co. v. J.T. Gibbons, Inc.,* 482 U.S. 437, 107 S.Ct. 2494, 96 L.Ed.2d 385 (1987). Since none of these categories can possibly be construed to include the fees of law clerks and paralegals, I would also hold that reimbursement for these expenses may not be separately awarded at actual cost.

I would therefore reverse the award of reimbursement for law clerk and paralegal expenses.

The following case footnotes correspond to the portions of the case that are printed in the textbook. Although it may seem that other footnotes are missing, they are not presented because their corresponding portions of the court's opinion have been redacted.

[1]Section 1988 provides in relevant part:

In any action or proceeding to enforce a provision of sections 1981, 1982, 1983, 1985, and 1986 of this title, title IX of Public Law 92-318 [20 U.S.C. § 1681 et seq.], or title VI of the Civil Rights Act of 1964 [42 U.S.C. § 2000d et seq.], the court, in its discretion, may allow the prevailing party, other than the United States, a reasonable attorney's fee as part of the costs.

[8]The attorney who bills separately for paralegal time is merely distributing her costs and profit margin among the hourly fees of other members of her staff, rather than concentrating them in the fee she sets for her own time.

[9]A variant of Missouri's "windfall" argument is the following: "If paralegal expense is reimbursed at a rate many times the actual cost, will attorneys next try to bill separately—and at a profit—for such items as secretarial time, paper clips, electricity, and other expenses?" Reply Brief for Petitioners 15–16. The answer to this question is, of course, that attorneys seeking fees under § 1988 would have no basis for requesting separate compensation of such expenses unless this were the prevailing practice in the local community. The safeguard against the billing at a profit of secretarial services and paper clips is the discipline of the market.

[10]It has frequently been recognized in the lower courts that paralegals are capable of carrying out many tasks, under the supervision of an attorney, that might otherwise be performed by a lawyer and billed at a higher rate. Such work might include, for example, factual investigation, including locating and interviewing witnesses; assistance with depositions, interrogatories, and document production; compilation of statistical and financial data;

(continues)

CASE LAW *Missouri v. Jenkins* (continued)

checking legal citations; and drafting correspondencex. Much such work lies in a gray area of tasks that might appropriately be performed either by an attorney or a paralegal. To the extent that fee applicants under § 1988 are not permitted to bill for the work of paralegals at market rates, it would not be surprising to see a greater amount of such work performed by attorneys themselves, thus increasing the overall cost of litigation. Of course, purely clerical or secretarial tasks should not be billed at a paralegal rate, regardless of who performs them. What the court in Johnson v. Georgia Highway Express, Inc., 488 F.2d 714, 717 (CA5 1974), said in regard to the work of attorneys is applicable by analogy to paralegals:

"It is appropriate to distinguish between legal work, in the strict sense, and investigation, clerical work, compilation of facts and statistics and other work which can often be accomplished by non-lawyers but which a lawyer may do because he has no other help available. Such non-legal work may command a lesser rate. Its dollar value is not enhanced just because a lawyer does it."

[11]Amicus National Association of Legal Assistants reports that 77 percent of 1,800 legal assistants responding to a survey of the association's membership stated that their law firms charged clients for paralegal work on an hourly billing basis. Brief for National Association of Legal Assistants as Amicus Curiae 11.

Case Questions

1. How many hours of paralegal time were billed? Did the prevailing party bill to the state of Missouri?

2. Why did Missouri argue that it should not have to pay for what the Court collectively called paralegal fees?

3. Why did the Court include paralegal fees as an allowable recovery under the statute that allows for the recovery of "reasonable attorney's fees"?

4. Why did the Court determine that the paralegal market rate, rather than the actual cost of the paralegal time, would be the allowable recovery?

5. What is the difference between the market rate and the actual cost?

6. Under what conditions did the Court find that paralegal fees would be recoverable?

7. Why did Chief Justice Rehnquist disagree with the Court's decision?

8. If, as Justice Rehnquist stated, a prudent attorney will include the cost of paralegals in the attorney's hourly rate, then would there be any practical difference between the Court's decision and Justice Rehnquist's dissent?

Following *Missouri v. Jenkins*, the Supreme Court dealt with several cases involving the recovery of attorney's fees under federal fee-shifting provisions, but did not revisit the issue of the recovery of paralegal fees—and at what rate. That is, until November 2007, when the high court granted certiorari in *Richlin Security Service Co. v. Chertoff*, (06-1717), a case involving the question of what is the correct method of paralegal fee recovery under the Equal Access to Justice Act (5 U.S.C. § 504, and 28 U.S.C. § 2412(d)) and its fee-recoverability provision.

In *Richlin*, a company that did business with the Homeland Security Office (and its predecessor, the Immigration and Naturalization Service), sued Homeland Security for underpayment of services rendered. After a successful but lengthy nine-year legal battle, the company asked for attorney's fees, and paralegal fees at the market rate. Because, in part, the fee-recovery statute at issue capped the hourly rate of attorney's fees, the Federal Circuit Court of Appeals distinguished *Missouri v. Jenkins*, and held that paralegal fees were recoverable only at cost, which was set at $35 an hour, rather than the requested $50–$90 an hour range. 472 F.3d 1370 (2006). Such a result conflicted with other federal circuits, who concluded that the Equal Access to Justice Act does provide for the recovery of paralegal fees "at market rates:" *Jean v. Nelson*, 863 F.2d 759 (11th Cir. 1988); *Miller v. Alamo*, 983 F.2d 856 (8th Cir. 1993); *Hyatt v. Barnhart*, 315 F.3d 239 (4th Cir. 2002); *Role Models America, Inc. v. Brownlee*, 353 F.3d 962 (D. C. Cir. 2004). The U.S. Supreme Court took the appeal because of this division among the federal circuits on interpreting the same statute, and will resolve the conflict in 2008.

Separate Recovery of Legal Assistant Fees in State Cases

Some states have avoided the dilemma of *Missouri v. Jenkins* by expressly stating, through legislation, that where the law allows for the recovery of attorney's fees, it also includes paralegal fees. For example, Ind. Code § 1-1-4-6 (b) states, "A reference in the Indiana Code to attorney's fees includes paralegal's fees." Illinois's statute, following the line of reasoning in *Missouri v. Jenkins*, specifically allows for the recovery of paralegal fees at "market rates." 5 Ill. Comp. Stat. 70/1.35. Other states expressly provide for the recovery of legal assistant fees where attorney fees are recoverable. *See* Ala. R. Civ. Pro., Rule 79(g) (1)(C); Cal. Prob. Code §10811(b); Fla. Stat. ch. 57.104; N.J. R. Ct., Rule 4:42–9 (b); N.Y. Sur. Ct. Proc. Law ○ 2110.4. In fact, New York reaffirmed its position on the recovery of legal assistant fees, extending it to a statute that allows for the recovery of legal fees for court-appointed defense attorneys in death penalty cases. *Mahoney v. Pataki*, 772 N.E.2d 1118 (N.Y. 2002).

It is important to realize that *Missouri v. Jenkins* allows for the recovery of paralegal fees where the work done by the paralegal is substantive legal work, which an attorney would do if not for the paralegal's efforts. Clerical or secretarial work is not the kind of work that courts are likely to allow as recoverable, even if done by a paralegal and even where a statute allows for the recovery of paralegal fees. In a case that predates *Missouri v. Jenkins,* a federal court refused to allow the recovery of paralegal costs, not because the statute failed to mention paralegals but because there was insufficient evidence that the employee in question, who was called a paralegal, was, in fact, a paralegal. Not only did the employee have no paralegal training, but she mostly performed clerical duties. *Jones v. Armstrong Cork Co.,* 630 F.2d 324 (11th Cir. 1980). It is interesting that Florida's statute on the recovery of attorney's fees allows the trial court to consider the work of "any legal assistants who contributed nonclerical, meaningful legal support to the matter involved and are working under the supervision of an attorney." Fla. Stat. ch. 57.104. See Exhibit 7-11 for information on what makes a paralegal fee recoverable.

EXHIBIT 7–11   WHAT MAKES A PARALEGAL'S FEE RECOVERABLE?

1. The paralegal's work must be substantive legal work (not clerical).

2. The paralegal's work must be adequately supervised.

3. The paralegal's qualifications must be sufficiently shown in the fees request.

4. The paralegal's work must be specifically shown in the fees request.

5. The paralegal's billable hours must be adequately accounted for and reasonable.

6. The paralegal's hourly rate should reflect community standards.

The following state case involves a request for the recovery of legal assistant fees under a state statute that only mentions the recovery of attorney fees. Notice the logical progression of the court's analysis concerning the recovery of legal assistant fees.

CASE LAW   *Absher Const. Co. v. Kent School Dist.*

No. 415, 917 P.2d 1086 (Wash. App. 1995)

PER CURIAM.

Kent School No. 415 (Kent) has requested an attorney fee award which includes payment for the time of non-lawyer personnel. We hold that such time may be compensable as part of an attorney fee award and set out guidelines for determining when such fees are appropriate. We find, however, that the total amount requested by Kent is not reasonable under the circumstances of this case and therefore award a lesser amount.

(continues)

CASE LAW *Absher Const. Co. v. Kent School Dist.* *(continued)*

The appellants sued Kent for amounts they claimed were owing under a public works contract, approximately $205,000. Kent won on summary judgment and was awarded $34,648.86 in fees and costs. Kent also prevailed on appeal and now seeks an additional $36,911.54 in fees and costs. The basis for the award is RCW 39.04.240.

The fee request includes time for the following individuals:

1. A partner in practice for 20 years billed 104.2 hours at $225.00 per hour ($23,445);

2. A fourth-year associate billed 53.1 hours at $130.00 per hour ($6,903);

3. A sixth-year associate billed 4.5 hours at $155.00 per hour ($697.50);

4. A legal assistant billed 39.5 hours at $67.00 per hour ($2,646.50);

5. A legal editor billed 4 hours at $62.00 per hour ($248); and

6. A legal clerk billed 8.5 hours at $35.00 per hour ($297.50).

The latter three are not attorneys. No case in Washington specifically addresses whether the time of non-lawyer personnel may be included in an attorney fee award.

We find persuasive the reasoning of the Arizona court in Continental Townhouses East Unit One Ass'n v. Brockbank, 152 Ariz. 537, 733 P.2d 1120, 73 A.L.R.4th 921 (1986). Properly employed and supervised non-lawyer personnel can decrease litigation expense. Lawyers should not be forced to perform legal tasks solely so that their time may be compensable in an attorney fee award. The question then becomes what sort of work performed by non-lawyer personnel is compensable. Regardless of the name given to the category of person who performs the work, we believe, as did the Arizona court, that the definition of legal assistant formulated by the American Bar Association Standing Committee on Legal Assistants provides appropriate guidance. Under that definition:

A legal assistant is a person, qualified through education, training, or work experience, who is employed or retained by a lawyer, law office, governmental agency, or other entity in a capacity or function which involves a performance, under the ultimate direction and supervision of an attorney, of specifically delegated substantive legal work, which work, for the most part, requires a sufficient knowledge of legal concepts that, absent such assistant, the attorney would perform the task.

The following criteria will be relevant in determining whether such services should be compensated: (1) the services performed by the non-lawyer personnel must be legal in nature; (2) the performance of these services must be supervised by an attorney; (3) the qualifications of the person performing the services must be specified in the request for fees in sufficient detail to demonstrate that the person is qualified by virtue of education, training, or work experience to perform substantive legal work; (4) the nature of the services performed must be specified in the request for fees in order to allow the reviewing court to

(continues)

determine that the services performed were legal rather than clerical; (5) as with attorney time, the amount of time expended must be set forth and must be reasonable; and (6) the amount charged must reflect reasonable community standards for charges by that category of personnel.

Employing these criteria, we allow only part of the fees requested for the legal assistant's services. He has requested compensation for preparing pleadings for duplication, preparing and delivering copies, requesting copies, and obtaining and delivering a docket sheet. We do not view this time as work which falls within these guidelines. We do allow an award for time spent preparing the briefs and related work. In computing the time we allow for him, we will assume, absent any other evidence in the record, that the hourly rate of $67.00 is reasonable for this type of work. We allow an award of $2,110.50 for 31.5 hours. We allow the recovery of fees for the time claimed by the legal editor for verifying citations and quotations. We disallow the time claimed for the legal clerk, which appears to consist primarily of obtaining copies of pleadings and organizing working copies of the pleadings. . . .

[The portion of the opinion dealing with the review of the attorneys' fees has been deleted.]

In sum, we conclude that the fees of non-lawyer personnel may be properly requested as part of an attorney fee award. In this case, applying the factors and considerations listed above, we award $23,055.50 plus $1,633.74 as a reasonable attorney fee on appeal, together with $134.65 costs on appeal.

Case Questions

1. What is the general theory put forward supporting the notion that legal assistant time can be recovered under a statute that does not specifically authorize it?

2. What specific qualifications would a legal assistant have to possess to meet the Court's test?

3. Why did the Court refuse certain portions of the bill that were allocated to the work of legal assistants?

4. How did the community standards come into play in this case?

Hawaii is another jurisdiction that allows legal assistant fees to be included with lawyer's fees in fee-shifting situations, even though its fee-shifting statute only mentions attorney's fees. *Blair v. Ing*, 31 P.3d 184 (Haw. 2001). Following the approach of *Missouri v. Jenkins* and state cases, the Hawaii Supreme Court concluded that it served the public interest to allow legal assistant fees to be separately recoverable, particularly because they are lower than the lawyer's fees that would obviously increase if they were the only allowable fees. But, the court refused to allow those fees that were secretarial in nature. Being a bit too voracious and inattentive for his own good, however, the requesting lawyer asked for fees for the three hours it took his paralegal to "prepare the record on appeal," an activity the Hawaii Supreme Court noted was always performed by the clerk of the court, per appellate rule, and thus denied the spurious request. *Id* at 191.

A more traditional approach to awarding legal assistant fees when the authorizing statute only mentions attorney's fees is the following case, which involved a suit for breach of contract, innocent misrepresentation, and **promissory estoppel** (a doctrine from the law of equity that allows one who relied on a promise of another to recover what was promised even though no enforceable contract existed under contract law). Although the court reached the opposite decision to that made in *Absher Const. Co. v. Kent School Dist. No. 415*, it did so with misgivings.

■ **promissory estoppel**

An exception to the requirement of "consideration," which is a required element to a valid contract. Generally, promissory estoppel allows a party who relied on the promise of another party to recover what was promised, even though the relying party would be unable to recover under contract law.

CASE LAW   *Joerger v. Gordon Food Service, Inc., 568*

N.W.2d 365 (Mich. App. 1997)

[The lawsuit involved Joerger suing Gordon Food Service for breach of contract, innocent misrepresentation, and promissory estoppel. Although Joerger won at trial, the jury awarded plaintiff no damages, and then the trial court granted Gordon Food Service's motion to award it attorney's fees as a sanction against Joerger for failing to settle the case following a mediation evaluation. State law allowed such a sanction, and the trial judge granted Gordon Food Service's request of $131,540 in attorney fees and also $7,348.95 in costs. Joerger appealed the verdict as well as the mediation sanction. The appellate court ruled against Joerger on almost all the issues presented in the appeal; these are not featured here in the text. The remaining issue, as the excerpts show, dealt with paralegal fees.] . . .

Plaintiffs also challenge the billings attributable to two individuals identified only by the initials "NAS" and "LAD." Plaintiffs argue that the individuals were not identified and no billing rate was provided for these individuals. Contrary to plaintiffs' assertions, the record reveals that these individuals were identified, by name, as two paralegals employed by defense counsel. Defendant also informed plaintiffs and the court that their hourly rate was $75. Accordingly, these arguments are without merit.

We do find merit, however, in plaintiffs' argument that the independent expenses attributable to the use of paralegals is not recoverable as costs. For purposes of mediation sanctions, "actual costs" include "those costs taxable in any civil action." MCR 2.403(O)(6). Chapter 24 of the Revised Judicature Act, M.C.L. § 600.2401 et seq.; M.S.A. § 27A.2401 et seq., governs costs. Taylor v. Anesthesia Associates of Muskegon, PC, 179 Mich.App. 384, 387, 445 N.W.2d 525 (1989). M.C.L. § 600.2405; M.S.A. § 27A.2405 provides that the following items may be taxed and awarded unless otherwise directed:

(continues)

CASE LAW *Joerger v. Gordon Food Service, Inc., 568* (continued)

1. Any of the fees of officers, witnesses, or other persons mentioned in this chapter or [M.C.L. § 600.2501 et seq.; M.S.A. § 27A.2501 et seq.] unless a contrary intention is stated.

2. Matters specially made taxable elsewhere in the statutes or rules.

3. The legal fees for any newspaper publication required by law.

4. The reasonable expense of printing any required brief and appendix in the supreme court, including any brief on motion for leave to appeal.

5. The reasonable costs of any bond required by law, including any stay of proceeding or appeal bond.

6. Any attorney fees authorized by statute or by court rule.

Our review of the provisions of the statute indicates nothing supporting an award of costs for expenses generated by paralegals. In the absence of statutory authorization, costs may not be awarded to recompense for a claimed litigation expense. Taylor, supra at 387–388, 445 N.W.2d 525.

Expenses generated by paralegals are also not recoverable as a separate component of mediation sanctions. Both MCR 2.403(O)(6) and M.C.L. § 600.2405; M.S.A. § 27A.2405 use the phrases "attorney fee" and "attorney fees." . . .

Clearly, attorney fees are not meant to compensate only work performed personally by members of the bar. Rather, the term must refer to a reasonable fee for the work product of an attorney that necessarily includes support staff. The rule allowing an award of attorney fees has traditionally anticipated the allowance of a fee sufficient to cover the office overhead of an attorney together with a reasonable profit. The inclusion of factor 5, the expenses incurred, reflects the traditional understanding that attorney fees should be sufficient to recoup at least a portion of overhead costs. Johnston v. Detroit Hoist & Crane Co., 142 Mich.App. 597, 601, 370 N.W.2d 1 (1985); Detroit Bank & Trust Co. v. Coopes, 93 Mich.App. 459, 468, 287 N.W.2d 266 (1979). Fixed overhead costs include such items as employee wages, rent, equipment rental, and so forth. *Id.* Thus, until a statute or a court rule specifies otherwise, the attorney fees must take into account the work not only of attorneys, but also of secretaries, messengers, paralegals, and others whose labor contributes to the work product for which an attorney bills a client, and it must also take account of other expenses and profit. We therefore must rule, albeit reluctantly, that the reasonable "attorney fees" should already include the work of paralegals, as well as that of attorneys and other factors underlying the fee. Accordingly, we remand in order for the trial court to reduce the award of attorney fees by the amount attributable to the independent paralegal billings.

(continues)

CASE LAW *Joerger v. Gordon Food Service, Inc., 568* (continued)

We, however, find it noteworthy that a growing number of our sister states have allowed an independent recovery of paralegal or legal assistant time in attorney fee awards under statute, rules of court, or decisional law authorizing awards of attorney fees. In most cases, with respect to paralegals and legal assistants, recovery is available "if a legal assistant performs work that has traditionally been done by any attorney." See, e.g., *Gill Savings Ass'n v. Int'l Supply Co., Inc.,* 759 S.W.2d 697, 702 (Tex.App., 1988). To qualify for such recovery, the evidence must establish: (1) that the legal assistant is qualified through education, training, or work experience to perform substantive legal work; (2) that substantive legal work was performed under the direction and supervision of an attorney; (3) the nature of the legal work that was performed; (4) the hourly rate being charged for the legal assistant; and (5) the number of hours expended by the legal assistant. *Id.*

We find that the increasing practice of allowing an independent recovery of paralegal or legal assistant time in attorney's fee awards has merit. We recognize that the day-to-day duties of a legal assistant will vary from law firm to law firm. If, however, the paralegal performs work that has traditionally been done by an attorney, we believe that it follows that a separate expense should be allowable. Neither statute nor court rule, however, currently allow such expenses as separate billable items. It is not our task to rewrite statutes. We therefore encourage the Legislature to change the statute or the Supreme Court to change the court rule to provide for appropriate billing for paralegal fees.

Affirmed in part, reversed in part, and remanded.

TAYLOR, Presiding Judge (concurring in part and dissenting in part).

I concur with the majority opinion except for that portion of part IV that holds that independent expenses attributable to the use of paralegals are not recoverable as mediation sanctions. Thus I would affirm the trial court's award of mediation sanctions that included costs attributable to paralegals.

The majority remands this case to the trial court with instructions that it reduce the award of attorney fees by the amount attributable to the independent paralegal billings because "attorney fees" must take into account the work not only of attorneys, but also of secretaries, messengers, paralegals, and others whose labor contributes to the work product for which an attorney bills a client. . . .

The flaw in the majority opinion is that its holding is dependent on how a law firm prepares its bills for the court. As I understand the holding, if the firm billed its client separately for paralegals or any other cost, such as secretaries or messengers, but, pursuant to prior agreed-to arrangements with the client, when submitting the billings to the trial court for mediation sanctions, folded those into "attorney fees," they would not run afoul of

(continues)

CASE LAW   *Joerger v. Gordon Food Service, Inc., 568* (continued)

the majority's holding. Presumably, all sophisticated firms who anticipate possible mediation sanctions will now adopt that procedure. We have, then, another puzzling fiction in a field where there are far too many now. . . .

Case Questions

1. Why did the court refuse to award paralegal fees even though it appeared to want to?

2. Why did the presiding judge disagree with the court's reasoning?

3. Which of the two preceding opinions do you find more legally persuasive?

On October 24, 2000, the Michigan Supreme Court amended Court Rule 2.626, which concerns attorney fees, so that it states the following:

"An award of attorney fees may include an award for the time and labor of any legal assistant who contributed nonclerical, legal support under the supervision of an attorney, provided the legal assistant meets the criteria set forth in Article 1, § 6 of the Bylaws of the State Bar of Michigan."

The Staff Comment to the new rule states that the change was made in response to *Joerger v. Gordon Food Service, Inc.*

ETHICAL CONSIDERATIONS FOR THE PARALEGAL

"When it comes to fees, the paralegal needs to keep two key thoughts in mind: do not set—or appear to set—legal fees, and be sure to accurately report billable time. Although the source of these directives is the operable lawyer ethics rules, the legal assistant ethics codes also speak to these concerns."

The Paralegal May Not Establish Fees

As discussed in Chapter 3, one of the acts commonly agreed to constitute the unauthorized practice of law is the establishment of legal fees. Almost all the national organizations that have created codes of ethics for legal assistants or paralegals specifically mention the prohibition against establishing fees. ABA Model Guidelines for the Utilization of Paralegal, Guideline 3(b); NALA Code of Ethics and Professional Responsibility, Canon 3(b); NALA Model Standards and Guidelines for Utilization of Legal Assistants, Guideline 2; NFPA Model Disciplinary Rules and Ethical Considerations, Rule 1.8. (This Rule is a general prohibition of the unauthorized practice of law.)

For those paralegals who engage in initial client interviews or who have regular client contact, it is especially critical that questions about legal fees or about the bill be directed to the supervising attorney. If a firm charges a fixed fee for certain kinds of work, some would say that a legal assistant is not establishing fees by answering a general question related to the amount of a fixed fee (or, for that matter, responding to a question about a particular lawyer's hourly rate). Nevertheless, erring on the side of caution is a safer way to deal with the billing questions of a client or prospective client. Concerning the preparation of the client's bill, at least one ethics opinion has stated that a firm may delegate to a non-lawyer the final authority for preparing the client's bill, but that the firm remains responsible for the ethics compliance of the bill (such as ensuring it is reasonable) and should supervise the non-lawyer accordingly. New York City Bar Association, Ethics Op. 94–9 (1994).

The Paralegal Must Report Accurate Hours

It is a fact of economics that profits increase as worker productivity increases and that productivity increases through speed and efficiency. The hamburger joint that serves twice as many customers in a day as its competitor will make twice as much money, assuming it does not employ twice as many employees as its competitor. Efficient employees are the key because efficiency increases productivity, which in turn increases profits.

The cloud in the silver lining to increased productivity is that one can only work so fast. Average billable hours for lawyers have increased dramatically in the last 40 years, and it is not uncommon for associates in large firms to bill more than 2,000 hours a year. As stated earlier in the chapter, billable hours for paralegals have also increased, and are approaching 1,500 hours a year, and even higher for some paralegals. And the temptation that faces lawyers under ever-present expectations to increase their billable hours can likewise face paralegals: pad their billable hours or double-bill. Such unethical activity is a two-headed monster. Not only is it illegal and wrong in and of itself, but it also can result in sanctions against the firm because lawyers are responsible for the misconduct of their non-lawyer employees.

The NFPA Model Disciplinary Rules and Ethical Considerations cuts right to the chase when speaking to honesty in billing. EC–1.2(c), says, "A paralegal shall ensure that all timekeeping and billing records prepared by the paralegal are thorough, accurate, and honest." Also, EC–1.2(d) states:

A paralegal shall not knowingly engage in fraudulent billing practices. Such practices may include, but are not limited to: inflation of hours billed to a client or employer; misrepresentation of the nature of tasks performed; and/or submission of fraudulent expense and disbursement documentation.

When paralegals and legal assistants have been caught engaging in dishonest billing practices, the result is the same as when lawyers get caught—the client gets a reduced bill or a refund. But because legal assistants are unlicensed, they cannot be subject to professional discipline unless issued by legal assistant or paralegal organizations. Regarding the pressure on paralegals to maintain their billable hours, Ohio does not allow law firms to pay its non-lawyer employees based on a percentage of their billable hours. Ohio State Bar Association, Ethics Op. 97–4 (1997). See Exhibit 7-12 for ethical considerations for paralegals and legal assistants.

EXHIBIT 7–12   ETHICAL CONSIDERATIONS FOR PARALEGALS AND LEGAL ASSISTANTS

- Paralegals and legal assistants may not establish legal fees.

- Paralegals and legal assistants must accurately report their billable hours:
  - No bill padding
  - No double billing

- Applicable Ethics Rules:
  - ABA Model Guidelines for the Utilization of Paralegal Services, Guideline 3 (b)
  - NALA Code of Ethics and Professional Responsibility, Canon 3(b)
  - NALA Model Standards and Guidelines for Utilization of Legal Assistants, Guideline 2
  - NFPA Model Disciplinary Rules and Ethical Considerations, EC-1.2(c),(d),(e)

Unbelievable Dedication to One's Job

A curious example of overeager diligence is the bankruptcy case, *In re Maruko Inc.*, 160 B.R. 633 (S.D. Cal. 1993). The case involved the bankruptcy judge's review of almost $2 million in requested attorneys' fees and costs. The fees were attributed to thirteen attorneys, three paralegals, and a few courier services. While the court reduced some portion of the fees for all of the lawyers and paralegals due to inappropriate or double billing, the first paralegal discussed in the case really caught the attention of the judge. After attempting to make sense of all the handwritten notes, arrows, and circles made by the paralegal to her original time sheet after the bankruptcy trustee's protests, the judge compared the mess to a diagram for a football play, and found her makeshift justification for her bill to be "incomprehensible." *Id* at 643. Furthermore, the judge noted that the paralegal billed in excess of 24 hours a day *three times! Id.* Needless to say, the judge reduced that paralegal's portion of the bill in the amount of $20,700. *Id.* And there were still two paralegals' bills yet to be reduced because of duplicity. Fortunately for all the paralegals, their names were withheld. One wonders if they were members of any paralegal or legal assistant organizations and, if so, whether they were sanctioned for their considerable contrivances.

SUMMARY

There are three prevalent kinds of legal fees. An hourly rate is charged for the lawyer's time, measured in increments. Hourly rates vary throughout the country, but more experienced attorneys and partners charge more per hour than associates. A blended rate is an average rate of higher and lower hourly rates that is applied to the work of all lawyers working on a matter. A contingency fee is a percentage of whatever the lawyer recovers for the client or, in certain situations, saves for the client. Contingency fee percentages increase as the lawyer's efforts for the client increase, with percentages ranging from 25 percent at settlement to 45 percent after appeal. Contingency fees are controversial when they appear to exploit the client or harm the general welfare of the country because of their sheer size. A fixed fee is a predetermined amount that is charged for the lawyer's services. Fixed fees are more common for routine legal services, such as the preparation of basic wills.

The key rules that govern legal fees are the Model Rules' Rule 1.5 and the Model Code's Rule DR 2–106. MR 1.5 prohibits fees and expenses that are unreasonable, while DR 2–106 prohibits fees that are clearly excessive. Both versions list eight nonexclusive variables that factor into the equation of what makes a fee reasonable, and some of those factors include the following: the time and labor involved; whether the lawyer will be precluded from taking other cases while working on the client's case; the results obtained; and the experience, reputation, and ability of the lawyer involved. Not everything a lawyer does can be billed to the client, and overhead expenses for a law office are usually not billable. Where statutes place caps on legal fees, a lawyer may not exceed those limits, even if the client agrees to the higher fee.

Despite the fee agreement reached between the lawyer and client, courts always have jurisdiction to review the fee for reasonableness. Courts generally find fees to be unreasonable or excessive if the lawyer has taken advantage of the client. Such instances of overreaching involve the lawyer failing to reduce the bill if it turns out that very little effort is needed to obtain the client's objectives or if the lawyer works exceptionally slowly to increase the bill. A lawyer also may not bill the client for his own incompetence or for acts that could have been done by the lawyer's legal assistant, but instead were done by the lawyer so those acts could be billed at a higher hourly rate.

Legal fees must be clearly explained to the client. Although neither the Model Rules nor the Model Code require that all legal fees be explained to the client in writing, it is recommended. Three critical areas of explanation the client should receive concerning fees involve: the explanation the new client should receive; the difference between fees and costs; and the difference between an advance and a retainer. The rules require that the fee agreement be promptly explained to the new client, although, again, there is no requirement that the fees be explained in writing. Fees are what the lawyer expects to be paid for the representation, while costs are expenses incurred during the representation and which the client is usually expected to pay. Courts favor the client when confusion arises over his understanding about fees versus costs. If the paralegal's time is billed on an hourly rate, then the lawyer must explain to the client the paralegal's contribution to the bill. If the client is expected to pay any money up front, then the lawyer also must clearly explain to the client the difference between an advance and a retainer. An advance is a prepayment of the lawyer's fee. Because a prepayment is yet to be earned, an advance is subject to being returned. A retainer, often called a general retainer, is a payment made to secure the lawyer's availability. Because of the nature of a retainer, it is earned upon payment, which traditionally makes it a nonrefundable payment, although jurisdictions are starting to oppose that payments made to lawyers be considered nonrefundable.

MR 1.15 and DR 9–102 concern the keeping of the client's money and require that it be kept separately from the lawyer's money. Such commingling can lead to conversion of the client's property. Therefore, lawyers set up client trust accounts to keep the client's money separate. The rules on keeping the client's money separate apply whenever the lawyer possesses property in which the client has an interest, including cases where the lawyer and client dispute the lawyer's bill. Every jurisdiction has in place an IOLTA program that requires the interest earned on client trust accounts that are nominal or of a short duration to be turned over to the bar association, which uses the funds for low-cost legal services.

There are specific rules, found in MR 1.5, that concern contingent fees. First, contingent fee agreements are required to be in writing, and under Ethics 2000 are required to be signed by the client. The current version of 1.5 also requires that the written contingent fee agreement discuss how expenses will be billed to the client. The Model Code, however, does not require that contingent fee agreements be in writing, but certain jurisdictions that operate under the Model Code do require written contingent fee agreements. Contingent fee agreements also need to clearly detail how the fee is to be determined. Both the Model Rules and the Model Code prohibit contingent fee agreements in criminal cases, and the Model Rules also prohibit contingency fees in domestic relations cases.

Lawyers in different firms are allowed to share legal fees under certain circumstances, including when the client agrees to the fee sharing. The rules, however, prohibit lawyers from sharing legal fees with non-lawyers. The policy behind such a prohibition—whether the non-lawyer is an independent contractor, paralegal, or any other non-lawyer employee—is the protection of the lawyer's professional judgment and independence. Illegal fee-sharing contracts between a lawyer and a non-lawyer are generally considered to be void. An exception is made for the non-lawyer employee, allowing them to be compensated with bonuses or retirement plans, as long as the extra compensation comes from the net proceeds of legal fees and no bonus is given with respect to a specific case.

Paralegal and legal assistant fees can be recovered under statutes that provide for lawyer fees to be recovered by the opposing party. At the federal level, the U.S. Supreme Court declared, in *Missouri v. Jenkins*, that legal assistant fees could be recovered at the market rate in federal lawsuits, even though the statute only mentions the recovery of lawyer fees. At the state level, many jurisdictions also allow for the recovery of paralegal fees through statutes or case law. In cases where paralegal fees are recoverable, they are generally only recoverable if the efforts of the paralegal are substantive, rather than clerical.

As mentioned in the Model Rules and the Model Code, as well as the national rules of ethics for paralegals and legal assistants, non-lawyer employees may not establish legal fees. Those paralegals who have client contact must be careful to avoid discussing a client's bill in ways that violate that prohibition. Furthermore, all paralegals who engage in hourly billing must report accurate and honest time sheets and must not engage in double billing or padding the bill.

ETHICS IN ACTION

1. Katie is suing her sister Mimi over their mother's will, which left everything to Mimi, including the lake house that had been in their mother's family for two generations. Calling it a house is rather generous; it is really a shanty with two bedrooms, a small living room, a galley kitchen, a weather-worn porch, and one and a half baths—with the half serving as a tiny pantry for the kitchen. The house was used in summers, as were most such cottages since they were built in the 1950s. That was before folks got the idea that lake properties were for year-round living, and before real estate brokers got the idea that lake cottages should be called houses, and should then be torn down and replaced by narrow McMansions. Katie believes her mother's Alzheimer's disease caused her to leave a will that provided only for Mimi. She is attempting to have her mother's estate put into intestacy, so that she can inherit half of the estate, which really consists of the lake cottage, now worth about $1 million. Katie's lawyer Nicole is taking the case under the following arrangement: If Katie wins, Nicole will be paid one-third of whatever Katie inherits. Ultimately, Katie is hoping to force a sale of the lake property, so she can get the cash.

   Is this an allowable contingency fee arrangement?

2. Tony is a noted divorce lawyer with a reputation for aggressive tactics toward opposing lawyers and their clients. If you want to make your spouse rue the day he ever met you, much less left you, call Tony and hope that your spouse hasn't hired

   (continues)

ETHICS IN ACTION *(continued)*

him first. In return for making your former mate wretched, Tony will charge you an exorbitant sum. You will likely decide to never remarry, just to be certain you'll never need Tony again. Because of his reputation and results, Tony charges $500 an hour, and requires a $15,000 advance payment. He has cases throughout the state, and, while driving, Tony constantly makes cell phone calls and uses his Blackberry at red lights and highway construction delays. His clients know that he charges for travel time, but they don't know that he engages in billable activities while traveling.

Can Tony bill the clients for whom he is traveling, and bill the other clients for whom he is making phone calls and other communication? If not, whose bill should get cut?

3. Heidi is a tax attorney who represents individuals and businesses. She advises them about changes in tax law, assists their accountants with preparations of their tax forms, and represents them when the IRS claims they should have paid more taxes. When she signs a new client, she informs them of her billing rate ($300 an hour), explains what costs are and how they are billed, and provides them with a written fee agreement. Heidi also introduces her clients to her paralegals, and explains the role they serve in her firm, which includes tax law research and client contact. Nothing is said about whether the paralegals' work is billed separately or is part of Heidi's hourly rate. Heidi does bill her paralegals' work separately, at the rate of $75 an hour, which reduces the overall fee considerably, although she doesn't list it separately in the clients' bills.

Is this method of billing a client allowed in your jurisdiction?

4. Keith works at a law firm with ten lawyers, where he is one of seven paralegals. Three of the paralegals work primarily for the firm's personal injury attorneys, three work for the estate planning attorneys, and Keith works for the two bankruptcy attorneys. As a result of the massive overhaul in the federal bankruptcy act, the bankruptcy attorneys have been swamped. Scores of new clients have come through the doors trying to file bankruptcy before the new bankruptcy laws go into effect, because it was been reported in the news that the new laws will be much stricter and more onerous on debtors. In the months leading up to the effective date of the new bankruptcy act, the two attorneys have filed hundreds of bankruptcies. Naturally, Keith's workload was also increased, and during that time, he probably averaged over 65 hours a week. Keith's firm does not pay overtime, even though the federal overtime exemptions do not apply to any of the firm's paralegals. However, the firm does pay its paralegals an annual bonus, tied to their performance reviews. Keith's two lawyers believe that his work during this client deluge warrants more than the maximum annual bonus he can receive. They get permission to have him

(continues)

ETHICS IN ACTION   *(continued)*

granted an extra week of vacation, and then Keith's two supervising lawyers send him on an all-expenses-paid skiing trip to Colorado, which includes air fare, a rental car, five nights in a ski lodge, and lift tickets. The firm's other paralegals are unaware that Keith's bosses have paid for his trip.

Does this vacation violate the prohibition against fee sharing between lawyers and non-lawyers?

5. Efficiency is rewarded at Carolyn's job, so much so that at the law firm where she works, Carolyn can earn almost as much as she likes. Carolyn's law firm works exclusively on filing worker's compensation claims for employees who have been denied benefits, and the firm is located downtown near the federal courthouse in a large city. The firm advertises heavily on radio, and on billboards located strategically near industrial parks. As prospective clients come through the doors of her firm, Carolyn gives them a worker's compensation information form to complete and later interviews those persons, taking down any pertinent information not included on the intake form. She types a summary of key facts regarding the prospective clients she has interviewed, and then provides those documents to her boss Russ, who decides whether he should take the case. The key to his practice is volume, and the key to volume is organization. Russ pays Carolyn an hourly rate, plus a flat rate of $10 for every person she interviews, and another $15 for every person who becomes Russ's client.

Does that compensation package violate the prohibition on fee sharing with lawyers and non-lawyers?

6. Maureen knows the dangers of practicing law, having been sued for malpractice once, and having had three grievances filed against her. Thankfully, Maureen successfully defended herself against the malpractice claim, and all three grievances went her way. What has remained with Maureen, however, was the fright she experienced when she realized that the clients she tried so hard to represent turned on her. In the grievance cases, the clients (about whom Maureen had a strange feeling) complained about their bills, demanding the bills be greatly reduced, and then filed a complaint with the disciplinary commission, alleging Maureen had neglected their cases or charged too much. The malpractice case resulted from Maureen trying to collect an unpaid fee from a client who then decided the best way to respond to the collection agency was to sue Maureen. Maureen has a new policy: If a client complains about their bill twice, after the second complaint, Maureen will reduce the bill 10 percent in an attempt to keep the client from doing what the former clients did to her. Maureen has informed her paralegal Cassidy of this secret

(continues)

ETHICS IN ACTION   *(continued)*

policy and has told Cassidy that Cassidy has the authority to reduce a client's bill by the same percentage and under the same circumstances as Maureen would choose to reduce the bill, if Maureen is out of the office when the client contacts the firm to complain.

Would Cassidy be establishing legal fees by doing this?

7. Samuel won an age discrimination claim in federal court for a female news anchor. The anchor was fired from a local television news station because the station manager thought the woman's best days were behind her. The trial judge allowed Samuel to turn his bill in to the court as part of the process of having the defendant pay Samuel's bill. This fee-shifting request includes the paralegal portion of Samuel's bill. According to Samuel's request, his two paralegals worked a total of 250 hours on the case. Their average market rate is $80 an hour (which is about 10 percent more than similar lawyers in Sam's county charge for their paralegals' time) and their average cost is $20 an hour. The request for fee shifting states that Andrew, Samuel's newest paralegal, worked about 100 hours on the case. Andrew has no paralegal education, but did attend a semester of law school. The request also states that Katie, Samuel's most senior paralegal, worked about 150 hours on the case. Katie has an associate's degree in paralegal studies and a bachelor's degree in political science. There is little detail on what each paralegal did, although they both filed affidavits stating they did substantive legal work on the case. Nothing presented in the fees request shows how the paralegals' work was supervised. The defendant has opposed Samuel's fee request, arguing that his portion of the bill is unreasonable, equaling 50 percent of the plaintiff's judgment. Included in his opposition is the claim that Samuel's paralegals' fees should not be recoverable because they aren't lawyers.

What, if any, of Samuel's paralegals' fees should be recoverable?

■ POINTS TO PONDER

1. Do you think the idea of prepaid legal insurance makes sense?

2. What is a contingent fee? What distinguishes a lawful contingent fee from an unlawful one?

3. Do you think the government should place limits on all contingency fees or eliminate them altogether? Why or why not?

4. What goes into determining whether a lawyer's fee is reasonable? Which of the eight factors listed in MR 1.5(a) or DR 2–106(B) do you think is the most relevant?

5. Why is it that a lawyer cannot bill the client for everything the lawyer does? What kinds of acts would qualify as being nonbillable?

6. Does your jurisdiction place caps on fees collected in certain kinds of cases? Are statutory limits on fees a violation of someone's freedom to make a contract?

7. What would make a lawyer's fee unreasonable or excessive simply because it is too high?

8. Assuming a fee agreement was put in writing, what kinds of information should it include, particularly if the client was new?

9. What is the difference between legal fees and costs? Why is it important that the distinction be made?

10. What is the difference between an advance and a retainer, and why does it matter?

11. When a client makes an advance payment to their lawyer, where should the money go?

12. What is an IOLTA program, and how does it work? What is your view on the constitutionality of an IOLTA?

13. Why is it that the Model Rules require contingency fee agreements to be in writing and signed by the client? If you are in a Model Code jurisdiction, does your set of rules still require written contingent fee agreements?

14. What information should a contingent fee agreement contain?

15. What kinds of cases are generally prohibited from being taken on a contingent fee, and why? What kind of domestic relations case could be taken on a contingent fee?

16. Why do you think the client must consent to fee sharing between lawyers of different firms?

17. How could the lawyer's judgment be negatively affected if the lawyer were allowed to share fees with a non-lawyer?

18. What exceptions to the fee-sharing rules apply to the non-lawyer employee? What parameters determine whether such exceptions are appropriate?

19. At the end of the film *Erin Brockovich* (as in the real-life case on which the film was based), Erin's lawyer made her a millionaire. Was that an appropriate payment?

20. Do you think a lawyer should be required to honor a fee-sharing agreement made with a paralegal even if it violates the rules on fee sharing?

21. Does your jurisdiction have a court rule or statute that expressly allows for the recovery of paralegal fees where the law allows for the recovery of attorney fees?

22. Given that the U.S. Supreme Court decided *Missouri v. Jenkins*, under what circumstances could a court still refuse to award paralegal fees?

23. What kind of statements, if any, could the legal assistant make to the prospective client concerning the lawyer's fee while still avoiding the establishment of fees?

24. Do you think paralegals should not work under a billable hours format, so as to avoid the pressure to engage in some of the false billing practices in which lawyers occasionally engage?

25. What significant changes did Ethics 2000 make to the rules on fees?

26. Is there anything not covered by the rules on fees that you think should be addressed?

■ KEY CONCEPTS_____

Advance	Litigation costs
Bill padding	Nonbillable activities
Commingling	Non-lawyer fee sharing
Contingent fee	Prepaid legal insurance
Double billing	Reasonable fee
Fixed fee	Recovery of paralegal/legal assistant fees
Hourly rate	Reverse contingent fee
Interest on lawyers' trust account	Statutorily limited fees

■ KEY TERMS_____

401k plan	conversion	promissory estoppel
advance	double billing	public policy
alimony	equity partner	quantum merit
bill padding	fixed fee	reverse contingent fee
certificates of deposits (CDs)	gross revenue	subrogation
commingling	legal treatise.	
contingent fee	NOW account	

Online Companion™
For additional resources, please go to
http://www.paralegal.delmar.cengage.com

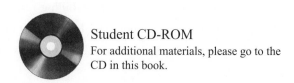

Student CD-ROM
For additional materials, please go to the
CD in this book.

8

Miscellaneous Ethics Issues

INTRODUCTION

There are some rules of ethics, as well as corresponding ethics opinions and cases, which are beyond the scope of this book because they do not closely relate to paralegals and legal assistants. There are also rules of ethics that should be of concern to non-lawyer employees, but are not neatly organized in discrete fashion, as are the confidentiality rules or the conflicts of interest rules. This chapter will explore a variety of those miscellaneous ethics rules, many of which concern litigation. First, there will be an analysis of the legal team's duty to provide the client with competent representation, including the need to adequately communicate with the client. Next, there will be an examination of ethics rules that concern the legal team's duty to be truthful with courts, clients, represented persons, and unrepresented persons. A summary of the rules that apply to those who work for prosecuting attorneys' offices will be reviewed. There will also be an inquiry into if there are circumstances under which a non-lawyer, including a paralegal, could be personally liable for legal malpractice. Finally, this chapter will close by examining the obligation on lawyers and paralegals that they reach out to their communities by providing pro bono services.

COMPETENCE

The very first rule of the ABA Model Rules of Professional Conduct is not about confidentiality or conflicts of interest, but rather concerns competence. ABA Model Rule 1.1 states, "A lawyer shall provide competent representation to

> "After twenty-five years' observation, I can give it as the condensed history of most, if not all, good lawyers, that they lived well and died poor."

DANIEL WEBSTER, NINETEENTH-CENTURY LAWYER AND STATESMAN EXTRAORDINAIRE

> "I have watched with great sadness the decline in esteem held by our society of lawyers."

SANDRA DAY O'CONNOR, UNITED STATES SUPREME COURT JUSTICE, 1981–2006

a client. Competent representation requires the legal knowledge, skill, thoroughness and preparation reasonably necessary for the representation." The ABA Model Code of Professional Responsibility has a similar provision; ABA DR 6–101(A) prohibits a lawyer from taking a case that "he knows or should know that he is not competent to handle, without associating himself with a lawyer who is competent to handle it." There are no Ethics 2000 changes to the text of MR 1.1, except for a few additions to the Comments. See Exhibit 8–1 on an overview of what is meant by the requirement that the legal team be "competent."

EXHIBIT 8–1   COMPETENCE AND THE LEGAL TEAM

- ABA Model Rule 1.1 – "A lawyer shall provide competent representation to a client."
- <u>What does competence require?</u>
  - **Preparation** – *Possessing the legal skills and knowledge necessary to adequately represent the client*
  - **Diligence** – *ABA Model Rule 1.3*
  - **Communication** – *ABA Model Rule 1.4*
- The lawyer's duty of communication <u>may not be completely delegated to the paralegal</u>.

Preparation

Obviously, a lawyer must be prepared to handle the client's needs, be they litigation related or transactional, (such as creating an **estate plan**). And as the Rules and Comments attest, a lawyer must possess the legal knowledge and skills needed to be competent. The legal knowledge required to adequately represent a client involves more than knowing the substantive law of the underlying matter (for instance, knowing the difference between a partnership and a limited partnership), but also knowing the procedural minutiae of the jurisdiction, including the state and local court rules. **Forms books** that help lawyers draft pleadings or motions and professional practice series volumes that help lawyers apply statutes and court rules to specific areas of practice can be valuable tools in bringing one up to speed. Remember from Chapter 7, however, that the client should not be billed for the time it takes a practitioner to reach a stage of competence.

For a Tennessee lawyer representing a murder defendant, being incompetent would have been quite an accomplishment. Despite never representing anyone accused of a felony, much less murder, he neither sought the assistance

---

■ **estate plan**

A legal structure designed to pass on one's assets to others in life and at death, and to minimize estate taxes and probate costs.

■ **forms books**

Books that have samples of various kinds of complaints, answers, and other litigation documents.

of an experienced criminal lawyer nor even the rules of criminal procedure. Astonishingly, he filed an answer and an amended answer to the indictment, which actually helped the prosecution because, like an answer (a pleading meant for a civil case), it set forth the defendant's version of events! In another matter, the same lawyer, never having been admitted to practice in federal court nor having cracked open the Federal Rules of Civil Procedure, filed a civil rights case in federal court, alleging that his client was libeled and his civil rights were violated because he received pornography in the mail. Not surprisingly, his case was dismissed. The lawyer's license was suspended for two years as a result of his glaring incompetence in those and two other cases. *Office of Disciplinary Counsel v. Henry*, 664 S.W.2d 62 (Tenn, 1983).

For the new lawyer, as with anyone who is attempting something new, there is the dreaded learning curve. If one's first day on the job is one's worst day on the job, then things can only get better with experience. Unfortunately, however, the new lawyer is bound by the same competency requirement that affects the most experienced lawyer in the jurisdiction. That leaves new lawyers with a disproportionate competency burden, for which courts will still hold them accountable. (See *Lewis v. State Bar*, 621 P.2d 258 (Cal. 1981), where, in a concurring opinion, a Justice stated that law schools should do more to prepare students for law practice.) Even in a firm where the new lawyer is expected to sink or swim, it is incumbent on her to ask for help. In a tragicomedy from Indiana, a new lawyer was severely disciplined for a web of deceit created to cause his clients—who were contesting a will—to think he was proceeding with their case. Greed was not the cause of his deceit, ignorance was. He was assigned the case by partners in his firm and had no earthly idea what to do. His ever-escalating, three-year sham included telling his clients of the progress in their case and telling them that a trial had been scheduled and then postponed, none of which was true. Eventually, he took his clients to the statehouse in Indianapolis, telling them he had an appointment concerning their case with the Indiana Supreme Court, and then telling them, after entering and reentering different doors of the statehouse, that the appointment had been postponed. As he eventually acknowledged in the disciplinary matter that somewhere in his gut he knew what was coming, his troubles stemmed not just from the fact that he lacked the skills to handle the litigation, but because he was embarrassed to ask others in his firm for help. *In re Deardorff*, 426 N.E. 2d 689 (Ind. 1981).

Diligence

Connected to the duty of competence is diligence, and ABA Model Rule 1.3 states, "A lawyer shall act with reasonable diligence and promptness in representing a client." The Model Code's DR 6–101(A)(3) mandates that a lawyer should not "[n]eglect a legal matter entrusted to him." And Ethical

Consideration 6–4 states that a lawyer needs to "give appropriate attention to his legal work." The Ethics 2000 Commission made no changes to Model Rule 1.3, but proposed a few more Comments to the rule, which were accepted by the House of Delegates.

Diligence is a necessary component of competence because, regardless of a lawyer's superior legal knowledge and skill, the duty of competence would be violated if a lawyer neglects the client's matter, fails to meet deadlines, or seeks unreasonable delays. One of the Comments to Model Rule 1.3 puts it plainly: "Perhaps no professional shortcoming is more widely resented than procrastination."

Reasonable diligence applies throughout all stages of the client's case, from investigating the facts and law sufficiently to know the applicable statute of limitations, to staying abreast of discovery timetables and court dates and completing tasks necessary to protect the client's interests in the event of a positive or negative judgment. In a case that would make a dead turtle look fast by comparison, a New York lawyer who filed a personal injury complaint on behalf of his client neglected the case for 14 years. Upon being investigated for his dilatory tactics, the lawyer claimed that it was his litigation strategy to delay the case until the opposing party's best witness was no longer available. The court took the view that such a strange strategy would have been impossible for the lawyer to concoct because he never investigated the client's case after filing the complaint; thus, he could not have known who that witness was. *In re Kovitz*, 504 N.Y.S.2d 400 (App. Div. 1986).

A lawyer's duty to be diligent also extends to the ending of the lawyer-client relationship, requiring that she inform the client if intending to withdraw from the case. Failure to do so subjects a lawyer to sanction. An extreme example of this failure is a Colorado case in which a lawyer was disbarred in absentia for leaving 60 clients in the lurch after he abandoned his law practice and left the state. *People v. Crist*, 948 P.2d 1020 (Colo. 1997).

As a result of both the tireless efforts of paralegal organizations to promote the value of its members and the growing acknowledgment of those members by employing lawyers, much substantive legal work is assigned to paralegals and legal assistants. But assigning work to one's paralegals does not relieve the lawyer of the obligation to follow through on the matter. Where lawyers simply assign their cases to their non-lawyer employees without any direction or supervision, disciplinary courts have considered those lawyers to have inappropriately withdrawn from representation. *See Matter of Robinson*, 495 S.E.2d 28 (Ga. 1998).

Communication

Are you old enough to remember a certain line of books on improving relationships and interpersonal communication skills, all with some form of the title, *Men Are from Mars, Women Are from Venus*. Pop psychologist John Gray sold millions of his *Mars...Venus* books in the 1990s in bookstores and on infomercials. Well, how long will it be before there is a *Lawyers Are from Mars, Clients . . .* book on communication for legal professionals? It would seem that if one were to read all the books on improving one's communication skills, there would be no time left over to actually talk to anyone. But, in fact, poor communication is a significant cause of client grievances filed with bar associations or disciplinary committees. In Indiana, for example, the state Supreme Court's disciplinary commission reports that about 35 percent of the grievances filed against lawyers involve allegations of lack of client communication, which includes nondiligence in the representation. (The upside to that data may be that it is better that the largest category of client complaints against lawyers concern communication and diligence failures instead of misdeeds such as fraud or illegal conduct.)

The duty to communicate with clients is expressly covered in ABA Model Rule 1.4, which in its Ethics 2000 version states:

  a. A lawyer shall:

> 1. promptly inform the client of any decision or circumstance with respect to which the client's informed consent, as defined in Rule 1.0(e), is required by these Rules;
>
> 2. reasonably consult with the client about the means by which the client's objectives are to be accomplished;
>
> 3. keep the client reasonably informed about the status of a matter;
>
> 4. promptly comply with reasonable requests for information; and
>
> 5. consult with the client about any relevant limitation on the lawyer's conduct when the lawyer knows that that the client expects assistance not permitted by the Rules of Professional Conduct or other law.

  b. A lawyer shall explain a matter to the extent reasonably necessary to permit the client to make informed decisions regarding the representation.

This current version is much more elongated than its prior version. The ABA Model Code has no singular counterpart, although a variety of Disciplinary Rules and Ethical Considerations discuss the lawyer's duty to not neglect a client's case, and to promptly inform a client about material developments. *See* DR 6–101(A)3; EC 7–8; EC 9–2.

The duty to communicate with the client becomes more difficult to honor as a lawyer's caseload increases, but nonetheless, she must maintain open lines of communication with the client through all stages of the case. There are many disciplinary cases with instances of lawyers being sanctioned for inadequate client communication, from failing to inform the client of the legal proceedings undertaken or material changes in the case and failing to respond to the client's requests for information about the status of the case in a timely manner, to failing to inform the client of mistakes made or about the conclusion of the case, and even failing to inform the client that the lawyer has withdrawn from the case or left the law firm.

Often in litigation, settlement negotiations take place in the absence of the parties as the lawyers haggle over settlement offers or the language of the settlement agreement. Nevertheless, the Rules, the Comments, and the case law make it clear that a lawyer must communicate all settlement offers with the client unless she knows the client will reject the offer. And because the client is the decision maker concerning the substance of her case, the lawyer must keep her reasonably well informed so that she can make informed decisions.

Competence and the Legal Assistant

As a member of the legal team, the legal assistant has a corresponding duty to provide competent and diligent services. As discussed in Chapter 2, ABA Model Rule 5.3, which is operative in most jurisdictions, requires partners and supervising lawyers to make reasonable efforts to ensure that their non-lawyer employees comport themselves with the same professional obligations as if they were lawyers.

What Makes a Legal Assistant Competent?

Canon 6 of the NALA Code of Ethics and Professional Responsibility requires a legal assistant to "maintain integrity and a high degree of competency through education and training . . . and through continuing education." The NALA Model Standards and Guidelines for Utilization of Legal Assistants discusses competency in its section on standards and lists seven different standards, many of them education related, that help determine a legal assistant's minimum qualifications. The NFPA Model Disciplinary Rules and Ethical Considerations speaks to the issue of competence in Rule 1.1, where it states, "A paralegal shall achieve and maintain a high level of competence." Three Ethical Considerations amplify the preceding maxim. EC–1.1(a) states that competency is achieved through education, training, and work experience; EC–1.1(b) requires a paralegal to participate in continuing education; and EC–1.1(c) concerns diligence, requiring a paralegal to "perform all assignments promptly and efficiently."

The law has such a broad horizon that the **West Digest System**, a research tool every paralegal should know how to use, is organized under 400-plus separate topics and has over 100,000 individual lines. There are federal and state statutes, federal and state administrative rules, and federal and state rules of court, not to mention local versions of the previously described kinds of primary authority. Because an overwhelming majority of American jurisdictions do not require certain prerequisites for one to work as a paralegal or legal assistant, or to use those titles, competence may be in the eye of the beholder—the employer.

■ **west digest system**
A method for researching case law, in which the law is divided into 400-plus topics, which are then divided into thousands of subtopics. When matched together, each topic and subtopic is known by its title and "key number" and corresponds to the key numbers of the headnotes for the cases, which are found by using a Thomson West-published digest.

For more information on the multiplicity of research assistance and guides offered by Westlaw®, including how to use digests, engage in legal research, and legal writing, click on "Free Westlaw User Guides" when you are on the following link from Westlaw's Web site: http://www.westgroup.com/westlaw/. Westlaw's competitor, Lexis, offers its own version of user-friendly legal research services, and one can learn about all that Lexis has to offer by accessing http://www.lexisnexis.com.

Despite an acknowledgment that "competence" can be an amorphous concept, there are certain competency factors about which all paralegal and legal assistant organizations are in agreement. First, one should get a high-quality education from an accredited college whose legal program is a member of the American Association for Paralegal Education and is either ABA approved or in compliance with ABA curriculum standards. Second, all those who work in a legal environment need to take **continuing legal education (CLE)** courses. Lawyers must earn a minimum number of CLE credits annually to maintain their law licenses. In Indiana, for instance, lawyers need to earn 36 hours in a three-year cycle, with a minimum of six hours per year. The procrastinating Hoosier lawyer who gets the minimum in the first two years will need to find and attend enough approved seminars to meet the remaining 24 hours.

Paralegals and legal assistants should try to do the same, although it can be difficult for them to earn annual CLE credits if their employers will not subsidize the cost of those courses. Both the NALA and NFPA require certification-bearing members to earn continuing legal education credits and, as discussed in Chapter 2, jurisdictions that offer paralegal or legal assistant memberships in their bar associations almost always require annual CLE requirements, including legal ethics CLEs. Considering that a half-day seminar can cost upward of several hundred dollars, it takes considerable commitment to stay current, even if required, to maintain one's certification.

The Paralegal and Client Communication

Because the economics of paralegal–client contact are favorable, paralegals often communicate with clients on behalf of lawyers. Interviewing clients, assisting clients in discovery matters, taking client phone calls, and writing correspondence to clients are just some of the ways in which the use of paralegals is beneficial both to clients and to law firms. Little things, such as returning client phone calls in a timely way and sending the client courtesy copies of all documents prepared on her behalf, can go a long way to prevent her from becoming disgruntled and in the mood to file a grievance against the lawyer.

Nevertheless, a lawyer's duty to communicate with clients cannot be completely delegated to non-lawyer employees because the responsibility for honoring the communication duty rests with the lawyer. For example, in a Kansas case, a lawyer with a high-volume bankruptcy practice ran his law firm through hiring over a dozen paralegals but giving them very little training. Judges repeatedly cautioned the lawyer about his shoddy law practice, to which he responded by repeatedly blaming his employees. Eventually, three of those

continuing legal education (cle)

A lawyer must earn certain annual CLE credits, as determined by the jurisdiction in which she is licensed. CLE credits, commonly called CLEs, are earned by attending bar-sponsored or bar-approved seminars that concern different practice areas of the law. Lawyers must also earn continuing legal ethics credits as part of their annual CLE requirements.

former employees contacted the state bar's disciplinary administrator, telling of their former employer's practices. The evidence showed the lawyer's complete lack of supervision of his paralegals and failure to communicate with his clients. It was stupefying that on one occasion the lawyer divided 30 days' worth of past phone messages among his employees, telling them to find out what the callers wanted. He was suspended from the practice of law indefinitely. *In re Farmer*, 950 P.2d 713 (Kan. 1997).

In the following case, a lawyer was held responsible for failing to communicate with his client and allowing his non-lawyer employees to commit the unauthorized practice of law because of his failure to supervise them and his sole reliance on their contact with his client.

CASE LAW *Mays v. Neal*

938 S.W.2d 830 (Ark. 1997)

GLAZE, Justice

This dispute arose after Mays's law firm, Mays & Crutcher, P.A., undertook to represent Vanessa Conley, who on July 18, 1994, was involved in a motor vehicle accident in Little Rock. The other vehicle involved in the accident was a rental car, which was insured by Empire Insurance Company. At the scene of the accident, a man, later known to be Tim Mason, approached Conley, asking her who caused the accident. Conley said that Mason identified himself as an investigator, and suggested Conley needed legal representation. This interchange resulted in Conley signing a contract employing Mays as her attorney. Mason gave Conley a business card bearing the name of Catherine Stevens and instructed Conley that Stevens was the person Conley should call.[1] Stevens later sent a copy of Conley's contract to Empire, along with her business card.

Conley said that, on July 19, 1994, Stevens called Conley's home and spoke with her husband, and Conley says she returned the call on July 20, 1994. Conley claims that, during her conversation with Stevens, Stevens referred her to the Price Chiropractic Clinic. Conley was subsequently treated by the Price Clinic from about July 25, 1994, to October 21, 1994. In November 1994, negotiations to settle Conley's claim took place between Stevens and Chuck Traylor, who was the claims adjuster with Empire Insurance Co. Some confusion and differences occurred between Stevens and Conley over the method and amount of payment Conley would approve before reaching any settlement. Conley also expressed that, although she had been released by the Price Clinic, she was still having pain and needed to see another doctor. Conley became dissatisfied with the manner in which her case was being handled, and on November 30, 1994, she went to Mays's office to retrieve her file. While Stevens retained possession of Conley's file because Mays was not present, it

(continues)

CASE LAW *Mays v. Neal* (continued)

is clear the Mays-Conley relationship had been severed by December 6, 1994—the date Stevens had notified Empire Insurance by letter (with a copy to Conley) that Mays no longer represented Conley. The letter also reflected that Conley had rejected Empire's $9,000.00 offer to settle, but Mays had retained an attorney's lien on any proceeds to be paid Conley in the future. Conley later claimed she had been unaware of any $9,000.00 offer until she received a copy of the December 6 letter.

Conley subsequently pursued her claim without the assistance of an attorney, and sought information from Empire Insurance by writing that Company on March 26, 1995. Empire's adjuster, Traylor, responded, indicating that he had not received the December 6 letter written by Mays, that he had already settled Conley's claim by having spoken with "Jim," who was with Mays's firm, and that Conley would have to obtain a letter reflecting Mays no longer represented her. In May of 1995, Conley forwarded to Traylor a copy of Mays's earlier December 6 letter, and informed Traylor that she had since contacted the Supreme Court Professional Conduct Committee and complained about Mays's representation. She further asked Traylor for a copy of the $9,000.00 check dated November 30, 1994, which purportedly had been sent to Mays in settlement of her claim. Upon receipt of Conley's May 1995 letter, Traylor sent Conley another letter, wherein he forwarded her a copy of the $9,000.00 check. The check had never been cashed. In August of 1995, Conley filed her formal complaint against Mays with the Professional Conduct Committee, alleging eight violations of the Model Rules of Professional Conduct, two of which the Committee eventually found meritorious. Besides complaining to the Committee about her initial confusion concerning the manner in which Mays established his contractual relationship with Conley, she also complained he failed to communicate and keep her informed concerning the law firm's negotiations with Empire Insurance Company in her behalf. . . .

We first address the Committee's decision that Mays violated Rule 1.4(b) by failing to communicate properly with his client, Conley. Rule 1.4(b) provides, "[A] lawyer shall explain a matter to the extent reasonably necessary to permit the client to make informed decisions regarding the representation." Adequacy of communication depends in part on the kind of advice or assistance involved. See Comment to Rule 1.4(b). The Comment further offers the example that, in negotiations where there is time to explain a proposal, the lawyer should review all important provisions with the client before proceeding to an agreement.

In the present case, such a review did not happen. In fact, from the beginning, there is proof that Mays's law firm failed to explain its contract with Conley or make clear early in the employment relationship the objectives of that legal representation. While Mays testified that he initially tries to make contact with his clients, he conceded that he never met with Conley or spoke to her by telephone. Mays further conceded that Conley's only contact

(continues)

CASE LAW   *Mays v. Neal* (continued)

with his firm was through his staff, and Stevens admitted that she had worked on Conley's case before Mays knew Conley was a client. In addition, Conley averred that her only contact with the firm was through Stevens even though, on several occasions, Conley had asked for an appointment with Mays. Each time Conley was told she should communicate with Stevens. In sum, although Mays and Stevens both related that Mays had instructed Stevens how Conley's case should be settled, the evidence is undisputed that Conley was afforded no opportunity to communicate directly with Mays and to ask him questions about her case. Obviously, the record supports the view that Mays had relied entirely upon his non-lawyer staff member to communicate with Conley even though Conley had posed questions concerning her legal representation, and was denied the opportunity to resolve those questions by meeting with him. . . .

[The portion of the opinion dealing with the lawyer's violation of MR 5.3 and 5.5, assisting others in the unauthorized practice of law, has been deleted.]

From the foregoing rules and principles, it is clear that, while a lawyer may delegate certain tasks to his assistants, he or she, as supervising attorney, has the ultimate responsibility for compliance by the non-lawyer with the applicable provisions of the Model Rules. In reviewing the record, we conclude Mays failed in this respect both in his firm's initial contracting with Conley and when negotiating her claim.

We again review in more detail the events leading to the signing of Conley as a client. In fact, Conley's testimony reflects she was confused and dissatisfied with her legal representation beginning when she signed Mays's contract at the scene of her accident on July 18, 1994. She said that she did not know who Mason was or what she had signed. She thought the paper she signed was for Mason to investigate the accident and to authorize him to get information. Mays testified that he did not employ, nor did he know Tim Mason, even though Mason possessed Stevens's business card and the law firm's employment contract which Conley signed. Ray Keech, an investigator and process server hired by the Committee, testified that in his attempts to locate Mason he was given a phone number, which turned out to be that for Mays & Crutcher. When Keech called the number, the person answering indicated that Mason only came into the office about once a month. . . .

We also note that there was substantial evidence that Mays had provided inadequate supervision over the manner in which his assistants negotiated Conley's claim. Mays testified that he monitored Conley's personal injury claim and evaluated it after receiving medical reports, bills, and wage-loss statements. He stated that he met with Stevens and Morris, and established a high and low range within which to settle. Mays said that Jimmy Morris had most of the contacts with Empire Insurance, and Stevens mostly dealt with Conley. Because

(continues)

CASE LAW *Mays v. Neal* (continued)

Conley's injury was a "soft-tissue" injury and she had incurred medical expenses of $2,700.00 to $2,800.00, Mays said he set a settlement range between $6,500.00 and $10,500.00.

Contrary to Stevens's version, Conley testified that she had never told Stevens how much she wished to net and never authorized a settlement in any amount. Nonetheless, Mays stated that he had authorized settlement for $9,000.00 because he could make some money and satisfy Conley as well. Without obtaining Conley's approval, Morris called Traylor at Empire Insurance, and the Company sent Mays a check for $9,000.00. While Conley had advised Stevens she would not settle for the Company's offer, Conley was unaware the Company had sent a $9,000.00 check until months after she had terminated Mays's firm.

Also adding to Conley's confusion was that, while Conley knew of Stevens, she was wholly unaware of the role Morris played in the negotiations with Empire Insurance, and only learned of Morris's existence after the insurance company later told her it had settled Conley's claim with "Jim." Unlike with Stevens, Morris's name was never disclosed as an assistant on the law firm stationery.

In sum, we must conclude, as did the Committee, that Mays failed to properly delegate his legal work and responsibilities and failed to properly supervise work delegated to his assistants. If he had, he would have been in the position at the least to have tried to resolve the questions that continued to resurface during his legal representation of Conley. For these reasons, we affirm the Committee's decisions.

The following case footnote corresponds to the portion of the case that is printed in the textbook. Although it may seem that other footnotes are missing, they are not presented because their corresponding portions of the court's opinion have been redacted.

¹The business card reflected the Mays & Crutcher Law Offices and showed Catherine Stevens as "Senior Claims Manager."

Case Questions

1. What solicitation and other violations were committed by Tim Mason?

2. What violations were committed by Catherine Stevens?

3. Empire Insurance believed it had settled the case with "Jim." Who was he?

4. How could attorney Mays contend he did not know who Tim Mason was, when Mason was the one who signed Conley as a client for Mays?

5. Mays settled a claim on behalf of a client he had never met (who had requested to talk with him) and then Mays placed a lien on his client's future settlement. In light of that and the other activities of his agents, explain how it was that he was only reprimanded.

Protecting Yourself Against Charges of Incompetence

Because competence is expected, and not simply encouraged, those who want to be competent must be willing to do whatever is necessary to achieve it. Often, that requires paralegals and legal assistants to spend personal time learning about the nuances of the area of the law in which they work, brushing up on legal software, perusing forms books, and scanning legal periodicals for practice-specific updates or changes. Another important item to bear in mind is that asking someone for assistance is a sign of competence, not inadequacy; a paralegal who fails to ask for help could later be the reason a lawyer's representation is found to be incompetent. And because language is the tool used by legal professionals, every paralegal should know how to use the English language effectively, including punctuation.

Mistakes happen, to put it politely, even among those who get paid to be correct. The following link is to Regret the Error, a Web site that reports on errors and misstatements made by the print and electronic media: http://www.regrettheerror.com/.

Paying attention to detail is, perhaps, the most important component of competent work. Scores of paralegals work in litigation, and litigation is rife with competence pitfalls. Although trials are so often the sole focus of fictionalized accounts of litigation, in reality the trial is the tip, while the discovery process is the iceberg. The volumes of papers that need to be date-stamped, processed, and indexed can be mind-boggling. Much of that work, including summarizing depositions, drafting pleadings, researching and drafting motions, working with accountants and other litigation consultants, and maintaining contact with the client and with opposing counsels or their employees, falls on the desks of paralegals. Throughout what can seem to be an endless process, paralegals and legal assistants must manage those details, remembering that failure to sufficiently follow the procedural rules can result in a negative judgment for the client, not to mention a negative employee review.

When lawyers formally defend against disciplinary charges of incompetence by blaming their non-lawyer employees, courts turn their collective ears away for two reasons: (a) Model Rule.5.3 makes lawyers responsible for the conduct of their non-lawyer employees; and (b) even if such a defense was factually accurate, non-lawyers cannot be professionally disciplined by a court. If it is true that the duty of competence imposes a disproportionate burden to the new lawyer, it could be said that the burden is even greater to the paralegal and legal assistant. Here is why: although the lawyer is formally responsible to the client, it is possible that when explaining an error to the client, the lawyer might place the brunt of the blame on her non-lawyer employee, regardless of whether that person is at fault. As unfair as it may be, for the sake of saving face, blame is often passed down the hierarchy. Therefore, it is critical that non-lawyer employees, through vigilant efforts of professional work, protect themselves as much as is possible against accusations of incompetent handling of client affairs. See Exhibit 8–2 for evidence of what makes a paralegal competent.

EXHIBIT 8–2   WHAT MAKES A PARALEGAL OR LEGAL ASSISTANT COMPETENT?

- Competence is required in the Ethics Codes:
  - NALA Code of Ethics, Canon 6
  - NFPA Model Disciplinary Code, Rule 1.1
- Some Indicia of Competence include the following:
  - A quality paralegal education
  - Continuing legal education courses
  - Knowing your jurisdiction's rules of professional conduct
  - Doing what is necessary to stay on top of your area of work or specialty
- Ultimately, competence is in the eye of the beholder: the employer.

Two Perspectives on Competence and Professionalism

High-ranking officials from the NALA and the NFPA have each written an essay for this chapter on the following topic: What makes a legal assistant or paralegal competent and professional, and what do you think the future holds for the profession?

Tita Brewster, ACP, President, National Association of Legal Assistants [Tita Brewster, ACP, a Senior Paralegal Specialist, is serving her second term as President of the National Association of Legal Assistants (NALA), is presently freelancing, and most recently was employed at Dechert, LLP in their new Austin, Texas office, assisting in the start-up of the new office, implementation of litigation paralegal protocols, case management, and trial preparation of patent litigation cases. Prior to that, she worked for Morgan Lewis & Bockius, LLP as a Senior Litigation Specialist preparing two patent infringement cases for trial in Utah and Delaware. She also recently worked at Ropers, Majeski, Kohn & Bentley in Redwood City, CA and Los Angeles, CA, but has worked for over 12 years at Ropers, Majeski, Kohn & Bentley. She attended the University of Texas at El Paso, obtained her Paralegal Certificate from West Valley College, in Saratoga, California, and is an Advanced Certified Paralegal in Discovery and Trial Preparation. Concentrating now on intellectual property litigation, Ms. Brewster has over 29 years of paralegal experience. She has been an active member of PASCCO (Paralegal Association of Santa Clara County) for 22 years, where she served two terms as President and recently completed a term as First Vice President and Director at Large. She served three terms as Liaison to the National Association of Legal Assistants and four terms as Bar Association Liaison. Ms. Brewster served two terms as the President of the California Alliance of Paralegal Associations (CAPA), where she was instrumental in promoting such goals as initiating the legislative groundwork for a statutory definition of "paralegal/legal assistant," which is now California Business and Professions Code § 6450. She completed two terms as National Ethics Chair for NALA. She was recently elected to her second term as the President of NALA after having served two terms as First Vice President, Second Vice President, Secretary, and Treasurer. She was the first honoree of the Mary Ann Pickrell Award, which is PASCCO's Paralegal of the Year award, and has served on the Paralegal Program Advisory Boards for numerous educational institutions. She has spoken before the ABA Commission on Non-Lawyer Practice and co-authored several litigation chapters of the *NALA Manual for Legal Assistants.*]

There are a great many "givens" in considering what makes a paralegal professional and competent. These givens are end results of many factors that go into defining a true "pro." It is a given that paralegal professionals must have first-rate training and a strong work ethic. It is a given that they have a natural affinity for attention to detail and a keen sense of legal ethics. It is also a given that their dedication to the profession and reliability to their employers is paramount.

Few of the givens that define professional paralegals are actually given—they are earned with hard work and perseverance. First-rate training can be accomplished through formal schooling and/or on the job, but in either case it is the paralegal who is the key factor in determining whether the preparation is actually first rate or just going through the drill. Training does not end with graduation from a paralegal curriculum. The dynamic nature of the legal system demands that paralegals stay abreast of changes through continuing legal education programs.

Fortunately, there has been an equally dynamic change in continuing legal education. The Internet has made CLE economically accessible to many paralegals who would find it nearly impossible to attend the number of live seminars and short courses needed to stay current in the field. Not all continuing paralegal education on the Web is created equal, however, and it is important to choose carefully. A solid benchmark in this regard is the online education offered by NALA. As the nation's preeminent professional association for paralegals, NALA has the resources to present online programs that can be relied upon for accuracy of material, superior pedagogy, and cutting-edge timeliness. Whether logging on for 'round-the-clock self-paced learning at NALAcampus. com, signing in for "live" presentations on NALA Campus LIVE!, or pursuing the new online Advanced Paralegal Certification program, these programs represent the highest quality in continuing paralegal education.

There is no better way to demonstrate dedication to the profession and dependability to employers than to secure voluntary certification as a Certified Paralegal (CP), or to achieve advanced certification in a specialty area through the new curriculum-based APC program. Being involved in local, state, and national paralegal association activities is another way true professionals stay on top of their game. Individual expertise and enthusiasm is admirable, but sharing those traits with others through participation in professional organizations is a self-stoking cycle that benefits the entire profession as well as the individual.

The prospects for professional paralegals are tied intimately to staying abreast of changes in the legal field, and to making the most of technology in continuing legal education. The choices of continuing paralegal education and voluntary certification offered by NALA richly demonstrate that the future of the paralegal profession is well underway.

Anita G. Hayworth, RP, President, National Federation of Paralegal Associations [Anita Hayworth is a senior litigation paralegal at Campbell Kyle Proffitt LLP in Carmel, Indiana, with over 22 years of experience. Ms. Hayworth has a B.S. in Criminal Justice with a minor in psychology, and a paralegal certificate from Indiana University–Kokomo. She became a PACE Registered Paralegal in September of 1999. Anita is currently serving as the President of National Federation of Paralegal Associations, Inc. (NFPA) for the 2006–2008 term. She previously served as NFPA Treasurer & Director of Finance, Region III Director, and held various coordinator positions including Roles & Responsibilities; Ethics & Professional Responsibility; Assistant PACE Coordinator-Public Relations. Anita has also been a member of the PACE Development Committee since February of 2001. A member of Indiana Paralegal Association (IPA), Anita received Paralegal of the Year and Outstanding Board Member awards from Indiana Paralegal Association in 2000. She was a member of IPA's Board of Directors for several years as its Primary Representative to NFPA and was instrumental in the drafting and implementation of several policy resolutions adopted by NFPA. She is also an affiliate member of the Indiana State Bar Association, and sits on the Paralegal Advisory Board at Indiana Vocational Technical College in Indianapolis. Anita is a member of the Paralegal Advisory Board at Thomas Edison State College, in Trenton, NJ.]

What is it that makes a paralegal competent and professional? First, let us take a look at what it means to be competent. Competency involves knowledge, experience, and the ability to apply that knowledge and experience to a particular task or set of tasks.

Education is the essential first step to becoming a paralegal. It is the foundation upon which to build knowledge through the application of what has been learned. Through the practical application of what has been learned (i.e., working as a paralegal), you gain the skills and experience necessary to become competent. One's education does not end upon graduation. Rather, it continues throughout one's career. To remain competent, a paralegal must continually strive to maintain and increase her knowledge of the law and changes in the law, then apply that knowledge to the work at hand. Attending continuing legal education seminars, networking with other legal professionals, and actively participating in a paralegal association provide the opportunities needed to remain competent.

The single most significant thing to remember about being a paralegal is this: the paralegal performs substantive legal work that involves legal concepts and is customarily (but not exclusively) performed by a lawyer. This means the paralegal is often doing work that would otherwise be performed by the lawyer.

To become a lawyer, one must attend college, then law school, then pass a bar exam in order to become licensed to practice law. Therefore, it stands to reason that the paralegal should also have an advanced education and meet certain minimum criteria in order to perform the substantive tasks delegated to her by the lawyer. NFPA defines "substantive" as work requiring recognition, evaluation, organization, analysis, and communication of relevant facts and legal concepts.

So, what makes a paralegal "professional?" Integrity and maturity in all situations is essential. Adherence to, and an understanding of, the code of ethics of the paralegal's association, and the jurisdiction in which the paralegal practices, is basic to becoming a professional. Respect for the law and for the tribunal process is absolutely necessary. One's personal conduct must reflect high moral and ethical standards in both public and private situations. Competency and compassion are essential elements of professionalism as is the understanding of the unauthorized practice of law—in other words, knowing and respecting the boundaries in which we perform legal services. A paralegal must know when and how to perform the duties we have been given so that there is not even the appearance of an impropriety. For example, there is a fine line between providing information and giving legal advice, and it takes time and experience to understand the difference. This takes us back to the point that education provides a foundation, and one must build upon that foundation through experience in order to gain competency and become a professional.

Finally, there is a difference between belonging to a profession and being professional. Graduating from a paralegal program and getting a paralegal job brings one into the paralegal profession. Being professional means making a commitment to oneself to grow and learn, to adhere to standards of conduct, and to respect the law. In other words, being professional becomes a way of life.

TRUTHFULNESS

More than a few rules of ethics concern the lawyer's—and by extension, the paralegal's—duty to be truthful. Although it might go without saying that a lawyer should be truthful, the rules formalize the appropriate conduct of the lawyer in certain situations, many of which have to do with litigation. Also, the comments to the rules help explain what it means to be untruthful.

The General Rule on Truth

ABA Model Rule 4.1 clearly states the following:
In the course of representing a client a lawyer shall not knowingly:

   a. make a false statement of material fact or law to a third person; or

b. fail to disclose a material fact to a third person when disclosure is necessary to avoid assisting a criminal or fraudulent act by a client, unless disclosure is prohibited by Rule 1.6.

That language is nearly identical to the language in MR 3.3(a)(1) and (2), which concerns truthfulness to a tribunal. Model Rule 4.1 is nearly identical to two provisions in DR 7–102(A) in the ABA Model Code. DR 7–102(A)(3) states that a lawyer shall not "[c]onceal or knowingly fail to disclose that which he is required by law to reveal." And DR 7–102(A)(5) states, "In his representation of a client, a lawyer shall not . . . [k]nowingly make a false statement of law or fact." The Ethics 2000 version of MR 4.1 is the same as the prior version, although there are some new Comments to the rule.

The basic rule on truthfulness has a multitude interpretive layers. Of those, paralegals should remember three important concepts associated with the truthfulness duty. First, it is only a "knowing" **misrepresentation**. Silence can be considered misrepresentation when there is a duty to speak. Misrepresentation can be negligent, as well as intentional that is in violation of the ethics rules. While negligent misrepresentations may be the cause of other legal problems, intentional misrepresentations are the kinds that the professional responsibility rules consider untruthful. Second, an intentional misrepresentation must be "material" in order to be unethical. Without splitting hairs unnecessarily, not all falsehoods are created equal, and a material misrepresentation is one that is significant in proportion to the statement in full. Third, failure to disclose what should be disclosed is as much a misrepresentation as stating something falsely. This concept is a delicate one. Although a paralegal may not use silence to help a client commit a crime or fraudulent act, a paralegal may also not disclose anything that would violate the lawyer-client confidentiality rule. Exhibit 8–3 summarizes the key concepts associated with the ethics concept of truthfulness.

■ **misrepresentation**
A false or untruthful statement.

EXHIBIT 8–3 KEY CONCEPTS ASSOCIATED WITH TRUTHFULNESS

- ABA Model Rule 4.1 is the starting point on truthfulness.

- Three key concepts associated with truthfulness are the following:
    1. MR 4.1 concerns *intentional misrepresentations*.
    2. MR 4.1 concerns *material misrepresentations*.
    3. Silence can be as untruthful as speaking falsely.

Clients and Truthfulness

All clients want their lawyers to be zealous—part pit bull and part Franciscan monk. Zealous representation of the client is mentioned in Canon 7 of the ABA Model Code and also discussed in the Comments to ABA Model Rule 1.3, but zealousness must be tempered by fairness to the other side and its legal team, as well as fidelity to the administration of justice. Two areas of violations with respect to clients will be discussed: bringing frivolous claims and putting forth false evidence.

NOT QUITE LINCOLN

While She Was at It, She Should Have Also Forged a "Get Out Of Jail Free" Card

In 2004, Idaho attorney Jeannie Braun was representing a client in a domestic relations dispute. That dispute included a fight over custody of the client's son, who was at that time living with his father, the client's ex-husband. One supposes Ms. Braun either lacked faith in her legal skills or the legal system, or perhaps she just wanted to reduce her client's bill by working quickly. What she did was remarkably brazen: she forged a judge's signature stamp on an "Ex-Parte Order For Temporary Custody and Restraining Order." Ms. Braun then gave the forged document to her client with instructions that the client would get custody of her son by giving the document to the police.

As described on the Order's title, the client got *temporary custody* of her son. Once the fraud was discovered, Ms. Braun was indicted for forgery. She then pled guilty and was sentenced to 14 years in prison. All but one year was suspended. In 2006, she was disbarred.

Frivolous Claims

Edward Brewer committed an act so vile, it is hard to comprehend. In 1998, he raped a mentally challenged, a cerebral palsy patient suffering from cancer, while she lay in her hospital bed. What he did afterward is not as awful as his crime, but is as shocking all the same: in 2002 he sued the hospital in Ohio where he raped his victim. Filing a federal lawsuit on his own behalf, Brewer alleged that the negligence of the hospital and its own security in allowing him to rape a woman who was unable to defend herself against his attack, and who would die weeks later, caused him "pain and suffering." And for that, he wanted $2 million. This from a man who plea bargained the original rape charges down to sexual battery and was sentenced to five years in prison. He then won an appeal that granted him a new trial, which resulted him in being convicted of rape and sentenced to 10 years. Thankfully, his lawsuit was dismissed.

Was that a frivolous lawsuit? That one was too easy. Try this one. While camping in Mt. Hood National Park in Oregon, in 2006, 23-year-old Jerry Mersereau left his tent in the middle of the night for bladder relief purposes, which sometimes can be a difficult trip to make at home. The reason Jerry sued the United States government over his late-night urgency is most succinctly stated in his complaint: "While finding a place to relieve himself, plaintiff walked off the unguarded and unprotected cliff falling approximately 20 to 30 feet to the creek bed below." Alleging that our government should have done more to combat the dangers of cliffs to campers, Jerry demanded compensation for his physical injuries and mental anguish. Is that a frivolous claim?

What about Stella Liebeck, who suffered third-degree burns in 1992 on her thighs and genitals after spilling the McDonald's coffee that was resting between her legs as she sat in a car? Was her lawsuit against McDonald's frivolous? After the trial judge reduced the jury verdict, Ms. Liebeck was awarded $640,000, but the parties eventually reached a confidential settlement. In the minds of many Americans, her case was ridiculous. However, not many of those who cast aspersions on her were aware that McDonald's had been the recipient of over 700 complaints about its coffee temperature in the 10-year period before the infamous lawsuit about her severe coffee burns. Nor did many know that McDonald's held its coffee at a temperature between 180° and 190° F, about 40 degrees hotter than coffee made at home.

Almost everyone bearing an axe to grind with the American legal system starts their argument with a favorite story about a frivolous lawsuit that wastes court resources and was filed by a money-hungry lawyer with no hint of ethics. Even Ann Landers once recounted as true what turned out to be a myth—a so-called urban legend. A column of hers included a harangue on the legal system by discussing a case in which a woman sued a pharmacy for negligence because she purchased a tube of contraceptive jelly at the pharmacy, went home and made some toast, put the jelly on the toast and ate it, had sex, and got pregnant. As the story goes, her lawsuit proceeded along the line that the pharmacy should have done more to alert her to the fact that contraceptive jelly is not...that kind of jelly.

For more on urban legends, check out the following link to a Web site that categorizes them, including a few legal doozies: http://www.snopes.com/.

The following Web site offers its own take on the high costs of litigation and frivolous lawsuits, offering examples of what it believes are frivolous lawsuits: http://www.overlawyered.com/index.html.

The Ethics 2000 version of ABA Model Rule 3.1 does not define what constitutes a frivolous claim, but it does state that a lawyer should not bring or defend a claim, "unless there is a basis in law and fact for doing so that is not frivolous...." MR 3.1 also states that in criminal cases, a lawyer may defend a client (including one who has committed acts that constitute the crime) so as to force the prosecution to prove every element of the charges. DR 7–102(A)(1) of the ABA Model Code states that a lawyer may not "[f]ile a suit, assert a position, conduct a defense, delay a trial, or take other action on behalf of his client when he knows or when it is obvious that such action would serve merely to harass or maliciously injure another." Other rules touch the prohibition of the frivolous, including Model Rule 3.4(d), which forbids the bringing of frivolous discovery requests. Frivolousness is a highly subjective concept because there is little specific instruction on what makes a case frivolous. Part of the confusion is because the chance of success is considered an inadequate litmus test, because even a long-shot case has a right to be filed. But there are two types of claims that courts will often find lacking in merit. First, claims made in **bad faith** are considered frivolous. A bad faith claim has historically included one that is made for no other purpose than to harass or embarrass someone else. An example of a bad faith case comes from North Dakota, where a lawyer was publicly reprimanded for harassing his ex-wife by groundlessly suing her for invasion of privacy and slander. *In re Bard*, 519 N.W.2d 286 (N.D. 1994). In 2002, however, the Ethics 2000 Commission deleted language in the Comments that explicitly tied bad client motives to a frivolous lawsuit, which leaves more emphasis on the nature of the claim instead of its purpose.

Second, claims are considered frivolous if they are so devoid of substance that there could be no legitimate basis for relief or remedy. Often, courts refer to these types of cases as having no basis in law or facts. Such was the case in an example from New York, where a lawyer was sanctioned with a $1,500 fine for what the appellate court called leveling a "frontal assault" against a trial judge. This frontal assault involved the lawyer seeking a **writ of mandamus** against a newly assigned trial judge for not responding to the lawyer's trial motions quickly enough to suit his tastes, when the case was one the lawyer had been grooming for 19 years. *Public Administrator of County of New York v. Cohen*, N.Y.S.2d 106 (App. Div. 1995).

Consider Caesar Barber, the New York resident who filed a suit in July 2002, claiming that fast food was the "legal" cause of his obesity and related health problems. Is he responsible for his own health? Is he showing his true gluttony by trying to reap millions from the four largest fast-food chains by claiming they should have told him that items like triple cheeseburgers with bacon and large orders of french fries contribute to health problems? Or, does he have a legitimate lawsuit when he blames the provider of his favorite foods for enticing him to eat their food, but failing to inform him of the actual fat content in it? His lawsuit was seeking other plaintiffs so it could be certified as a class action, and the way one views that lawsuit—frivolous or legitimate—might have as much to do with one's political views as one's legal views.

Distinct from the professional responsibility rules, sanctions can be issued against lawyers who file frivolous claims because of Civil Procedure Rule 11, operative in the federal and state civil procedure rules. That rule requires that the attorney of record (i.e., the one who signs the pleadings, motions, or other litigation filings) be responsible to ensure that the filings are well grounded in fact and not made for any improper purpose. Sanctions are also available under the federal and state versions of Civil Procedure Rule 37 against lawyers who are found to have abused the discovery process. Furthermore, Rule 38 of the Federal Rules of Appellate Procedure provides, "If a court of appeals shall determine that an appeal is frivolous, it may...award just damages and single or double costs to the appellee."

bad faith

Something done in bad faith is done dishonestly, or with ulterior motives.

writ of mandamus

An order issued by a court, ordering some official to do a particular act that was requested by the party seeking the writ of mandamus.

A federal statute provides for sanctions against an attorney, or other person permitted to conduct cases in federal court, who "multiplies the proceedings in any case unreasonably and vexatiously." 28 U.S.C. § 1927. California has a statute designed to prevent vexatious litigation. It defines a such a litigant in different categories, including one who has in a seven-year period brought at least five non–small claims actions that have ended in negative judgments or have not been brought to adjudication within two years. Cal. Code of Civil Proc. § 391(b)(1). Once the determination is made that someone is a vexatious litigant, that person must obtain court approval before bringing another suit or else be found in contempt of court. Cal. Code of Civil Proc. § 391.7(b). Legislation that restricts one's right to sue is controversial, but California's vexatious litigation statute has been upheld on appeal against claims that it is unconstitutional. *Wolfgram v. Wells Fargo Bank*, 61 Cal.Rptr.2d 694 (Cal. App. 1997). And in another California case where a dental patient who was disgruntled over a $60 fee for a crown, sued the dentist...and 30 federal agencies and judges in 10 lawsuits for conspiracy, extortion, perjury, and violation of his rights. The appellate court upheld the trial court's conclusion that the pro se plaintiff was vexatious. *Bravo v. Ismaj*, 120 Cal.Rptr.2d 879 (Cal.App. 2002). See Exhibit 8–4 for general principles on frivolous litigation.

EXHIBIT 8–4 WHAT MAKES A LAWSUIT FRIVOLOUS?

The Key Rules	Claims Made in Bad Faith	Claims Devoid of Substance
• ABA Model Rule 3.1 and 3.4(d) • ABA Model Code DR 7-102 (A) • 28 U.S.C. §1927 • 28 U.S.C. §1912	• A lawsuit made solely with the intention of harassing or maligning someone • *Example*: Repeatedly suing a neighbor in an attempt to get them to move	• A lawsuit that has no basis in law or in fact • *Example*: Suing someone, while knowing that the statute of limitations has long since passed

---

False Evidence

ABA Model Rule 3.3(a)(1)(2), and (4) prohibit a lawyer from making material misrepresentations to a tribunal, failing to disclose material facts when disclosure is necessary to prevent assisting the client in committing a criminal or fraudulent act, and offering evidence the lawyer knows is false. The Model Code has nearly identical prohibitions in DR 7–102(A)(5), DR 7–102(A)(3), and DR 7–102(A)(4). Included in the Ethics 2000 version of Model Rule 3.3 is the

NOT QUITE LINCOLN

Can't Anybody on That School Board Read or Do Basic Math?

In 1997, Orange County, California, attorney Maureen Graves agreed to take a case which was over 400 miles north. The case was located in Calaveras County, the place Mark Twain put on the map with his 1867 short story—the one about the famous jumping frog named Daniel Webster. The real Daniel Webster was one of America's most famous lawyers and statesmen, and was a remarkably indefatigable orator. But even Webster might have grown weary of what attorney Graves had to endure. Her client, who attended a public high school, was a special needs student who was suing the school district to get increased special education services, such as additional tutoring. This case was so straightforward that Ms. Graves agreed to represent the student and his mother *pro bono*.

Lozano Smith, the law firm representing the school district, was so dishonest, however, that it tied up the case in federal court for over seven years. According to Ms. Graves's estimate, the school district paid Lozano Smith almost $500,000 dollars to fight her client's requests, which would have cost around $8,000 dollars to provide.

Graves finally prevailed in 2003, and in 2004 the federal judge who granted her request for summary judgment disciplined Lozano Smith for its intentionally dilatory tactics. In his 83-page opinion, Judge Oliver Wanger expressed his dissatisfaction at Lozano Smith's repeated misstatements of the law and facts throughout the litigation, and for what he called the firm's "concerted effort to distort, if not outright deceive, the court."

For starters, Judge Oliver Wanger issued a $5,000 fine against the school district, Lozano Smith, and Ms. Elaine Yama, the attorney from the firm who handled the case. He then ordered Ms. Yama to take 20 hours of continuing legal education ethics courses by the end of that year. Judge Wanger also ordered Lozano Smith to provide six hours of ethics courses for all 81 of its attorneys.

It is a good thing that 2004 was a leap year; one imagines the attorneys at Lozano Smith needed the extra day to complete their required ethics courses.

removal of the word "material" from 3.3(a)(1), as well as an expansion of the lawyer's duty to take remedial action if she becomes aware that someone is engaging, or has engaged, in fraudulent activity with respect to the case.

Problems in this area can occur when the lawyer knows the client wants to testify falsely. If the case is a civil matter, the lawyer may not allow the client to testify falsely, preventing this by going so far as to inform the judge about the intended perjury if, after discussing the matter with the client, it is clear that the latter still insists on testifying falsely.

The answer is not so easy in a criminal matter, however, because of a criminal defendant's constitutional rights. Although a lawyer may not put a criminal defendant on the stand and assist her in committing perjury, there is a line of thinking that says that a lawyer may, like King Solomon, "cut the baby in two" by allowing the defendant to take the stand to present her testimony in a narrative. This approach involves the defendant talking from the witness stand, but without any direct examination by the defense lawyer. During the closing argument, the lawyer will also avoid referring to the defendant's testimony. Courts have given their approval to this narrative approach to perjured testimony because, as one court put it, "the narrative approach best accommodates the competing interests of the defendant's constitutional right to testify and the attorney's ethical obligations." *People v. Johnson*, 72 Cal.Rptr.2d 805, 818 (Cal.App. 1998). (Also in the case, the court cited other jurisdictions that approved of the narrative approach.)

Not all jurisdictions agree with the narrative approach to perjured testimony in criminal cases. The Comments to MR 3.3 criticize the narrative approach, and the ABA reaffirmed its opposition in an ethics opinion that states that if all attempts at dissuading the client from lying on the stand fail, the lawyer must disclose the intended perjury to the court. ABA Commission on Ethics and Professional Responsibility, Formal Op. 87–353 (1987). Also, the United States Supreme Court took a case on perjured testimony in *Nix v. Whiteside*, 475 U.S. 157 (1986). In *Nix*, a murder defendant planned on testifying falsely about whether the victim was holding a gun at the time of the attack, and the defendant's lawyer explained that he would have to inform the trial court of the defendant's actions if the latter insisted on testifying falsely. The defendant testified truthfully and then, after being convicted, appealed on the grounds that he was denied effective assistance of counsel because his counsel prevented his intended testimony. The Supreme Court affirmed the conviction, finding that, although the constitutional right to testify is certain, "it is elementary that such a right does not extend to testifying falsely." *Nix*, at 173. However, *Nix v. Whiteside* does not mean that a jurisdiction is prohibited from adopting the narrative approach; it does mean that a defendant cannot cry foul in those jurisdictions that refuse to allow for the narrative approach.

Other problems can arise when working with clients in discovery matters or helping them gather information in transactional matters, such as estate planning. There will be occasions when clients will express or imply a desire to hide information or assets or bend the truth. Although clients are allowed to seek every lawful advantage possible, they may not use the legal process for fraudulent purposes or as a refuge against the truth. For example, in a Social Security case, a lawyer was sanctioned for submitting a doctor's report that the lawyer knew had been changed in parts that concerned the extent of her client's injuries, as well as the dates of treatments. *In re Watkins*, 656 So.2d 984 (La. 1995). Therefore, when a paralegal has a reasonable suspicion that the client is being deceitful, it is imperative that those suspicions be reported to the supervising lawyer, because the lawyer is responsible for the paralegal's conduct, including any failure to take preventative or remedial action. Remember, if the client's presentation of fraudulent information is discovered, the lawyer, despite being unaware of the fraud, could be sanctioned for failing to adequately supervise the paralegal who was aware of it and failed to report it to the lawyer.

Unfortunately, there are occasions where lawyers violate the rules, not by allowing their clients to present false information, but by altering their clients' information. In an Arizona case, a lawyer changed the draft answers of his client's interrogatories before turning the final answers over to the opposing party, who had submitted the interrogatory questions. The client did not become aware of the changes until over a year later and, in the disciplinary proceedings, the lawyer argued that he did not violate MR 3.3 stating that the reason he had changed his client's draft answers was because they were originally incorrect. The court, in sanctioning the lawyer, stated that it was troubled by the lawyer's novel argument. *In re Shannon*, 876 P.2d 548 (Ariz. 1994). And in another case, a lawyer representing the **personal representative** of an **intestate estate** submitted a final account to the estate (which now had a different personal representative), which included attorney's fees. The new personal representative verified the account and mailed it back to the attorney for filing with the probate court. Upon receiving the verified account, the lawyer realized that she had underestimated her legal fees, so she instructed her legal assistant to alter the document by changing the legal fees portion. The legal assistant questioned the lawyer about the appropriateness of that and was told that the lawyer would contact the personal representative to get permission. That was not done, however. The legal assistant did change the document as instructed, but mailed it to the personal representative with a cover letter stating that changes had been made to the final account. Unfortunately, the representative never read the letter or altered account, which postponed the inevitable controversy by three months. In the disciplinary proceedings, the court considered the lawyer's actions a violation of several rules on honesty and suspended her for 120 days. However, it offered no view on the complicity of the legal assistant. *In re Morris*, 953 P.2d 387 (Or. 1998).

Anyone who has ever tried to purchase a car or, worse, sell a used car, recognizes the bullfight-dance that is negotiation. The buyer stampedes forward with informational demands. ("Has it been in a wreck?" "Why are you selling it?" "Does it need any work?") The seller sidesteps the charge. ("I've never wrecked it." "I'm looking for a minivan because I'm thinking about having kids." "It's not brand new, but it's in good shape and I hate to give it up.") Truth is often a commodity in precious supply when parties are negotiating, including when parties in a lawsuit are in settlement discussions or mediation. The ABA spoke to

■ personal representative

Someone appointed to manage the legal affairs of another person, or of an estate.

■ intestate estate

The personal and real property of a person who died without leaving a valid will to direct the transfer of that property.

that issue in 2006, issuing an ethics opinion reiterating that a lawyer may not make a materially false statement to a third party during settlement discussion. But the ABA also concluded that broad statements about the client's willingness to settle or settlement goals are not statements covered by the material falsity of the ethics rules. ABA Formal Ethics Op. 06–439.

Represented Persons and Truthfulness: The Anticontact Rule

The Ethics 2000 version of Model Rule 4.2 concerns under what circumstances a member of a legal team may contact a person represented by a lawyer, and states, "In representing a client, a lawyer shall not communicate about the subject of the representation with a person the lawyer knows to be represented by another lawyer in the matter, unless the lawyer has the consent of the other lawyer or is authorized to do so by law or a court order." This rule, known as the anticontact rule, is designed to protect against a lawyer taking unfair advantage of someone outside the presence of that person's lawyer. As stated in ABA Commission on Ethics and Professional Responsibility, Formal Op. 95–396 (1995), one of the purposes of this type of rule is to protect a represented person from unwittingly divulging privileged or harmful information that would not have been disclosed if the other lawyer were present.

This rule has a broader application. It goes beyond lawsuits and also applies when a lawyer knows the person to be contacted is represented by a lawyer in connection with the reason the first lawyer wants to make contact. For instance, a lawyer could not directly contact a person from whom the lawyer's client wants to purchase a piece of property *if* the other person has retained a lawyer for the purposes of assisting in the sale of the property. The Ethics 2000 version of 4.2 has an addition that allows a lawyer to directly contact a represented person if the lawyer is authorized by a court order, and 4.2 has some new Comments.

The ABA Model Code's anticontact rule is nearly identical, but the difference is significant. Not only does DR 7–104(A)(1) prohibit a lawyer from making inappropriate contact, but it also prohibits a lawyer from causing another person to make inappropriate contact. That language expressly covers the conduct of paralegals. More important, DR 7–104(A)(1) uses the word "party" instead of "person." That distinction is significant because in jurisdictions that operate under the Model Code, a lawyer or legal assistant would only be prohibited from directly contacting the other party (which might require that there be formal legal proceedings underway). The prohibition is not to others related to the legal matter, such as the party's family members or employees who have retained lawyers concerning the legal matter. Moreover, some jurisdictions that have adopted the Model Rules still use the word *party* in the language of MR 4.2 (which was used in the original ABA version of MR 4.2, prior to 1995), even though the title of MR 4.2 uses the word *person*. Some of the Model Rules jurisdictions whose version of MR 4.2 concerns parties rather than persons include: Alaska (which concerns "a party or person" in its rule), Arizona, Colorado, Connecticut, Illinois, Indiana, Kansas, Michigan, and Pennsylvania. California, which uses a set of ethics rules that are not modeled formally after either the Model Rules or Model Code, also has an anticontact rule that applies to parties, instead of persons. Therefore, legal assistants should be careful to learn whether their jurisdiction prohibits direct contact with represented persons or represented parties.

The Paralegal and the Anticontact Rules

When a lawyer is prohibited from making direct contact with a represented person, then so is the non-lawyer agent or employee of the lawyer, because neither can do what the principal is prohibited from doing. In a California case, a lawyer attempted to contact another attorney's clients in connection with a legal matter involving both lawyers' clients. After being warned by the other lawyer not to do so, the first lawyer sent a threatening letter to the other party. Then, after being caught, the first lawyer claimed that his legal assistant sent the letter, despite that the letter purported to bear the lawyer's signature. Without disputing the lawyer's claim that his employee sent the letter, the court found him in violation of the anticontact rule, regardless of who sent the letter. *Crane v. State Bar*, 635 P.2d 163 (Cal. 1981).

Exceptions to the Anticontact Rules

Regardless whether one's jurisdiction prohibits direct contact with represented persons or parties, there are some common exceptions that apply. One exception not mentioned in the text of Model Rule 4.2, but mentioned in the Comments, is that parties (or persons) are allowed to have direct contact with one another outside the presence of their lawyers, but only if the client making contact is not, in essence, reading from a script devised by his or her lawyer. In an Ohio case, an attorney had his personal injury client, who was the plaintiff, call the defendant three days before the trial to tell the defendant what the plaintiff planned to testify. To make matters worse, during the conversation the plaintiff handed the phone to his lawyer who, forgetting that the defendant was represented, discussed the case with the defendant. Fortunately, for the sake of his law license, the lawyer withdrew from the case. *Trumball County Bar Association v. Makridis*, 671 N.E. 2d 31 (Ohio 1996). And in an odd case from Alabama, after a man walked into a posthole in his mother's backyard, he sued her for $100,000, and when she was in a nursing home, he and his lawyer went to "visit" her, without her attorney's presence. Her attorney was not amused by the bedside visitation, and neither was the court, which disqualified the son's lawyer from the case. *Ex parte Lammon*, 688 So.2d 836 (Ala.Civ.App. 1996).

When lawyers represent themselves pro se, they are wearing two hats: lawyer and party. Because the rules allow represented parties or persons to have direct contact with each other, it might seem that a self-represented lawyer would fall under that anticontact exception. That is not necessarily the case; some jurisdictions, such as Idaho, Oregon, and Wyoming, have concluded that a self-represented lawyer may not make direct contact with a represented person because it would be impossible to take off the lawyer hat. *See Runsvold v. Idaho State Bar*, 925 P.2d 1118 (Idaho 1996); *Sandstrom v. Sandstrom*, 880 P.2d 103 (Wyo. 1994); and *In re Conduct of Smith*, 861 P.2d 1013 (Or. 1993). Oregon, in fact, amended its anticontact rule when it was a Model Code jurisdiction to expressly cover a "lawyer representing a lawyer's own interest." Or. R. CPR DR 7–104(A)(1). (As of 2005, it follows Model Rule 4.2.) Even in those jurisdictions that forbid pro se lawyers from making direct contact with any represented party or person, such a prohibition would not apply to any non-lawyer who was pro se in a case and wanted to communicate directly with the other party, even if the other party was represented.

Members of one legal team can also make direct contact with a represented person if the purpose of the communication is outside the scope of the representation. For instance, a lawyer representing a client suing a city government in a zoning permit matter may directly contact a representative of the city to discuss the quality of the city's snow removal system. Members of one legal team may also make direct contact with intended witnesses to the legal matter, such as doctors or other experts. ABA Commission of Ethics and Professional Responsibility, Formal Op. 93–378 (1993). And, as stated in Model Rule 4.2, members of one legal team may make direct contact with a represented person if the other lawyer gives consent or if the contact is authorized by law. Those contacts that are authorized by law include cases in which statutes or rules of court provide permission, such as court rules that authorize for service of process on a party. ABA Commission and Professional Responsibility, Formal Op. 95–396 (1995).

In the criminal litigation context, the anticontact rules get very confusing when juxtaposed with criminal procedure law, both in the investigative phase and the adjudicative phase. For instance, in 1989, Attorney General Richard Thornburgh issued a controversial memorandum that stated federal prosecutors were not bound by state anticontact rules and could not be sanctioned for violating them. That position then became part of the Code of Federal Regulations in 1994 in 28 C.F.R. § 77 et seq. After much friction between the Justice Department, the ABA, and the states, the U.S. Congress got involved in 1998, enacting legislation called The Citizens Protection Act that expressly makes federal prosecutors subject to the ethics rules of the states wherein they work. The U.S. Congress then ordered the attorney general (then Janet Reno) to amend the Department of Justice Rules in accordance with the statute. 28 U.S.C. § 530B(a) and (b). Those changes were then made to 29 C.F.R. § 77.3. Exhibit 8–5 provides an overview of the anticontact rule.

EXHIBIT 8–5 THE ANTICONTACT RULE

What Is it?	Model Rules vs. Model Code?	Exceptions?
• ABA MR 4.2 and ABA MC DR 7–104 prevent a member of one legal team from having contact concerning the legal matter with someone represented by counsel for the legal matter.	• The Model Rules's version prohibits one legal team's contact with a represented "person" (anyone connected to the litigation). • The Model Code's version prohibits one legal team's contact with a represented "party" (someone involved in the litigation).	• Parties can have contact with each other, but not necessarily when lawyers represent themselves in litigation. • Contact can be made for purposes outside the scope of the representation. • Contact can be made if consent is given by the represented person's lawyer. • Contact can be made if it is authorized by law. • Contact can be made if it is authorized by a court order (Ethics 2000 addition).

Unrepresented Persons and Truthfulness

During the course of representing a client, the lawyer and the lawyer's staff will have contact with those who are, or might be, connected to the case. Often those persons will be unrepresented, such as someone who worked with the client or who may have witnessed an accident that is the cause of the litigation. A variety of ethical issues are involved when contact is made with those persons who do not have legal representation. Foremost of those considerations is the requirement that those contacting unrepresented persons may not state or imply neutrality.

ABA Model Rule 4.3 requires that a lawyer making contact with an unrepresented person clearly explain to that person that she is not disinterested. Furthermore, the rule requires that the lawyer make a reasonable effort to clear up any misunderstanding the unrepresented person may have about the purpose of his or her contact. The ABA Model Code has no similar rule, although DR 7–104(A)(2) prohibits a lawyer from giving "advice to a person who is not represented by a lawyer, other than the advice to secure counsel." The Ethics 2000 version of MR 4.3 has a new sentence that is reminiscent of the Model Code and the Comment to MR 4.3, in that it says, "The lawyer shall not give legal advice to an unrepresented person, other than the advice to secure counsel, if the lawyer knows or reasonably should know that the interests of such a person are or have a reasonable possibility of being in conflict with the interests of the client."

Not only is it misleading to imply neutrality to an unrepresented party, it also could be unfair because the information gleaned from the unrepresented party might actually turn it into an adverse party who unwittingly helped give information to the other side. For example, such a veiled projection of neutrality would be inappropriate if the person being contacted is known by the lawyer or legal assistant to be someone who will be served a complaint soon, once enough information is gathered. False impressions of disinterest in the litigation can also be made when the legal team contacts employees of the other party. In a lawsuit involving an airline crash, a consultant of the plaintiff's lawyer sent a deceptive letter and questionnaire to the pilots of the airline (the defendant), the stated purpose being to identify the training and experience of the pilots. What the pilots were not told was that the questionnaire was sent to gather information that might be used against the airline in the pending litigation. Upon learning of the tactic, the trial court sanctioned the plaintiff's attorney for violating the federal district court version of Model Rule 4.3 by excluding from evidence the information learned from the questionnaires. *In re Air Crash Disaster,* 909 F. Supp. 1116 (N.D. Ill. 1995).

NOT QUITE LINCOLN

The Mother of all "Do the Ends Justify the Means?" Dilemmas

In 1998, three Colorado women were murdered in an astonishingly brutal manner, and a fourth woman was tied down by the murderer and forced to watch one of the killings. But as the killer, William "Cody" Neal, left his hostage victim in the blood-splattered apartment, he gave her his pager number and told her to contact the police.

Although sheriff's deputies had made cellular phone contact with Neal, they were unable to determine his location. During several phone conversations, Neal confessed to the murders, uttering rambling statements about his connection to the CIA and FBI, and made statements law enforcement perceived to be threatening.

Then Neal stated he wanted to talk to a particular lawyer before turning himself in. When that lawyer couldn't be located, Neal requested to talk to a public defender. At that point, chief deputy district attorney Mark Pautler devised a scheme whereby he would pretend to be a public defender in order to get Neal's surrender. Telling his boss that exigent circumstances warranted such a tactic, Pautler was given permission, and then facilitated Neal's surrender after talking to him on the phone.

No one from the public defender's office was told of this deceitful tactic. Therefore, when the chief public defender approached Neal, Neal told him he was already represented. He gave his lawyer's name as "Mark Palmer," the fake name Pautler gave himself for the phone calls.

Upon realizing the government had deceived him, this already conspiracy-challenged defendant eventually fired his actual public defender, represented himself, pled guilty to the murder charges, represented himself at the sentencing proceedings, and was sentenced to death.

After being accused of violating Colorado's Rules of Professional Conduct for having engaged in a knowing deceit, Pautler argued that his conduct was warranted by the gravity and emergency of the situation. He said that he was justified in deceiving a murderer into getting him to surrender without hurting anyone else.

Despite the forcefulness of Pautler's argument, the Colorado Supreme Court disagreed. The Court concluded that prosecuting attorneys have a higher duty of honesty than the average lawyer, and that Pautler "violated duties owed to the legal system, the profession, and the public." Finding it troubling that Pautler said he would do it all over again if he had to, the Court suspended him for three months. However, it stayed the suspension and put him on 12 months probation, ordered him to retake an ethics exam, to take an extra 29 hours of continuing legal education credits, and required him to be directly supervised by an experienced attorney.

The codes of conduct drafted by paralegal organizations also require their members to be forthright when communicating with unrepresented persons. Guideline 1 of the NALA Model Standards and Guidelines for Utilization of Legal Assistants states, "Legal assistants should: 1. Disclose their status as legal assistants at the outset of any professional relationship with a client, other attorneys, a court or administrative agency or personnel thereof, *or members of the general public*." (Emphasis added.) Furthermore, Canon 1 of the NALA Code of Ethics and Professional Responsibility provides that "A legal assistant . . . [may not] take any actions that attorneys may not take," while Canon 5 restates Guideline 1 of the NALA Model Standards. EC–1.7(a) of the NFPA Model Disciplinary Rules and Ethical Considerations states, "A paralegal's title shall clearly indicate the individual's status and shall be disclosed in all business and professional communications *to avoid misunderstandings and misconceptions about the paralegal's role and responsibilities*." (Emphasis added.)

When communicating with witnesses who are unrepresented, paralegals and legal assistants must keep two important maxims in mind: (a) do not give legal advice; and (b) do not tell witnesses what to do or say. Refraining from giving legal advice is hard to do when in contact with unrepresented witnesses because once they know the interviewer works for a lawyer, they are likely to ask, "What should I do?" Lawyers must be careful that their information gathering does not cross the line into causing the witness to think that the lawyer-client relationship has been created. Paralegals also need to be especially careful when communicating with unrepresented witnesses, not only in identifying their role and status, but also in how they deal with the witness's questions.

In addition to previously cited rules on honesty, ABA Model Rule 3.4(a) prohibits a lawyer from unlawfully obstructing another party's access to evidence or unlawfully destroying or hiding things that have evidentiary value. MR 3.4(b) and (f) also prohibit a lawyer from assisting a witness in testifying falsely or counseling someone, including a prospective witness, to refuse to give relevant information to the other side. That prohibition also would include advising a prospective witness person to leave the jurisdiction. Witness preparation is an acknowledged part of trial preparation, but not much is stated in the rules about what would cross the line from appropriate preparation into inappropriate coaching, other than to say that lawyers may not assist witnesses in offering perjured testimony. When interviewing witnesses or assisting them in preparing for deposition or trial testimony, paralegals must not tell witnesses—including clients—what to say or what the legal impact of their testimony would be.

Advising a witness to leave the jurisdiction is considered to be an obstruction of justice, even if the lawyer claims a good faith reason for such advice. An Ohio lawyer, after completing the direct examination of his client, advised his client (during a recess) to leave the courthouse and not go directly home, so that the client, by his absence, could not be subject to cross-examination. To the trial court's astonishment, the lawyer claimed the advice was given because the lawyer believed that, after the recess was over, the unfinished case was barred by operation of a statutory timetable and, therefore, the court no longer had jurisdiction over the case. Neither the trial court nor the disciplinary panel was impressed by the tactic, and the lawyer was sanctioned. *Office of Disciplinary Counsel v. Slodov*, 660 N.E.2d 1164 (Ohio 1996).

Ex Parte Communication and Truthfulness

Although lawyers are duty bound to zealously represent their clients, all actions performed on their clients' behalf must be within the bounds of fairness. Included in this notion of fairness is the prohibition on lawyers having **ex parte communication** (i.e., private or outside the presence of opposing counsel) with judges or jury members. The Ethics 2000 version of ABA Model Rules 3.5(a) and (b) state,

1. "A lawyer shall not: (a) seek to influence a judge, juror, prospective juror or other official by means prohibited by law;

2. communicate ex parte with such a person during the proceeding unless authorized to do so by law or court order."

The Ethics 2000 version includes rephrasing MR 3.5(b) to limit its application to "during the proceeding." Also, the prohibition on communicating with a juror was moved to a new MR 3.5(c), and the prohibition was rephrased to allow post-verdict communications with jurors unless prohibited by court order, or the juror declares a desire not to communicate, or if the communication involves deceit, duress, or harassment. This relaxing of the prohibition against juror communication was prompted because some courts have ruled that the former MR 3.5(b) was unconstitutionally overbroad because it applied to all juror communications, including even after the trial was over.

ex parte communication
Communication made to the court during litigation in the absence of the other party or the other party's attorney.

venire

A member of the legal process, including the jury.

The Model Code has a similar prohibition. DR 7–108(A) states, "Before the trial of a case a lawyer . . . shall not communicate with . . . anyone he knows to be a member of the **venire**," and DR 7–108(B) prohibits a lawyer from communicating with "any member of the jury" during the trial of a case; and DR 7–110(B) prohibits a lawyer from "communicat[ing] . . . as to the merits of the cause with a judge or an official before whom the proceeding is pending, except . . . upon adequate notice to opposing counsel" unless "otherwise authorized by law."

Contacting a judge without the knowledge of the opposing counsel is wrong, even if the contact is not made for the purposes of trying to influence the judge. Recall from Chapter 7 that one of the violations that contributed to F. Lee Bailey's disbarment was his ex parte letter to the trial judge overseeing the plea bargain and sentence of Bailey's drug-dealing client. In fact, the court acknowledged that Bailey's ex parte communication with the judge was, by itself, sufficient to warrant disbarment.

The rules on juror-communication are even stricter than those concerning judges because, although many jurisdictions allow a lawyer to communicate with a judge during a case if the contact is unrelated to the case (such as a social contact), contact with a juror, even in a social setting, can result in a mistrial. In an Iowa case, a trial verdict in favor of the defendant was overturned because two of the defendant's lawyers had shared a drink with the jury foreman before the trial was over, after coincidentally meeting in a restaurant on a Friday night. Even though the juror was the one who initiated the contact and there was no evidence that the trial was discussed during the social contact, the appellate court found such contact projected an appearance of impropriety that cast doubt on the jury system. *Omaha Bank for Cooperatives v. Siouxland Cattle Cooperative*, 305 N. W.2d 458 (Iowa 1981). Beyond that, some jurisdictions prohibit lawyers or their employees from contacting jurors even after the trial is complete (*L.S. Mississippi Bar*, 649 So. 2d 810 (Miss. 1995)), or require court permission before making post-trial contact with jurors (*Florida Bar v. Newhouse*, 489 So. 2d 935 (Fla. 1986)), or prohibit post-trial contact if designed to influence the juror in future trials (*Commission for Lawyer Discipline v. Benton*, 980 S.W.2d 425 (Tex. 1998)). Even before the ABA modified its stance on juror contact, some ethics opinions did allow for post-trial juror contact, including one ethics opinion allowing a firm to assign a paralegal the responsibility of contacting the jurors, as long as the contact involves no harassment or intimidation. Pa. State Bar Association, Ethics Op. 91–52 (1991).

The NFPA Model Disciplinary Rules and Ethical Considerations clearly states in EC–1.2(a): "A paralegal shall not engage in any ex parte communications involving the courts or any other adjudicatory body in an attempt to exert undue influence or to obtain advantage or the benefit of only one party." Because paralegals can be valuable members of the trial team, the opportunity for inappropriate contact is equally available to them. From **voir dire** through the trial, paralegals need to do more than avoid discussing the case with the jurors;

voir dire

The process of picking jurors by questioning prospective jurors on matters related to the case, including biases and prejudices.

they must stay away from them. Furthermore, a paralegal must speak up if she knows anyone in the jury pool or on the jury. An extreme example of lawyer misconduct involved a prospective juror who was married to the legal secretary of one of the parties' lawyers. Not only did the prospective juror lie about his wife's employment, but the lawyer was also complicit in the fraud, failing to truthfully question the prospective juror about his relationships with any of the parties. When the fraud was discovered, the lawyer was suspended for six months. *Matter of Roberts*, 442 N.E.2d 986 (Ind. 1982).

Although lawyers can use jury consultants to help identify favorable prospective jurors (but certainly not to the extent shown in the film *Runaway Jury*), lawyers and their employees cross the line when trying to make contact with prospective jurors. Courts even sanction lawyers when their associates have made intentional contact with the relatives of prospective jurors or jurors to determine the jurors' views on matters related to the litigation. *See In re Two Anonymous Members of the South Carolina Bar*, 298 S.E.2d 450 (S.C. 1982). In a federal patent infringement case, the district court sanctioned a lawyer who employed a private investigator to investigate jurors on the lawyer's trial. The private investigator used a telephone survey as the pretext to contact the jurors. Although the investigator concocted the telephone survey scheme, the lawyer's culpability was attributed to that he delegated to his "poorly trained" paralegal the responsibility to contact the investigator. It was fitting that part of the sanctions included a requirement that the law firm formulate a seminar to train its paralegals about the ethical pitfalls of litigation. *Hill-Rom Company, Inc. v. Kinetic Concepts, Inc.* (S.C. Jan. 14, 1999).

Contact with jurors can go beyond the stupid to the criminal and become jury tampering. All states and the federal government have jury-tampering statutes. For instance, federal law criminalizes the threatening or intimidation of jurors, as well as attempts to influence them, including in writing, and provides for punishments that can include many years in prison. 18 U.S.C. § 1503 and § 1504. See Exhibit 8–6 for a summary of the ex parte communication rule.

EXHIBIT 8–6   EX PARTE COMMUNICATION

- **What is it?**
  - *Communicating with a judge, juror, or prospective juror in the absence of the other party or that party's attorney.*

- **Why does it matter?**
  - *Ex parte communication is prohibited by ABA Model Rule 3.5 and ABA Model Code DR 7–108, and NFPA Model Disciplinary Rules, EC–1.2(a).*
  - *The Ethics 2000 version of 3.5 even puts limitation on contacting a juror at the conclusion of a case.*
  - *If a paralegal or legal assistant engages in ex parte communication, it can lead to a mistrial, a reversal, ethics charges, and even sanctions.*

Legal Research and Truthfulness

Both the ABA Model Rules and Model Code make it clear that, when citing legal authority to a court, either orally or in writing, a lawyer must disclose authority that is directly adverse to the lawyer's client when the authority comes from the court's jurisdiction and the other lawyer fails to cite it. MR 3.3(a)(2) (Ethics 2000); DR 7–106(B)(1). At first blush, it seems antithetical to the competitive nature of litigation to require one lawyer to do what might be described as the other lawyer's work. If, during the course of representing a client, a lawyer fails to discover a statute or case that is directly helpful, how unhappy would the other lawyer's client be to find out that his or her advocate shared that helpful statute or case with the judge? It seems evident that if such directly adverse authority were found by the lawyer whose client would be hurt by its discovery, then the lawyer whose client would be helped by such a discovery should have been able to find it in the first place.

This ethical dilemma is a conflict of duties, but because lawyers are officers of the court, their duty to the administration of justice is paramount to their duty to their clients. Courts make decisions based on the applicable law, and lawyers are expected to provide courts with all applicable law. In fact, the Comment to MR 3.3 that concerns this duty to provide directly adverse authority says, "The underlying concept is that legal argument is a discussion seeking to determine the legal premises properly applicable to the case." Because legal research is one of the authorized tasks that legal assistants can perform, it is incumbent on those legal researchers to make their supervising attorneys aware of directly adverse, controlling authority. To qualify, such primary authority would: (1) have to come from the same jurisdiction of the court who has authority over the litigation (e.g., a Kansas Supreme Court case being contemplated for litigation occurring in a Kansas court); and (2) be directly adverse (i.e., a holding that is specifically negative to the client's position). Even if the legal researcher is unsure whether the discovered authority is directly adverse, it is better to err on the side of caution and show the research to the supervising attorney.

Some critics argue that such a rule is much ado about nothing because in order to sanction a lawyer for failing to disclose directly adverse controlling authority, a court would first have to establish that the lawyer knew of the directly adverse authority, not simply that the lawyer did not cite it. For example, in a case from Texas, a lawyer representing a defendant convicted of murder cited to the appellate court one case that had become moot due to a change in an operative statute. At the oral arguments, that lawyer supported his argument by citing a case that had been expressly overruled six years earlier by a controlling case. Although the court advised the lawyer to do better research in the future, no sanction was given because there was no evidence that the lawyer knowingly violated Texas's rule on citing directly adverse authority. *Geter v. State* 1996 WL 459767 (Tex.App.-Dallas 1996, not designated for publication). A court, however, can conclude that a case or statute *should have been found* by a lawyer, as was the case in Florida where an appellate court concluded that a lawyer was wrong in citing to a trial court a statute the lawyer should have known was not in effect at the time of the underlying matter. *Dilallo By and Through Dilallo v. Riding Safely, Inc.* 687 So.2d 353 (Fla. App. 1997). Others argue that such a rule is almost irrelevant because there are few cases where lawyers have been professionally disciplined for violating Model Rule 3.3(a)(2) (which was 3.3(a) in its prior version). However, there are more than a few cases, particularly federal cases, where lawyers have been sanctioned under civil procedure Rule 11 for failing to cite directly adverse authority.

Not every jurisdiction expresses concern about whether its lawyers are failing to cite directly adverse, controlling authority. Alabama, the first state to have a code of lawyer ethics, has dispensed altogether with the requirement that its lawyers cite to the court directly adverse authority, as has Kentucky. Ala. Rules of Prof. Conduct, 3.3; Kentucky Rules of Prof. Conduct, 3.3.

In the following case, the appellate court has little difficulty concluding that the lawyers in question *knowingly* failed to cite directly adverse authority that was controlling in the jurisdiction.

CASE LAW 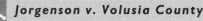 *Jorgenson v. Volusia County*

846 F.2d 1350 (11th Cir. 1988)

PER CURIAM

The appellants, attorneys Eric Latinsky and Fred Fendt, were sanctioned by the district court pursuant to Fed.R.Civ.P. 11 for failing to cite adverse, controlling precedent in a memorandum filed in support of an application for a temporary restraining order and a preliminary injunction. In the appellants' initial appeal to this court, the case was remanded to the district court because the court had failed to notify the attorneys in advance that it was considering sanctions, and did not give them an opportunity to respond. Jorgenson v. County of Volusia, 824 F.2d 973 (11th Cir.1987) (unpublished opinion). On remand, the district court reaffirmed the imposition of sanctions, and the attorneys appeal. We affirm.

Appellants filed an application in the district court for a temporary restraining order and a preliminary injunction on behalf of their clients, who own and operate a lounge known as "Porky's." In support of the application, appellants filed a memorandum of law which challenged the validity of a Volusia County ordinance prohibiting nude or semi-nude entertainment in commercial establishments at which alcoholic beverages are offered for sale or consumption. The memorandum failed to discuss or cite two clearly relevant cases: *City of Daytona Beach v. Del Percio*, 476 So.2d 197 (Fla.1985) and *New York State Liquor Authority v. Bellanca*, 452 U.S. 714, 101 S.Ct. 2599, 69 L.Ed.2d 357 (1981). We find that this failure supports the imposition of Rule 11 sanctions in the circumstances of this case.

(continues)

CASE LAW   *Jorgenson v. Volusia County* (continued)

The field of law concerning the regulation of the sale and consumption of alcohol in connection with nude entertainment is a narrow and somewhat specialized field. Prior to the opinion of the Supreme Court of Florida in Del Percio, the critical question of whether the state of Florida had delegated its powers under the Twenty-First Amendment to counties and municipalities had gone unanswered. In some circles, that decision was long-awaited. If the state had delegated the authority, local ordinances regulating the sale or consumption of alcohol would be entitled to a presumption in favor of their validity which is conferred by the Twenty-First Amendment. *See Bellanca,* 452 U.S. at 718, 101 S.Ct. at 2601. If the state had not delegated the authority, the ordinances would be subject to the stricter review applicable to exercises of the general police power. *See Krueger v. City of Pensacola,* 759 F.2d 851, 852 (11th Cir.1985).

The question regarding Florida's delegation of its powers under the Twenty-First Amendment was answered by the Supreme Court of Florida in *Del Percio,* a case in which one of the appellants, Latinsky, participated. The court held that the powers had been delegated. Less than one year later, on or about January 13, 1986, Latinsky and an associate brought the instant suit seeking a declaration that a similar ordinance was unconstitutional and requesting a temporary restraining order and a preliminary injunction. In their presentation to the court, the appellants cited a number of cases describing the limits on the exercise of the general police power. However, they did not advise the court in any way that *Del Percio* had been decided, despite the fact that *Del Percio* required that the validity of the ordinance be judged in light of powers retained under the Twenty-First Amendment rather than the general police power.

The appellants purported to describe the law to the district court in the hope that the description would guide and inform the court's decision. With apparently studied care, however, they withheld the fact that the long-awaited decision by the Supreme Court of Florida had been handed down. This will not do. The appellants are not redeemed by the fact that opposing counsel *subsequently* cited the controlling precedent. The appellants had a duty to refrain from affirmatively misleading the court as to the state of the law. They were not relieved of this duty by the possibility that opposing counsel might find and cite the controlling precedent, particularly where, as here, a temporary restraining order might have been issued *ex parte.*

In this court, appellants argue that the cases were not cited because they are not controlling. We certainly acknowledge that attorneys are legitimately entitled to press their own interpretations of precedent, including interpretations which render particular cases inapplicable. It is clear, however, that appellants' attempts to show that *Del Percio* and *Bellanca* are not controlling are simply post hoc efforts to evade the imposition of sanctions. Neither the original complaint nor the memorandum of law filed by appellants in the district

(continues)

> **CASE LAW**   *Jorgenson v. Volusia County* (continued)
>
> court reflect or support the arguments they now raise. Indeed, it is likely that the arguments were not raised previously because they are completely without merit. In the circumstances of this case, the imposition of Rule 11 sanctions by the district court was warranted. The judgment of the district court is AFFIRMED.
>
> ### Case Questions
>
> 1. How could the court safely conclude that the sanctioned lawyers knowingly failed to cite controlling authority?
>
> 2. Why would the *Del Percio* case be controlling in a federal court if that case came from a state appellate court?
>
> 3. If the opposing counsel cited both key cases to the District Court, why would the District Court and the Eleventh Circuit of Appeals bother to take the time to sanction the lawyers who failed to do so?

Prosecuting Attorney's Offices and the Truth

Prosecuting attorneys occupy a unique place in the legal system: they are advocates without clients, at least in the sense that "client" is used in the legal profession; the chief prosecutors in local and state offices run for office, which makes them politicians (the double shot of stiff drinks – one part politician, one part lawyer, no ice); prosecutors have the full authority of government and its unlimited resources behind them; and, with rare exception, prosecutors are protected from liability for their own mistakes. This last distinction is owed to the doctrine of **governmental immunity**, which stems from English common law and the famous phrase from the 18th Century's most famous and quoted legal commentator, William Blackstone, that the king can do no wrong. Although there are various types and levels of immunity, personal immunity often covers the official acts of government employees, like prosecuting attorneys, when those actions are accompanied by a good faith belief in their correctness. Thus, the lawsuit that awaits the private practice attorney for her errors of practice or judgment is unlikely to be wielded against the government attorney.

Although attorneys in prosecutor's offices are generally insulated from personal liability, their licenses are not so immune, because they are still subject to the rules of ethics in their jurisdiction. Therefore, paralegals who work in prosecuting attorney's offices (and in similar government legal offices) must be acquainted with the key rules that are directly applicable. As already discussed earlier in the text, the screening allowances for government attorneys and their

■ governmental immunity

Also known as sovereign immunity, a doctrine from English common law that holds that government may not be sued for its actions unless it first gives permission to be sued. This doctrine traditionally protects governments and their employees against being sued for their official actions.

non-lawyer employees were historically more liberal than for those in private practice. And the rules on truth discussed in the prior sections equally apply to government attorneys and paralegals.

There also exists a separate rule specifically directed to prosecuting attorneys, Rule 3.8 of the ABA Model Rules of Professional Conduct. It has six sections, but all of them concern obligations toward being fair and truthful to those accused of a crime. Rule 3.8(a) forbids a prosecutor from charging someone with a crime when there is no **probable cause** for doing so, while 3.8(b) and (c) require prosecutors to protect a defendant's constitutional rights to a defense lawyer and against a mistaken waiver of the right against self-incrimination. Prosecutors have unlimited discretion; their decisions to charge, or not charge, someone with a crime is theirs alone. However, when prosecutors abuse their discretion, they can find themselves on the receiving end of a similar discretion, the decision to bring disciplinary charges against them. In an Indiana case, a prosecuting attorney decided the best chance at reelection was to threaten his likely opponent with the bringing of dormant criminal charges that the opponent had falsified a client's statements. The Indiana Supreme Court found this "thinly veiled" threat to be an abuse of prosecutorial discretion and suspended the attorney for 30 days. *Matter of Christoff,* 690 N.E.2d 1135 (Ind. 1997). And the chief deputy prosecutor was publicly reprimanded for his role in the matter. *Id.* at 1141.

Rule 3.8(d) is a rule relating to discovery and shows that the obligation to be fair and truthful is a serious obligation. It requires a prosecuting attorney to, in a timely fashion, give to the defendant any evidence which would tend to be "exculpatory," which means would negate his or her guilt, as well as disclose to the court and a convicted defendant any unprivileged mitigating information that could affect sentencing. This duty is one that can be traced to U.S. Supreme Court decisions. *See Brady v. Maryland,* 373 U.S. 83 (1963); *United States v. Bagley,* 473 U.S. 667 (1985); *Kyles v. Whitley,* 514 U.S. 419 (1995). In a Colorado case where an assistant district attorney had a letter in her possession, written by the alleged victim of domestic violence and which recanted her earlier statements and corroborated the defendant's version of events, the attorney held onto the letter until after the preliminary hearing, believing the letter would not change the outcome of the hearing. Although the Colorado Supreme Court held that its Rule 3.8(d) requires prosecutors to turn over any exculpatory evidence *before any critical stage of the proceeding,* it found that the attorney's misconduct was not an intentional violation. *In re Attorney C,* 47 P.3d 1167 (Colo. 2002).

ABA Model Rule 3.8(e) discusses the propriety of a prosecuting attorney issuing a subpoena to another attorney in a grand jury or other criminal proceeding. It prohibits a subpoena from being issued with respect to the receiving attorney's current or past client unless three conditions are met: 1) the subpoena seeks information not protected by a privilege; 2) the evidence sought is "essential" to an ongoing investigation or prosecution; and 3) there is no

probable cause

A sufficient legal reason, based on the known facts and circumstances, for arresting or indicting someone, as well as for obtaining a warrant.

feasible alternative to subpoenaing the lawyer. This rule can be read in conjunction with ABA Rule 3.7, which establishes strict guidelines on when a lawyer may testify in a trial where the lawyer is representing someone.

Because so much news coverage is dedicated to legal news (or, at least, legal stories involving celebrities and the infamous), and with the advent of Court TV (renamed "truTV"), who would think there is a rule regarding what lawyers may publicly say regarding their current cases? Actually, there is more than one. Rule 3.8(f) states that:

> except for statements that are necessary to inform the public of the nature and extent of the prosecutor's action and that serve a legitimate law enforcement purpose, [prosecutors shall] refrain from making extrajudicial comments that have a substantial likelihood of heightening public condemnation of the accused and exercise reasonable care to prevent investigators, law enforcement personnel, employees or other persons assisting or associated with the prosecutor in a criminal case from making an extrajudicial statement that the prosecutor would be prohibited from making under Rule 3.6 or this Rule.

Rule 3.6 of the ABA Model Rules, referenced in 3.8(f), is a lengthy rule that describes when lawyers are allowed to make "extrajudicial" statements that are intended or likely to be disseminated in the media. Notice that 3.8(f) expressly puts under its coverage (and the coverage of 3.6) those persons who work for or with prosecuting attorneys. This portion of 3.8(f) is the work of Ethics 2000, as is the last paragraph in the Comments, which makes reference to Rule 5.3, the critical rule for paralegals. So, prosecutorial paralegals have been warned.

The U. S. Supreme Court heard a case in 1991 dealing with Nevada's rule on extrajudicial statements. Although it narrowly concluded that Nevada's then-version of 3.6 was unconstitutionally vague, it also decided that the First Amendment was not violated by prohibiting a lawyer from making extrajudicial statements that created a "substantial likelihood of materially prejudicing" the proceedings. *Gentile v. State Bar of Nevada*, 501 U.S. 1030 (1991). Often, the timing of the public statement is the most important factor in determining if the speaker has violated the rule. See, for instance, *Iowa Supreme Court Board of Professional Ethics and Conduct v. Visser*, 629 N.W.2d 376 (Iowa 2001), where a lawyer's statements to a reporter that were put in a newspaper article two years before the trial began, and in a newspaper published in a town 50 miles from the trial, were ruled to be not in violation of the extrajudicial statement rule (ABA Model Code DR 7-107 back then).

The Duke Rape Case: Miscarriage of Justice or Worse?

Does anyone still cling to the belief that David Evans, Reade Seligmann, and Collin Finnerty raped an exotic dancer in the upstairs bathroom of their rented house in Durham, North Carolina on March 13, 2006? That the alleged victim and a second dancer went to the house on that evening is not in dispute;

photographs from that evening show a house full of Duke lacrosse players partying with the help of the two strippers. What happened later that evening is no longer up to conjecture, although as the story began to first unfold and then unravel, there were two opposing views. Those with one view believed, like former Durham District Attorney Mike Nifong publicly claimed, that the three rich, white students from the prestigious, private university brutally assaulted the black, public college student working part-time as an exotic dancer. Those with the opposing view believed that the three men were assaulted by a prosecuting attorney, who, either grossly negligently or intentionally, foisted a nonexistent case as a means for his reelection. Not since Tom Wolfe's *Bonfire of the Vanities* has such a perfect storm of privilege, prejudice, and politics converged on the legal system in such a distressing way.

Unlike the harsh days of the common law, a rape victim's uncorroborated testimony of a rape is sufficient to convict. And DNA evidence is not required in any jurisdiction to prove that the accused committed the crime. But the case against the Duke students, based on the statements of the alleged victim and her friend, began to shift and contradict itself almost the first time its original version was told. And not only did the DNA evidence not establish what District Attorney Nifong said it would, it was withheld from the defense until after the grand jury indicted the young men.

The changes in the alleged victim's story ranged from the number of men who attacked her, to how long she was attacked, to the physical descriptions of the attackers, to the role played by her colleague, and eventually to the essential aspect of the attack. Considering that her accusation was one alleging violence and brutality, a lack of physical evidence of injury would have been troubling, especially because she recanted her initial claim, as did the other dancer, who claimed to be a witness and then not a witness. When a time-stamped ATM photograph was released showing Reade Seligmann to be nowhere near the house at the time of the alleged attack (any version), Mr. Nifong still pressed on, despite his claim in December, 2006, that he had yet to personally talk to the alleged victim, whose testimony would have to be the sole evidence in any trial.

DNA samples were taken in April of 2006 from all 46 white Duke lacrosse players, by result of a court application Nifong filed that said, "the DNA evidence requested will immediately rule out any innocent persons." But when the results proved negative (none of the 46 samples, including the three defendants', matched the DNA in or on the body of the alleged victim, despite the presence of several other men's DNA), the case still went forward. And, perhaps most troubling of all, the results of the DNA tests were withheld from the defendants until November. At that time, it was long after the felony indictments were handed down, and long after Mr. Nifong won a difficult primary reelection on May 2 that pitted him against two opponents, including one of his former employees. Mr. Nifong also won the general election that fall (again, before the DNA results were presented).

The campaign connection is critical, because during the months after the arrests, Mr. Nifong made numerous public statements on the pending investigation and prosecutions. He referred to the defendants as "hooligans" and said their "daddies" would buy them expensive lawyers. He alleged that there were racial overtones to the attack, including the defendants' use of racial slurs. In March of 2006, he talked to a reporter from ESPN and, in an astonishing remark, questioned why these three young men accused of a crime second only to first-degree murder in North Carolina would even want a lawyer: "And one would wonder why one needs an attorney if one was not charged and had not done anything wrong." And as it concerned the DNA tests, he publicly claimed that the lack of incriminating physical evidence was because the accused were wearing condoms—even though his own files had a statement from the accuser that the men were not wearing condoms and that as a result of their attack she spit out semen from her mouth.

By December of 2006, the accuser's story had changed again, and she claimed to not be certain that she was physically raped. Nifong withdrew the rape charges, but continued to prosecute the defendants for kidnapping and other sexual crimes. Adding to the sureality of it all, Nifong withdrew himself from the case in January, 2007, and requested the North Carolina Attorney General's Office to take over, which it did. And on April 11, 2007, state Attorney General Roy Cooper held a press conference to announce that all charges against the three students had been dropped, and called the three students "innocent." During his press conference, he referred to Mike Nifong as a "rogue prosecutor."

Why would an elected official, sworn to search for the truth in representing the people of his county, use all of his resources in a case that went from wobbly to broken, and then request to be removed from it? Mr. Nifong had another case to prepare: his own. On December 28, 2006, the North Carolina Bar Association filed ethics charges against Nifong, accusing him of repeatedly making extrajudicial statements that were "prejudicial to the administration of justice," a violation of the state's version of Rules 3.8(f) and 3.6(a). The 17-page filing also accused the district attorney of engaging in "conduct involving dishonesty, fraud, deceit or misrepresentation in violation of Rule 8.4(c)," which relates to the public statements he made that the defendants had worn condoms when they raped the accuser.

One month later, the bar association amended its complaint, adding even more serious charges. The bar accused Nifong of intentionally withholding potentially exculpatory evidence from the defense, in violation of North Carolina's Rule 3.8(d). Specifically, the bar alleged that Nifong ordered the private company he hired to test the DNA samples to keep the specific, negative results out of its official report, and then withheld those results until November, 2006. Beyond that, the bar accused Nifong of lying about the cover-up to the defense lawyers and also to the trial judge, whom Nifong told during a discovery hearing in May, 2006, "I've turned over everything I have." Furthermore, the bar accused Nifong of lying to the grievance commission in his responses to its initial ethics complaint. The amended complaint also re-accuses Nifong of violating Rule 3.6(a) and 8.4(c), as well as various violations of 3.3, and 3.4, rules on truthfulness to the tribunal and fairness to the opposing party and counsel.

Mr. Nifong's defense amounted to stressing that he did not intentionally violate the ethics rules. Mistakes happen. But such a defense did not prevent the North Carolina disciplinary committee from unanimously voting to disbar him in June 2007. The three-member-panel concluded that he was guilty of fraud, deceit, misrepresentations of material facts, and lying about withholding exculpatory evidence, "a clear case of intentional, prosecutorial misconduct," the committee declared. Perhaps sensing the inevitable hammer about to be dropped and hoping for a drop of goodwill, Nifong announced the day of the disbarment decision that he thought disbarment would be appropriate and that he would not appeal the panel's decision.

Nifong's legal troubles did not end with his disbarment and the July 2007 resignation of his office as Durham District Attorney. He was also charged with criminal contempt of court because of false statements he made at an evidentiary hearing during his original prosecution. In August 2007, he was convicted and sentenced to one day in jail, which he served. And still Mike Nifong is likely to be a defendant in court once again, because the three former students filed suit in October 2007, seeking unspecified damages against the city of Durham, Nifong, and the police detectives involved in the case. This federal lawsuit was filed approximately one month after the students' families sought a $30 million settlement and prosecutorial reforms from the city of Durham.

There is so much information to be sifted on this matter, no one or two Web links will suffice. But one can find many of the official documents from the cases on the Smoking Gun Web site: http://www.thesmokinggun.com/.

The most thorough and compelling source on the Duke Lacrosse debacle is a Web log created by KC Johnson, a historian who, with the country's leading legal journalist, Stuart Taylor, co-authored a book on the case, *Until Proven Innocent: Political Correctness and the Shameful Injustices of the Duke Lacrosse Rape Case.* Mr. Johnson's blog is: http://www.durhamwonderland.blogspot.com/.

MALPRACTICE LIABILITY FOR THE NONLAWYER

■ **malpractice**

Improper or harmful conduct committed by a professional in the course of their profession.

Malpractice is the bane of doctors and lawyers, the threat of which causes the purchase and careful renewal of malpractice liability insurance. And like any insurance, malpractice insurance is only needed by those who face the danger of liability. Can a non-lawyer be held liable for legal malpractice? The short answer is yes—although there are few cases that discuss the issue, and even fewer that involve paralegals. Logically, one might think that, because non-lawyers are unlicensed, they could not be held liable for malpractice, because malpractice is generally defined as the improper or negligent conduct of a professional in the performance of her profession. But there are occasions where courts have found non-lawyers liable for malpractice, despite their status.

What Constitutes Malpractice?

The cause of action for legal malpractice based on negligence has four elements: (1) a duty owed by the defendant to the plaintiff; (2) a breach of that duty, shown through a failure to exercise reasonable care; (3) losses suffered by the plaintiff; and (4) **proximate cause** between the defendant's negligent conduct and the plaintiff's losses. Concerning element 2, a failure to exercise reasonable care involves determining whether the lawyer's conduct was less than what a similarly situated, reasonable lawyer would have done. And, as is the case with any claim of negligence, there must be proximate cause: a direct link between the unreasonable act and the alleged harm. As a general rule, making a mistake, even a big mistake, would not result in malpractice if the plaintiff could not prove that the loss suffered was caused by the lawyer's misconduct. For instance, if a lawyer were to incompetently draft a will for a client who ended up spending every last penny before dying, there would be no malpractice case because a correctly drafted will would have resulted in the same outcome for the heirs—no inheritance.

■ **proximate cause**
A sufficient legal reason, based on the known facts and circumstances, for arresting or indicting someone, as well as for obtaining a warrant.

Sometimes, clients sue their lawyers for malpractice after a litigation loss, but just because a client lost a lawsuit does not necessarily mean that the lawyer was negligent. And even if the lawyer acted negligently, that does not mean there will be a finding of malpractice. To win such a malpractice claim, the client is generally required to show that the outcome would have been different "but for" the lawyer's blunder. Such a standard is akin to the client retrying the case in a "what if?" world. (What if a different lawyer had done things differently?) And if a court were to find that a case would have been unwinnable in any reasonable lawyer's hands, then the client's malpractice claim is thwarted.

In a case from Kansas illustrating that principle—as well as an example of a non-lawyer being liable for legal malpractice—a couple sued a lawyer and his brother for malpractice. It seems that the Webbs, fearing losing their house and 56 acres to foreclosure, transferred their property to some friends who put up some money to prevent the foreclosure. The Webbs used the services of Charles Pomeroy (the person who did their taxes) to draft the documents transferring title to their friends. Charles, however, failed to draft a written repurchase agreement so the Webbs could get their property back when they had the money. Following the title transfer, the Webbs made the monthly payments on the loan their friends had secured to forestall the foreclosure. But a few years later, the friends, in an unfriendly move, decided to sell the property, and the Webbs, now using E. Pomeroy (the lawyer-brother of Charles) lost the eventual lawsuit to get their title back. The Webbs then sued both brothers for malpractice. The Kansas Court of Appeals ruled in favor of E. Pomeroy in the malpractice lawsuit because the prior suit was lost because there was no written evidence of the repurchase agreement, and the suit to get the title back would have been lost regardless of E. Pomeroy's litigation tactics. However, the court reversed the trial court's directed verdict in favor of Charles Pomeroy. Upon holding Charles to the same standard as if he were a lawyer (because he wrongfully engaged in legal transactions), the court declared that he could be liable for his negligence in failing to secure a written repurchase agreement, which he had continued to tell the Webbs he would do. *Webb v. Pomeroy*, 655 P.2d 465 (Kan. App. 1982).

The Theory Behind Non-Lawyer Malpractice

If non-lawyer members of the legal team, such as paralegals, are so unregulated as to be unlicensed in their own profession—much less unlicensed to practice law—how could they be held liable as professionals for their misdeeds? The answer lies in the fact that malpractice is a tort; it is a particular kind of negligence. A court will not refuse to hold someone liable for negligence simply because that person had no legal right to do what she did incompetently. If that were the case, driving without a license might be a good idea. A professional license entitles one to engage in a profession, but it does not insulate the professional against professional negligence. Likewise, the lack of a license does not prevent a tortfeasor from being accountable for performing improper acts. Remember from Chapter 3 that a jurisdiction's highest court cannot sanction a non-lawyer for engaging in the unauthorized practice of law because the non-lawyer is not a member of the bar and, therefore, not subject to professional discipline. It can, however, issue a cease and desist order to the non-lawyer practicing law without a license and then hold her in contempt of court for a violation of the court's order.

Despite the lack of a regulating court's ability to discipline a non-lawyer, a jury could still find that her incompetent, unauthorized practice of law constituted negligence. In a Washington State case, property owners sold a piece of real estate with the assistance of a non-lawyer escrow agent who drafted the closing documents. Those documents failed to make the property a security interest in the transaction, and when the buyer eventually filed for bankruptcy and disappeared, the sellers lost $35,000. After finding that the escrow agent had engaged in the unauthorized practice of law, the Washington Supreme Court declared that the escrow agent's failure to explain to the sellers the significance of an unsecured real estate sale constituted legal negligence for which the escrow agent was liable. *Bowers v. Transamerica Title Ins. Co.*, 675 P.2d 193 (Wash. 1983). Other courts have held that non-lawyers may be liable for malpractice: *Torres v. Fiol*, 441 N.E.2d 1300 (Ill. App.1982) (non-lawyer holding himself out as provider of legal services errantly prepared mortgage documents); *Wright v. Langdon*, 623

S.W.2d 823 (Ark. 1981) (non-lawyer mistakenly drafted sales contract for house trailer); *Mattieligh v. Poe*, 356 P.2d 328 Wash. 1960) (real estate broker accused of negligently preparing sales contract).

The following landmark case involving a non-lawyer sued for malpractice has been cited in scores of cases, many of those concerning whether a beneficiary of a contract between a lawyer and a client can sue the lawyer for negligence.

CASE LAW *Biakanja v. Irving*

320 P.2d 16 (Cal. 1958)

GIBSON, Chief Justice.

Plaintiff's brother, John Maroevich, died, leaving a will which devised and bequeathed all of his property to plaintiff. The will, which was prepared by defendant, a notary public, was denied probate for lack of sufficient attestation. Plaintiff, by intestate succession, received only one-eighth of the estate, and she recovered a judgment against defendant for the difference between the amount which she would have received had the will been valid and the amount distributed to her.

Defendant, who is not an attorney, had for several years written letters and prepared income tax returns for Maroevich. The will was typed in defendant's office and "subscribed and sworn to" by Maroevich in the presence of defendant, who affixed his signature and notarial seal to the instrument. Sometime later Maroevich obtained the signatures of two witnesses to the will neither of whom was present when Maroevich signed it. These witnesses did not sign in the presence of each other, and Maroevich did not acknowledge his signature in their presence.

An attorney who represented Maroevich's stepson in the probate proceedings testified that he had a telephone conversation with defendant shortly after Maroevich's death, in which defendant said he prepared the will and notarized it. According to the attorney, defendant, in discussing how the will was witnessed, "admonished me to the effect that I was a young lawyer, I'd better go back and study my law books some more, that anybody knew a will which bore a notarial seal was a valid will, didn't have to be witnessed by any witnesses." The court found that defendant agreed and undertook to prepare a valid will and that it was invalid because defendant negligently failed to have it properly attested. The findings are supported by the evidence.

The principal question is whether defendant was under a duty to exercise due care to protect plaintiff from injury and was liable for damage caused plaintiff by his negligence even though they were not in privity of contract. In *Buckley v. Gray*, 1895, 110 Cal. 339, 42 P. 900, 31 L.R.A. 862, it was held that a person who was named as a beneficiary under a will could not recover damages from an attorney who negligently drafted and directed the execution of the will with the result that the intended beneficiary was deprived of substantial benefits.

(continues)

CASE LAW *Biakanja v. Irving (continued)*

The court based its decision on the ground that the attorney owed no duty to the beneficiary because there was no privity of contract between them. *Mickel v. Murphy*, 147 Cal.App.2d 718, 305 P.2d 993, relying on *Buckley v. Gray, supra*, held that a notary public who prepared a will was not liable to the beneficiary for failing to have it properly executed. When Buckley v. Gray, supra, was decided in 1895, it was generally accepted that, with the few exceptions noted in the opinion in that case, there was no liability for negligence committed in the performance of a contract in the absence of privity. Since that time the rule has been greatly liberalized, and the courts have permitted a plaintiff not in privity to recover damages in many situations for the negligent performance of a contract.

Liability has been imposed, in the absence of privity, upon suppliers of goods and services which, if negligently made or rendered, are "reasonably certain to place life and limb in peril." [citations omitted]... Prosser, Torts (2d ed. 1955), ss 84–85, p. 497 et seq. There is also authority for the imposition of liability where there is no privity and where the only foreseeable risk is of damage to tangible property [citations omitted]....[S]ee *Prosser, supra*, s 84, pp. 501–502....

The determination whether in a specific case the defendant will be held liable to a third person not in privity is a matter of policy and involves the balancing of various factors, among which are the extent to which the transaction was intended to affect the plaintiff, the foreseeability of harm to him, the degree of certainty that the plaintiff suffered injury, the closeness of the connection between the defendant's conduct and the injury suffered, the moral blame attached to the defendant's conduct, and the policy of preventing future harm. Cf. Prosser, Torts (2d ed. 1955), ss 36, 88, 107, pp. 168, 172, 544–545, 747; 2 Harper and James, Torts (1956), s 18.6, p. 1052. Here, the "end and aim" of the transaction was to provide for the passing of Maroevich's estate to plaintiff. See *Glanzer v. Shepard*, 233 N.Y. 236, 135 N.E. 275, 23 A.L.R. 1425. Defendant must have been aware from the terms of the will itself that, if faulty solemnization caused the will to be invalid, plaintiff would suffer the very loss which occurred. As Maroevich died without revoking his will, plaintiff, but for defendant's negligence, would have received all of the Maroevich estate, and the fact that she received only one-eighth of the estate was directly caused by defendant's conduct.

Defendant undertook to provide for the formal disposition of Maroevich's estate by drafting and supervising the execution of a will. This was an important transaction requiring specialized skill, and defendant clearly was not qualified to undertake it. His conduct was not only negligent but was also highly improper. He engaged in the unauthorized practice of the law (Bus. & Prof.Code, s 6125; cf. *People v. Merchants' Protective Corp.*, 189 Cal. 531, 535, 209 P. 363; *People v. Sipper*, 61 Cal.App.2d Supp. 844, 848, 142 P.2d 960; *Grand Rapids Bar Ass'n v. Denkema*, 290 Mich. 56, 287 N.W. 377, 380; *State ex rel. Wyoming State Bar v. Hardy*, 61 Wyo. 172, 156 P.2d 309, 313, which is a misdemeanor in violation of section 6126 of the

(continues)

CASE LAW   *Biakanja v. Irving* (continued)

Business and Professions Code. Such conduct should be discouraged and not protected by immunity from civil liability, as would be the case if plaintiff, the only person who suffered a loss, were denied a right of action.

We have concluded that plaintiff should be allowed recovery despite the absence of privity, and the cases of *Buckley v. Gray*, 110 Cal. 339, 42 P. 900, 31 L.R.A. 862, and *Mickel v. Murphy*, 147 Cal.App.2d 718, 305 P.2d 993, are disapproved insofar as they are in conflict with this decision.

The judgment is affirmed.

Case Questions

1. Aside from the fact that the notary should not have drafted and executed someone's will, what did she do that was negligent?

2. What is privity of contract, and why would it matter that the plaintiff lacked it?

3. Of the factors the court listed as decisive on whether someone should be liable to another without there being privity of contract, which factor do you think applied most directly here?

4. In addition to the negligence, what else convinced the court that the notary should be liable to the plaintiff for the loss of seven-eighths of the plaintiff's inheritance?

5. Does your jurisdiction allow non-lawyers to draft and execute wills or trusts?

When a court allows a law office employee to be held liable for legal malpractice, such an allowance flows first from a finding that the non-lawyer was engaging in the unauthorized practice of law, especially where the client is unaware of the non-lawyer's status. Then, if the client suffers from the incompetent acts of the non-lawyer's unauthorized performance, a court will hold the non-lawyer to the same standards of conduct to which a lawyer is held. A case from New York typifies the preceding doctrine, as well as the theme for this text: a paralegal or legal assistant is one who engages in substantive legal work for, and under the direction of, a licensed attorney. In *Sussman v. Grado*, 746 N.Y. S.2d 548 (N.Y. Dist. Ct. 2002), Sussman went to Grado, who called herself an independent paralegal, for assistance in collecting on an unpaid judgment, paying Grado $45 for the services. When Grado realized she did not know how to accomplish the collection, she returned the fee to Sussman, telling him that his business "will not be welcome here." *Id* at 550. Thinking the judgment became unenforceable because of Grado's inaction, Sussman sued Grado for negligence. The court concluded that Grado was not liable because the judgment was still alive and capable of being enforced, quite a "whew" moment for her. But it also ruled that she had committed the unauthorized practice of law, and awarded Sussman damages for Grado's deceptive business practices, and referred the case to the New York State Attorney General's Office. *Id* at 553.

The good news is, a paralegal or legal assistant *who is working under the supervision of a lawyer and in furtherance of lawyer's representation of the client* and who commits a negligent act would generally not be liable for malpractice. The bad news is, the lawyer would be, and that would be unpleasant for all involved.

In the following case, a law clerk was sued for malpractice by a client who believed that the law clerk was a lawyer. While reading it, notice the dissenting opinion's different view on the facts in the case.

CASE LAW *Busch v. Flangas*

837 P.2d 438 (Nev. 1992)

PER CURIAM

Appellant Mary Busch is the former owner of the Busch Bavarian Pastry Shop. In 1984, Busch agreed to sell the shop. A customer suggested that Busch contact respondent Delwin Potter, who worked for respondent Peter Flangas, to help draw up documents pertaining to the sale of the bakery. Believing Potter to be a lawyer, Busch contacted Flangas' law office and made an appointment with Potter. Potter was in fact a law clerk employed by Flangas. The necessary documents for the sale of the bakery were prepared, but a UCC-1 financing statement necessary to the perfecting of Busch's security interest in the bakery equipment pending final payment was never filed. The buyers failed to satisfy their financial obligation to Busch and eventually filed bankruptcy. Busch, as an unsecured creditor, lost her interest in the bakery equipment. Busch instituted a malpractice action against Potter and Flangas, alleging that Potter's negligence caused her to lose her security interest in the bakery equipment. Busch claimed that Flangas was also liable for his employee's negligence. Potter and Flangas claimed that another attorney had supervised Potter's work, thus relieving both of them of any liability. The district court granted summary judgment in favor of Potter and Flangas, and Busch appealed. We reverse. . . .

Even though both parties moved for summary judgment, this did not relieve the district court of its responsibility to determine whether genuine issues of fact existed. *Ardmore Leasing Corp. v. State Farm Mut. Auto. Ins. Co.*, 106 Nev. 513, 796 P.2d 232 (1990). Our review of the record reveals the existence of disputed material facts concerning the issue of Potter's and Flangas' liability. Summary judgment was therefore improper.

[The court first determined that the district court erred in concluding that Busch's bakery had been leased, instead of sold, and was, therefore, outside the scope of the Uniform Commercial Code.]

(continues)

CASE LAW   *Busch v. Flangas* (continued)

Busch presented substantial evidence indicating that the transaction required a UCC-1 financing statement, which Potter failed to file, to secure her interest in the bakery equipment. Although Potter is not an attorney, he can be subject to a legal malpractice claim if he attempts to provide legal services. See *Bowers v. Transamerica Title Ins. Co.*, 100 Wash.2d 581, 675 P.2d 193 (1983). Therefore, summary judgment was improperly granted as to Potter.

Flangas contends that he cannot be liable for malpractice because he never met Busch nor attempted to provide legal services for her. Clearly, this contention is without merit. Busch's claim against Flangas states a cause of action on a respondeat superior theory. Thus, Flangas may be liable for Potter's negligence if Potter was acting within the scope of his employment when he performed services for Busch. *Molino v. Asher*, 96 Nev. 814, 618 P.2d 878 (1980). Respondents concede that Potter was employed by Flangas, but claim that on this occasion Potter was supervised by another attorney 1 who maintains a separate practice, but who nevertheless occasionally utilized the services of Potter or Flangas' secretaries.

Busch claims that Flangas was responsible for supervising Potter's work, and attached to her opposition to the motions for summary judgment copies of Potter's paychecks from Flangas covering the period of time when Potter performed services for Busch. At a minimum, Busch raised a genuine issue below as to Flangas' liability. Therefore, summary judgment was improperly granted as to Flangas. NRCP 56(c).

After careful consideration, we have determined that the other issues raised by the parties are without merit. The summary judgment in favor of respondents is reversed, and the case is remanded to the district court for a trial on the merits.

SPRINGER, Justice, with whom LEAVITT, District Judge, agrees, dissenting:

I conclude that the trial court was correct in granting summary judgment; therefore, I respectfully dissent.

The Flangas Judgment

The case against Flangas is based on actual negligence on his part and not on vicarious liability. An employer is liable for an employee's acts which the employer authorized or ratified, upon familiar principles of negligence and agency. Vicarious liability, on the other hand, is based on conduct which is not the conduct of the employer but which extends to any and all tortious conduct which an agent performs within the "scope of employment." Busch does not plead a case for vicarious liability nor does she aver that all of Potter's tortious acts were done in the scope of his employment for Flangas. Rather than trying to impute Potter's negligence to Flangas under the doctrine of respondeat superior, Busch's complaint charges specific and independent negligence on the part of Flangas. According to the complaint, "Flangas knew that Defendant Potter was representing himself as an attorney

(continues)

CASE LAW   *Busch v. Flangas* (continued)

and performing legal services on behalf of Defendant Flangas." In other words, Flangas knowingly let a non-lawyer work in his office as a lawyer. There is no evidence that this charge is true.

Busch argues in her "Opposition to Motion for Summary Judgment" that Potter is guilty of "malpractice per se." This may be true, but absent an allegation that such untoward and outrageous action by Potter was done in the scope and power of his employment by Flangas, no vicarious liability can exist.| Because there is no claim for vicarious liability and because there is no evidence to support actual negligence on the part of Flangas, I would affirm the trial court's summary judgment in his favor.

The Potter Judgment

The gist of Busch's claim against Potter is that Potter "represented himself to Plaintiff as an attorney and further represented that he was competent and able to prepare all documents . . . and . . . to protect the Plaintiff 's [legal] interests," and that Potter was then guilty of legal malpractice when he "negligently failed and omitted to cause the UCC-1 Financing Statement to be filed with the appropriate agency."

If, as is clearly the case, Potter had not "represented himself to Plaintiff as an attorney," he could not, of course, have undertaken the duty "to prepare all documents" nor "to fully protect the Plaintiff 's [legal] interests." By Busch's own testimony, neither Flangas nor Potter ever represented that Potter was a lawyer. Busch "assumed" that Potter was a lawyer because one of her customers at the bakery told her so. There is no evidence that Potter was either acting as a lawyer or representing himself to be a lawyer. According to Potter's affidavit, he prepared the documents in question at the behest of and under the supervision of another attorney, John Stone. I believe that the trial court was correct in concluding that there was no evidence to support the allegation that Potter "represented himself to Plaintiff as an attorney" or that as a non-attorney working for attorney Stone, Potter owed a duty to Busch relative to the preparation and filing of the UCC documents. I would affirm the trial court's summary judgment in favor of Potter.

The following case footnotes correspond to the portions of the case that are printed in the textbook. Although it may seem that other footnotes are missing, they are not presented because their corresponding portions of the court's opinion have been redacted.

| The statute of limitations has run against this other attorney, precluding a claim against him.

| In the mentioned Opposition papers, Busch tardily mentions "the theory of respondeat superior," but neither the complaint nor the motion documents support this kind of claim of liability.

(continues)

CASE LAW **Busch v. Flangas** *(continued)*

Case Questions

1. If Potter worked for attorney Flangas, why did the court say that Potter could be separately liable for malpractice?

2. What evidence showed that Potter worked for Flangas?

3. Why does the dissent believe that the summary judgment in favor of Flangas should be affirmed?

4. Why does the dissent believe that the summary judgment in favor of Potter should be affirmed?

5. Do you think Potter held himself out as a lawyer to Busch?

See Exhibit 8–7 for a summary of the issue concerning paralegals and malpractice liability.

NOT QUITE LINCOLN

Boy Oh Boies! One Paralegal's Brush with Career Death

"This appeal represents a lawyer's nightmare." That could be the hackneyed opening of a legal potboiler written by any number of lawyers turned authors. Unfortunately, that quote is the very first sentence in an opinion by the Ninth Circuit Court of Appeals in 2004, in an appeal brought by David Boies, superlawyer and, in this case, supplicant of the court's mercy.

However, the nightmare was not only a lawyer's; it also belonged to one of Boies's paralegals, whose neglect made it necessary to ask an appellate court to disregard the rules on timely filing an appeal.

Fifteen years earlier, two jockeys sued their business managers for racketeering violations under federal law—RICO, as it is known. Mr. Boies and his firm represented the defendants, who lost at trial in 1992.

The plaintiffs, however, chose a remedy that was barred by the statute of limitations (a small affliction that would prove to be contagious). Thus, an appellate court sent the case back to the trial court for another bite at the damages apple. When the plaintiffs made their amended claim for damages, the court entered a judgment against the defendants on July 3, 2002.

However, Mr. Boies's paralegal, whose job it was to keep track of deadlines for filing notices of appeals, misread the Federal Rules of Appellate Procedure, believing that Rule 4 (a)(1)(B) provided 60 days to file an appeal. But 60 days is only given when the government is a party, and Rule 4(a)(1)(A), which clearly applied, provides only 30 days.

Somewhere between 30 and 60 days after the judgment was issued, Mr. Boies discovered the error and asked for an extension of time, under the doctrine of "excusable neglect," to file an appeal. The District Court granted his request, so the victorious plaintiffs went to the Ninth Circuit. There, a three-judge panel dismissed Mr. Boies's appeal, concluding that he inappropriately delegated the critical function of scheduling to his paralegal. The judges held, as matter of law, that Mr. Boies's reliance on his paralegal was inexcusable.

Showing the kind of mettle that helped Vice President Gore protest the 2000 presidential election almost to Christmas, Mr. Boies then requested the entire panel of Ninth Circuit justices to hear his case *en banc*. The panel agreed to do so, and then it ruled in Mr. Boies's favor, reversing the three-judge panel version of itself in *Pincay v. Andrews*, 389 F.3d 853 (9th Cir. 2004). Namely, the Ninth Circuit reexamined the strict rule of the earlier decision, that delegating such a scheduling task to a paralegal was impermissible.

Applying the U.S. Supreme Court's standard on excusable neglect in *Pioneer Investment Services v. Brunswick Associates*, 507 U.S. 380 (1993), the *en banc* court concluded that more flexibility was called for. Despite calling the error "egregious" and both the lawyer and the paralegal "negligent," the Ninth Circuit found no reason to overturn the District Court's ruling that the missed deadline, although neglectful, was still excusable.

EXHIBIT 8-7 MALPRACTICE LIABILITY AND THE PARALEGAL

- **Can a Non-Lawyer Be Liable for Malpractice?**
  - *YES!*
  - *A non-lawyer's liability is predicated on the non-lawyer's commission of the unauthorized practice of law.*
  - *Courts take the view that if non-lawyers acts like lawyers, then they will be held to the professional standards of lawyers.*
- **What About Paralegals?**
  - *If a paralegal engages in UPL, independent of a lawyer-supervisor, and commits a negligent act, it is possible that the paralegal could be sued for malpractice.*
  - *But if a paralegal engages in work under the direction and supervision of a lawyer, then even negligent acts wouldn't result in a finding of "paralegal malpractice."*
  - *The paralegal would not be in the clear with the supervising lawyer, though.*

Non-Lawyer Malpractice Is Not a Universal View

Not all jurisdictions subscribe to the view that a non-lawyer can be found liable for legal malpractice. For instance, Ohio does not allow a paralegal to be sued for malpractice. In an Ohio case, the president of a corporation sued the corporation's attorney and the attorney's paralegal for malpractice, and the case was dismissed on summary judgment. While affirming the trial court's summary judgment, the Ohio Court of Appeals noted that because the paralegal was not an attorney, "she could not be charged with malpractice." *Palmer v. Westmeyer*, 549 N.E.2d 1202,1209 (Ohio App. 1988). (On a related note, Ohio parts company with the famous California case, *Biakanja v. Irving*, discussed earlier, and expressly holds that a beneficiary under a will may not bring a negligence claim against the attorney who drafted it because there is no privity of contract between them. *Simon v. Zipperstein*, 512 N.E.2d 636 (Ohio 1987)).

Similarly, in *In re Estate of Divine*, 635 N.E.2d 581 (Ill. App. 1994), discussed in Chapter 5 on conflicts of interest, the Illinois Court of Appeals refused to adopt the view that a paralegal has a fiduciary duty to the client because the paralegal works for the lawyer who does have a fiduciary duty to the client. In that case, the court refused to hold the paralegal liable to the heirs of an elderly client with whom that paralegal had become quite close, including being named a co-owner of the client's extremely large bank accounts and inheriting money under the client's will. And in Alabama, the Supreme Court ruled in a case with a similar, non-lawyer malpractice issue that there was no state right to sue a union for legal malpractice. The case involved disgruntled union members who sued their union for legal malpractice after the union inadequately represented the members in a discrimination suit. *United Steelworkers of America, AFL-CIO v. Craig*, 571 So.2d 1101 (Ala. 1990). (Although that case did not involve a paralegal, it did involve a non-lawyer being sued for malpractice.)

Even in California, where *Biakanja v. Irving* held that a non-lawyer could be liable for legal malpractice, there is a different view concerning negligent legal representation by non-lawyers in administrative adjudications. The case taking this position involved a steelworker who was injured on the job and was awarded over $8,000 by the state Industrial Accident Commission. The steelworker (named Bland) sued a fellow union member (named Reed), claiming that Reed's advice negligently caused Bland to miss out on suing an industrial company that Bland believed caused his injuries. The California Court of Appeals acknowledged that non-lawyers were engaging in legal practice when appearing before the Industrial Accident Commission, but it was authorized because state law allowed it. Nevertheless, the court ruled it was improper to hold a nonlawyer practicing before the commission to the same standard of care as that of a lawyer. *Bland v. Reed*, 67 Cal.Rptr. 859 (Cal. Ct. App. 1968).

PRO BONO SERVICES

Sharing is a virtue, and although *virtuous* is an adjective the public might rarely use when thinking about lawyers, the legal profession has a history of sharing its legal services with the less fortunate. In fact, one could make the argument that the indigent have more access to lawyers than does the middle class, at least as it concerns the right to state-provided representation in criminal cases and entry to state-sponsored legal aid. Within the lawyer culture, the idea of serving the public good is expressed formally in the rules concerning pro bono services. *Pro bono* is the short version of *pro bono publico*, which is Latin, meaning *for the public good or welfare.* Paralegals and legal assistants also have a heritage rich with benevolence and a hand outstretched, not to take but to give. Assisting lawyers in the provision of pro bono services is one of the key characteristics that puts paralegals in the ranks with true professionals.

The Evolution of the Pro Bono Rules

The ABA Model Code (the predecessor to the ABA Model Rules) has no Disciplinary Rules on pro bono services, but there are a few Ethical Considerations that discussed them. EC 2–25, following Canon 2, titled "A Lawyer Should Assist the Legal Profession in Fulfilling Its Duty to Make Legal Counsel Available," states:

The basic responsibility for providing legal services for those unable to pay ultimately rests upon the individual lawyer, and personal involvement in the problems of the disadvantaged can be one of the most rewarding experiences in the life of a lawyer. Every lawyer, regardless of professional prominence or professional workload, should find time to participate in serving the disadvantaged.

And EC 8–3, following Canon 8, titled "A Lawyer Should Assist in Improving the Legal System," declares, "Those persons unable to pay for legal services should be provided needed services."

The original version of the ABA Model Rules took a more definite position than did the Model Code by stating:

A lawyer should render public interest legal service. A lawyer may discharge this responsibility by providing professional services at no fee or a reduced fee to persons of limited means or to public service or charitable groups or organizations by service in activities for improving the law, the legal system, or the legal profession, and by financial support for organizations that provide legal services to persons of limited means. ABA MR 6.1 (1983 version).

The revised Model Rules version of 6.1 is more specific than the original version and states, "A lawyer should aspire to render at least (50) hours of pro bono publico legal services per year." MR 6.1 then lists ways in which a lawyer can fulfill that responsibility, including providing free or substantially discounted legal services to charitable or similar organizations, or persons of limited means. The current Ethics 2000 version of 6.1 has an additional opening sentence to the rule that states, "Every lawyer has a professional responsibility to provide legal services to those unable to pay." Some states have modified the 50-hour contribution stated in the ABA's 6.1 and have reduced the amount to between 20–30 hours (Florida, Massachusetts, Mississippi, Washington), while some have increased it, such as Nevada, which has a 60-hour recommendation. For an overview of the history of the ABA's pro bono rules, see Exhibit 8–8.

EXHIBIT 8–8   THE EVOLUTION OF THE PRO BONO RULES

ABA Model Code	ABA Model Rules (1983)	ABA Model Rules (Amended Version)	ABA Model Rules (Ethics 2000)
• No disciplinary rule on pro bono services. • Canon 2 said, "A lawyer should assist the legal profession in fulfilling its duty to make legal counsel available."	• Rule 6.1 said that a lawyer should render pro bono services, and listed ways that could be accomplished.	• Rule 6.1 was changed to say, "A lawyer should aspire to render at least (50) hours of pro bono publico legal services per year."	• Rule 6.1 now has an additional sentence: "Every lawyer has a professional responsibility to provide legal services to those unable to pay."

Despite the changes made to the original version of MR 6.1, many jurisdictions that have adopted the Model Rules (including much of Ethics 2000) still retain the language of the original MR 6.1, which has no language on how many pro bono hours per year should be given, including the following: Alabama, Connecticut, Delaware, Indiana, Kansas, Michigan, Nebraska, Oklahoma, Pennsylvania, South Carolina, West Virginia, and Wisconsin.

New York, a rare jurisdiction that follows the Model Code, has modified the language of its pro bono rule, EC 2–25, to include a 20-hours aspirational standard for annual pro bono services. Ohio, a former Model Code jurisdiction, has no version of 6.1, but is considering what to adopt. And Oregon, another former Model Code jurisdiction, has yet to adopt any version of 6.1, but still has an Aspirational Standard, 13.1 (not found in the Oregon Rules of Professional Conduct but in the Board of Bar Governors Policies) from its Model Code days, which states that every Oregon attorney should endeavor to annually provide 80 hours of pro bono services, including 20 to 40 hours of free representation to the poor.

In addition to recommending an annual service contribution of pro bono hours, some jurisdictions encourage their lawyers to provide annual financial contributions, often as an alternative to providing legal services. Massachusetts recommends its lawyers to provide $250 to 1 percent of their annual taxable, professional income to pro bono causes. The District of Columbia encourages the giving of the lesser of either $400 or 1 percent of the lawyer's earned income. Florida's recommended annual pro bono contribution is $350, while Nevada and Utah recommend $500.

Should Lawyers Be Required to Perform Pro Bono Services?

If one is not obligated to follow a rule, then there is no rule. Although MR 6.1 is part of the Model Rules, it is not mandatory because all versions use the word *should*. But, the original draft of the first version of MR 1.6 did use the word *shall*, instead of *should*. That language failed to survive the ABA legislative process because of a concern that requiring pro bono work was unconstitutional and unworkable. In fact, even the members of the Ethics 2000 Commission invited comments on whether its version of MR 6.1 should be changed to require lawyers to engage in pro bono activities, but such a significant change was not made. Jurisdictions, of course, have the power to mandate pro bono services, just as states have mandated that interest on lawyer trust accounts be transferred to bar associations to help fund legal aid services (discussed in Chapter 7).

Although lawyers are not required to perform pro bono services, the trend has been moving toward that direction since the advent of the ABA Model Code. The State Bar of Nevada Board of Governors, for instance, unanimously voted in 1994 to implement a mandatory pro bono requirement, with the failure to comply subjecting an attorney to discipline, including license revocation. However, the reaction by some of the rank and file of the Nevada bar was so hostile that the plan was dropped in 1995. New York experienced similar reaction by its bar members when, in 2005, the state bar association expanded its definition of pro bono and suggested alternative methods of accomplishment, including the giving of money. Many New York lawyers, especially those working in small firms, objected, raising concerns that this expanded approach to pro bono was a sly step toward eventually requiring it. Others were bothered that the new definition allowed lawyers to "buy out" their obligation, something wealthy New Yorkers could do during the Civil War draft days, to avoid serving, provided they paid $300 for others to replace them in uniform. And others objected that the expanded definition placed less emphasis on helping the poor and more on promoting legal causes, civil rights and others, for which there is already a pool of available lawyers. Ultimately, the expanded pro bono definition was passed, but the 20 hours per year recommendation remained, which is less than half what the ABA recommends. At least one New York firm in Albany (Gordon, Siegel, Mastro, Mullaney, Gordon & Galvin) made the changed rule unnecessary, because, in 2004, it required pro bono services of all partners and associates. The annual requirement is 24 hours, and partners who fail to provide must pay up.

Florida's version of Model Rule 6.1 (4–6.1) comes close to requiring pro bono services, at least indirectly. Rule 4-6.1(a) includes a statement in favor of pro bono services that is different from the Model Rules, and is one that specifically exempts judges and other members of the bar who cannot practice law. Rule 4–6.1(b) states that pro bono is not mandatory, but then goes on to list two ways in which lawyers can fulfill their pro bono responsibility: (1) annually providing at least 20 hours of pro bono legal service to the poor; or (2) annually giving at least $350 to a legal aid organization. But 4–6.1(d) increases the mandatory nature of pro bono services by requiring every Florida lawyer to complete a form (at the time of paying one's yearly bar fees) that certifies whether the lawyer has or has not fulfilled their annual pro bono responsibility. The form also provides room for the lawyer to describe how the pro bono responsibility was met in ways other than those listed in 4–6.1(b). And 4–6.1(e) allows a lawyer to bank for up to two years' worth any pro bono hours in excess of the annual 20 hours. Although MR 6.1(b) states that failure to fulfill one's responsibilities does not subject a lawyer to discipline, MR 6.1 (d) states that failure to complete and return the form does subject a lawyer to discipline. Florida is not alone in requiring the annual reporting of pro bono services. Four other states have similar requirements: Illinois, Maryland, Mississippi, and Nevada.

In 1994, Florida attorney Thomas Schwarz filed suit in federal court, arguing that Florida's reporting requirement and exemption for judges were unconstitutional. The federal lawsuit was preceded by a suit in the Florida Supreme Court, as well as a separate request made by the Florida Bar that the mandatory part of the pro bono reporting rule be amended. But the Florida Supreme Court dismissed Mr. Schwarz's suit, and denied the Bar's request in 1997. His claim that the Florida Supreme Court—the creator of the rule—had a conflict of interest that prevented it from deciding the rule's constitutionality also fell on deaf ears. So he sued in federal court and, in 1998, the Eleventh Circuit Court of Appeals also ruled against him. *Schwarz v. Kogan*, 132 F.3d 1387 (11th Cir. 1998). It found that there was a "sound basis" for the rule's aspirational $350 pro bono option, as well as the mandatory reporting requirement. The Eleventh Circuit also upheld the district court's ruling that there was nothing unconstitutional with the pro bono rule exempting judges and their law clerks from its application. *Id.* at 1393.

Those opposed to mandatory pro bono argue that such a requirement is unconstitutional in that requiring lawyers to work free of charge violates the equal protection clause of the Fourteenth Amendment, because no other occupation or profession is required to give away their labor or services. Furthermore, it is argued that a pro bono requirement violates the Fifth Amendment's Takings Clause because the government (courts that regulate the bar) cannot take private property (a lawyer's time and skill) without "just compensation," as is required. Another anti-mandatory pro bono argument is that it is un-American to force anyone, lawyer or otherwise, to do good deeds, not to mention that it is presumptuous to think that all lawyers can afford—after paying their law school bills, bar fees, overhead, and taxes—to provide a unilaterally determined number of free hours of labor.

Those in favor of mandatory pro bono service point out that because the practice of law is a monopoly, those who make up part of the monopoly should appropriately handle such power by providing some services that benefit the common good without expectation of compensation. Another supporting argument is that mandatory pro bono service is the best way to combat the growing legal needs of the poor. As noted in 1997 by a New York state court report, fewer than half the state's lawyers provided the recommended 20 hours per year of pro bono services, which prompted consideration on mandating pro bono. There is also the argument that the practice of law is a profession and not purely a business, so that a comparison of lawyers to plumbers, for instance, for the purposes of anti-mandatory pro bono arguments, is miscast. Finally, one could argue that mandatory pro bono programs could do a great deal to combat the general disdain the public has for lawyers, whose hourly rates have exceeded inflation and whose billable hours have dramatically increased since the ethics rules first got serious about "encouraging" lawyers to use their talents to help the poor.

Although lawyers are not required to provide pro bono services, more than a few law schools require pro bono service as a prerequisite to graduation. Tulane University School of Law became the first law school to adopt a mandatory program in 1987 and, according to the American Association of Law Schools, since Tulane instituted its program, 13 other law schools instituted mandatory programs, including Columbia University School of Law, Florida State University School of Law, Southern Methodist University School of Law, Valparaiso University School of Law, and the University of Washington School of Law. Another mandatory pro bono school, the University of Pennsylvania Law School, has a public service program that requires students to perform 70 hours of law-related services as a condition of graduation eligibility. Penn law students can fulfill their requirements in a variety of ways, including providing services at legal aid offices, government legal departments, and political action committee offices. Students can also provide assistance to professors, as well as lawyers in private practice who are working on pro bono cases.

The following link is to the ABA's Standing Committee on Pro Bono and Public Service, which includes the Center for Pro Bono. It provides a multitude of pro bono information: http://www.abanet.org/legalservices/probono/.

The Pro Bono Institute, which is part of the Georgetown Law Center, provides information, resources, and support to those in and out of the legal profession who want to expand low-cost legal services to the poor. Its Web site address is: http://www.probonoinst.org/.

Pro Bono and the Paralegal

As the phrase goes, what is good for the goose is good for the gander. All the national ethics codes designed specifically for paralegals and legal assistants mention pro bono services. Guideline 10 of the ABA Model Guidelines for the Utilization of Paralegal Services states, "A lawyer who employs a paralegal should facilitate the paralegal's participation in appropriate continuing education and pro bono publico activities." It is interesting that the Comment to Guideline 10 discusses the benefits that will accrue to the lawyer who includes the legal assistant in the pro bono legal services the lawyer is obligated to provide under Model Rule 6.1, and then states, "*where appropriate, the paralegal is encouraged to provide such services independently.*" (Emphasis added.) Furthermore, the ABA's Standing Committee on Paralegals created a brochure in 1995 entitled "How to Use Legal Assistants in Pro Bono Publico Programs." This brochure discusses the advantages of legal assistants engaging in pro bono activities and lists ways in which legal assistants across the country are participating, including serving as intake interviewers and screeners at government-funded legal services programs and local bar association pro bono programs, as well as participating as client advocates in court-approved special advocacy (CASA) programs. The brochure acknowledges that any legal assistant pro bono program must include attorney supervision of the work being done and should carry professional liability insurance. The ABA's Standing Committee on Pro Bono has a Web page that discusses the importance of involving paralegals in pro bono activities. It also has links to other Web sites and pages that encourage or award paralegal pro bono services.

The ABA's Standing Committee on Pro Bono Services, referenced earlier in the Chapter, has a page dedicated to paralegals and pro bono services. It can be found by using the "Resources Just for You," feature found on the Pro Bono Services Web page: http://www.abanet.org/legalservices/probono/.

Paralegal pro bono activities are also encouraged through the rules of court or statutes that formally approve of the use of paralegals and legal assistants, because those guidelines borrow heavily from any of the previously mentioned paralegal or legal assistant codes of ethics. *See* Indiana Rules of Professional Conduct, Use of Legal Assistants, Guideline 9.9; Michigan Guidelines for the Utilization of Legal Assistant Services, Guideline 8; State Bar of Montana, Paralegal Rules of Professional Responsibility, Rule 3; Nebraska Guidelines for the Utilization of Legal Assistants, Article II (P)(5); and Washington State Bar Association Guidelines for the Utilization of Legal Assistant Services, Guideline 10.

The NFPA Model Disciplinary Rules and Ethical Considerations encourage pro bono activities in Rule 1.4, by stating, "A paralegal shall serve the public interest by contributing to the delivery of quality legal services and the improvement of the legal system, including pro bono publico services and community services." Following Rule 1.4 is EC–1.4(b), which states, "A paralegal shall support **bona fide** efforts to meet the need for legal services by those unable to pay reasonable or customary fees; for example, participation in pro bono

■ **bona fide**

Genuine, or good faith.

projects and volunteer work." Furthermore, EC–1.4 (d) calls for paralegals to contribute 24 hours annually to properly supervised pro bono activities. All NFPA members are annually asked to complete the NFPA Pro Bono Reporting Form, certifying that they contributed 24 hours of service. The NFPA also has a pro bono committee to coordinate NFPA's pro bono vision, has a national pro bono conference, and gives a national award to an NFPA member association that has made significant contributions to community pro bono efforts. The revised Model Disciplinary Rules includes a new rule, EC–1.4(e), which carries the pro bono idea one step further by stating that paralegals should aspire to provide 24 hours annually in community service. Distinguishing community service from pro bono, EC–1.4(e) gives examples of such activities, for example, working at homeless shelters, soup kitchens, and women's shelters, and providing natural disaster relief.

The NFPA's Web site, http://www.paralegals.org, has an opening page link to "Pro Bono," which then leads to a multitude of pro bono information, including NFPA's history with pro bono services, annual pro bono awards given to NFPA members, and regional NFPA associations that provide pro bono services.

The National Association of Legal Assistants is also a formal supporter of pro bono services, and has held forums on promoting pro bono activities. Guideline 4 of the NALA Model Standards and Guidelines for Utilization of Legal Assistants states, "In the supervision of a legal assistant, consideration should be given to: . . . 5. Encouraging and supporting memberships and active participation in professional organizations." The Comment to Guideline 4 discusses the working relationship between lawyers and legal assistants extending to cooperative efforts on public services activities, and also makes reference to the pro bono encouragement in Guideline 10 of the ABA Model Guidelines. See Exhibit 8–9 on pro bono services and the paralegal ethics codes.

EXHIBIT 8–9 PRO BONO AND THE PARALEGAL ETHICS CODES

- ABA Model Guidelines for the Utilization of Paralegal Services, Guideline 10
  - *"A lawyer...should facilitate the paralegal's participation in...pro bono publico activities."*

- NFPA Model Disciplinary Rules and Ethical Considerations, EC 1.4(b),(d)
  - *Recommends member annually contributing 24 hours of pro bono services under the supervision of an attorney or as authorized by legal authority.*

- NALA Model Standards and Guidelines for Utilization of Legal Assistants, Guideline 4, and accompanying Comment
  - *Encourages the relationship between lawyer and legal assistant to extend to cooperating on pro bono services where possible.*

Many state and local paralegal associations take an active role in promoting pro bono activities. For instance, the Paralegal Division of the State Bar of Texas annually gives its "Exceptional Pro Bono Award" to one of its members who has provided extraordinary charitable paralegal services. Formerly, a joint project between the Paralegal Division and the Texas Bar Foundation called "Pro Bono Partners" which was funded by a grant from the Texas Bar Foundation, teamed a paralegal or legal assistant with a lawyer on either an ad hoc or continuing basis so that both could work together on pro bono services. The team with the greatest number of pro bono hours was recognized at the annual state bar convention. It speaks highly of those paralegal and legal assistants who volunteer their time helping those who could not otherwise afford it, particularly because paralegals and legal assistants, earning much less money than lawyers, could argue they cannot afford to contribute. But if one were to wait until it was affordable to help others, help would be long in arriving.

SUMMARY

Lawyers are required to provide competent representation. Competency is defined by having the legal knowledge and skill necessary to represent the client's interests. Even the new lawyer is held to the same competency standard that applies to the experienced lawyer. Connected to the duty of competence is the requirement that lawyers act with reasonable diligence on behalf of their clients. Despite the fact that the rules of ethics also require that lawyers keep their clients reasonably informed about their cases, lack of communication is the significant cause of client complaints against lawyers. The communication duty includes the need to pass along to the client settlement offers made by the opposing party, because the client is the one with the right to accept or reject such offers.

As a member of the legal team, the legal assistant has a corresponding duty to provide competent and diligent services. Competence requires that legal assistants be prepared to handle the matters assigned to them, and all the national paralegal ethics codes speak to the issue of competence and diligence. Meeting the requirement of competence and professionalism involves legal assistants being properly educated and trained, as well as regularly earning Continuing Legal Education (CLE) credits. Because paralegals often have a lot of client contact, they need to be especially careful to communicate effectively, which includes promptly returning phone calls and possessing effective writing skills. However, a lawyer's duty to communicate with clients cannot be completely delegated to non-lawyer employees because the responsibility for honoring the communication duty rests with the lawyer. Legal assistants, particularly those who work in litigation firms, must strive to maintain a standard that is as competent as possible to protect themselves against being blamed for incompetent representation.

More than a few rules of ethics concern a lawyer's—and by extension, a paralegal's—duty to be truthful. The rules make it clear that a lawyer may not make a material misrepresentation in the course of representing a client. Failure to disclose what is needed to prevent the commission of a fraud or crime would also be a violation of the ethics rules. To commit a violation, the lawyer or legal assistant would first have to know of the misrepresentation and the misrepresentation would have to be material.

Lawyers are prohibited from bringing frivolous claims on behalf of their clients. A frivolous claim is not one that has a slim chance of winning; rather, it is a claim (or defense) that has no basis in law or fact. Also, claims are considered frivolous when they are made in bad faith or for the purpose of harassing the other party. Not only do the ethics rules prohibit frivolous claims, but a variety of civil and appellate procedure rules and statutes prohibit them as well.

Lawyers are prohibited from putting forth false evidence. The most extreme example of this is false testimony, and the rules require lawyers to do everything possible to prevent their clients from testifying falsely. Even in criminal cases, clients do not have a constitutional right to testify falsely. Paralegals must consult with their supervising attorneys whenever there is a reasonable suspicion that clients are not being forthcoming, such as in discovery matters, because even if lawyers are unaware of their clients' deceit, they could still be subject to discipline for failing to adequately supervise their employees.

Members of the legal team should avoid directly communicating with persons who are represented by counsel, unless permission has been given or the law authorized the contact. This type of rule is designed to protect a person from being taken advantage of by the other side's lawyer when the contacted person is without the assistance of his or her own lawyer. However, some jurisdictions still use the language from either the anticontact rule of the Model Code or that of the Model Rules and only prohibit the direct contact of represented parties. There are exceptions to the anticontact rule, including the right of parties to directly communicate with one another and the right to make direct contact with the intended witnesses of a party. Because the anticontact rule applies equally to all members of the legal team, paralegals must be careful about contacting represented persons.

A variety of ethical issues are involved when contact is made with those persons who do not have legal representation. Foremost of those considerations is the requirement in jurisdictions that operate under a version of the Model Rules that those contacting unrepresented persons may not state or imply neutrality. The rules require that a member of the legal team making contact with an unrepresented person clearly explain to that person that the lawyer is not disinterested and clear up any misunderstanding the unrepresented person may have about the neutrality of the person contacting them. The purpose behind such a rule is fairness to those who, unless they are lawyers, are at a disadvantage when discussing matters related to a case with a lawyer or another member of the legal team. The Model Code has no similar prohibition other than requiring that the only advice a lawyer should give to an unrepresented person is to get a lawyer. All of the paralegal ethics codes require that paralegals disclose their status at the outset of any professional communication. Paralegals should also make sure not to give legal advice—or imply it—to unrepresented persons or advise them to leave the jurisdiction.

Because the interests of fairness in litigation are so important, the rules prohibit lawyers from having any ex parte communication with any judge or jury member involved in the litigation. While attempts at inappropriately influencing a judge or jury member are clearly wrong (and are very often criminalized), the simple act of having inappropriate contact with a judge or jury member could be the cause of professional discipline. The paralegal codes of ethics, likewise, prohibit ex parte communication, and those paralegals who go to court with their attorneys must have no contact with members of the jury during the course of the legal proceedings.

An area of litigation fairness that may seem a bit odd is the requirement that lawyers must cite directly controlling adverse authority to the court when the opposing party has failed to cite it. To be sanctioned for such a legal research violation, it must be established that the lawyer was aware the adverse legal authority existed. Some argue that such a rule is much ado about nothing, and two jurisdictions have abandoned the requirement altogether. Nevertheless, legal assistants conducting legal research must make their supervising attorneys aware of any negative legal authority.

Government lawyers, specifically those who work in prosecuting attorney's offices, are bound by rules that require fairness in the execution of their duties. Specifically, prosecuting attorneys are prohibited from making statements that are designed to prejudice defendants, and are required to turn over to defendants any evidence that may tend to negate guilt, referred to as exculpatory evidence. Paralegals who work for government or prosecuting attorneys must remember that the same duties of fairness that apply to their supervisors also apply to them.

Malpractice is the failure of a lawyer to exercise reasonable care with respect to the client's case, and a resulting harm to the client caused by the lawyer's negligence. While it is clear that lawyers can be found liable for their own negligence and for the negligence of their non-lawyer employees, it is also possible for a non-lawyer to be the subject of a legal malpractice lawsuit because malpractice is a tort and is distinct from professional discipline. The starting point for any case of non-lawyer malpractice starts with the unauthorized practice of law because, despite the lack of a regulating court's ability to discipline a non-lawyer, a jury could still find that the non-lawyer's incompetent, unauthorized practice of law constituted negligence. Not all jurisdictions, however, agree that a legal assistant or other non-lawyer can be liable for malpractice, particularly when the one suing for malpractice was not deceived about the non-lawyer's status.

Although nothing in the Model Code or Model Rules requires a lawyer to provide pro bono services, lawyers, as a group, have a history of providing pro bono services to the public. The most recent version of the Model Rules encourages lawyers to provide a minimum of 50 annual pro bono hours, and some jurisdictions' pro bono rules suggest up to 80 annual hours. Some law schools make pro bono services a prerequisite to graduation.

Despite being a relatively young profession, paralegalism has a strong history of involving itself in pro bono services. Starting with the ABA Model Guidelines for the Utilization of Paralegal Services, all paralegal codes of conduct and many state legal assistant organizations specifically mention and sponsor pro bono activities. Paralegals and legal assistants engage in a variety of pro bono activities, including assisting at legal aid offices and volunteering in court-appointed special advocacy programs. In most situations, legal assistants must perform their pro bono activities under the supervision of lawyers, so as not to engage in a charitable form of the unauthorized practice of law.

ETHICS IN ACTION

1. Darlene and Daryl Jenkins lived in their home for 25 years. It sat by a little creek in town, and was one of the rare homes that didn't seem like a city home. As the city's population grew, the city needed space for things such as wider streets and larger schools. The elementary school next to Darlene and Daryl had always been separated by a thicket of trees that ran along the curve of the creek. But now the city needed all that space, including the lot on which the Jenkins' home sat. The city had the right to take the home by way of eminent domain, but was required under the law to pay a reasonable price for it. The Jenkins naturally thought their little home was worth more than the city offered. In fact, they thought it was worth twice as much. But the Jenkins' opinion was tied to factors that weren't recognized by real estate brokers or the city, such as the proximity of their home to downtown, as well as the memories of living there. The Jenkins were represented by attorney Mark in the negotiations with the city. Unfortunately, Mark was too busy planning his run for a county council seat to give the Jenkins much consideration. Mark's paralegal Barb, however, had really connected with the Jenkins, and it was she with whom they spoke on a regular basis. The city had made a final counter offer that would only be open until Friday and the Jenkins asked Barb's opinion on this. Although Barb told them she couldn't advise them what to do, the Jenkins asked, "What would you do if you were us?" Barb told them she would take the money and avoid the upcoming arbitration. So, the Jenkins said, "Okay. We're done with this. Tell the city we'll take their lousy money." Barb then contacted the city.

(continues)

ETHICS IN ACTION   *(continued)*

Has Mark comported with the duty to effectively communicate with the Jenkins? Why or why not?

2. Bart works feverishly for Arnold, who has a busy litigation practice, but Arnold recently tried to foray into some appellate work. A client Arnold represented in a divorce a few years ago came to Arnold because the client had been denied a promotion at the state department of transportation. From the interview, Arnold believed that he needed to appeal the transportation board's decision by bringing an action in the venue-appropriate trial court, as was the case for many administrative decisions. What he didn't realize was that when the department of transportation made a hiring decision for the position level Arnold's client had applied, the required appeal was to the court of appeals. So, after Arnold had Bart file the required pleadings, the time for correctly filing the appeal passed, and Arnold's client found himself without recourse. Panic struck Arnold after realizing his error, and he called the client to come to the office for a face-to-face mea culpa. When the client arrived, he told Arnold how losing that promotion was the best thing to happen to him, because it caused him to look elsewhere for similar employment, which he found at an engineering company that is paying him more than he would have made had he gotten the promotion. Relieved by this serendipity, Arnold told the client what happened, but blamed Bart for the error, telling the client that Bart had been so overworked, he wasn't paying attention to details like he used to. Following the client meeting, Arnold told Bart that Bart was blamed for incorrectly filing the appeal. Arnold's theory was that the bad news, which seemed to become a moot point anyway, would go down better if a paralegal were blamed for it. Arnold then chuckled and said, "Don't worry about it. The guy loves his new job and didn't seem to care too much once I told him I wasn't going to bill him for any work done on the matter."

    What can Bart do? Should he do anything?

3. The trial between two business partners splitting up was every bit as nasty as a divorce between two spiteful spouses. What had begun with so much promise 10 years earlier ended almost violently, and now all that was left was for a jury to decide how much of the business went to each partner. Their landscaping business had been a wild success and had grown to 20 employees who did everything from mowing to tree planting and trimming, to installing water gardens and pools. But Ray and Dave, the partners, had come to hate each other, with each believing the other had nothing to do with the business's success. In truth, Ray was more responsible for the success because he was the one with the green thumbs and the great

(continues)

ETHICS IN ACTION   *(continued)*

landscaping ideas their clients wanted. But Dave, who had an M.B.A., was able to steer the business through its early, lean years, masterfully managing cash flow, and obsessing about expenses. He also had a knack for hiding some of the business's retained earnings in a secret account. To cover this up, he needed to create false accounting records that showed the business was making less than it actually had. Dave's brother-in-law Randy was Dave's attorney and was fully aware of the fraud, as was Ann, Randy's paralegal. She was bothered by it all, but her guilt was assuaged by her paycheck. That disappeared a week after the case ended, when Ann was fired for mismanaging the firm's trust account. So, she called Ray on the phone to tell him what she knew, and then she faxed to Ray's attorney a letter telling him that she had helped her boss falsify evidence. It really hit the fan then. Ray and his attorney went ballistic and attempted to get a new trial. And Dave and Randy sued Ann for defamation.

Was Ann right to contact Ray and his attorney? Can she be sued for defamation, or does she have immunity? Can she be sued by Ray for fraud?

4. Nancy is a paralegal working at a firm where one of the attorneys represents a neighborhood association seeking to force a homeowner to repaint his house. Association bylaws state that a house may not be painted blue or red, and Sandy, the homeowner in question, painted her house Boston Red Sox-red, in honor of their long-overdue World Series victory. Sandy claims her home isn't bound by the association's bylaws because her home was built before the original subdivision was platted, even though it was bought by the subdivision developer before Nancy became the owner. Nancy doesn't work for the attorney who represents the association, but is aware of the case due to the office scuttlebutt. While attending her daughter's dance recital, Nancy is introduced to Sandy, the woman who lives in the Red Sox house. When Sandy realizes the coincidence, the conversation turns from ballet to the lawsuit. Sandy tells Nancy that it's unfair that she has to spend thousands of dollars defending her choice to live the way she wants to, and that she isn't harming anyone by painting her house the way she wants to. Nancy agrees that it does seem odd that anybody could control someone else's house color, but tells Sandy that from what she has seen at work, the homeowners associations always win in cases like this. "For what it's worth," Nancy says, "I would think the association should only care if you paint your house in Yankee pinstripes."

Has Nancy violated the anticontact rule?

5. Going to court is the best thing about Jane's job. The excitement and unpredictability of trials—the tension that everyone involved feels just as the judge enters the courtroom, the fight over whose evidence is more credible and reliable—

(continues)

ETHICS IN ACTION   *(continued)*

it is everything Jane hoped being a paralegal would involve. Her boss Grace is quite the litigator who gets nauseous at the thought of having to attend a mediation and risk losing another case to a milquetoast conclusion. Presently, the two of them are involved in a knock-down-drag-out fight with a pharmaceutical company, alleging that the company's weight loss drug causes high blood pressure and strokes. The defense contends there is no scientific evidence to support the allegation. Furthermore, it argued that high blood pressure and strokes are part of what comes with being overweight in the first place. The trial was winding down on Good Friday, and the judge ended court early so everyone could get a head start on the Easter holiday. At the nicest Easter brunch in town, Jane was standing in line for the prime rib slicing when she was tapped on the shoulder. Turning around, Jane saw juror no. 5 smiling at her while stuffing his face full of an omelet made just to his liking (cheese, ham, onions, no tomatoes). "Hi!" juror no. 5 somehow managed to get past his teeth. "I thought I recognized you when you came in." He then started to make small talk while others walked around Jane to get their own slices of prime rib. Jane smiled and nodded back, telling juror no. 5 that she was there with her family for the sixth Easter brunch in a row. Talk turned to the trial when juror no. 5 said, "How long do you think this case is going to last? My boss is really itching for me to come back to work. Oh—by the way—your boss is a great lawyer. She really gave it to that defense expert the last week." Jane agreed, mumbling something about Grace being the best, and then said goodbye after telling juror no. 5 that the case should probably be done by Tuesday.

Has Jane violated the rule against ex parte communication? What should she do?

6. Jason is doing research for an appellate brief for his boss Troy. The appeal involves an esoteric question of contract law unlikely to matter to all that many people in the state. The issue involves interpreting a peculiar part of that state's Uniform Commercial Code (UCC) and Troy is taking a position that is in line with the official comments of the UCC. Jason's research showed that not only was there no case on point in this matter, but there was no precedent in the jurisdiction dealing with the question. After "key citing" that section of the official UCC version on Westlaw®, Jason noticed that two other state's highest courts had dealt with the question at hand and had reached identical conclusions—the exact opposite of the position Troy was taking in this appeal. In fact, the second court expressly followed the line of reasoning the earlier court had taken on the matter. Jason copied both cases and provided them to Troy with the word, "Ouch!" written on a cover sheet that summarized both cases. Troy filed his appellate brief without citing either of those

(continues)

ETHICS IN ACTION   *(continued)*

cases. When asked by Jason about not including those two cases, Troy said, "Ignorance is bliss. And, why would I do the heavy lifting for the other side?" As it turned out, the other side in the appeal never found those cases.

Has Troy violated either MR 3.3(a)(3) or DR 7-106(B)? Is Jason obligated to do anything, if he believes Troy violated that ethics doctrine?

7. Tiffany is a paralegal at a large law firm specializing in intellectual property law. Her boss represents inventors, authors, and businesses that are trying to protect their patents, copyrights, and trademarks. Tiffany doesn't work for the money, because she is the wealthiest person at her firm. Her great grandmother created a bakery company following World War II that had a catchy slogan and a logo of two happy children eating the company's bread and cookies. In fact, it was a trademark infringement case that her family's company waged against a small, start-up bakery that got Tiffany interested in intellectual property law. Spurning a job at the company, a decision made easier by Tiffany's yeast allergy, she took a job at the law firm that represented her family's company a few years earlier. Tiffany's boss Amber had assigned Tiffany primary responsibility to assist a small drug company protect the patent on its Parkinson's disease medication. Unfortunately, Tiffany mistook the deadline requirements on filing a patent renewal, due to a recent change in the law. As a result, the medication went off-patent and the small drug company was squeezed to the breaking point by the large pharmaceutical companies that made a generic version of the same medication. The small drug company brought a malpractice claim against Tiffany's boss and then amended its complaint to include Tiffany after learning in discovery that, technically, it was Tiffany's fault. Finding out how rich she was also had a little something to do with her being added as a defendant.

Has Amber committed malpractice? In your jurisdiction, could Tiffany be liable for malpractice?

■ POINTS TO PONDER_____

1. What does it mean to say that a lawyer must be competent?

2. In addition to the substantive law, what else must a lawyer know in order to be competent?

3. What kinds of activities would qualify as satisfying the lawyer's duty to communicate with the client?

4. What can paralegals do to improve the lines of communication between lawyers and clients?

5. What determines whether a paralegal is competent?

6. Lawyers are required to obtain continuing legal education credits. Do you think that legal assistants should also be required to do the same?

7. What different rules concern the legal team's duty to be truthful?

8. Can you think of an example of an untruth that would not have to be disclosed because it is not a material misrepresentation?

9. How do you think one can balance the duty of confidentiality with the duty to be honest to opposing parties and courts?

10. What makes a claim a frivolous one? Do you think the case of Jerry Mersereau, who fell down a cliff during the night, looking for the bathroom while camping in a national forest, or the McDonald's coffee spill case are examples of frivolous suits?

11. Does your jurisdiction have a statute that concerns vexatious litigation?

12. What steps should be followed when a member of the legal team believes that the client wants to testify falsely? Other than in a litigation context, what might a client do that could qualify as false and, therefore, require lawyer intervention?

13. Do you think the narrative approach for putting on false testimony in criminal cases is more fair to the defendant or more unfair to the legal system?

14. What is the general rule on dealing with represented persons?

15. What are some of the exceptions to the rule in question 14?

16. What is the significance to distinguishing between represented persons and represented parties in an anticontact rule?

17. Does your jurisdiction cover represented persons?

18. What is expected when a paralegal makes contact with an unrepresented person?

19. What is ex parte communication and why is it not allowed?

20. What is wrong with a paralegal talking to a member of the jury during the lunch break, as long as the case is not discussed?

21. What changes did the Ethics 2000 Commission propose to the ex parte rule?

22. Do you think that lawyers should be sanctioned for failing to cite directly adverse, controlling legal authority? Why or why not?

23. What ethical issues should be of concern to paralegals and legal assistants working in prosecuting attorney's offices or other government law offices?

24. Do you think the ethics charges against District Attorney Mike Nifong are legitimate or unfounded?

25. What is legal malpractice? Why is it that a negative result for a client does not necessarily mean that the lawyer will be found to have committed malpractice?

26. How can non-lawyers be liable for legal malpractice if they are unlicensed to practice law?

27. Can a legal assistant who works under the supervision of a lawyer be found liable for malpractice?

28. In what different ways can a lawyer fulfill pro bono obligations?

29. Do you think that pro bono activities or contributions should be mandatory for lawyers?

30. Do you think that pro bono services should be mandatory for paralegals? Should pro bono activities be required for students as a condition to graduating?

■ KEY CONCEPTS

Anticontact Rule

Competence and client representation

Diligence and client representation

Directly adverse authority

Ex parte communication

Frivolous lawsuits

Malpractice

Narrative approach to perjured testimony

Non-lawyer malpractice

Preparation and client representation

Pro bono

Truthfulness and client representation

Vexatious litigant

■ KEY TERMS

bad faith

bona fide

continuing legal education (cle)

estate plan

ex parte communication

forms books

governmental immunity

intestate estate

malpractice

misrepresentation

personal representative

probable cause

proximate cause

venire

voir dire

west digest system

writ of mandamus

Online Companion™
For additional resources, please go to
http://www.paralegal.delmar.cengage.com

Student CD-ROM
For additional materials, please go to the
CD in this book.

A

ABA Model Guidelines for the Utilization of Paralegal Services

PREAMBLE

The Standing Committee on Paralegals of the American Bar Association drafted, and the ABA House of Delegates adopted, the ABA Model Guidelines for the Utilization of Legal Assistant Services in 1991. Most states have also prepared or adopted state-specific recommendations or guidelines for the utilization of services provided by paralegals.[1] All of these recommendations or guidelines are intended to provide lawyers with useful and authoritative guidance in working with paralegals.

This 2003 revision of the Model Guidelines is intended to reflect the legal and policy developments that have taken place since the first draft in 1991 and may assist states in revising or further refining their own recommendations and guidelines. Moreover, the Standing Committee is of the view that these and other guidelines on paralegal services will encourage lawyers to utilize those services effectively and promote the continued growth of the paralegal profession.[2]

The Standing Committee has based these 2003 revisions on the American Bar Association's Model Rules of Professional Conduct but has also attempted to take into account existing state recommendations and guidelines, decided authority and contemporary practice. Lawyers, of course, are to be first directed by Rule 5.3 of the Model Rules in the utilization of paralegal services, and nothing contained in these Model Guidelines is intended to be inconsistent with that rule. Specific ethical considerations and case law in particular states must also be taken into account by each lawyer that reviews these guidelines. In the commentary after each Guideline, we have attempted to identify the basis for the Guideline and any issues of which we are aware that the Guideline may present. We have also included selected references to state and paralegal association guidelines where we believed it would be helpful to the reader.

Guideline 1: **A lawyer is responsible for all of the professional actions of a paralegal performing services at the lawyer's direction and should take reasonable measures to ensure that the paralegal's conduct is consistent with the lawyer's obligations under the rules of professional conduct of the jurisdiction in which the lawyer practices.**

Comment to Guideline 1: The Standing Committee on Paralegals ("Standing Committee") regards Guideline 1 as a comprehensive statement of general principle governing the utilization of paralegals in the practice of law. As such, the principles contained in Guideline 1 are part of each of the remaining Guidelines. Fundamentally, Guideline 1 expresses the overarching principle that although a lawyer may delegate tasks to a paralegal, a lawyer must always assume ultimate responsibility for the delegated tasks and exercise independent professional judgment with respect to all aspects of the representation of a client.

Under principles of agency law and the rules of professional conduct, lawyers are responsible for the actions and the work product of the nonlawyers they employ. Rule 5.3 of the Model Rules of Professional Conduct ("Model Rules")[3] requires that supervising lawyers ensure that the conduct of nonlawyer assistants is compatible with the lawyer's professional obligations. Ethical Consideration 3-6 of the Model Code encourages lawyers to delegate tasks to paralegals so that legal services can be rendered more economically and efficiently. Ethical Consideration 3-6, however, provides that such delegation is only proper if the lawyer "maintains a direct relationship with his client, supervises the delegated work, and has complete professional responsibility for the work product." The adoption of Rule 5.3, which incorporates these principles, reaffirms this encouragement.

To conform to Guideline 1, a lawyer must give appropriate instruction to paralegals supervised by the lawyer about the rules governing the lawyer's professional conduct, and require paralegals to act in accordance with those rules. *See* Comment to Model Rule 5.3; *see also* National Association of Legal Assistant's Model Standards and Guidelines for the Utilization of Legal Assistants, Guidelines 1 and 4 (1985, revised 1990, 1997) (hereafter "NALA Guidelines"). Additionally, the lawyer must directly supervise paralegals employed by the lawyer to ensure that, in every circumstance, the paralegal is acting in a manner consistent with the lawyer's ethical and professional obligations. What constitutes appropriate instruction and supervision will differ from one state to another and the lawyer has the obligation to make adjustments accordingly.

Guideline 2: **Provided the lawyer maintains responsibility for the work product, a lawyer may delegate to a paralegal any task normally performed by the lawyer except those tasks proscribed to one not licensed as a lawyer by statute,**

court rule, administrative rule or regulation, controlling authority, the applicable rules of professional conduct of the jurisdiction in which the lawyer practices, or these Guidelines.

Comment to Guideline 2: The essence of the definition of the term "legal assistant" first adopted by the ABA in 1986[4] and subsequently amended in 1997[5] is that, so long as appropriate supervision is maintained, many tasks normally performed by lawyers may be delegated to paralegals. EC 3-6 under the Model Code mentioned three specific kinds of tasks that paralegals may perform under appropriate lawyer supervision: factual investigation and research, legal research, and the preparation of legal documents. Various states delineate more specific tasks in their guidelines including attending client conferences, corresponding with and obtaining information from clients, witnessing the execution of documents, preparing transmittal letters, and maintaining estate/guardianship trust accounts. *See, e.g.,* Colorado Bar Association Guidelines for the Use of Paralegals (the Colorado Bar Association has adopted guidelines for the use of paralegals in 18 specialty practice areas including civil litigation, corporate law and estate planning); NALA Guideline 5.

While appropriate delegation of tasks is encouraged and a broad array of tasks is properly delegable to paralegals, improper delegation of tasks will often run afoul of a lawyer's obligations under applicable rules of professional conduct. A common consequence of the improper delegation of tasks is that the lawyer will have assisted the paralegal in the unauthorized "practice of law" in violation of Rule 5.5 of the Model Rules, DR 3-101 of the Model Code, and the professional rules of most states. Neither the Model Rules nor the Model Code defines the "practice of law." EC 3-5 under the Model Code gave some guidance by equating the practice of law to the application of the professional judgment of the lawyer in solving clients' legal problems. This approach is consistent with that taken in ABA Opinion 316 (1967) which states: "A lawyer . . . may employ nonlawyers to do any task for him except counsel clients about law matters, engage directly in the practice of law, appear in court or appear in formal proceedings as part of the judicial process, so long as it is he who takes the work and vouches for it to the client and becomes responsible for it to the client." As a general matter, most state guidelines specify that paralegals may not appear before courts, administrative tribunals, or other adjudicatory bodies unless the procedural rules of the adjudicatory body authorize such appearances. *See, e.g.,* State Bar of Arizona, Committee on the Rules of Prof'l Conduct, Opinion No. 99-13 (December 1999) (attorney did not assist in unauthorized practice of law by supervising paralegal in tribal court where tribal court rules permit non-attorneys to be licensed tribal advocates).[6] Additionally, no state permits paralegals to conduct depositions or give legal advice to clients. *E.g.,* Guideline 2, Connecticut Bar Association Guidelines for Lawyers Who Employ or Retain Legal Assistants (the "Connecticut Guidelines"); Guideline 2, State Bar of Michigan Guidelines for Utilization of Legal Assistants; State Bar of Georgia, State Disciplinary Board Advisory Opinion No. 21 (September 16, 1977); *Doe v. Condon,* 532 S.E.2d 879 (S.

C. 2000) (it is the unauthorized practice of law for a paralegal to conduct educational seminars and answer estate planning questions because the paralegal will be implicitly advising participants that they require estate planning services). *See also* NALA Guidelines II, III, and V.

Ultimately, apart from the obvious tasks that virtually all states argue are proscribed to paralegals, what constitutes the "practice of law" is governed by state law and is a fact specific question. *See, e.g.*, Louisiana Rules of Prof'l Conduct Rule 5.5 which sets out specific tasks considered to be the "practice of law" by the Supreme Court of Louisiana. Thus, some tasks that have been specifically prohibited in some states are expressly delegable in others. *Compare*, Guideline 2, Connecticut Guidelines (permitting paralegal to attend real estate closings even though no supervising lawyer is present provided that the paralegal does not render opinion or judgment about execution of documents, changes in adjustments or price or other matters involving documents or funds) *and* The Florida Bar, Opinion 89-5 (November 1989) (permitting paralegal to handle real estate closing at which no supervising lawyer is present provided, among other things, that the paralegal will not give legal advice or make impromptu decisions that should be made by a lawyer) *with* Supreme Court of Georgia, Formal Advisory Opinion No. 86-5 (May 1989) (closing of real estate transactions constitutes the practice of law and it is ethically improper for a lawyer to permit a paralegal to close the transaction). It is thus incumbent on the lawyer to determine whether a particular task is properly delegable in the jurisdiction at issue.

Once the lawyer has determined that a particular task is delegable consistent with the professional rules, utilization guidelines, and case law of the relevant jurisdiction, the key to Guideline 2 is proper supervision. A lawyer should start the supervision process by ensuring that the paralegal has sufficient education, background and experience to handle the task being assigned. The lawyer should provide adequate instruction when assigning projects and should also monitor the progress of the project. Finally, it is the lawyer's obligation to review the completed project to ensure that the work product is appropriate for the assigned task. *See* Guideline 1, Connecticut Guidelines; *See also, e.g., Spencer v. Steinman*, 179 F.R.D. 484 (E.D. Penn. 1998) (lawyer sanctioned under Rule 11 for paralegal's failure to serve subpoena duces tecum on parties to the litigation because the lawyer "did not assure himself that [the paralegal] had adequate training nor did he adequately supervise her once he assigned her the task of issuing subpoenas").

Serious consequences can result from a lawyer's failure to properly delegate tasks to or to supervise a paralegal properly. For example, the Supreme Court of Virginia upheld a malpractice verdict against a lawyer based in part on negligent actions of a paralegal in performing tasks that evidently were properly delegable. *Musselman v. Willoughby Corp.*, 230 Va. 337, 337 S.E. 2d 724 (1985). *See also* C. Wolfram, Modern Legal Ethics (1986), at 236, 896. Disbarment and suspension from the practice of law have resulted from a lawyer's failure to properly supervise the work performed by paralegals. *See Matter of Disciplinary Action Against Nassif*, 547 N.W.2d 541 (N.D. 1996) (disbarment for failure to supervise which resulted in the unauthorized practice of law by office paralegals); *Attorney Grievance Comm'n of Maryland v. Hallmon*, 681 A.2d 510 (Md. 1996) (90-day suspension for, among other things, abdicating responsibility for a case to paralegal without supervising or reviewing the paralegal's work). Lawyers have also been subject to monetary and other sanctions in federal and state courts for failing to properly utilize and supervise paralegals. *See In re Hessinger & Associates*, 192 B.R. 211 (N.D. Cal. 1996) (bankruptcy court directed to reevaluate its $100,000 sanction but district court finds that law firm violated Rule 3-110(A) of the California Rules of Professional Conduct by permitting bankruptcy paralegals to undertake initial interviews, fill out forms and complete schedules without attorney supervision).

Finally, it is important to note that although the attorney has the primary obligation to not permit a nonlawyer to engage in the unauthorized practice of law, some states have concluded that a paralegal is not relieved from an independent obligation to refrain from illegal conduct and to work directly under an attorney's supervision. *See In re Opinion No. 24 of the Committee on the Unauthorized Practice of Law*, 607 A.2d 962, 969 (N.J. 1992) (a "paralegal who recognizes that the attorney is not directly supervising his or her work or that such supervision is illusory because the attorney knows nothing about the field in which the paralegal is working must understand that he or she is engaged in the unauthorized practice of law"); Kentucky Supreme Court Rule 3.7 (stating that "the paralegal does have an independent obligation to refrain from illegal conduct"). Additionally, paralegals must also familiarize themselves with the specific statutes governing the particular area of law with which they might come into contact while providing paralegal services. *See, e.g.*, 11 U.S.C. § 110 (provisions governing non-lawyer preparers of bankruptcy petitions); *In Re Moffett*, 263 B.R. 805 (W.D. Ky. 2001) (nonlawyer bankruptcy petition preparer fined for advertising herself as "paralegal" because that is prohibited by 11 U.S.C. § 110(f)(1)). Again, the lawyer must remember that any independent obligation a paralegal might have under state law to refrain from the unauthorized practice of law does not in any way diminish or vitiate the lawyer's obligation to properly delegate tasks and supervise the paralegal working for the lawyer.

Guideline 3: **A lawyer may not delegate to a paralegal:**

(a) Responsibility for establishing an attorney-client relationship.

(b) Responsibility for establishing the amount of a fee to be charged for a legal service.

(c) Responsibility for a legal opinion rendered to a client.

Comment to Guideline 3: Model Rule 1.4 and most state codes require lawyers to communicate directly with their clients and to provide their clients information reasonably necessary to make informed decisions and to effectively participate in the representation. While delegation of legal tasks to nonlawyers may benefit clients by enabling their lawyers to render legal services more economically and efficiently, Model Rule 1.4 and Ethical Consideration 3-6 under the Model Code emphasize that delegation is proper only if the lawyer "maintains a direct relationship with his client, supervises the delegated work and has complete professional responsibility for the work product." The National Association of Legal Assistants ("NALA"), Code of Ethics and Professional Responsibility, Canon 2, echoes the Model Rule when it states: "A legal assistant may perform any task which is properly delegated and supervised by an attorney as long as the attorney is ultimately responsible to the client, maintains a direct relationship with the client, and assumes professional responsibility for the work product." Most state guidelines also stress the paramount importance of a direct attorney-client relationship. *See* Ohio EC 3-6 and New Mexico Rule 20-106. The direct personal relationship between client and lawyer is critical to the exercise of the lawyer's trained professional judgment.

Fundamental to the lawyer-client relationship is the lawyer's agreement to undertake representation and the related fee arrangement. The Model Rules and most states require lawyers to make fee arrangements with their clients and to clearly communicate with their clients concerning the scope of the representation and the basis for the fees for which the client will be responsible. Model Rule 1.5 and Comments. Many state guidelines prohibit paralegals from "setting fees" or "accepting cases." *See, e.g.*, Pennsylvania Eth. Op. 98-75, 1994 Utah Eth. Op. 139. NALA Canon 3 states that a paralegal must not establish attorney-client relationships or set fees.

EC 3-5 states: "The essence of the professional judgment of the lawyer is his educated ability to relate the general body and philosophy of law to a specific legal problem of a client; and thus, the public interest will be better served if only lawyers are permitted to act in matters involving professional judgment." Clients are entitled to their lawyers' professional judgment and opinion. Paralegals may, however, be authorized to communicate a lawyer's legal advice to a client so long as they do not interpret or expand on that advice. Typically, state guidelines phrase this prohibition in terms of paralegals being forbidden from "giving legal advice" or "counseling clients about legal matters." *See, e.g.*, New Hampshire Rule 35, Sub-Rule 1, Kentucky SCR 3.700, Sub-Rule 2. NALA Canon 3 states that a paralegal must not give legal opinions or advice. Some states have more expansive wording that prohibits paralegals from engaging in any activity that would require the exercise of independent legal judgment. *See, e.g.*, New Mexico Rule 20-103. Nevertheless, it is clear that all states and the Model Rules encourage direct communication between clients and a paralegal insofar as the paralegal is performing a task properly delegated by a lawyer. It should be noted that a lawyer who permits a paralegal to assist in establishing the attorney-client relationship, in communicating the lawyer's fee, or in preparing the lawyer's legal opinion is not delegating responsibility for those matters and, therefore, is not in violation of this guideline.

Guideline 4: **It is the lawyer's responsibility to take reasonable measures to ensure that clients, courts, and other lawyers are aware that a paralegal, whose services are utilized by the lawyer in performing legal services, is not licensed to practice law.**

Comment to Guideline 4: Since, in most instances, a paralegal is not licensed as a lawyer, it is important that those with whom the paralegal communicates are aware of that fact. The National Federation of Paralegal Associations, Inc. ("NFPA"), Model Code of Professional Ethics and Responsibility and Guidelines for Enforcement, EC 1.7(a)-(c) requires paralegals to disclose their status. Likewise, NALA Canon 5 requires a paralegal to disclose his or her status at the outset of any professional relationship. While requiring the paralegal to make such disclosure is one way in which the lawyer's responsibility to third parties may be discharged, the Standing Committee is of the view that it is desirable to emphasize the lawyer's responsibility for the disclosure under Model Rule 5.3 (b) and (c). Lawyers may discharge that responsibility by direct communication with the client and third parties, or by requiring the paralegal to make the disclosure, by a written memorandum, or by some other means. Several state guidelines impose on the lawyer responsibility for instructing a paralegal whose services are utilized by the lawyer to disclose the paralegal's status in any dealings with a third party. *See, e.g.,* Kentucky SCR 3.700, Sub-Rule 7, Indiana Guidelines 9.4, 9.10, New Hampshire Rule 35, Sub-Rule 8, New Mexico Rule 20-104. Although in most initial engagements by a client it may be prudent for the attorney to discharge this responsibility with a writing, the guideline requires only that the lawyer recognize the responsibility and ensure that it is discharged. Clearly, when a client has been adequately informed of the lawyer's utilization of paralegal services, it is unnecessary to make additional formalistic disclosures as the client retains the lawyer for other services.

Most guidelines or ethics opinions concerning the disclosure of the status of paralegals include a proviso that the paralegal's status as a nonlawyer be clear and that the title used to identify the paralegal not be deceptive. To fulfill these objectives, the titles assigned to paralegals must be indicative of their status as nonlawyers and not imply that they are lawyers. The most common titles are "paralegal" and "legal assistant" although other titles may fulfill the dual purposes noted above. The titles "paralegal" and "legal assistant" are sometimes coupled with a descriptor of the paralegal's status, e.g., "senior paralegal" or "paralegal coordinator," or of the area of practice in which the paralegal works, e.g., "litigation paralegal" or "probate paralegal." Titles that are commonly used to identify lawyers, such as "associate" or "counsel," are misleading and inappropriate. *See, e.g.,* Comment to New Mexico Rule 20-104 (warning against the use of the title "associate" since it may be construed to mean associate-attorney).

Most state guidelines specifically endorse paralegals signing correspondence so long as their status as a paralegal is clearly indicated by an appropriate title. *See* ABA Informal Opinion 1367 (1976).

Guideline 5: **A lawyer may identify paralegals by name and title on the lawyer's letterhead and on business cards identifying the lawyer's firm.**

Comment to Guideline 5: Under Guideline 4, above, a lawyer who employs a paralegal has an obligation to ensure that the status of the paralegal as a nonlawyer is fully disclosed. The primary purpose of this disclosure is to avoid confusion that might lead someone to believe that the paralegal is a lawyer. The identification suggested by this guideline is consistent with that objective while also affording the paralegal recognition as an important member of the legal services team.

ABA Informal Opinion 1527 (1989) provides that nonlawyer support personnel, including paralegals, may be listed on a law firm's letterhead and reiterates previous opinions that approve of paralegals having business cards. *See also* ABA Informal Opinion 1185 (1971). The listing must not be false or misleading and "must make it clear that the support personnel who are listed are not lawyers."

All state guidelines and ethics opinions that address the issue approve of business cards for paralegals, so long as the paralegal's status is clearly indicated. *See, e.g.,* Florida State Bar Ass'n. Comm. on Prof'l Ethics, Op. 86-4 (1986); Kansas Bar Ass'n, Prof'l Ethical Op. 85-4; State Bar of Michigan Standing Comm. on Prof'l and Judicial Ethics, RI-34 (1989); Minnesota Lawyers' Prof'l Responsibility Bd., Op. 8 (1974). Some authorities prescribe the contents and format of the card or the title to be used. *E.g.,* Georgia Guidelines for Attorneys Utilizing Paralegals, State Disciplinary Board Advisory Op. No. 21 (1977); Iowa State Bar Ethical Guidelines for Legal Assistants in Iowa, Guideline 4; South Carolina Bar Ethics Op. 88-06; and Texas General Guidelines for the Utilization of the Services of Legal Assistants by Attorneys, Guideline VIII. All agree the paralegal's status must be clearly indicated and the card may not be used in a deceptive way. Some state rules, such as New Hampshire Supreme Court Rule 7, approve the use of business cards noting that the card should not be used for unethical solicitation.

Most states with guidelines on the use of paralegal services permit the listing of paralegals on firm letterhead. A few states do not permit attorneys to list paralegals on their letterhead. *E.g.,* State Bar of Georgia Disciplinary Board Opinion Number 21 "Guidelines for Attorneys Utilizing Paralegals," 1(b); New Hampshire Supreme Court Rule 35, Sub-Rule 7; New Mexico Supreme Court Rule 20-113 and South Carolina Bar Guidelines for the Utilization by Lawyers of the Services of Legal Assistants Guideline VI. These states rely on earlier ABA Informal Opinions 619 (1962), 845 (1965), and 1000 (1977), all of which were expressly withdrawn by ABA Informal Opinion 1527. These earlier opinions interpreted the predecessor Model Code DR 2-102 (A), which, prior to *Bates v. State Bar of Arizona,* 433 U.S. 350 (1977), had strict limitations on the information that could be listed on letterheads. In light of the United States Supreme Court opinion in *Peel v. Attorney Registration and Disciplinary Comm'n of Illinois,* 496 U.S.

91 (1990), it may be that a restriction on letterhead identification of paralegals that is not deceptive and clearly identifies the paralegal's status violates the First Amendment rights of the lawyer.

More than 20 states have rules or opinions that explicitly permit lawyers to list names of paralegals on their letterhead stationery, including Arizona, Connecticut, Florida, Illinois, Indiana, Kentucky, Michigan, Mississippi, Missouri, Nebraska, New York, North Carolina, Oregon, South Dakota, Texas, Virginia, and Washington.

The Model Code of Ethics and Professional Responsibility of the National Federation of Paralegal Associations indicates that the paralegal's "title shall be included if the paralegal's name appears on business cards, letterheads, brochures, directories, and advertisements." Canon 6, EC-6.2. NFPA Informal Ethics and Disciplinary Opinion No. 95-2 provides that a paralegal may be identified with name and title on law firm letterhead unless such conduct is prohibited by the appropriate state authority.

Guideline 6: **A lawyer is responsible to take reasonable measures to ensure that all client confidences are preserved by a paralegal.**

Comment to Guideline 6: A fundamental principle in the client-lawyer relationship is that the lawyer must not reveal information relating to the representation. Model Rule 1.6. A client must feel free to discuss whatever he/she wishes with his/her lawyer, and a lawyer must be equally free to obtain information beyond that volunteered by his/her client. The ethical obligation of a lawyer to hold inviolate the confidences and secrets of the client facilitates the full development of the facts essential to proper representation of the client and encourages laypersons to seek early legal assistance. EC 4-1, Model Code. "It is a matter of common knowledge that the normal operation of a law office exposes confidential professional information to nonlawyer employees of the office. . . this obligates a lawyer to exercise care in selecting and training employees so that the sanctity of all confidences and secrets of clients may be preserved." EC 4-2, Model Code.

Model Rule 1.6 applies not only to matters communicated in confidence by the client, but also to all information relating to the representation, whatever its source. Pursuant to the rule, a lawyer may not disclose such information except as authorized or required by the Rules of Professional Conduct or other law. Further, a lawyer must act competently to safeguard information relating to the representation of a client against inadvertent or unauthorized disclosure by the lawyer or "other persons who are participating in the representation of the client or who are subject to the lawyer supervision." Model Rule 1.6, Comment 15. It is therefore the lawyer's obligation to instruct clearly and to take reasonable steps to ensure that paralegals preserve client confidences.

Model Rule 5.3 requires a lawyer having direct supervisory authority over a paralegal to make reasonable efforts to ensure that the person's conduct is compatible with the professional obligations of the lawyer. Comment 1 to Model Rule 5.3 makes it clear that a lawyer must give "such assistants appropriate instruction and supervision concerning the ethical aspects of their employment, particularly regarding the obligation not to disclose information relating to the representation of the client, and should be responsible for their work product." Disciplinary Rule 4-101(D) under the Model Code provides that: "A lawyer shall exercise reasonable care to prevent his employees, associates and others whose services are utilized by him from disclosing or using confidences or secrets of a client. . . ." Nearly all states that have guidelines for utilization of paralegals require the lawyer "to instruct legal assistants concerning client confidences and to exercise care to ensure the legal assistants comply with the Code in this regard." *See, e.g.* New Hampshire Rule 35, Sub-Rule 4; Kentucky Supreme Court Rule 3.700, Sub-Rule 4; Indiana Rules of Prof'l Responsibility, Guideline 9.10.

Model Rule 5.3 further extends responsibility for the professional conduct of paralegals to a "partner, and a lawyer who individually or together with other lawyers possesses comparable managerial authority in a law firm." Lawyers with managerial authority within a law firm are required to make reasonable efforts to establish internal policies and procedures designed to provide reasonable assurance that paralegals in the firm act in a way compatible with the relevant rules of professional conduct. Model Rule 5.3(a), Comment 2.

The NFPA Model Code of Professional Ethics and Responsibility and Guidelines for Enforcement, EC-1.5 states that a paralegal "shall preserve all confidential information provided by the client or acquired from other sources before, during, and after the course of the professional relationship." Further, NFPA EC-1.5(a) requires a paralegal to be aware of and abide by all legal authority governing confidential information in the jurisdiction in which the paralegal practices and prohibits any use of confidential information to the disadvantage of a client. Likewise, the NALA Code of Ethics and Professional Responsibility, Canon 7 states that, "A legal assistant must protect the confidences of the client and must not violate any rule or statute now in effect or hereafter enacted controlling the doctrine of privileged communications between a client and an attorney." Likewise, NALA Guidelines state that paralegals should "preserve the confidences and secrets of all clients; and understand the attorney's code of professional responsibility and these guidelines in order to avoid any action which would involve the attorney in a violation of that code, or give the appearance of professional impropriety." NALA Guideline 1 and Comment.

Guideline 7: **A lawyer should take reasonable measures to prevent conflicts of interest resulting from a paralegal's other employment or interests.**

Comment to Guideline 7: Loyalty and independent judgment are essential elements in the lawyer's relationship to a client. Model Rule 1.7, comment 1. The independent judgment of a lawyer should be exercised solely for the benefit of his client and free from all compromising influences and loyalties. EC 5.1. Model Rules 1.7 through 1.13 address a lawyer's responsibility to prevent conflicts of interest and potential conflicts of interest. Model Rule 5.3 requires lawyers with direct supervisory authority over a paralegal and partners/lawyers with manage-rial authority within a law firm to make reasonable efforts to ensure that the conduct of the paralegals they employ is compatible with their own professional obligations, including the obligation to prevent conflicts of interest. Therefore, paralegals should be instructed to inform the supervising lawyer and the management of the firm of any interest that could result in a conflict of interest or even give the appearance of a conflict. The guideline intentionally speaks to "other employment" rather than only past employment because there are instances where paralegals are employed by more than one law firm at the same time. The guideline's reference to "other interests" is intended to include personal relationships as well as instances where the paralegal may have a financial interest (i.e., as a stockholder, trust beneficiary, or trustee, etc.) that would conflict with the clients in the matter in which the lawyer has been employed.

"Imputed Disqualification Arising from Change in Employment by Non-Lawyer Employee," ABA Informal Opinion 1526 (1988), defines the duties of both the present and former employing lawyers and reasons that the restrictions on paralegals' employment should be kept to "the minimum necessary to protect confidentiality" in order to prevent paralegals from being forced to leave their careers, which "would disserve clients as well as the legal profession." The Opinion describes the attorney's obligations (1) to caution the paralegal not to disclose any information and (2) to prevent the paralegal from working on any matter on which the paralegal worked for a prior employer or respecting which the employee has confidential information.

Disqualification is mandatory where the paralegal gained information relating to the representation of an adverse party while employed at another law firm and has revealed it to lawyers in the new law firm, where screening of the paralegal would be ineffective, or where the paralegal would be required to work on the other side of the same or substantially related matter on which the paralegal had worked while employed at another firm. When a paralegal moves to an opposing firm during ongoing litigation, courts have held that a rebuttable presumption exists that the paralegal will share client confidences. *See, e.g.,* *Phoenix v. Founders*, 887 S.W.2d 831, 835 (Tex. 1994) (the presumption that confidential information has been shared may be rebutted upon showing that sufficient precautions were taken by the new firm to prevent disclosure including that it (1) cautioned the newly-hired paralegal not to disclose any information relating to representation of a client of the former employer; (2) instructed the paralegal not to work on any matter on which he or she worked during prior employment or about which he or she has information relating to the former employer's representation; and (3) the new firm has taken reasonable measures to ensure that the paralegal does not work on any matter on which he or she worked during the prior employment, absent the former client's consent). But, adequate and effective screening of a paralegal may prevent disqualification of the new firm. Model Rule 1.10, comment 4. Adequate and effective screening gives a lawyer and the lawyer's firm the opportunity to build and enforce an "ethical wall" to preclude the paralegal from any involvement in the client matter that is the subject of the conflict and to prevent the paralegal from receiving or disclosing any information concerning the matter. ABA Informal Opinion 1526 (1988). The implication of the ABA's informal opinion is that if the lawyer, and the firm, do not implement a procedure to effectively screen the paralegal from involvement with the litigation, and from communication with attorneys and/or co-employees concerning the litigation, the lawyer and the firm may be disqualified from representing either party in the controversy. *See In re Complex Asbestos Litigation*, 232 Cal. App. 3d 572, 283 Cal. Rptr. 732 (1991) (law firm disqualified from nine pending asbestos cases because it failed to screen paralegal that possessed attorney-client confidences from prior employment by opposing counsel). Some courts hold that paralegals are subject to the same rules governing imputed disqualification as are lawyers. In jurisdictions that do not recognize screening devices as adequate protection against a lawyer's potential conflict in a new law firm, neither a "cone of silence" nor any other screening device will be recognized as a proper or effective remedy where a paralegal who has switched firms possesses material and confidential information. *Zimmerman v. Mahaska Bottling Company*, 19 P.3d 784, 791-792 (Kan. 2001) ("[W]here screening devices are not allowed for lawyers, they are not allowed for non-lawyers either."); *Koulisis v. Rivers*, 730 So. 2d 289 (Fla. Dist. Ct. App. 1999) (firm that hired paralegal with actual knowledge of protected information could not defeat disqualification by showing steps taken to screen the paralegal from the case); Ala. Bar R-02-01, 63 Ala. Law 94 (2002). These cases do not mean that disqualification is mandatory whenever a nonlawyer moves from one private firm to an opposing firm while there is pending litigation. Rather, a firm may still avoid disqualification if (1) the paralegal has not acquired material or confidential information regarding the litigation, or (2) if the client of the former firm waives disqualification and approves the use of a screening device or ethical wall. *Zimmerman*, 19 P.3d at 822.

Other authorities, consistent with Model Rule 1.10(a), differentiate between lawyers and nonlawyers. In *Stewart v. Bee Dee Neon & Signs, Inc.*, 751 So. 2d 196 (Fla. Dist. Ct. App. 2000) the court disagreed with the *Koulisis* rule that paralegals should be held to the same conflicts analyses as lawyers when they change law firms. In *Stewart*, a secretary moved from one law firm to the opposing firm in mid-litigation. While Florida would not permit lawyer screening to defeat disqualification under these circumstance, the *Stewart* court emphasized that "it is important that non-lawyer employees have as much mobility in employment opportunity as possible" and that "any restrictions on the non-lawyer's employment should be held to the minimum necessary to protect confidentiality of client information." *Stewart*, 751 So. 2d at 203 (citing ABA Informal Opinion 1526 (1988)). The analysis in *Stewart* requires the party moving for disqualification to prove that the nonlawyer actually has confidential information, and that screening has not and can not be effectively implemented. *Id.* at 208. In

Leibowitz v. The Eighth Judicial District Court of the State of Nevada, 79 P.3d 515 (2003), the Supreme Court of Nevada overruled its earlier decision in *Ciaffone v. District Court,* 113 Nev. 1165, 945 P.2d 950 (1997), which held that screening of nonlawyer employees would not prevent disqualification. In *Leibowitz,* the court held that when a firm identifies a conflict, it has an absolute duty to screen and to inform the adversarial party about the hiring and the screening mechanisms. The Court emphasized that disqualification is required when confidential information has been disclosed, when screening would be ineffective, or when the affected employee would be required to work on the case in question.

Still other courts that approve screening for paralegals compare paralegals to former government lawyers who have neither a financial interest in the outcome of a particular litigation, nor the choice of which clients they serve. *Smart Industries Corp. v. Superior Court County of Yuma,* 876 P.2d 1176, 1184 (Ariz. App. 1994) ("We believe that this reasoning for treating government attorneys differently in the context of imputed disqualification applies equally to nonlawyer assistants . . ."); *accord, Hayes v. Central States Orthopedic Specialists, Inc.,* 51 P.3d 562 (Okla. 2002); Model Rule 1.11(b) and (c).

Comment 4 to Model Rule 1.10(a) states that the rule does not prohibit representation by others in the law firm where the person prohibited from involvement in a matter is a paralegal. But, paralegals "ordinarily must be screened from any personal participation in the matter to avoid communication to others in the firm of confidential information that both the nonlawyers and the firm have a legal duty to protect." *Id.*

Because disqualification is such a drastic consequence for lawyers and their firms, lawyers must be especially attuned to controlling authority in the jurisdictions where they practice. *See generally,* Steve Morris and Christina C. Stipp, Ethical Conflicts Facing Litigators, ALI SH009ALI-ABA 449, 500-502 (2002).

To assist lawyers and their firms in discharging their professional obligations under the Model Rules, the NALA Guidelines requires paralegals "to take any and all steps necessary to prevent conflicts of interest and fully disclose such conflicts to the supervising attorney" and warns paralegals that any "failure to do so may jeopardize both the attorney's representation and the case itself." NALA, Comment to Guideline 1. NFPA Model Code of Professional Ethics and Responsibility and Guidelines for Enforcement, EC-1.6 requires paralegals to avoid conflicts of interest and to disclose any possible conflicts to the employer or client, as well as to the prospective employers or clients. NFPA, EC-1.6 (a)-(g).

Guideline 8: **A lawyer may include a charge for the work performed by a paralegal in setting a charge for legal services.**

Comment to Guideline 8: In *Missouri v. Jenkins,* 491 U.S. 274 (1989), the United States Supreme Court held that in setting a reasonable attorney's fee under 28 U.S.C. § 1988, a legal fee may include a charge for paralegal services at "market rates" rather than "actual cost" to the attorneys. In its opinion, the Court stated that, in setting recoverable attorney fees, it starts from "the self-evident proposition that the 'reasonable attorney's fee' provided for by statute should compensate the work of paralegals, as well as that of attorneys." *Id.* at 286. This statement should resolve any question concerning the propriety of setting a charge for legal services based on work performed by a paralegal. *See also,* Alaska Rules of Civil Procedure Rule 79; Florida Statutes Title VI, Civil Practice & Procedure, 57.104; North Carolina Guideline 8; Comment to NALA Guideline 5; Michigan Guideline 6. In addition to approving paralegal time as a compensable fee element, the Supreme Court effectively encouraged the use of paralegals for the cost-effective delivery of services. It is important to note, however, that *Missouri v. Jenkins* does not abrogate the attorney's responsibilities under Model Rule 1.5 to set a reasonable fee for legal services, and it follows that those considerations apply to a fee that includes a fee for paralegal services. *See also,* South Carolina Ethics Advisory Opinion 96-13 (a lawyer may use and bill for the services of an independent paralegal so long as the lawyer supervises the work of the paralegal and, in billing the paralegal's time, the lawyer discloses to the client the basis of the fee and expenses).

It is important to note that a number of court decisions have addressed or otherwise set forth the criteria to be used in evaluating whether paralegal services should be compensated. Some requirements include that the services performed must be legal in nature rather than clerical, the fee statement must specify in detail the qualifications of the person performing the service to demonstrate that the paralegal is qualified by education, training or work to perform the assigned work, and evidence that the work performed by the paralegal would have had to be performed by the attorney at a higher rate. Because considerations and criteria vary from one jurisdiction to another, it is important for the practitioner to determine the criteria required by the jurisdiction in which the practitioner intends to file a fee application seeking compensation for paralegal services.

Guideline 9: **A lawyer may not split legal fees with a paralegal nor pay a paralegal for the referral of legal business. A lawyer may compensate a paralegal based on the quantity and quality of the paralegal's work and the value of that work to a law practice, but the paralegal's compensation may not be contingent, by advance agreement, upon the outcome of a particular case or class of cases.**

Comment to Guideline 9: Model Rule 5.4 and DR 3-102(A) and 3-103(A) under the Model Code clearly prohibits fee "splitting" with paralegals, whether characterized as splitting of contingent fees, "forwarding" fees, or other sharing of legal fees. Virtually all guidelines adopted by state bar associations have continued this prohibition in one form or another. *See, e.g.,* Connecticut Guideline 7, Kentucky Supreme Court Rule 3.700, Sub-Rule 5; Michigan Guideline 7; Missouri Guideline III; North Carolina Guideline 8; New Hampshire Rule 35, Sub-Rules 5 and 6; R.I. Sup. Ct. Art. V. R. 5.4; South Carolina Guideline V. It appears clear that a paralegal may not be compensated on a contingent basis for a particular case or be paid for "signing up" clients for representation. Having stated this prohibition, however, the guideline attempts to deal with the practical consideration of how a paralegal may be compensated properly by a lawyer or law firm. The linchpin of the prohibition seems to be the advance agreement of the lawyer to "split" a fee based on a pre-existing contingent arrangement.[7] *See, e.g., Matter of Struthers*, 877 P.2d 789 (Ariz. 1994) (an agreement to give to nonlawyer all fees resulting from nonlawyer's debt collection activities constitutes improper fee splitting); *Florida Bar v. Shapiro*, 413 So. 2d 1184 (Fla. 1982) (payment of contingent salary to nonlawyer based on total amount of fees generated is improper); State Bar of Montana, Op. 95-0411 (1995) (lawyer paid on contingency basis for debt collection cannot share that fee with a nonlawyer collection agency that worked with lawyer).

There is no general prohibition against a lawyer who enjoys a particularly profitable period recognizing the contribution of the paralegal to that profitability with a discretionary bonus so long as the bonus is based on the overall success of the firm and not the fees generated from any particular case. *See, e.g.,* Philadelphia Bar Ass'n Prof. Guidance Comm., Op. 2001-7 (law firm may pay nonlawyer employee a bonus if bonus is not tied to fees generated from a particular case or class of cases from a specific client); Va. St. Bar St. Comm. of Legal Ethics, Op. 885 (1987) (a nonlawyer may be paid based on the percentage of profits from all fees collected by the lawyer). Likewise, a lawyer engaged in a particularly profitable specialty of legal practice is not prohibited from compensating the paralegal who aids materially in that practice more handsomely than the compensation generally awarded to paralegals in that geographic area who work in law practices that are less lucrative. Indeed, any effort to fix a compensation level for paralegals and prohibit great compensation would appear to violate the federal antitrust laws. *See, e.g., Goldfarb v. Virginia State Bar*, 421 U.S. 773 (1975).

In addition to the prohibition on fee splitting, a lawyer also may not provide direct or indirect remuneration to a paralegal for referring legal matters to the lawyer. *See* Model Guideline 9; Connecticut Guideline 7; Michigan Guideline 7; North Carolina Guideline 8. *See also, Committee on Prof'l Ethics & Conduct of Iowa State Bar Ass'n v. Lawler*, 342 N.W. 2d 486 (Iowa 1984) (reprimand for lawyer payment of referral fee); *Trotter v. Nelson*, 684 N.E.2d 1150 (Ind. 1997) (wrongful to pay to nonlawyer five percent of fees collected from a case referred by the nonlawyer).

Guideline 10: **A lawyer who employs a paralegal should facilitate the paralegal's participation in appropriate continuing education and pro bono publico activities.**

Comment to Guideline 10: For many years the Standing Committee on Paralegals has advocated that formal paralegal education generally improves the legal services rendered by lawyers employing paralegals and provides a more satisfying professional atmosphere in which paralegals may work. Recognition of the employing lawyer's obligation to facilitate the paralegal's continuing professional education is, therefore, appropriate because of the benefits to both the law practice and the paralegals and is consistent with the lawyer's own responsibility to maintain professional competence under Model Rule 1.1. *See also* EC 6-2 of the Model Code. Since these Guidelines were first adopted by the House of Delegates in 1991, several state bar associations have adopted guidelines that encourage lawyers to promote the professional development and continuing education of paralegals in their employ, including Connecticut, Idaho, Indiana, Michigan, New York, Virginia, Washington, and West Virginia. The National Association of Legal Assistants Code of Ethics and Professional Responsibility, Canon 6, calls on paralegals to "maintain a high degree of competency through education and training . . . and through continuing education. . . ." and the National Federation of Paralegal Associations Model Code of Ethics and Professional Responsibility, Canon 1.1, states that a paralegal "shall achieve and maintain a high level of competence" through education, training, work experience and continuing education.

The Standing Committee is of the view that similar benefits accrue to the lawyer and paralegal if the paralegal is included in the pro bono publico legal services that a lawyer has a clear obligation to provide under Model Rule 6.1 and, where appropriate, the paralegal is encouraged to provide such services independently. The ability of a law firm to provide more pro bono publico services is enhanced if paralegals are included. Recognition of the paralegal's role in such services is consistent with the role of the paralegal in the contemporary delivery of legal services generally and is also consistent with the lawyer's duty to the legal profession under Canon 2 of the Model Code. Several state bar associations, including Connecticut, Idaho, Indiana, Michigan, Washington and West Virginia, have adopted a guideline that calls on lawyers to facilitate paralegals' involvement in pro bono publico activities. One state, New York, includes pro bono work under the rubric of professional development. (*See* Commentary to Guideline VII of the New York State Bar Association Guidelines for the Utilization by Lawyers of the Service of Legal Assistants, adopted June 1997.) The National Federation of Paralegal Associations Model Code of Ethics and Professional Responsibility and Guidelines for Enforcement, Canon 1.4, states that paralegals "shall serve the public interest by contributing to the improvement of the legal system and delivery of quality legal services, including pro bono publico legal services." In the accompanying Ethical Consideration 1.4(d), the Federation asks its members to aspire to contribute at least 24 hours of pro bono services annually.

Copyright ©2004 American Bar Association. Reprinted by permission.

NOTES

[1] In 1986, the ABA Board of Governors approved a definition for the term "legal assistant." In 1997, the ABA amended the definition of legal assistant by adopting the following language: "A legal assistant or paralegal is a person qualified by education, training or work experience who is employed or retained by a lawyer, law office, corporation, governmental agency or other entity who performs specifically delegated substantive legal work for which a lawyer is responsible." To comport with current usage in the profession, these guidelines use the term "paralegal" rather than "legal assistant," however, lawyers should be aware that the terms legal assistant and paralegals are often used interchangeably.

[2] While necessarily mentioning paralegal conduct, lawyers are the intended audience of these Guidelines. The Guidelines, therefore, are addressed to lawyer conduct and not directly to the conduct of the paralegal. Both the National Association of Legal Assistants (NALA) and the National Federation of Paralegal Associations (NFPA) have adopted guidelines of conduct that are directed to paralegals. *See* NALA, "Code of Ethics and Professional Responsibility of the National Association of Legal Assistants, Inc." (adopted 1975, revised 1979, 1988 and 1995); NFPA, "Affirmation of Responsibility" (adopted 1977, revised 1981).

[3] The Model Rules were first adopted by the ABA House of Delegates in August of 1983. To date, some 43 states and two jurisdictions have adopted the Model Rules to govern the professional conduct of lawyers licensed in those states. However, because several states still utilize a version of the Model Code of Professional Responsibility ("Model Code"), these comments will refer to both the Model Rules and the predecessor Model Code (and to the Ethical Considerations and Disciplinary Rules found under the canons in the Model Codes). In 1997, the ABA formed the Commission on Evaluation of the Rules of Professional Conduct ("Ethics 2000 Commission") to undertake a comprehensive review and revision of the Model Rules. The ABA House of Delegates completed its review of the Commission's recommended revisions in February 2002. Visit http://www.abanet.org/cpr/jclr/jclr_home.html for information regarding the status of each state Supreme Court's adoption of the Ethics 2000 revisions to the Model Rules.

[4] The 1986 ABA definition read: "A legal assistant is a person, qualified through education, training or work experience, who is employed or retained by a lawyer, law office, governmental agency, or other entity, in a capacity or function which involves the performance, under the ultimate direction and supervision of an attorney, of specifically delegated substantive legal work, which work, for the most part, requires a sufficient knowledge of legal concepts that, absent such assistant the attorney would perform the task."

[5] In 1997, the ABA amended the definition of legal assistant by adopting the following language: "A legal assistant or paralegal is a person qualified by education, training or work experience who is employed or retained by a lawyer, law office, corporation, governmental agency or other entity who performs specifically delegated substantive legal work for which a lawyer is responsible."

[6] It is important to note that pursuant to federal or state statute, paralegals are permitted to provide direct client representation in certain administrative proceedings. While this does not obviate the lawyer's responsibility for the paralegal's work, it does change the nature of the lawyer's supervision of the paralegal. The opportunity to use such paralegal services has particular benefits to legal services programs and does not violate Guideline 2. *See generally* ABA Standards for Providers of Civil Legal Services to the Poor Std. 6.3, at 6.17-6.18 (1986).

[7] In its Rule 5.4 of the Rules of Professional Conduct, the District of Columbia permits lawyers to form legal service partnerships that include non-lawyer participants. Comments 5 and 6 to that rule, however, state that the term "nonlawyer participants" should not be confused with the term "nonlawyer assistants" and that "nonlawyer assistants under Rule 5.3 do not have managerial authority or financial interests in the organization."

NFPA Model Code of Ethics and Professional Responsibility and Guidelines for Enforcement

PREAMBLE

The National Federation of Paralegal Associations, Inc. ("NFPA") is a professional organization comprised of paralegal associations and individual paralegals throughout the United States and Canada. Members of NFPA have varying backgrounds, experiences, education and job responsibilities that reflect the diversity of the paralegal profession. NFPA promotes the growth, development and recognition of the paralegal profession as an integral partner in the delivery of legal services.

In May 1993 NFPA adopted its Model Code of Ethics and Professional Responsibility ("Model Code") to delineate the principles for ethics and conduct to which every paralegal should aspire. Many paralegal associations throughout the United States have endorsed the concept and content of NFPA's Model Code through the adoption of their own ethical codes. In doing so, paralegals have confirmed the profession's commitment to increase the quality and efficiency of legal services, as well as recognized its responsibilities to the public, the legal community, and colleagues.

Paralegals have recognized, and will continue to recognize, that the profession must continue to evolve to enhance their roles in the delivery of legal services. With increased levels of responsibility comes the need to define and enforce mandatory rules of professional conduct. Enforcement of codes of paralegal conduct is a logical and necessary step to enhance and ensure the confidence of the legal community and the public in the integrity and professional responsibility of paralegals.

In April 1997 NFPA adopted the Model Disciplinary Rules ("Model Rules") to make possible the enforcement of the Canons and Ethical Considerations contained in the NFPA Model Code. A concurrent determination was made that the Model Code of Ethics and Professional Responsibility, formerly aspirational in nature, should be recognized as setting forth the enforceable obligations of all paralegals.

The Model Code and Model Rules offer a framework for professional discipline, either voluntarily or through formal regulatory programs.

§1. NFPA MODEL DISCIPLINARY RULES AND ETHICAL CONSIDERATIONS

1.1 A Paralegal Shall Achieve and Maintain a High Level of Competence

Ethical Considerations

EC–1.1(a) A paralegal shall achieve competency through education, training, and work experience.

EC–1.1(b) A paralegal shall participate in continuing education in order to keep informed of current legal, technical, and general developments.

EC–1.1(c) A paralegal shall perform all assignments promptly and efficiently.

1.2 A Paralegal Shall Maintain a High Level of Personal and Professional Integrity

Ethical Considerations

EC–1.2(a) A paralegal shall not engage in any ex parte communications involving the courts or any other adjudicatory body in an attempt to exert undue influence or to obtain advantage or the benefit of only one party.

EC–1.2(b) A paralegal shall not communicate, or cause another to communicate, with a party the paralegal knows to be represented by a lawyer in a pending matter without the prior consent of the lawyer representing such other party.

EC–1.2(c) A paralegal shall ensure that all timekeeping and billing records prepared by the paralegal are thorough, accurate, honest, and complete.

EC–1.2(d) A paralegal shall not knowingly engage in fraudulent billing practices. Such practices may include, but are not limited to: inflation of hours billed to a client or employer; misrepresentation of the nature of tasks performed; and/or submission of fraudulent expense and disbursement documentation.

EC–1.2(e) A paralegal shall be scrupulous, thorough, and honest in the identification and maintenance of all funds, securities, and other assets of a client and shall provide accurate accounting as appropriate.

EC–1.2(f) A paralegal shall advise the proper authority of non-confidential knowledge of any dishonest or fraudulent acts by any person pertaining to the handling of the funds, securities, or other assets of a client. The authority to whom the report is made shall depend on the nature and circumstances of the possible misconduct (e.g., ethics committees of law firms, corporations and/or paralegal associations, local or state bar associations, local prosecutors, administrative agencies, etc.). Failure to report such knowledge is in itself misconduct and shall be treated as such under these rules.

1.3 A Paralegal Shall Maintain a High Standard of Professional Conduct

Ethical Considerations

EC–1.3(a) A paralegal shall refrain from engaging in any conduct that offends the dignity and decorum of proceedings before a court or other adjudicatory body and shall be respectful of all rules and procedures.

EC–1.3(b) A paralegal shall avoid impropriety and the appearance of impropriety and shall not engage in any conduct that would adversely affect his/her fitness to practice. Such conduct may include, but is not limited to: violence, dishonesty, interference with the administration of justice, and/or abuse of a professional position or public office.

EC–1.3(c) Should a paralegal's fitness to practice be compromised by physical or mental illness, causing that paralegal to commit an act that is in direct violation of the Model Code/Model Rules and/or laws governing the jurisdiction in which the paralegal practices, that paralegal may be protected from sanction upon review of the nature and circumstances of that illness.

EC–1.3(d) A paralegal shall advise the proper authority of non-confidential knowledge of any action of another legal professional that clearly demonstrates fraud, deceit, dishonesty, or misrepresentation. The authority to whom the report is made shall depend on the nature and circumstances of the possible misconduct (e.g., ethics committees of law firms, corporations and/or paralegal associations, local or state bar associations, local prosecutors, administrative agencies, etc.). failure to report such knowledge is in itself misconduct and shall be treated as such under these rules.

EC–1.3(e) A paralegal shall not knowingly assist any individual with the commission of an act that is in direct violation of the Model Code/Model Rules and/or the rules and/or laws governing the jurisdiction in which the paralegal practices.

EC–1.3(f) If a paralegal possesses knowledge of future criminal activity, that knowledge must be reported to the appropriate authority immediately.

1.4 A Paralegal Shall Serve the Public Interest by Contributing to the Delivery of Quality Legal Services and the Improvement of the Legal System, Including Pro Bono Publico Services and Community Service

Ethical Considerations

EC–1.4(a) A paralegal shall be sensitive to the legal needs of the public and shall promote the development and implementation of programs that address those needs.

EC–1.4(b) A paralegal shall support efforts to improve the legal system and access thereto and shall assist in making changes.

EC–1.4(c) A paralegal shall support and participate in the delivery of Pro Bono Publico services directed toward implementing and improving access to justice, the law, the legal system or the paralegal and legal professions.

EC–1.4(d) A paralegal should aspire annually to contribute twenty-four (24) hours of Pro Bono Publico services under the supervision of an attorney or as authorized by administrative, statutory or court authority to:

1. persons of limited means; or

2. are designed primarily to address the legal needs of persons with limited means; or

3. individuals, groups or organizations seeking to secure or protect civil rights, civil liberties or public rights.

The twenty-four (24) hours of Pro Bono Publico services contributed annually by a paralegal may consist of such services as detailed in this EC-1.4(d), and/or administrative matters designed to develop and implement the attainment of this aspiration as detailed above in EC-1.4(a) B (c), or any combination of the two.

EC-1.4(e)   A paralegal should aspire to contribute twenty-four (24) hours of Community

Service on an annual basis. For purposes of this EC, "Community Service" shall be defined as: volunteer activities that have the effect of providing a valuable service or benefit to a local community, as distinguished from those services which fall within the traditional definition of *pro bono publico*. By way of example and not limitation, several examples of Community Service may include: working with Habitat for Humanity, volunteering with local women's shelters, volunteering for hurricane relief, serving meals at local soup kitchens or local homeless shelters.

1.5   A Paralegal Shall Preserve All Confidential Information Provided by the Client or Acquired from Other Sources before, during, and after the Course of the Professional Relationship

Ethical Considerations

EC–1.5(a)   A paralegal shall be aware of and abide by all legal authority governing confidential information in the jurisdiction in which the paralegal practices.

EC–1.5(b)   A paralegal shall not use confidential information to the disadvantage of the client.

EC–1.5(c)   A paralegal shall not use confidential information to the advantage of the paralegal or of a third person.

EC–1.5(d)   A paralegal may reveal confidential information only after full disclosure and with the client's written consent; or, when required by law or court order; or, when necessary to prevent the client from committing an act that could result in death or serious bodily harm.

EC–1.5(e)   A paralegal shall keep those individuals responsible for the legal representation of a client fully informed of any confidential information the paralegal may have pertaining to that client.

EC–1.5(f)   A paralegal shall not engage in any indiscreet communications concerning clients.

1.6   A Paralegal Shall Avoid Conflicts of Interest and Shall Disclose Any Possible Conflict to the Employer or Client, as Well as to the Prospective Employers or Clients

Ethical Considerations

EC–1.6(a)   A paralegal shall act within the bounds of the law, solely for the benefit of the client, and shall be free of compromising influences and loyalties. Neither the paralegal's personal or business interest, nor those of other clients or third persons, should compromise the paralegal's professional judgment and loyalty to the client.

EC–1.6(b)   A paralegal shall avoid conflicts of interest that may arise from previous assignments, whether for a present or past employer or client.

EC–1.6(c)   A paralegal shall avoid conflicts of interest that may arise from family relationships and from personal and business interests.

EC–1.6(d)   In order to be able to determine whether an actual or potential conflict of interest exists a paralegal shall create and maintain an effective recordkeeping system that identifies clients, matters, and parties with which the paralegal has worked.

EC–1.6(e)   A paralegal shall reveal sufficient non-confidential information about a client or former client to reasonably ascertain if an actual or potential conflict of interest exists.

EC–1.6(f) A paralegal shall not participate in or conduct work on any matter where a conflict of interest has been identified.

EC–1.6(g) In matters where a conflict of interest has been identified and the client consents to continued representation, a paralegal shall comply fully with the implementation and maintenance of an Ethical Wall.

1.7 A Paralegal's Title Shall Be Fully Disclosed

Ethical Considerations

EC–1.7(a) A paralegal's title shall clearly indicate the individual's status and shall be disclosed in all business and professional communications to avoid misunderstandings and misconceptions about the paralegal's role and responsibilities.

EC–1.7(b) A paralegal's title shall be included if the paralegal's name appears on business cards, letterhead, brochures, directories, and advertisements.

EC–1.7(c) A paralegal shall not use letterhead, business cards, or other promotional materials to create a fraudulent impression of his/her status or ability to practice in the jurisdiction in which the paralegal practices.

EC–1.7(d) A paralegal shall not practice under color of any record, diploma, or certificate that has been illegally or fraudulently obtained or issued or which is misrepresentative in any way.

EC–1.7(e) A paralegal shall not participate in the creation, issuance, or dissemination of fraudulent records, diplomas, or certificates.

1.8 A Paralegal Shall Not Engage in the Unauthorized Practice of Law

Ethical Considerations

EC–1.8(a) A paralegal shall comply with the applicable legal authority governing the unauthorized practice of law in the jurisdiction in which the paralegal practices.

§2. GUIDELINES FOR THE ENFORCEMENT OF THE MODEL CODE OF ETHICS AND PROFESSIONAL RESPONSIBILITY

2.1 Basis for Discipline

2.1(a) Disciplinary investigations and proceedings brought under authority of the Rules shall be conducted in accord with obligations imposed on the paralegal professional by the Model Code of Ethics and Professional Responsibility.

2.2 Structure of Disciplinary Committee

2.2(a) The Disciplinary Committee ("Committee") shall be made up of nine (9) members including the Chair.

2.2(b) Each member of the Committee, including any temporary replacement members, shall have demonstrated working knowledge of ethics/professional responsibility-related issues and activities.

2.2(c) The Committee shall represent a cross-section of practice areas and work experience. The following recommendations are made regarding the members of the Committee.

1. At least one paralegal with one to three years of law-related work experience.

2. At least one paralegal with five to seven years of law-related experience.

3. At least one paralegal with over ten years of law-related experience.

4. One paralegal educator with five to seven years of work experience; preferably in the area of ethics/professional responsibility.

5. One paralegal manager.

6. One lawyer with five to seven years of law-related work experience.

7. One lay member.

2.2(d) The Chair of the Committee shall be appointed within thirty (30) days of its members' induction. The Chair shall have no fewer than ten (10) years of law-related work experience.

2.2(e) The terms of all members of the Committee shall be staggered. Of those members initially appointed, a simple majority plus one shall be appointed to a term of one year, and the remaining members shall be appointed to a term of two years. Thereafter, all members of the Committee shall be appointed to terms of two years.

2.2(f) If for any reason the terms of a majority of the Committee will expire at the same time, members may be appointed to terms of one year to maintain continuity of the Committee.

2.2(g) The Committee shall organize from its members a three-tiered structure to investigate, prosecute, and/or adjudicate charges of misconduct. The members shall be rotated among the tiers.

2.3 Operation of Committee

2.3(a) The Committee shall meet on an as-needed basis to discuss, investigate, and/or adjudicate alleged violations of the Model Code/Model Rules.

2.3(b) A majority of the members of the Committee present at a meeting shall constitute a quorum.

2.3(c) A Recording Secretary shall be designated to maintain complete and accurate minutes of all Committee meetings. All such minutes shall be kept confidential until a decision has been made that the matter will be set for hearing as set forth in Section 6.1 below.

2.3(d) If any member of the Committee has a conflict of interest with the Charging Party, the Responding Party, or the allegations of misconduct, that member shall not take part in any hearing or deliberations concerning those allegations. If the absence of that member creates a lack of a quorum for the Committee, then a temporary replacement for the member shall be appointed.

2.3(e) Either the Charging Party or the Responding Party may request that, for good cause shown, any member of the Committee not participate in a hearing or deliberation. All such requests shall be honored. If the absence of a Committee member under those circumstances creates a lack of a quorum for the Committee, then a temporary replacement for that member shall be appointed.

2.3(f) All discussions and correspondence of the Committee shall be kept confidential until a decision has been made that the matter will be set for hearing as set forth in Section 6.1 below.

2.3(g) All correspondence from the Committee to the Responding Party regarding any charge of misconduct and any decisions made regarding the charge shall be mailed certified mail, return receipt requested, to the Responding Party's last known address and shall be clearly marked with a "Confidential" designation.

2.4 Procedure for the Reporting of Alleged Violations of the Model Code/ Disciplinary Rules

2.4(a)   An individual or entity in possession of non-confidential knowledge or information concerning possible instances of misconduct shall make a confidential written report to the Committee within thirty (30) days of obtaining same. This report shall include all details of the alleged misconduct.

2.4(b)   The Committee so notified shall inform the Responding Party of the allegation(s) of misconduct no later than ten (10) business days after receiving the confidential written report from the Charging Party.

2.4(c)   Notification to the Responding Party shall include the identity of the Charging Party, unless, for good cause shown, the Charging Party requests anonymity.

2.4(d)   The Responding Party shall reply to the allegations within (10) business days of notification.

2.5 Procedure for the Investigation of a Charge of Misconduct

2.5(a)   Upon receipt of a Charge of Misconduct ("Charge"), or on its own initiative, the Committee shall initiate an investigation.

2.5(b)   If, upon initial or preliminary review, the Committee makes a determination that the charges are either without basis in fact or, if proven, would not constitute professional misconduct, the Committee shall dismiss the allegations of misconduct. If such determination of dismissal cannot be made, a formal investigation shall be initiated.

2.5(c)   Upon the decision to conduct a formal investigation, the Committee shall:

1. mail to the Charging and responding Parties within three (3) business days of that decision notice of the commencement of a formal investigation. That notification shall be in writing and shall contain a complete explanation of all Charge(s), as well as the reasons for a formal investigation and shall cite the applicable codes and rules;

2. allow the Responding Party thirty (30) days to prepare and submit a confidential response to the Committee, which response shall address each charge specifically and shall be in writing; and

3. upon receipt of the response to the notification, have thirty (30) days to investigate the Charge(s). If an extension of time is deemed necessary, that extension shall not exceed ninety (90) days.

2.5(d)   Upon conclusion of the investigation, the Committee may:

1. dismiss the Charge upon the finding that it has no basis in fact;

2. dismiss the Charge upon the finding that, if proven, the Charge would not constitute Misconduct;

3. refer the matter for hearing by the Tribunal; or

4. in the case of criminal activity, refer the Charge(s) and all investigation results to the appropriate authority.

2.6 Procedure for a Misconduct Hearing before a Tribunal

2.6(a)   Upon the decision by the Committee that a matter should be heard, all parties shall be notified and a hearing date shall be set. The hearing shall take place no more than thirty (30) days from the conclusion of the formal investigation.

2.6(b)   The Responding Party shall have the right to counsel. The parties and the Tribunal shall have the right to call any witnesses and introduce any documentation that they believe will lead to the fair and reasonable resolution of the matter.

2.6(c)   Upon completion of the hearing, the Tribunal shall deliberate and present a written decision to the parties in accordance with procedures as set forth by the Tribunal.

2.6(d)   Notice of the decision of the Tribunal shall be appropriately published.

2.7 Sanctions

2.7(a)   Upon a finding of the Tribunal that misconduct has occurred, any of the following sanctions, or others as may be deemed appropriate, may be imposed upon the Responding Party, either singularly or in combination:

1. letter of reprimand to the Responding Party; counseling;

2. attendance at an ethics course approved by the Tribunal; probation;

3. suspension of the license/authority to practice; revocation of license/authority to practice;

4. imposition of a fine; assessment of costs; or

5. in the instance of criminal activity, referral to the appropriate authority.

2.7(b)   Upon the expiration of any period of probation, suspension, or revocation, the Responding Party may make application of reinstatement. With the application for reinstatement, the Responding Party must show proof of having complied with all aspects of the sanctions imposed by the Tribunal.

2.8 Appellate Procedures

2.8(a)   The parties shall have the right to appeal the decision of the Tribunal in accordance with the procedure as set forth by the Tribunal.

Appellate Body means a body established to adjudicate an appeal to any decision made by a Tribunal or other decision-making body with respect to formally-heard Charges of Misconduct.

Charge of Misconduct means a written submission by any individual or entity to an ethics committee, paralegal association, bar association, law enforcement agency, judicial body, government agency, or other appropriate body or entity, that sets forth non-confidential information regarding any instance of alleged misconduct by an individual paralegal or paralegal entity.

Charging Party means any individual or entity who submits a Charge of Misconduct against an individual paralegal or paralegal entity.

Competency means the demonstration of: diligence, education, skill, and mental, emotional, and physical fitness reasonably necessary for the performance of paralegal services.

Confidential Information means information relating to a client, whatever its source, that is not public knowledge nor available to the public. ("Non-Confidential Information" would generally include the name of the client and the identity of the matter for which the paralegal provided services.)

Disciplinary Committee means any committee that has been established by an entity such as a paralegal association, bar association, judicial body, or government agency to: (a) identify, define and investigate general ethical considerations and concerns with respect to paralegal practice; (b) administer and enforce the Model Code and Model Rules and; (c) discipline any individual paralegal or paralegal entity found to be in violation of same.

Disciplinary Hearing means the confidential proceeding conducted by a committee or other designated body or entity concerning any instance of alleged misconduct by an individual paralegal or paralegal entity.

Disclose means communication of information reasonably sufficient to permit identification of the significance of the matter in question.

Ethical Wall means the screening method implemented in order to protect a client from a conflict of interest. An Ethical Wall generally includes, but is not limited to, the following elements: (1) prohibit the paralegal from having any connection with the matter; (2) ban discussions with or the transfer of documents to or from the paralegal; (3) restrict access to files; and (4) educate all members of the firm, corporation, or entity as to the separation of the paralegal (both organizationally and physically) from the pending matter. For more information regarding the Ethical Wall, see the NFPA publication entitled "The Ethical Wall—Its Application to Paralegals."

Ex parte means actions or communications conducted at the instance and for the benefit of one party only, and without notice to, or contestation by, any person adversely interested.

Investigation means the investigation of any charge (s) of misconduct filed against an individual paralegal or paralegal entity by a Committee.

Letter of Reprimand means a written notice of formal censure or severe reproof administered to an individual paralegal or paralegal entity for unethical or improper conduct.

Misconduct means the knowing or unknowing commission of an act that is in direct violation of those Canons and Ethical Considerations of any and all applicable codes and/or rules of conduct.

Paralegal is synonymous with "Legal Assistant" and is defined as a person qualified through education, training, or work experience to perform substantive legal work that requires knowledge of legal concepts and is customarily, but not exclusively, performed by a lawyer. This person may be retained or employed by a lawyer, law office, governmental agency, or other entity or may be authorized by administrative, statutory, or court authority to perform this work.

Pro Bono Publico means providing or assisting to provide quality legal services in order to enhance access to justice for persons of limited means; charitable, religious, civic, community, governmental and educational organizations in matters that are designed primarily to address the legal needs of persons with limited means; or individuals, groups or organizations seeking to secure or protect civil rights, civil liberties or public rights.

Proper Authority means the local paralegal association, the local or state bar association, Committee (s) of the local paralegal or bar association(s), local prosecutor, administrative agency, or other tribunal empowered to investigate or act upon an instance of alleged misconduct.

Responding Party means an individual paralegal or paralegal entity against whom a Charge of Misconduct has been submitted.

Revocation means the recision of the license, certificate or other authority to practice of an individual paralegal or paralegal entity found in violation of those Canons and Ethical Considerations of any and all applicable codes and/or rules of conduct.

Suspension means the suspension of the license, certificate or other authority to practice of an individual paralegal or paralegal entity found in violation of those Canons and Ethical Considerations of any and all applicable codes and/or rules of conduct.

Tribunal means the body designated to adjudicate allegations of misconduct.

Reprinted by permission of the National Federation of Paralegal Associations, Inc. ©2006.

NALA Model Standards and Guidelines for Utilization of Legal Assistants

INTRODUCTION

The purpose of this annotated version of the National Association of Legal Assistants, Inc. Model Standards and Guidelines for the Utilization of Legal Assistants (the "Model," "Standards" and/or the "Guidelines") is to provide references to the existing case law and other authorities where the underlying issues have been considered. The authorities cited will serve as a basis upon which conduct of a legal assistant may be analyzed as proper or improper.

The Guidelines represent a statement of how the legal assistant may function. The Guidelines are not intended to be a comprehensive or exhaustive list of the proper duties of a legal assistant. Rather, they are designed as guides to what may or may not be proper conduct for the legal assistant. In formulating the Guidelines, the reasoning and rules of law in many reported decisions of disciplinary cases and unauthorized practice of law cases have been analyzed and considered. In addition, the provisions of the American Bar Association's Model Rules of Professional Conduct, as well as the ethical promulgations of various state courts and bar associations have been considered in the development of the Guidelines.

These Guidelines form a sound basis for the legal assistant and the supervising attorney to follow. This Model will serve as a comprehensive resource document and as a definitive, well-reasoned guide to those considering voluntary standards and guidelines for legal assistants.

I
PREAMBLE

Proper utilization of the services of legal assistants contributes to the delivery of cost-effective, high-quality legal services. Legal assistants and the legal profession should be assured that measures exist for identifying legal assistants and their role in assisting attorneys in the delivery of legal services. Therefore, the National Association of Legal Assistants, Inc., hereby adopts these Standards and Guidelines as an educational document for the benefit of legal assistants and the legal profession.

Comment

The three most frequently raised questions concerning legal assistants are (1) How do you define a legal assistant; (2) Who is qualified to be identified as a legal assistant; and (3) What duties may a legal assistant perform? The definition adopted in 1984 by the National Association of Legal Assistants answers the first question. The Model sets forth minimum education, training and experience through standards which will assure that an individual utilizing the title "legal assistant" has the qualifications to be held out to the legal community and the public in that capacity. The Guidelines identify those acts which the reported cases hold to be proscribed and give examples of services which the legal assistant may perform under the supervision of a licensed attorney.

These Guidelines constitute a statement relating to services performed by legal assistants, as defined herein, as approved by court decisions and other sources of authority. The purpose of the Guidelines is not to place limitations or restrictions on the legal assistant profession. Rather, the Guidelines are intended to outline for the legal profession an acceptable course of conduct. Voluntary recognition and utilization of the Standards and Guidelines will benefit the entire legal profession and the public it serves.

II
HISTORY

The National Association of Legal Assistants adopted this Model in 1984. At the same time the following definition in of a legal assistant was adopted:

Legal assistants, also known as paralegals, are a distinguishable group of persons who assist attorneys in the delivery of legal services. Through formal education, training, and experience, legal assistants have knowledge and expertise regarding the legal system and substantive and procedural law which qualify them to do work of a legal nature under the supervision of an attorney.

Historically, there have been similar definitions adopted by various legal professional organizations. Recognizing the need for one clear definition the NALA membership approved a resolution in July 2001 to adopt the legal assistant definition of the American Bar Association. This definition continues to be utilized today.

III
DEFINITION

A legal assistant or paralegal is a person qualified by education, training or work experience who is employed or retained by a lawyer, law office, corporation, governmental agency or other entity who performs specifically delegated substantive legal work for which a lawyer is responsible. (Adopted by the ABA in 1997 and by NALA in 2001)

Comment

This definition emphasizes the knowledge and expertise of legal assistants in substantive and procedural law obtained through education and work experience. It further defines the legal assistant or paralegal as a professional working under the supervision of an attorney as distinguished from a non-lawyer who delivers services directly to the public without any intervention or review of work product by an attorney. Such unsupervised services, unless authorized by court or agency rules, constitute the unauthorized practice of law.

Statutes, court rules, case law and bar association documents are additional sources for legal assistant or paralegal definitions. In applying the Standards and Guidelines, it is important to remember that they were developed to apply to the legal assistant as defined herein. Lawyers should refrain from labeling those as paralegals or legal assistants who do not meet the criteria set forth in this definition and/or the definitions set forth by state rules, guidelines or bar associations. Labeling secretaries and other administrative staff as legal assistants/paralegals is inaccurate.

For billing purposes, the services of a legal secretary are considered part of overhead costs and are not recoverable in fee awards. However, the courts have held that fees for paralegal services are recoverable as long as they are not clerical functions, such as organizing files, copying documents, checking docket, updating files, checking court dates and delivering papers. As established in *Missouri v. Jenkins*, 491 U.S.274, 109 S.Ct. 2463, 2471, n.10 (1989) tasks performed by legal assistants must be substantive in nature which, absent the legal assistant, the attorney would perform.

There are also case law and Supreme Court Rules addressing the issue of a disbarred attorney serving in the capacity of a legal assistant.

IV
STANDARDS

A legal assistant should meet certain minimum qualifications. The following standards may be used to determine an individual's qualifications as a legal assistant:

1. Successful completion of the Certified Legal Assistant ("CLA") certifying examination of the National Association of Legal Assistants, Inc.;

2. Graduation from an ABA approved program of study for legal assistants;

3. Graduation from a course of study for legal assistants which is institutionally accredited but not ABA approved, and which requires not less than the equivalent of 60 semester hours of classroom study;

4. Graduation from a course of study for legal assistants, other than those set forth in (2) and (3) above, plus not less than six months of in-house training as a legal assistant;

5. A baccalaureate degree in any field, plus not less than six months in-house training as a legal assistant;

6. A minimum of three years of law-related experience under the supervision of an attorney, including at least six months of in-house training as a legal assistant; or

7. Two years of in-house training as a legal assistant.

For purposes of these Standards, "in-house training as a legal assistant" means attorney education of the employee concerning legal assistant duties and these Guidelines. In addition to review and analysis of assignments, the legal assistant should receive a reasonable amount of instruction directly related to the duties and obligations of the legal assistant.

Comment

The Standards set forth suggest minimum qualifications for a legal assistant. These minimum qualifications, as adopted, recognize legal related work backgrounds and formal education backgrounds, both of which provide the legal assistant with a broad base in exposure to and knowledge of the legal profession. This background is necessary to assure the public and the legal profession that the employee identified as a legal assistant is qualified.

The Certified Legal Assistant (CLA) /Certified Paralegal (CP) examination established by NALA in 1976 is a voluntary nationwide certification program for legal assistants. (*CLA and CP are federally registered certification marks owned by NALA.*) The CLA/CP designation is a statement to the legal profession and the public that the legal assistant has met the high levels of knowledge and professionalism required by NALA's certification program. Continuing education requirements, which all certified legal assistants must meet, assure that high standards are maintained. The CLA/CP designation has been recognized as a means of establishing the qualifications of a legal assistant in supreme court rules, state court and bar association standards and utilization guidelines.

Certification through NALA is available to all legal assistants meeting the educational and experience requirements. Certified Legal Assistants may also pursue advanced certification in specialty practice areas through the APC, Advanced Paralegal Certification, credentialing program. Legal assistants/paralegals may also pursue certification based on state laws and procedures in California, Florida, Louisiana, North Carolina, and Texas.

V
GUIDELINES

These Guidelines relating to standards of performance and professional responsibility are intended to aid legal assistants and attorneys. The ultimate responsibility rests with an attorney who employs legal assistants to educate them with respect to the duties they are assigned and to supervise the manner in which such duties are accomplished.

Comment

In general, a legal assistant is allowed to perform any task which is properly delegated and supervised by an attorney, as long as the attorney is ultimately responsible to the client and assumes complete professional responsibility for the work product.

ABA Model Rules of Professional Conduct, Rule 5.3 provides:

With respect to a non-lawyer employed or retained by or associated with a lawyer:

> (a) a partner in a law firm shall make reasonable efforts to ensure that the firm has in effect measures giving reasonable assurance that the person's conduct is compatible with the professional obligations of the lawyer;

> (b) a lawyer having direct supervisory authority over the non-lawyer shall make reasonable efforts to ensure that the person's conduct is compatible with the professional obligations of the lawyer; and

> (c) a lawyer shall be responsible for conduct of such a person that would be a violation of the rules of professional conduct if engaged in by a lawyer if:

>> (1) the lawyer orders or, with the knowledge of the specific conduct ratifies the conduct involved; or

>> (2) the lawyer is a partner in the law firm in which the person is employed, or has direct supervisory authority over the person, and knows of the conduct at a time when its consequences can be avoided or mitigated but fails to take remedial action.

There are many interesting and complex issues involving the use of legal assistants. In any discussion of the proper role of a legal assistant, attention must be directed to what constitutes the practice of law. Proper delegation to legal assistants is further complicated and confused by the lack of an adequate definition of the practice of law.

Kentucky became the first state to adopt a Paralegal Code by Supreme Court Rule. This Code sets forth certain exclusions to the unauthorized practice of law:

For purposes of this rule, the unauthorized practice of law shall not include any service rendered involving legal knowledge or advice, whether representation, counsel or advocacy, in or out of court, rendered in respect to the acts, duties, obligations, liabilities or business relations of the one requiring services where:

> A. The client understands that the paralegal is not a lawyer;

> B. The lawyer supervises the paralegal in the performance of his or her duties; and

> C. The lawyer remains fully responsible for such representation including all actions taken or not taken in connection therewith by the paralegal to the same extent as if such representation had

been furnished entirely by the lawyer and all such actions had been taken or not taken directly by the attorney. Paralegal Code, Ky.S.Ct.R3.700, Sub-Rule 2.

South Dakota Supreme Court Rule 97–25 Utilization Rule a(4) states: "The attorney remains responsible for the services performed by the legal assistant to the same extent as though such services had been furnished entirely by the attorney and such actions were those of the attorney."

Guideline I

Legal assistants should:

1. Disclose their status as legal assistants at the outset of any professional relationship with a client, other attorneys, a court or administrative agency or personnel thereof, or members of the general public;

2. Preserve the confidences and secrets of all clients; and

3. Understand the attorney's Rules of Professional Responsibility and these Guidelines in order to avoid any action which would involve the attorney in a violation of the Rules, or give the appearance of professional impropriety.

Comment

Routine early disclosure of the legal assistant's status when dealing with persons outside the attorney's office is necessary to assure that there will be no misunderstanding as to the responsibilities and role of the legal assistant. Disclosure may be made in any way that avoids confusion. If the person dealing with the legal assistant already knows of his/her status, further disclosure is unnecessary. If at any time in written or oral communication the legal assistant becomes aware that the other person may believe the legal assistant is an attorney, immediate disclosure should be made as to the legal assistant's status.

The attorney should exercise care that the legal assistant preserves and refrains from using any confidence or secrets of a client, and should instruct the legal assistant not to disclose or use any such confidences or secrets.

The legal assistant must take any and all steps necessary to prevent conflicts of interest and fully disclose such conflicts to the supervising attorney. Failure to do so may jeopardize both the attorney's representation of the client and the case itself.

Guidelines for the Utilization of Legal Assistant Services adopted December 3, 1994 by the Washington State Bar Association Board of Governors states:

Guideline 7: A lawyer shall take reasonable measures to prevent conflicts of interest resulting from a legal assistant's other employment or interest insofar as such other employment or interests would present a conflict of interest if it were that of the lawyer.

In Re Complex Asbestos Litigation, 232 Cal. App. 3d 572 (Cal. 1991), addresses the issue wherein a law firm was disqualified due to possession of attorney-client confidences by a legal assistant employee resulting from previous employment by opposing counsel.

In Oklahoma, in an order issued July 12, 2001, in the matter of *Mark A. Hayes, M.D. v. Central States Orthopedic Specialists, Inc.*, a Tulsa County District Court Judge disqualified a law firm from representation of a client on the basis that an ethical screen was an impermissible device to protect from disclosure confidences gained by a non-lawyer employee while employed by another law firm. In applying the same rules that govern attorneys, the court found that the Rules of Professional Conduct pertaining to confidentiality apply to non-lawyers who leave firms with actual knowledge of material, confidential information and a screening device is not an appropriate alternative to the imputed disqualification of an incoming legal assistant who has moved from one firm to another during ongoing litigation and has actual knowledge of material, confidential information. The decision was appealed and the Oklahoma Supreme Court determined that, under certain circumstances, screening is an appropriate management tool for non-lawyer staff.

In 2004 the Nevada Supreme Court also addressed this issue at the urging of the state's paralegals. The Nevada Supreme Court granted a petition to rescind the Court's 1997 ruling in *Ciaffone v. District Court*. In this case, the court clarified the original ruling, stating "mere opportunity to access confidential information does not merit disqualification." The opinion stated instances in which screening may be appropriate, and listed minimum screening requirements. The opinion also set forth guidelines that a district court may use to determine if screening has been or may be effective. These considerations are:

1. substantiality of the relationship between the former and current matters

2. the time elapsed between the matters

3. size of the firm

4. number of individuals presumed to have confidential information

5. nature of their involvement in the former matter

6. timing and features of any measures taken to reduce the danger of disclosure

7. whether the old firm and the new firm represent adverse parties in the same proceeding rather than in different proceedings.

The ultimate responsibility for compliance with approved standards of professional conduct rests with the supervising attorney. The burden rests upon the attorney who employs a legal assistant to educate the latter with respect to the duties which may be assigned and then to supervise the manner in which the legal assistant carries out such duties. However, this does not relieve the legal assistant from an independent obligation to refrain from illegal conduct. Additionally, and notwithstanding that the Rules are not binding upon non-lawyers, the very nature of a legal assistant's employment imposes an obligation not to engage in conduct which would involve the supervising attorney in a violation of the Rules.

The attorney must make sufficient background investigation of the prior activities and character and integrity of his or her legal assistants.

Further, the attorney must take all measures necessary to avoid and fully disclose conflicts of interest due to other employment or interests. Failure to do so may jeopardize both the attorney's representation of the client and the case itself.

Legal assistant associations strive to maintain the high level of integrity and competence expected of the legal profession and, further, strive to uphold the high standards of ethics.

NALA's Code of Ethics and Professional Responsibility states, "A legal assistant's conduct is guided by bar associations' codes of professional responsibility and rules of professional conduct."

Guideline 2

Legal assistants should not:

1. Establish attorney-client relationships; set legal fees; give legal opinions or advice; or represent a client before a court, unless authorized to do so by said court; nor

2. Engage in, encourage, or contribute to any act which could constitute the unauthorized practice law.

Comment

Case law, court rules, codes of ethics and professional responsibilities, as well as bar ethics opinions now hold which acts can and cannot be performed by a legal assistant. Generally, the determination of what acts constitute the unauthorized practice of law is made by State Supreme Courts.

Numerous cases exist relating to the unauthorized practice of law. Courts have gone so far as to prohibit the legal assistant from preparation of divorce kits and assisting in preparation of bankruptcy forms and, more specifically, from providing basic information about procedures and requirements, deciding where information should be placed on forms, and responding to questions from debtors regarding the interpretation or definition of terms.

Cases have identified certain areas in which an attorney has a duty to act, but it is interesting to note that none of these cases state that it is improper for an attorney to have the initial work performed by the legal assistant. This again points out the importance of adequate supervision by the employing attorney.

An attorney can be found to have aided in the unauthorized practice of law when delegating acts which cannot be performed by a legal assistant.

Guideline 3

Legal assistants may perform services for an attorney in the representation of a client, provided:

1. The services performed by the legal assistant do not require the exercise of independent professional legal judgment;

2. The attorney maintains a direct relationship with the client and maintains control of all client matters;

3. The attorney supervises the legal assistant;

4. The attorney remains professionally responsible for all work on behalf of the client, including any actions taken or not taken by the legal assistant in connection therewith; and

5. The services performed supplement, merge with and become the attorney's work product.

Comment

Legal assistants, whether employees or independent contractors, perform services for the attorney in the representation of a client. Attorneys should delegate work to legal assistants commensurate with their knowledge and experience and provide appropriate instruction and supervision concerning the delegated work, as well as ethical acts of their employment. Ultimate responsibility

for the work product of a legal assistant rests with the attorney. However, a legal assistant must use discretion and professional judgment and must not render independent legal judgment in place of an attorney.

The work product of a legal assistant is subject to civil rules governing discovery of materials prepared in anticipation of litigation, whether the legal assistant is viewed as an extension of the attorney or as another representative of the party itself. Fed. R. Civ. P. 26 (b)(3) and (5).

Guideline 4

In the supervision of a legal assistant, consideration should be given to:

1. Designating work assignments that correspond to the legal assistant's abilities, knowledge, training and experience;

2. Educating and training the legal assistant with respect to professional responsibility, local rules and practices, and firm policies;

3. Monitoring the work and professional conduct of the legal assistant to ensure that the work is substantively correct and timely performed;

4. Providing continuing education for the legal assistant in substantive matters through courses, institutes, workshops, seminars and in-house training; and

5. Encouraging and supporting membership and active participation in professional organizations.

Comment

Attorneys are responsible for the actions of their employees in both malpractice and disciplinary proceedings. In the vast majority of cases, the courts have not censured attorneys for a particular act delegated to the legal assistant, but rather, have been critical of and imposed sanctions against attorneys for failure to adequately supervise the legal assistant. The attorney's responsibility for supervision of his or her legal assistant must be more than a willingness to accept responsibility and liability for the legal assistant's work. Supervision of a legal assistant must be offered in both the procedural and substantive legal areas. The attorney must delegate work based upon the education, knowledge and abilities of the legal assistant and must monitor the work product and conduct of the legal assistant to insure that the work performed is substantively correct and competently performed in a professional manner.

Michigan State Board of Commissioners has adopted Guidelines for the Utilization of Legal Assistants (April 23, 1993). These guidelines, in part, encourage employers to support legal assistant participation in continuing education programs to ensure that the legal assistant remains competent in the fields of practice in which the legal assistant is assigned.

The working relationship between the lawyer and the legal assistant should extend to cooperative efforts on public service activities wherever possible. Participation in pro bono activities is encouraged in ABA Guideline 10.

Guideline 5

Except as otherwise provided by statute, court rule or decision, administrative rule or regulation, or the attorney's rules of professional responsibility, and within the preceding parameters and proscriptions, a legal assistant may perform any function delegated by an attorney, including, but not limited to the following:

1. Conduct client interviews and maintain general contact with the client after the establishment of the attorney-client relationship, so long as the client is aware of the status and function of the legal assistant, and the client contact is under the supervision of the attorney.

2. Locate and interview witnesses, so long as the witnesses are aware of the status and function of the legal assistant.

3. Conduct investigations and statistical and documentary research for review by the attorney.

4. Conduct legal research for review by the attorney.

5. Draft legal documents for review by the attorney.

6. Draft correspondence and pleadings for review by and signature of the attorney.

7. Summarize depositions, interrogatories and testimony for review by the attorney.

8. Attend executions of wills, real estate closings, depositions, court or administrative hearings and trials with the attorney.

9. Author and sign letters providing the legal assistant's status is clearly indicated and the correspondence does not contain independent legal opinions or legal advice.

Comment

The United States Supreme Court has recognized the variety of tasks being performed by legal assistants and has noted that use of legal assistants encourages cost-effective delivery of legal services, *Missouri v. Jenkins*, 491 U.S.274, 109 S.Ct. 2463, 2471, n.10 (1989). In *Jenkins*, the court further held that legal assistant time should be included in compensation for attorney fee awards at the rate in the relevant community to bill legal assistant time.

Courts have held that legal assistant fees are not a part of the overall overhead of a law firm. Legal assistant services are billed separately by attorneys, and decrease litigation expenses. Tasks performed by legal assistants must contain substantive legal work under the direction or supervision of an attorney, such that if the legal assistant were not present, the work would be performed by the attorney.

In *Taylor v. Chubb*, 874 P.2d 806 (Okla. 1994), the Court ruled that attorney fees awarded should include fees for services performed by legal assistants and, further, defined tasks which may be performed by the legal assistant under the supervision of an attorney including, among others: interview clients; draft pleadings and other documents; carry on legal research, both conventional and computer aided; research public records; prepare discovery requests and responses; schedule depositions and prepare notices and subpoenas; summarize depositions and other discovery responses; coordinate and manage document production; locate and interview witnesses; organize pleadings, trial exhibits and other documents; prepare witness and exhibit lists; prepare trial notebooks; prepare for the attendance of witnesses at trial; and assist lawyers at trials.

Except for the specific proscription contained in Guideline 1, the reported cases do not limit the duties which may be performed by a legal assistant under the supervision of the attorney.

An attorney may not split legal fees with a legal assistant, nor pay a legal assistant for the referral of legal business. An attorney may compensate a legal assistant based on the quantity and quality of the legal assistant's work and value of that work to a law practice.

CONCLUSION

These Standards and Guidelines were developed from generally accepted practices. Each supervising attorney must be aware of the specific rules, decisions and statutes applicable to legal assistants within his/her jurisdiction.

© Copyright 1997; Adopted 1984; Revised 1991, 1997, 2007; National Association of Legal Assistants, Inc. Reprinted with permission of the National Association of Legal Assistants, *www.nala.org*, 1516 S. Boston, #200, Tulsa, OK 74119.

NALA Code of Ethics and Professional Responsibility

Each NALA member agrees to follow the canons of the NALA Code of Ethics and Professional Responsibility. Violations of the Code may result in cancellation of membership. First adopted by the NALA membership in May of 1975, the Code of Ethics and Professional Responsibility is the foundation of ethical practices of paralegals in the legal community.

A paralegal must adhere strictly to the accepted standards of legal ethics and to the general principles of proper conduct. The performance of the duties of the paralegal shall be governed by specific canons as defined herein so that justice will be served and goals of the profession attained. (See Model Standards and Guidelines for Utilization of Legal Assistants, Section II [Appendix C.])

The canons of ethics set forth hereafter are adopted by the National Association of Legal Assistants, Inc., as a general guide intended to aid paralegals and attorneys. The enumeration of these rules does not mean there are not others of equal importance although not specifically mentioned. Court rules, agency rules and statutes must be taken into consideration when interpreting the canons.

Definition: Legal assistants, also known as paralegals, are a distinguishable group of persons who assist attorneys in the delivery of legal services. Through formal education, training and experience, legal assistants have knowledge and expertise regarding the legal system and substantive and procedural law which qualify them to do work of a legal nature under the supervision of an attorney.

In **2001**, NALA members also adopted the ABA definition of a legal assistant/paralegal, as follows:

A legal assistant or paralegal is a person qualified by education, training or work experience who is employed or retained by a lawyer, law office, corporation, governmental agency or other entity who performs specifically delegated substantive legal work for which a lawyer is responsible. (Adopted by the ABA in 1997)

CANON 1

A paralegal must not perform any of the duties that attorneys only may perform nor take any actions that attorneys may not take.

CANON 2

A paralegal may perform any task which is properly delegated and supervised by an attorney, as long as the attorney is ultimately responsible to the client, maintains a direct relationship with the client, and assumes professional responsibility for the work product.

CANON 3

A paralegal must not: (a) engage in, encourage, or contribute to any act which could constitute the unauthorized practice of law; and (b) establish attorney-client relationships, set fees, give legal opinions or advice or represent a client before a court or agency unless so authorized by that court or agency; and (c) engage in conduct or take any action which would assist or involve the attorney in a violation of professional ethics or give the appearance of professional impropriety.

CANON 4

A paralegal must use discretion and professional judgment commensurate with knowledge and experience but must not render independent legal judgment in place of an attorney. The services of an attorney are essential in the public interest whenever such legal judgment is required.

CANON 5

A paralegal must disclose his or her status as a paralegal at the outset of any professional relationship with a client, attorney, a court or administrative agency or personnel thereof, or a member of the general public. A paralegal must act prudently in determining the extent to which a client may be assisted without the presence of an attorney.

CANON 6

A paralegal must strive to maintain integrity and a high degree of competency through education and training with respect to professional responsibility, local rules and practice, and through continuing education in substantive areas of law to better assist the legal profession in fulfilling its duty to provide legal service.

CANON 7

A paralegal must protect the confidences of a client and must not violate any rule or statute now in effect or hereafter enacted controlling the doctrine of privileged communications between a client and an attorney.

CANON 8

A paralegal must disclose to his or her employer or prospective employer any pre-existing client or personal relationship that may conflict with the interests of the employer or prospective employer and/or their clients.

CANON 9

A paralegal must do all other things incidental, necessary, or expedient for the attainment of the ethics and responsibilities as defined by statute or rule of court.

CANON 10

A paralegal's conduct is guided by bar associations' codes of professional responsibility and rules of professional conduct.

APPENDIX E

Legal Ethics and Related Web Sites

SPECIFIC LEGAL ETHICS WEB SITES

ABA Center for Professional Responsibility
http://www.abanet.org/cpr/home.html

American Legal Ethics Library
http://www.law.cornell.edu/ethics

Georgetown Journal of Legal Ethics
http://www.law.georgetown.edu/journals/ethics/

Legalethics.com
http://www.legalethics.com

STATE BAR ASSOCIATIONS (SOME POST THEIR ETHICS OPINIONS ON-LINE)

Alabama State Bar Association
http://www.alabar.org/

Alaska State Bar Association
http://www.alaskabar.org/

Arizona State Bar Association
http://www.azbar.org/

Arkansas Bar Association
http://www.arkbar.com/

California State Bar Association
http://www.calbar.org/

Colorado State Bar Association
http://www.cobar.org/

Connecticut State Bar Association
http://www.ctbar.org/

Delaware State Bar Association
http://www.dsba.org/

District of Columbia Bar
http://www.dcbar.org/

Florida State Bar Association
http://www.flabar.org/

Georgia State Bar Association
http://www.gabar.org/

Hawaii State Bar Association
http://www.hsba.org/

Idaho State Bar Association
http://www2.state.id.us/isb/index.htm

Illinois State Bar Association
http://www.illinoisbar.org/

Indiana State Bar Association
http://www.inbar.org/

Iowa State Bar Association
http://www.iowabar.org/main.nsf

Kansas Bar Association
http://www.ksbar.org/

Kentucky Bar Association
http://www.kybar.org/

Louisiana State Bar Association
http://www.lsba.org/

Maine State Bar Association
http://www.mainebar.org/

Maryland State Bar Association
http://www.msba.org/index.htm

Massachusetts State Bar Association
http://www.massbar.org/

State Bar of Michigan
http://www.michbar.org/

Minnesota State Bar Association
http://www.mnbar.org/

Mississippi State Bar Association
http://www.msbar.org/

Missouri Bar Association
http://www.mobar.org/

State Bar of Montana
http://www.montanabar.org/

Nebraska State Bar Association
http://www.nebar.com/

Nevada State Bar Association
http://www.nvbar.org/

New Hampshire State Bar Association
http://www.nhbar.org/

New Jersey State Bar Association
http://www.njsba.com/

State Bar of New Mexico
http://www.nmbar.org/

New York State Bar Association
http://www.nysba.org/

North Carolina State Bar Association
http://www.ncbar.com/index.asp

State Bar Association of North Dakota
http://www.sband.org/

Ohio State Bar Association
http://www.ohiobar.org/

Oklahoma State Bar Association
http://www.okbar.org/

Oregon State Bar Association
http://www.osbar.org/

Pennsylvania State Bar Association
http://www.pa-bar.org/

Colegio de Abogados de Puerto Rico
http://www.capr.org/

Rhode Island State Bar Association
http://www.ribar.com/

South Carolina Bar Association
http://www.scbar.org/

South Dakota State Bar Association
http://www.sdbar.org/

Tennessee Bar Association
http://www.tba.org/

Texas State Bar Association
http://www.sbot.org/

Utah State Bar Association
http://www.utahbar.org/

Vermont State Bar Association
http://www.vtbar.org/

Virgin Islands Bar Association
http://www.vibar.org/

Virginia State Bar Association
http://www.vsb.org/

Washington State Bar Association
http://www.wsba.org/

West Virginia State Bar Association
http://www.wvbar.org/

Wisconsin State Bar Association
http://www.wisbar.org/

Wyoming State Bar Association
http://www.wyomingbar.org/

PARALEGAL/LEGAL ASSISTANT AND RELATED WEB SITES

ABA Standing Committee for Paralegal Services
http://www.abanet.org/legalservices/paralegals/

The American Alliance of Paralegals, Inc.
http://www.aapipara.org/

American Association for Paralegal Education
http://www.aafpe.org

U.S. Department of Labor, Bureau of Labor
Statistics Paralegals and Legal Assistants
Occupational Outlook Handbook
http://www.bls.gov/oco/ocos114.htm

International Paralegal Management Association
http://www.paralegalmanagement.org/ipma/

Legal Assistant Today
http://www.legalassistanttoday.com/index.htm

National Association of Legal Assistants
http://www.nala.org

National Federation of Paralegal Associations
http://www.paralegals.org

Paralegal Division of the State Bar of Texas
http://txpd.org/default.asp

MISCELLANEOUS LEGAL WEB SITES THAT CAN AID IN ETHICS RESEARCH

CrossingtheBar.Com
http://www.crossingthebar.com

FindLaw
http://www.findlaw.com/

HierosGamos World Wide Legal Directories
http://www.hg.org/

Law.com
http://www.law.com/

LawIDEA
http://www.lawidea.com/

Law Guru
http://www.lawguru.com/index.php

Lawyers.com
http://www.lawyers.com/

Lexis/Nexis
http://www.lexis-nexis.com/default.asp

Loislaw
http://www.loislaw.com/

NOLO
http://www.nolo.com

Overlawyered
http://www.overlawyered.com/

Palidan Legal Resources
http://www.palidan.com

The 'Lectric Law Library
http://www.lectlaw.com/

The Public Library of Law
http://www.plol.org/Pages/Search.aspx

Versus Law
http://www.versuslaw.com

Westlaw
http://www.west.thomson.com/westlaw/

APPENDIX F

Legal Ethics Movie Guide

This guide is neither exhaustive nor definitive. It is just for fun. I am a movie fan, and thought it would be interesting to include in the textbook a list of certain movies whose themes are connected, even if peripherally, to the subject of legal ethics. What follows is a quick description of a few great, and not so great, movies in which legal ethical dilemmas are a part of the story. But be advised: movies about the legal system and its members are no more accurate than war movies or more realistic than musicals; they may be, but that is unlikely. The reader is advised not to judge these movies solely on their real-life legal accuracy. For example, if the Ashley Judd film, *Double Jeopardy*, were supposed to be a legally authentic interpretation of the Fifth Amendment's protection, it wouldn't have been nearly as entertaining. That *Jaws* presented a far-fetched depiction of a shark bearing grudges in no way lessens its greatness as a film. Finally, although many of these movies are derivatives of books, they are placed on this list without consideration of their book version. Readers are encouraged to contact me for suggestions on movies that should be added to the list.

ANATOMY OF A MURDER (NR 1959)

Decades before Scott Turow and John Grisham wrote best-selling legal thrillers that morphed into films, Michigan Supreme Court Justice John D. Voelker, using the pen name Robert Traver, wrote the novel, *Anatomy of a Murder*, which was then made into this film. Shot on location in the Upper Peninsula of

571

Michigan, this superb movie was years ahead of its time, in both the subject matter and the way with which the subject is dealt. Jimmy Stewart stars as Paul Biegler, a small-town defense lawyer who recently lost his reelection as district attorney. Paul Biegler's office is his home—literally. As the movie unfolds, Biegler is asked to represent an army lieutenant named Manion (Ben Gazzara), accused of murdering the owner of an area bar. Manion claims he shot and killed Mr. Quill, the bar owner, because Quill raped Manion's wife on the night of the murder. Because of the hour-long difference between Manion's awareness of the alleged rape and his homicidal response, Biegler tells Manion in the initial interview there is no justification defense available to him. But, as this interview progresses, Biegler helps Manion realize that his defense should be insanity, in that he was so angry his wife was raped by Quill that he had an irresistible impulse to kill Quill. And so, what seems a dishonest defense then proceeds. Biegler's interview of Mrs. Manion (played deliciously by Lee Remick) reveals her to be, at the least, quite the flirt, casting some doubt on her claim of having been ravished by the bar owner. As Biegler tries to prepare for a high-profile trial on behalf of a client he doesn't really like, whose defense is one that Biegler doesn't really believe, a few plot twists are provided for good measure. Along the way, Biegler relies on the assistance of his secretary (who is much more a paralegal) and his mentor (who is much more a drunk). Jimmy Stewart's small-town persona is a dodge; he outwits the prosecution at every turn. He puts the dead victim on trial, often over the protest of the prosecution and rebuke of the trial judge, while the prosecutor (George C. Scott) puts Mrs. Manion on trial for being coquettish. In key parts of the trial, the lawyers use words like *sperm* and *panties*, a notable choice of frank language for a film from 1959. We know that Lieutenant Manion, with his seething anger, was not insane when he shot a man to death, but we don't know if Mrs. Manion was raped and beaten—at least by the bar owner. So, why would Jimmy Stewart defend such a creep, and with such questionable tactics? It certainly wasn't for the money.

AND JUSTICE FOR ALL (R 1979)

What does it say about a legal movie when the characters who are the oddest and most loathsome are the judges and the members of the ethics committee? This is not to say that the lawyers in this movie are normal or above reproach; it is just that they are more normal by comparison to the judges and the ethics committee. Even though this film was less than favorably reviewed by the professional movie critics, I love it. Al Pacino does a devil of a job advocating for his clients in a Baltimore criminal justice system that is as bleak and broken down as a metaphor for legal and political cancer could ever be. Without giving away the pivotal points in the plot, what you find in *And Justice for All* is a month or so in the life of a gritty, idealistic, but not naive, defense lawyer who is not above going to jail to make a point. As he confronts the injustice in the system, while trying to comfort his panicked clients, Pacino is forced by the blackmail of an ethics charge to defend a client whom he despises. While watching Pacino emote his ever-mounting frustration at what he is facing, you forget that he played mafioso Michael Corleone, the master of steely composure. And for sheer visceral satisfaction, few scenes in a movie compare to the end of this one.

BODY HEAT (R 1981)

Be aware, *Body Heat* more than earned its R rating, and tells the type of infidelity-murder-mystery story more popular during the 1930s and 1940s, but tells it without any of that time period's innuendo. When Ned Racine (William Hurt), a small-minded lawyer in a steamy Florida coastal town, comes across the obviously married Mattie Walker (Kathleen Turner), she says something to him in their flirtation that portends Ned's ruination, "You're not too smart; I like that in a man." Drawn in by her sexual power over him, Ned foolishly comes to think that she loves him. His infatuation blocks him from realizing that it was her idea —not his—to murder Mattie's older, rich husband (Richard Crenna). Why a woman with that much voltage would be interested in a 60-watt man never occurs to Ned, a lawyer whose only professional notoriety is the malpractice he committed a few years earlier when drafting a will. Ned thinks he is devising the perfect murder of Mattie's husband, and even advises her against fraudulently writing a new will for her husband, making Mattie the sole beneficiary. He tells her that such an oddly timed replacement will look too suspicious. He's smart all right, but, like she said, *not too smart.* And for that, he will pay. Nothing goes as planned, or at least as Ned planned, and as Ned's friends—cops investigating the murder—warn him to stay away from Mattie, the movie heads to its inevitability, brought on by a second act of malpractice Ned didn't realize he had committed. But who can remember the rule against perpetuities? Ned hasn't been framed, because he is the murderer, but he can't prove that he didn't act alone, or that Mattie slipped away with the money. This movie serves to remind us all that a lawyer who has an affair with a scheming trophy wife who used to work in a law office deserves to be punished. Small consolation as it is, because Ned's affair with Mattie began before she became his client, at least he didn't break that ethics rule.

CHANGING LANES (R 2002)

Changing Lanes is a poignant and distressing film. Two men are driving to court on the FDR expressway on Good Friday. One, Doyle Gibson, is a new convert to Alcoholics Anonymous on his way to family court for a hearing where he will try to keep his ex-wife from moving far away with their two boys. The other, attorney Gavin Banek, is a recent convert to blind ambition. Banek is on his way to probate court. There, he plans to close the estate of a dead philanthropist whose granddaughter is alleging lacked testamentary capacity to remove the board members from his huge foundation shortly before his death, thus giving control over the assets to two senior partners at Banek's firm. After a minor fender bender with Gavin, Doyle is intent upon following the proper insurance procedures. Gavin simply writes him a blank check and drives away in his Mercedes, offering a "better luck next time" cliché. But in the rush of the moment, Gavin has left with Doyle a red folder containing the power of appointment documents that are critical to Gavin's hearing. When Gavin gets to his courtroom, and realizes the key legal documents transferring control over a hundred million dollar foundation are missing, he gets (after lying) a day-long reprieve from the judge to get the file back. When Doyle gets to his courtroom 20 minutes late, custody has just been granted to his ex-wife in his absence. To get the file back, Gavin—with the help of a computer hacker—ruins Doyle's financial history, but only as a threat. Doyle gets the threat, but Gavin doesn't get the file. Mutually assured destruction is sure to result from each man's escalating revenge tactics. But something else is awry. It finally dawns on Gavin that he shouldn't have been in probate court that morning, but that one or both of the partners named as the foundation's new trustees should have been there instead. One of those partners just happens to be Gavin's father-in-law (played by Sydney Pollack, famed director of *The Way We Were, Tootsie, Out of Africa,* and *The Firm,* who is always good playing the confident alpha-male, as he does in *A Civil Action, Michael Clayton,* and here). Realizing he was denied access to the case file, and was only given the signature document, Gavin suspects—and then learns—that the two partners defrauded an old man near death and granted themselves a million-dollar fee in the process. Despite Gavin's and Doyle's increasing mutual animus, there are poignant moments of contemplation and redemptive action. Gavin's father-in-law, however, is not feeling so repentant, and the partners' solution to the problem of the missing power of appointment is priceless in its brazenness. *Changing Lanes* is worthy of multiple viewings because, like a prism, there are multiple images to notice, all in need of reflection.

A CIVIL ACTION (R 1998)

This wonderful but sad film is based on an even sadder nonfiction book. Hotshot attorney Jan Schlictmann, played by John Travolta, drives a black Porsche and is on Boston's top-ten bachelors list. He has gotten rich and famous by smartly choosing the right kind of personal injury cases for his small firm and often settling them. Against his better judgment, he agrees to take the collective cases of some Woburn, Massachusetts families who believe their children have suffered disease and death due to poisons in their drinking water as a result of toxic waste dumping. Jan knows better, that this case is an orphan for a reason, but he takes it after meeting with the families. He focuses his sights on two large, industrial companies, Beatrice Foods and W.R. Grace. Jan makes two critical decisions upon which the movie hinges. First, he and his firm front the litigation costs; and second, he refuses a couple of settlement opportunities because he wants to take the case all the way to trial. The families want to tell the jury and the world their story, and Jan wants them on the stand because he knows what compelling witnesses they will make. As the case twists and turns through the discovery process, Jan's small firm is bled white working on its only case, and paying for experts and geological studies. Jerome Facher, wonderfully portrayed by Robert Duval, W.R. Grace's attorney, realizes Jan's dilemma and uses it to his advantage, while devising a strategy to keep the plaintiffs from ever setting foot in the jury box. The trial judge, played by John Lithgow, seems to be less than impartial, almost like a third defense team. Like Don Quixote and Captain Ahab, Jan loses his perspective as his single-minded fervor increases. Eventually, he loses his firm. The case Jan never wanted becomes the one he can't give up. And all the while, there are the poor families waiting and waiting for their view of justice—an apology and a cleaned-up environment. There are so many memorable performances by so many talented actors, and there is so much going on—and going wrong—that *A Civil Action* deserves to be purchased. There is even a follow-up book for the movie, *A Documentary Companion to A Civil Action*, used in many law schools, that contains the litigation documents from the actual case.

CLASS ACTION (PG-13 1991)

This overlooked movie is interesting on many levels. On one level, *Class Action* is an interesting character study of a famous tort lawyer, played by Gene Hackman, who sees himself as the last best hope for the little guy, fighting corporate or government Goliaths. Hackman's character is suing a car company for what is reminiscent of the Ford Pinto scandal from decades ago. The Ford Motor Company was accused of putting the Pinto into the market while aware that it would blow up upon rear impact, rather than recalling it, because recalling the car was thought to be more expensive than settling with those who would be injured, or worse. On another level this movie is, like *The Sopranos*, a story of family tension. The law firm defending the car company has a lawyer, played by Mary Elizabeth Mastrantonio, working on the case. In a curious twist, the lawyer also happens to be Hackman's daughter. It takes but a few minutes to see them together to realize they are highly flammable in each other's presence, and for deeper reasons than his politics and her career path. Adding to the tension, Mastrantonio, an associate, is in a semi-secret relationship with her supervising partner, whose prior actions have affected the car company's problems. As Mastrantonio comes to believe her value to the firm is for reasons beyond her talent as a litigator, she devises quite a solution, which is both litigation-daring and ethically unique, to say the least. Besides the family tensions and office romances, there are discovery abuses, courtroom histrionics, and the most stunning senior partner law office one could imagine.

THE CLIENT (PG-13 1994)

Watching a man commit suicide is awful enough. However, for Mark Swayne (played by Brad Renfro, who tragically died of his own hands in 2008), the older of two young brothers exploring the woods near their house, it is even worse, because he was in a car with the man just before the man took his life. As it turns out, the man was the lawyer for notorious New Orleans mob hit man "The Blade" (Anthony LaPaglia), who is about to go on trial for the murder of a Louisiana senator, even though there is no body. Because that lawyer knew where the body was buried, and had been threatened with a subpoena by the famed federal prosecutor "Rev. Roy," played by Tommy Lee Jones, the mob lawyer figured it was better to die at his own hands before The Blade got to him. The investigation shows that Mark was in the car with that terrified lawyer before his death, so the police and The Blade believe the boy knows the lawyer's secret. Because Mark and his brother are poor and have only one parent, their mother, Rev. Roy believes it shouldn't be that hard to get Mark to testify about what the mob lawyer told him, even though the mob is trying to kill Mark. Rightfully believing he needs his own lawyer, Mark ends up in the dingy downtown office of Reggie Love, played by Susan Sarandon, who Mark at first mistakes for a secretary. Reggie takes his case for the fee of one dollar. So begins a cat and mouse game, as Reggie tries to protect her client from Rev. Roy, who tries to cajole and threaten Mark into testifying for the government. Reggie also tries to protect Mark from The Blade, who is doing everything possible to prevent Mark from having any say in the matter. Because this movie comes from a John Grisham book, there is little doubt that Mark will survive his legal and physical dangers, and that Reggie Love will use barely legal and ethical tactics to navigate Mark through it all. What might go unnoticed in *The Client* is that the lawyer's suicide is prompted by the threat of a subpoena to testify against his client concerning the whereabouts of the missing senator's body. This is a curious setup for a movie about attorney-client confidentiality, especially because the ethics rules on confidentiality, as well as evidentiary statutes on attorney-client privilege, cover a client's prior crimes. Notice also that Anthony Edward's character is Sarandon's paralegal, a welcome role reversal.

CRIMINAL LAW (R 1989)

When a movie about a criminal defense lawyer begins with a Nietzsche quote, you know you are in for something over the top. ("Whoever fights monsters should see to it that in the process he does not become a monster.") After watching *Criminal Law*, you might be tempted to say, "What doesn't kill me makes me stronger." Resist the temptation. Ben Chase (Gary Oldman), formally of the prosecutor's office, is an up-and-coming criminal defense attorney in Boston who is defending Martin Thiel IV (Kevin Bacon), a rich preppie accused of the grisly rape and murder of a young woman. The key evidence against

Martin is eyewitness testimony. Ben succeeds in providing reasonable doubt through his cross-examination of the key witness, and through a sneaky trial tactic. After securing his smug client's freedom, Ben's peacock-like strut is cut short when, a few nights later, another grisly rape and murder is committed and Ben is left with the inescapable conclusion that the murderer is his client. Wracked with guilt, Ben contacts a sex crimes detective and former colleague and, after violating every version of the rule on confidentiality, tells her of his plan for atonement: he is going to represent Martin again and gather *evidence against* his client. Obviously, such a strategy is not only ludicrous and career ending, but it is miscast, because Ben bears no personal responsibility for the second and third murders. As cheesy legal movies go, this one sprays from a can, but it's not bland.

ERIN BROCKOVICH (R 2000)

Erin Brockovich might be the film on this list that is capable of generating the most energetic class discussion, and not simply because its title character is the country's most famous—and beloved—paralegal. Julia Roberts won a best actress Oscar for poignantly capturing the desperation and ingenuity of Erin Brockovich, a woman who fights demographic prejudice to keep alive an otherwise unwinnable case against a powerful corporation. But, like a hero from Greek tragedy, Ms. Brockovich's flaws make her more than one-dimensional. Those interested in pursuing beyond the film's version of events might start with an April 14, 2000, Salon.com article that claims only the positive half of the *Erin Brockovich* story was presented, and that some of the actual plaintiffs have less than charitable feelings toward their legal team. After getting T-boned at a red light and suing the doctor who hit her, Erin Brockovich loses at trial, in no small measure due to her foul-mouthed performance on the witness stand. Somehow, she talks her way into a job with Ed Masry, played by Albert Finney, her lawyer from the car accident suit. Having a never-take-no-for-an-answer attitude trumps having no education or legal experience, and it is that attitude that leads her to the biggest tort case of its time. While going through a pro bono real estate file, Erin notices medical records for persons in Hinkley, California, whose homes are being purchased by Pacific Gas & Electric (PG&E), a utility company operating a nearby facility. Using charm and her feminine wiles in her investigation (to put it mildly), Erin comes to believe that PG&E's use of chromium 6 has polluted the water, resulting in cancers and other illness for many of Hinkley's residents. After Ed fires and rehires Erin, they begin their representation of the Hinkley residents, all of whom are so significant to Erin she has memorized their personal information and history. Initially, Ed's strategy is to avoid a lawsuit against PG&E (for fear of it being dismissed out of hand) and, instead, to negotiate better real estate settlements. Finally convinced by Erin's persistence, Ed files suit against PG&E. As the burdens of the case mount against Ed and his small firm, Erin tries to balance motherhood, work, and a relationship with a gentle and longsuffering neighbor. Ultimately, Erin's and Ed's efforts are so fruitful, the plaintiffs are awarded $333 million, and Erin is awarded a $2 million bonus. *Erin Brockovich* is definitely not *A Civil Action*.

A FEW GOOD MEN (R 1992)

I considered leaving this movie off the list because it concerns, not the American legal system, but the American Military Justice System, something about which I know almost nothing. But, taking my own advice about the purpose of this legal movie guide, I decided not to worry about what I did not know. Tom Cruise and Demi Moore star in this legal drama as young navy lawyers appointed to defend two Marines accused of killing another Marine in a hazing incident at a Marine base in Guantanamo Bay, Cuba. Because Tom Cruise settles cases, rather than litigates them, we are supposed to get the hint that he was given the case for just that reason. Things are strictly business between Cruise and Moore, who do not like each other, as they investigate Moore's theory that there is more to the story, namely, that someone (from Jack Nicholson through Kiefer Sutherland) ordered the hazing incident that went awry. The movie is too obvious a preparation for the inevitable courtroom fireworks between Cruise and Nicholson, but the fireworks are still bright and loud. On an ethics level, a point is made in the movie about whether Cruise will be charged with a crime by the prosecutor (Kevin Bacon) if Cruise, without evidence and in cross-examination, accuses the much higher ranking Nicholson of lying. This Rob Reiner film is quite good, but it approaches propaganda (unlike his following film, *The American President,* which is good and clearly propaganda).

THE FIRM (R 1993)

One of the first John Grisham novels to be made into a movie, *The Firm* is outstanding. Tom Cruise plays eager law school grad Mitch McDeere, who is seduced by a rich offer from a Memphis firm that seems to have family values. This would be wonderful except for the fact that the family the firm values is the mafia. This firm loses lawyers to accidental deaths like the "rock band" Spinal Tap loses drummers. Poor Mitch and his lovely wife, played by Jeanne Tripplehorn, come to realize they are pawns in this chess game between the firm and the government. With a huge supporting cast punctuated by Gene Hackman (this time a diabolical lawyer), Holly Hunter (a private investigator's girlfriend/secretary), and Ed Harris (the FBI agent working on Mitch), this long film travels from the idyllic to the horrific. Can Mitch catch the bad guys, save his life, and keep his law license? If you have not seen the movie, let me just say that the principles of fair billing and confidentiality have never been so fascinating.

THE GINGERBREAD MAN (R 1998)

An oddly titled film from a John Grisham script that quickly went to video, this thriller involves the law simply because its protagonist is a Savannah attorney played by Kenneth Branagh. This maelstrom, occurring during a hurricane, asks the question: how bad can things get when a lawyer sleeps with someone he barely knows who then becomes his client, who happens to have a stereotyped, Pentecostal-crazy father, eerily played by Robert Duvall? The answer to the preceding question is: things can get really bad. While watching this film, I wondered why, if Branagh's character would risk his career, and more, for the pleasure of dating his client, then why didn't he just date the character played by Daryl Hannah, who worked in his firm? Wouldn't that have been the lesser of two evils? Such a movie is a guilty pleasure for those who like films reminiscent of Alfred Hitchcock.

JAGGED EDGE (R 1985)

A few years before terrorizing Michael Douglas in *Fatal Attraction*, Glenn Close co-starred in this movie. In it, she plays a lawyer who agrees to represent a super-rich newspaper publisher, played by Jeff Bridges, who is accused of brutally murdering his wife (her death is the reason he became rich). Having left criminal law due to guilt over a past case, Close's character only begrudgingly gives in to her senior partner's wishes that she represent the publisher if she can be convinced that he didn't do it. Imagine that. Adding to the movie's tension, Close goes up against a politically minded district attorney, someone with whom she committed a serious ethics violation years ago, and who also is the reason she stopped practicing criminal law. Set in San Francisco, this courtroom thriller is both a whodunit and a love story—that is, if a lawyer falling in love with her murder-defendant client, who might be a sociopath, is your kind of a love story. And along with the murderous clues, the film happens to be sprinkled with a few gaffes, including one where Close wears two different suits in the same courtroom scene.

LIAR LIAR (PG-13 1997)

How do you know when a lawyer is lying? His mouth starts moving. That joke essentially sets up the premise for this fairy tale about Fletcher Reede, a lawyer played bombastically by Jim Carrey, who has no choice but to be absolutely honest for 24 hours. *Liar Liar* shows us we might not always want to learn the truth, especially if it involves sharing an elevator ride, or a bed, with Fletcher. Fletcher's life as a lawyer is seamless only because it is stitched with constant fabrications. But his life as an ex-husband and sort-of-father becomes increasingly disappointing to his former wife and five-year-old son. After his little boy's birthday wish comes true, Fletcher soon discovers that he can speak only the truth, the whole truth, and nothing but the truth. While attempting to represent a sleazy spouse involved in a divorce and to become a partner in his law firm—and at the same time avoid the former object of his affection (his boss)—Fletcher loses valuable time with his son. Can Fletcher win an ugly case without telling any lies? Can he even keep his job without telling any lies? Can anyone deny that Jim Carrey is much more than a one-note performer? Be honest.

MICHAEL CLAYTON (R 2007)

When a tale is told well, it matters little that the narrative has been told many times before. Shakespeare didn't invent the themes of jealousy, remorse, longing, tragedy, conspiracy, or blood lust. But he spun those fibers into the most vibrant tapestries of the English language. And with all due respect to the Bard, *Michael Clayton* does something similarly difficult: it takes two old clichés—that giant corporations are evil, and that big, soulless law firms enable corporate destruction of the innocent in exchange for huge sums of money—and refashions them into such a powerful and tension-filled drama that the viewer feels completely spent by the end. In contrast to *A Civil Action* or *The Verdict*, superb and mournful dramas whose focus is on flawed men working on big cases, *Michael Clayton* uses a big case to focus on flawed men, and one flawed woman.

In the film, three people are coming undone. The first is Arthur Edens, played by Tom Wilkinson, the chief litigator of a mega-law firm in Manhattan, who has billed enough hours to equal 12% of his aged life to UNorth, a huge agro-chemical company fighting a toxic poisoning class-action lawsuit. While off his bipolar medication, Edens has an epiphany that he has been defending a murderer, and suffers a nervous breakdown during a deposition. The second is the chief in-house counsel for UNorth, who absolutely knows her employer is covering up a deadly secret, but tries to keep everything under control through her steely resolve and detached compartmentalization. The third is Michael Clayton himself, played by George Clooney. He is also employed by the mega firm, but only as a "fixer," meaning he is the kind of lawyer you don't want to have listed as a partner, but who you want around to handle the kind of client problems not easily solved by using the courts. Michael Clayton knows where on the firm's ladder his rung is found. It shows in the term he uses for himself: the janitor. Clayton realizes he needs an employment backup plan, and has bought a corner bar with his loser-brother, but whose quick failure has left him with debts he can't pay and debt collectors he can't avoid.

In the span of four days, each of those lawyers has a metamorphosis. Arthur Edens loses his sanity, but gains a child-like clarity, and so his guilt-cleansing confessions to his friend Michael Clayton ring like crazy talk. Clayton, who's been dispatched to Milwaukee, has been given the job of quieting Edens down for the sake of the firm. To make matters worse, the senior partner, played by Sidney Pollack, is quietly planning a merger with another mega firm, and the merger will implode if news leaks that the world's best litigator had a naked meltdown in Milwaukee and is now helping one of the plaintiff's win her case. But when Arthur Edens escapes from Clayton and returns to New York, UNorth and the law firm are desperate to find him and keep him quiet. Clayton is running out of time to fix this problem, or else he won't be able to solve his own problem with the debt collectors, all the while aware that if he fixes his firm's problem, which will provide cover for the merger to take place, he'll likely be out of a job at the new firm.

Karen Crowder, UNorth's chief counsel, played by Tilda Swinton (and who won an Academy award for her performance), is also running out of time to end this decade-long lawsuit before her company is exposed by its own hired-gun, defense lawyer. The metamorphosis she experiences is Machiavellian, and the methods she uses to fix her employer's problem are so cold-hearted, they make her sweat through her clothing.

Each of these lawyers unravels in their own way, and Clooney's portrayal of someone whose self-loathing is masked by somber focus to the tasks at hand is something special to watch. Surprisingly, for all his experience in cleaning up messes, Michael Clayton is perilously unaware that his law firm and its biggest client might view him as part of the problem. Tony Gilroy, the writer of the *Bourne* films, wrote and directed this movie, and it has that kind of claustrophobic feel, without the shaky camera action. And in an odd way, *Michael Clayton* brings to mind the books and movies of master spy-author John LeCarre, whose very un-James-Bond-like characters use dialogue as a weapon, and hide for cover behind vague notions of a different kind of company loyalty.

MY COUSIN VINNY (R 1992)

When Ralph Macchio's character and Macchio's friend get wrongly arrested for murder while traveling through the Deep South, Cousin Vinny, played by Joe Pesci, gets their phone call. Cousin Vinny then drives down from Brooklyn with his fiancé, played by Marisa Tomei, to save the day. There's just one problem. Vinny has only just passed the bar after many attempts. He is no more capable of defending the two against murder charges than he is of being comfortable spending time in the hayseed town where his clients await their trial. Although this movie pokes a little fun at a stereotyped southern culture, it also does not shy away from lampooning the northerners. Not only does Vinny lie about his identity to the judge, but he puts his fiancé on the stand—as a tire track expert. (It worked so well that Tomei won an Oscar.) Fred Gwynne, who was TV's Herman Munster, gives a warm performance as the conservative trial judge. Remember, this is a comedy, so don't critique the courtroom scenes too harshly.

PHILADELPHIA (R 1993)

Tom Hanks won an Academy Award for this movie. In it, Hanks plays Andrew Beckett, a rising associate in a blue-blood, downtown law firm in the City of Brotherly Love, who sues the firm after he is fired, purportedly for incompetence and attitude problems. Beckett rightly believes his termination was arranged after the partners discovered he is gay and suffering from the complications of AIDS, two facts that Beckett had kept to himself. As other firms give Beckett the cold shoulder—not because he has AIDS, but because he wants to sue a powerful law firm—which is yet another ethics issue—Beckett turns to another attorney, excellently played by Denzel Washington. He is the opposite of Beckett, not because of race, but because he is a television-advertising ambulance chaser who also initially discriminates against Beckett because of his illness. *Philadelphia* is as much about Denzel Washington's personal journey as it is about the case. The movie would have been more poignant had it been made five or ten years earlier, but nevertheless, it raises important issues and handles them with dignity and pathos. With a strong supporting cast including Antonio Banderas, Mary Steenburgen, and Jason Robards, the movie follows a predictable path that many "wronged versus wrong" trial stories take. It is nice to see Beckett using a paralegal for substantive work, as he does early in the movie. (The film *In and Out,* from 1997, is based on Tom Hanks's acceptance speech at the 1994 Academy Awards for his role in *Philadelphia. In and Out* is about a high school drama teacher "outed" by his former pupil. When the pupil wins an Oscar playing a homosexual, he credits his gay teacher.)

PRESUMED INNOCENT (R 1990)

Before there was John Grisham, there was Scott Turow, a lawyer whose novels are more densely plotted and whose characters are more complex. If you like your legal movies dark and emotionally painful, this one is for you. This gripping mystery stars Harrison Ford, in one of his few non-heroic roles, as Rusty Sabich, the assistant district attorney given the unfortunate assignment of solving the vicious murder of a woman with whom he had been involved and obsessed, who also worked in his office. As the evidence points to Rusty, he is thrown overboard by his friend, the district attorney, who is in a tight re-election campaign against a former assistant district attorney. As his strangely loyal wife stands by her man, Rusty seeks the help of a superstar defense attorney Sandy Stern, played marvelously by Raul Julia. Sandy Stern is a character that appears in at least two more novels, including being the main character in *The Burden of Proof.* This plot thickens like a roux; everyone seems to have something to hide. Is the prosecution cheating? Is the defense cheating? Is the judge cheating? Is the —you get the picture. And if you do get this picture, keep the children away. *Presumed Innocent* has some racy moments. The trial tactics taken by Sandy are doubly cunning and part red herring, but press against the ethical boundaries. Part of the pleasure of watching this excellent movie is seeing Harrison Ford in such a dark role, something we rarely see.

PRIMAL FEAR (R 1996)

Since that day in 1841 when delusional Daniel M'Naghten shot at the British Prime Minister, killing the Prime Minister's personal secretary instead, the insanity defense has been nothing if not controversial. *Primal Fear* uses this controversy to tell quite a story about a lawyer's desire to promote himself in a murder case involving the Catholic Church and a sex scandal, and which might include a government conspiracy. When the beloved Chicago archbishop is found sliced to death with a mysterious call number carved onto his chest, and a young man—covered in blood and seen running from the scene—is arrested, to the rescue comes Martin Vail (Richard Gere), Chicago's most famous defense lawyer. Martin visits the accused Aaron Stampler (Edward Norton) in jail and offers to represent Aaron pro bono. Prosecuting the case is Martin's ex-girlfriend (Laura Linney), whose bosses are pressuring her to get a death penalty verdict. Although the evidence drips with Aaron's guilt, Martin believes Aaron's story: that a third person was in the room with the archbishop, and that Aaron was passed out before the killing. Why a lawyer (who earlier tells a man in a bar that a good defense lawyer never even asks his client if he did it) would believe such an alibi makes little sense, except in a movie. So Martin's strategy is to dig deep into the archbishop's background to find who would have a motive for murdering him. Martin's investigator and paralegal proceed to dig up dirt on the dead priest. Meanwhile, a psychiatrist begins digging at the mild-mannered, stammering defendant, who was an altar boy in the archbishop's parish. What is discovered on those fronts is shocking. Martin's solution to his client's defense difficulties is a fiendish trial strategy triangulating the insanity defense, multiple personality disorder, and big-city politics. His victory is pyrrhic, as the film's final scenes show just how sick Aaron really is.

THE RAINMAKER (PG-13 1997)

Nearly perfect for a classroom setting, *The Rainmaker* is rich with professional responsibility quandaries. Unlikely as it may be that a brand new lawyer could take on an insurance company, which is backed by a high-powered legal team, there is much to be gained by watching this film, originally a John Grisham novel, and directed by the great Francis Ford Coppola. Fresh and broke from law school, former idealist Rudy Baylor, played by Matt Damon, can't avoid working for a personal injury lawyer named Bruiser (Mickey Rourke). Bruiser's office is in a strip mall, and his cases are scrounged up by a self-proclaimed "paralawyer" who has flunked the bar six times, but who seems the driving force, or at least the work horse, in the law office. Danny DeVito's performance as the paralawyer is delightful. Bruiser's arrangement with Rudy is that Rudy must pay his own way by bringing cases to Bruiser, who will give Rudy a cut of the fees. Fortunately, Rudy has brought a few cases with him. He is working on a will for an old widow who claims to be worth millions. He also has the case of a poor family whose son is dying of leukemia and were denied repeated requests for medical treatment coverage by Great Benefits Insurance Company. After signing up these clients, and while studying for the bar exam, Rudy is sent with paralawyer Deck Shiffler to fish for clients at a Memphis hospital. After catching a client, Rudy and Deck catch wind of Bruiser's impending federal indictment. Before they get roped into the mess, Rudy and Deck decide to split with their cases and start their own little firm. In the meantime, Rudy rents an apartment from the not-so-rich widow for whom he has written a will, and he falls in love with a young, abused married girl (Claire Danes), who eventually becomes his client.

Rudy faces a Herculean task as he and Deck—one who has never represented a client in court and one who has no right to do so—try to prepare their case against the obviously greedy insurance company. The insurance company is defended by the loathsome Leo Drummond, played by John Voight, whose dirty tricks range from colluding with the first judge on the case in an attempt to convince Rudy that the case should settle for a low amount, to having witnesses disappear just before scheduled depositions, to bugging Rudy's office. However, Rudy and Deck are not as pure as the wind-driven snow, and use some of their own tricks to try to even the playing field. The second judge, played gracefully by Danny Glover, senses what Rudy is up against, and gives the new lawyer as much leeway as is reasonable. Proving that Great Benefits wrongfully denied Donny Ray Black's claim as a matter of business practice is difficult, especially because the key witness and internal documents are missing. But thanks to Deck's chicanery and unique legal research, and a wrenching closing argument made by the dead boy, Rudy gives to Mrs. Black the victory she desires. And that victory brings Rudy's fast-tracked career to a quick end.

RUNAWAY JURY (PG-13 2003)

This film comes from a long list of John Grisham novels turned into movies. But where the source material centered on a big tobacco lawsuit, the film version of *Runaway Jury* makes gun manufacturers the bad guys. When a former day trader goes on a rampage at a brokerage firm and murders a stockbroker, the broker's widow sues the gun manufacturer. The suit alleges the manufacturer is liable for negligently making such assault-type weapons so readily available without any compunction. One would expect the stakes to be skyscraper-high for such a groundbreaking case, so it is no surprise when the defense uses the services of a jury consultant. But, to have the infamous consultant Rankin Finch (Gene Hackman) on your side means that you can almost guarantee a victory, considering he and his crack staff employ technology and tactics that would make James Bond jealous. Not only does Vicksburg Arms believe it will have the jury on its side, but it and a few other gun manufacturers also have conspired to pay a fee into the tens of millions of dollars, if needed, to ensure the outcome. The plaintiff's attorney, Wendell Rohr (Dustin Hoffman), has his own jury consultant, sort of, but not someone with the ammo of Rankin Finch. However, being outgunned doesn't bother attorney Rohr, because he believes he has justice on his side. Nick Easter (John Cusack) seems a little too nonplussed about the prospects of being on this jury, but becomes juror no. 9 on the biggest public policy case in decades. Rankin is rankled that Easter made it on the jury. His hunch is accurate because Easter sets about subtly influencing the other jurors even before the opening statements begin. Before long, a mysterious woman (Rachel Weisz) sends a message to Finch that she can guarantee a defense verdict for $10 million. Then the woman, intimately connected to Easter, makes the same extortion to Wendell Rohr. The mystery of *Runaway Jury* isn't for whom the jury will vote, but who Nick Easter is and what is motivating him. Although wrapped too neatly with the implication being that the ends justify the means, *Runaway Jury* does raise important issues about the intrusion of jury consulting into the system of justice. It also raises the question of whether it is ever right to render a verdict because the cause it represents is greater than the evidence would allow.

THE STAR CHAMBER (R 1983)

Beginning in 1487, a not-so-secret court called The Star Chamber met at the Royal Palace of Westminster for about 150 years. Distinct from other courts, the Star Chamber was initially well regarded as an efficient judicial forum. Its misuse of power led to its eventual dismissal. In today's parlance, "star chamber" refers to any tribunal that renders its decisions (and enforcements) in secret and without procedural safeguards. Borrowing loosely from this historical antecedent, this hard-to-find film is a worthy morality tale on the tension between justice and legal technicalities, but the film unfortunately ends as a thriller. As if made for a critic of the Warren Court's decisions in search and seizure cases, this movie is set in Los Angeles—Earl Warren's city of birth—as news reports spill the details of the heinous murders of elderly women. After the police capture the suspect red-handed, the defendant's lawyer gets all the evidence, and then the charges are thrown out on what seems to be a minor technicality. Although the prosecutor tells him that this decision will release a serial murder, Judge Hardin, played by Michael Douglas, believes the law requires such a result. Later, two suspected child murderers are arrested and find themselves in Judge Hardin's court. Once again, he follows the law, excluding key evidence, but not after considerable soul searching. His decision results in a dismissal of the charges. The dead boy's grief-stricken father then takes the law into his own hands, for which he is jailed. "What happened to right and wrong?" Judge Hardin asks his wife as he contemplates his role in freeing the defendants. Hardin's mentor and fellow judge, played by Hal Holbrook (who would join Michael Douglas a few years later in the huge hit *Wall Street*), has an answer. Sensing Hardin's desperation, Holbrook, the seasoned judge, says to Hardin, "Someone has kidnapped justice and hidden it in the law." Holbrook's character then invites the younger judge to join a cadre of judges who meet in secret to decide the fates of prior defendants whose obvious guilt was protected by legal technicalities. After hearing a summary of the dismissed cases, the cadre of judges vote and then send a hit man to carry out the sentences. Preposterous as that is, authenticity is strived for in what is really an agenda-film, because excellent police work shows that the two child murderer suspects released by Judge Hardin's procedural decisions were, in fact, innocent. Judge Hardin is then faced with quite a dilemma: do nothing and chalk up that mistake as the cost of doing business; or, do something and risk exposing himself and the others as conspirators and murderers.

SUSPECT (R 1987)

This movie starts with a tragic bang, as an important judge commits suicide. The suicide then becomes part of the backdrop to this legal thriller starring Cher as an overworked, underpaid, Washington, D.C., public defender who is desperately in need of a vacation. A mean judge, played by John Mahoney (the lovable Dad from *Frazier*), appoints Cher's character to represent a deaf-mute homeless man (portrayed by Liam Neeson), who is accused of murdering a legal secretary. Although she is not expected to do much with her client or his case, Cher starts to prepare a defense that seems, in some odd way, to lead to political intrigue and treachery. Viewers can be thankful that this is not one of those movies where the lawyer gets romantically involved with her client. She gets involved with a member of the jury instead. Dennis Quaid plays that juror, a slick lobbyist who begins to act like one of the Hardy Boys while in cahoots with Cher, who frets over all the ethics violations she is committing. Sure the plot has holes in it, and the ending seems forced, but the movie has a pace that keeps one wondering what is going to happen next, includes strong performances, and is fun to watch.

A TIME TO KILL (R 1996)

One of the more difficult movies on this list to watch, *A Time to Kill* tells the story of Carl Lee Haley, a poor black man portrayed by Samuel L. Jackson. Haley shoots and kills two white men who brutally raped and almost murdered his little daughter. Because the slayings are vigilantism, Carl Lee is charged with first-degree murder. Jake Bergantz, played by Matthew McConaughey, defends Haley. The question in the film is not whether Carl Lee did it, but whether he can get a fair trial in his small Mississippi hometown, which is deeply racially divided. Even after multiple viewings, one is left with the impression that this film is so over-the-top it seems like a caricature. Even after the rape and courthouse killings, there are Ku Klux Klan attacks, police abuses, a race riot, a fire-bombing, a sniper attack, a bomb planting, a house burning, cheating prosecutors, cheating defense lawyers, cheating jurors, a kidnapping, and more. There is, early in the film, an interesting ethical dilemma involving whether Bergantz is somehow responsible for the killings because, before killing the rapists, Carl Lee discusses with Bergantz the prospect of killing them. Concerning the trial, ask yourself whether Bergantz is violating the rules of ethics by putting his client on the stand to support a defense (insanity) that both he and his client know is inapplicable.

TO KILL A MOCKINGBIRD (UNRATED 1962)

To state the obvious, this is a thoroughly rewarding film to watch and is much more than a courtroom drama. It is also the only film on this list to be part of the American Film Institute's "100 Greatest American Movies" (at number 34). Gregory Peck won an Oscar playing Atticus Finch, a widowed southern lawyer in a Depression-era small town, raising two adventurous children—a daughter named Scout, and a son named Jem—who call their father by his first name. Atticus is appointed to defend a black man, Tom Robinson (played with much distinction by Brock Peters), wrongfully accused of raping a white woman. At the same time, Finch's children are on a hunt to get a good look at the supposedly scary man down the street, Boo Radley (one of Robert Duvall's first roles). This compelling story, both tragic and uplifting, is told by Scout. The movie focuses more on the children than on their lawyer father. While Atticus and his family endure the hatred of some of the racist folks in town because he is representing Tom Robinson, Atticus never wavers in showing his children how to live a dignified life through quiet courage. The courtroom scenes and Atticus's closing argument are quite compelling, particularly because Atticus's children are watching the trial from the balcony. Jem and Scout are seated with the black members of the community who welcome them in the "Negroes Only" section of the courthouse. If you have not seen this movie, watch it. If you have seen it, watch it again.

12 ANGRY MEN (UNRATED 1957)

This is a must-see movie, no matter how old it is. Henry Fonda stars as a member of a jury deliberating after the murder trial of a Puerto Rican boy accused of murdering his father in a rage-filled stabbing. This black-and-white film, shot like a play and consisting of frank dialogue in a steamy, New York City jury room, forces the viewer to confront what appears to be obvious guilt with the nuances of reasonable doubt raised by one dissenting juror. As the deliberations begin, we can see that many of the jurors are prejudiced. Fonda brilliantly combats that prejudice by avoiding it directly, and instead tackles the other jurors' notions about the evidence with an approach as methodical as the architect he is, and with a bit of Clarence Darrow-styled sleight of hand. Finally, when most of the other jurors have changed their verdicts, the last holdouts can only cling to their bigotry and bitterness. Throughout the film, Fonda's character never insists the defendant didn't do it; he asks the jurors to consider that it's possible the evidence isn't all that it seemed to be. By the film's end, reasonable doubt has been found, which doesn't necessarily mean an innocent man has been freed. This movie has an all-star cast with many recognizable faces, including Jack Klugman and Jack Warden. It is no more a coincidence that Henry Fonda's suit is white than it is predictable what the film's conclusion will be. However, it is the journey that makes this film so enjoyable. It is a good thing that justice is blind, or else the hero's own unethical sleight of hand would have been noticed.

THE VERDICT (R 1982)

Here is a movie that may be hard to find, but is well worth the search. Before *The Rainmaker* and *A Civil Action*, movies about forlorn lawyers up against deep-pocketed defendants with armies of litigators, there was *The Verdict*. Five Oscar nominations were awarded to *The Verdict*, including Best Picture, Best Actor for Paul Newman, and Best Supporting Actor for James Mason, who plays the lead defense attorney. Although criticized by some lawyers at the time of it release for being unfairly unrealistic, this movie succeeds at providing a magnificent legal drama. Frank Galvin, skillfully played by Paul Newman, is a pathetic, alcoholic, nearly disbarred lawyer who goes to funerals and hands his business card to the bereaved. The reason Galvin was nearly disbarred helps to explain the alcoholism, which helps to explain why he only has one client, a young woman left brain-dead after general anesthesia was administered to her while in a Catholic hospital in Boston. Galvin's only friend and mentor, played by Jack Warden, gave Galvin the case because it is such a clear candidate for settling, and it might help Galvin get back on his feet. Galvin has ignored the case for 18 months, and it is headed for trial soon, so he hurriedly talks up the prospects of a settlement while meeting with the woman's sister and guardian. Galvin then takes some Polaroid pictures of his client in her bed in the hospital ward, planning to use the photos in his settlement conference with the Boston archdiocese. However, Galvin sees his only chance for redemption in those photos. So, he refuses the $210,000 offer and then begs his only friend to help him get this case ready for trial in two weeks. Opposing Galvin is the brilliant and silky Ed Concannon (James Mason), the senior partner of a large defense firm, who will stop at nothing to win his case, including using a spy against Galvin. As Galvin labors to get hostile nurses who were on the scene that day to agree to help him, he loses his expert witness, who was bought off by the defense at the very last minute. Because the trial judge evidently favors the defense, he refuses to grant Galvin an extension and scolds Galvin about his foolish refusal of the Catholic Church's settlement offer. Galvin is now left with nothing holding his case together but himself, which is the worst dilemma for a man whose bottle of self-worth is empty. If only he could summon the skill and clarity he once had before everything in his life and career went so badly. While it is easy to notice the dirty tricks pulled by the defense lawyer, one must also realize that Galvin could be severely sanctioned for the many ethics violations he commits: miscommunication with the client's guardian regarding a settlement offer; wrongful solicitations; lying; deceit with unrepresented persons; and more. Then again, saints don't need redemption.

YOUNG MR. LINCOLN (G 1939)

Perhaps no one in American history is more revered than Abraham Lincoln. Thrust from relative anonymity and lukewarm support as he entered the White House during America's most trying time, reviled for much of his presidency, and then martyred at the dawn of peace, Lincoln's shadow has never waned. And through all the political failures Lincoln endured prior to the 1860 election, Lincoln's greatness as an Illinois lawyer was never in doubt. Moving through a 10-year time period in which Lincoln loses his beloved Ann Rutledge and becomes a lawyer (thanks to being given a set of *Blackstone's Commentaries*), the focus in *Young Mr. Lincoln* is on a famous criminal trial believed by some never to have occurred. In that trial, Lincoln, wonderfully played by Henry Fonda, defends two brothers accused of murdering a town bully late on the night of a town fair. According to the contemporaneous accounts, Lincoln defended one man, not two brothers, wrongfully accused of murder, late in Lincoln's legal career, not early in it. The movie's inclusion of Lincoln's 1858 Senatorial opponent Stephen Douglas as a possible suitor to a young Mary Todd is corny, and the trial scenes are presented with Hollywood histrionics. However, the scenes still are priceless examples of Lincoln's razor-sharp wit and shrewd legal mind. *Young Mr. Lincoln* is a love letter of a film, more hagiography than biography. But the essence of the film, which is that Lincoln was both good and a good lawyer, rings true. And couldn't we all use a little reminder, even one told with the license fiction affords, of the value that an ethical lawyer adds to society?

Glossary

401(k) plan An employee retirement plan authorized by Section 401 of the Internal Revenue Code, sometimes called a salary reduction plan. In a 401k plan, an employee's pre-tax contributions are matched in some percentage by his employer's contributions.

A

accident runners Persons hired by lawyers to find personal injury clients, usually by going to the scene of accidents or disasters. Accident runners are respected even less than ambulance chasers.

adjudication The process of formally resolving a controversy, based on evidence presented.

admiralty Admiralty law involves the traditional rules and practices associated with the navigation of the sea or commercial transaction conducted on navigable waterways. Admiralty law is also known as maritime law.

advance A prepayment for future legal services made to an attorney at the beginning of the representation. As the lawyer works on the case, the advance is being earned.

affidavit A written statement of declaration made under oath and very often in the course of litigation.

affirm The decision of an appellate court that maintains the status quo and keeps the lower court's decision in place.

aggregate settlement A settlement made by all parties on the same side of a case. Sometimes called a joint settlement.

alimony Payments of support made by one spouse to another spouse, following a divorce. Some states have eliminated alimony as a general requirement in divorce.

Alternative dispute resolution (ADR) Method of resolving conflict outside the traditional method of litigation and a trial. Forms of ADR include negotiation, mediation, and arbitration.

amicus curiae A Latin phrase that means "friend of the court." An amicus curiae brief is a brief filed by one who is not a party to the lawsuit, or appeal but who believes the court needs to read the legal perspective presented in the amicus brief in order to make a correct decision.

annotated When a rule of court or statute is annotated, that means it is privately published and comes with research material in addition to the statute or rule.

antifederalist A founding father who opposed the design of the Constitution because it provided for an unlimited federal government.

appearance of impropriety A standard of ethical conduct, found in the Model Code of Professional Responsibility, in which lawyers are advised to avoid certain activities because those activities look bad, rather than actually being bad.

arbitration An alternative dispute resolution mechanism where parties agree to submit their dispute to a neutral third party, called an arbitrator, who renders a decision, which is usually binding. Arbitration, usually a creature of contract, is quicker and, therefore, less expensive than traditional litigation.

associate A lawyer in a law firm who has not reached partnership status, but may be on a partnership track.

B

bad faith Something done in bad faith is done dishonestly, or with ulterior motives.

barratry Historically, barratry was the crime of stirring up frivolous, or groundless, litigation.

bill padding A dishonest billing practice that involves one exaggerating the time spent working on a client's case.

black letter law Legal principles that have become so accepted and unequivocal that they are cited as truisms.

bona fide Genuine, or good faith.

C

cause of action Facts that are sufficient to entitle a party to claim a legal wrong, entitling the claimant to a remedy. Lawsuits are based on causes of action and can be dismissed if they fail to state a cause of action.

certificates of deposits (CDs) A type of conservative investment wherein someone gives money to a bank or other financial institution in exchange for promissory notes from the institutions detailing the interest to be paid on the money and the date on which the principal and interest will be paid to the investor.

champerty An agreement between the lawyer and client where the lawyer agrees to pay the costs of the litigation in exchange for the client transferring to the lawyer the client's ownership in any future judgment. The historical prohibition of champerty has been relaxed by the allowances of contingency fees.

circulars Notices or advertisements sent to certain groups of people.

class action A lawsuit brought by a representative of a large group of plaintiffs (or prospective plaintiffs) on behalf of the group. Rule 23 of the Federal Rules of Civil Procedure governs class actions.

comments In this context, a comment is the official commentary of the rules committee that follows specific rules of court. Comments are designed to give meaning to the specific rules.

commercial speech Communications made for business purposes. Speech made in the pursuit of capitalism is commercial speech, and it is less protected under free speech doctrines than religious or political speech.

commingling The unlawful mixing of one person's money with another person's money in the same account.

common law This phrase has three related definitions. In this context, common law refers to judge-made law, or the process whereby appellate courts make precedent that lower courts must follow. Because of our colonial history with England, America is known as a common law country.

companion cases Two or more appellate cases that are connected because they involve the same parties in similar legal situations, or different parties with the same legal issue.

constituent A part of something else that is a distinct entity.

contempt Also known as contempt of court, this is an act or omission that tends to obstruct the administration of justice or shows disrespect for the court; it can include disobeying the instructions or orders of the court.

contingent fee A fee paid to a lawyer that is paid only if the lawyer succeeds in recovering a settlement or judgment for the client. The contingent fee is a percentage of what the client obtains.

continuing legal education (CLE) A lawyer must earn certain annual CLE credits, as determined by the jurisdiction in which she is licensed. CLE credits, commonly called CLEs, are earned by attending bar-sponsored or bar-approved seminars that concern different practice areas of the law. Lawyers must also earn continuing legal ethics credits as part of their annual CLE requirements.

conversion A tortuous act that involves one exercising authority over another's property, to the deprivation, and without the permission, of the innocent party.

D

declaratory judgment A judgment granted by the court that, without ordering any performance or determining damages, is close to an "advisory opinion" (which courts do not issue). A declaratory judgment is designed to allow a party to ask a court to resolve a controversy before it becomes a full-blown case.

deposition A litigation discovery device, similar to testifying at trial, whereby the deponent is put under oath and subject to lawyer's questions. Depositions occur in law offices or conference rooms, but not in courtrooms.

disciplinary commission A panel consisting mostly of lawyers and authorized by a state's highest court to investigate and prosecute lawyer misconduct.

discovery A pre-trial procedure used in litigation where parties gain information from each other. Discovery is designed to promote open disclosure of relevant evidence and is supposed to operate without court involvement.

double billing A dishonest billing practice that involves billing two clients for the same time.

E

engagement letter A letter from a lawyer to a client that formally acknowledges that the firm has accepted the client's case and sets forth the terms of the representation.

equity partner A partner in a law firm who is a shareholder, having voting rights.

estate plan A legal structure designed to pass on one's assets to others in life and at death, and to minimize estate taxes and probate costs.

ex parte communication Communication made to the court during litigation in the absence of the other party or the other party's attorney.

F

federalist A founding father who believed in the need for the federal government to have unlimited power, as designed in the Constitution.

fiduciary One who has a legal duty to act in the best interests of another. Lawyers are fiduciaries to their clients, as parents are to their minor children.

fixed fee A predetermined fee that covers all of the lawyer's efforts in services rendered for a particular client matter. A fixed fee is distinguished from an hourly rate.

foreclosure The act of a creditor to take ownership and control of property that was used as collateral by the debtor.

forms books Books that have samples of various kinds of complaints, answers, and other litigation documents.

fraud An intentional deception that results in a legal injury to another. Fraud usually involves a material misrepresentation (which can include silence) made to deceive the other party, reliance by the other party on the misrepresentation, and resulting harm.

G

governmental immunity Also known as sovereign immunity, a doctrine from English common law that holds that government may not be sued for its actions unless it first gives permission to be sued.

This doctrine traditionally protects governments and their employees against being sued for their official actions.

grievance One's allegation that something denies some equitable or legal right, or causes injustice.

gross revenue Sometimes called gross income, this is the total revenue received before deductions, such as expenses.

I

immunity A grant of protection made by prosecutors to witnesses, which prevents them from being prosecuted for their testimony or written statements, except where their assertions are lies.

independent contractor One who is self-employed, but hired to do work for others as needed, such as an attorney, an accountant, or a caterer.

independent counsel A special prosecutor, authorized by specific statute with a broad scope of authority to investigate and, if necessary, criminally prosecute high government officials.

indigent Poor, determined to be incapable of paying for a lawyer's services.

informed consent Giving one's agreement to take a certain action, including doing nothing, after having received a full explanation of the possible ramifications and consequences of taking that action.

injunction A court order forbidding a party to do something or ordering the party to start doing something.

insider trading The buying or selling of a company's stock by the company's insiders, based on information the insiders know, and before that information is released to the public. Insiders are usually defined as executive officers, directors, or shareholders of a corporation owning at least 10 percent of the corporation's stock.

inter alia A Latin phrase that means "among other things."

interrogatories A discovery device that involves one party sending to the other party a set, or sets, of questions that are to be answered under oath and in writing.

intestate The legal status of someone who dies without having left a will, which includes having a will that is later deemed invalid.

intestate estate The personal and real property of a person who died without leaving a valid will to direct the transfer of that property.

J

judicial review The doctrine from *Marbury v. Madison* that gives appellate courts the right to review the constitutionality of the acts of the legislative and executive branches, in addition to reviewing the decision of lower courts.

jurisdiction In this context, jurisdiction means a particular place over which a court has authority, usually a state.

L

legal treatise A form of secondary authority, much like a legal textbook, but which is often accorded higher status because of its longstanding reputation in the legal community.

libelous Libel is a false written statement that is published and made in order to harm the reputation of another. Slander is the spoken form of libel. Libel and slander are different forms of defamation.

liquidated damages clause A part of a contract that predetermines the monetary damages one party would owe the other in the event of breach of contract. Liquidated damages need to be a reasonable estimate of the damages suffered in order to be valid.

M

malfeasance A wrongful or unlawful act.

malpractice Improper or harmful conduct committed by a professional in the course of her profession.

mediation A form of ADR in which a third party, known as a neutral, assists the opposing parties in the process of trying to reach a settlement.

memorandum of law An internal memorandum of law is legal analysis on the merits of a client's case. An external memorandum of law is an advocacy document, similar to a trial or appellate brief, presented to a court.

misdemeanor Generally, a lower classified crime in comparison to a felony.

misrepresentation A false or untruthful statement.

motions Formal applications to a court (such as a motion for summary judgment), requesting the court to issue an order.

multi-state bar exam A bar exam that allows the successful applicant to be licensed in more than one jurisdiction. Such an exam is a result of a reciprocity agreement between the jurisdictions.

N

NOW account Negotiable order of withdrawal account. A NOW account is an account that allows the depositor to withdraw sums of money from the account at will. NOW accounts are also called demand deposit accounts.

O

Office of Independent Counsel (OIC) A statutorily created special legal office empowered to investigate and prosecute misconduct by members of the executive branch of government and other high-ranking government officials.

original jurisdiction The authority an appellate court has to hear a case directly, before the case proceeds through the trial court and then is appealed.

P

partner A lawyer who has been granted ownership status in a firm, having been voted in as a partner by the other partners. Partners generally share in the firm's profits.

patent The grant of ownership in an invention, giving the owner exclusive rights over the invention for a certain number of years.

pecuniary That which concerns money.

personal representative Someone appointed to manage the legal affairs of another person or of an estate.

plea bargaining Negotiating in a criminal case, resulting in the prosecutor and the defendant agreeing to dispose of the charges through a settlement in which the defendant pleads guilty to a lesser charge.

pleadings Formal allegations of facts that consist of the plaintiff's claim (the complaint) or the defendant's response (the answer).

positive law A phrase that refers to law made through political, governmental means.

prenuptial agreement A contract entered into by two people intending to marry each other, in which the people agree in writing to their respective property rights in the event of divorce or death.

prima facie On its face or on the surface.

pro bono Legal services provided to a client free of charge, or at a reduced rate. The original Latin form was pro bono publico, which means for the public good or welfare.

pro se A Latin phrase that refers to one representing oneself in a legal matter.

probable cause A sufficient legal reason, based on the known facts and circumstances, for arresting or indicting someone, as well as for obtaining a warrant.

promissory estoppel An exception to the requirement of "consideration," which is a required element to a valid contract. Generally, promissory estoppel allows a party who relied on the promise of another party to recover what was promised, even though the relying party would be unable to recover under contract law.

proximate cause A sufficient legal reason, based on the known facts and circumstances, for arresting or indicting someone, as well as for obtaining a warrant.

public policy Generalized views about the American culture or ideals upon which specific laws are made.

puffing A real word used in sales contexts to mean an opinion or belief that is not meant to be taken as a statement of fact or warranty.

Q

quantum merit A Latin phrase that means "as much as deserved." Quantum merit is an equitable principle used in contract cases by plaintiffs attempting to recover something for their efforts when courts have already determined that operative legal principles deny the validity of a contract.

R

real estate closing The formal consummation of a sale of real estate, which usually involves the signing of many documents, payment of the real estate, and delivery of the deed or title.

recuse When someone, such as a judge or other person of influence, removes him or herself from participation in a matter because of a conflict of interest.

remand A remand occurs when an appellate court sends at least part of an appeal back to a lower court to reexamine the evidence or damages in light of the higher court's decision.

respondeat superior A Latin phrase that means "let the superior reply." This is a legal doctrine that makes employers (or principals) liable for the misconduct of their employees (or agents) that is committed within the scope of the employment.

restatement Unified, systematic statements on the common law created by the American Law Institute. There are many restatements, including the Restatement of Contracts, the Restatement of Agency, and the Restatement of Torts.

retainer A payment, similar to an advance, made to an attorney that is made to secure the lawyer's availability. When a retainer is called a general retainer, it is usually nonrefundable because the

lawyer has earned the retainer upon payment. When a retainer is called a special retainer, it is usually a refundable payment, much like an advance.

reverse The opposite of affirm.

reverse contingent fee A type of contingent fee arrangement that involves the lawyer being paid a percentage of what the lawyer saves the client from losing, as opposed to a percentage of what the lawyer obtains for the client.

rules of court Sets of rules that are adopted by the highest appellate court of a jurisdiction and apply to the practice of law, unlike statutes, which are passed by a legislature and apply to all.

S

Securities Exchange Commission (SEC) An agency of the U.S. government created in 1934, and charged with enforcing federal securities (investments) laws and regulating the securities markets.

security interest Where a creditor secures the repayment of a loan by taking legal title to certain property of the debtor, known as collateral. In the event of default, the creditor has rights to the collateral. A mortgage is an example of a security interest.

shareholder's derivative lawsuit A lawsuit in which a shareholder of a corporation, on behalf of the corporation, sues the corporation's board of directors, alleging that their actions have harmed the corporation. Any benefits from the derivative lawsuit flow to the corporation, not personally to the shareholder.

solicitor general The third ranking member of the U.S. Justice Department. The solicitor general represents the federal government before the U.S. Supreme Court.

status conference A pretrial meeting required under the federal rules of procedure and many state and local procedure rules, attended by the attorney, and designed to inform the trial court of where things are in the pretrial stage (discovery, witnesses, settlement negotiations, estimated length of a trial).

subrogation When someone who has made a payment on another's behalf has the legal or equitable right to be paid back from the party who was originally liable for the payment. Subrogation often occurs when an insurance company pays its insured party under the terms of the insurance contract, and then is subrogated in the insured party's lawsuit against the defendant.

summary judgment A litigation strategy in which a trial is prevented because the judge dismisses the case due to two prerequisites: (a) there are no material facts concerning the case that are in disagreement by both parties; and (b) the law applying to the case is on the side of the party who has asked the judge for a summary judgment.

surety bond A written instrument filed with a court in which one promises to be liable up to the amount stated in the bond in the event of negligence or failure to perform.

T

trust A legal mechanism where property is held by one party for the benefit of another. A trust is created when the Donor transfers the property into the trust where the Trustee holds the legal title to the property, while the Beneficiary of the trust has the equitable title in the property, which means the benefits (income) of the trust are provided to the beneficiary.

trust accounts A special bank account where the property of the client is held and maintained by the attorney.

U

undue influence Where one party, in a position of strength over another party who is in a position of weakness, causes that party to enter into a contractual relationship with the superior party, or causes that party to give a gift to the superior party.

Undue influence takes away the free will of the weaker party because of the unfair influence of the superior party.

unified bar association A bar association whose members must join upon being admitted to the practice of law in a particular jurisdiction. It is also known as an integrated bar association.

V

vacate Similar to a remand, but sometimes a higher court vacates a lower court's decision to temporarily set a matter aside with instructions that the lower court rewrite its opinion in light of the higher court's opinion.

venire A member of the legal process, including the jury.

voir dire The process of picking jurors by questioning prospective jurors on matters related to the case, including biases and prejudices.

W

waived To waive a right or prerogative is to give it up. A waiver can be implied.

warranty A statement that amounts to a promise of quality or the assurance of certain facts.

West Digest System A method for researching case law, in which the law is divided into 400-plus topics, which are then divided into thousands of subtopics. When matched together, each topic and subtopic is known by its title and "key number" and corresponds to the key numbers of the headnotes for the cases, which are found by using a Thomson West-published digest.

writ of mandamus An order issued by a court, ordering some official to do a particular act that was requested by the party seeking the writ of mandamus.

Index

IMPORTANT! READ CAREFULLY: This End User License Agreement ("Agreement") sets forth the conditions by which Cengage Learning will make electronic access to the Cengage Learning-owned licensed content and associated media, software, documentation, printed materials, and electronic documentation contained in this package and/or made available to you via this product (the "Licensed Content"), available to you (the "End User"). BY CLICKING THE "I ACCEPT" BUTTON AND/OR OPENING THIS PACKAGE, YOU ACKNOWLEDGE THAT YOU HAVE READ ALL OF THE TERMS AND CONDITIONS, AND THAT YOU AGREE TO BE BOUND BY ITS TERMS, CONDITIONS, AND ALL APPLICABLE LAWS AND REGULATIONS GOVERNING THE USE OF THE LICENSED CONTENT.

1.0   SCOPE OF LICENSE

1.1   Licensed Content. The Licensed Content may contain portions of modifiable content ("Modifiable Content") and content which may not be modified or otherwise altered by the End User ("Non-Modifiable Content"). For purposes of this Agreement, Modifiable Content and Non-Modifiable Content may be collectively referred to herein as the "Licensed Content." All Licensed Content shall be considered Non-Modifiable Content, unless such Licensed Content is presented to the End User in a modifiable format and it is clearly indicated that modification of the Licensed Content is permitted.

1.2   Subject to the End User's compliance with the terms and conditions of this Agreement, Cengage Learning hereby grants the End User, a nontransferable, nonexclusive, limited right to access and view a single copy of the Licensed Content on a single personal computer system for noncommercial, internal, personal use only. The End User shall not (i) reproduce, copy, modify (except in the case of Modifiable Content), distribute, display, transfer, sublicense, prepare derivative work(s) based on, sell, exchange, barter or transfer, rent, lease, loan, resell, or in any other manner exploit the Licensed Content; (ii) remove, obscure, or alter any notice of Cengage Learning's intellectual property rights present on or in the Licensed Content, including, but not limited to, copyright, trademark, and/or patent notices; or (iii) disassemble, decompile, translate, reverse engineer, or otherwise reduce the Licensed Content.

2.0   TERMINATION

2.1   Cengage Learning may at any time (without prejudice to its other rights or remedies) immediately terminate this Agreement and/or suspend access to some or all of the Licensed Content, in the event that the End User does not comply with any of the terms and conditions of this Agreement. In the event of such termination by Cengage Learning, the End User shall immediately return any and all copies of the Licensed Content to Cengage Learning.

3.0   PROPRIETARY RIGHTS

3.1   The End User acknowledges that Cengage Learning owns all rights, title and interest, including, but not limited to all copyright rights therein, in and to the Licensed Content, and that the End User shall not take any action inconsistent with such ownership. The Licensed Content is protected by U.S., Canadian and other applicable copyright laws and by international treaties, including the Berne Convention and the Universal Copyright Convention. Nothing contained in this Agreement shall be construed as granting the End User any ownership rights in or to the Licensed Content.

3.2   Cengage Learning reserves the right at any time to withdraw from the Licensed Content any item or part of an item for which it no longer retains the right to publish, or which it has reasonable grounds to believe infringes copyright or is defamatory, unlawful, or otherwise objectionable.

4.0   PROTECTION AND SECURITY

4.1   The End User shall use its best efforts and take all reasonable steps to safeguard its copy of the Licensed Content to ensure that no unauthorized reproduction, publication, disclosure, modification, or distribution of the Licensed Content, in whole or in part, is made. To the extent that the End User becomes aware of any such unauthorized use of the Licensed Content, the End User shall immediately notify Cengage Learning. Notification of such violations may be made by sending an e-mail to delmarhelp@Cengage.com.

5.0   MISUSE OF THE LICENSED PRODUCT

5.1   In the event that the End User uses the Licensed Content in violation of this Agreement, Cengage Learning shall have the option of electing liquidated damages, which shall include all profits generated by the End User's use of the Licensed Content plus interest computed at the maximum rate permitted by law and all legal fees and other expenses incurred by Cengage Learning in enforcing its rights, plus penalties.

6.0   FEDERAL GOVERNMENT CLIENTS

6.1   Except as expressly authorized by Cengage Learning, Federal Government clients obtain only the rights specified in this Agreement and no other rights. The Government acknowledges that (i) all software and related documentation incorporated in the Licensed Content is existing commercial computer software within the meaning of FAR 27.405(b)(2); and (2) all other data delivered in whatever form, is limited rights data within the meaning of FAR 27.401. The restrictions in this section are acceptable as consistent with the Government's need for software and other data under this Agreement.

7.0   DISCLAIMER OF WARRANTIES AND LIABILITIES

7.1   Although Cengage Learning believes the Licensed Content to be reliable, Cengage Learning does not guarantee or warrant (i) any information or materials contained in or produced by the Licensed Content, (ii) the accuracy, completeness or reliability of the Licensed Content, or (iii) that the Licensed Content is free from errors or other material defects. THE LICENSED PRODUCT IS PROVIDED "AS IS," WITHOUT ANY WARRANTY OF ANY KIND AND CENGAGE LEARNING DISCLAIMS ANY AND ALL WARRANTIES, EXPRESSED OR IMPLIED, INCLUDING, WITHOUT LIMITATION, WARRANTIES OF MERCHANTABILITY OR FITNESS FOR A PARTICULAR PURPOSE. IN NO EVENT SHALL CENGAGE LEARNING BE LIABLE FOR: INDIRECT, SPECIAL, PUNITIVE OR CONSEQUENTIAL DAMAGES INCLUDING FOR LOST PROFITS, LOST DATA, OR OTHERWISE. IN NO EVENT SHALL CENGAGE LEARNING'S AGGREGATE LIABILITY HEREUNDER, WHETHER ARISING IN CONTRACT, TORT, STRICT LIABILITY OR OTHERWISE, EXCEED THE AMOUNT OF FEES PAID BY THE END USER HEREUNDER FOR THE LICENSE OF THE LICENSED CONTENT.

8.0   GENERAL

8.1   Entire Agreement. This Agreement shall constitute the entire Agreement between the Parties and supercedes all prior Agreements and understandings oral or written relating to the subject matter hereof.

8.2   Enhancements/Modifications of Licensed Content. From time to time, and in Cengage Learning's sole discretion, Cengage Learning may advise the End User of updates, upgrades, enhancements and/or improvements to the Licensed Content, and may permit the End User to access and use, subject to the terms and conditions of this Agreement, such modifications, upon payment of prices as may be established by Cengage Learning.

8.3   No Export. The End User shall use the Licensed Content solely in the United States and shall not transfer or export, directly or indirectly, the Licensed Content outside the United States.

8.4   Severability. If any provision of this Agreement is invalid, illegal, or unenforceable under any applicable statute or rule of law, the provision shall be deemed omitted to the extent that it is invalid, illegal, or unenforceable. In such a case, the remainder of the Agreement shall be construed in a manner as to give greatest effect to the original intention of the parties hereto.

8.5   Waiver. The waiver of any right or failure of either party to exercise in any respect any right provided in this Agreement in any instance shall not be deemed to be a waiver of such right in the future or a waiver of any other right under this Agreement.

8.6   Choice of Law/Venue. This Agreement shall be interpreted, construed, and governed by and in accordance with the laws of the State of New York, applicable to contracts executed and to be wholly preformed therein, without regard to its principles governing conflicts of law. Each party agrees that any proceeding arising out of or relating to this Agreement or the breach or threatened breach of this Agreement may be commenced and prosecuted in a court in the State and County of New York. Each party consents and submits to the nonexclusive personal jurisdiction of any court in the State and County of New York in respect of any such proceeding.

8.7   Acknowledgment. By opening this package and/or by accessing the Licensed Content on this Web site, THE END USER ACKNOWLEDGES THAT IT HAS READ THIS AGREEMENT, UNDERSTANDS IT, AND AGREES TO BE BOUND BY ITS TERMS AND CONDITIONS. IF YOU DO NOT ACCEPT THESE TERMS AND CONDITIONS, YOU MUST NOT ACCESS THE LICENSED CONTENT AND RETURN THE LICENSED PRODUCT TO CENGAGE LEARNING (WITHIN 30 CALENDAR DAYS OF THE END USER'S PURCHASE) WITH PROOF OF PAYMENT ACCEPTABLE TO CENGAGE LEARNING, FOR A CREDIT OR A REFUND. Should the End User have any questions/comments regarding this Agreement, please contact Cengage Learning at delmar.help@cengage.com.